"Cliff Dwellers" by George Bellows

THE ANNALS
OF
AMERICA

THE ANNALS OF AMERICA

Volume 12

1895 - 1904

Populism, Imperialism, and Reform

William Benton, *Publisher*

ENCYCLOPÆDIA BRITANNICA, INC.
Chicago London Toronto Geneva Sydney Tokyo Manila

The editors wish to express their gratitude for permission to reprint
material from the following sources:

Harvard University Press for Selection 18, from *The
Letters of Theodore Roosevelt*, ed. by Elting E. Morison,
Vol. I, Cambridge, Mass.: Harvard University Press,
Copyright 1951 by the President and Fellows of Harvard College.

Houghton Mifflin Company for Selection 71, from
Letters of Charles Eliot Norton, Copyright 1913 by Sara
Norton.

The University of Minnesota Press for Selection 5,
from *The Welsh in America: Letters from the Immigrants*, ed. by Alan Conway, Minneapolis: The University of Minnesota Press, © Copyright 1961 by the
University of Minnesota.

Yale University Press for Selection 108, from *War and
Other Essays*, by William Graham Sumner, ed. by Albert Galloway Keller.

CODED SOURCES IN THIS VOLUME

157 Indiana 324

Reports of Cases Argued and Determined in the Supreme Court of Judicature of the State of Indiana. Vol. 157, pp. 324ff.

Malloy

[Senate Foreign Relations Committee] *Treaties, Conventions, International Acts, Protocols and Agreements between the United States of America and other Powers 1776-1909.* Edited by William M. Malloy. In 2 vols. Washington, 1910.

PRFA

[United States Department of State] *Papers Relating to Foreign Affairs.* Compiled annually since 1861 except for 1869 with supplements issued periodically. Title changed to *Papers Relating to Foreign Relations of the United States* in 1870 and to *Foreign Relations of the United States* in 1947. Washington, 1862 *et seq.*

Record

Congressional Record. A record of the proceedings of Congress from March 3, 1873, to date, arranged by number of Congress and by session. Washington, 1874 *et seq.*

Richardson

A Compilation of the Messages and Papers of the Presidents 1789-1897. Edited by James D. Richardson. In 10 vols. Washington, 1896-1899. New edition extended to 1908. Washington, 1909.

United States Reports [Supreme Court].

156 U.S. 1	Vol. 156, pp. 1ff.;
158 U.S. 564	Vol. 158, pp. 564ff.;
163 U.S. 537	Vol. 163, pp. 537ff.;
193 U.S. 197	Vol. 193, pp. 197ff.

Contents

POPULISM, IMPERIALISM, AND REFORM
In Pictures

As America's leading city, its financial center and its main point
of contact with other nations, New York developed and
diversified most rapidly and extensively. Novelty was always
likely in New York; progress and new problems alike were
apt to appear here earlier than elsewhere. New York was
to serve often as both a model and a laboratory for new social
and political techniques in the modern city.

The spirit of Manifest Destiny outlived its original continental
goals and led the United States into an active role in world
politics. "Gunboat diplomacy" in the Caribbean, based on the
Monroe Doctrine, and the Open Door policy in the Far East,
based on the possibility of trade and influence via the possession
of the Philippines, were both expressions of a new style of
American politics. There was implicit in all this a departure from
tradition that closely approached the radical in degree.

The closing of the frontier marked the end of physical expansion;
there remained the new and in some ways even greater challenge
of economic exploitation and internal development. Rude settlements
grew into towns and towns into cities as civilization and the
ambiguous "culture" came into the former frontier.

The economic development of the West depended upon ending
the dominance of simple extractive industries and attracting
permanent enterprises — agriculture, commerce, manufacturing.
Newly settled areas gradually achieved the stability necessary
to attract investment capital and, in the richer areas, economic
autonomy was soon within grasp. Those who could not adjust to
a tamer sort of life could recapture the frontier in distant Alaska.

The South began gradually to modernize its economy. With the aid
of capital from the rich East, industry grew up slowly and began
to create an alternative to the traditional Southern agrarianism.
Though the day when the South could claim to be economically
sound and self-sufficient was yet far off, auspicious signs could
be seen in new cities like Birmingham, Knoxville, Miami. As a
new social order began to seem imminent, the traditions of the
post-Civil War South were written into a wave of legal segregation.

The last years of innocent, self-contained America have come to
seem, in retrospect, something of a Golden Age. In its first flush
of real wealth and strength, confident and as yet untouched by
a older world across the Atlantic, America was also in the last
days of a rural and small-town culture. Looking back from not
always pleasant cities across two World Wars, it is not surprising
that a golden glow seems to surround such a period.

Introduction

The Panic of 1893 led to the most severe depression the country suffered between the 1870s and 1929 (see, for example, Volume 11, Selection 95). The Panic itself did not last long, and during the first McKinley administration (1897-1901) stock prices reached new highs. But even in the relatively prosperous years before 1893 and after 1895 the real wages of workers fell, at the same time that the cost of living rose. The workers knew this, whatever the economic figures and indices seemed to show, and it was one reason for the continuing labor unrest that marked the period. (See Selections 5-7, 9, 48, 64, 82, 92, 94, 97-99, 104, 111, 115, and 120-123.)

Factory workers in the cities were well off compared to the farmers. It was the latter who suffered most, and their plight was of long standing. Up until about 1880 a land boom in the West and continuing high prices for wheat and corn had maintained the belief in eternal prosperity; but, as the 1880s revealed, it was based on two decades of abnormally mild, wet weather. In 1885 the law of averages began to take its toll, when one of the worst winters in history almost destroyed the cattle industry. And in 1887 there came a summer so dry that almost the entire wheat crop in western Kansas and Nebraska was lost. During the next four years half the people who had confidently entered this area trekked eastward again. Whichever direction they were moving, the Conestoga wagons of the period were usually adorned with signs, the best known of which comes from another migration: "Pikes Peak or Bust." The wagons of these returning Kansans carried such signs as "In God We Trusted, In Kansas We Busted."

There was distress in other agricultural regions as well — in the East, in the Midwest, in the South. As Washington Gladden wrote in 1890, "the American farmer is steadily losing ground. His burdens are heavier every year and his gains are more meager; he is beginning to fear that he may be sinking into a servile condition." (See Volume 11, Selection 68; see also, in Volume 11, Selections 44, 66-67, 69, and 90; and in this volume see, among others, Selection 58.)

Things were especially bad in the South, more dependent than ever on its one crop, cotton (see Selection 100). One rather perverse result was the passage, in almost every one of the states of the old Confederacy, of Jim Crow laws (as they came to be called) that not only institutionalized the previously informal segregation of the races, but also subjected the Negro to humiliations that he had hardly suffered under slavery. Indeed it has been said that the darkest period for the Negro in American history was the three decades from 1890 to 1920. The Negro's position during these years was so perilous, in fact, that he was fortunate if he suffered nothing more than humiliation and escaped being lynched. In 1892, 155 Negroes were lynched, and although from that date the number slowly dropped off, at least 50 Negroes were lynched in every year until 1913. Despite the common excuse that lynching was justified to protect Southern womanhood, rape or sexual assault was not even charged in four-fifths of the recorded cases, and Negroes could be lynched, and were, for such "offenses" as refusing to sell their crop at a white man's price. And 2 percent of the victims were women. (For discussions of the situation of Negroes during this period, see Volume 11, Selections 11, 46-47, and 53, and, in this volume, Selections 4-5, 52, 88, and 112; see also Selection 21, which is an extract from the Supreme Court's decision in *Plessy* v. *Ferguson*, the famous case that upheld the legality of Negro segregation for nearly sixty years.)

The farmers (and at first the Negroes, though they were later shut out of the movement) did not take the situation lying down. As Gladden had said in 1890, "whatever [the farmer] can do by social combination or by united political action to remove the disabilities under which he is suffering, he intends to do at once and with all his might." One action was the founding of the Peoples' or Populist Party in 1892, which combined elements of the earlier Farmers' Alliances and the nearly defunct Knights of Labor as well as other minor groups. The Populists were in favor of "free silver" (which would be inflationary, they thought, and thus helpful to the debtor class in society — see Selection 16), government ownership of railroads, an eight-hour day, and restrictions on immigration to maintain the level of wages. They were also for a graduated income tax. The 1894 Tariff Law included a 2 percent tax on incomes above $4,000, but it was short-lived, the Supreme Court declaring it unconstitutional in *Pollock* v. *Farmers' Loan and Trust Co.* in 1895 (see Selection 15, and also Selection 113). The Sixteenth Amendment to the Constitution thereby became necessary (it was ratified in 1913) before the government could legally enact such a "direct tax."

As a third party the Populists never got very far, but their policies and programs had an important influence on American politics for a generation and longer. William Jennings Bryan, who electrified the Democratic convention in 1896 with his famous "Cross of Gold" speech (see Selection 22), and thereby won the nomination though he was only thirty-six, was a Populist at heart, and drew much of his support from those who had voted Populist four years before. He was defeated by the Republican William McKinley, but he made the campaign one of the most remarkable ones in our history. Ostensibly fought over the silver issue (McKinley was a high tariff, gold standard candidate), it was really a conflict, the first in a generation, between a nominee who stood for the people and one who stood for the privileged few. There were more of the former, as there are today, but too many of them wanted to be among the few to elect Bryan. Nevertheless, the campaign was significant. It "was at once the last protest of the old agrarian order against industrialism," wrote Samuel Eliot Morison, "and the first attempt of the new order to clean house. Bryan was the bridge between Andrew Jackson and Theodore Roosevelt."

The dominant event of the relatively short period covered by this volume was not economic or political, though it had ramifications in both realms. It was the Spanish-American War, which raised serious questions not only about America's practical foreign policy, but also about its ultimate role in world affairs.

The war itself was a simple matter enough, and for the details the reader is referred to the Chronology of the years 1896-1899. But the questions were not simple at all. The war began partly as a device to raise circulation revenues of a couple of newspapers, but it quickly became a crusade for liberty. So far so good; and if the conflict had been confined to the freeing of Cuba and Puerto Rico from Spanish colonial rule, most Americans would probably have continued to approve it, as by and large they did in 1896 and 1897. But the adventure in the Philippines was another matter; there we seemed to be putting down a revolution, instead of supporting one, and the specter of imperialism naturally raised its head. The debate raged, and became acrimonious; reputations were made and broken; and imperialism became the touchstone (just as free silver had been half a decade before) by which to judge the politics and indeed the virtue of public and private men alike.

The upshot of the war was that the United States acquired some important Pacific bases that, on the whole, were well and fairly administered, so that many of the evils that had been feared did not come to pass. Nevertheless, the acquisition of Manila and Pearl Harbor (the Hawaiian question was a closely related one) probably made a clash with Japan inevitable, a fact that the families of many American boys would eventually rue. (This volume is rich in writings of every kind dealing with the Spanish-American War and the question of America's so-called imperialist ambitions. For the Cuba affair, see Selections 2-3, 18-19, 26-27, 36-44, and 108-109; and for the Philippines and the question of empire see Selections 53-57, 71-75, and 125. And for the background of the controversy over Hawaii, see Volume 11, Selection 89.)

The reader of this volume cannot fail to note the importance of the Spanish-American War in these years around the turn of the century, nor is he likely to miss the continuing relevance of the statements by men of all degrees and opinions to recent events like the war in Vietnam, the problem of European defense and of NATO, the question of the American contributions to the emergent nations of Africa and South America, and so forth. But the volume also deals extensively with another subject of considerable importance, the pointers to which are perhaps not so clear. This is the problem of the city, which, in this volume, comes to the forefront of American attention in a way that it had never done before.

The 1890s did not invent the city, of course, nor were the perennial problems of urban life first recognized during the period. But they were probably talked about in a different way, and above all, they were considered to have a higher priority than had been the case even in the previous decade. (However, see Volume 11, Selections 39, 52, 57, and 93.)

For example, Henry Fletcher discusses the drift to the cities in Selection 12. This was not, strictly speaking, a new phenomenon; the percentage of Americans living in urban rather than rural environments steadily increased from 1800 on. But it is probably fair to say that the phenomenon, as such, was not recognized until the end of the century — nor was it seriously considered as a problem, as something that had to be taken account of, until that time. F. J. Kingsbury's "defense" of the city (see Selection 13) is another example of the new attitude toward the city. Cities were not defended before the 1890s; they did not have to be; no one thought of defending them. It was only when cities became the preeminent American social institution they still are today (though there are perhaps hints that the great age of the city is coming to an end) that men began to attack them, and therefore to defend them. (For a somewhat different viewpoint, see Selection 49.)

Similarly, the problems of city government — of corruption, of protection and the special kind of security that city life may afford but does not necessarily afford, of justice and injustice — also began to be widely discussed in this period. Theodore Roosevelt, then police commissioner of New York, discussed the subject in 1895 (see Selection 14); Josiah Phillips Quincy discussed it (though from a different point of view) in 1897 (see Selection 31); and Robert Woods, Samuel Jones, George Washington Plunkitt, and Lincoln Steffens made contributions, too (see Selections 50, 67, 102, 114, and 116-117). The special problems created by, and for, the swelling immigrant population of cities like New York were also much talked about during this period — see, for example, Jane Addams' comments on the schooling of the children of the foreign-born (Selection 29) and the extract from Jacob Riis' famous work on the New York slums, *How the Other Half Lives* (Selection 93).

The special American contribution to the appearance of cities also began to be widely noticed at this time. The school of architects, led by Louis Sullivan, who changed the face of Chicago in less than a generation and made it the first truly modern-looking city in the country, and perhaps in the world, is treated from several points of view in this and the preceding volume (see Volume 11, Selection 10, and in this volume, Selections 11, 80, and 86). And what can be called the sound of the city is heard here for the first time. Not the whole sound; not the great blooming clackety confusion that every twentieth-century city dweller knows; but the songs of the city, at least, several of which date from this period. George M. Cohan's love for Broadway ("When you are away from old Broadway," he used to say, "you are only camping out") is urban to the core (see Selection 118). The errant ladies whose adventures are recounted in Selection 33 were city girls at heart, whether or not they had been born in the country and only recently exposed to urban pressures and trials. And Paul Dresser's lovely song, "On the Banks of the Wabash, Far Away" (Selection 63), although it is about the country, was written for a city audience — a nostalgic and sentimental one — and was vastly popular among such people. (For other songs about New York in the '90s, see Volume 11, Selection 94.)

The reforming movement — and spirit — known as Progressivism is discussed in the Introduction to the next volume, but the greatest of all Progressives requires mention here, standing out, as he does, head and shoulders — and round eyeglasses — above the rest. This is Theodore Roosevelt, who was mentioned above as New York's police commissioner and who also might have been named as one of the popular heroes of the Spanish-American War (Finley Peter Dunne's Mr. Dooley dubbed him "the President of the Society of the First Man Up San Juan Hill"). Roosevelt's calls for honesty in public life led the Republicans, who thought him an annoying gadfly, to give him the vice-presidential nomination in 1900. Their idea was to rid themselves of a pest; but the assassination of President McKinley in September 1901 put T. R. into the White House. "I told William McKinley it was a mistake to nominate that wild man at Philadelphia," said Republican "Kingmaker" Mark Hanna on the train carrying McKinley's body back to Washington. "Now look, that damned cowboy is President of the United States."

It had been difficult for many people to imagine Roosevelt as chief executive, but he soon showed that he could remain the ebullient Teddy and be President at the same time. He exemplified the "strenuous life" by playing tennis, riding horseback on icy roads (to show the "swivel-chair generals" how it was done), boxing (he lost the sight of an eye in one match), and hunting for big game with old cronies John Burroughs and Thomas Alva Edison. His Cabinet meetings were interrupted, like John F. Kennedy's half a century later, by children bursting in with news that couldn't wait, and he did not blanch when one of them took a pony up in the White House elevator. He liked to entertain, and he made his home a meeting place for whoever happened to interest him. He lived life to the hilt, and the country loved it. Everyone talked and wrote about him. One poem went like this:

> T. R. is spanking a Senator,
> T. R. is chasing a bear,
> T. R. is busting an awful Trust,
> And dragging it from its lair.
> They're calling T. R. a lot of things —
> The men in the private car —
> But the day-coach likes exciting folks
> And the day-coach likes T. R.

It was as if someone had opened a window and let in the fresh air when Theodore Roosevelt got down to running the country. He crowded the trusts; strengthened the legislation to regulate railroads; enacted pure food and drug laws; in general, shook his fist in the face of the startled industrialists. It would be wrong to assume that he was a deeply committed reformer who made war on his own class. He rarely carried any program to its apparently logical conclusion, and he was always ready to accept half a loaf rather than hold out for the whole. (Taft, who succeeded him, and who was considered a traitor to the movement in his time, actually produced more "progressive" legislation than Roosevelt.) Nevertheless, with his colorful personality and his gift for phrase-making — "muckrakers," "certain malefactors of great wealth," "square deal," "speak softly and carry a big stick" — he roused dormant sentiments in many people, and set in motion a crusade that lasted for two decades and, although it suffered a hiatus under the presidents of Roosevelt's own Republican Party during the 1920s, revived again under Franklin Roosevelt and was carried on by his successors.

Theodore Roosevelt was not the radical that many Americans expected, and some feared. Often his most spectacular actions seemed aimed primarily at saving the capitalists from their own foolishness. At other times, he went just far enough to take the sting out of more radical demands. Some historians, indeed, make much of the negative quality of his reforms. As they see it, he did many of the right things for the wrong reasons. It is true that the propertied interests of the country learned to tolerate Roosevelt, and to recognize that his bark was worse than his bite. He was even supported in his campaign for reelection in 1904 by such men as Morgan, Rockefeller, Harriman, Frick, Gould, and Depew.

To leave it at this, however, would also be wrong. By almost any standard, Roosevelt was a great reforming President. He might have done more; but his record of achievement was the best since Lincoln. Moreover, many of his accomplishments had great symbolic importance. His intervention on behalf of the miners in the anthracite strike of 1902, for example, had a profound effect on the labor movement, even though he did not actually do very much for the miners. What mattered is that for the first time a President had announced the people's sovereignty over the great corporations. The principle would sometimes be blurred, but never again lost. Above all, Roosevelt infected the country with a spirit and an enthusiasm that soon flamed independently of him. In a sense, he deserves credit for all of the achievements of Progressivism, for they resulted, in the last analysis, from a national confidence that he more than any other man produced and nourished. (For various writings by and about Theodore Roosevelt in this volume, see Selections 14, 18, 34, 92, 108, 114, 121, and 125; and in Volume 13, Selections 1, 37-39, 51, 62, 69, 77, and 98.)

Chronology : 1895 - 1904

1895

Jan. 22. National Association of Manufacturers holds its first meeting in Cincinnati; meeting is attended by hundreds of manufacturing companies.

March 5. A minority of House Democrats signs "Appeal of the Silver Democrats," framed by Richard P. Bland of Missouri and William Jennings Bryan of Nebraska. Appeal demands immediate return to free coinage of silver at a silver-to-gold ratio of 16 to 1 and increases split between silver and gold advocates in Democratic Party.

October. Stephen Crane at age 23 publishes his second novel, *The Red Badge of Courage*, which wins him international fame; based on one battle of the Civil War, it is an uncannily realistic account written by a man who has never known war. In a decade of popular romances, such as *When Knighthood Was in Flower, The Prisoner of Zenda*, and *Quo Vadis*, Crane's intense realism is especially notable.

First U.S. Supreme Court case involving Sherman Antitrust Act of 1890 is *U.S. v. E. C. Knight Company*. By distinguishing manufacturing from commerce and holding that the Sherman Act does not apply to manufacturing combinations within states, the Court greatly weakens enforcement of the law and removes federal control from all but interstate monopolies.

U.S. Supreme Court invalidates federal income tax in *Pollock v. Farmers' Loan and Trust Company* on ground that personal property taxes are direct taxes.

U.S. Supreme Court upholds use of federal troops and of labor injunctions to maintain movement of U.S. mails and interstate transportation in Pullman Strike of 1894, thus sanctioning the injunction as a strike-breaking device. Decision in effect removes protection of laws extended to labor unions since 1842.

George Westinghouse builds huge power generators at Niagara Falls. Although hydroelectric power has been manufactured there earlier, the Westinghouse generators are the first capable of producing hydroelectric power for a wide area.

Sears, Roebuck Company opens mail-order business; this company and Montgomery Ward and Company, which has been established in 1872 in response to farm, and especially Grange, resentment of profits taken by middlemen, as well as difficulty in reaching urban markets, soon revolutionize rural retailing. Rural free delivery postal service, established in the following year, helps end isolation of farm communities.

Republican editor William Allen White buys the *Emporia* (Kansas) *Daily and Weekly Gazette* and in the following year writes editorial "What's the Matter with Kansas?", a strong criticism of Populism that makes him and his paper famous.

Woodville Latham demonstrates his moving-picture projector, the Pantoptikon, which combines Thomas Edison's Kinetoscope with the magic lantern. Other devices of this and the next few years are the Cinematograph, Phantascope, Vitascope, Kineoptican, Animatograph, Nickelodeon, and Biograph; none run films of more than a few minutes' duration.

Negro Baptist groups, meeting in Atlanta, Georgia, merge to form National Baptist Convention of the U.S.A.

1895 - 1896

Feb. 8, 1895. Since U.S. bond issues of 1894 have produced little public response, and gold reserve has continued to shrink as it is used not only for redeeming bonds but also for operational expenses of government, the secretary of the treasury is forced to buy with bonds $62 million in gold from banking syndicate of J. P. Morgan and August Belmont. Measure is strongly criticized by Populists and bimetallists. **Jan. 6, 1896.** In spite of loan, gold reserve declines to $79 million, and Treasury issues $100 million worth of bonds for purchase. It is quickly bought up, but since Treasury must continue to redeem bonds in gold, the reserve declines to below $90 million in July. By this time, financial depression is waning, but gold hoarding continues until fall election victory of gold-standard advocates.

Feb. 24. Oppressed by Spain and in midst of financial depression resulting from Panic of 1893 and U.S. high protective tariff on sugar, native Cubans begin fight for independence. **June 12.** President Cleveland calls upon sympathetic Americans to avoid giving help to rebels, but savage countermeasures undertaken by Spain and "yellow journalism" of William Randolph Hearst's *New York Morning Journal* and Joseph Pulitzer's *New York World* fan American sympathy for rebels almost to war pitch. **April 6, 1896.** Congress passes resolution granting belligerent rights to Cuba and offering Spain peace arbitration by President. **May 22.** Spain rejects offer.

1895 - 1899

Feb. 20, 1895. Congress approves President Cleveland's recommendation that the U.S. attempt to be named arbitrator of 56-year-old British-Venezuelan dispute over boundary between British Guiana and Venezuela that has continued since 1840. **Nov. 26.** Offer to Great Britain, which cites Monroe Doctrine as justification for U.S. intervention, is rejected by British foreign secretary. **Dec. 17.** President Cleveland presents British-U.S. correspondence to Congress with a statement so belligerent that Great Britain, considering dispute relatively unimportant, consents to appointment of boundary commission. **Feb. 2, 1897.** Great Britain and Venezuela agree to submit dispute to arbitration. **Oct. 3, 1899.** Settlement places boundary at line of first British claims but gives mouth of Orinoco River to Venezuela.

1896

Jan. 4. Utah becomes forty-fifth state of the United States after five unsuccessful attempts, starting in 1856; federal government has been unwilling to consider Utah constitutions until Mormon Church itself outlaws polygamy. Name of state is derived from that of Ute Indians.

April 6. American athlete James B. Connolly, winner of the hop, step, and jump, becomes first Olympic champion in 1,500 years at revival of Olympic Games in Athens, Greece; U.S. team, arriving on day of opening after long sea voyage, wins 9 of the 12 track and field events. Australian E. Flack's winning time in metric mile (1,500 meters), 4 min. 33.2 sec.

April 23. Koster and Bial's Music Hall in New York City holds first public exhibition of moving pictures, a series of short pieces ranging from blond dancers to surf on a beach. It is called "the crown and flower of nineteenth-century magic."

May 27. Prohibition Party meets and nominates Joshua Levering of Maryland for President. National Party (a minority of free-silverites) nominates Charles E. Bentley of Nebraska. **June 18.** Republicans, in convention maneuvered by Marcus A. Hanna, Cleveland industrialist, nominate William McKinley of Ohio for President, with Garret A. Hobart of New Jersey as his running mate. Platform backs gold standard but seeks to appease free-silver faction by promising international free-silver policy. **July 9.** Socialist Labor Party nominates Charles H. Matchett of New York. **July 11.** Free-silver-dominated Democrats, after hearing William Jennings Bryan's impassioned "cross of gold" speech, nominate him for President and Arthur Sewall of Maine for Vice-President. Platform backs free coinage of silver and attacks trusts, the high protective tariff, Supreme Court income tax ruling, and labor injunctions. **July 24.** National Silver Republicans, who have bolted Republicans on adoption of gold platform, back Democratic candidates. **July 25.** People's (Populist) Party also nominates Bryan. **Sept. 3.** National Democratic Party, consisting of gold advocates who have bolted Democratic convention because of free-silver issue, nominates John M. Palmer of Illinois. In campaign Bryan travels 18,000 miles and makes 600 speeches, earning name "the boy orator of the Platte." McKinley conducts "front-porch" campaign, addressing thousands of visitors who come

to his Ohio home, while Hanna, as his campaign manager, distributes millions of leaflets and hires thousands of campaign speakers. Both candidates concentrate almost entirely on money issues.

Nov. 3. In election McKinley wins by popular vote of 7,102,000 to Bryan's 6,493,000; electoral vote is McKinley, 271; Bryan, 176; McKinley carries East and Middle West, and Bryan wins South and West. Republicans keep control of House and Senate.

U.S. Supreme Court in *Plessy* v. *Ferguson* accepts "separate but equal" doctrine of race relations. Distinguishing legal from social rights, Court rules that separate, equal treatment of Negroes under state laws is not discrimination as prohibited by Fourteenth Amendment to Constitution. Decision marks beginning of Jim Crow era.

Duryea brothers, whose automobiles have won most speed competitions in past two years, turn out 10 automobiles in their factory during the year.

Sarah Orne Jewett publishes the last of her revelations of problems in fading Maine settlements, *The Country of the Pointed Firs*, a collection of short stories. *The Damnation of Theron Ware* by Harold Frederic deals with religious hypocrisy of small-town Methodists and creates a sensation.

New York World publishes "The Yellow Kid," forerunner of modern comic strips; words are printed on bright yellow shirt of boy instead of outside of frame as in earlier cartoons.

Former baseball player William Ashley ("Billy") Sunday begins career of evangelism; he conducts 300 revivals in major cities and is heard by 100 million people before his death in 1935.

1896 - 1898

Aug. 6, 1896. Gold is discovered on Bonanza Creek in Yukon Territory, northwest Canada. **June 1897.** News reaches U.S., and thousands of gold seekers join rush to Canada. **July 14.** First large Klondike gold shipment, $750,000, arrives in San Francisco. By 1898 this inaccessible and hitherto almost unpopulated area contains 18,000 people. In spite of frozen ground and other difficult mining conditions, $22 million is mined in peak production year 1900.

1897

Jan. 12. National Monetary Conference, meeting at Indianapolis, endorses existing gold standard and appoints commission that later submits to Congress a plan for U.S. monetary system. U.S. begins period of prosperity with settlement of free-silver question in previous year's election.

March 2. Immigration bill that requires literacy tests for immigrants is vetoed by President Cleveland on the ground that it is a "radical departure from our national policy."

July 7. Dingley Tariff raises duties to new high levels, averaging almost 60 percent on the value of goods imported.

In *U.S. v. Trans-Missouri Freight Association*, the Supreme Court rules that association of 18 railroads formed to fix transportation rates is in violation of the Sherman Antitrust Act; railroads' argument that only combinations that restrain commerce unreasonably are illegal is rejected at this time, but it later becomes the policy of the Court.

First practical subway in the U.S. is completed in Boston. Plans for New York City subway have been rejected the year before as too great a financial burden on the city.

Congregational minister Charles M. Sheldon publishes *In His Steps,* a collection of his sermons in which he has shown young people what they would do if for a year they emulated Jesus Christ. To the present day, book has sold about 8 million copies in 20 languages.

Edwin Arlington Robinson publishes *The Children of the Night,* which includes poems from *The Torrent and the Night Before* of the previous year.

1897 - 1902

William James, leader of Pragmatist movement, publishes collections of his lectures and essays: *The Will to Believe and Other Essays in Popular Philosophy; Human Immortality; Talks to Teachers on Psychology and to Students on Some of Life's Ideals;* and *The Varieties of Religious Experience.*

1898

Jan. 12. Cubans loyal to Spain riot in Havana in protest against policy of new Spanish government, which has made extensive concessions to rebels in civil war. Policy is also disapproved by rebels, who want independence, and by interventionists in the U.S., who believe U.S. control of Cuba is vital to U.S. domination of the Caribbean.

Feb. 9. William Randolph Hearst's *New York Journal,* rabidly interventionist, publishes private letter from Spanish minister to the U.S., Dupuy de Lôme, that has been stolen by Cuban revolutionists; letter describes President McKinley as weak and further inflames U.S. anti-Spanish sentiment. De Lôme resigns his post immediately.

Feb. 15. U.S. battleship *Maine,* which has arrived at Havana in January to protect

American residents and property during revolution in Cuba, is blown up in the harbor, with a loss of 260 men. Perpetrator of explosion is never discovered, but American people are persuaded that Spain is responsible, and incident inflames U.S. anti-Spanish feeling, making intervention in revolution a certainty. "Remember the Maine!" becomes cry of interventionists.

Feb. 25. Pacific fleet, under Commodore George Dewey, is ordered to the Philippines by Assistant Secretary of the Navy Theodore Roosevelt, with instructions to engage the Spanish fleet there if war breaks out. .

March 27. In spite of strong interventionist feeling in the U.S., President McKinley, in effort to maintain peace, orders minister to Spain, Stewart L. Woodford, to deny that U.S. desires annexation of Cuba but wants only cessation of brutalities, with armistice until October 1. **April 9.** Spain agrees to U.S. demands.

April 11. Yielding to public and political pressure, McKinley, in reversal of his anti-war policy, asks for congressional resolution authorizing use of U.S. Army and Navy to force Spain to leave Cuba and declares Cuba independent. **April 20.** McKinley signs resolution passed by Congress, but Spain breaks off diplomatic relations with the U.S. before Woodford can deliver ultimatum.

April 22. U.S. orders blockade of all Cuban ports, seizes one Spanish ship as first capture of war, and authorizes a volunteer force of 200,000 men to build up Army. One unit formed under Volunteer Army Act is "Rough Riders," commanded by Colonel Leonard Wood and Lieutenant Colonel Theodore Roosevelt, who has been a notably ardent advocate of annexation and has resigned his post as assistant secretary of the navy. At this time, U.S. Navy is rela-

tively strong and well equipped, with both Atlantic and Pacific squadrons, but Army consists of only 28,000 men commanded by 2,100 officers and is inadequately equipped, especially for campaign in tropics.

April 24. Refusing to recognize Cuban independence as demanded by U.S. Congress, Spain declares war on U.S. **April 25.** U.S. declares war on Spain retroactively to April 21, when Spain has broken off diplomatic relations.

May 1. U.S. Pacific fleet destroys, captures, or cripples all 10 ships of the Spanish Pacific fleet at Manila in seven-hour battle that results in more than 300 Spanish deaths and 7 wounded for the U.S.

May 12. Louisiana continues Southern reaction against Reconstruction when it adopts new constitution that virtually disfranchises Negroes by property and literacy tests for voting; whites, however, are protected against restrictions by grandfather clause, which exempts descendants of men who voted before 1867.

May 19. Spanish Atlantic fleet, four cruisers and three destroyers, having sailed from Cape Verde Islands, arrives in harbor of Santiago de Cuba and anchors under protection of Cuban artillery. **May 29.** U.S. naval force from Key West, Florida, blocks entrance to harbor, bottling up Spanish ships.

May 24. U.S. battleship *Oregon* arrives at Key West after dramatic run from Pacific to join Atlantic fleet; 67-day journey, necessary for route around Cape Horn, arouses the U.S. to importance of a canal across the Isthmus of Panama.

June 1. Congress passes Erdman Arbitration Act, which authorizes federal mediation in disputes between interstate carriers and their employees and prohibits blacklisting of union members by interstate transportation companies.

June 10. Congress passes War Revenue Bill that authorizes taxes on such items as tobacco, liquor, and flour and a government bond issue of $400 million; sale of bonds, however, reaches only half the authorized amount.

June 15. Six hundred U.S. Marines defeat Spanish forces in Battle of Guantanamo Bay, Cuba.

June 20. Island of Guam in the Pacific Ocean surrenders to commander of U.S.S. *Charleston;* on previous day, island has been shelled, but Spanish commander, unaware of war, has apologized to Captain Glass of the *Charleston* for not returning the salute, saying that there is no ammunition on the island.

June 22. Expeditionary force of 17,000 men under General William Shafter arrives in Cuba and begins landing operations east of Santiago. **July 1.** In attack on well-defended village of El Caney, about 7,000 U.S. troops battle 600 defenders for one day before capturing it. On same day, Theodore Roosevelt leads his "Rough Riders" (unmounted) in impetuous charge up Kettle Hill in attack on San Juan Hill that is successful, but casualties of two battles are nearly 1,600 men. Roosevelt becomes a national hero for attack but does not endear himself to his superiors. With capture of hills overlooking Santiago, U.S. can use artillery against city, as well as against Spanish fleet in the harbor.

July 3. Spanish fleet, ordered not to surrender, tries to run blockade of five U.S. battleships and two cruisers. In four-hour battle along coast, Spanish ships are destroyed, with more than 2,000 killed, wounded, and captured. American casualties are 1 killed and 1 wounded.

July 7. President McKinley signs annexation of Hawaii bill, passed by joint resolution in Congress; previously blocked by Cleveland and the Senate, annexation has been favored by President McKinley, especially after Japan has protested it. Joint resolution, which requires only a simple majority, is resorted to in order to avoid defeat by the Senate. Hawaii becomes a U.S. territory in 1900.

July 17. Santiago's 24,000 defenders surrender to U.S.

July 21. Four U.S. ships bombard and take Nipe, in last Cuban sea battle of the war.

July 25. General Wesley Merritt arrives with land reinforcements at Manila Bay to join U.S. fleet, which, lacking army support, has been blockading Manila since naval victory.

July 25-Aug. 12. U.S. forces take Puerto Rico, having met only minor resistance.

Aug. 4. U.S. War Department orders Cuban expeditionary force back to Long Island, New York, to escape further spread of food poisoning and disease, which has attacked 4,200 troops, 3,000 of whom have yellow fever.

Aug. 12. U.S. proposal, agreed to by Spain, calls for: Paris as place of treaty negotiations; end of hostilities; relinquishment of sovereignty by Spain over Cuba; cession by Spain of Puerto Rico and one of the Ladrone Islands to the U.S.; and U.S. occupation of Manila until control of the Philippines can be decided by treaty.

Aug. 13. U.S. forces and Filipino guerrillas, unaware that hostilities have ceased, fight battle for Manila. Surrender of the city on following day marks the end of 100 years of Filipino rebellion against Spain.

Oct. 25. Although U.S. opinion on the Philippines has been divided at beginning of Paris meeting on October 1, President McKinley decides to demand that Spain cede the islands to the U.S. **Dec. 10.** Final terms of treaty, although Spain has strongly opposed Philippine demand, are: cession of the Philippines for payment of $20 million; surrender of all claims to Cuba, making it independent; Spanish assumption of the Cuban public debt of $400 million; and cession of Guam and Puerto Rico to the U.S. Treaty of Paris marks the end of Spanish rule in the Western Hemisphere.

Almost all important battles in Spanish-American War have been naval actions. Although the U.S. Army has been undermanned, poorly commanded, inadequately supplied, and insufficiently trained, the Navy has been vastly superior to Spain's. Of almost 5,500 U.S. deaths, fewer than 400 men have been killed in battle. More than 90 percent are victims of disease. Direct cost of war has been $250 million.

In *Holden* v. *Hardy,* a decision that becomes precedent for validity of state control of labor conditions, the U.S. Supreme Court upholds Utah law that sets maximum hours for miners, pointing out that mining is an especially dangerous industry.

The Supreme Court finds that a child born of Chinese parents in the U.S. may not be deported under the Chinese Exclusion Act, since native citizenship is not dependent on race or color.

Adolphus Busch builds the first Diesel engine in U.S., using foreign patents rights.

Observations of Finley Peter Dunne's Mr. Dooley, homely philosopher, for the first time attract national attention on publication of his comments on Dewey's victory at Manila, although observations have appeared regularly in Chicago papers for six years. Mr. Dooley's Irish-dialect comments on public affairs have enormous influence in following period. *David Harum,* novel of rural life, is published after death of its author, Edward Noyes Westcott; popular up to the present day, it is the beginning of so-called b'gosh school of fiction.

First group exhibit by American Impressionist painters, New York City. Group calling itself "Ten American Painters" includes some artists who have participated in 1877 exhibit of Society of American Artists.

1899

Jan. 15. Edwin Markham publishes social protest poem, "The Man with the Hoe," in the *San Francisco Examiner;* within one week it appears in newspapers throughout the U.S.; it becomes the most popular poem published up to this date in the U.S.

Feb. 6. Treaty of Paris is ratified by the Senate after heated debate between imperialists, who emphasize strategic advantage of U.S. control of the Philippines and fear that other nations will establish themselves on the islands, and anti-imperialists, who fight against acquiring territory peopled by alien races and believe that acquisition is contrary to self-government principles of the U.S. William Jennings Bryan is finally able to persuade opponents to vote for treaty, since by its terms resolution of Philippine question can be postponed.

Feb. 17. Anti-Imperialist League is founded; it unites liberal leaders of all U.S. parties to oppose expansion beyond the continental limits into foreign territories.

May 18-July 29. U.S. attends disarmament and arbitration conference at The Hague with 25 other nations invited by Czar Nicholas II of Russia. No agreement on arms results, but Permanent Court of Arbitration is established. Arbitration is not made compulsory, however, and U.S. insists on its right to uphold the Monroe Doctrine when disputes involving the Western Hemisphere occur.

Dec. 2. Britain, Germany, and the U.S. sign Samoan treaty, dividing Samoa between Germany and the U.S., after Britain has withdrawn its claims in exchange for German territory in other Pacific areas and in West Africa. U.S. part of Samoa, governed by the Navy, becomes an important naval base.

The U.S. formally claims Wake Island, an atoll in the Central Pacific Ocean, for use as a cable station; it has been mapped in 1841 by a U.S. exploring expedition.

Educator John Dewey, head of University of Chicago's Laboratory School, begins revolution in American education with publication of *The School and Society*, which expresses, among other concepts, his belief that education must begin with actual experience rather than with the learning of traditional subjects.

Economist Thorstein Veblen publishes his first book, *The Theory of the Leisure Class*, while teaching at the University of Chicago.

Louis Sullivan designs Schlesinger & Mayer (now Carson, Pirie Scott & Company) department store in Chicago; it is the first major commercial modern-style building in the U.S.

1899 - 1902

Feb. 4. Filipinos, incensed at failure of the U.S. to grant them immediate independence, begin armed revolt against U.S. occupation forces; about 70,000 men on each side are engaged. Organized resistance ends by December, but guerrilla warfare continues until the spring of 1902 despite capture of Filipino leader in March 1901 and

American assurances that military occupation will cease and that independence will be granted after Filipinos have learned to govern themselves.

1900

March 6. Social Democrats meet in Indianapolis and nominate Eugene V. Debs of Indiana for President and Job Harriman of California for Vice-President. May 10. People's (Anti-Fusion) Party meets at Cincinnati and nominates Wharton Barker of Pennsylvania for President and Ignatius Donnelly of Minnesota for Vice-President. May 10. Fusion Populist Party nominates William Jennings Bryan for President and Charles A. Towne (who later withdraws in favor of Adlai E. Stevenson) for Vice-President. June 2. Socialist Laborites at New York nominate Joseph P. Maloney of Massachusetts for President, with Valentine Remmel of Pennsylvania as his running mate. June 19. Republicans at Philadelphia renominate President McKinley and, against his will, Theodore Roosevelt as his running mate. Roosevelt fears that he will be buried politically in the Vice-Presidency. Platform is pro-gold standard and pro-administration foreign policy and stresses need for canal across Panamanian isthmus. June 27. Prohibitionists nominate John G. Woolley of Illinois and Henry B. Metcalf of Rhode Island. July 5. Democrats also nominate William Jennings Bryan, but with Adlai E. Stevenson as his running mate. Platform is anti-imperialist and again demands free coinage of silver. McKinley repeats pattern of previous campaign, never leaving his home, but Roosevelt travels 21,000 miles, making 700 speeches, frequently wearing his "Rough Rider" hat.

March 14. Congress passes Gold Standard Act, making gold the only currency standard in the U.S. Act is made possible by increase in production of gold in the Klondike and South Africa. The U.S. dollar is valued at 25.8 grains of gold, and gold reserve of $150 million is to be held separately from other funds. Small-town national banks are authorized in order to appease farm interests.

March 20. Secretary of State John Hay announces that Germany, Russia, Britain, France, Italy, and Japan have accepted the Open Door Policy for China. Weakness of China has enabled foreign countries to force commercial and territorial concessions from it, and the U.S. has feared that they will discriminate against other powers in areas under their influence. In the previous year Hay has asked the powers to agree to protect Chinese independence and commercial equality for all powers in Chinese trade. Assurances have been vague, but Hay accepts them as approval.

April 12. Congress passes Foraker Act, which creates civil government for Puerto Rico, makes the island an unorganized territory, and extends the Dingley Tariff to include the island.

June. Peking, China, is occupied by Chinese groups known as Boxers, who are rebelling against foreign intrusion in China. Boxers besiege foreign legations of the city for several months and, with the encouragement of the empress dowager of China, kill scores of foreign missionaries, thousands of Chinese Christians ("secondary foreign devils"), and the German minister to China.

July 3. Secretary Hay, afraid that other powers will withdraw support of the Open Door Policy using the Boxer Rebellion as justification, sends circular letter stating that the U.S. desires a solution that will bring permanent safety and peace to China and safeguard equal and impartial world trade in all parts of the empire.

Aug. 14. International military expedi-

tion, including the U.S., occupies Peking, loots the city, rescues missionaries, and disperses remnants of Boxers.

September. Orville and Wilbur Wright fly their first full-scale glider at Kitty Hawk, North Carolina; its "warped wings" are first successful device built for lateral control in flying.

Nov. 6. President McKinley and Theodore Roosevelt win election with popular vote of 7,218,000 to Bryan's 6,357,000. Electoral vote is McKinley, 292; Bryan, 155; Republicans keep control of House and Senate.

Nov. 15. Andrew Carnegie founds the Carnegie Institute of Technology in Pittsburgh.

Dr. Walter Reed is named head of U.S. Army Yellow Fever Commission; he and his associates experiment with volunteers in Cuba and prove that yellow fever is transmitted by mosquitoes. Their findings make possible the virtual elimination of yellow fever from Cuba, the U.S., and, later, the Panama Canal Zone.

International Ladies' Garment Workers' Union is founded in New York City to fight a 70-hour workweek and a home-sewing system in which women earn a maximum of 30 cents per day.

Olds Company of Detroit begins first mass production of automobiles, turning out 400 cars in first year. Production in second year is 1,600 and in third, 4,000.

Doubleday and Company publishes first novel of Theodore Dreiser, *Sister Carrie*, realistic story of the deterioration of a man caused by an immoral girl. Probably because of disapproval of publisher's wife, Company prints only 1,000 copies and fails

to promote book. Effect on Dreiser is a nervous breakdown and thoughts of suicide; he does not write another novel for 11 years.

First "little theater" in the U.S. is built in Chicago for the Hull House Players, a group sponsored by Jane Addams' social settlement, whose residents include actors, musicians, and artists, as well as social workers.

Carry Nation, prompted by her marriage to an alcoholic, begins her crusade of "hatchetation" of "joints"; singing hymns, praying, and smashing equipment with her hatchet, she wrecks many saloons in Kansas and moves on to San Francisco and the East. Arrested 30 times for disturbing the peace, she is an embarrassment to the temperance organizations, which do not support her, although she contributes to them.

At the turn of the century, census shows population of 75,995,000, an increase of almost 21 percent over 1890; figure includes 3,688,000 immigrants arrived since 1890. About 40 percent of population lives in places of 2,500 or more. New York is the largest city, with a population of 3,437,000; Chicago is second, with 1,699,000, followed by Philadelphia, with 1,294,000. Since 1890 almost 4 million more people have moved west of the Mississippi River than to the East. At this time life expectancy at birth is 48 years for males and 51 years for females.

Illiteracy of persons over 10 years old in the U.S. has decreased to 10.7 percent as compared with 20 percent in 1870. About 72 percent of children between 5 and 17 years old are enrolled in schools.

Immigration to the U.S. since 1820 has been 17,286,000 from Europe, 370,000 from Asia, 1,219,000 from Canada and Lat-

in America, and 249,000 from all other places.

Since 1870, 430 million acres of land have been occupied by settlers, and 225 million acres have been improved and cultivated; this is more than in the entire period prior to 1870, beginning with settlement at Jamestown in 1607.

In period since the Civil War, railroad lines have increased from 37,000 miles to 193,000; three and a half times as much freight is carried by rail; tonnage of ships in coastal and internal trade has almost doubled, notably Great Lakes shipping, which now carries ores, as well as grains.

By this year the U.S. has about 150,000 miles of surfaced roads, and 8,000 passenger automobiles are registered.

Although electric power is produced by various means, its use is limited because of difficulty of transmission. By this year the longest electric power line in the U.S. is from Santa Ana, California, to Los Angeles, a distance of 35 miles.

Steel output is about 10 million tons, with steel for structural and other products exceeding steel for rails by two to one. More steel is produced by the open-hearth process than by the Bessemer process at this time. Hydraulic presses rather than steam hammers are in general use for forging.

Total value of farm machinery has tripled since 1870, with the invention of binders, specialized harrows, various plows, cream separators, and giant combines for harvesting and threshing. Almost nine times as much commercial fertilizer is used as in 1870.

Number of farms and farm acreage in the U.S. have doubled since 1870, and farm regions have become specialized. About half the wheat and barley, 40 percent of the corn, and almost all the flaxseed are grown in the west North Central states; most wool is produced in the Mountain states; a third of the oats is produced in the Middle West; three-quarters of the buckwheat is grown in New York and Pennsylvania; three-quarters of the peanuts in North Carolina and Virginia; three-quarters of the tobacco in the Southern border states; three-quarters of the rice in Louisiana; more than half the milk in Illinois, Wisconsin, Iowa, and New York. Meat-packing is concentrated in the Middle West, especially since the invention of refrigerator cars.

By 1900 the U.S. is exporting three times as much as at the end of the Civil War; major exports are cotton, meat, grain and grain products, petroleum products, and machinery; about three-quarters of U.S. exports go to Europe, and remainder is about evenly divided among the other continents. Imports, about half of which are from Europe, in 1900 are double those of 1866.

Dime novels have been enormously successful during this period; books such as those written under the pen name "Nick Carter" are turned out by many otherwise serious writers; publishers of these books have been inspired by the success of the penny dreadfuls in England.

1900 - 1901

April 7. President McKinley instructs the second (Taft) Philippine Commission to bear in mind that the government that is being established "is designed . . . for the happiness, peace, and prosperity of the people of the Philippine Islands." In following year government, staffed by Filipinos as well as the Commission, becomes well enough organized so that military government is withdrawn in July 1901, except in areas where guerrilla fighting continues.

1901

Jan. 10. First significant oil strike in Texas when Spindletop gusher blows in near Beaumont; discovery marks the beginning of change from domination of the state by cattle and railroad interests to control by oilmen.

Sept. 6. Although extraordinary precautions have been taken because an assassination attempt is suspected, President McKinley is shot by anarchist Leon Czolgosz while at the Pan-American Exposition in Buffalo, New York. Sept. 14. Although doctors have at first thought his condition not serious, gangrene affects two stomach wounds, and McKinley dies. Vice-President Theodore Roosevelt takes oath of office as twenty-sixth President.

Sept. 7. U.S. and other involved nations sign agreement placing Boxer Rebellion indemnity at $333 million. U.S. share is nearly $25 million, but the U.S. later cancels $18 million of debt. China spends this $18 million of U.S. share to send Chinese students to U.S. colleges and universities.

Oct. 16. President Roosevelt arouses wide resentment in the South by giving a luncheon for Negro educator Booker T. Washington.

October. Citizenship is granted to Indians of Five Civilized Tribes (Cherokees, Creeks, Choctaws, Chickasaws, and Seminoles), who have been moved to Oklahoma from the Southeast and later deprived of much of their land by unscrupulous practices of settlers and U.S. government agencies.

Nov. 18. U.S. and Britain sign second Hay-Pauncefote Treaty, which replaces Clayton-Bulwer Treaty of 1850 for joint rights in any canal across the Isthmus of Panama. Treaty of 1901 and related agreements grant the U.S. the right to build, operate, and fortify canal, while providing equal access for peaceful purposes to all nations.

Nov. 27. Secretary of War Elihu Root, in reorganization of the Army because of shortcomings revealed by the Spanish-American War, establishes Army War College to provide advanced instruction and training for officers.

Dec. 3. First annual message of President Roosevelt announces campaign for regulation of large business combinations, proposing to retain combinations but prevent abuses by them.

In "Insular Cases" Supreme Court holds that territories gained by the U.S. in the Spanish-American War are neither parts of the U.S. nor foreign countries; that congressional authorization is necessary to impose duties on goods shipped to the U.S. from Puerto Rico; that goods shipped to Puerto Rico from the U.S. are duty free; and that citizens of such territories do not automatically have the rights of U.S. citizens, since such rights must be granted by Congress.

Social Democratic Party under Eugene V. Debs and reform arm of Socialist Labor Party merge to form Socialist Party.

U.S. Steel Corporation is organized by financiers headed by Elbert H. Gary and J. P. Morgan; it consolidates Carnegie Company and other properties, such as coal mines, iron ore mines, and railroads. Capitalized at over $1 billion, it is the world's largest industrial combination up to this time.

Reginald A. Fessenden patents radio transmitter in the U.S., although first wireless transmission has been achieved by Guglielmo Marconi six years earlier in Europe.

Fessenden's improvement is the beginning of radio communication across water, especially with ships.

John D. Rockefeller and his son, John D. Rockefeller, Jr., found, as one of many philanthropic organizations they create, the Rockefeller Institute for Medical Research.

King C. Gillette begins manufacture of modern safety razor with disposable blades.

1901 - 1903

March 2, 1901. Army Appropriation Bill, including provisions relating to Cuba known as the Platt Amendment, is passed by Congress. Cuban constitution drawn up in the same year, prior to planned evacuation by American troops, does not include provisions for future relations with the U.S. Cuba has been informed that the U.S. will not withdraw unless such provisions are included. **June 12.** Cuba adds provisions to constitution that make the island unofficially a protectorate of the U.S. **May 20, 1902.** U.S. withdraws from Cuba. **May 22, 1903.** Platt Amendment is added to U.S.-Cuban treaty to prevent its being dropped from Cuban constitution.

Frank Norris publishes *The Octopus,* which deals with struggle between wheat growers and the railroads; it is first novel of planned wheat trilogy. Second book, *The Pit,* is based on Chicago grain market. Norris dies before writing third novel, *The Wolf,* in which he has planned to picture a European famine relieved by wheat.

Jan. 24. U.S. signs treaty with Denmark for purchase of the Danish West Indies, but treaty fails in Danish Parliament. The transaction for the Virgin Islands (as they are known after purchase) is finally completed in 1917.

Feb. 19. Attorney General Philander C.

Knox announces that at the request of President Roosevelt the U.S. will prosecute the Northern Securities Company, a railroad holding company headed by J. P. Morgan, John D. Rockefeller, James J. Hill, and E. H. Harriman, for restraint of interstate commerce under the Sherman Antitrust Act. McKinley has failed to enforce the Act in spite of the extensive growth of holding companies during his administration.

1902

February. Dr. Charles W. Stiles, heavily supported by the Rockefeller Foundation, instigates antihookworm campaign throughout the South when he discovers that poor whites are not lazy but are weakened by the widespread invasion of the parasite.

March 6. Office of Permanent Bureau of the Census is established; it later becomes a part of the Department of Commerce.

May 12. Following refusal of mine operators to arbitrate when anthracite coal miners of Pennsylvania ask 20 percent wage increase and eight-hour day, about 150,000 United Mine Workers strike. **Oct. 16.** In first federal government action on behalf of labor, President Roosevelt appoints commission to settle strike. **Oct. 21.** Strike is discontinued, with miners, in March 1903, being awarded 10 percent wage increase but not recognition of union. Mine owners' stand against arbitration at beginning of strike arouses public opinion against large trusts.

June 2. Oregon becomes the first state in the U.S. to adopt general initiative and referendum, by which the people can override legislative rulings and initiate popular vote on legislation. Groups hostile to machine rule put through similar reforms, as well as reforms in primary elections, in other states in following few years.

June 17. Reclamation (Newlands) Act reserves funds from sale of public lands in 16 Southern and Western states to finance irrigation in dry areas; since Act also gives the President the right to retain public lands for the public, it is the beginning of systematic establishment of public parks.

June 28. Congress passes Spooner (Isthmian Canal) Act, which authorizes the financing and construction of the Panama Canal and appropriates $40 million for the purpose; in case the U.S. is unable to reach agreement for lease of Colombian area from New Panama Canal Company of France and negotiate treaty with Colombia (Panama being a province of Colombia), Act authorizes building of canal through Nicaragua.

July 1. Congress passes Philippine Government Act, which sets up a civil government under aid and supervision of the U.S.; islands become an unorganized territory. Taft Commission, appointed earlier by President McKinley, becomes supervisory agency.

Dec. 12. At the request of Venezuelan dictator Cipriano Castro, President Roosevelt intervenes in dispute between Venezuela and Britain, Germany, and Italy. During Castro's regime, Venezuela has become heavily indebted to the European nations, and they have finally sent warships to blockade Venezuelan ports. Bombardment of ports has led Castro to request that the U.S. propose arbitration. Settlement of dispute is achieved by the Hague Court in 1904.

Maryland passes the first workmen's compensation law, but it is invalidated later by the Supreme Court.

Arthur D. Little with his associates patents rayon (cellulose ester) and artificial silk; manufacture by the American Viscose Company in 1910 makes rayon the first commercially successful synthetic textile fiber.

Henry James, returning to his earlier theme, Americans abroad, after a period of portraying English society, publishes *The Wings of the Dove* and, in the next two years, *The Ambassadors* and *The Golden Bowl.*

Theodore Roosevelt publishes *Outdoor Pastimes of an American Hunter,* marking the beginning of an open-air-living vogue. He is joined by Stewart Edward White, John Muir, and John Burroughs, who publish many books and articles on outdoor living. Owen Wister publishes *The Virginian,* a novel of outdoor life in Wyoming; it becomes a best seller immediately.

1903

Jan. 24. Great Britain and the U.S. agree to form joint commission to settle dispute over ownership of Alaskan panhandle, claimed by both U.S. and Canada. During deliberations of commission, President Roosevelt hints at use of military force if the U.S. is not satisfied with decision. **Oct.** Commission accepts U.S. claims, giving U.S. ocean outlets of panhandle.

Feb. 11. Expedition Act is passed to speed up action on federal antitrust suits; it gives antitrust cases precedence over others on Circuit Court schedules.

Feb. 14. Congress establishes U.S. Army General Staff Corps with the responsibility of preparing and carrying out military plans to eliminate conflict that has hitherto existed between commanding general and the secretary of war.

Feb. 14. Ninth Cabinet office is created

when President Roosevelt forms Department of Commerce and Labor; it includes Bureau of Corporations, authorized to investigate companies involved in interstate commerce. Department becomes two separate agencies ten years later.

Feb. 19. Elkins Act prohibits railroads from varying published rates and specifies punishment for shippers, agents, and railway personnel who accept or give rebates, a device that has been used to avoid prosecution for rate deviations in interstate commerce.

Feb. 23. For the first time a federal police power is ruled greater than that of the states when the Supreme Court upholds federal ruling that lottery tickets cannot be transported by mail from one state to another; up to this time, the federal government has regulated but not prohibited interstate commerce.

March 17. U.S. Senate ratifies Hay-Herran Treaty, which provides for a $10 million initial payment and renewable 99-year lease of land for the Panama Canal at rental of $250,000 per year. **Aug. 12.** Colombian Senate rejects Treaty because money is to be paid to New Panama Canal Company, and Senate wants delay until Company's charter expires, so that Colombia will receive payment.

May 23. Wisconsin enacts first direct primary election system in the U.S. Eventually system is adopted by almost all states, but procedures differ widely.

July 4. First service on Pacific cable is established when President Roosevelt sends around-the-world message that returns to him in 12 minutes.

Aug. 1. First transcontinental automobile journey is completed; Packard car arrives in New York 52 days after leaving San Francisco, having traveled all the way under its own power.

Nov. 2. President Roosevelt orders warships to Panama to protect right of "free and uninterrupted transit" across the isthmus; Roosevelt has given tacit approval to revolution brewing in Colombia that has been instigated by members of New Panama Canal Company and native elements. **Nov. 3.** Province of Panama declares itself independent of Colombia. **Nov. 6.** The U.S. recognizes the Republic of Panama. **Nov. 13.** Minister from Panama, formerly an officer of New Panama Canal Company, is received in Washington.

Nov. 18. The U.S. signs Hay-Bunau-Varilla Treaty with Panama. Treaty gives the U.S. perpetual lease on 10-mile strip across the isthmus for payment of $10 million and $250,000 annually to begin nine years later. The U.S. is to guarantee Panamanian independence and neutrality of the Canal Zone.

Jack London publishes his most popular book, *The Call of the Wild,* and in the next year *The Sea-Wolf.* Kate Douglas Wiggin publishes *Rebecca of Sunnybrook Farm;* a sentimental book for girls, it eventually sells more than a million copies in the U.S. and is widely translated.

The Great Train Robbery, produced by Edwin Porter, is first movie to use motion of camera, as well as of actors, the first "Western," and the first film with a plot.

Alfred Stieglitz founds magazine *Camera Work* to advance photography as a fine art.

1903 - 1906

Dec. 17, 1903. Orville Wright is first man to fly a powered heavier-than-air machine when he stays aloft for 12 seconds in an airplane designed by himself and his brother Wilbur. Improved airplane flown in 1905 stays up for 38 minutes and travels 24 miles. Machine is patented in 1906.

Ida M. Tarbell, pioneer muckraker, begins publishing *The History of the Standard Oil Company* in *McClure's* magazine. Lincoln Steffens publishes *The Shame of the Cities,* also in *McClure's,* which, like other widely read magazines, publishes in this period exposures of graft and corruption in government and industry. Name "muckrakers" originates with Theodore Roosevelt, who, when pure sensationalism begins to replace efforts at reform, compares some authors with the man with the muckrake in *Pilgrim's Progress.*

1904

Jan. 4. U.S. Supreme Court holds that although citizens of Puerto Rico are not citizens of the U.S., neither are they aliens, and they may not be denied admission to the continental U.S.

Feb. 29. President Roosevelt appoints seven-man commission to take charge of construction of the Panama Canal. **May 4.** Canal strip is legally transferred to the U.S.

March 11. Morton Street Tunnel under the Hudson River nears completion when the shield from the New Jersey end touches that of the New York end, and William G. McAdoo becomes first man to cross the river below the surface.

March 14. In *Northern Securities* v. *United States,* first of more than 30 antitrust actions begun by Roosevelt administration, Supreme Court dissolves holding company formed by means of stock transaction to control four of the six railroad systems running from the Central states to the Pacific Coast; no criminal prosecutions follow. This case and previous one against Trans-Missouri Freight Association in 1897 revive the Sherman Antitrust Act of 1890.

May 5. Socialist Party nominates Eugene V. Debs of Indiana for President at Chicago. **June 21.** Republicans meet at Chicago and nominate Theodore Roosevelt by acclaim, with Charles W. Fairbanks of Indiana as his running mate; platform is conservative Republican line. **June 29.** Prohibition Party meets at Indianapolis and nominates Dr. Silas C. Swallow of Pennsylvania. **July 2.** Socialist Labor Party meets and nominates Charles H. Corregan of New York. **July 5.** People's Party nominates Thomas E. Watson of Georgia. **July 9.** Democrats at St. Louis nominate Alton B. Parker of New York for President and Henry G. Davis of West Virginia for Vice-President; platform favors antitrust action and increased powers for Interstate Commerce Commission. **Aug. 31.** Continental Party meets at Chicago and nominates Austin Holcomb of Georgia.

Oct. 27. First section of New York City subway begins service from City Hall to 145th Street; line later becomes first subway in the world to run both underground and underwater.

Nov. 8. President Roosevelt and Fairbanks win election with popular vote of 7,628,000 to 5,084,000 for Parker and Davis. Five minor parties poll only 6 percent of vote. Electoral vote is Roosevelt, 336, Parker, 140; Parker wins only states of the Solid South, and Republicans are still in control of House and Senate. On election night, Roosevelt promises that he will consider his first partial term a first term and will not accept another nomination for the Presidency.

Unity Temple in Chicago, designed by Frank Lloyd Wright, is completed; it is first building designed entirely for poured concrete construction. Architect Bertram Goodhue's "Gothic" chapel, built for U.S. Military Academy at West Point, gives impetus to vogue for Gothic churches and academic buildings.

1904 - 1907

Dec. 6, 1904. President Roosevelt, when European powers threaten to intervene in Caribbean to collect debts owed by the Dominican Republic, asserts right of the U.S. to exercise international police powers in the Western Hemisphere when forced to do so by international conflicts. Statement, later called the Roosevelt Corollary to the Monroe Doctrine, changes Doctrine from prohibition of intervention by European powers to right of intervention by the U.S. **Jan. 20, 1905.** U.S. and the Dominican Republic sign agreement giving the U.S. charge of debt payments and customs finances of the Dominican Republic, which President Roosevelt carries out, although agreement is rejected by the U.S. Senate. **Feb. 25, 1907.** Permanent treaty is ratified between the U.S. and the Dominican Republic, which includes 1905 agreement, and U.S. withdraws from the island in following July.

Agriculture and Natural Resources

Farming came to North America with colonization and, until well into the period of mass industrialization, agriculture was recognized as the greatest single economic resource of the United States. The grains of the middle and northern states and the tobacco and cotton of the South dominated both domestic and foreign commerce. Apart from lumber, which seemed more of a nuisance than a resource to the expanding, westward moving population, the nation's other resources — coal, iron, copper, petroleum, silver, gold, and numerous other metals of more recent utility — were discovered and put to use as the frontier moved west and industrialization increased. It was the wide availability of natural resources as well as the willingness to use them that made the United States the land of opportunity.

The resources were not always wisely used. The continent seemed so vast, and its contents so unlimited, that the population tended to exploit rather than utilize much of what was available. Land was frequently farmed until it was exhausted, whereupon the farmers moved to uncultivated soil to begin again. Vast stands of timber were destroyed and not replaced. Mines were worked, depleted, and forgotten. Wildlife was killed off with no thought of its eventual extinction. It was only gradually that conservation measures were accepted and put to use, and this often against powerful opposition. Since World War II the manifold threats to the environment have been more widely recognized and steps taken under government sponsorship to rehabilitate our surroundings to assure long-term use of a still abundant supply of natural and agricultural resources.

Maps prepared by Uni-Map Inc., Palatine, Ill.
for Encyclopaedia Britannica, Inc.

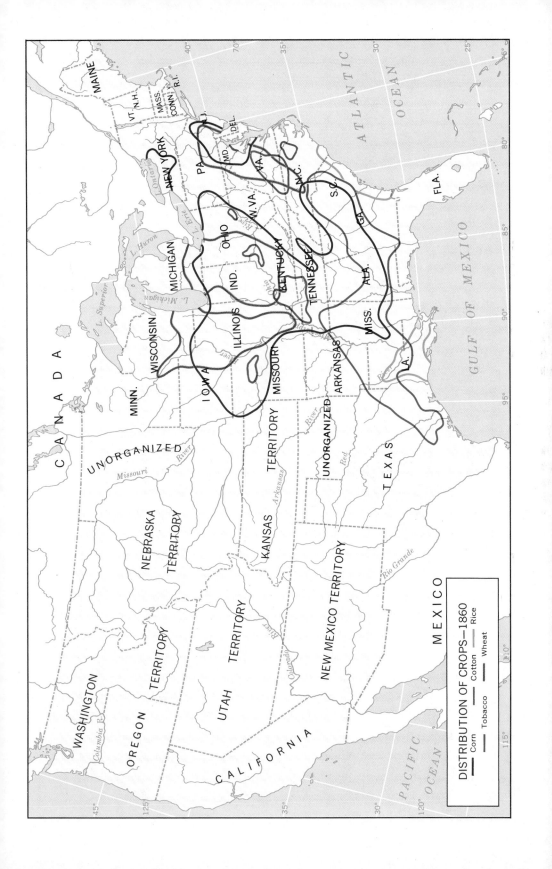

DISTRIBUTION OF CROPS—1860

Corn ——— Cotton ——— Rice

Tobacco ——— Wheat

MAINE

VT. N.H.
MASS.
CONN. R.I.

NEW YORK

PA. N.J.
MD. DEL.

N. VA. VA.

N.C.

S.C.

GA.

FLA.

MICHIGAN

OHIO

IND.

KENTUCKY

TENNESSEE

ALA.

MISS.

WISCONSIN

ILLINOIS

IOWA

MISSOURI

ARKANSAS

LA.

MINN.

CANADA

UNORGANIZED

NEBRASKA TERRITORY

KANSAS TERRITORY

UNORGANIZED

TEXAS

WASHINGTON

OREGON TERRITORY

UTAH TERRITORY

NEW MEXICO TERRITORY

CALIFORNIA

MEXICO

ATLANTIC OCEAN

GULF OF MEXICO

PACIFIC OCEAN

L. Superior

L. Michigan

L. Huron

L. Erie

L. Ontario

Ohio River

Missouri River

Missouri

Red River

Arkansas

Colorado River

Rio Grande

Columbia R.

40°

70°

35°

30°

25°

80°

85°

90°

95°

115°

120°

125°

45°

35°

30°

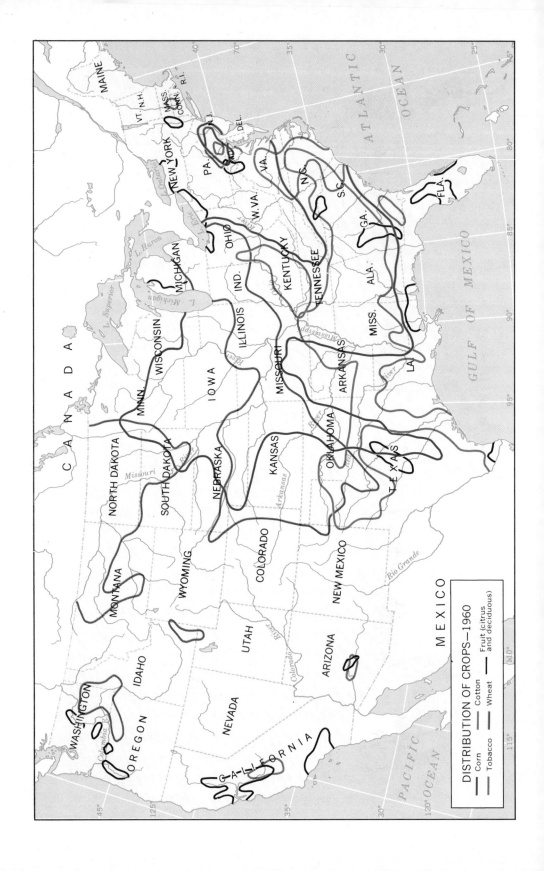

DISTRIBUTION OF CROPS—1960

Corn
Tobacco
Cotton
Wheat
Fruit (citrus
and deciduous)

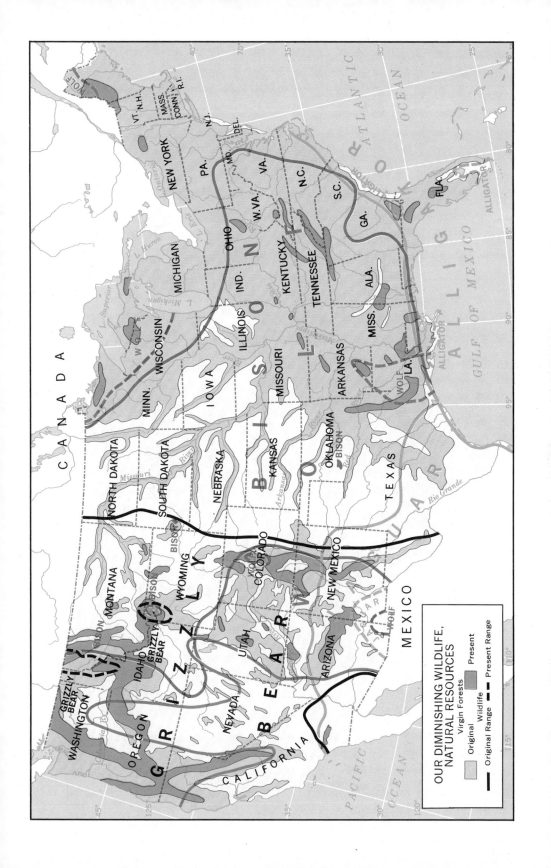

OUR DIMINISHING WILDLIFE,
NATURAL RESOURCES

Virgin Forests

Original

Present

Wildlife

Original Range

Present Range

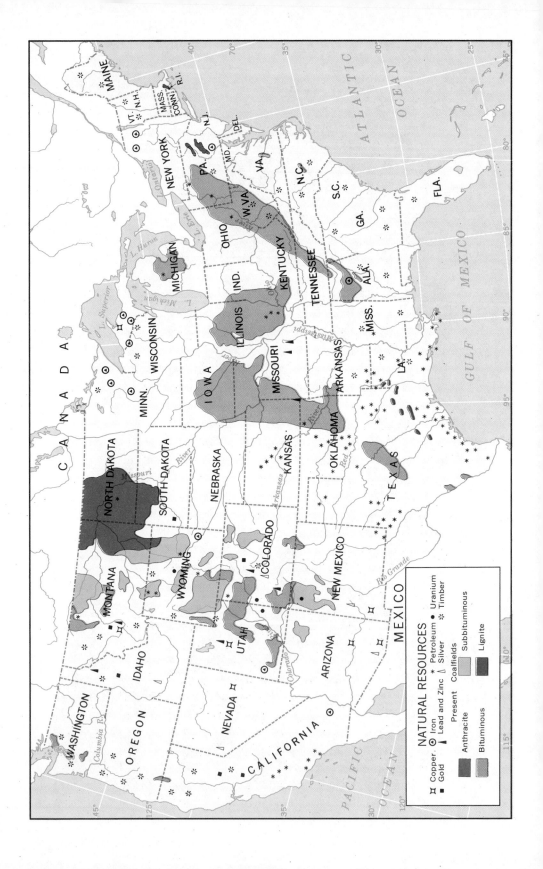

1895

1.

KATHARINE LEE BATES: "America the Beautiful"

"America the Beautiful" is sung almost as often as the national anthem and is regarded by many Americans as a second national song. The composer, Samuel A. Ward, had written a great deal of music that was not of much consequence, but when Katharine Lee Bates put words to one of his melodies in 1895, a moving song resulted. Written at a time when national patriotism was running high, "America the Beautiful" expressed the widespread belief that this country was indeed chosen by God to be the promised land. The version reprinted is the original one and differs somewhat from the version that is usually sung.

Source: *Famous Songs and Those Who Made Them*, Helen K. Johnson and Frederic Dean, eds.,
New York, 1895.

AMERICA THE BEAUTIFUL

O beautiful for halcyon skies,
   For amber waves of grain,
For purple mountain majesties
   Above the enameled plain!
     America! America!
   God shed His grace on thee
Till souls wax fair as earth and air
   And music-hearted sea!

O beautiful for Pilgrim feet,
   Whose stern, impassioned stress
A thoroughfare for freedom beat
   Across the wilderness!
     America! America!
   God shed His grace on thee
Till paths be wrought through wilds
   of thought
   By Pilgrim foot and knee!

O beautiful for glory tale
   Of liberating strife,
When once and twice, far man's avail,
   Men lavished precious life!
     America! America!
   God shed His grace for thee,
Till selfish gain no longer stain
   The banner of the free!

O beautiful for patriot dream
   That sees beyond the years
Thine alabaster cities gleam
   Undimmed by human tears!
     America! America!
   God shed His grace for thee,
Till nobler men keep once again
   Thy whiter jubilee!

2.

HENRY CABOT LODGE: Overseas Expansion and the National Future

Henry Cabot Lodge was first elected to the U.S. Senate from Massachusetts in 1893 — he would remain for nearly thirty-two years — and from the beginning spoke frequently and forcefully for his views. Early in his career, he became known as an advocate of overseas expansion. In company with friends such as Theodore Roosevelt, Lodge criticized Democratic President Cleveland's hesitancy in annexing Hawaii and his unwillingness to establish outposts in the Pacific. In a magazine article of March 1895, a portion of which appears below, Lodge explained his position. Later that year he urged, concerning the Venezuelan crisis, that the Monroe Doctrine should be invoked, "peaceably if we can, forcibly if we must."

Source: *Forum*, March 1895: "Our Blundering Foreign Policy."

ALL THE GREAT constructive legislation of this country, with hardly an exception, has been the work of the Republican Party and its predecessors. The Federalists organized the government; the Whigs developed our industries and set on foot our great system of internal improvements; the Republicans maintained the Union, abolished slavery, placed the last great amendments on the Constitution, and established our credit and our tariff.

The record of the Democratic Party for constructive legislation, on the other hand, despite their many years of power, is singularly barren. But there is one direction where the Democratic Party has done a great work. The Republicans, under the lead of Charles Sumner, added Alaska to our domain, but with this exception all our great acquisitions of territory have been the work of Democrats. To them we owe the Louisiana Purchase, Florida, Texas, and the Mexican cession. If the Democratic Party has had one cardinal principle beyond all others, it has been that of pushing forward the boundaries of the United States.

Under this administration, governed as it is by free-trade influences, this great principle of the Democratic Party during nearly a century of existence has been utterly abandoned. Thomas Jefferson, admitting that he violated the Constitution while he did it, effected the Louisiana Purchase, but Mr. Cleveland has labored to overthrow American interests and American control in Hawaii. Andrew Jackson fought for Florida, but Mr. Cleveland is eager to abandon Samoa. The Democratic Party, in its leaders at least, has been successfully Cobdenized, and that is the underlying reason for their policy of retreat.

It is the melancholy outcome of the doctrine that there is no higher aim or purpose for men or for nations than to buy and sell, to trade jackknives, and make everything cheap. No one underrates the importance of the tariffs or the still greater importance of a sound currency. But of late years we have been so absorbed in these economic questions that we have grown unmindful of others. We have had something too much of these disciples of the Manchester school, who think the price of calico more important than a nation's honor, the duties on pig iron of more moment than the advance of a race.

It is time to recall what we have been tending to forget: that we have always had and that we have now a foreign policy which is of great importance to our national well-being. The foundation of that policy was Washington's doctrine of neutrality. To him and to Hamilton we owe the principle that it was not the business of the United States to meddle in the affairs of Europe. When this policy was declared, it fell with a shock upon the Americans of that day, for we were still colonists in habits of thought and could not realize that the struggles of Europe did not concern us. Yet the establishment of the neutrality policy was one of the greatest services which Washington and Hamilton rendered to the cause of American nationality.

The corollary of Washington's policy was the Monroe Doctrine, the work of John Quincy Adams, a much greater man than the President whose name it bears. Washington declared that it was not the business of the United States to meddle in the affairs of Europe, and John Quincy Adams added that Europe must not meddle in the Western Hemisphere. As I have seen it solemnly stated recently that the annexation of Hawaii would be a violation of the Monroe Doctrine, it is perhaps not out of place to say that the Monroe Doctrine has no bearing on the extension of the United States, but simply holds that no European power shall establish itself in the Americas or interfere with American governments.

The neutrality policy and the Monroe Doctrine are the two great principles established at the outset by farseeing statesmen in regard to the foreign relations of the United States. But it would be a fatal mistake to suppose that our foreign policy stopped there, or that these fundamental propositions in any way fettered the march of the American people. Washington withdrew us from the affairs of Europe, but at the same time he pointed out that our true line of advance was to the west. He never for an instant thought that we were to remain stationary and cease to move forward. He saw, with prophetic vision, as did no other man of his time, the true course for the American people. He could not himself enter into the promised land, but he showed it to his people, stretching from the Blue Ridge to the Pacific Ocean.

We have followed the teachings of Washington. We have taken the great valley of the Mississippi and pressed on beyond the Sierras. We have a record of conquest, colonization, and territorial expansion unequaled by any people in the 19th century. We are not to be curbed now by the doctrines of the Manchester school, which have never been observed in England and which, as an importation, are even more absurdly out of place here than in their native land.

It is not the policy of the United States to enter, as England has done, upon the general acquisition of distant possession in all parts of the world. Our government is not adapted to such a policy, and we have no need of it, for we have an ample field at home; but at the same time it must be remembered that while in the United States themselves we hold the citadel of our power and greatness as a nation, there are outworks essential to the defense of that citadel which must neither be neglected nor abandoned.

There is a very definite policy for American statesmen to pursue in this respect if they would prove themselves worthy inheritors of the principles of Washington and Adams. We desire no extension to the south, for neither the population nor the lands of Central or South America would be desirable additions to the United States. But from the Rio Grande to the Arctic Ocean there should be but one flag and one country. Neither race nor climate forbids this extension, and every consideration of national growth and national welfare demands it.

In the interests of our commerce and of our fullest development, we should build the Nicaragua Canal, and for the protection of that canal and for the sake of our commercial supremacy in the Pacific we should control the Hawaiian Islands and maintain our influence in Samoa. England has studded the West Indies with strong places which are a standing menace to our Atlantic seaboard. We should have among those islands at least one strong naval station, and when the Nicaragua Canal is built, the island of Cuba, still sparsely settled and of almost unbounded fertility, will become to us a necessity. Commerce follows the flag, and we should build up a navy strong enough to give protection to Americans in every quarter of the globe and sufficiently powerful to put our coasts beyond the possibility of successful attack.

The tendency of modern times is toward consolidation. It is apparent in capital and labor alike, and it is also true of nations. Small states are of the past and have no future. The modern movement is all toward the concentration of people and territory into great nations and large dominions. The great nations are rapidly absorbing for their future expansion and their present defense all the waste places of the earth. It is a movement which makes for civilization and the advancement of the race. As one of the great nations of the world, the United States must not fall out of the line of march.

For more than thirty years we have been so much absorbed with grave domestic questions that we have lost sight of these vast interests which lie just outside our borders. They ought to be neglected no longer. They are not only of material importance but they are matters which concern our greatness as a nation and our future as a great people. They appeal to our national honor and dignity and to the pride of country and of race. If the humiliating foreign policy of the present administration has served to call attention to these questions and to remind us that they are quite as important, at least, as tariffs or currency, it will perhaps prove to have been a blessing in disguise. When we face a question of foreign relations, it should never be forgotten that we meet something above and beyond party politics, something that rouses and appeals to the patriotism and the Americanism of which we never can have too much, and of which during the last two years our government has shown altogether too little.

3.

Richard Olney: On American Jurisdiction in the Western Hemisphere

In 1895 a boundary dispute between Great Britain and Venezuela became the basis for a heated debate in the United States. President Grover Cleveland was silent at first and remained neutral. However, when Richard Olney, a vocal defender of American interests in the hemisphere, became secretary of state in June 1895, everyone expected a change in American foreign policy. They were not disappointed. Olney's note to Ambassador Thomas F. Bayard (a portion of which is reprinted below), written on July 20, 1895, instructed Bayard, in clear and unequivocal language, to inform the British government of the vital interests of the United States in the Venezuela affair.

Source: PRFA, 1895, I, pp. 545-562.

Sir:

I am directed by the President to communicate to you his views upon a subject to which he has given much anxious thought and respecting which he has not reached a conclusion without a lively sense of its great importance as well as of the serious responsibility involved in any action now to be taken.

It is not proposed, and for present purposes is not necessary, to enter into any detailed account of the controversy between Great Britain and Venezuela respecting the western frontier of the colony of British Guiana. . . .

The important features of the existing situation . . . may be briefly stated.

1. The title to territory of indefinite but confessedly very large extent is in dispute between Great Britain on the one hand and the South American republic of Venezuela on the other.

2. The disparity in the strength of the claimants is such that Venezuela can hope to establish her claim only through peaceful methods — through an agreement with her adversary either upon the subject itself or upon an arbitration.

3. The controversy, with varying claims on the part of Great Britain, has existed for more than half a century, during which period many earnest and persistent efforts of Venezuela to establish a boundary by agreement have proved unsuccessful.

4. The futility of the endeavor to obtain a conventional line being recognized, Venezuela for a quarter of a century has asked and striven for arbitration.

5. Great Britain, however, has always and continuously refused to arbitrate, except upon the condition of a renunciation of a large part of the Venezuelan claim and of a concession to herself of a large share of the territory in controversy.

6. By the frequent interposition of its good offices at the instance of Venezuela, by constantly urging and promoting the restoration of diplomatic relations between the

two countries, by pressing for arbitration of the disputed boundary, by offering to act as arbitrator, by expressing its grave concern whenever new alleged instances of British aggression upon Venezuelan territory have been brought to its notice, the government of the United States has made it clear to Great Britain and to the world that the controversy is one in which both its honor and its interests are involved, and the continuance of which it cannot regard with indifference.

The accuracy of the foregoing analysis of the existing status cannot, it is believed, be challenged. It shows that status to be such that those charged with the interests of the United States are now forced to determine exactly what those interests are and what course of action they require. It compels them to decide to what extent, if any, the United States may and should intervene in a controversy between and primarily concerning only Great Britain and Venezuela, and to decide how far it is bound to see that the integrity of Venezuelan territory is not impaired by the pretensions of its powerful antagonist.

Are any such right and duty devolved upon the United States? If not, the United States has already done all, if not more than all, that a purely sentimental interest in the affairs of the two countries justifies, and to push its interposition further would be unbecoming and undignified and might well subject it to the charge of impertinent intermeddling with affairs with which it has no rightful concern. On the other hand, if any such right and duty exist, their due exercise and discharge will not permit of any action that shall not be efficient and that, if the power of the United States is adequate, shall not result in the accomplishment of the end in view. The question thus presented, as matter of principle and regard being had to the settled national policy, does not seem difficult of solution. Yet the momentous practical consequences dependent upon its determination require that it should be carefully considered and that the grounds of the conclusion arrived at should be fully and frankly stated.

That there are circumstances under which a nation may justly interpose in a controversy to which two or more other nations are the direct and immediate parties is an admitted canon of international law. The doctrine is ordinarily expressed in terms of the most general character and is perhaps incapable of more specific statement. It is declared in substance that a nation may avail itself of this right whenever what is done or proposed by any of the parties primarily concerned is a serious and direct menace to its own integrity, tranquillity, or welfare. The propriety of the rule when applied in good faith will not be questioned in any quarter.

On the other hand, it is an inevitable though unfortunate consequence of the wide scope of the rule that it has only too often been made a cloak for schemes of wanton spoliation and aggrandizement. We are concerned at this time, however, not so much with the general rule as with a form of it which is peculiarly and distinctively American. Washington, in the solemn admonitions of the Farewell Address, explicitly warned his countrymen against entanglements with the politics or the controversies of European powers:

> Europe has a set of primary interests which to us have none or a very remote relation. Hence she must be engaged in frequent controversies, the causes of which are essentially foreign to our concerns. Hence, therefore, it must be unwise in us to implicate ourselves by artificial ties in the ordinary vicissitudes of her politics or the ordinary combinations and collisions of her friendships or enmities. Our detached and distant situation invites and enables us to pursue a different course.

During the administration of President Monroe this doctrine of the Farewell Address was first considered in all its aspects and with a view to all its practical consequences. The Farewell Address, while it took America out of the field of European politics, was silent as to the part Europe might be permitted to play in America. Doubtless it was thought the latest addition to the family of nations should not make haste to prescribe rules for the guidance of its older members, and the expediency and propriety of serving the powers of Europe with notice of a complete and distinctive American policy excluding them from interference with American political affairs might well seem dubious to a generation to whom the French alliance, with its manifold advantages to the cause of American independence, was fresh in mind.

Twenty years later, however, the situation had changed. The lately born nation had greatly increased in power and resources, had demonstrated its strength on land and sea, and as well in the conflicts of arms as in the pursuits of peace, and had begun to realize the commanding position on this continent which the character of its people, their free institutions, and their remoteness from the chief scene of European contentions combined to give to it. The Monroe administration therefore did not hesitate to accept and apply the logic of the Farewell Address by declaring in effect that American nonintervention in European affairs necessarily implied and meant European nonintervention in American affairs. . . .

There is, then, a doctrine of American public law, well founded in principle and abundantly sanctioned by precedent, which entitles and requires the United States to treat as an injury to itself the forcible assumption by a European power of political control over an American state. The application of the doctrine to the boundary dispute between Great Britain and Venezuela remains to be made and presents no real difficulty. Though the dispute relates to a boundary line, yet, as it is between states, it

necessarily imports political control to be lost by one party and gained by the other. The political control at stake, too, is of no mean importance, but concerns a domain of great extent — the British claim, it will be remembered, apparently expanded in two years some 33,000 square miles — and, if it also directly involves the command of the mouth of the Orinoco, is of immense consequence in connection with the whole river navigation of the interior of South America.

It has been intimated, indeed, that in respect of these South American possessions, Great Britain is herself an American state like any other, so that a controversy between her and Venezuela is to be settled between themselves as if it were between Venezuela and Brazil or between Venezuela and Colombia, and does not call for or justify United States intervention. If this view be tenable at all, the logical sequence is plain.

Great Britain as a South American state is to be entirely differentiated from Great Britain generally, and if the boundary question cannot be settled otherwise than by force, British Guiana, with her own independent resources and not those of the British Empire, should be left to settle the matter with Venezuela — an arrangement which very possibly Venezuela might not object to. But the proposition that a European power with an American dependency is for the purposes of the Monroe Doctrine to be classed not as an European but as an American state will not admit of serious discussion. If it were to be adopted, the Monroe Doctrine would be too valueless to be worth asserting. Not only would every European power now having a South American colony be enabled to extend its possessions on this continent indefinitely but any other European power might also do the same by first taking pains to procure a fraction of South American soil by voluntary cession.

The declaration of the Monroe message

— that existing colonies or dependencies of a European power would not be interfered with by the United States — means colonies or dependencies then existing, with their limits as then existing. . . .

Thus . . . the British demand that her right to a portion of the disputed territory shall be acknowledged before she will consent to an arbitration as to the rest seems to stand upon nothing but her own *ipse dixit* [pronouncement]. She says to Venezuela, in substance: "You can get none of the debatable land by force, because you are not strong enough; you can get none by treaty, because I will not agree; and you can take your chance of getting a portion by arbitration only if you first agree to abandon to me such other portion as I may designate." It is not perceived how such an attitude can be defended nor how it is reconcilable with that love of justice and fair play so eminently characteristic of the English race.

It in effect deprives Venezuela of her free agency and puts her under virtual duress. Territory acquired by reason of it will be as much wrested from her by the strong hand as if occupied by British troops or covered by British fleets. It seems therefore quite impossible that this position of Great Britain should be assented to by the United States; or that, if such position be adhered to with the result of enlarging the bounds of British Guiana, it should not be regarded as amounting, in substance, to an invasion and conquest of Venezuelan territory.

In these circumstances, the duty of the President appears to him unmistakable and imperative. Great Britain's assertion of title to the disputed territory combined with her refusal to have that title investigated being a substantial appropriation of the territory to her own use, not to protest and give warning that the transaction will be regarded as injurious to the interests of the people of the United States as well as oppressive in itself would be to ignore an established policy with which the honor and welfare of this country are closely identified. While the measures necessary or proper for the vindication of that policy are to be determined by another branch of the government, it is clearly for the executive to leave nothing undone which may tend to render such determination unnecessary.

You are instructed, therefore, to present the foregoing views to Lord Salisbury by reading to him this communication (leaving with him a copy should he so desire), and to reinforce them by such pertinent considerations as will doubtless occur to you. They call for a definite decision upon the point whether Great Britain will consent or will decline to submit the Venezuelan boundary question in its entirety to impartial arbitration.

It is the earnest hope of the President that the conclusion will be on the side of arbitration, and that Great Britain will add one more to the conspicuous precedents she has already furnished in favor of that wise and just mode of adjusting international disputes. If he is to be disappointed in that hope, however — a result not to be anticipated and in his judgment calculated to greatly embarrass the future relations between this country and Great Britain — it is his wish to be made acquainted with the fact at such early date as will enable him to lay the whole subject before Congress in his next annual message.

The white man cannot keep the Negro in the ditch without sitting down there with him.

BOOKER T. WASHINGTON

4.

Booker T. Washington: The Road to Negro Progress

On September 18, 1895, Booker T. Washington delivered a speech at the Cotton States and International Exposition in Atlanta, Georgia, that made him a national figure. He was introduced by former governor Rufus Bullock as a "representative of Negro enterprise and Negro civilization." His speech allayed any fears his white audience might have had about the ambitions of the Southern Negro. Washington emphasized that the Negro wanted responsibilities rather than rights and proposed a program of accommodation that pleased all white Southerners. The result was that Washington assumed the role of national Negro leader, and his words were considered representative of Negro thought for a generation.

Source: *The Story of My Life and Work,* Revised edition, Naperville, Ill. and Atlanta, Ga., 1900, pp. 165-171.

Mr. President and Gentlemen of the Board of Directors and Citizens:

One-third of the population of the South is of the Negro race. No enterprise seeking the material, civil, or moral welfare of this section can disregard this element of our population and reach the highest success. I but convey to you, Mr. President and Directors, the sentiment of the masses of my race when I say that in no way have the value and manhood of the American Negro been more fittingly and generously recognized than by the managers of this magnificent exposition at every stage of its progress. It is a recognition that will do more to cement the friendship of the two races than any occurrence since the dawn of our freedom.

Not only this, but the opportunity here afforded will awaken among us a new era of industrial progress. Ignorant and inexperienced, it is not strange that in the first years of our new life we began at the top instead of at the bottom; that a seat in Congress or the state legislature was more sought than real estate or industrial skill; that the political convention or stump speaking had more attractions than starting a dairy farm or truck garden.

A ship lost at sea for many days suddenly sighted a friendly vessel. From the mast of the unfortunate vessel was seen a signal: "Water, water; we die of thirst." The answer from the friendly vessel at once came back: "Cast down your bucket where you are." A second time the signal, "Water, water, send us water!" ran up from the distressed vessel, and was answered: "Cast down your bucket where you are." And a third and fourth signal for water was answered: "Cast down your bucket where you are." The captain of the distressed vessel, at last heeding the injunction, cast down his bucket, and it came up full of fresh, sparkling water from the mouth of the Amazon River.

To those of my race who depend on bettering their condition in a foreign land or who underestimate the importance of cultivating friendly relations with the Southern white man, who is their next-door neighbor, I would say: Cast down your bucket where you are; cast it down in making friends, in every manly way, of the people of all races by whom we are surrounded. Cast it down in agriculture, mechanics, in commerce, in domestic service, and in the professions. And in this connection it is well to bear in mind that whatever other sins the South may be called to bear, when it comes to business, pure and simple, it is in the South that the Negro is given a man's chance in the commercial world, and in nothing is this exposition more eloquent than in emphasizing this chance.

Our greatest danger is that, in the great leap from slavery to freedom, we may overlook the fact that the masses of us are to live by the productions of our hands and fail to keep in mind that we shall prosper in proportion as we learn to dignify and glorify common labor, and put brains and skill into the common occupations of life; shall prosper in proportion as we learn to draw the line between the superficial and the substantial, the ornamental gewgaws of life and the useful. No race can prosper till it learns that there is as much dignity in tilling a field as in writing a poem. It is at the bottom of life we must begin, and not at the top. Nor should we permit our grievances to overshadow our opportunities.

To those of the white race who look to the incoming of those of foreign birth and strange tongue and habits for the prosperity of the South, were I permitted I would repeat what I say to my own race, "Cast down your bucket where you are." Cast it down among the 8 million Negroes whose habits you know, whose fidelity and love you have tested in days when to have proved treacherous meant the ruin of your firesides. Cast down your bucket among these people who have, without strikes and labor wars, tilled your fields, cleared your forests, builded your railroads and cities, and brought forth treasures from the bowels of the earth and helped make possible this magnificent representation of the progress of the South. Casting down your bucket

among my people, helping and encouraging them as you are doing on these grounds, and, with education of head, hand, and heart, you will find that they will buy your surplus land, make blossom the waste places in your fields, and run your factories.

While doing this, you can be sure in the future, as in the past, that you and your families will be surrounded by the most patient, faithful, law-abiding, and unresentful people that the world has seen. As we have proved our loyalty to you in the past, in nursing your children, watching by the sick-bed of your mothers and fathers, and often following them with tear-dimmed eyes to their graves, so in the future, in our humble way, we shall stand by you with a devotion that no foreigner can approach, ready to lay down our lives, if need be, in defense of yours; interlacing our industrial, commercial, civil, and religious life with yours in a way that shall make the interests of both races one. In all things that are purely social we can be as separate as the fingers, yet one as the hand in all things essential to mutual progress.

There is no defense or security for any of us except in the highest intelligence and development of all. If anywhere there are efforts tending to curtail the fullest growth of the Negro, let these efforts be turned into stimulating, encouraging, and making him the most useful and intelligent citizen. Effort or means so invested will pay a thousand percent interest. These efforts will be twice blessed — "blessing him that gives and him that takes."

There is no escape, through law of man or God, from the inevitable:

The laws of changeless justice bind
Oppressor with oppressed;
And close as sin and suffering joined
We march to fate abreast.

Nearly 16 million hands will aid you in pulling the load upward, or they will pull against you the load downward. We shall constitute one-third and more of the ignorance and crime of the South, or one-third its intelligence and progress; we shall contribute one-third to the business and industrial prosperity of the South, or we shall prove a veritable body of death, stagnating, depressing, retarding every effort to advance the body politic.

Gentlemen of the exposition, as we present to you our humble effort at an exhibition of our progress, you must not expect overmuch. Starting thirty years ago with ownership here and there in a few quilts and pumpkins and chickens (gathered from miscellaneous sources), remember: the path that has led from these to the invention and production of agricultural implements, buggies, steam engines, newspapers, books, statuary, carving, paintings, the management of drugstores and banks, has not been trodden without contact with thorns and thistles. While we take pride in what we exhibit as a result of our independent efforts, we do not for a moment forget that our part in this exhibition would fall far short of your expectations but for the constant help that has come to our educational life, not only from the Southern states but especially from Northern philanthropists who have made their gifts a constant stream of blessing and encouragement.

The wisest among my race understand that the agitation of questions of social equality is the extremest folly, and that progress in the enjoyment of all the privileges that will come to us must be the result of severe and constant struggle rather than of artificial forcing. No race that has anything to contribute to the markets of the world is long in any degree ostracized. It is important and right that all privileges of the law be ours, but it is vastly more important that we be prepared for the exercise of those privileges. The opportunity to earn a dollar in a factory just now is worth infinitely more than the opportunity to spend a dollar in an opera house.

In conclusion, may I repeat that nothing in thirty years has given us more hope and

Library of Congress

Booker T. Washington, first principal and chief developer of Tuskegee Institute in Alabama

encouragement and drawn us so near to you of the white race as this opportunity offered by the exposition; and here bending, as it were, over the altar that represents the results of the struggles of your race and mine, both starting practically empty-handed three decades ago, I pledge that, in your effort to work out the great and intricate problem which God has laid at the doors of the South, you shall have at all times the patient, sympathetic help of my race; only let this be constantly in mind that, while from representations in these buildings of the product of field, of forest, of mine, of factory, letters, and art, much good will come — yet far above and beyond material benefits will be that higher good, that let us pray God will come, in a blotting out of sectional differences and racial animosities and suspicions, in a determination to administer absolute justice, in a willing obedience among all classes to the mandates of law. This, coupled with our material prosperity, will bring into our beloved South a new heaven and a new earth.

5.

John R. Williams: Immigrant and Negro Labor in the Coal Mines

*The letters of immigrants to their friends and relations in the Old Country have
provided historians with a rich source of knowledge about the personal attitudes
as well as the material conditions of newcomers to America. This letter by
John R. Williams to his friend William Thomas, written November 10, 1895,
is a good example. Williams was a Welshman who became a coal miner in
Algoma, West Virginia, after working elsewhere. In his letter he provided a
perceptive and detailed analysis of working conditions in the mines as well as
a description of the Negro mine workers that was quite unlike the ordinary
American estimate of the Negroes.*

Source: *The Welsh in America*, Alan Conway, ed., Minneapolis, 1961, pp. 204-210.

You will, I am sure, be surprised to find I
am in the wilds of West Virginia; well, I
came down here in the middle of June last
and I like to be here very much and I am
getting on all right.

Up at Wilkes-Barre, I failed to get a
show anyhow; the mining homes there
block an Englishman; a foreigner has no
chance in that state unless he is a citizen of
the U.S.A., and that means residence in the
country five years.

I worked for months at the Lehigh and
Wilkes-Barre Coal Company's Stanton colliery with a timberman and repairers gang.
We were three in the gang and had the
main engine planes to keep in repair. It was
very hard work as the timbering had to be
very heavy, not a stick allowed under eighteen inches in diameter, the arms averaging
nine feet long with twelve-foot collars, the
seam we worked in being the celebrated
Baltimore Vein, which is eighteen feet in
thickness in all. I never saw such splendid
timbering in my life as is done in America.
All the notching and dressing of the timber
is done with the crosscut saw and adze, and

must fit to a nicety, and that is the only
good thing I have seen in American mining.

As for everything else, they are as ancient
as Adam. The head of the gang was getting
$2.50 but my partner and I were only get-
ting $1.88 (per day). The collieries of this
company got to run so badly that I left and
went to work in the No. 4 shaft of the
Kingstone collieries. There again two
worked with a timberman and earned more
money, inasmuch that the miners were kept
working more regular than Stanton.

The coal trade in the anthracite districts
has been extremely dull all through the
year, the production overwhelmingly over-
balancing the demand. Labor is so plentiful
that operators can do just what they please.
Pennsylvania is swarming with foreigners
— Poles, Hungarians, Slavish, Swedes, and
Italians, etc. — who are fast driving the English, Welsh, and Scotch miners out of
competition. Noticeably, the Poles and
Hungarians are a harder working people
and physically stronger men than the English and Welsh. They live much harder
and at about half the cost and can stand

more and harder work than our country-men.

Before the influx of the foreigners I have named into this country, the Welsh had the best show in the mines here, but in consequence of their foolhardy and unreasonable impositions in pretty well everything, they at length became perfectly unmanageable and the operators had no alternative but to send and get whole cargoes of the foreigners I have named, who now practically monopolize the business, and no longer will America hold out a friendly hand to the British miner who must stay at home and do the best he can there or come here and starve. There are in America today, and especially in the West, thousands upon thousands of our countrymen who would gladly return to England and Wales if they could only do so, but they cannot find the money.

Our mines are situated in the Elkhorn about 18 miles up from Pocahontas, the latter place being about 650 miles from Norfolk on the Atlantic Coast. The only railway communication for this coalfield is the Norfolk and Western Railroad. We are on what is called the Pocahontas Flat Top Coalfield, which comprises a very large area. The major part of this coalfield belongs to a company called the Flat Top Coal Land Association, who own something like 200,000 acres and upward.

The coal is let at 10 cents per ton, with all timber free for mining purposes. As the name implies, the seam is nearly dead level in all directions and crops out to the surface nearly all over the field. The average thickness of the seam is seven and a half feet of clean coal in one block. It is the prettiest seam of coal I have ever seen.

This coalfield is mixed up with a number of zigzag valleys all over the shop and the slopes all covered with beautiful timber in great abundance, being pine, maple, oak, hickory, and ash. The climate of this state is different to that of Pennsylvania. In the summer the heat is very great during the day but beautifully cool in the mornings and evenings. In Pennsylvania it is unbearably hot at nights and a fellow can't sleep anyhow. I was jolly glad to clear out of it, if only for that very reason alone.

All over this Flat Top coalfield the various companies work the same seam of coal, which is called the Pocahontas No. 3 Seam. The quality of this seam of coal is excellent, smokeless steam coal of remarkably fine quality. The various English analysts who have analyzed it one and all pronounce it to be equal to the very best Cardiff steam coal. There is not a particle of gas in this seam — that is, gas given off in working — and that is the salvation of the place. Had it been otherwise they could not compete in the market, as the coal in that event could not be blasted and another mode of working would be too expensive.

We work the coal on the pillar and stall system, drawing the pillars back, the headings being narrow, twelve feet wide, and the stalls six yards wide, with pillars fourteen yards wide. The miners hole under the coal about six feet and then blast it down, sending all out. The miners are paid 60 cents per car for all stall coal and 75 cents per car for all adze coal. The cars hold three tons. No yardage is paid on anything. The miners find all lights, tools, and explosives and stand their own props.

Usually, two men work together in every place and fill out on an average six to eight cars per day. All other class of labor is daywork. The average cost of production including everything is 40 to 48 cents per ton free on truck at colliery.

The company I am with hold nearly 3,000 acres of coal, all leased from the Flat Top Association.

We have three openings on the coal and are now working on an average of 800 tons per day, but in six months time we can turn out 2,000 tons per day if trade will allow it. We have 200 coke ovens and turn out an excellent article. Our haulage from the main double partings underground is done by steam locomotives, which do the work splendidly and there is no unpleasant effect from fumes, etc., as the coal is practically smokeless.

Unfortunately, we have about four feet of fine clay on top of our coal, the clay being in three beds. This clay roof is full of kettle bottoms, as they are called here (bells at home), and we have also an abundance of the fossil remains of huge trees in this roof. It is a most dangerous roof and we have to watch it for our lives. Those bells are often eight feet in diameter and don't give the slightest warning but simply drop out without any warning whatever. We can't bring our props nearer than ten or twelve feet of the face, on account of blasting the coal.

We have three gangs of men under the charge of slatemen doing nothing but clearing falls, etc.

In America they work ten hours per day exclusive of the one-hour dinner time. We commence working coal at 7 A.M. and knock off at 6 P.M.

All our face haulage is done by mules and it is truly wonderful the hard work they stand. No horse can stand the same amount of work. All our cars (trams) have brakes, so it is all pulling or chain work and no shafting. They could not stand shafting on account of the great weight of the loads.

Now let me tell you something about the people we have in this country. About two-thirds are niggars and practically all our miners are niggars. There are a few white ones among them.

Before I came here I was told the niggars were a most treacherous, devilish lot of people to deal with and the only way to manage them was to knock them down with anything at hand, at any slight offense on their part. This was told me by several people in Pennsylvania who had had a great deal of experience with them, so when I came here I expected to have a jabbering, semiwild lot of people to deal with.

I started from Wilkes-Barre on a Monday and came by the Pennsylvania Railroad, who booked me through for $17, and came via Harrisburg, Hagerstown, and Roanoke and got into Pocahontas at noon on Wednesday. We had four hours to wait there to get up to Algoma. Being beastly tired of the train, I got into a large dining saloon. Presently two niggar young women came to me: they were about eighteen years old and they had delightfully melodious sweet voices and spoke in most guarded and beautiful English. "By jove," says I to myself, "if all the niggars are like these girls, I am jolly glad I came down here." Talking about modest and respectful behavior, why every other place I have ever been to both at home and America, were not in it.

I came in contact with several of them, men this time, while waiting at Poco and found them all extremely well-behaved and enlightened people. I am extremely fond of them and have not had the slightest trouble with them since I have been here. And I would rather manage 500 of them than half a dozen of the white people of this country. In dealing with a niggar, you have to be very firm with them and insist upon having your instructions carried out to the letter. I treat them very respectfully and show them that I respect their race and they appreciate that more than words can tell, for most white people treat them otherwise, which is the greatest mistake.

I had not been at the mine a week before I found they were telling one another that the new colonel likes niggars, he don't say you damned black son of a bitch but he say kind things to us. There is not a niggar on the job who won't try to jump out of his skin if I ask him to.

The poor niggar has been shamefully abused and ill-treated by white men, more the shame to them. Even the niggar children when you meet them on the road are different to white children; the former are polite and thoroughly well-behaved, with no coarse language, the white children, quite the reverse, a filthy low set.

The niggar though is not without his

faults. By nature he is an awful thief, especially in the eatable line, chickens and turkeys a specialty, but if you catch him in the act, he is not a vicious thief; he will only turn round and make up some cock-and-bull story to account for it. He is an awful liar but not a mean one. He lies for fun, bravado, because it's natural to him.

He is outrageously lazy too and like the boa constrictor will not work while his belly is full; consequently we are obliged to keep about double the number we require about the mines to enable us to have a decent working force at any one time. They live in huts, shacks they are called here, around the mines, and the highest standard of morality is not very strictly observed by them. They eat, cook, and sleep all through and through — men, women, girls, and boys, makes no difference to them. Few of them go through the form of legal marriage but the greater number live in adultery and when they get tired of one another they change partners. In America living in adultery is punishable by law, and every now and then lots of them get indicted just to show that there is just such a law in existence. The penalty is that they must at once marry or go to jail.

The white man of this state and adjoining states is about the most contemptible person on the face of God's earth. He is unbearably ignorant and does not know it. He has generally been brought up on the mountains, hog fashion, and when they come to the mines and earn a lot of money, they swell out and don't know themselves. He is a small ferrety eyed fellow, with hollow, lanky cheeks, a thin, pointed nose, with about seventeen hairs on his chin and thirteen hairs on his upper lip which he insultingly calls a moustache. That is the best description I can give you of the native white man of the South.

These detestable cranks seem to think that the poor niggar was made to receive their insults and brutality; so when they meet at those saloons where they sell poison for whiskey and vitriol for brandy, those fearful rows begin. The white men start by clubbing the niggar on the head with a revolver, for everybody is obliged to carry his shooting iron here, and then business is busy and the shooting becomes general, everyone firing away regardless of object, friend or foe. It is nothing unusual here to find four or five fellows shot dead, and it is quite unusual if this is not the case on pay nights, which, thank God, only comes but once a month. After doing the fiendish work they clear out to some other place and there is an end to it unless the authorities come across the villain accidentally.

Such is life in West Virginia. I have seen about a score of fellows shot; fellows at home dread a hammering with the fists more than those fellows dread a pistol shot. A short time ago, one of our fellows got shot through the neck for cheating at cards, and when the doctor told him "this was a pretty narrow shave, Sam," he just grinned and said, "Yes, Doc, dis was powerful close, de devil nearly kissed me dis time."

It is forbidden by law to carry concealed firearms in the state, but in the face of it everybody carries one and indeed would not be safe to go without one. When I came here they told me I must buy a good revolver and always carry it with me, so I got one and planted it in my hip pocket and I did not like the feeling of this thing at all; I felt as if I carried a gallows in my pocket all the time, but, like everything else, I got accustomed to it and the thing comes as natural to me now as putting my hat on.

All over the Union the election of public officials is now going on, and the Republicans are going in wholesale, the Democrats making a very bad show; and when the presidential election takes place in about two years time, the Americans will be happy again, for they will then have a Republican President and not a Democrat.

6.

Frederick Taylor: A Piece-Rate System of Wages

Frederick Taylor's theories about manufacturing methods helped to revolutionize production as well as business management. Taylor, a mechanical engineer, first presented the results of his researches at a meeting of the American Society of Mechanical Engineers in June 1895. His paper, a portion of which appears below, impressed his colleagues and quickly led to the implementation of his ideas in various industrial operations. One of Taylor's assistants described his system as one in which "the employer attempts to do justice to the employee, and in return requires the employee to be honest." Taylor's analysis of the most efficient ways to pay workers for their efforts appealed to industrialists because of its "scientific" nature as well as its commonsensical approach to human relations. "Taylorization," which was widely copied after 1900, was the forerunner of present-day industrial management, especially in the area of time and motion studies.

Source: *Transactions of the American Society of Mechanical Engineers,* New York, 1895, pp. 856-903: "A Piece-Rate System."

THE ORDINARY PIECEWORK SYSTEM involves a permanent antagonism between employers and men, and a certainty of punishment for each workman who reaches a high rate of efficiency. The demoralizing effect of this system is most serious. Under it, even the best workmen are forced continually to act the part of hypocrites to hold their own in the struggle against the encroachments of their employers.

The system introduced by the writer, however, is directly the opposite, both in theory and in its results. It makes each workman's interests the same as that of his employer, pays a premium for high efficiency, and soon convinces each man that it is for his permanent advantage to turn out each day the best quality and maximum quantity of work.

The writer has endeavored in the following pages to describe the system of manage-ment introduced by him in the works of the Midvale Steel Company, of Philadelphia, which has been employed by them during the past ten years with the most satisfactory results.

The system consists of three principal elements: (1) an elementary rate-fixing department; (2) the differential rate system of piecework; (3) what he believes to be the best method of managing men who work by the day.

Elementary rate fixing differs from other methods of making piecework prices in that a careful study is made of the time required to do each of the many elementary operations into which the manufacturing of an establishment may be analyzed or divided. These elementary operations are then classified, recorded, and indexed, and, when a piecework price is wanted for work, the job is first divided into its elementary operations, the time required to do each elementary operation is found from the records, and the total time for the job is summed up from these data. While this method seems complicated at the first glance, it is, in fact, far simpler and more effective than the old method of recording the time required to do whole jobs of work, and then, after looking over the records of similar jobs, guessing at the time required for any new piece of work.

The differential rate system of piecework consists briefly in offering two different rates for the same job; a high price per piece, in case the work is finished in the shortest possible time and in perfect condition, and a low price, if it takes a longer time to do the job or if there are any imperfections in the work. (The high rate should be such that the workman can earn more per day than is usually paid in similar establishments.) This is directly the opposite of the ordinary plan of piecework; in which the wages of the workmen are reduced when they increase their productivity.

The system by which the writer proposes managing the men who are on daywork consists in paying *men* and not *positions*. Each man's wages, as far as possible, are fixed according to the skill and energy with which he performs his work and not according to the position which he fills. Every endeavor is made to stimulate each man's personal ambition. This involves keeping systematic and careful records of the performance of each man as to his punctuality, attendance, integrity, rapidity, skill, and accuracy, and a readjustment from time to time of the wages paid him in accordance with this record.

The advantages of this system of management are:

First, that the manufactures are produced cheaper under it, while at the same time the workmen earn higher wages than are usually paid.

Second, since the rate fixing is done from accurate knowledge instead of more or less by guesswork, the motive for holding back on work, or "soldiering," and endeavoring to deceive the employers as to the time required to do work is entirely removed, and with it the greatest cause for hard feelings and war between the management and the men.

Third, since the basis from which piecework as well as day rates are fixed is that of exact observation instead of being founded upon accident or deception, as is too frequently the case under ordinary systems, the men are treated with greater uniformity and justice, and respond by doing more and better work.

Fourth, it is for the common interest of both the management and the men to cooperate in every way so as to turn out each day the maximum quantity and best quality of work.

Fifth, the system is rapid, while other systems are slow, in attaining the maximum productivity of each machine and man; and when this maximum is once reached, it is automatically maintained by the differential rate.

Sixth, it automatically selects and attracts the best men for each class of work, and it develops many first-class men who would otherwise remain slow or inaccurate, while at the same time it discourages and sifts out men who are incurably lazy or inferior.

Finally, one of the chief advantages derived from the above effects of the system is that it promotes a most friendly feeling between the men and their employers, and so renders labor unions and strikes unnecessary.

There has never been a strike under the differential rate system of piecework, although it has been in operation for the past ten years in the steel business, which has been during this period more subject to strikes and labor troubles than almost any other industry.

7.

David J. Brewer: *In Re Debs*

The Pullman Strike in Chicago in 1894 raised all kinds of legal, political, economic, and social questions. Could a labor union interfere with the operation of an entire industry in order to obtain its aims? Could, or should, the government act on behalf of industry? How could the wage earner express his discontent without incurring the wrath of big business and government? Many of these questions were answered, at least temporarily, by the swift government action that broke the strike. When the injunction served on the union in 1894 was disobeyed by Eugene Debs and the other leaders of the American Railway Union, it was reaffirmed by the Supreme Court (U.S. v. Debs, 1894), and the union was declared to be acting illegally in restraint of trade under the Sherman Antitrust Act of 1890. In addition, an appeal for a writ of habeas corpus for Debs, who was sentenced to six months in jail, was denied. Justice Brewer, speaking for the Court, explained the denial in a ruling delivered on May 27, 1895, a portion of which appears below.

Source: 158 U.S. 564.

THE CASE PRESENTED by the bill is this: The United States, finding that the interstate transportation of persons and property, as well as the carriage of the mails, is forcibly obstructed, and that a combination and conspiracy exists to subject the control of such transportation to the will of the conspirators, applied to one of their courts, sitting as a court of equity, for an injunction to restrain such obstruction and prevent carrying into effect such conspiracy. Two questions of importance are presented: First, are the relations of the general government to interstate commerce and the transportation of the mails such as authorize a direct interference to prevent a forcible obstruction thereof? Second, if authority exists, as authority in governmental affairs implies both power and duty, has a court of equity jurisdiction to issue an injunction in aid of the performance of such duty? . . .

What are the relations of the general government to interstate commerce and the transportation of the mails? They are those of direct supervision, control, and management. While under the dual system which prevails with us the powers of government are distributed between the state and the nation, and while the latter is properly styled a government of enumerated powers, yet, within the limits of such enumeration, it has all the attributes of sovereignty, and, in the exercise of those enumerated powers, acts directly upon the citizen and not through the intermediate agency of the state. . . .

Obviously these powers given to the national government over interstate commerce and in respect to the transportation of the mails were not dormant and unused. Congress had taken hold of these two matters and, by various and specific acts, had assumed and exercised the powers given to it, and was in the full discharge of its duty to regulate interstate commerce and carry the mails. The validity of such exercise and the exclusiveness of its control had been again and again presented to this Court for consideration.

It is curious to note the fact that in a large proportion of the cases in respect to interstate commerce brought to this Court the question presented was of the validity of state legislation in its bearings upon interstate commerce, and the uniform course of decision has been to declare that it is not within the competency of a state to legislate in such a manner as to obstruct interstate commerce. If a state with its recognized powers of sovereignty is impotent to obstruct interstate commerce, can it be that any mere voluntary association of individuals within the limits of that state has a power which the state itself does not possess?

As, under the Constitution, power over interstate commerce and the transportation of the mails is vested in the national government, and Congress by virtue of such grant has assumed actual and direct control, it follows that the national government may prevent any unlawful and forcible interference therewith. But how shall this be accomplished? Doubtless, it is within the competency of Congress to prescribe by legislation that any interference with these matters shall be offenses against the United States, and prosecuted and punished by indictment in the proper courts. But is that the only remedy? Have the vast interests of the nation in interstate commerce and in the transportation of the mails no other protection than lies in the possible punishment of those who interfere with it?

To ask the question is to answer it. By Article III, Section 2, Clause 3 of the federal Constitution, it is provided: "The trial of all crimes except in cases of impeachment shall be by jury; and such trial shall be held in the state where the said crime shall have been committed." If all the inhabitants of a state, or even a great body of them, should combine to obstruct interstate commerce or the transportation of the mails, prosecutions for such offenses had in such a community would be doomed in advance to failure. And if the certainty of such failure was known, and the national government had no other way to enforce the freedom of interstate commerce and the transportation of the mails than by prosecution and punishment for interference therewith, the whole interests of the nation in these respects would be at the absolute mercy of a portion of the inhabitants of that single state.

But there is no such impotency in the national government. The entire strength of the nation may be used to enforce in any part of the land the full and free exercise of all national powers and the security of all rights entrusted by the Constitution to its care. The strong arm of the national government may be put forth to brush away all obstructions to the freedom of interstate commerce or the transportation of the mails. If the emergency arises, the Army of the nation, and all its militia, are at the service of the nation to compel obedience to its laws.

But passing to the second question, is there no other alternative than the use of force on the part of the executive authorities whenever obstructions arise to the freedom of interstate commerce or the transportation of the mails? Is the Army the only instrument by which rights of the public can be enforced and the peace of the nation preserved? Grant that any public nuisance may be forcibly abated either at the instance of the authorities or by any individual suffering private damage therefrom, the existence of this right of forcible abatement is not inconsistent with nor does it destroy the right of appeal in an orderly way to the courts for a judicial determination, and an exercise of their powers by writ of injunction and

Eugene V. Debs, socialist labor leader; photographed as a young man

otherwise to accomplish the same result. . . .

So, in the case before us, the right to use force does not exclude the right of appeal to the courts for a judicial determination and for the exercise of all their powers of prevention. Indeed, it is more to the praise than to the blame of the government that, instead of determining for itself questions of right and wrong on the part of these petitioners and their associates and enforcing that determination by the club of the policeman and the bayonet of the soldier, it submitted all those questions to the peaceful determination of judicial tribunals and invoked their consideration and judgment as to the measure of its rights and powers and the correlative obligations of those against whom it made complaint. And it is equally to the credit of the latter that the judgment of those tribunals was by the great body of them respected, and the troubles which threatened so much disaster terminated.

Neither can it be doubted that the government has such an interest in the subject matter as enables it to appear as party plaintiff in this suit. It is said that equity only interferes for the protection of property and that the government has no property interest. A sufficient reply is that the United States have a property in the mails, the protection of which was one of the purposes of this bill. . . .

We do not care to place our decision upon this ground alone. Every government, entrusted, by the very terms of its being, with powers and duties to be exercised and discharged for the general welfare, has a right to apply to its own courts for any proper assistance in the exercise of the one and the discharge of the other, and it is no sufficient answer to its appeal to one of these courts that it has no pecuniary interest in the matter. The obligations which it is under to promote the interest of all, and to prevent the wrongdoing of one resulting in injury to the general welfare, is often of itself sufficient to give it a standing in court. This proposition in some of its relations has heretofore received the sanction of this Court. In *United States* v. *San Jacinto Tin Co.,* 125 U.S. 273, 285, was presented an application of the United States to cancel and annul a patent for land on the ground that it was obtained by fraud or mistake. The right of the United States to maintain such a suit was affirmed, though it was held that if the controversy was really one only between individuals in respect to their claims to property, the government ought not to be permitted to interfere. . . .

It is obvious from these decisions that while it is not the province of the government to interfere in any mere matter of private controversy between individuals, or to use its great powers to enforce the rights of one against another, yet, whenever the wrongs complained of are such as affect the public at large, and are in respect of matters which by the Constitution are entrusted to the care of the nation, and concerning which the nation owes the duty to all the citizens of securing to them their common rights, then the mere fact that the government has no pecuniary interest in the controversy is not sufficient to exclude it from the courts or prevent it from taking measures therein to fully discharge those constitutional duties.

The national government, given by the Constitution power to regulate interstate commerce, has by express statute assumed jurisdiction over such commerce when carried upon railroads. It is charged, therefore, with the duty of keeping those highways of interstate commerce free from obstruction, for it has always been recognized as one of the powers and duties of a government to remove obstructions from the highways under its control. . . .

Up to a recent date, commerce, both interstate and international, was mainly by water, and it is not strange that both the legislation of Congress and the cases in the courts have been principally concerned therewith. The fact that in recent years interstate commerce has come mainly to be carried on by railroads and over artificial highways has in no manner narrowed the scope of the constitutional provision or abridged the power of Congress over such commerce. On the contrary, the same fullness of control exists in the one case as in the other, and the same power to remove obstructions from the one as from the other.

Constitutional provisions do not change, but their operation extends to new matters as the modes of business and the habits of life of the people vary with each succeeding generation. The law of the common carrier is the same today as when transportation on land was by coach and wagon, and on water by canalboat and sailing vessel, yet in its actual operation it touches and regulates transportation by modes then unknown, the railroad train and the steamship. Just so is it with the grant to the national government of power over interstate commerce. The

Constitution has not changed. The power is the same. But it operates today upon modes of interstate commerce unknown to the fathers, and it will operate with equal force upon any new modes of such commerce which the future may develop. . . .

That the bill filed in this case alleged special facts calling for the exercise of all the powers of the court is not open to question. The picture drawn in it of the vast interests involved, not merely of the city of Chicago and the state of Illinois but of all the states, and the general confusion into which the interstate commerce of the country was thrown; the forcible interference with that commerce; the attempted exercise by individuals of powers belonging only to government, and the threatened continuance of such invasions of public right, presented a condition of affairs which called for the fullest exercise of all the powers of the courts. If ever there was a special exigency, one which demanded that the court should do all that courts can do, it was disclosed by this bill, and we need not turn to the public history of the day, which only reaffirms with clearest emphasis all its allegations. . . .

We have given to this case the most careful and anxious attention, for we realize that it touches closely questions of supreme importance to the people of this country. Summing up our conclusions, we hold that the government of the United States is one having jurisdiction over every foot of soil within its territory, and acting directly upon each citizen; that while it is a government of enumerated powers, it has within the limits of those powers all the attributes of sovereignty; that to it is committed power over interstate commerce and the transmission of the mail; that the powers thus conferred upon the national government are not dormant but have been assumed and put into practical exercise by the legislation of Congress; that in the exercise of those powers it is competent for the nation to remove all obstructions upon highways, natural or artificial, to the passage of interstate commerce or the carrying of the mail; that while it may be competent for the government (through the executive branch and in the use of the entire executive power of the nation) to forcibly remove all such obstructions, it is equally within its competency to appeal to the civil courts for an inquiry and determination as to the existence and character of any alleged obstructions, and if such are found to exist, or threaten to occur, to invoke the powers of those courts to remove or restrain such obstructions; that the jurisdiction of courts to interfere in such matters by injunction is one recognized from ancient times and by indubitable authority; that such jurisdiction is not ousted by the fact that the obstructions are accompanied by or consist of acts in themselves violations of the criminal law; that the proceeding by injunction is of a civil character and may be enforced by proceedings in contempt; that such proceedings are not in execution of the criminal laws of the land; that the penalty for a violation of injunction is no substitute for and no defense to a prosecution for any criminal offenses committed in the course of such violation; that the complaint filed in this case clearly showed an existing obstruction of artificial highways for the passage of interstate commerce and the transmission of the mail —

an obstruction not only temporarily existing, but threatening to continue; that under such complaint the Circuit Court had power to issue its process of injunction; that it having been issued and served on these defendants, the Circuit Court had authority to inquire whether its orders had been disobeyed, and when it found that they had been, then to proceed under Section 725, Revised Statutes, which grants power "to punish, by fine or imprisonment . . . disobedience . . . by any party . . . or other person, to any lawful writ, process, order, rule, decree, or command," and enter the order of punishment complained of; and, finally, that, the Circuit Court, having full jurisdiction in the premises, its finding of the fact of disobedience is not open to review on habeas corpus in this or any other court. . . .

We enter into no examination of the act of July 2, 1890 . . . upon which the Circuit Court relied mainly to sustain its jurisdiction. It must not be understood from this that we dissent from the conclusions of that court in reference to the scope of the act, but simply that we prefer to rest our judgment on the broader ground which has been discussed in this opinion, believing it of importance that the principles underlying it should be fully stated and affirmed.

The petition for a writ of habeas corpus is *denied*.

While there is a lower class, I am in it.
While there is a criminal element, I am of it.
While there is a soul in jail, I am not free.

EUGENE V. DEBS

8.

M. W. Fuller and J. M. Harlan: *United States v. E. C. Knight Company*

The Sherman Antitrust Act of 1890 prohibited combinations in "restraint of trade or commerce among the several states." A critical test of the law occurred in 1895 in the Knight case. E. C. Knight Company was a combination of sugar-refining companies that comprised 98 percent of the sugar-refining capacity of the country. Its major operation was located in Pennsylvania, but it owned refineries elsewhere as well. Chief Justice Fuller, speaking for the Court, interpreted the law very narrowly and declared that the Knight Company was not in violation of the Sherman Act. He reasoned that Congress had authority over interstate commerce, but not over manufacturing, and thus held that the Sugar Trust could not come under federal control. Portions of Fuller's ruling and of the lone dissent of Justice John M. Harlan are reprinted below.

Source: 156 U.S. 1.

Mr. Chief Justice Fuller: The fundamental question is, whether conceding that the existence of a monopoly in manufacture is established by the evidence that monopoly can be directly suppressed under the act of Congress in the mode attempted by this bill. . . . The argument is that the power to control the manufacture of refined sugar is a monopoly over a necessary of life, to the enjoyment of which by a large part of the population of the United States interstate commerce is indispensable, and that, therefore, the general government, in the exercise of the power to regulate commerce, may repress such monopoly directly and set aside the instruments which have created it. But this argument cannot be confined to necessaries of life merely, and must include all articles of general consumption.

Doubtless the power to control the manufacture of a given thing involves in a certain sense the control of its disposition, but this is a secondary and not the primary sense; and although the exercise of that power may result in bringing the operation of commerce into play, it does not control it, and affects it only incidentally and indirectly. Commerce succeeds to manufacture and is not a part of it. The power to regulate commerce is the power to prescribe the rule by which commerce shall be governed and is a power independent of the power to suppress monopoly. But it may operate in repression of monopoly whenever that comes within the rules by which commerce is governed or whenever the transaction is itself a monopoly of commerce.

It is vital that the independence of the commercial power and of the police power, and the delimitation between them, however sometimes perplexing, should always be recognized and observed, for, while the one furnishes the strongest bond of union, the other is essential to the preservation of the autonomy of the states as required by our dual form of government; and acknowledged evils, however grave and urgent they may appear to be, had better be borne than the risk be run, in the effort to suppress them, of more serious consequences by re-

John Marshall Harlan, who served on the Supreme Court for 34 years and gained recognition for his dissenting position on some of the major cases of his era

sort to expedients of even doubtful constitutionality. . . .

It was in the light of well-settled principles that the act of July 2, 1890, was framed. Congress did not attempt thereby to assert the power to deal with monopoly directly as such; or to limit and restrict the rights of corporations created by the states or the citizens of the states in the acquisition, control, or disposition of property; or to regulate or prescribe the price or prices at which such property or the products thereof should be sold; or to make criminal the acts of persons in the acquisition and control of property which the states of their residence or creation sanctioned or permitted. Aside from the provisions applicable where Congress might exercise municipal power, what the law struck at was combinations, contracts, and conspiracies to monopolize trade and commerce among the several states or with foreign nations; but the contracts and acts of the defendants related exclusively to the acquisition of the Philadelphia refineries and the business of sugar refining in Pennsylvania, and bore no direct relation to commerce between the states or with foreign nations. The object was manifestly private gain in the manufacture of the commodity, but not through the control of interstate or foreign commerce.

It is true that the bill alleged that the products of these refineries were sold and distributed among the several states, and that all the companies were engaged in trade or commerce with the several states and with foreign nations; but this was no more than to say that trade and commerce served manufacture to fulfill its function. Sugar was refined for sale, and sales were probably made at Philadelphia for consumption, and undoubtedly for resale by the first purchasers throughout Pennsylvania and other states, and refined sugar was also forwarded by the companies to other states for sale. Nevertheless, it does not follow that an attempt to monopolize, or the actual monopoly of the manufacture was an attempt, whether executory or consummated, to monopolize commerce, even though, in order to dispose of the product, the instrumentality of commerce was necessarily invoked.

There was nothing in the proofs to indicate any intention to put a restraint upon trade or commerce, and the fact, as we have seen, that trade or commerce might be indirectly affected was not enough to entitle complainants to a decree. The subject matter of the sale was shares of manufacturing stock, and the relief sought was the surrender of property which had already passed and the suppression of the alleged monopoly in manufacture by the restoration of the status quo before the transfers; yet the act of Congress only authorized the Circuit courts to proceed by way of preventing and restraining violations of the act in respect of contracts, combinations, or conspiracies in restraint of interstate or international trade or commerce.

Mr. Justice Harlan: The power of Congress covers and protects the absolute freedom of such intercourse and trade among the states as may or must succeed manufacture and precede transportation from the place of purchase. This would seem to be conceded; for, the Court in the present case expressly declare that "*contracts to buy, sell, or exchange goods to be transported among the several states,* the transportation and its instrumentalities, and articles bought, sold, or exchanged for the purpose of such transit among the states, or put in the way of transit, *may be regulated,* but this is *because they form part of interstate trade or commerce.*" Here is a direct admission — one which the settled doctrines of this Court justify — that contracts to buy and the purchasing of goods *to be transported from one state to another,* and transportation, with its instrumentalities, are all *parts* of interstate trade or commerce. Each part of such trade is then under the protection of Congress.

And yet, by the opinion and judgment in this case, if I do not misapprehend them, Congress is without power to protect the commercial intercourse that such purchasing necessarily involves against the restraints and burdens arising from the existence of *combinations* that meet purchasers, from whatever state they come, with the threat — for it is nothing more nor less than a threat — that they *shall not* purchase what they desire to purchase, *except at the prices fixed by such combinations.*

A citizen of Missouri has the right to go in person, or send orders, to Pennsylvania and New Jersey for the purpose of purchasing refined sugar. But of what value is that right if he is confronted in those states by a vast *combination* which absolutely controls the price of that article by reason of its having acquired all the sugar refineries in the United States in order that they may fix prices in their own interest exclusively?

In my judgment, the citizens of the several states composing the Union are entitled, of right, to buy goods in the state where they are manufactured, or in any other state, without being confronted by an illegal combination whose business extends throughout the whole country, which by the law everywhere is an enemy to the public interests, and which prevents such buying, except at prices arbitrarily fixed by it. I insist that the free course of trade among the states cannot coexist with such combinations. When I speak of trade I mean the buying and selling of articles of every kind that are recognized articles of interstate commerce.

Whatever improperly obstructs the free course of interstate intercourse and trade, as involved in the buying and selling of articles to be carried from one state to another, may be reached by Congress, under its authority to regulate commerce among the states. The exercise of that authority so as to make trade among the states, in all recognized articles of commerce, absolutely free from unreasonable or illegal restrictions imposed by combinations is justified by an express grant of power to Congress and would redound to the welfare of the whole country. I am unable to perceive that any such result would imperil the autonomy of the states, especially as that result cannot be attained through the action of any one state.

Undue restrictions or burdens upon the purchasing of goods, in the market for sale, to be transported to other states, cannot be imposed even by a state without violating the freedom of commercial intercourse guaranteed by the Constitution. But if a *state* within whose limits the business of refining sugar is exclusively carried on may not constitutionally impose burdens upon purchases of sugar *to be transported to other states,* how comes it that combinations of corporations or individuals, within the same state, may not be prevented by the national government from putting unlawful restraints upon the purchasing of that article *to be carried from the state in which such purchases are made?*

If the national power is competent to repress *state* action in restraint of interstate trade as it may be involved in purchases of refined sugar to be transported from one state to another state, surely it ought to be deemed sufficient to prevent unlawful restraints attempted to be imposed by combinations of corporations or individuals upon those identical purchases; otherwise, illegal combinations of corporations or individuals may — so far as national power and interstate commerce are concerned — do, with impunity what no state can do. . . .

It may be that the means employed by Congress to suppress combinations that restrain interstate trade and commerce are not all or the best that could have been devised. But Congress, under the delegation of authority to enact laws necessary and proper to carry into effect a power granted, is not restricted to the employment of those means "without which the end would be entirely unattainable." "To have prescribed the means," this Court has said,

> by which government should, in all future time, execute its powers, would have been to change entirely the character of that instrument and give it the properties of a legal code. It would have been an unwise attempt to provide, by immutable rules for exigencies which, if foreseen at all, must have been seen dimly and which can be best provided for as they occur. To have declared that the best means shall not be used, but those alone without which the power given would be nugatory, would have been to deprive the legislature of the capacity to avail itself of experience, to exercise its reason, and to accommodate its legislation to circumstances. . . .

Where the law is not prohibited and is really calculated to effect any of the objects entrusted to the government, to undertake here to inquire into the degree of its necessity would be to pass the line which circumscribes the judicial department, and to tread on legislative ground (*M'Culloch* v. *Maryland*). . . .

By the Act of 1890, Congress subjected to forfeiture "any property owned under any contract or by any combination, or pursuant to any conspiracy (and being the subject thereof) mentioned in Section 1 of this act, and being in the course of transportation from one state to another, or to a foreign country." It was not deemed wise to subject such property to forfeiture before transportation began or after it ended. If it be suggested that Congress might have prohibited the *transportation* from the state in which they are manufactured of any articles, by whomsoever at the time owned, that had been manufactured by combinations formed to monopolize some designated part of trade or commerce among the states, my answer is that it is not within the functions of the judiciary to adjudge that Congress shall employ particular means in execution of a given power simply because such means are, in the judgment of the courts, best conducive to the end sought to be accomplished.

Congress, in the exercise of its discretion as to choice of means conducive to an end to which it was competent, determined to reach that end through civil proceedings instituted to prevent or restrain these obnoxious combinations in their attempts to burden interstate commerce by obstructions that interfere *in advance of transportation* with the free course of trade between the people of the states. In other words, Congress sought to prevent the coming into existence of combinations, the purpose or tendency of which was to impose unlawful restraints upon interstate commerce. . . .

The question here relates to restraints upon the freedom of interstate trade and commerce imposed by illegal combinations. After the fullest consideration I have been able to bestow upon this important question, I find it impossible to refuse my assent to this proposition: whatever a state may do to protect its completely interior traffic or trade against unlawful restraints, the general government is empowered to do for the protection of the people of all the states — for this purpose one people — against unlawful restraints imposed upon interstate traffic or trade in articles that are to enter into commerce among the several states.

If, as already shown, a state may prevent or suppress a *combination,* the effect of which is to subject its domestic trade to the restraints necessarily arising from their obtaining the absolute control of the sale of a particular article in general use by the community, there ought to be no hesitation in allowing to Congress the right to suppress a similar *combination* that imposes a like unlawful restraint upon interstate trade and traffic in that article. While the states retain, because they have never surrendered, full control of their completely internal traffic, it was not intended by the framers of the Constitution that any part of interstate commerce should be excluded from the control of Congress. Each state can reach and suppress combinations so far as they unlawfully restrain its interior trade, while the national government may reach and suppress them so far as they unlawfully restrain trade among the states.

While the opinion of the Court in this case does not declare the Act of 1890 to be unconstitutional, it defeats the main object for which it was passed. For it is, in effect, held that the statute would be unconstitutional if interpreted as embracing such unlawful restraints upon the purchasing of goods in one state to be carried to another state as necessarily arise from the *existence* of combinations formed for the purpose and with the effect, not only of monopolizing the ownership of all such goods in every part of the country but of controlling the prices for them in all the states. This view of the scope of the act leaves the public, so far as national power is concerned, entirely at the mercy of combinations which arbitrarily control the prices of articles purchased to be transported from one state to another state.

I cannot assent to that view. In my judgment, the general government is not placed by the Constitution in such a condition of helplessness that it must fold its arms and remain inactive while capital combines, under the name of a corporation, to destroy competition, not in one state only but throughout the entire country, in the buying and selling of articles — especially the necessaries of life — that go into commerce among the states. The doctrine of the autonomy of the states cannot properly be invoked to justify a denial of power in the national government to meet such an emergency, involving as it does that freedom of commercial intercourse among the states which the Constitution sought to attain.

It is said that there are no proofs in the record which indicate an *intention* upon the part of the American Sugar Refining Company and its associates to put a restraint upon trade or commerce. Was it necessary that formal proof be made that the persons engaged in this combination admitted, in words, that they intended to restrain trade or commerce? Did anyone expect to find in the written agreements which resulted in the formation of this combination a distinct expression of a purpose to restrain interstate trade or commerce? Men who form and control these combinations are too cautious and wary to make such admissions orally or in writing.

Why, it is conceded that the object of this combination was to obtain control of the business of making and selling refined sugar throughout the entire country. Those interested in its operations will be satisfied with nothing less than to have the whole population of America pay tribute to them. That object is disclosed upon the very face of the transactions described in the bill. And it is proved — indeed, is conceded — that that object has been accomplished to the extent that the American Sugar Refining Company now controls 98 percent of all the sugar-refining business in the country, and therefore controls the price of that article everywhere.

Now, the *mere existence* of a combination having such an object and possessing such extraordinary power is itself, under settled principles of law — there being no adjudged case to the contrary in this country — a direct restraint of trade in the article for the control of the sales of which in this country that combination was organized. And that restraint is felt in all the states for the reason, known to all, that the article in question goes, was intended to go, and must always go into commerce among the several states and into the homes of people in every condition of life.

A decree recognizing the freedom of commercial intercourse as embracing the right to buy goods to be transported from one state to another, without buyers being burdened by unlawful restraints imposed by combinations of corporations or individuals, so far from disturbing or endangering, would tend to preserve the autonomy of the states and protect the people of all the states against dangers so portentous as to excite apprehension for the safety of our liberties. If this be not a sound interpretation of the Constitution, it is easy to perceive that interstate traffic, so far as it involves the price to be paid for articles necessary to the comfort and well-being of the people in all the states, may pass under the absolute control of overshadowing combinations having financial resources without limit and an audacity in the accomplishment of their objects that recognizes none of the restraints of moral obligations controlling the action of individuals — combinations governed entirely by the law of greed and selfishness; so powerful that no single state is able to overthrow them and give the required protection to the whole country, and so all-pervading that they threaten the integrity of our institutions.

We have before us the case of a combination which absolutely controls or may, at its discretion, control the price of all refined sugar in this country. Suppose another *combination*, organized for private gain and to control prices, should obtain possession of all the large flour mills in the United States; another, of all the grain elevators; another, of all the oil territory; another, of all the salt-producing regions; another, of all the cotton mills; and another, of all the great establishments for slaughtering animals, and the preparation of meats. What power is competent to protect the people of the United States against such dangers except a national power — one that is capable of exerting its sovereign authority throughout every part of the territory and over all the people of the nation?

To the general government has been committed the control of commercial intercourse among the states, to the end that it may be free at all times from any restraints except such as Congress may impose or permit for the benefit of the whole country. The common government of all the people is the only one that can adequately deal with a matter which directly and injuriously affects the entire commerce of the country, which concerns equally all the people of the Union, and which, it must be confessed, cannot be adequately controlled by any one state. Its authority should not be so weakened by construction that it cannot reach and eradicate evils that, beyond all question, tend to defeat an object which that government is entitled, by the Constitution, to accomplish.

"Powerful and ingenious minds," this Court has said, "taking, as postulates, that the powers expressly granted to the government of the Union are to be contracted by construction into the narrowest possible compass, and that the original powers of the states are retained if any possible construction will retain them, may, by a course of well-digested but refined and metaphysical reasoning, founded on these premises, explain away the Constitution of our country, and leave it a magnificent structure, indeed, to look at, but totally unfit for use. They may so entangle and perplex the understanding as to obscure principles which were before thought quite plain, and induce doubts where, if the mind were to pursue its own course, none would be perceived" (*Gibbons* v. *Ogden*).

9.

Lester F. Ward: Plutocracy or Paternalism

Sociology was a new branch of the social sciences in 1895; it had received little recognition from the academic world and less from the public at large. One early sociologist whose views were destined to shape all later work in the field was Lester Ward. Advocating a "sociocracy,". Ward wrote many books in support of the thesis that "the individual has reigned long enough. The day has come for society to take its affairs into its own hands and shape its own destinies." A suggestion of what the proper relationship should be between the individual and government was presented in his article, "Plutocracy and Paternalism," published in November 1895.

Source: *Forum*, November 1895.

To judge from the tone of the popular press, the country would seem to be between the devil of state interference and the deep sea of gold. The two epithets "plutocracy" and "paternalism," so freely applied, are intended to characterize the worst tendencies of the times in these two opposite directions, and are calculated to engender the bitterest feelings in the public mind. If such a thing were possible, it would certainly be useful, standing aloof from the contest, to make a cool, unbiased analysis of the true meaning of these terms in their relation to the existing state of affairs. While it may be admitted that this is impossible, such an approximation to it as the conditions will allow can certainly do no harm. . . .

Justly or unjustly, society has made wealth a measure of worth. It is easy on general principles to prove that it is not such a measure. Everyone is personally cognizant of numerous cases to the contrary. All will admit that, taken in the abstract, the principle is unsound, and yet all act upon it. Not rationally, not perhaps consciously, but still they do it. It is "human nature" to respect those who have and to care little for those who have not. There is a sort of feeling that if one is destitute there must be a reason for it. It is inevitably ascribed to some personal deficit. In a word, absence of means is, in one form or another, made to stand for absence of merit.

Its cause is looked for in character. This is most clearly seen in the marked contrast between the indisposition to help the unsuccessful and the willingness to help the successful. Aside from the prospect of a *quid pro quo*, no one wants to waste time, energy, or money on what is worthless — and possession is the primary test of worth. . . .

Thus it comes about that wealth, in the existing state of society, is a tremendous power. It gives not only ease, plenty, luxury, but, what is infinitely more, the respect of all and the envy of the less favored. It gives, in a word, superiority; and the strongest craving of man's nature is, in one way or another, to be set over his fellows. When all this is considered, the futility of the proposal of certain reformers to eradicate the passion for proprietary acquisition becomes apparent. It may be assumed that this passion will continue for an indefinite period to be the ruling element of the industrial state. That it has done and is still doing incalculable service to society few will deny. That it may continue to be useful to the end of our present industrial era will probably be admitted by all but a small class.

If the accumulation of wealth, even for the benefit of individuals, were all that is involved in the term "plutocracy," the indictment would not be serious. If the governing power implied in the last component of the word were nothing more than the normal influence that wealth exerts, no great injury to society could accrue. Even the amassing of colossal fortunes is not an evil in itself, since the very activity which it requires stimulates industry and benefits a large number. There is, it is true, a danger — in the transmission of such fortunes to inactive and nonproductive heirs — of creating a nonindustrial class in perpetuity; but this could be remedied, without hardship to any worthy person, by a wise limitation of inheritance.

So much for plutocracy. Let us now turn to the other pole of public opinion and inquire into the meaning of "paternalism." Literally, of course, paternalism in government would be restricted to cases in which the governing power is vested in a single person, who may be regarded as well-disposed and seeking to rule his subjects for their own good, as a father governs his children. But a ruling family, or even a large ruling class, may be supposed to govern from similar motives. In either case the governed are not supposed to have any voice in the matter, but are cared for like children by the assumed wisdom of their rulers. How far from true paternalism is anything that exists in this or any other civilized country today may therefore be readily seen.

No one will claim that there is any danger, in a representative government with universal suffrage, of any such state being brought about. This shows at the outset that the term is not used in its original and correct sense but is merely borrowed and applied as a stigma to certain tendencies in republican governments which the users of it do not approve. What are these tendencies? In general it may be said that they are tendencies toward the assumption by the state of functions that are now entrusted to private enterprise.

On the one hand, it is logically argued that the indefinite extension of such powers would eventuate in the most extreme socialistic system — the conduct of all business by the state. On the other hand, it is shown with equal logic that the entire relinquishment of the functions which the state has already assumed would be the abolition of government itself. The extremists of one party would land us in socialism; those of the other, in anarchy. But on one side it is said by the more moderate that the true function of government is the protection of society; to which it is replied by the other that such extension of governmental powers is in the interest of protection, viz., protection against the undue rapacity of private enterprise. Here, as almost everywhere else in the realm of politics, it is a question of quantity and not of quality. It is not a difference in principle, but in policy. It is the degree to which the fundamental principle of all government is to be carried out. . . .

The first law of economics is that everyone may be depended upon at all times to seek his greatest gain. It is both natural and right that the individual should be ever seeking to acquire for himself and his; and this rather irrespective of the rest of the world. . . . Any advantage gained by force is promptly met by the law; but advantage gained by cunning, by superior knowledge — if it be only of the technicalities of the law — is not a crime, though its spirit be as bad as that of highway robbery and its consequences a thousand times worse.

From this point of view, then, modern society is suffering from the very opposite of paternalism — from under-government, from the failure of government to keep pace with the change which civilization has wrought in substituting intellectual for physical qualities as the workers of injustice. . . . The true function of government is not to fetter but to liberate the forces of society, not to diminish but to increase their effectiveness. Unbridled competition destroys itself. The only competition that endures is that which goes on under judicious regulation.

If, then, the danger of plutocracy is so largely due to insufficient government, where is the tendency to paternalism in the sense of too much government? This opens up the last and most important aspect of the subject. If there were no influences at work in society but those of unaided nature; if we had a pure physiocracy or government of nature such as prevails among wild animals, and the weak were thereby sacrificed that the strong might survive to beget the strong and thus elevate the race along the lines of evolution — however great the hardship, we might resign ourselves to it as part of the great cosmic scheme. But unfortunately this is not the case.

Without stopping to show that, from the standpoint of a civilized society, the qualities which best fit men to gain advantage over their fellows are the ones least useful to society at large, it will be sufficient for the present purpose to point out that in the actual state of society it is not even those who, from this biological point of view, are the fittest that become in fact the recipients of the greatest favors at the hands of society. This is due to the creation, by society itself, of artificial conditions that destroy the balance of forces and completely nullify all the beneficial effects that are secured by the operation of the natural law on the lower plane. Indeed, the effect is reversed, and instead of developing strength, either physical or mental, through activity incident to emulation, it tends to parasitic degeneracy through the pampered idleness of the favored classes.

What, in the last analysis, are these social conditions? They are at bottom integral parts of government. They are embodied in law. Largely they consist of statute law. Where this is wanting they rest on judicial decisions, often immemorial, and belonging to the *lex non scripta*. In a word, they constitute the great system of jurisprudence relating to property and business, gradually built up through the ages to make men secure in their possessions and safe in their business transactions, but which in our day, owing to entirely changed industrial conditions, has become the means of throwing unlimited opportunities in the way of some and of barring out the rest from all opportunities. This system of artificial props, bolsterings, and scaffoldings has grown so perfect as to make exertion needless for the protected class and hopeless for the neglected mass. In a word, it has become the bulwark of monopoly. . . .

And thus we have the remarkable fact, so persistently overlooked in all the discussions of current questions, that government which fails to protect the weak is devoting all its energies to protecting the strong. It legalizes and promotes trusts and combinations; subsidizes corporations and then absolves them from their obligations; sustains stock-watering schemes and all forms of speculation; grants without compensation the most valuable franchises, often in perpetuity; and in innumerable ways creates, defends, and protects a vast array of purely parasitic enterprises, calculated directly to foster the worst forms of municipal corruption. The proofs of each one of these counts lie about us on every hand. Only those who are blinded by interest or prejudice can fail to see them. . . .

The charge of paternalism is chiefly made

by the class that enjoys the largest share of government protection. Those who denounce state interference are the ones who most frequently and successfully invoke it. The cry of laissez faire mainly goes up from the ones who, if really "let alone," would instantly lose their wealth-absorbing power.

A significant example of this is found in some of the provisions of the so-called Pooling Bill. In a paper read by the Hon. Carroll D. Wright before the American Economic Association in December last, he characterizes this as "state-socialistic," and says:

> This pending legislation is demanded at the instance of the shippers and the railroads of the country, and its passage is being aided by a powerful lobby in their service. The railroads base their advocacy of the bill on the claim that it will be for the interest of the shippers to have such a law.

And he predicts that it will be followed by a demand that the government shall take charge of the roads and guarantee dividends to the stockholders. He further says:

> All this will be at the demand and in the interest of the railroads and of the shippers, and not of the labor involved in carrying on the work of transportation, as the demand of today for the enactment of the Pooling Bill is alleged to be largely in the interest of the shippers and the public welfare.

Nothing is more obvious today than the signal inability of capital and private enterprise to take care of themselves, unaided by the state; and while they are incessantly denouncing "paternalism" — by which they mean the claim of the defenseless laborer and artisan to a share in this lavish state protection — they are all the while besieging legislatures for relief from their own incompetency and "pleading the baby act" through a trained body of lawyers and lobbyists. The dispensing of national pap to this class should rather be called "maternalism," to which a square, open, and dignified paternalism would be infinitely preferable.

Still all these things must be regarded as perfectly natural, that is, inherent in the nature of man, and not as peculiar to any class. Therefore, personalities and vituperation are entirely out of place. It is simply a question of whether they are going to be permitted to go on. The fault is altogether with the system. Nor should anyone object to state protection of business interests. Even monopoly may be defended against aggressive competition on the ground of economy. The protection of the strong may not be too great, but there should be at the same time protection of the weak against the protected strong.

It is not the purpose of this article to point out remedies, but tendencies; and it seems clear that right here are to be located the two greatest dangers to modern society. Here lies the only plutocracy, and here the only paternalism. The two are really one and are embodied in the joint fact of state-protected monopoly.

The degree to which the citizen is protected in the secure enjoyment of his possessions is a fair measure of the state of civilization, but this protection must apply as rigidly to the poor man's possessions as to those of the rich man. In the present system, the latter is not only encouraged but actually tempted to exploit the former. Every trust, every monopoly, every carelessly granted franchise has or may have this effect; and the time has arrived when a part at least of this paternal solicitude on the part of government should be diverted from the monopolistic element and bestowed upon the general public. If we must have paternalism, there should be no partiality shown in the family.

10.

Antonín Dvořák: Music in America

*At the end of the nineteenth century, loyal American patrons of the arts praised
America for her increasing numbers of orchestra halls, art museums, and theaters,
but critics argued that the increase was more in quantity than in quality. In the field
of music, Americans had made contributions — for example, ragtime and Negro
spirituals — but they were not noted for their innovations in "serious" music. The
famous Bohemian composer, Antonín Dvořák, who had based his symphony*
From the New World *on American folk themes, was asked by* Harper's New
Monthly *magazine to evaluate the state of music in America for its readers.
His analysis, reprinted here in part, discussed some of the weaknesses and strengths
of American life that played a role, in his view, in blocking the development of
a flourishing musical tradition.*

Source: *Harper's New Monthly*, February 1895.

It is a difficult task at best for a foreigner
to give a correct verdict of the affairs of another country. With the United States of
America this is more than usually difficult,
because they cover such a vast area of land
that it would take many years to become
properly acquainted with the various localities, separated by great distances, that
would have to be considered when rendering a judgment concerning them all. It
would ill become me, therefore, to express
my views on so general and all-embracing a
subject as music in America were I not
pressed to do so, for I have neither traveled
extensively, nor have I been here long
enough to gain an intimate knowledge of
American affairs. I can only judge of it from
what I have observed during my limited experience as a musician and teacher in America, and from what those whom I know
here tell me about their own country.
Many of my impressions therefore are those
of a foreigner who has not been here long
enough to overcome the feeling of strangeness and bewildered astonishment which

must fill all European visitors upon their
first arrival. . . .

When I see how much is done in every
other field by public-spirited men in America — how schools, universities, libraries,
museums, hospitals, and parks spring up out
of the ground and are maintained by generous gifts — I can only marvel that so little
has been done for music. After 200 years of
almost unbroken prosperity and expansion,
the net results for music are a number of
public concert halls of most recent growth;
several musical societies with orchestras of
noted excellence, such as the Philharmonic
Society in New York, the orchestras of Mr.
Thomas and Mr. Seidl, and the superb orchestra supported by a public-spirited citizen of Boston; one opera company, which
only the upper classes can hear or understand; and a national conservatory, which
owes its existence to the generous forethought of one indefatigable woman.

It is true that music is the youngest of
the arts and must therefore be expected to
be treated as Cinderella; but is it not time

that she were lifted from the ashes and given a seat among the equally youthful sister arts in this land of youth, until the coming of the fairy godmother and the prince of the crystal slipper? . . .

The great American republic alone, in its national government as well as in the several governments of the states, suffers art and music to go without encouragement. Trades and commerce are protected, funds are voted away for the unemployed, schools and colleges are endowed, but music must go unaided and be content if she can get the support of a few private individuals. . . .

It is one of the anomalies of this country that the principle of protection is upheld for all enterprises but art. By protection I do not mean the exclusion of foreign art. That, of course, is absurd. But just as the state here provides for its poor industrial scholars and university students, so should it help the would-be students of music and art. As it is now, the poor musician not only cannot get his necessary instruction, in the first place, but if by any chance he has acquired it, he has small prospects of making his chosen calling support him in the end. Why is this? Simply because the orchestras in which first-class players could find a place in this country can be counted on one hand; while of opera companies where native singers can be heard, and where the English tongue is sung, there are none at all.

Another thing which discourages the student of music is the unwillingness of publishers to take anything but light and trashy music. European publishers are bad enough in that respect, but the American publishers are worse. Thus, when one of my pupils last year produced a very creditable work, and a thoroughly American composition at that, he could not get it published in America but had to send it to Germany, where it was at once accepted. The same is true of my own compositions on American subjects, each of which hitherto has had to be published abroad.

No wonder American composers and musicians grow discouraged and regard the more promising condition of music in other countries with envy! Such a state of affairs should be a source of mortification to all truly patriotic Americans. Yet it can be easily remedied. What was the situation in England but a short while ago? Then they had to procure all their players from abroad, while their own musicians went to the Continent to study. Now that they have two standard academies of music in London, like those of Berlin, Paris, and other cities, the national feeling for music seems to have been awakened, and the majority of orchestras are composed of native Englishmen who play as well as the others did before. A single institution can make such a change, just as a single genius can bestow an art upon his country that before was lying in unheeded slumber. . . .

If the old commonwealths of Greece and Italy and the modern republics of France and Switzerland have been able to do this, why cannot America follow their example? The money certainly is not lacking. Constantly we see great sums of money spent for the material pleasures of the few, which, if devoted to the purposes of art, might give pleasure to thousands. . . .

In answer to such arguments I am told that there is no popular demand for good music in America. That is not so. Every concert in New York, Boston, Philadelphia, Chicago, or Washington, and most other cities, no doubt, disproves such a statement. American concert halls are as well filled as those of Europe, and, as a rule, the listeners — to judge them by their attentive conduct and subsequent expression of pleasure — are not a whit less appreciative. How it would be with opera I cannot judge, since American opera audiences, as the opera is conducted at present, are in no sense representative of the people at large. I have no doubt, however, that if the Americans had a chance to hear grand opera sung in their own language they would enjoy it as well and appreciate it as highly as the opera goers of Vienna, Paris, or Munich enjoy theirs. The change from Italian and French to English will scarcely have an injurious effect on the present good voices of the singers, while it may have the effect of improving the voices of American singers, bringing out more clearly the beauty and strength of the *timbre*, while giving an intelligent conception of the work that enables singers to use a pure diction, which cannot be obtained in a foreign tongue.

The American voice, so far as I can judge, is a good one. When I first arrived in this country I was startled by the strength and the depth of the voices in the boys who sell papers on the street, and I am still constantly amazed at its penetrating quality.

In a sense, of course, it is true that there is less of a demand for music in America than in certain other countries. Our common folk in Bohemia know this. When they come here, they leave their fiddles and other instruments at home, and none of the itinerant musicians with whom our country abounds would ever think of trying their luck over here. Occasionally, when I have met one of my countrymen whom I knew to be musical in this city of New York or in the West, and have asked him why he did not become a professional musician, I have usually received the answer, "Oh, music is not wanted in this land." This I can scarcely believe. Music is wanted wherever good people are, as the German poet has sung. It only rests with the leaders of the people to make a right beginning.

When this beginning is made, and when those who have musical talent find it worth their while to stay in America, and to study and exercise their art as the business of their life, the music of America will soon become more national in its character. This, my conviction, I know, is not shared by many who can justly claim to know this country better than I do. Because the population of the United States is composed of many different races in which the Teutonic element

predominates, and because, owing to the improved methods of transmission of the present day, the music of all the world is quickly absorbed by this country, they argue that nothing specially original or national can come forth. According to that view, all other countries which are but the results of a conglomeration of peoples and races, as, for instance, Italy, could not have produced a national literature or a national music.

A while ago I suggested that inspiration for truly national music might be derived from the Negro melodies or Indian chants. I was led to take this view partly by the fact that the so-called plantation songs are indeed the most striking and appealing melodies that have yet been found on this side of the water, but largely by the observation that this seems to be recognized, though often unconsciously, by most Americans. All races have their distinctively national songs, which they at once recognize as their own, even if they have never heard them before. . . .

It is a proper question to ask, what songs, then, belong to the American and appeal more strongly to him than any others? What melody could stop him on the street if he were in a strange land and make the home feeling well up within him, no matter how hardened he might be or how wretchedly the tune were played? Their number, to be sure, seems to be limited. The most potent as well as the most beautiful among them, according to my estimation, are certain of the so-called plantation melodies and slave songs, all of which are distinguished by unusual and subtle harmonies, the like of which I have found in no other songs but those of old Scotland and Ireland.

The point has been urged that many of these touching songs, like those of Foster, have not been composed by the Negroes themselves but are the work of white men, while others did not originate on the plantation but were imported from Africa. It seems to me that this matters but little.

One might as well condemn the *Hungarian Rhapsody* because Liszt could not speak Hungarian. The important thing is that the inspiration for such music should come from the right source and that the music itself should be a true expression of the people's real feelings. To read the right meaning, the composer need not necessarily be of the same blood, though that, of course, makes it easier for him. . . .

The white composers who wrote the touching Negro songs which dimmed Thackeray's spectacles so that he exclaimed, "Behold, a vagabond with a corked face and a banjo sings a little song, strikes a wild note, which sets the whole heart thrilling with happy pity!" had a similarly sympathetic comprehension of the deep pathos of slave life. If, as I have been informed, they were, these songs were adopted by the Negroes on the plantations, they thus became true Negro songs. Whether the original songs which must have inspired the composers came from Africa or originated on the plantations matters as little as whether Shakespeare invented his own plots or borrowed them from others.

The thing to rejoice over is that such lovely songs exist and are sung at the present day. I, for one, am delighted by them. Just so it matters little whether the inspiration for the coming folk songs of America is derived from the Negro melodies, the songs of the Creoles, the red man's chant, or the plaintive ditties of the homesick German or Norwegian.

Undoubtedly the germs for the best of music lie hidden among all the races that are commingled in this great country. The music of the people is like a rare and lovely flower growing amidst encroaching weeds. Thousands pass it, while others trample it underfoot, and thus the chances are that it will perish before it is seen by the one discriminating spirit who will prize it above all

else. The fact that no one has as yet arisen to make the most of it does not prove that nothing is there. . . .

My own duty as a teacher, I conceive, is not so much to interpret Beethoven, Wagner, or other masters of the past, but to give what encouragement I can to the young musicians of America. I must give full expression to my firm conviction and to the hope that just as this nation has already surpassed so many others in marvelous inventions and feats of engineering and commerce, and has made an honorable place for itself in literature in one short century, so it must assert itself in the other arts, and especially in the art of music.

Already there are enough public-spirited lovers of music striving for the advancement of this their chosen art to give rise to the hope that the United States of America will soon emulate the older countries in smoothing the thorny path of the artist and musician. When that beginning has been made, when no large city is without its public opera house and concert hall, and without its school of music and endowed orchestra, where native musicians can be heard and judged, then those who hitherto have had no opportunity to reveal their talent will come forth and compete with one another, till a real genius emerges from their number who will be as thoroughly representative of his country as Wagner and Weber are of Germany, or Chopin of Poland.

To bring about this result we must trust to the ever youthful enthusiasm and patriotism of this country. When it is accomplished and when music has been established as one of the reigning arts of the land, another wreath of fame and glory will be added to the country which earned its name, the "Land of Freedom," by unshackling her slaves at the price of her own blood.

Unloading banana boats in New York Harbor, 1905

METROPOLIS

New York entered the 20th century as the undisputed financial and commercial center of the nation. Land annexations in 1874 and 1895, which took in territory beyond the original island of Manhattan, resulted in the incorporation of Greater New York City in 1898 under a single metropolitan government. The development of the city rested largely on an improving technology. By 1904 the steam railways had been converted to electricity, new water sources were being developed, street construction was advancing rapidly, the first subway was completed; the city was organizing itself into something more than an overgrown town. With size and importance came new problems as well. A rich city with a rich government was tempting to politicians and public servants of less than perfect honesty. In the aftermath of the Tweed Ring exposures, Tammany candidates and reformers practically alternated as mayor; regular investigations and scandals, particularly in the police department, accelerated political turnover and often catapulted relatively unknown men — Theodore Roosevelt, for example — into national prominence. Problems of the slum and the ghetto, of race and poverty, were already well-developed, but were as yet widely ignored.

(Above) South Ferry, New York, terminal for the Staten Island Ferry and elevated train lines, 1890s; (below left) Wall Street and Trinity Church; (below right) Chamber of Commerce Building

(Above left) Gillinder Building; (above right) Temple Emanuel, oldest Reform synagogue in New York City; photographed in 1896 by J. S. Johnston; (below) Washington Square Arch at the entrance to Greenwich Village. It was designed by Stanford White and erected about 1895

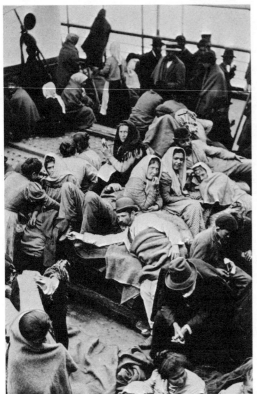

(Above left) Immigrants photographed aboard ship en route to America, 1902; (above right) dining room on Ellis Island for immigrants awaiting admission to America; (below) main building on Ellis Island, center for processing immigrants, in 1905

(Top) Mulberry Street on New York's east side, 1904; (center) English class being conducted for immigrants; (bottom) sweatshop in Ludlow Street, photo by Jacob Riis

(Above) Rear of tenement building in Roosevelt Street; photograph by Jacob Riis

(Left and below) Fifth Street before and after the campaign to get garbage off city streets. Theodore Roosevelt, governor of the state, and Tammany Hall joined forces in this movement. Both photographs by Jacob Riis

(Above) Street preaching; (below left) clam seller in Mulberry Bend; (below right) two rag collectors on a New York street, photograph by Alice Austen, 1897

(Above left) Customers in a Bowery dive at midnight, 1898; (above right) a "fashionable barroom" of the same period; (below) policeman arresting a hobo in New York in 1898

(Above) Newsstand oper-
ated by immigrants near
an entrance to the elevated train in uptown Man-
hattan

(Left) Easter crowds on
Fifth Avenue outside St.
Patrick's Cathedral in
1904; photo by the Detroit
Publishing Company; (be-
low) strolling along the
Mall in Central Park in
1894; photo by J. S. Johnston

(Above) Waldorf-Astoria
Hotel on Fifth Avenue,
photographed in 1899

(Right) Francois I bed-
room in the State apart-
ment at the Waldorf-As-
toria, 1900. (Below)
Metropolitan Club Read-
ing Room photographed in
1895 by James Breese

(Above) View of residences along Upper Fifth Avenue; (left) Mrs. George Jay Gould, wife of Jay Gould's son

(Above) Lady alighting from her carriage; photographed in 1902; (left) J. P. Morgan participating in university commencement

Dancing class in the playground of a "Letter H-plan" school in New York. Photo by Jacob Riis

(Above) Outdoor school for tubercular children; (below) backyard playground in Nurse's Settlement; both photographs by Jacob Riis

Class being held in the condemned Essex Market School; photo by Jacob Riis

A growing interest on the part of reformers and philosophers in the education of children developed into the movement for "progressive" education. New York was a center for experimentation; the New York College for the Training of Teachers, founded in 1889, became a division of Columbia University in 1898 and was a leading force in the movement. New York also had new and difficult problems; beyond organizing, financing, and staffing a massive urban school system, the city had to deal with the fact that a large proportion — as high as 70 percent — of the children were immigrants, often with little knowledge of the language or customs of America. Schoolwork had also to compete with child labor; it usually lost.

(Above) Night school for working children at the Seventh Avenue Lodging House; (below) boys in a manual training class in a public school; both photographs by Jacob Riis

(Top) The Short Tail gang under the pier at the foot of Jackson Street, 1888; (center left) Sunday services in the Tombs, New York; (center right) unidentified thief; (bottom) penitentiary lockstep at Blackwell's Island

11.

Montgomery Schuyler: The Chicago Architects

*The first "skyscraper" was designed by W. L. B. Jenney in 1884 for a Chicago
insurance company, and such buildings soon became the distinctive mark of the
architecture of that city. Following Jenney's lead, other Chicago architects, notably
Louis Sullivan and Frank Lloyd Wright, built bold twenty-story buildings, with iron
frameworks and characterized by stark lines, in the city's business section.*
*Although the Chicago school was praised by many for having taken an exciting step
forward in urban buildings, there were also many critics. A moderate and thoughtful
appraisal was prepared by Montgomery Schuyler for his "Great American Architects"
series. The introductory section of one of these articles, published in December 1895,
appears below.*

Source: *Architectural Record*, December 1895: "Architecture in Chicago."

It is impossible fairly to estimate the work of the leading architects of Chicago without some preliminary reference to the conditions of their work. In part, perhaps in the main, these are the same conditions that preside over the evolution of American architecture in general, but some of them are really local, and those of them that are general are applied in Chicago with a peculiar strictness and intensity. It is from this stringency of application that the characteristics of Chicago building come, and that it comes that the individuality of that building is so much more local than it is general that from the first sight in a photograph of a new Chicago building one can "place" it so much more readily than one can assign it to its particular author. Here, more than elsewhere, "the individual withers, and the world is more and more."

Of course, what I have in mind in saying this is "the heart of Chicago," the business quarter, for it is by that that Chicago is characterized, especially in its architecture.

Its architectural expressions are twofold only, places of business and places of residence. It would be impossible to mention another great city of which this is so strictly true. It is indeed curious how the composite image of Chicago that remains in one's memory as the sum of his innumerable individual impressions is made up exclusively of the skyscraper of the city and the dwellings of the suburbs. Not a church enters into it, so as to count, as churches count for so much elsewhere. Scarcely a public building enters into it. There is the old Art Institute; indeed, excellent and impressive building. There is the new Art Institute, scholarly and academic, and the new library, of a more modern and exuberant as well as of a more vigorous aspect, and there is the city and county building which is exuberant exclusively. Still later, there is the Newberry Library at one end of the town and the Chicago University at the other.

But this brief list, which must be very nearly exhaustive, is not a list of characteristic buildings. In spite of the respectable dimensions of several of these in longitude and latitude their inferiority in the third and most characteristic dimension of altitude denotes that they are incidental and episodical to the real task of the architects, which is to produce skyscrapers and homes — and factories, indeed, which architecturally are neither here nor there, but which occupy much of the attention and contribute much to the incomes of the busiest architects. The deficiency of churches, which in magnitude and costliness are commensurate with the populousness and wealth of the city, and in architectural interest are comparable with its utilitarian structures, is a fact that must strike every stranger.

The men who project and "finance" the utilitarian buildings are the same men who are ready to incur expenditures for public purposes with a generosity and a public spirit that are elsewhere unparalleled, and that constitute one of the justest of the boasts of the place. But it seems that churches do not enter into their scheme of public benefaction, and any lavishness of expenditure on churches appears to strike them as a little frivolous and dilettante.

There is a kernel of real meaning and applicability in the legend of the inhabitant of a "boom town" further to the West who was bragging about the hotels and the saloons and the "opera house" of it to a stranger, who at last inquired about the churches. "Well, no," Occidentalis gloriosus [Glory of the West] had to own; "there was some talk about one, but the boys thought it would look too dudish." Whether the Chicago man thinks that he can do without monumental churches, or is only postponing them till a more convenient season, the lack of them restricts the range of architectural practice to a simplicity unknown in older cities.

Theaters would elsewhere constitute a variation and a relief, and Chicago is a very play-going place, but it no more possesses a monumental theater than a monumental church. It has no more a Nouvel Opera than it has a Notre Dame. Burke, speaking of the new London theaters of a century ago, described them as "large and lofty piles, which lift their broad shoulders in gigantic pride, almost emulous of the temples of God," and in more than one modern capital the emulation has been carried further. In Chicago the theaters are housed in "huge and lofty piles," but they are not altogether monumental for the reason that they are but incidents of the piles.

The two theaters that are of the chief architectural interest interiorly, and one of them is of the greatest architectural interest, are enclosed and in great part concealed, the one in a hotel and the other in an office building. The fact is very characteristic. It is the characteristic fact, for in the dwellings there is little of strictly local color. They might be in Buffalo, or in St. Paul, or in a suburb of any American city. Hardly in New York, because the expanse of Chicago permits a spaciousness and a detachment that the projector of a townhouse upon cramped Manhattan Island cannot afford, or thinks he cannot, which comes to the same thing. It is only "the heart of Chicago" that is straitened for room. It is accordingly only in the heart of Chicago that we find Chicago buildings.

Even before the introduction of the "Chicago construction," which first appeared in the Home Insurance Building some six years ago, the skyscrapers were noticeable for two Chicagoan characteristics, their extreme altitude and their strictly utilitarian treatment. Now that the Chicago construction has come to prevail, they are still noteworthy in comparison with the skyscraper of other towns for these same qualities.

And this brings me to remark upon the very great share which the Chicago "businessman" has had in the evolution of commercial architecture in Chicago, a share not less important than that of the architects, and not less important for being in the main negative. We all like to hear the intelligent foreigner upon the characteristic manifestations of our national spirit, if he be candid as well as intelligent, to see ourselves as others see us, and it gives me pleasure to quote a very intelligent and a very candid foreigner, M. Paul Bourget, in *Outre Mer,* upon the commercial architecture of Chicago, what he says is so true and so well put:

> At one moment you have around you only "buildings." They scale the sky with their eighteen, with their twenty stories. The architect who has built, or rather who has plotted them, has renounced colonnades, moldings, classical embellishments. He has frankly accepted the condition imposed by the speculator; multiplying as many times as possible the value of the bit of ground at the base in multiplying the supposed offices. It is a problem capable of interesting only an engineer, one would suppose. Nothing of the kind. The simple force of need is such a principle of beauty and these buildings so conspicuously manifest that need that in contemplating them you experience a singular emotion. The sketch appears here of a new kind of art, an art of democracy, made by the crowd and for the crowd, an art of science in which the certainty of natural laws gives to audacities in appearance the most unbridled the tranquillity of geometrical figures.

It is noteworthy that the observer had seen and described New York before he saw Chicago. The circumstance makes more striking his recognition that it is in Chicago that the type of office building has been most clearly detached and elucidated. One is arrested by the averment that this art, so evidently made "for the crowd," is also made "by the crowd," since a crowd cannot be an artist, one is inclined to say. But there is not only the general consideration that in architecture an artist cannot even produce without the cooperation of his public, and cannot go on producing without being popular. There is the particular consideration that in this strictly utilitarian building the requirements are imposed with a stringency elsewhere unknown in the same degree, and very greatly to the advantage of the architecture.

Elsewhere, the designer of a business building commonly attempts to persuade or to hoodwink his client into sacrificing something of utility to "art," and, when he succeeds, it is commonly perceptible that the sacrifice has been in vain and that the building would have been better for its artistic purpose if it had been better for its practical purpose. There used to be an absurd story current in New York of how that the owner of two examples of florid classic in cast iron (the Gilsey Building in lower Broadway and the Gilsey House in upper Broadway, they were) exclaimed, when the second was finished, that now he had done enough for art and henceforth he meant to build as a matter of business.

Commercial architecture in Chicago is long past that stage, and that it is so is due rather to the businessman than to the architect. In this way and to this extent the architecture is made "by the crowd," is an architecture of the people and by the people as well as for the people. I asked one of the successful architects of Chicago what would happen if the designer of a commercial building sacrificed the practical availableness of one or more of its stories to the assumed exigencies of architecture, as has often been done in New York and as has been done in several aggravated and conspicuous instances that will readily occur to the reader familiar with recent building there. His answer was suggestive: "Why, the word would be passed and he would never get another to do. No, we never try those tricks on our businessmen. They are too wide-awake."

Another successful architect explained to me his procedure in designing a skyscraper. "I get from my engineer a statement of the minimum thickness of the steel post and its enclosure of terra cotta. Then I establish the minimum depth of floor beam and the minimum height of the sill from the floor to accommodate what must go between them. These are the data of my design." It is not the question whether the piers would not look better for somewhat more of massiveness, whether the skeleton could not be more "padded round with flesh and fat" to its aesthetic advantage, without too serious an infringement upon its suitableness for its purpose, whether the designer could not make a workable compromise between what it might please him to call his artistic conscience and the duty he owes as the agent and adviser of the owner in directing an investment for the largest possible return.

Modern commercial architecture in general, when it is done by artistic designers, is such a compromise. It bears the scars of a conflict, if not between the architect and the client, between the claims of utility and of art, or I should prefer to say between the facts of the case and the notions of the architect. It is only the work of the "architect," the work that nobody looks at twice or thinks of once, or cares to talk about, that evinces a purpose, not indeed to fulfill perfectly the real requirements of the building, but to carry out the "architect's" confused notion of the owner's confused notion of the manner of satisfying those requirements. That is as different a matter as possible from putting the resources of a trained and artistic intelligence absolutely at the service of an employer, and the results are as different as possible.

The architects of Chicago are not so radically different as all this from architects elsewhere. They are different on compulsion. They have "frankly accepted the conditions imposed by the speculator," (the word I translate "frankly" is *brutalement* [brutally], and I wish that M. Bourget had chosen to say "loyally" instead), because they are really imposed, and there is no getting away from them, if one would win and keep the reputation of a "practical" architect.

And mark that the businessmen who impose these conditions are not the most private-spirited; they are the most public-spirited body of businessmen of any commercial city in the world. They are willing to make the most generous sacrifices for their city to provide it with ornaments and trophies which shall make it something more than a center of pig-sticking and grain-handling. They are willing to play the part of Maecenas to the fine arts, only they insist that they will not play it "during business hours." They are too clear-headed to allow themselves or their architects to confuse their several and distinct capacities of money-makers and Maecenases.

If they allow themselves to be confused upon this point, in the first place they would not have so much money to do their public benefactions withal, and in the second place their commercial architecture would not have the character that in fact it has, and that comes from their insistence upon a rigid adherence to the real requirements of their commercial undertakings. Into that architecture, then, their influence enters as a very potent factor, and, whatever the architect beginning his practice in Chicago with his head full of "classical embellishments" may have thought or said, it enters, as every discerning beholder must now perceive, as a very beneficent factor.

In one respect, and this a respect that more or less affects commercial architecture everywhere, the influence is not beneficial. The architect is too much pressed for time. His client is aware that parsimony is not economy and is willing to give him all the money that he really needs. He is aware, also, that mere greediness defeats its own purpose, that to erect a very lofty building on a very restricted site is to increase the comparative cost both of building and of maintenance, and that to occupy with rentable apartments space that is needed for light and air is a very costly proceeding. In all such things he shows a spirit of large and intelligent liberality.

But it is especially true of him, what our French critic has noted as a national characteristic, that he cannot spare time. From the hour that the ground for a new building is put at his disposal the work of construction must go on at the highest rate of speed. If the plans are not matured at that moment, they must be executed in their immaturity, or with such ripening only as can be allowed while the work is actually going forward. There is after that no time left for the leisurely correction and completion upon which artistic perfection depends. There is no atmosphere in the world that less resembles "the still air of delightful studies" than that of the heart of Chicago.

And so the successful practitioner of architecture in Chicago is primarily an administrator. He absolutely must be that. If he be secondarily an artist, all the better; but in that case he is an artist working under pressure, a condition which is peculiarly abhorrent to the "artistic temperament." All the questions of arrangement of construction and of design which enter into the design of that very complicated organism, the modern office building, are presented at once, with a peremptory demand for an immediate answer. In the answer to them must concur the constructor, the designer, and the "practical man." Whether these three are united in one person or distributed among three, the primary and coordinating qualification is that of an administrator. "The readiness is all."

A busy practitioner must have his professional apparatus, including his professional library, at his fingers' ends. The irrefutable criticism in the *Vicar of Wakefield* that "the picture would have been better if the artist had taken more pains" is irrelevant. It is not a question whether the study of another month might not invigorate the masses and chasten the detail. The foundation plans must be ready as soon as the ground is cleared, and the building must not at any stage wait a day for drawings.

Here, it is true, the general uniformity of the problem is a great resource to the designer. An architect who lives by and upon office buildings has always, it is to be presumed, designs adumbrated in his mind — alternative designs, very possibly, for past buildings, rejected as less eligible for the past purpose than the design executed, but more eligible for the future purpose, or designs entirely ideal, drawn from a consideration of the abstract skyscraper. Much of the preliminary and general work of design may thus be done before the commission arrives, much more than if the practice were more varied.

But with whatever mitigations there may be of the conditions, the conditions are so especially stringent in Chicago as to make the successes all the more remarkable. And, indeed, it would be worse than idle to find fault with the conditions because, as we have seen, the successes have been won by an absolute loyalty to the conditions and by the frank abandonment of every architectural convention that comes in conflict with them.

The good Lord gave me my money, and how could I withhold it from the University of Chicago?

JOHN D. ROCKEFELLER, to first graduating class of the university

12.

HENRY J. FLETCHER: Migration to the Cities

The last half of the nineteenth century saw an unprecedented growth of American cities, along with a marked increase in the problems, both political and economic, that such growth entails. Many people discussed the phenomenon, and in 1895, when Henry Fletcher published the following analysis of the shift from country to city, most sociologists, though they may have lamented the loss of the virtues associated with rural life, at the same time appreciated the deep social needs that underlay the trend. Fletcher's derisive remarks about the "smoky city" as opposed to the "pure sky" of the countryside placed him in the small group of traditionalists who, as we can see in retrospect, were hoping for the impossible: a reversal of the worldwide urbanization that is an unmistakable feature of our time. His article is reprinted here in part.

Source: *Forum,* August 1895: "The Drift of Population to Cities: Remedies."

THE CLOSING DECADES of this century are witnessing no more remarkable phenomenon than that shown in the migration of population, not so much from country to country as from place to place in the same country. This interior migration is most noticeable in the most progressive lands. . . .

The smaller towns are not conscious of the full extent of their loss, because, as regards the number of residents, it is partly or wholly repaired by reinforcements from the surrounding country. The newest portions of the Western states, which are still in process of settlement, have not as yet felt the full effect of the centripetal attraction, for population tends to spread out into a more or less uniform density; but wherever immigration has ceased, the new forces quickly begin to tell, and throughout the older settled states, in New York as well as in Illinois and Iowa, a universal and all-powerful current has set in, sweeping everything toward the centers. . . .

It may be declared to be the general rule that, wherever the land is fully occupied, all the people not actually needed to cultivate the soil are being drawn into the towns, while the productive industries of the towns, together with those identified with them, are being transferred to the largest cities. For a certain number of years the country steadily grew more and more densely populated; this process came to a standstill, and now the tide is running swiftly in the opposite direction.

This transplantation has most far-reaching effects. Politically, it transfers a preponderance of power to the great cities, changing the results of important elections and increasing the urgency of municipal problems. Socially, it swells the number of the classes most exposed to agitation and discontent, intensifies the dangers to be apprehended from social upheavals, and widens the growing chasm between the classes. It concentrates the wealth of the nation into fewer hands, and reacts profoundly upon the material, social, and political life of the entire nation. The importance of this migration, therefore, is hardly to be overestimated.

It is a striking characteristic of our period that it is a period of universal transition, in which large masses of people, apparently against their own interests, leave the country where homes are cheap, the air pure, all men equal, and extreme poverty unknown, and crowd into cities where all these conditions are reversed. When this movement has proceeded too fast and the cities have become swollen with a surplus population for whom there is no employment, when urban expansion has far outrun the growth of the contributory territory and this condition has become excessive and universal, a panic interrupts this concentration for a time, until the proper balance between town and country is reestablished. The more rapid, therefore, the process of centralization, the more frequent and intense must be the periods of depression needed to correct it. . . .

In comparing the evils and advantages resulting from this striking migratory tendency, a distinction must be kept in mind between the interests of the individual and those of society at large. In changing his place of residence, every man undoubtedly acts on his best judgment of his own needs and cares nothing about its effects on society. But the student of social science, observing so stupendous a movement, asks whether society is to be the gainer or the loser by it. On the one side, he trembles — especially if he be an American — at the prospect of adding enormously to the burden of the municipal governments in the large cities, already almost breaking down through corruption and inefficiency. He realizes that in times of social disturbance the great cities are an ever growing menace to the public authority and even to the existing social order. He knows that crime is increasing, like the cities, out of all proportion

to everything else; and that the massing of dense populations means impaired public health and morals.

The constant depletion of the smaller towns and of the country, steadily draining away the best, producing absenteeism and local stagnation, must be regarded as an evil of great magnitude. It lowers the tone of village and farm life, prevents the rapid diffusion throughout the country of improvements in education, and tends to exclude the inhabitants of the rural districts from participation in the great ameliorations of modern life which ought to be common to all. . . .

In America, even the poorest of the working people refuse to go into the country to live. Labor is benefited in many ways by association; school advantages are better, wages higher, capital receives better returns, ambition has a wider field, where the rivers of people have their confluence. Yet, on the whole, the conclusion seems unavoidable that the evils and dangers, present and prospective, of the excessive massing of the people in the cities far outweigh the benefits. . . .

Doubtless the chief cause of this remarkable concentration is the natural superiority, under existing conditions, of large centers for all the processes of production and exchange. Here the manufacturer and the jobber come into direct contact with their customers. The retailer finds all the different articles needed to replenish his stock. Competition between producers raises the quality of goods while lowering prices, buyers are attracted by the great variety offered, and thus all the makers of a given article find it to their advantage to get together, and the greater the market the more powerfully it attracts both buyer and seller. Cheap freights and passenger fares, improved postal and telegraph service, and all the devices to facilitate business between distant places help the movement. . . .

Against such competition the small

towns, with their population largely composed of industrial noncombatants, have but little chance. It has been the history of the last few years that a large number of these assisted removals has come to grief. In the case of Minneapolis, the development of Minnesota and the Dakotas has induced the transfer to that city of many producers in order to be nearer to the consumers, but in nearly every case the removal has been at the expense of some smaller town. The great mills, like those of Minneapolis, can produce flour more economically than any small mill, however well-equipped, and can sell it at a smaller margin of profit. They therefore engross the export trade and supply the market except for local consumption. This explains in part the remarkable diminution in the number of local flouring mills during the last decade, but there are other causes. . . .

Chicago, with its suburbs, has swallowed the factories and workshops and work people of villages and minor cities within a radius of many hundred miles. Multitudes flock to the cities because the drift is that way, because business is dull in the villages, often without any distinct analysis of reasons, but in reality because production and exchange, insofar as it is not by its nature local, is being rapidly removed thither.

Ample allowance must be made also for the influence of various social motives. Many successful men desire better social opportunities for their families than the small towns afford; there are those who propose to live on their accumulated gains and want to be near the centers of fashion and amusement. Undeniably the city has superior attractions as a place of residence for the well-to-do; even the poorest classes, who live in filthy tenements and are completely shut out from the enjoyments of nature, seem to find in the noises, the crowds, the excitements, even in the sleepless anxieties of the daily struggle for life, a charm they are powerless to resist.

Against these multiplied influences ceaselessly operating in favor of the great cities, the country and the lesser towns contend in vain. They are like the laws of nature, and are submitted to patiently. But in league with them has been another potent agency — the transportation system of the country, whose management in the past engaged actively in the work of helping the strong to absorb the weak.

Prior to the passage of the Interstate Commerce Law in 1887, the bitter competition of the railways for business reduced through rates to a figure out of all proportion to those charged to and from intermediate points. It was a cardinal principle with the managers that business must be obtained at whatever price. Freight was sometimes carried between important terminal points, not merely for less than it cost but actually for nothing. Freight rates kept perpetually falling, until they became lower, on the average, than anywhere in the world; and in the terrible struggle to maintain their solvency, it was the settled policy of the managers to make up the deficiencies on business carried at unremunerative rates by stiffly holding up the rates that were not competitive. Many able railway men saw that this policy was a ruinous one, both from the standpoint of their local communities and themselves, for it sacrificed a large number of places whose interests needed to be fostered until they were strong enough to stand alone. But they insisted that they were powerless to resist the influence of competition; that in the absence of effective pooling arrangements it was impossible to maintain proper rates at competitive points, and at the same time the necessary revenues must be derived from some source.

The long-and-short-haul clause of the Interstate Commerce Law was designed to compel them to solve this problem; they were practically required to cut down their local or raise their through rates, but were still strictly forbidden to form pools for the

Elevated train over Herald Square in New York City at the turn of the century

maintenance of through rates. Before the passage of the law there can be no question that nearly universal discrimination was practised against the defenseless small towns, with the result of checking their growth and blasting their prosperity. . . .

Such was the state of things prior to the adoption of the law. The railways declare that they are now obeying its provisions, and no doubt they are doing so as regards intermediate stations on main lines, where the applicability of the law is unquestioned. But a large portion of the business of the country is done over railways which are but parts of through routes leading to great centers, and as to through business on such railways, the courts now hold that the law does not apply. . . .

It appears from what has already been said that for some of the conditions that are operating so unfavorably against the country there is no remedy. So far as the concentration is the result of the natural superiority of the city as a place for business or residence, so long as human nature continues to crave the stimulus of social contact, there can be no remedy until the accumulated miseries of overgrown cities drive the

people back to the land. Some sanguine observers, seeing the temporary check caused by the present depression, think that that time has now arrived. Others look to the recent extraordinary extension of the system of electric street railways into the country districts, to give relief by making it more convenient to live and work outside the cities.

This movement, however, appears to be suburban only. It can hardly stop the rush to the cities, but it will enable the cities to spread out over a wider territory, materially reduce the overcrowding, and raise greatly the standard of health and comfort for the poorer citizens. This suburban movement is universal, and is one of the most significant features of modern town life. It is introducing great changes in the condition of the people and will deeply affect all the elements of the city question. It is another proof of the important part which transportation plays in developing and molding the form of the modern commonwealth. But this countermovement can hardly affect the rush from the country toward the center, and possibly it may even accelerate it by ameliorating the condition of the city's poorer classes. More is to be expected from the transmission of electric power for manufactories, both in offering cheaper rents and ampler accommodations in the country, and also, perhaps, by diminishing the superiority which the factory now enjoys over the small shop.

With these exceptions, the only remedy that can avail to moderate existing conditions is equality in transportation rates; that is, such a readjustment as shall treat the railroad system as a unit and all the people as equally entitled to its benefits. In such an adjustment of rates, competition between the different parts of the system must be reduced to the lowest terms and the welfare of all sections of the country must be considered. So long as railroads are permitted to wage warfare upon each other, they will obtain the sinews of war by taxing their own people, whose situation leaves them no choice in the selection of a route. What system will be devised to secure equality remains to be developed in the future. At the present time it would seem that some comprehensive method of government supervision must be adopted, or the railroads will solve the problem for themselves by first securing the legal right to form pools, and afterward organizing themselves into a federation strong enough neither to need nor to fear the law.

One lesson which seems to lie upon the surface is that agriculture is not reaping the advantages promised by the early advocates of the protective system. Protection was to place the factory and the farm side by side; the farmer was assured that he should be reimbursed for the higher prices he was to pay for manufactured articles by the growth in his neighborhood of a busy population of workers who would buy his products at enhanced prices. This promise has not been redeemed. The farmer has found the articles he needed made artificially dear, but there are every year fewer factories in his vicinity

and lower prices for his products. The universal depression of agriculture East and West, the dwindling population of agricultural communities, would seem to indicate that the cultivators of the soil are being exploited for the benefit of manufacturers, and that the cities are appropriating the largest part of the profit. The loyalty and tenacity with which the farmers have so long clung to the doctrine of protection in the face of declining prosperity is remarkable.

It is not pleasant to believe that in the future development of our country dullness, isolation, and monotony are to be the permanent lot of the tillers of the soil. It will be unfortunate for our national life if agriculture shall come to be shunned by the intelligent and abandoned to a class of peasants. For centuries the real strength and glory of England has been in her sturdy yeomanry; the passion to own land and live upon it is today the chief cause of the prosperity of France. We in the United States cherish a deep love for the farms and villages from which most of us have sprung, and whence we must chiefly recruit the energies of a race that is consuming its strength in smoky cities.

Is it not possible that the fierceness of the rage for wealth will one day abate and the people begin to look about them for the sweetness and serenity which human nature longs for in its highest moments, and which are best found under a pure sky, amid the quietness of nature? When the farmer and villager begin to study more how to enrich and beautify farm and village life, when perfect roads, daily mails, the telephone, the electric railway, the manual-training school shall have carried into the remotest corners the blessings of the new civilization, it may be that the incentive to live in cities will be largely removed. If the dwellers in the smaller towns and country want to counteract the existing tendencies, they must be alert to seize and appropriate the agencies which are now transforming modern life.

13.

F. J. KINGSBURY: In Defense of the City

After the Civil War, the trend toward city living was accelerated. By 1900, forty percent of all Americans lived in communities of 2,500 or more. This significant change in living and working habits caused writers, sociologists, and preachers to comment upon the virtues and vices of urbanization. F. J. Kingsbury contributed his views on the subject in his 1895 presidential address before the American Social Science Association. A portion of the address is reprinted below.

Source: *Journal of Social Science*, No. 33, November 1895: "The Tendency of Men to Live in Cities."

THE FEATURE OF CITIES which is perhaps at present attracting more attention than any other is their misgovernment. . . . At least three times within forty years the municipal government of New York has been so bad that it was felt that every interest in the city, except perhaps the liquor interest, was seriously threatened; and relief has only come through the interference of the state legislature, which is a kind of interference that, however necessary and useful it may occasionally be, does not belong logically to our system of government. Perhaps here the real question is whether a republican form of government, or self-government, was ever intended for those who are clearly not fit to govern themselves or anybody else.

It is right to add, as a matter of fairness to New York, that Philadelphia and Chicago are just as bad, and that every little municipality through our whole land has to struggle with some "boss" who has learned his trade or taken his cue from successful rascals in our larger towns. "A public office is an opportunity for public plunder" is the way their motto reads, if they hang it right side out.

One would think after reading all this about the evils of cities from the time of Cain to the last New York election — or, rather, let us say, to the last but one — and especially when we must admit that we know everything that is said to be true, and that even then not the half nor the tenth part has been told, and we are almost driven to the conclusion that nothing short of the treatment applied to Sodom and Gomorrah will meet the necessities of the case; that every sane man and woman should flee without stopping for the open country; and the women especially should be careful how they look behind them, and be sure to remember Lot's wife, and nothing should induce them to turn their faces cityward again.

Now, in spite of all this, precisely the reverse is true; and, while there has always been a strong tendency in humanity cityward, this nineteenth century sees it intensified beyond all former experience. . . .

Aside from all questions of mutual defense and protection and mutual helpfulness in various ways, and industrial convenience, doubtless one of the very strongest of forces in the building of the city is the human instinct of gregariousness. This underlies ancient as well as modern, military as well as industrially founded, aggregations, and the hamlet or the village as well as the city. But there is always a craving to get where there are more people. The countryman, boy or girl, longs for the village, the villager for the larger town, and the dweller in the larger town for the great city; and, having once gone, they are seldom satisfied to return to a place of less size. In short, whatever man may have been or may be in his prognathous or troglodyte condition, ever since we have known much about him he has been highly gregarious, even under unfavorable conditions.

As long ago as 1870, Mr. Frederick Law Olmsted, in a paper read before this Association, said, "There can be no doubt that in all our modern civilization, as in that of the ancients, there is a strong drift townward"; and he quotes the language of an intelligent woman, whose early life had been spent in one of the most agreeable and convenient farming countries in the United States: "If I were offered a deed of the best farm I ever saw on condition of going back to the country to live, I would not take it. I would rather face starvation in town."

The life of the great city would seem to bear hardest of all on the very poor, and the country, or at least suburban, life to present the strongest attraction, by contrast, to this class. Pure air, plenty of water, room for children to play, milk on which to feed them, room to sleep, wholesome food for adults — these things, almost impossible to the poor in the city, are nearly all of easy attainments in the country; yet the overmastering desire for a city life seems to be stronger with this class than with any other.

Perhaps you are familiar with the story of the kind lady who found a widow with a great family of children living in the depths of poverty and dirt in the city, and moved them all to a comfortable country home, where, with a moderate amount of exertion, they were sure of a living. At the end of six

weeks her country agent reported that the family had suddenly disappeared, no one knew where. Going back to the neighborhood of their old haunts, she found them all reestablished there in the same circumstances of dirt and destitution as of old. "Why *did* you leave that comfortable home and come back here?" was her astonished inquiry. "Folks is more company nor sthoomps, anyhow," was the answer. Poor food, and little of it, dirt and discomfort, heat and cold — all count as nothing in competition with this passion of gregariousness and desire for human society, even where that means more or less of a constant fight as the popular form of social intercourse.

Doubtless one of the most potent factors in the modern growth of cities has been the immense improvement in the facilities for travel, which has been such a marked characteristic of the last half century. But, after all, what is this but saying that it has been made easier for people to go where they wished to be? Facilities for travel make it as easy to get from city to country as from country to city; but the tide, except for temporary purposes, all sets one way.

Nevertheless, there is no question that this case of locomotion has been availed of to a surprising extent in transporting each year in the summer season a very large portion, not of the rich alone but of nearly every class, not only from our great cities but from our moderately large towns, to the woods and lakes and seashore for a time. The class of people who, fifty years since, lived in the same house the year round, without thought of change, now deem a six or twelve weeks' residence in the country a vital necessity; and this fact is a great alleviation and antidote to some of the unfavorable influences of city life.

All modern industrial life tends to concentration as a matter of economy. It has long been remarked that the best place to establish or carry on any kind of business is where that business is already being done. For that reason we see different kinds of manufactures grouping themselves together — textiles in one place, metals in another; and, of the textiles, cottons in one place, woolens in another; and of the metals, iron in one place, copper in another, and so on.

The reason of this is obvious. In a community where a certain kind of business is carried on, the whole population unconsciously become, to a certain extent, experts. They know a vast deal more of it than people who have had no such experience. Every man, woman, and child in a fishing village is much superior in his or her knowledge of fish, bait, boats, wind, and weather to the inhabitants of inland towns. This is true of all the arts, so that, besides the trained hands which may be drawn upon when needed, there is a whole population of half-trained ones ready to be drawn upon to fill their places.

Then, every kind of business is partly dependent on several other kinds. There must be machine makers, blacksmiths, millwrights, and dealers in supplies of all sorts. Where there is a large business of any kind, these subsidiary trades that are supported by it naturally flock around it; whereas in an isolated situation the central establishment must support all these trades itself or go a considerable distance when it needs their assistance. Fifty or sixty years ago small manufacturing establishments in isolated situations and on small streams were scattered all through the Eastern states. The condition of trade at that time rendered this possible. Now they have almost wholly disappeared, driven out by economic necessity; and their successors are in the cities and large towns.

If you will examine any city newspaper of fifty or sixty years ago, you will find frequent advertisements for boys as clerks in stores; and almost always they read "one from the country preferred." Now you never see this. Why is it? I think mainly because the class of boys which these advertisements were expected to attract from the country are no longer there. This was really a call for the well-educated boys of the well-to-do farmers of native stock who thought they could better themselves by going to a city. They went, and did better themselves; and those who stayed behind, fell behind. The country people deteriorated, and the country boy was no longer, for business purposes, the equal of the boy who had been trained in city ways. Country boys still go to the city; but they are not advertised for and have to find their own way.

Our great Civil War compelled us to find out some way in which to replace the productive power of a million men sent into the field and suddenly changed from producers into consumers. Their places had to be filled in the lines of agriculture and of all the mechanic arts, in the counting room, in the pulpit, at the bar, and everywhere else where a soldier was to be found. A hundred thousand of these places, more or less, in shops, in mechanic industries, in counting rooms, in the medical profession, even at the pulpit and the bar, were filled with women; and the deficit left by the remainder of the million was supplied by newly invented machinery to do their work. The result was that, when the war was over, a million of men, or as many as came back, found their places filled. They were no longer needed.

In all rural occupations this was especially the case; and, being driven out of the country by want of work, they flocked to the city as the most likely place to find it. The disturbing influence in financial, economic, and industrial matters of this sudden change of a million men from producers to consumers and back again to producers, followed as it was soon after by the disturbing influences of the Franco-Prussian War, have never been given their due weight by students of sociology.

We must remember, too, that cities as places of human habitation have vastly improved within half a century. About fifty years ago neither New York nor Boston had public water, and very few of our cities had either water or gas, and horse railroads had not been thought of. When we stop to think what this really means in sanitary matters, it seems to me that the increase of cities is no longer a matter of surprise.

A few years since the great improvement of the lift, or elevator, added probably 10 percent, actually, and much more than that theoretically, to the possibilities of population on a given amount of ground; and now within a very recent period three new factors have been suddenly developed which promise to exert a powerful influence on the problems of city and country life. These are the trolley, the bicycle, and the telephone. It is impossible at present to foresee just what their influence is to be on the question of the distribution of population; but this much is certain, that it adds from five to fifteen miles to the radius of every large town, bringing all this additional area into new relations to business centers. Places five or ten miles apart and all the intervening distances are rendered accessible and communicable for all the purposes of life as if they were in the next street.

Already the bicycle has done more toward directing attention and effort to the improvement of ordinary highways than all that has been done before since the days of Indian paths. It is affecting the legislation of the country on the subject of roads. When we think of what this minimizing of distance means, we cannot help seeing that its influence must be immense, but just what no man can foretell. It is by such apparently unimportant, trifling, and inconspicuous forces that civilization is swayed and molded in its evolutions, and no man can foresee them or say whither they lead.

Cities, as desirable places of human habitation, seem to have touched low-water mark — as did almost everything else — in that miserable period of comparative cessation in human progress known to us in European history as the "Dark" or "Middle Ages." . . . Yet in these medieval cities, miserable places as many of them often were for human dwellings, there were certain forces at work which have done as much for humanity and for modern civilization as any that can be named. Cities have always been nurseries of freemen. . . .

It must be noticed that it is always in cities that those who can afford it get the best food; and, if you are living in the country, you are largely dependent on the city for your supply. The summer seashore visitor usually finds, if he takes the trouble to investigate, that his fresh fish comes from the nearest great city, also his meat, and quite likely his butter and eggs, and nearly everything except perhaps his milk. To be sure, they came from the country first in many cases; but they seek the best market and are to be best found at it.

It is also only in great cities, as a rule, that the best medical skill can be obtained. There we all go or send to have our most serious diseases treated and our most critical surgical operations performed. It is almost wholly owing to the unsanitary condition among the children of the very poor that the city death rate is so high. . . .

I have been fairly familiar with the streets of New York and Boston for the last fifty years, and there is no fact in that connection with which I have been more impressed than the physical improvement which has taken place in both men and women during that period. The men are more robust and more erect, the women have greatly improved both in feature and carriage; and in the care and condition of the teeth in both sexes a surprising change has taken place. In Boston streets and streetcars, it seems to me that you see a hundred good-looking women where you formerly saw one. Whether this would hold good in the slums and low parts of the town may be doubted, but there, of course, one looks for the refuse and cast-off material of society.

A few years since I stood by the grave of a prominent man in one of our rural towns. By my side stood a man who had achieved a reputation both in literature and law. He said to me, "Who is that man opposite?" calling my attention to a tall, fine-looking man. "That," I replied, "is General H." "Ah!" said my friend with accents of enthusiasm, "one needs to come into the rural districts to see the finest specimens of manhood." I said, "Look about, and see if you find any more." He did not find them. Then I said, "You have picked out the one man here who is in no sense a rural product. It is true this is his home, but his life is metropolitan or cosmopolitan; and those prematurely old, bowed, rheumatic, decrepit, and uninteresting people who make up most of the gathering are the true representatives of our rural population." I think I shattered an ideal, but the logic of facts was too strong to be resisted.

Perhaps this is as good a place as any to remark that, when any occupation or calling in life or in a community becomes relatively less remunerative than the average, there begins at once by natural selection a process of personal deterioration of those engaged in it. In other words, success is the stepping-stone to improvement. And in the rural districts of the Eastern states this deterioration has been going on now for fifty years. . . .

I think it is Dr. Strong who says: "When population decreases and roads deteriorate, there is an increasing isolation, with which comes a tendency toward demoralization and degeneration. The mountain whites of the South afford an illustration of the results of such a tendency operating through several generations. Their heathenish degradation is not due to their antecedents, but primarily to their isolation." He also mentions communities in New England where like causes have produced a similar result. I think isolated rural life, where people seldom come in contact with dwellers in large towns, always tends to barbarism. I believe that poorer people in our cities, if planted in isolated situations in the country, would deteriorate and grow barbaric in habit and thought even though they might be physically in better condition. What very unattractive people most of our rural population are!

It is to be noted that the attrition and constant opportunity for comparison which city life makes possible, and even compulsory, tend to make all the people who are subjected to its influence alike. They do and see and hear and smell and eat the same things. They wear similar clothes, they read the same books, and their minds are occupied with the same objects of thought. In the end they even come to look alike, as married people are sometimes said to do, so that they are at once recognized when they are seen in some other place; while people who live isolated lives think their own thoughts, pursue different objects, and are compelled to depend upon their own judgments and wills for the conduct of their daily lives.

The consequence is that they develop and increase peculiarities of character and conduct to the verge of eccentricity, if not beyond it, and present all that variety and freshness of type, which we call originality, or individuality. They are much more dramatic, picturesque, and interesting in literature, perhaps not always in real life. I mention this in passing, without any attempt to estimate fully the value of either development. Doubtless something is lost and something gained in either case, and probably much could be said in favor of each. Many persons have a great desire to get, as they say, "back to nature"; while others prefer mankind in the improved state, even with some sameness. . . .

The country is a good place to rest in, especially if one can control his surroundings. The quiet, the calm, the peace, the pleasant color, the idyllic sights and sounds, all tend to allay nervous irritation, to tranquilize the soul, to repress the intellectual, and to invigorate the animal functions in a very remarkable degree. But this is not rustic life; it is only the country life of the city resident. But the tranquil appearance of a country town, the apparent simplicity and serenity of rural life, the sweet idyllic harmony of rural surroundings, are, as everyone must know who has much experience, very deceptive. . . .

The small jealousies and rivalries, the ambitions, bickerings, and strifes of a small rural community, are greatly intensified by the circumscribed area in which they find their vent, and, compared with the same human frailties in a larger sphere, have all the drawbacks of temper in a cart. . . . It would seem, then:

1. That for economic reasons a large part of the work of the world must be done in cities, and the people who do that work must live in cities.

2. That almost everything that is best in life can be better had in the city than elsewhere; and that, with those who can command the means, physical comforts and favorable sanitary conditions are better obtained there.

3. That a certain amount of change from city to country is desirable, and is also very universally attainable to those who desire it, and is constantly growing more so.

4. That the city is growing a better place to live in year by year; that in regard to the degenerate portion of mankind, the very poor, the very wicked, or the very indifferent, it is a question whether they are better off in the country; but, whether they are or not, their gregarious instincts will lead them to the city, and they must be dealt with there as part of the problem.

5. That efforts to relieve the congested conditions of the city poor by deportation of children to the country are good and praiseworthy, but only touch the surface of things, and that city degeneration must mainly be fought on its own ground.

Perhaps, too, the country needs some of our sympathy and care. It appears clear that here is a constant process of deterioration. Deserted farms and schools and churches mark the progress of ignorance and debasement, and threaten to again make the villagers *pagani,* as they were in the days of old. And improvement here is not the hopeless thing it might seem; but it must be on economic, and not on sentimental, lines.

The problems here discussed have but recently attracted general attention, and doubtless much is yet to be learned; but the progress already made is by no means small, and all the signs are signs of promise.

———◆———

Some civilized women would lose half their charm without dress, and some would lose all of it.

SAMUEL L. CLEMENS ("MARK TWAIN")

No civilized person ever goes to bed the same day he gets up.

RICHARD HARDING DAVIS

14.

Theodore Roosevelt: Police Reform in New York City

Theodore Roosevelt, as president of the Board of Police Commissioners of New York City from 1895 to 1897, had his eyes opened to the more sordid aspects of life in the city. Relying heavily on reports by Jacob Riis and Lincoln Steffens, two muckraking journalists who admired Roosevelt and were more than willing to acquaint him with New York's corruption, Roosevelt spoke out often and with effect against the practices of the political bosses and the patronage system. Critics claimed that Roosevelt's bark was worse than his bite, but in fact his reforms so embarrassed "Boss" T. C. Platt that he managed to have Roosevelt "kicked upstairs" to the Republican vice-presidential nomination in 1900. It was thought that the young reformer would thereby be silenced — but the assassination of McKinley in 1901 made him President of the United States. Roosevelt's article, reprinted here in part, was originally titled "The Enforcement of Law."

Source: *Forum*, September 1895.

THE QUESTION AT ISSUE in New York City just at present is much more important than the question of a more or less liberal Sunday excise law. The question is as to whether public officials are to be true to their oaths of office, and see that the law is administered in good faith. The Police Board stands squarely in favor of the honest enforcement of the law. Our opponents of every grade and of every shade of political belief take the position that government officials who have sworn to enforce the law shall violate their oaths whenever they think it will please a sufficient number of the public to make the violation worthwhile.

It seems almost incredible that in such a controversy it should be necessary to do more than state in precise terms both propositions. Yet it evidently is necessary. Not only have the wealthy brewers and liquor sellers, whose illegal business was interfered with, venomously attacked the commissioners for enforcing the law but they have been joined by the major portion of the New York press and by the very large mass of voters who put the gratification of appetite above all law.

These men have not dared to meet the issue squarely and fairly. They have tried to befog it and to raise false issues. They have especially sought to change the fight from the simple principle of the enforcement of law into a contest as to the extent of the restrictions which should properly be placed on the sale of liquors. They do not deny that we have enforced the law with fairness and impartiality, but they insist that we ought to connive at lawbreaking.

Very many friends of the reform movement and very many politicians of the party to which I belong have become frightened at the issue thus raised; and the great bulk of the machine leaders of the Democracy profess to be exultant at it and to see in it a chance for securing their own return to power. Senator Hill and Tammany in particular have loudly welcomed the contest. On the other hand, certain Republican politicians and certain Republican newspapers have contended that our action in honestly doing our duty as public officers of the municipality of New York will jeopardize the success of the Republican Party, with which I, the president of the Board, am identified. The implication is that for the sake of the Republican Party, a party of which I am a very earnest member, I should violate my oath of office and connive at lawbreaking.

To this I can only answer that I am far too good a Republican to be willing to believe that the honest enforcement of law by a Republican can redound to the discredit of the party to which he belongs. This applies as much to the weak-kneed municipal reformers who fear that we have hurt the cause of municipal reform as it does to the Republicans. I am not an impractical theorist; I am a practical politician. But I do not believe that practical politics and foul politics are necessarily synonymous terms. . . .

When such are the fears of our friends and the hopes of our foes, it is worthwhile briefly to state exactly what the condition of affairs was when the present Board of Police Commissioners in New York took office, and what that course of conduct was which has caused such violent excitement. The task is simple. On entering office we found, what indeed had long been a matter of common notoriety, that various laws, and notably the Excise Law, were enforced rigidly against people who had no political pull, but were not enforced at all against the men who had a political pull, or who possessed sufficient means to buy off the high officials who controlled, or had influence in, the Police Department.

All that we did was to enforce these laws, not against some wrongdoers, but honestly and impartially against all wrongdoers. We did not resurrect dead laws; we did not start a crusade to enforce blue laws. All that we did was to take a law which was very much alive, but which had been used only for purposes of blackmail, and to do away entirely with the blackmail feature by enforcing it equitably as regards all persons. Looked at soberly, this scarcely seems a revolutionary proceeding; and still less does it seem like one which needs an elaborate justification.

In an authorized interview with Mr. J. P. Smith, the editor of the *Wine and Spirit Gazette,* the position of the former Police Board — and of Senator Hill and his political allies as well — toward the enforcement of the Excise Law has been set forth with such clearness that I cannot do better than quote it. Mr. Smith's statement appeared on July 18 last. No attempt whatever has been made to controvert its truth, and it may be accepted as absolute. What makes it all the more important is that it was evidently made, not at all as an attack upon the persons implicated but as a mere statement of fact to explain certain actions of the liquor sellers in the past. The interview runs in part as follows:

> Governor Flower, as well as the legislature of 1892, was elected upon distinct pledges that relief would be given by the Democratic Party to the liquor dealers, especially of the cities of the state. In accordance with this promise a Sunday-opening clause was inserted in the Excise Bill of 1892. Governor Flower then said that he could not approve the Sunday-opening clause; whereupon the Liquor Dealers' Association, which had charge of the bill, struck the Sunday-opening clause out.
>
> After Governor Hill had been elected for the second term, I had several interviews with him on that very subject. He told me, "Do you know, I am the friend of the liquor dealers and will go to almost any length to help them and give them relief; but do not ask me to recommend to the legislature the passage of the law opening the saloons on Sunday. I cannot do it, for it will ruin the Democratic Party in the state." He gave the same interview to various members of the State Liquor Dealers' Association, who waited upon him for the purpose of

getting relief from the blackmail of the police, stating that the lack of having the Sunday question properly regulated was at the bottom of the trouble.

Blackmail had been brought to such a state of perfection and had become so oppressive to the liquor dealers themselves that they communicated first with Governor Hill and then with Mr. Croker. The *Wine and Spirit Gazette* had taken up the subject because of gross discrimination made by the police in the enforcement of the Sunday-closing law. The paper again and again called upon the Police Commissioners to either uniformly enforce the law or uniformly disregard it. A committee of the Central Association of Liquor Dealers of this city then took up the matter and called upon Police Commissioner Martin.

An agreement was then made between the leaders of Tammany Hall and the liquor dealers according to which the monthly blackmail paid to the police should be discontinued in return for political support. In other words, the retail dealers should bind themselves to solidly support the Tammany ticket in consideration of the discontinuance of the monthly blackmail by the police. This agreement was carried out. Now what was the consequence? If the liquor dealer, after the monthly blackmail ceased, showed any signs of independence, the Tammany Hall district leader would give the tip to the police captain, and that man would be pulled and arrested on the following Sunday.

Continuing, Mr. Smith inveighs against the law, but says:

The Police Commissioners [the present Police Commissioners] are honestly endeavoring to have the law impartially carried out. They are no respecters of persons. And our information from all classes of liquor dealers is that the rich and the poor, the influential and the uninfluential are required equally to obey the law.

I call particular attention to the portion of the interview which I have italicized above. It shows conclusively that the Sunday-closing feature was deliberately left in by Senator Hill and his aides because they did not believe they could afford to strike it out. It is idle to talk of a provision thus embodied in statute law as being a dead letter. Still more idle is it to talk of a law as "antiquated" when it was enacted only three years ago.

Mr. Smith's statement shows moreover that Tammany heartily approved of keeping the law in its present condition because, by so doing, they kept a sword suspended over the neck of every recalcitrant saloonkeeper. The law was never dead at all. It was very much alive. We revived it only in the sense that we revived the forgotten habit of administering it with decency and impartiality. . . .

The corrupt and partial enforcement of the law under Tammany turned it into a gigantic implement for blackmailing a portion of the liquor sellers and for the wholesale corruption of the Police Department. The high Tammany officials, and the police captains and patrolmen blackmailed and bullied the small liquor sellers without a pull and turned them into abject slaves of Tammany Hall. On the other hand, the wealthy and politically influential liquor sellers absolutely controlled the police, and made or marred captains, sergeants, and patrolmen at their pleasure. Many causes have tended to corrupt the police administration of New York, but no one cause was so potent as this. . . .

When we entered office the law was really enforced at the will of the police officials. In some precincts most of the saloons were closed; in others, almost all were open. In general, the poor man without political influence and without money had to shut up, while his rich rival who possessed a "pull" was never molested. Half of the liquor sellers were allowed to violate the law. Half of them were not allowed to violate it. Under the circumstances we had one of two courses to follow. We could either instruct the police to allow all the saloonkeepers to become lawbreakers or else we could instruct them to stop all lawbreaking. It is unnecessary to say that the latter course was the only one possible to officials who had respect for their oaths of office.

The clamor that followed our action was deafening; and it was also rather amusing in view of the fact that all we had done was to perform our obvious duty. At the outset the one invariable statement with which we were met was that we could not enforce the law. A hundred — aye, a thousand — times we were told by big politicians, by newspapers, by private individuals that the Excise Law could not be enforced; that Mayor Hewitt had tried it and failed; that Superintendent Byrnes had tried it and failed; that nobody could succeed in such a task. Well, the answer is simple. We *have* enforced the law, so far.

It is very badly drawn, so as to make it extremely difficult of enforcement; and some of the officials outside the Police Department hamper instead of aiding the police in their efforts to enforce it. However, we understand well that we must do the best we can with the tools actually at hand, if we cannot have the tools we wish. We cannot stop all illegal drinking on Sunday, anymore than we can stop all theft; but so far we have succeeded in securing a substantial compliance with the law.

The next move of our opponents was to adopt the opposite tack, and to shriek that, in devoting our attention to enforcing the Excise Law, we were neglecting all other laws; and that, in consequence, crime was on the increase. We met this by publishing the comparative statistics of the felonies committed and of the felons arrested under our administration and under the previous administration. These showed that for a like period of time about one felony less a day occurred under our administration, while the number of arrests for felonies increased at the rate of nearly one a day. . . .

The next argument advanced was that Americans of German origin demanded beer on Sundays, and that the popular sentiment was with them and must be heeded.

To this we could only answer that we recognized popular sentiment only when embodied in law. . . .

The spirit shown by the men and the newspapers who denounce us for enforcing the law is simply one manifestation of the feeling which brings about and is responsible for lynchings and for all the varieties of Whitecap outrages. The men who head a lynching party and the officers who fail to protect criminals threatened with lynching always advance, as their excuse, that public sentiment sanctions their action. The chief offenders often insist that they have taken such summary action because they fear lest the law be not enforced against the offender. In other words, they put public sentiment ahead of law in the first place; and in the second they offer, as a partial excuse for so doing, the fact that too often laws are not enforced by the men elected or appointed to enforce them.

The only possible outcome of such an attitude is lawlessness, which gradually grows until it becomes mere anarchy. The one all-important element in good citizenship in our country is obedience to law. The greatest crimes that can be committed against our government are to put on the statute books, or to allow to remain there, laws that are not meant to be enforced and to fail to enforce the laws that exist. . . .

In the end we shall win, in spite of the open opposition of the forces of evil, in spite of the timid surrender of the weakly good, if only we stand squarely and fairly on the platform of the honest enforcement of the law of the land. But if we were to face defeat instead of victory, that would not alter our convictions and would not cause us to flinch one handsbreadth from the course we have been pursuing. There are prices too dear to be paid even for victory. We would rather face defeat as a consequence of honestly enforcing the law than win a suicidal triumph by a corrupt connivance at its violation.

15.

Edward B. Whitney: Political Dangers of the Income Tax Decision

During the second administration of Grover Cleveland, the Democratic Congress passed the Wilson-Gorman Tariff. The act lowered tariffs generally and included a provision for a 2 percent tax on incomes over $4,000. The following year, 1895, saw the defeat of the latter provision by the Supreme Court. Ruling that the tax was unconstitutional, the Court, in a narrow 5 to 4 decision, alienated many people by its action. One historian has called the decision the most unpopular one since the Dred Scott case. Edward Whitney, assistant U.S. attorney general, had argued in favor of the tax provision before the Court. He described what he called the "Political Dangers of the Income-Tax Decision," in an article published in August 1895.

Source: *Forum*, August 1895.

THE INCOME TAX CASES just decided will rank with the legal tender cases and the electoral commission as examples of the extraordinary power which one man may sometimes exercise under our system of government. Not only was a tax law, out of which a return of $30 million annually had been expected, declared null and void by a single vote but the question was so close that two judges changed in opinion on the reargument. On the first hearing, six out of eight judges held the law void as to so much of one's income as is derived from rentals, while four only of them held it void as a whole.

On the second hearing, a ninth judge being present, one of the six, together with the new judge, concluded that it was valid as to the rentals, and valid also as a whole. One judge, however, who had voted against it on the rentals question alone, now concluded to vote against it as a whole; and the final poll stood, therefore, five to four on each question. The decision of the Court

on the first hearing found not a single supporter on the second.

Like the legal tender cases, again, the decision reversed the previous ruling of the same Court upon a great and fundamental political question, which was the center of a hot political controversy. It differs from those cases in that the decisions which it overrules were unanimous and had long been acquiesced in.

It is the purpose here to consider not the merits of the decision but its probable effects. To do so, the decision itself and the controversy decided must first be explained. The case did not turn upon the points mainly discussed by the public. The charges so hotly urged against this income tax, that it was ununiform and inquisitorial, counted for nothing. The tax, as the Court decided that it should have been laid, would have been certainly less uniform and might have been no less inquisitorial.

The Constitution gives Congress the power to lay taxes and duties. It provides that direct taxes shall be apportioned among the several states according to their populations as shown by the census. It puts no such restriction upon duties, which are, on the contrary, to be uniform throughout the United States. The Court decided in 1880, in Judge Springer's case, by a unanimous vote of the seven judges then sitting, that an income tax essentially like the late one was a duty and not a direct tax, and therefore valid. A similar ruling had been made in 1868, by a unanimous decision of the eight judges then forming the tribunal, upon the validity of a corporation income tax; and in these and other cases the Court had said that the definitions had been substantially settled as early as the case of Mr. Hylton's carriage tax in 1796.

Congress, therefore, in enacting the Revenue Law of 1894, and providing that a certain portion of the existing deficit should be met by the proceeds of an income tax, acted in reliance upon very clear and definite rulings of the Supreme Court itself. It could not have laid any tax with greater assurance of safety. It could not foreknow the future actions of the Court. It had to shape its legislation by the decisions of the past.

Five judges now rule, however — and these five are entitled to speak for the Court — that the seven of 1880 and the eight of 1868, that Chief Justices Chase and Waite, Associate Justices Nelson, Miller, Strong, and Bradley and the rest, were all mistaken; and that an income tax is a direct tax, not a duty. . . .

Among the many duties revived by Congress during our Civil War as means of supporting the Union, and which would seem to be no longer available, are the duties on descents and devises of real property; on legacies and distributive shares of personal property; on carriages, yachts, billiard tables, watches, musical instruments, and gold and silver plate; on bonds and mortgages, on stocks, and on deeds and leases of land. The duties on the net incomes of corporations (as measured by the interest paid on their bonds, the dividends paid on their stock, and the sums carried annually to surplus account) must hereafter be subjected to large deductions, if they can be renewed at all.

The reasoning of the Court, in fact, exempts all wealth from effective federal taxation. For nobody denies that taxation on so large a scale by a system of apportionment is a lame and unsatisfactory proceeding at the best, sure to be seldom tried and little relied upon. Even in the case of a land tax, it has not proved well-fitted for emergencies. The federal government has never attempted to reach personal property in this way; nor can it be doubted that such an attempt would be a failure.

Suppose an attempt to levy an income tax by apportionment, exempting small incomes, as must be done in any proper income tax. The total amount of money to be raised must first be fixed. Then it must be divided up among the states in proportion to their population. Then the number of incomes in each state over the given amount must be ascertained and the quota of that state assessed upon the incomes *pro rata*. This would be unfair enough even if an income were a definite object with a fixed location, like a house. The taxpayers in some states would pay two or three times as much as taxpayers in other states.

An income, however, is not a tangible object, nor has it any fixed location. It is usually regarded by legal fiction as belonging wherever its owner chooses to plant his "legal residence." A large income thus wanders from county to county or from state to state, often for the sole purpose of avoiding taxation. One wealthy man moves into Rhode Island for that purpose; another into New Jersey. Moreover, under a system of apportionment many large incomes could never be reached at all. A woman, who is also a millionaire, marries an English duke or a French count. Her income, though entirely the product of American labor, instantly becomes free of taxation under such a system.

Queer questions also arise. A man gets rich in Nebraska, invests his property in land there and lives on the rents. Then, in order to escape taxation or to get into "society," or for whatever other reason, he moves to New York, or to Rhode Island, or to the District of Columbia. The court holds that a tax on rents is a tax on the land rented. Is his income to be taxed in Nebraska or at his new residence?

The principle of apportionment is grossly unfair as well as impracticable. The industries of our nation are closely intertwined. Each section is partly dependent on the others for its support. Wherever the men with large incomes choose to settle themselves, the incomes which they enjoy are really the joint product of the industry of the entire nation. Each man should, therefore, pay his own share; and to apportion according to legal residence would be to make a sectional tax, discriminating in favor of those parts of the country where wealthy people like to congregate.

It may safely be assumed that the nation will levy no income taxes under this new theory of the Constitution. Nor can the states levy such taxes efficiently. The sources of a large income are often scattered all over the Union, and the state which its fortunate possessor selects to reside in cannot tap them. To make the tax efficient, the owner and his property should both be within the jurisdiction. State income taxes never have been successful, and the result of this decision is probably to release individual incomes from all effective taxation.

What are its practical consequences? . . . Because the wealth of the country cannot be taxed effectively, the impositions upon the poor man will be doubled, and an immense debt again established for his descendants to pay. Part of this debt will probably be in the shape of more fiat money, to plague rich and poor alike for a generation to come.

Moreover, in time of stress, it is most important that the nation may have recourse to taxes which will be both certain and elastic; in other words, to taxes which may be increased or diminished with some certainty as to the amount of money which will thus be obtained. This is the case with income taxes. Great Britain, when it adds a penny in the pound to the tax, knows pretty nearly what additional revenue will come in. This is not the case with excises or customs duties, especially the latter. Increasing the duty on an imported article often means decreasing its importation. On the other hand, if the duty remains unchanged, or even is reduced, still its importation may decrease from decreased use or from growth of domestic manufactures. . . .

Should the nation rest satisfied with its now restricted power? I do not think so. I do not think that it is good for the poor man to be overtaxed. I do not think that it is good in the long run for the rich man, that the immense majority of the people in this country should have a just grievance against the fortunate holders of accumulated property. It is said that there are no classes in this country and that class distinctions should never be alluded to. Unfortunately, there is a distinction between rich and poor which cannot be wiped out under our present civilization. If individual ownership of accumulated property is a good thing — and I think it is, for, if it were abolished, the elements of aspiration and hope would largely be taken out of life — then care should be taken that such property should bear at least its full share of every public burden. It should never be placed for a moment in the wrong.

It is said that there is really a balance struck in this regard by state and local taxation. That is true to a certain extent. Real property there bears a large part of the burden, but it is the real property of rich and poor alike. And personal property still almost wholly escapes. But assume that state taxes are a compensation in times of peace. Where is the compensation for the immense mass of additional taxation, nearly all laid by the federal government, in time of war? The volunteer army which marches out to protect all our property is filled up by poor men or men of moderate means. Are they to bear as well a ninefold share of the expense in proportion to their means? They are to bear it unless the Constitution shall in some way be restored to the place where it was supposed to be for the first century of its life. . . .

The reasoning which segregates the nine judges of today from the nine judges of thirty years ago, which charges the present judges with the responsibility of reviewing the errors of their predecessors, destroys the continuity of the Court in the public mind. The same reasoning segregates each individual judge from his eight associates and properly places his individual portrait at the head of the column which sets forth his individual opinion or records his individual change of mind.

But the public is not satisfied with an unlimited veto power in any individual. If the Court establishes the doctrine of change, the people, by adding new justices, can control and direct the movement. They can bring up again this question of the taxability of wealth. That, probably, is inevitable. They can bring up again the national bank, the control of commerce, the legal tender notes. They can inquire into the constitutionality of the Fourteenth and Fifteenth amendments. When some new socialistic law is wanted, they can demand a convenient constitutional power from their packed Supreme Court, as a congressional majority looks to its speaker for a convenient parliamentary rule.

Will wealth, for the present moment released from a small pecuniary assessment, profit or lose in the end by the new gospel of instability? It may be well for the wealthy reader, laying aside for an hour the newspaper which daily reflects his ideas, to think this question over by himself. . . .

The question whether an income tax can properly be levied in time of peace is one that cannot be decided by a court. Congress is the judge of the necessity, at any given time, for any tax which can be levied at all. Our ancestors made many promises when they were trying to secure the ratification of the Constitution as to the rarity with which direct taxation would be imposed. As soon as they began work, however, they admitted that it was a subject as to which policy must be the only guide. Any tax levied may properly be called a war tax so long as the Treasury is struggling with an immense annual deficit, where, but for pensions to veterans of the Civil War, we should have an annual surplus of double the amount.

———————◆———————

The savings of many in the hands of one.

EUGENE V. DEBS, of wealth

It is wrong to assume that men of immense wealth are always happy.

JOHN D. ROCKEFELLER, to his Sunday school class

16.

James Laurence Laughlin: Against Free Coinage of Silver

*The Populist Party, outraged by President Cleveland's repeal of the Sherman Silver
Purchase Act in 1893, propagandized continuously on the virtues of free silver.
The party accepted the formula proposed by one of its most effective spokesmen,
W. H. "Coin" Harvey, and proclaimed that farmers and workers would benefit greatly
by adopting the coinage of silver at a ratio of 16 to 1 (of gold). "The bimetallic
standard," Harvey declared, "will make the United States the most prosperous nation
on the globe." James Laughlin, a professor of political economy at the University of
Chicago and one of the staunchest critics of free silver, debated the issue with Harvey
in 1895. Laughlin's views are reprinted here.*

Source: *Facts About Money*, Chicago, 1895, pp. 223-238.

MONEY IS USED as a common denominator to which other things are referred for comparison. In order to compare goods with money, there is no more need of as many pieces of money as there are articles to be compared than there is of having a quart cup for every quart of milk in existence, or of having a yardstick in a dry goods store for every yard of cloth on the shelf. The idea that it is necessary to multiply the measurements of value is absurd; but it is of the foremost importance that the measure of values should not be tampered with and should not be changed by legislation to the damage of all transactions based upon it. Right here is the whole secret of the opposition to silver as money. Silver has lost its stability of value. It is no better than any ordinary metal for stability. The action of India in June 1893 sends it down 20 percent. The mere rumor of the Chinese indemnity sends it up 10 percent.

The greater or less quantity of money there is roaming about in circulation is no reason why anyone gets more of it. Money, like property, is parted with for a consider-ation. No matter how many more coins there are coming from the mint under free coinage and going into the vaults of the banks to the credit of the mine owners who own the bullion, there are no more coins in the pockets of Weary Waggles, who is cooling his heels on the sidewalk outside the bank.

The increased number of handsome horses and carriages on Michigan Avenue does not imply that I can get them if I have not the wealth to purchase them with. I must produce, work, turn out goods, and labor. I must get gold or silver or something equivalent to the value of the goods, and in that way I shall get them and in no other way. There is no way of getting rich by short cuts or by legislation or by merely increasing the means of exchanging goods, when goods themselves are the principal thing.

Money is the only machine by which goods are exchanged against one another. No matter how valuable, it is not wanted for itself. It is only a means to an end, like a bridge over a river. Do you suppose that the farmers of this country really believe that with each ton of silver taken out of the mines by the silver lawmakers in the Senate that there are created bushels of wheat and bushels of corn and barrels of mess pork? The silver belongs to the mine owners. How will it get into our pockets or the pockets of anyone else? Do we insult anyone's penetration by supposing that the congressional silver kings are going coaching about the country distributing their money for nothing? Our farmers are no fools. They know they can get more money only by producing more commodities to be exchanged for it and for those commodities they want as good money as any other men in the country have got. . . .

As free coinage of silver would inevitably result in a rise of prices, it would immediately result in the fall of wages. Its first effect would be to diminish the purchasing power of all our wages. The man who gets $500 or $1,000 a year as a fixed rate of wages or salary will find he could buy just half as much as now. Yes, but someone will say, the employer will raise his wages. Now, will he? But the facts on that point are clear and indisputable. It has been one of the undisputed facts of history that, when prices rise, the wages of labor are the last to advance; and when prices fall, the wages of labor are the first to decline. Free coinage of silver would make all the articles of the laborer's consumption cost him 100 percent more unless he can get a rise in his wages by dint of strikes and quarrels and all the consequent dissatisfaction arising from friction between the employer and employee. He would be able to buy only one-half as many articles of daily consumption as he had before.

In short, a rise of prices necessarily results in a diminution of the enjoyments of the laboring class until they can force the employers, through a long process of agitation, to make an increase in their wages. Are we willing to sacrifice the interests of the labor-

ing classes to the demands of certain owners of silver mines who hope to hoodwink the people with the cry of more money? This would be, clearly enough, distinct and serious damage.

The damage runs in other directions, however. The proposal to adopt a depreciated standard of value is simply an attempt to transfer from the great mass of the community who have been provident, industrious, and successful, a portion of their savings and gains into the pockets of those who have been idle, extravagant, or unfortunate. The provision which has been made for old age, for sickness, for death, for widows and orphans, or by insurance will be depreciated in the same ratio. No invasion of hostile armies, burning and destroying as they advance, could by any possibility equal the desolation and ruin which would thus be forced upon the great mass of the American people.

Such a depreciation, however — as all experience and history has shown — does not fall alike upon the shrewd and the unsophisticated. The shrewd ones, the bankers, etc., will be easily able to take care of themselves; while we plain people will be robbed of our hard-won earnings without any hope of compensation.

Free coinage of silver at 16:1 would injure all those who wish to borrow because it would frighten lenders and make them unwilling to lend except at high rates of interest. Moreover, since the average term of mortgages, in general, is not over five or six years, present indebtedness of this kind does not run back to 1873. Free coinage is essentially dishonest.

If I have saved painfully $1,000 by many years of sacrifice and lend it to B on a mortgage; then, if B urges legislation by which he can pay me back in a cheaper money worth one-half of what he got from me, do you suppose I would ever again lend to B or renew my mortgage? If I had pinched or saved, gone without a new overcoat, or used a shabby parlor carpet in order to save something and invest it for my child, and then I gave it over to *B*, who has had the spending of it, isn't it fair and square that I should have back again what I gave? If *B* had the enjoyment from spending it, he is not thereby absolved from paying it back. No trick or sophistry can make the scaling of this debt to me anything but dishonesty and cheating.

Any state that enacts laws whereby debts can be scaled signs its own commercial doom. No one will invest where he foresees repudiation; loans cannot be made except at rates so high as to pay for the risks of loss. Cheating is bad business policy for man or state. . . .

The Sherman Act of July 4, 1890, unless it had been repealed, would have brought us to the silver standard as it was. The mere suspicion of it struck a blow at our measure of value, brought on a panic, made prices uncertain, and caused doubts as to future plans in every factory and shop in the land. Those who have silver mines, and who can by their wealth control political parties and legislatures, who make the very seat of our national government their private offices, and actually turn the national Senate into a bureau for bulling the prices of their product — to those men we say, beware.

Those of us who belong to the rank of plain citizens, who are thinking only of the country as a whole, who believe in the honesty and intelligence of the people, hold that when a question of right or wrong is presented in a campaign of education the people will decide for right and for justice. We cannot believe that a special interest, led by millionaires, can go on unchecked in their plan of sacrificing the taxpayers in order to heap up riches, especially when this is done on the most fallacious of all economic grounds — grounds which have been proved wrong by the experience of every country of modern times.

How long will it take to convince every man in the land that conditions of prosperity are those in which the honest man can best meet and pay his obligations? Unless a debtor can get employment or find a market for his goods, how can he pay interest or principal? Now, if tampering with the standard in the terms of which all transactions are drawn, all contracts made, all goods bought and sold brings industrial paralysis because no one knows what will happen ten days ahead, and no one will go on making goods for a changing market, except at ruinous profits, it is to the interest of every laborer, every debtor, every honest man, is it not, to keep and maintain the value of the standard so far as that may be done? The debtor will be no better off by free coinage. Even if we had it — which we never will — every lender would insert the gold clause in the contract. . . .

Is it true that, even laying aside all honor and justice, resorting to a single silver standard depreciated 50 percent, the debtor will sell his goods at 100 percent more, and the more easily pay off his debts? By no means. That is the most superficial of all views. Trickery is always sure to follow those who resort to it. And I do not myself feel it necessary only to appeal to the selfish motives of the American people. I for one am ready to appeal to that integrity, that sense of honor, and that uprightness in the American people which, whenever it has been appealed to, has decided rightly upon these great questions of justice.

In conclusion, gentlemen, extraordinary as is the proposal for free coinage, it is in truth only a huge deceit. It was born in the private offices of the silver kings, nursed at the hands of speculators, clothed in economic error, fed on boodle, exercised in the lobby of Congress, and as sure as there is honesty and truth in the American heart it will die young and be buried in the same ignominious grave wherein lies the now-forgotten infant once famous as the rag baby.

Free coinage is greenbackism galvanized into life. That heresy in its old form of a demand for more money has already been laid low. It will not long deceive us in its new form of a demand for more silver, or for silver fiatism. Nor in any other respect is it what it presumes to be. It is not a proposition for bimetallism. It is a wild leap in the dark for silver monometallism. Under the cry for more money are veiled the plans of a daring syndicate of mine owners and speculators who have hoodwinked the people in certain parts of the country and who, while deluding them with a specious argument for more money, are laughing in their sleeves at a constituency so easily gulled.

17.

JOHN L. SPALDING: Religion as an Essential Part of Education

Although he appreciated the great usefulness of public schools, the Roman Catholic bishop of Peoria, Illinois, John Spalding, maintained in many books that religious training should play a central role in education. He was concerned with teachers as well as with students, and believed that the only truly effective educator was a religious man. Spalding argued this and similar views in a book, Means and Ends of Education *(1895), from which a selection is reprinted here.*

Source: *Means and Ends of Education*, Chicago, 1903: "The Religious Element in Education."

THE CATHOLIC VIEW OF THE SCHOOL question is as clearly defined as it is well known. It rests upon the general ground that man is created for a supernatural end and that the church is the divinely appointed agency to help him to attain his supreme destiny. If education is a training for completeness of life, its primary element is the religious, for complete life is life in God. Hence we may not assume an attitude toward the child, whether in the home, in the church, or in the school, which might imply that life apart from God could be anything else than broken and fragmentary. A complete man is not one whose mind only is active and enlightened; but he is a complete man who is alive in all his faculties.

The truly human is found not in knowledge alone but also in faith, in hope, in love, in pure-mindedness, in reverence, in the sense of beauty, in devoutness, in the thrill of awe, which Goethe says is the highest thing in man.

If the teacher is forbidden to touch upon religion, the source of these noble virtues and ideal moods is sealed. His work and influence become mechanical, and he will form but commonplace and vulgar men. And if an educational system is established on this narrow and material basis, the result will be deterioration of the national type, and the loss of the finer qualities which make men many-sided and interesting which are the safeguards of personal purity and of unselfish conduct.

Religion is the vital element in character, and to treat it as though it were but an incidental phase of man's life is to blunder in a matter of the highest and most serious import. Man is born to act, and thought is valuable mainly as a guide to action. Now, the chief inspiration to action, and above all to right action, is found in faith, hope, and love, the virtues of religion, and not in knowledge, the virtue of the intellect. Knowledge, indeed, is effectual only when it is loved, believed in, and held to be a ground for hope. Man does not live on bread alone, and if he is brought up to look to material things, as to the chief good, his higher faculties will be stunted. If to do rightly rather than to think keenly is man's chief business here on earth, then the virtues of religion are more important than those of the intellect; for to think is to be unresolved, whereas to believe is to be impelled in the direction of one's faith. In epochs of doubt things fall to decay; in epochs of faith the powers which make for full and vigorous life hold sway. The education which forms character is indispensable, that which trains the mind is desirable.

The essential element in human life is conduct, and conduct springs from what we believe, cling to, love, and yearn for, vastly more than from what we know. The decadence and ruin of individuals and of societies come from lack of virtue, not from lack of knowledge. "The hard and valuable part of education," says Locke, "is virtue; this is the solid and substantial good, which the teacher should never cease to inculcate till the young man places his strength, his glory, and his pleasure in it." We may, of course, distinguish between morality and religion, between ethics and theology. As a

matter of fact, however, moral laws have everywhere reposed upon the basis of religion, and their sanction has been sought in the principles of faith. As an immoral religion is false, so, if there is no God, a moral law is meaningless.

Theorists may be able to construct a system of ethics upon a foundation of materialism; but their mechanical and utilitarian doctrines have not the power to exalt the imagination or to confirm the will. Their educational value is feeble. Here in America we have already passed the stage of social development in which we might hold out to the young, as an ideal, the hope of becoming President of the republic, or the possessor of millions of money. We know what sorry men presidents and millionaires may be. We cannot look upon our country simply as a wide racecourse with well-filled purses hanging at the goal for the prizewinners. We clearly perceive that a man's possessions are not himself and that he is or ought to be more than anything which can belong to him. Ideals of excellence, therefore, must be substituted for those of success.

Opinion governs the world, but ideals draw souls and stimulate to noble action. The more we transform with the aid of machinery the world of matter, the more necessary does it become that we make plain to all that man's true home is the world of thought and love, of hope and aspiration. The ideals of utilitarianism and secularism are unsatisfactory. They make no appeal to the infinite in man, to that in him which makes pursuit better than possession, and which, could he believe there is no absolute truth, love, and beauty, would lead him to despair.

Today, as of old, the soul is born of God and for God, and finds no peace unless it rest in Him. Theology, assuredly, is not religion; but religion implies theology, and a church without a creed is a body without articulation. The virtues of religion are indispensable. Without them, it is not well either with individuals or with nations; but these virtues cannot be inculcated by those who, standing aloof from ecclesiastical organizations, are thereby cut off from the thought and work of all who in every age have most loved God, and whose faith in the soul has been most living. Religious men have wrought for God in the church as patriots have wrought for liberty and justice in the nation; and to exclude the representatives of the churches from the school is practically to exclude religion — the power which more than all others makes for righteousness, which inspires hope and confidence, which makes possible faith in the whole human brotherhood, in the face even of the political and social wrongs which are still everywhere tolerated. To exclude religion is to exclude the spirit of reverence, of gentleness and obedience, of modesty and purity; it is to exclude the spirit by which the barbarians have been civilized, by which woman has been uplifted and ennobled and the child made sacred.

From many sides the demand is made that the state schools exercise a greater moral influence, that they may be efficient in forming character as well as in training the mind. It is recognized that knowing how to read and write does not insure good behavior. Since the state assumes the office of teacher, there is a disposition among parents to make the school responsible for their children's morals as well as for their minds, and thus the influence of the home is weakened. Whatever the causes may be, there seems to be a tendency, both in private and in public life, to lower ethical standards. The moral influence of the secular school is necessarily feeble, since our ideas of right and wrong are so interfused with the principles of Christianity that to ignore our religious convictions is practically to put aside the question of conscience. If the state may take no cognizance of sin, neither may its

school do so. But, in morals, sin is the vital matter; crime is but its legal aspect. Men begin as sinners before they end as criminals.

The atmosphere of religion is the natural medium for the development of character. If we appeal to the sense of duty, we assume belief in God and in the freedom of the will; if we strive to awaken enthusiasm for the human brotherhood, we imply a divine fatherhood. Accordingly, as we accept or reject the doctrines of religion, the sphere of moral action, the nature of the distinction between right and wrong, and the motives of conduct all change. In the purely secular school only secular morality may be taught; and whatever our opinion of this system of ethics may otherwise be, it is manifestly deficient in the power which appeals to the heart and the conscience.

The child lives in a world which imagination creates, where faith, hope, and love beckon to realms of beauty and delight. The spiritual and moral truths which are to become the very life-breath of his soul he apprehends mystically, not logically. Heaven lies about him; he lives in wonderland and feels the thrill of awe as naturally as he looks with wide-open eyes. Do not seek to persuade him by telling him that honesty is the best policy, that poverty overtakes the drunkard, that lechery breeds disease, that to act for the common welfare is the surest way to get what is good for oneself; for such teaching will not only leave him unimpressed, but it will seem to him profane and almost immoral. He wants to feel that he is the child of God, of the infinitely good and all-wonderful; that in his father, divine wisdom and strength are revealed; in his mother, divine tenderness and love. He so believes and trusts in God that it is our fault if he knows that men can be base.

In nothing does the godlike character of Christ show forth more beautifully than in His reverence for children. Shall we profess to believe in Him and yet forbid His name to be spoken in the houses where we seek to train the little ones whom He loved? Shall we shut out Him whose example has done more to humanize, ennoble, and uplift the race of man than all the teachings of the philosophers and all the disquisitions of the moralists? If the thinkers, from Plato and Aristotle to Kant and Pestalozzi, who have dealt with the problems of education, have held that virtue is its chief aim and end, shall we thrust from the school the one ideal character who, for nearly 1,900 years, has been the chief inspiration to righteousness and heroism; to whose words patriots and reformers have appealed in their struggles for liberty and right; to whose example philanthropists have looked in their labors to alleviate suffering; to whose teaching the modern age owes its faith in the brotherhood of men; by whose courage and sympathy the world has been made conscious that the distinction between man and woman is meant for the propagation of the race, but that as individuals they have equal rights and should have equal opportunities?

We all, and especially the young, are influenced by example more than by precepts and maxims, and it is unjust and unreasonable to exclude from the schoolroom the living presence of the noblest and best men and women, of those whose words and deeds have created our Christian civilization. In the example of their lives we have truth and justice, goodness and greatness in concrete form; and the young who are brought into contact with these centers of influence will be filled with admiration and enthusiasm; they will be made gentle and reverent; and they will learn to realize the ever-fresh charm and force of personal purity. Teachers who have no moral criteria, no ideals, no counsels of perfection, no devotion to God and godlike men cannot educate, if the proper meaning of education is the complete unfolding of all man's powers.

The school, of course, is but one of the many agencies by which education is given.

We are under the influence of our whole environment — physical, moral, and intellectual; political, social, and religious; and if, in all this, aught were different, we ourselves should be other. The family is a school and the church is a school; and current American opinion assigns to them the business of moral and religious education. But this implies that conduct and character are of secondary importance; it supposes that the child may be made subject to opposite influences at home and in the school, and not thereby have his finer sense of reverence, truth, and goodness deadened. The subduing of the lower nature, of the outward to the inner man, is a thing so arduous that reason, religion, and law combined often fail to accomplish it.

If one should propose to do away with schools altogether and to leave education to the family and the church, he would be justly considered ridiculous; because the carelessness of parents and the inability of the ministry of the church would involve the prevalence of illiteracy. Now, to leave moral and religious education to the family and the churches involves, for similar reasons, the prevalence of indifference, sin, and crime. If illiteracy is a menace to free institutions, vice and irreligion are a greater menace. The corrupt are always bad citizens; the ignorant are not necessarily so. Parents who would not have their children taught to read and write, were there no free schools, will as a rule neglect their religious and moral education. In giving religious instruction to the young, the churches are plainly at a disadvantage; for they have the child but an hour or two in seven days, and they get into their Sunday classes only the children of the more devout.

If the chief end of education is virtue; if conduct is three-fourths of life; if character is indispensable while knowledge is only useful, then it follows that religion — which, more than any other vital influence, has power to create virtue, to inspire conduct, and to mold character — should enter into all the processes of education. Our school system, then, does not rest upon a philosophic view of life and education. We have done what it was easiest to do, not what it was best to do; and in this, as in other instances, churchmen have been willing to sacrifice the interests of the nation to the whims of a narrow and jealous temper.

The denominational system of popular education is the right system. The secular system is a wrong system. The practical difficulties to be overcome that religious instruction may be given in the schools are relatively unimportant and would be set aside if the people were thoroughly persuaded of its necessity. An objection which Dr. Harris, among others, insists upon, that the method of science and the method of religion are dissimilar, and that therefore secular knowledge and religious knowledge should not be taught in the same school seems to me to have no weight. The method of mathematics is not the method of biology; the method of logic is not the method of poetry; but they are all taught in the same school. A good teacher, in fact, employs many methods. In teaching the child grammatical analysis, he has no fear of doing harm to his imagination or his talent for composition.

No system, however, can give assurance that the school is good. To determine this we must know the spirit which lives in it. The intellectual, moral, and religious atmosphere which the child breathes there is of far more importance, from an educational point of view, than any doctrines he may learn by rote, than any acts of worship he may perform.

The teacher makes the school; and when high, pure, devout, and enlightened men and women educate, the conditions favorable to mental and moral growth will be found, provided a false system does not compel them to assume a part and play a role, while the true self — the faith, hope, and love whereby they live — is condemned to inaction. The deeper tendency of the present age is not, I think, to exclude religion from any vital process but rather to widen the content of the idea of religion until it embrace the whole life of man.

The worship of God is not now the worship of infinite wisdom, holiness, and justice alone but is also the worship of the humane, the beautiful, and the industriously active. Whether we work for knowledge or freedom, or purity or strength, or beauty or health, or aught else that is friendly to completeness of life, we work with God and for God. In the school, as in whatever other place in the boundless universe a man may find himself, he finds himself with God, in Him moves, lives, and has his being.

———————◆———————

Always tell the truth, always take the humane and moral side, always remember that right feeling is the vital spark of strong writing, and that publicity, publicity, PUBLICITY is the greatest moral factor and force in our public life.
       JOSEPH PULITZER, advice to his editors on the *New York World*, Dec. 29, 1895

1896

18.

THEODORE ROOSEVELT: The Monroe Doctrine and the National Honor

*A dispute between England and Venezuela over the boundary of British Guiana
(now Guyana) became the concern of the United States in 1895 when the Venezuelan
ambassador to the U.S. requested its intervention. Recalling the memory
of the "immortal Monroe," the ambassador argued that the United States had a
traditional duty and a legitimate right to arbitrate the dispute. On December 17,
1895, President Grover Cleveland asked Congress for funds to defray the costs of
an investigation into the matter. Theodore Roosevelt, who had impatiently urged
American intervention for a long time, applauded Cleveland's action in the following
indignant letter to the* Harvard Crimson, *written January 2, 1896.*

Source: *The Letters of Theodore Roosevelt,* Elting E. Morison, ed., Cambridge, 1951, pp. 504-505.

I HAVE SEEN A NEWSPAPER statement that various professors and students of Harvard have urged, through your columns, the Harvard graduates and undergraduates to bring such pressure as they could upon senators and congressmen in order to prevent their upholding the honor and dignity of the United States by supporting the President and the secretary of state in their entirely proper attitude on the Venezuela question. I do not believe that any considerable number either of senators or congressmen would consent to betray the American cause, the cause not only of national honor but in reality of international peace, by abandoning our position in the peace, by abandoning our position in the Venezuelan matter; but I earnestly hope that Harvard will be saved from the discredit of advising such a course.

The Monroe Doctrine had for its first exponent Washington. In its present shape, it was in reality formulated by a Harvard man, afterward President of the United States, John Quincy Adams. John Quincy Adams did much to earn the gratitude of all Americans. Not the least of his services was his positive refusal to side with the majority of the cultivated people of New England and the Northeast in the period just before the War of 1812, when these cultivated people advised the same spiritless submission to improper English demands that some of their intellectual descendants are now advising.

The Monroe Doctrine forbids us to acquiesce in any territorial aggrandizement by a European power on American soil at the expense of an American state. If people wish to reject the Monroe Doctrine in its entirety, their attitude, though discreditable to their farsighted patriotism, is illogical; but let no one pretend that the present Venezuelan case does not come within the strictest view of the Monroe Doctrine. If we permit a European nation in each case itself to decide whether or not the territory which it wishes to seize is its own, then the Monroe Doctrine has no real existence; and if the European power refuses to submit the question to proper arbitration, then all we can do is to find the facts for ourselves and act accordingly. England's pretentions in this case are wholly inadmissible and the President and secretary of state and the Senate and House deserve the highest honor for the course they have followed.

Nothing will tend more to preserve peace on this continent than the resolute assertion of the Monroe Doctrine; let us make this present case serve as an object lesson, once for all. Nothing will more certainly in the end produce war than to invite European aggressions on American states by abject surrender of our principles. By a combination of indifference on the part of most of our people, a spirit of eager servility toward England in another smaller portion, and a base desire to avoid the slightest financial loss even at the cost of the loss of national honor by yet another portion, we may be led into a course of action which will for the moment avoid trouble by the simple process of tame submission to wrong.

If this is done, it will surely invite a repetition of the wrong; and in the end the American people are certain to resent this. Make no mistake. When our people, as a whole, finally understand the question, they will insist on a course of conduct which will uphold the honor of the American flag; and we can in no way more effectively invite ultimate war than by deceiving foreign powers into taking a position which will make us certain to clash with them once our people have been fully aroused.

The stock-jobbing timidity, the Baboo kind of statesmanship which is clamored for at this moment by the men who put monetary gain before national honor, or who are still intellectually in a state of colonial dependence on England, would in the end most assuredly invite war. A temperate but resolute insistence upon our rights is the surest way to secure peace. If Harvard men wish peace with honor they will heartily support the national executive and national legislature in the Venezuela matter; will demand that our representatives insist upon the strictest application of the Monroe Doctrine; and will farther demand that immediate preparation be made to build a really first-class navy.

------◆------

There is a homely adage which runs, "Speak softly and carry a big stick; you will go far." If the American nation will speak softly and yet build and keep at a pitch of the highest training a thoroughly efficient navy, the Monroe Doctrine will go far.

THEODORE ROOSEVELT, address at Minnesota State Fair, Sept. 2, 1901

19.

Henry Cabot Lodge: For Intervention in Cuba

Cuba's history during the latter part of the nineteenth century was marked by frequent insurrections, many of which involved bloodshed. Spain suppressed reform movements whenever they arose and maintained a rigid and unyielding policy toward all efforts to improve conditions on the island. The United States, for reasons both of commerce and security, was naturally interested in the fate of Cuba. Many Americans resented the Spanish presence so close to their shores. By 1896 it was apparent that a full-scale uprising was under way, and Congress, led by members of the Senate Foreign Relations Committee, passed a resolution urging Spain to mediate her differences with the rebels. Henry Cabot Lodge, a member of the committee, was one of the most articulate advocates of forceful action against Spain if she did not comply. Lodge's views were expressed in a speech delivered to the Senate on February 20, 1896.

Source: *Record*, 54 Cong., 1 Sess., pp. 1971-1972.

I UNITED WITH THE REST of the Committee on Foreign Relations, with a single exception, in reporting the concurrent resolution which is now before the Senate. I will say, however, with perfect frankness, that I for one should be very glad if the Senate should see fit to go further in this direction; for I believe that the time has come when the United States should use their good offices to bring to an end the deplorable condition of affairs which now exists in the island of Cuba. In my opinion, the course which would meet with universal approbation of our own people and command the respect of the world would be to offer our good offices to mediate between Spain and the Cubans in order to restore peace and give independence to the island which Spain can no longer hold.

I think there are very few matters which are of more immediate importance to the people of the United States than this, not merely because their sympathies are engaged but also because in the condition of

that island and in its future are involved large and most serious interests of the United States. . . .

We know that the railroad lines are cut; that the telegraph wires are down; that every report of a Spanish victory which comes to us in the newspapers is followed by the statement of a fresh insurgent advance. We know, as a matter of fact, that the whole of that island today, except where the Spanish fleets ride at anchor and where the Spanish armies are encamped, is in the hands of the insurgents. We know that they have formed a government; that they have held two elections; that every officer in the Army holds his commission from the civil government which they have established.

We know the terms of the provisional government, and in the presence of these facts, and of the fighting that those men have done, I think it is not unreasonable of them to ask some recognition at the hands of the people of the United States. They have risen against oppression, compared to which the oppression which led us to rebel against England is as dust in the balance and they feel that for this reason, if no other, they should have the sympathy of the people of the United States.

Martinez Campos, the ablest general in Spain, has been recalled because he failed to put down the insurrection — recalled when the insurgent troops had been actually in the suburbs of Havana — and in his place has been sent a man whose only reputation known to the world is that of the most cold-blooded brutality in the last war for liberty in that island. That is the actual condition of Cuba today, speaking broadly and without reference to the details of actions or skirmishes.

Now, Mr. President, the question arises, and I think the time has come and more than come to decide it — What are the duties of the United States in the presence of this war? What action should we take in regard to a condition of affairs which lies right at our threshold? We have heard a good deal in some of the recent debates of the ties of kindred, of our gratitude to other nations with whom we happen to be in controversy, and of how much consideration we should show for the nations of Europe in regard to matters where the interests of the United States are involved.

Whatever may be said as to our relations to some other countries, I think the relations of this country to Spain offer no ties of gratitude or of blood. If that for which the Spanish Empire has stood since the days of Charles V is right, then everything for which the United States stands and has always stood is wrong. If the principles that we stand for are right, then the principles of which Spain has been the great exponent in history are utterly wrong. . . . We have the right to look at this thing purely from the point of view of the interests of humanity and the interests of the United States. There are no ties, no obligations, no traditions to bind us.

Now turn to the other party in this conflict. Turn to the Cubans battling for their liberties. I think, Mr. President, that even the most bitter opponent of the Spanish-Americans would admit that free Cuba, under the constitution which now exists, would be an immense advance in civilization, in all that makes for the progress of humanity, over the government which Spain has given to that island.

The Cubans offer a free press and free speech. Both are suppressed there by Spain. Spain closed a Protestant chapel in the city of Matanzas. The Cubans by their constitution guarantee a free church in a free state. They guarantee liberty of conscience. Those are things in which Americans believe, and the Cubans, whatever their faults or deficiencies may be, stand also for those principles.

Our immediate pecuniary interests in the island are very great. They are being destroyed. Free Cuba would mean a great market to the United States; it would mean an opportunity for American capital, invited there by signal exemptions; it would mean an opportunity for the development of that splended island.

Cuba is but a quarter smaller than the island of Java, and the island of Java sustains 23 million people. Cuba has a population of 1,500,000 and she is one of the richest spots on the face of the earth. She has not grown or prospered because the heavy hand of Spain has been upon her.

Those, Mr. President, are some of the more material interests involved in this question, but we have also a broader political interest in the fate of Cuba. The great island lies there across the Gulf of Mexico. She commands the Gulf, she commands the channel through which all our coastwise traffic between the Gulf and our Northern and Eastern states passes. She lies right athwart the line which leads to the Nicaragua Canal. Cuba in our hands or in friendly hands, in the hands of its own people, attached to us by ties of interest and gratitude, is a bulwark to the commerce, to the safety, and to the peace of the United States.

We should never suffer Cuba to pass from the hands of Spain to any other European power. We may dismiss that aspect of the subject. The question is whether we shall permit the present condition of affairs to continue. The island today is lost to Spain. They may maintain a guerilla warfare for years. They may wipe out every plantation and deluge the island in blood. . . . Spain may ruin the island. She can never hold it or govern it again.

Cuba now is not fighting merely for independence. Those men are fighting, every one of them, with a price on their heads and a rope around their necks. They have shown that they could fight well. They are now fighting the battle of despair. That is the condition today in that island. And here we stand motionless, a great and powerful country not six hours away from these scenes of useless bloodshed and destruction.

I have spoken of our material interests. I have referred to our political interests in the future of Cuba. But, Mr. President, I am prepared to put our duty on a higher ground than either of those, and that is the broad ground of a common humanity. No useful end is being served by the bloody struggle that is now in progress in Cuba, and in the name of humanity it should be stopped. . . .

Of the sympathies of the American people, generous, liberty-loving, I have no question. They are with the Cubans in their struggle for freedom. I believe our people would welcome any action on the part of the United States to put an end to the terrible state of things existing there. We can stop it. We can stop it peacefully. We can stop it, in my judgment, by pursuing a proper diplomacy and offering our good offices. Let it once be understood that we mean to stop the horrible state of things in Cuba and it will be stopped. The great power of the United States, if it is once invoked and uplifted, is capable of greater things than that.

Mr. President, we have a movement in favor of peace and arbitration recently set on foot by some distinguished and very wealthy and eminent citizens of the city of New York and other great cities of the country. They are influenced beyond any question by devotion to the divine principle of "peace on earth and goodwill to men." I cannot suppose that for a moment they mean to confine their opposition to war merely to wars in which we are engaged. They must be opposed to all wars; and they are, I take it, but an expression of the general feeling of the American people that the mission of the great republic is one of peace.

Therefore, Mr. President, here is a war with terrible characteristics flagrant at our very doors. We have the power to bring it to an end. I believe that the whole American people would welcome steps in that direction.

Recognition of belligerency as an expression of sympathy is all very well. I think it is fully justified by the facts in Cuba, but I should like to see some more positive action taken than that. I think we cannot escape the responsibility which is so near to us. We cannot shrug our shoulders and pass by on the other side. If that war goes on in Cuba, with the added horrors which this new general brings with him, the responsibility is on us; we cannot escape it. We should exert every influence of the United States. Standing, as I believe the United States stands, for humanity and civilization, we should exercise every influence of our great country to put a stop to that war which is now raging in Cuba and give to that island once more peace, liberty, and independence.

20.

HENRY CABOT LODGE: For Immigration Restrictions

The Anglo-Saxon race, according to Senator Henry Cabot Lodge, possessed qualities that destined it for greatness. Quoting the French writer Gustave Le Bon, Lodge declared to his Senate colleagues on March 16, 1896, that the Anglo-Saxons in America were marked by "unconquerable energy, a very great initiative, an absolute empire over self, [and] a sentiment of independence." These laudatory remarks were included by Lodge in support of a bill he had introduced to restrict immigration, one of the provisions of which would require a literacy test for incoming foreigners. Lodge felt that this and other provisions of the bill would serve to keep the American race from being polluted by those whose cultural backgrounds seemed to him incompatible with the country's institutions. A portion of his speech is reprinted here.

Source: *Record,* 54 Cong., 1 Sess., pp. 2817-2820.

THIS BILL IS INTENDED to amend the existing law so as to restrict still further immigration to the United States. Paupers, diseased persons, convicts, and contract laborers are now excluded. By this bill it is proposed to make a new class of excluded immigrants and add to those which have just been named the totally ignorant.

The bill is of the simplest kind. The 1st Section excludes from the country all immigrants who cannot read and write either their own or some other language. The 2nd Section merely provides a simple test for determining whether the immigrant can read or write, and is added to the bill so as to define the duties of the immigrant inspectors, and to assure to all immigrants alike perfect justice and a fair test of their knowledge.

Two questions arise in connection with this bill. The first is as to the merits of this particular form of restriction; the second, as to the general policy of restricting immigration at all. I desire to discuss briefly these two questions in the order in which I have stated them.

The smaller question as to the merits of this particular bill comes first. The existing laws of the United States now exclude, as I have said, certain classes of immigrants who, it is universally agreed, would be most undesirable additions to our population. These exclusions have been enforced and the results have been beneficial, but the excluded classes are extremely limited and do not by any means cover all or even any considerable part of the immigrants whose presence here is undesirable or injurious, nor do they have any adequate effect in properly reducing the great body of immigration to this country. There can be no doubt that there is a very earnest desire on the part of the American people to restrict further and much more extensively than has yet been done foreign immigration to the United States.

The question before the committee was how this could best be done; that is, by what method the largest number of undesirable immigrants and the smallest possible number of desirable immigrants could be shut out. Three methods of obtaining this further restriction have been widely discussed of late years and in various forms have been brought to the attention of Congress. The first was the imposition of a capitation tax on all immigrants. There can be no doubt as to the effectiveness of this method if the tax is made sufficiently heavy. But although exclusion by a tax would be thorough, it would be undiscriminating, and your committee did not feel that the time had yet come for its application.

The second scheme was to restrict immigration by requiring consular certification of immigrants. This plan has been much advocated, and if it were possible to carry it out thoroughly and to add very largely to the number of our consuls in order to do so, it would no doubt be effective and beneficial. But the committee was satisfied that consular certification was, under existing circumstances, impractical; that the necessary machinery could not be provided; that it would lead to many serious questions with foreign governments, and that it could not be properly and justly enforced. It is not necessary to go further into the details which brought the committee to this conclusion. It is sufficient to say here that the opinion of the committee is shared, they believe, by all expert judges who have given the most careful attention to the question.

The third method was to exclude all immigrants who could neither read nor write, and this is the plan which was adopted by the committee and which is embodied in this bill. In their report the committee have shown by statistics, which have been collected and tabulated with great care, the emigrants who would be affected by this illiteracy test. . . . It is found, in the first place, that the illiteracy test will bear most heavily upon the Italians, Russians, Poles, Hungarians, Greeks, and Asiatics, and very lightly, or not at all, upon English-speaking emigrants or Germans, Scandinavians, and French. In other words, the races most affected by the illiteracy test are those whose emigration to this country has begun within the last twenty years and swelled rapidly to enormous proportions, races with which the English-speaking people have never hitherto assimilated, and who are most alien to the great body of the people of the United States.

On the other hand, immigrants from the United Kingdom and of those races which are most closely related to the English-speaking people, and who with the English-speaking people themselves founded the American colonies and built up the United States, are affected but little by the proposed test. These races would not be prevented by this law from coming to this country in practically undiminished numbers. These kindred races also are those who alone go to the Western and Southern states, where immigrants are desired, and take up our unoccupied lands. The races which would suffer most seriously by exclusion under the proposed bill furnish the immigrants who do not go to the West or South, where immigration is needed, but who remain on the Atlantic seaboard, where immigration is not needed and where their presence is most injurious and undesirable. . . .

It now remains for me to discuss the second and larger question, as to the advisability of restricting immigration at all. This is a subject of the greatest magnitude and the most far-reaching importance. It has two sides, the economic and the social. As to the former, but few words are necessary. There is no one thing which does so much to bring about a reduction of wages and to injure the American wage earner as the un-, limited introduction of cheap foreign labor through unrestricted immigration. Statistics show that the change in the race character of our immigration has been accompanied by a corresponding decline in its quality. The number of skilled mechanics and of persons trained to some occupation or pursuit has fallen off, while the number of those without occupation or training, that is, who are totally unskilled, has risen in our recent immigration to enormous proportions. This low, unskilled labor is the most deadly enemy of the American wage earner, and does more than anything else toward lowering his wages and forcing down his standard of living.

An attempt was made, with the general assent of both political parties, to meet this crying evil some years ago by the passage of what are known as the contract-labor laws. That legislation was excellent in intention but has proved of but little value in practice. It has checked to a certain extent the introduction of cheap, low-class labor in large masses into the United States. It has made it a little more difficult for such labor to come here, but the labor of this class continues to come, even if not in the same way, and the total amount of it has not been materially reduced. Even if the contract-labor laws were enforced intelligently and thoroughly, there is no reason to suppose that they would have any adequate effect in checking the evil which they were designed to stop. It is perfectly clear, after the experience of several years, that the only relief which can come to the American wage earner from the competition of low-class immigrant labor must be by general laws restricting the total amount of immigration and framed in such a way as to affect most strongly those elements of the immigration which furnish the low, unskilled, and ignorant foreign labor.

It is not necessary to enter further into a discussion of the economic side of the general policy of restricting immigration. In this direction the argument is unanswerable. If we have any regard for the welfare, the wages, or the standard of life of American workingmen, we should take immediate steps to restrict foreign immigration. There is no danger, at present at all events, to our workingmen from the coming of skilled mechanics or of trained and educated men with a settled occupation or pursuit, for immigrants of this class will never seek to lower the American standard of life and wages. On the contrary, they desire the same standard for themselves. But there is an ap-

palling danger to the American wage earner from the flood of low, unskilled, ignorant, foreign labor which has poured into the country for some years past, and which not only takes lower wages but accepts a standard of life and living so low that the American workingman can not compete with it.

I now come to the aspect of this question which is graver and more serious than any other. The injury of unrestricted immigration to American wages and American standards of living is sufficiently plain and is bad enough, but the danger which this immigration threatens to the quality of our citizenship is far worse. That which it concerns us to know and that which is more vital to us as a people than all possible questions of tariff or currency is whether the quality of our citizenship is endangered by the present course and character of immigration to the United States. To determine this question intelligently we must look into the history of our race. . . .

For practical purposes in considering a question of race and in dealing with the civilized peoples of western Europe and of America, there is no such thing as a race of original purity according to the divisions of ethnical science. In considering the practical problems of the present time, we can deal only with artificial races — that is, races like the English-speaking people, the French, or the Germans — who have been developed as races by the operation during a long period of time of climatic influences, wars, migrations, conquests, and industrial development. To the philologist and the ethnologist it is of great importance to determine the ethnical divisions of mankind in the earliest historic times. To the scientific modern historian, to the student of social phenomena, and to the statesman alike the early ethnic divisions are of little consequence, but the sharply marked race divisions which have been gradually developed by the conditions and events of the last thousand years are absolutely vital. . . .

The English-speaking race . . . has been made slowly during the centuries. Nothing has happened thus far to radically change it here. In the United States, after allowing for the variations produced by new climatic influences and changed conditions of life and of political institutions, it is still in the great essentials fundamentally the same race. The additions in this country until the present time have been from kindred people or from those with whom we have been long allied and who speak the same language. By those who look at this question superficially we hear it often said that the English-speaking people, especially in America, are a mixture of races. Analysis shows that the actual mixture of blood in the English-speaking race is very small, and that while the English-speaking people are derived through different channels, no doubt, there is among them nonetheless an overwhelming preponderance of the same race stock, that of the great Germanic tribes who reached from Norway to the Alps. They have been welded together by more than a thousand years of wars, conquests, migrations, and struggles, both at home and abroad, and in so doing they have attained a fixity and definiteness of national character unknown to any other people. . . .

When we speak of a race, then, we do not mean its expressions in art or in language, or its achievements in knowledge. We mean the moral and intellectual characters, which in their association make the soul of a race and which represent the product of all its past, the inheritance of all its ancestors, and the motives of all its conduct. The men of each race possess an indestructible stock of ideas, traditions, sentiments, modes of thought, an unconscious inheritance from their ancestors, upon which argument has no effect. What makes a race are their mental and, above all, their moral characteristics, the slow growth and accumulation of centuries of toil and conflict. These are the qualities which determine their social efficiency as a people, which make one race rise and another fall, which we draw out of a dim past through many generations of ancestors, about which we cannot argue, but in which we blindly believe, and which guide us in our short-lived generation as they have guided the race itself across the centuries. . . .

Those qualities are moral far more than intellectual, and it is on the moral qualities of the English-speaking race that our history, our victories, and all our future rest. There is only one way in which you can lower those qualities or weaken those characteristics and that is by breeding them out. If a lower race mixes with a higher in sufficient numbers, history teaches us that the lower race will prevail. The lower race will absorb the higher, not the higher the lower, when the two strains approach equality in numbers. In other words, there is a limit to the capacity of any race for assimilating and elevating an inferior race, and when you begin to pour in unlimited numbers people of alien or lower races of less social efficiency and less moral force, you are running the most frightful risk that any people can run. The lowering of a great race means not only its own decline but that of human civilization. . . .

Mr. President, more precious even than forms of government are the mental and moral qualities which make what we call our race. While those stand unimpaired, all is safe. When those decline, all is imperiled. They are exposed to but a single danger and that is by changing the quality of our race and citizenship through the wholesale infusion of races whose traditions and inheritances, whose thoughts and whose beliefs are wholly alien to ours and with whom we have never assimilated or even been associated in the past. The danger has begun. It is small as yet, comparatively speaking, but it is large enough to warn us to act while there is yet time and while it can be done easily and efficiently. There lies the peril at the portals of our land; there is pressing in the tide of unrestricted immigration.

The time has certainly come, if not to stop at least to check, to sift, and to restrict those immigrants. In careless strength, with generous hand, we have kept our gates wide open to all the world. If we do not close them, we should at least place sentinels beside them to challenge those who would pass through. The gates which admit men to the United States and to citizenship in the great republic should no longer be left unguarded.

21.

Henry B. Brown and John M. Harlan: *Plessy* v. *Ferguson*

By 1896 segregation in railway cars was in effect in all Southern states. In an effort to test the constitutionality of Louisiana's segregation laws, Homer A. Plessy, who was only one-eighth Negro and could easily pass for white, sat in a white car after having made it known that he was a Negro. When he was asked to move to a Negro car Plessy refused. He was arrested and tried, and he appealed his conviction to the Louisiana Supreme Court. The U.S. Supreme Court heard the case on a writ of error and, in a landmark decision, ruled that "separate but equal accommodations" were constitutional. The judgment sanctioned segregation in the South as well as the North for nearly sixty years. Justice Harlan delivered the sole dissenting opinion; portions of this and of Justice Brown's majority opinion are reprinted here.

Source: 163 U.S. 537.

Mr. Justice Brown:

This case turns upon the constitutionality of an act of the General Assembly of the state of Louisiana, passed in 1890, providing for separate railway carriages for the white and colored races. . . . The 1st Section of the statute enacts

That all railway companies carrying passengers in their coaches in this state shall provide equal but separate accommodations for the white and colored races, by providing two or more passenger coaches for each passenger train, or by dividing the passenger coaches by a partition so as to secure separate accommodations: *Provided,* that this section shall not be construed to apply to street railroads. No person or persons, shall be admitted to occupy seats in coaches, other than, the ones, assigned, to them on account of the race they belong to. . . .

By the 2nd Section it was enacted

That the officers of such passenger trains shall have power and are hereby required to assign each passenger to the coach or compartment used for the race to which such passenger belongs; any passenger insisting on going into a coach or compartment to which by race he does not belong shall be liable to a fine of $25, or, in lieu thereof, to imprisonment for a period of not more than twenty days in the parish prison; and any officer of any railroad insisting on assigning a passenger to a coach or compartment other than the one set aside for the race to which said passenger belongs shall be liable to a fine of $25, or, in lieu thereof, to imprisonment for a period of not more than twenty days in the parish prison; and should any passenger refuse to occupy the coach or compartment to which he or she is assigned by the officer of such railway, said officer shall have power to refuse to carry such passenger on his train, and for such refusal neither he nor the railway company which he represents shall be liable for damages in any of the courts of this state. . . .

The constitutionality of this act is attacked upon the ground that it conflicts both with the Thirteenth Amendment of the Constitution, abolishing slavery, and the Fourteenth Amendment, which prohibits certain restrictive legislation on the part of the states.

1. That it does not conflict with the Thirteenth Amendment, which abolished slavery and involuntary servitude except as a punishment for crime, is too clear for argument. . . . A statute which implies merely a legal distinction between the white and colored races — a distinction which is founded in the color of the two races, and which must always exist so long as white men are distinguished from the other race by color — has no tendency to destroy the legal equality of the two races or reestablish a state of involuntary servitude. Indeed, we do not understand that the Thirteenth Amendment is strenuously relied upon by the plaintiff in error in this connection.

2. By the Fourteenth Amendment, all persons born or naturalized in the United States and subject to the jurisdiction thereof are made citizens of the United States and of the state wherein they reside; and the states are forbidden from making or enforcing any law which shall abridge the privileges or immunities of citizens of the United States, or shall deprive any person of life, liberty, or property without due process of law, or deny to any person within their jurisdiction the equal protection of the laws.

The proper construction of this amendment was first called to the attention of this court in the *Slaughter-House Cases* . . . which involved, however, not a question of race but one of exclusive privileges. The case did not call for any expression of opin-

ion as to the exact rights it was intended to secure to the colored race, but it was said generally that its main purpose was to establish the citizenship of the Negro; to give definitions of citizenship of the United States and of the states, and to protect from the hostile legislation of the states the privileges and immunities of citizens of the United States as distinguished from those of citizens of the states.

The object of the amendment was undoubtedly to enforce the absolute equality of the two races before the law, but in the nature of things it could not have been intended to abolish distinctions based upon color, or to enforce social as distinguished from political equality, or a commingling of the two races upon terms unsatisfactory to either. Laws permitting, and even requiring, their separation in places where they are liable to be brought into contact do not necessarily imply the inferiority of either race to the other, and have been generally, if not universally, recognized as within the competency of the state legislatures in the exercise of their police power. The most common instance of this is connected with the establishment of separate schools for white and colored children, which has been held to be a valid exercise of the legislative power even by courts of states where the political rights of the colored race have been longest and most earnestly enforced. . . .

While we think the enforced separation of the races, as applied to the internal commerce of the state, neither abridges the privileges or immunities of the colored man, deprives him of his property without due process of law, nor denies him the equal protection of the laws, within the meaning of the Fourteenth Amendment, we are not prepared to say that the conductor, in assigning passengers to the coaches according to their race, does not act at his peril, or that the provision of the 2nd Section of the act, that denies to the passenger compensation in damages for a refusal to receive him into the coach in which he properly belongs, is a valid exercise of the legislative power. Indeed, we understand it to be conceded by the state's attorney, that such part of the act as exempts from liability the railway company and its officers is unconstitutional.

The power to assign to a particular coach obviously implies the power to determine to which race the passenger belongs, as well as the power to determine who, under the laws of the particular state, is to be deemed a white and who a colored person. This question, though indicated in the brief of the plaintiff in error, does not properly arise upon the record in this case, since the only issue made is as to the unconstitutionality of the act, so far as it requires the railway to provide separate accommodations and the conductor to assign passengers according to their race.

It is claimed by the plaintiff in error that, in any mixed community, the reputation of belonging to the dominant race, in this instance the white race, is *property*, in the same sense that a right of action, or of inheritance, is property. Conceding this to be so for the purposes of this case, we are unable to see how this statute deprives him of, or in any way affects, his right to such property. If he be a white man and assigned to a colored coach, he may have his action for damages against the company for being deprived of his so-called property. Upon the other hand, if he be a colored man and be so assigned, he has been deprived of no property since he is not lawfully entitled to the reputation of being a white man.

In this connection, it is also suggested by the learned counsel for the plaintiff in error that the same argument that will justify the state legislature in requiring railways to provide separate accommodations for the two races will also authorize them to require separate cars to be provided for people whose hair is of a certain color, or who are aliens, or who belong to certain nationalities, or to enact laws requiring colored people to walk upon one side of the street

and white people upon the other, or requiring white men's houses to be painted white and colored men's black, or their vehicles or business signs to be of different colors, upon the theory that one side of the street is as good as the other, or that a house or vehicle of one color is as good as one of another color. The reply to all this is that every exercise of the police power must be reasonable and extend only to such laws as are enacted in good faith for the promotion for the public good and not for the annoyance or oppression of a particular class. . . .

So far, then, as a conflict with the Fourteenth Amendment is concerned, the case reduces itself to the question whether the statute of Louisiana is a reasonable regulation, and with respect to this there must necessarily be a large discretion on the part of the legislature. In determining the question of reasonableness, it is at liberty to act with reference to the established usages, customs, and traditions of the people, and with a view to the promotion of their comfort, and the preservation of the public peace and good order. Gauged by this standard, we cannot say that a law which authorizes or even requires the separation of the two races in public conveyances is unreasonable or more obnoxious to the Fourteenth Amendment than the acts of Congress requiring separate schools for colored children in the District of Columbia, the constitutionality of which does not seem to have been questioned, or the corresponding acts of state legislatures.

We consider the underlying fallacy of the plaintiff's argument to consist in the assumption that the enforced separation of the two races stamps the colored race with a badge of inferiority. If this be so, it is not by reason of anything found in the act, but solely because the colored race chooses to put that construction upon it. The argument necessarily assumes that if, as has been more than once the case, and is not unlikely to be so again, the colored race should become the dominant power in the state legislature and should enact a law in precisely similar terms, it would thereby relegate the white race to an inferior position. We imagine that the white race, at least, would not acquiesce in this assumption.

The argument also assumes that social prejudices may be overcome by legislation and that equal rights cannot be secured to the Negro except by an enforced commingling of the two races. We cannot accept this proposition. If the two races are to meet upon terms of social equality, it must be the result of natural affinities, a mutual appreciation of each other's merits, and a voluntary consent of individuals. As was said by the Court of Appeals of New York in *People* v. *Gallagher* . . .

> This end can neither be accomplished nor promoted by laws which conflict with the general sentiment of the community upon whom they are designed to operate. When the government, therefore, has secured to each of its citizens equal rights before the law and equal opportunities for improvement and progress, it has accomplished the end for which it was organized and performed all of the functions respecting social advantages with which it is endowed.

Legislation is powerless to eradicate racial instincts or to abolish distinctions based upon physical differences, and the attempt to do so can only result in accentuating the difficulties of the present situation. If the civil and political rights of both races be equal, one cannot be inferior to the other civilly or politically. If one race be inferior to the other socially, the Constitution of the United States cannot put them upon the same plane.

It is true that the question of the proportion of colored blood necessary to constitute a colored person as distinguished from a white person is one upon which there is a difference of opinion in the different states, some holding that any visible admixture of black blood stamps the person as belonging to the colored race (*State* v. *Chavers,* 5 Jones, [N.C.]1, p.11); others that it depends

upon the preponderance of blood (*Gray* v. *State,* 4 Ohio, 354; *Monroe* v. *Collins,* 17 Ohio St. 665); and still others that the predominance of white blood must only be in the proportion of three-fourths (*People* v. *Dean,* 14 Michigan, 406; *Jones* v. *Commonwealth,* 80 Virginia, 538). But these are questions to be determined under the laws of each state and are not properly put in issue in this case. Under the allegations of his petition it may undoubtedly become a question of importance whether, under the laws of Louisiana, the petitioner belongs to the white or colored race.

The judgment of the court below is, therefore, *affirmed.*

Mr. Justice Harlan:

In respect of civil rights, common to all citizens, the Constitution of the United States does not, I think, permit any public authority to know the race of those entitled to be protected in the enjoyment of such rights. Every true man has pride of race, and, under appropriate circumstances, when the rights of others, his equals before the law, are not to be affected, it is his privilege to express such pride and to take such action based upon it as to him seems proper. But I deny that any legislative body or judicial tribunal may have regard to the race of citizens when the civil rights of those citizens are involved. Indeed, such legislation as that here in question is inconsistent, not only with that equality of rights which pertains to citizenship, national and state, but with the personal liberty enjoyed by everyone within the United States.

The Thirteenth Amendment does not permit the withholding or the deprivation of any right necessarily inhering in freedom. It not only struck down the institution of slavery as previously existing in the United States but it prevents the imposition of any burdens or disabilities that constitute badges of slavery or servitude. It decreed universal civil freedom in this country. This Court has so adjudged. But that amendment having been found inadequate to the protection of the rights of those who had been in slavery, it was followed by the Fourteenth Amendment, which added greatly to the dignity and glory of American citizenship and to the security of personal liberty by declaring that "all persons born or naturalized in the United States and subject to the jurisdiction thereof are citizens of the United States and of the state wherein they reside," and that "no state shall make or enforce any law which shall abridge the privileges or immunities of citizens of the United States; nor shall any state deprive any person of life, liberty, or property without due process of law, nor deny to any person within its jurisdiction the equal protection of the laws."

These two amendments, if enforced according to their true intent and meaning, will protect all the civil rights that pertain to freedom and citizenship. Finally, and to the end that no citizen should be denied on account of his race the privilege of participating in the political control of his country, it was declared by the Fifteenth Amendment that "the right of citizens of the United States to vote shall not be denied or abridged by the United States or by any state on account of race, color, or previous condition of servitude."

These notable additions to the fundamental law were welcomed by the friends of liberty throughout the world. They removed the race line from our governmental systems. They had, as this Court has said, a common purpose; namely, to secure "to a race recently emancipated, a race that through many generations have been held in slavery, all the civil rights that the superior race enjoy." They declared, in legal effect, this Court has further said, "that the law in the states shall be the same for the black as for the white; that all persons, whether colored or white, shall stand equal before the laws of the states, and, in regard to the colored race, for whose protection the amendment was primarily designed, that

no discrimination shall be made against them by law because of their color."

We also said: "The words of the amendment, it is true, are prohibitory, but they contain a necessary implication of a positive immunity, or right, most valuable to the colored race — the right to exemption from unfriendly legislation against them distinctively as colored — exemption from legal discriminations, implying inferiority in civil society, lessening the security of their enjoyment of the rights which others enjoy, and discriminations which are steps toward reducing them to the condition of a subject race." It was, consequently, adjudged that a state law that excluded citizens of the colored race from juries because of their race and however well-qualified in other respects to discharge the duties of jurymen was repugnant to the Fourteenth Amendment. . . .

The decisions referred to show the scope of the recent amendments of the Constitution. They also show that it is not within the power of a state to prohibit colored citizens, because of their race, from participating as jurors in the administration of justice.

It was said in argument that the statute of Louisiana does not discriminate against either race, but prescribes a rule applicable alike to white and colored citizens. But this argument does not meet the difficulty. Everyone knows that the statute in question had its origin in the purpose, not so much to exclude white persons from railroad cars occupied by blacks as to exclude colored people from coaches occupied by or assigned to white persons. Railroad corporations of Louisiana did not make discrimination among whites in the matter of accommodation for travelers. The thing to accomplish was, under the guise of giving equal accommodation for whites and blacks, to compel the latter to keep to themselves while traveling in railroad passenger coaches. No one would be so wanting in candor as to assert the contrary.

The fundamental objection, therefore, to

the statute is that it interferes with the personal freedom of citizens. "Personal liberty," it has been well said, "consists in the power of locomotion, of changing situation, or removing one's person to whatsoever places one's own inclination may direct, without imprisonment or restraint, unless by due course of law." . . . If a white man and a black man choose to occupy the same public conveyance on a public highway, it is their right to do so, and no government proceeding alone on grounds of race can prevent it without infringing the personal liberty of each.

It is one thing for railroad carriers to furnish, or to be required by law to furnish, equal accommodations for all whom they are under a legal duty to carry. It is quite another thing for government to forbid citizens of the white and black races from traveling in the same public conveyance, and to punish officers of railroad companies for permitting persons of the two races to occupy the same passenger coach. If a state can prescribe, as a rule of civil conduct, that whites and blacks shall not travel as passengers in the same railroad coach, why may it not so regulate the use of the streets of its cities and towns as to compel white citizens to keep on one side of a street and black citizens to keep on the other?

Why may it not, upon like grounds, punish whites and blacks who ride together in street cars or in open vehicles on a public road or street? Why may it not require sheriffs to assign whites to one side of a courtroom and blacks to the other? And why may it not also prohibit the commingling of the two races in the galleries of legislative halls or in public assemblages convened for the consideration of the political questions of the day? Further, if this statute of Louisiana is consistent with the personal liberty of citizens, why may not the state require the separation in railroad coaches of native and naturalized citizens of the United States, or of Protestants and Roman Catholics?

The answer given at the argument to these questions was that regulations of the kind they suggest would be unreasonable and could not, therefore, stand before the law. Is it meant that the determination of questions of legislative power depends upon the inquiry whether the statute whose validity is questioned is, in the judgment of the courts, a reasonable one, taking all the circumstances into consideration? A statute may be unreasonable merely because a sound public policy forbade its enactment. But I do not understand that the courts have anything to do with the policy or expediency of legislation. A statute may be valid, and yet, upon grounds of public policy, may well be characterized as unreasonable. Mr. Sedgwick correctly states the rule when he says that the legislative intention being clearly ascertained, "the courts have no other duty to perform than to execute the legislative will, without any regard to their views as to the wisdom or justice of the particular enactment." . . .

There is a dangerous tendency in these latter days to enlarge the functions of the courts by means of judicial interference with the will of the people as expressed by the legislature. Our institutions have the distinguishing characteristic that the three departments of government are coordinate and separate. Each must keep within the limits defined by the Constitution, and the courts best discharge their duty by executing the will of the lawmaking power, constitutionally expressed, leaving the results of legislation to be dealt with by the people through their representatives.

Statutes must always have a reasonable construction. Sometimes they are to be construed strictly; sometimes, liberally, in order to carry out the legislative will. But however construed, the intent of the legislature is to be respected if the particular statute in question is valid, although the courts, looking at the public interests, may conceive the statute to be both unreasonable and impolitic. If the power exists to enact a statute, that ends the matter so far as the courts are concerned. The adjudged cases in which statutes have been held to be void because unreasonable are those in which the means employed by the legislature were not at all germane to the end to which the legislature was competent.

The white race deems itself to be the dominant race in this country. And so it is, in prestige, in achievements, in education, in wealth, and in power. So, I doubt not, it will continue to be for all time if it remains true to its great heritage and holds fast to the principles of constitutional liberty. But in view of the Constitution, in the eye of the law, there is in this country no superior, dominant, ruling class of citizens. There is no caste here. Our Constitution is color-blind and neither knows nor tolerates classes among citizens.

In respect of civil rights, all citizens are equal before the law. The humblest is the peer of the most powerful. The law regards man as man and takes no account of his surroundings or of his color when his civil rights as guaranteed by the supreme law of the land are involved. It is therefore to be regretted that this high tribunal, the final expositor of the fundamental law of the land, has reached the conclusion that it is competent for a state to regulate the enjoyment by citizens of their civil rights solely upon the basis of race.

In my opinion, the judgment this day rendered will, in time, prove to be quite as pernicious as the decision made by this tribunal in the *Dred Scott Case.* It was adjudged in that case that the descendants of Africans who were imported into this country and sold as slaves were not included nor intended to be included under the word "citizens" in the Constitution and could not claim any of the rights and privileges which that instrument provided for and secured to citizens of the United States; that at the time of the adoption of the Constitution they were "considered as a subordinate and inferior class of beings who had been subju-

gated by the dominant race, and, whether emancipated or not, yet remained subject to their authority, and had no rights or privileges but such as those who held the power and the government might choose to grant them." . . .

The recent amendments of the Constitution, it was supposed, had eradicated these principles from our institutions. But it seems that we have yet, in some of the states, a dominant race — a superior class of citizens, which assumes to regulate the enjoyment of civil rights, common to all citizens, upon the basis of race. The present decision, it may well be apprehended, will not only stimulate aggressions, more or less brutal and irritating, upon the admitted rights of colored citizens, but will encourage the belief that it is possible, by means of state enactments, to defeat the beneficent purposes which the people of the United States had in view when they adopted the recent amendments of the Constitution, by one of which the blacks of this country were made citizens of the United States and of the states in which they respectively reside, and whose privileges and immunities as citizens the states are forbidden to abridge.

Sixty millions of whites are in no danger from the presence here of 8 million blacks. The destinies of the two races in this country are indissolubly linked together, and the interests of both require that the common government of all shall not permit the seeds of race hate to be planted under the sanction of law. What can more certainly arouse race hate, what more certainly create and perpetuate a feeling of distrust between these races than state enactments, which, in fact, proceed on the ground that colored citizens are so inferior and degraded that they cannot be allowed to sit in public coaches occupied by white citizens? That, as all will admit, is the real meaning of such legislation as was enacted in Louisiana.

The sure guarantee of the peace and security of each race is the clear, distinct, unconditional recognition by our governments, national and state, of every right that inheres in civil freedom and of the equality before the law of all citizens of the United States without regard to race. State enactments regulating the enjoyment of civil rights upon the basis of race, and cunningly devised to defeat legitimate results of the war under the pretense of recognizing equality of rights, can have no other result than to render permanent peace impossible and to keep alive a conflict of races, the continuance of which must do harm to all concerned.

This question is not met by the suggestion that social equality cannot exist between the white and black races in this country. That argument, if it can be properly regarded as one, is scarcely worthy of consideration; for social equality no more exists between two races when traveling in a passenger coach or a public highway than when members of the same races sit by each other in a streetcar or in the jury box, or stand or sit with each other in a political assembly, or when they use in common the streets of a city or town, or when they are in the same room for the purpose of having their names placed on the registry of voters, or when they approach the ballot box in order to exercise the high privilege of voting.

There is a race so different from our own that we do not permit those belonging to it to become citizens of the United States. Persons belonging to it are, with few exceptions, absolutely excluded from our country. I allude to the Chinese race. But by the statute in question, a Chinaman can ride in the same passenger coach with white citizens of the United States, while citizens of the black race in Louisiana, many of whom, perhaps, risked their lives for the preservation of the Union, who are entitled, by law, to participate in the political control of the state and nation, who are not excluded, by law or by reason of their race, from public stations of any kind, and who have all the legal rights that belong to white citizens,

are yet declared to be criminals, liable to imprisonment, if they ride in a public coach occupied by citizens of the white race.

It is scarcely just to say that a colored citizen should not object to occupying a public coach assigned to his own race. He does not object, nor, perhaps, would he object to separate coaches for his race, if his rights under the law were recognized. But he objects, and ought never to cease objecting to the proposition that citizens of the white and black races can be adjudged criminals because they sit, or claim the right to sit, in the same public coach on a public highway.

The arbitrary separation of citizens, on the basis of race, while they are on a public highway, is a badge of servitude wholly inconsistent with the civil freedom and the equality before the law established by the Constitution. It cannot be justified upon any legal grounds.

If evils will result from the commingling of the two races upon public highways established for the benefit of all, they will be infinitely less than those that will surely come from state legislation regulating the enjoyment of civil rights upon the basis of race. We boast of the freedom enjoyed by our people above all other peoples. But it is difficult to reconcile that boast with a state of law which, practically, puts the brand of servitude and degradation upon a large class of our fellow citizens, our equals before the law. The thin disguise of "equal" accommodations for passengers in railroad coaches will not mislead anyone, nor atone for the wrong this day done.

The result of the whole matter is that while this Court has frequently adjudged, and at the present term has recognized the doctrine, that a state cannot, consistently with the Constitution of the United States, prevent white and black citizens, having the required qualifications for jury service, from sitting in the same jury box, it is now solemnly held that a state may prohibit white and black citizens from sitting in the same passenger coach on a public highway, or may require that they be separated by a "partition," when in the same passenger coach. . . .

I am of opinion that the statute of Louisiana is inconsistent with the personal liberty of citizens, white and black, in that state, and hostile to both the spirit and letter of the Constitution of the United States. If laws of like character should be enacted in the several states of the Union, the effect would be in the highest degree mischievous. Slavery, as an institution tolerated by law, would, it is true, have disappeared from our country, but there would remain a power in the states, by sinister legislation, to interfere with the full enjoyment of the blessings of freedom; to regulate civil rights, common to all citizens, upon the basis of race; and to place in a condition of legal inferiority a large body of American citizens now constituting a part of the political community called the People of the United States, for whom, and by whom through representatives, our government is administered. Such a system is inconsistent with the guarantee given by the Constitution to each state of a republican form of government and may be stricken down by Congressional action or by the courts in the discharge of their solemn duty to maintain the supreme law of the land, anything in the constitution or laws of any state to the contrary notwithstanding.

For the reasons stated, I am constrained to withhold my assent from the opinion and judgment of the majority.

22.

William Jennings Bryan: The Cross of Gold

"We are unalterably opposed," declared the Republican Party platform in 1896, "to every measure calculated to debase our currency." A few weeks later the Democratic Party platform demanded "the free and unlimited coinage of both silver and gold." Thus a major debate on the currency issue seemed likely when, as the final speaker in defense of the Democratic platform, young William Jennings Bryan not only made it inevitable but also electrified the convention with his eloquent plea for the coinage of silver. His concluding sentence, "You shall not crucify mankind upon a cross of gold," became the battle cry of the silver Democrats, and is one of the most famous American political statements. Bryan's speech, delivered on July 8, 1896, catapulted him into a position of leadership in his party and won him its presidential nomination that year.

Source: *Official Proceedings of the Democratic National Convention Held in Chicago, Ill., July 7, 8, 9, 10, and 11, 1896*, Logansport, Ind., 1896, pp. 226-234.

I WOULD BE PRESUMPTUOUS, indeed, to present myself against the distinguished gentlemen to whom you have listened if this were but a measuring of ability; but this is not a contest among persons. The humblest citizen in all the land when clad in armor of a righteous cause is stronger than all the whole hosts of error that they can bring. I come to speak to you in defense of a cause as holy as the cause of liberty — the cause of humanity. When this debate is concluded, a motion will be made to lay upon the table the resolution offered in commendation of the administration and also the resolution in condemnation of the administration. I shall object to bringing this question down to a level of persons. The individual is but an atom; he is born, he acts, he dies; but principles are eternal; and this has been a contest of principle.

Never before in the history of this country has there been witnessed such a contest as that through which we have passed. Never before in the history of American politics has a great issue been fought out as this issue has been by the voters themselves.

On the 4th of March, 1895, a few Democrats, most of them members of Congress, issued an address to the Democrats of the nation asserting that the money question was the paramount issue of the hour; asserting also the right of a majority of the Democratic Party to control the position of the party on this paramount issue; concluding with the request that all believers in free coinage of silver in the Democratic Party should organize and take charge of and control the policy of the Democratic Party. Three months later, at Memphis, an organization was perfected, and the silver Democrats went forth openly and boldly and courageously proclaiming their belief and declaring that if successful they would crystallize in a platform the declaration which they had made; and then began the conflict with a zeal approaching the zeal which inspired the crusaders who followed Peter the Hermit. Our silver Democrats went forth from victory unto victory, until they are assembled now, not to discuss, not to debate, but to enter up the judgment rendered by the plain people of this country.

But in this contest, brother has been arrayed against brother, and father against son. The warmest ties of love and acquaintance and association have been disregarded. Old leaders have been cast aside when they refused to give expression to the sentiments of those whom they would lead, and new leaders have sprung up to give direction to this cause of freedom. Thus has the contest been waged, and we have assembled here under as binding and solemn instructions as were ever fastened upon the representatives of a people.

We do not come as individuals. Why, as individuals we might have been glad to compliment the gentleman from New York [Senator Hill], but we knew that the people for whom we speak would never be willing to put him in a position where he could thwart the will of the Democratic Party. I say it was not a question of persons; it was a question of principle; and it is not with gladness, my friends, that we find ourselves brought into conflict with those who are now arrayed on the other side. The gentleman who just preceded me [Governor Russell] spoke of the old state of Massachusetts. Let me assure him that not one person in all this convention entertains the least hostility to the people of the state of Massachusetts.

But we stand here representing people who are the equals before the law of the largest cities in the state of Massachusetts. When you come before us and tell us that we shall disturb your business interests, we reply that you have disturbed our business interests by your action. We say to you that you have made too limited in its application the definition of a businessman. The man who is employed for wages is as much a businessman as his employer. The attorney in a country town is as much a businessman as the corporation counsel in a great metropolis. The merchant at the crossroads store is as much a businessman as the merchant of New York. The farmer who goes forth in the morning and toils all day, begins in the spring and toils all summer, and by the application of brain and muscle to the natural resources of this country creates wealth, is as much a businessman as the man who goes upon the Board of Trade and bets upon the price of grain. The miners who go 1,000 feet into the earth or climb 2,000 feet upon the cliffs and bring forth from their hiding places the precious metals to be poured in the channels of trade are as much businessmen as the few financial magnates who in a backroom corner the money of the world.

We come to speak for this broader class of businessmen. Ah, my friends, we say not one word against those who live upon the Atlantic Coast; but those hardy pioneers who braved all the dangers of the wilderness, who have made the desert to blossom as the rose — those pioneers away out there, rearing their children near to nature's heart, where they can mingle their voices with the voices of the birds — out there where they have erected schoolhouses for the education of their children and churches where they praise their Creator, and the cemeteries where sleep the ashes of their dead — are as deserving of the consideration of this party as any people in this country.

It is for these that we speak. We do not come as aggressors. Our war is not a war of conquest. We are fighting in the defense of our homes, our families, and posterity. We have petitioned, and our petitions have been scorned. We have entreated, and our entreaties have been disregarded. We have begged, and they have mocked when our calamity came.

We beg no longer; we entreat no more; we petition no more. We defy them!

The gentleman from Wisconsin has said he fears a Robespierre. My friend, in this land of the free you need fear no tyrant who will spring up from among the people. What we need is an Andrew Jackson to stand as Jackson stood, against the encroachments of aggregated wealth.

They tell us that this platform was made to catch votes. We reply to them that changing conditions make new issues; that the principles upon which rest Democracy are as everlasting as the hills; but that they must be applied to new conditions as they arise. Conditions have arisen and we are attempting to meet those conditions. They tell us that the income tax ought not to be brought in here; that is not a new idea. They criticize us for our criticism of the Supreme Court of the United States. My friends, we have made no criticism. We have simply called attention to what you know. If you want criticisms, read the dissenting opinions of the Court. That will give you criticisms.

They say we passed an unconstitutional law. I deny it. The income tax was not unconstitutional when it was passed. It was not unconstitutional when it went before the Supreme Court for the first time. It did not become unconstitutional until one judge changed his mind; and we cannot be expected to know when a judge will change his mind.

The income tax is a just law. It simply intends to put the burdens of government justly upon the backs of the people. I am in favor of an income tax. When I find a man who is not willing to pay his share of the burden of the government which protects him, I find a man who is unworthy to enjoy the blessings of a government like ours.

He says that we are opposing the national bank currency. It is true. If you will read what Thomas Benton said, you will find that he said that in searching history he could find but one parallel to Andrew Jackson. That was Cicero, who destroyed the conspiracies of Cataline and saved Rome. He did for Rome what Jackson did when he destroyed the bank conspiracy and saved America.

We say in our platform that we believe that the right to coin money and issue money is a function of government. We believe it. We believe it is a part of sovereignty and can no more with safety be delegated to private individuals than can the power to make penal statutes or levy laws for taxation.

Mr. Jefferson, who was once regarded as good Democratic authority, seems to have a different opinion from the gentleman who has addressed us on the part of the minority. Those who are opposed to this proposition tell us that the issue of paper money is a function of the bank and that the government ought to go out of the banking business. I stand with Jefferson rather than with them, and tell them, as he did, that the issue of money is a function of the government and that the banks should go out of the governing business.

They complain about the plank which declares against the life tenure in office. They have tried to strain it to mean that which it does not mean. What we oppose in that plank is the life tenure that is being built up in Washington which establishes an officeholding class and excludes from participation in the benefits the humbler members of our society. . . .

Let me call attention to two or three great things. The gentleman from New York says that he will propose an amendment providing that this change in our law shall not affect contracts which, according to the present laws, are made payable in gold. But if he means to say that we cannot change our monetary system without protecting those who have loaned money before the change was made, I want to ask him where, in law or in morals, he can find authority for not protecting the debtors when the act of 1873 was passed when he now insists that we must protect the creditor. He says he also wants to amend this platform so as to provide that if we fail to maintain the parity within a year that we will then suspend the coinage of silver. We reply that when we advocate a thing which we believe will be successful we are not compelled to raise a doubt as to our own sincerity by trying to show what we will do if we are wrong.

I ask him, if he will apply his logic to us, why he does not apply it to himself. He

Lightfoot Collection

William Jennings Bryan

says that he wants this country to try to secure an international agreement. Why doesn't he tell us what he is going to do if they fail to secure an international agreement. There is more reason for him to do that than for us to expect to fail to maintain the parity. They have tried for thirty years — thirty years — to secure an international agreement, and those are waiting for it most patiently who don't want it at all.

Now, my friends, let me come to the great paramount issue. If they ask us here why it is we say more on the money question than we say upon the tariff question, I reply that if protection has slain its thousands the gold standard has slain its tens of thousands. If they ask us why we did not embody all these things in our platform which we believe, we reply to them that when we have restored the money of the Constitution, all other necessary reforms will be possible, and that until that is done there is no reform that can be accomplished.

Why is it that within three months such

a change has come over the sentiments of the country? Three months ago, when it was confidently asserted that those who believed in the gold standard would frame our platforms and nominate our candidates, even the advocates of the gold standard did not think that we could elect a President; but they had good reasons for the suspicion, because there is scarcely a state here today asking for the gold standard that is not within the absolute control of the Republican Party.

But note the change. Mr. McKinley was nominated at St. Louis upon a platform that declared for the maintenance of the gold standard until it should be changed into bimetallism by an international agreement. Mr. McKinley was the most popular man among the Republicans and everybody three months ago in the Republican Party prophesied his election. How is it today? Why, that man who used to boast that he looked like Napoleon, that man shudders today when he thinks that he was nominated on the anniversary of the Battle of Waterloo. Not only that, but as he listens he can hear with ever increasing distinctness the sound of the waves as they beat upon the lonely shores of St. Helena.

Why this change? Ah, my friends, is not the change evident to anyone who will look at the matter? It is because no private character, however pure, no personal popularity, however great, can protect from the avenging wrath of an indignant people the man who will either declare that he is in favor of fastening the gold standard upon this people, or who is willing to surrender the right of self-government and place legislative control in the hands of foreign potentates and powers. . . .

We go forth confident that we shall win. Why? Because upon the paramount issue in this campaign there is not a spot of ground upon which the enemy will dare to challenge battle. Why, if they tell us that the gold standard is a good thing, we point to their platform and tell them that their platform pledges the party to get rid of a gold standard and substitute bimetallism. If the gold standard is a good thing, why try to get rid of it? If the gold standard, and I might call your attention to the fact that some of the very people who are in this convention today and who tell you that we ought to declare in favor of international bimetallism and thereby declare that the gold standard is wrong and that the principles of bimetallism are better — these very people four months ago were open and avowed advocates of the gold standard and telling us that we could not legislate two metals together even with all the world.

I want to suggest this truth, that if the gold standard is a good thing we ought to declare in favor of its retention and not in favor of abandoning it; and if the gold standard is a bad thing, why should we wait until some other nations are willing to help us to let it go?

Here is the line of battle. We care not upon which issue they force the fight. We are prepared to meet them on either issue or on both. If they tell us that the gold standard is the standard of civilization, we reply to them that this, the most enlightened of all nations of the earth, has never declared for a gold standard, and both the parties this year are declaring against it. If the gold standard is the standard of civilization, why, my friends, should we not have it? So if they come to meet us on that, we can present the history of our nation. More than that, we can tell them this, that they will search the pages of history in vain to find a single instance in which the common people of any land ever declared themselves in favor of a gold standard. They can find where the holders of fixed investments have.

Mr. Carlisle said in 1878 that this was a struggle between the idle holders of idle capital and the struggling masses who produce the wealth and pay the taxes of the country; and my friends, it is simply a ques-

Culver Pictures, Inc.

"The Sacrilegious Candidate"; anti-Bryan cartoon in "Judge," 1896

broad and fertile prairies. Burn down your cities and leave our farms, and your cities will spring up again as if by magic. But destroy our farms and the grass will grow in the streets of every city in this country.

My friends, we shall declare that this nation is able to legislate for its own people on every question without waiting for the aid or consent of any other nation on earth, and upon that issue we expect to carry every single state in this Union.

I shall not slander the fair state of Massachusetts nor the state of New York by saying that when its citizens are confronted with the proposition, "Is this nation able to attend to its own business?" — I will not slander either one by saying that the people of those states will declare our helpless impotency as a nation to attend to our own business. It is the issue of 1776 over again. Our ancestors, when but 3 million, had the courage to declare their political independence of every other nation upon earth. Shall we, their descendants, when we have grown to 70 million, declare that we are less independent than our forefathers? No, my friends, it will never be the judgment of this people. Therefore, we care not upon what lines the battle is fought. If they say bimetallism is good but we cannot have it till some nation helps us, we reply that, instead of having a gold standard because England has, we shall restore bimetallism, and then let England have bimetallism because the United States have.

If they dare to come out and in the open defend the gold standard as a good thing, we shall fight them to the uttermost, having behind us the producing masses of the nation and the world. Having behind us the commercial interests and the laboring interests and all the toiling masses, we shall answer their demands for a gold standard by saying to them, you shall not press down upon the brow of labor this crown of thorns. You shall not crucify mankind upon a cross of gold.

tion that we shall decide upon which side shall the Democratic Party fight. Upon the side of the idle holders of idle capital, or upon the side of the struggling masses? That is the question that the party must answer first; and then it must be answered by each individual hereafter. The sympathies of the Democratic Party, as described by the platform, are on the side of the struggling masses, who have ever been the foundation of the Democratic Party.

There are two ideas of government. There are those who believe that if you just legislate to make the well-to-do prosperous that their prosperity will leak through on those below. The Democratic idea has been that if you legislate to make the masses prosperous their prosperity will find its way up and through every class that rests upon it.

You come to us and tell us that the great cities are in favor of the gold standard. I tell you that the great cities rest upon these

23.

Daniel De Leon: The Aims of Socialism

Daniel De Leon was a sincere and devoted Marxist who seems to have been more concerned with promulgating Marxist doctrines than with practical reforms. Although an energetic agitator who tried for years to convert the American labor movement to his radical views, his actual accomplishments were small compared to those of such men as Eugene Debs, who could present issues in such a way as to interest the average worker. Head of the Socialist Labor Party during the 1890s and editor of the radical newspaper The People, *De Leon delivered the following address, one of his best-known speeches, in Boston on January 26, 1896. It is reprinted here in part.*

Source: *Reform or Revolution*, n.p., n.d.

ORGANIZATION

IT HAS BECOME an axiom that, to accomplish results, organization is requisite. Nevertheless, there is "organization" and "organization." That this is so appears clearly from the fact that the pure-and-simplers have been going about saying to the workers: "Organize! Organize!" And after they have been saying that and have been "organizing" and "organizing" for the past thirty or forty years, we find that they are virtually where they started, if not worse off; that their "organization" partakes of the nature of the lizard whose tail destroys what his foreparts build up.

I think the best thing I can do to aid you in organizing is to give you the principles upon which the Socialist sections of New York City and Brooklyn are organized. To do that I shall go back to basic principles, and in explaining to you the difference there is between Reform and Revolution, I shall be able, step by step, to point out to you how it is we do it and how you ought to do.

I shall assume — it is a wise course for a speaker to adopt — that none in this audience knows what is "Reform" and what is "Revolution." Those who are posted will understand me all the better; those who are not will follow me all the easier.

We hear people talk about the "Reform Forces," about "Evolution," and about "Revolution" in ways that are highly mixed. Let us clear up our terms. Reform means a change of externals; Revolution — peaceful or bloody, the peacefulness or the bloodiness of it cuts no figure whatever in the essence of the question — means a change from within.

REFORM

TAKE, FOR INSTANCE, a poodle. You can reform him in a lot of ways. You can shave his whole body and leave a tassel at the tip of his tail; you may bore a hole through each ear, and tie a blue bow on the one and a red bow on the other; you may put a brass collar around his neck with your initials on and a trim little blanket on his back; yet, throughout, a poodle he was and a poodle he remains. Each of those changes probably wrought a corresponding change in the poodle's life. When shorn of all his hair except a tassel at the tail's tip, he was owned by a wag who probably cared only for the fun he could get out of his pet; when he appears gaily decked in bows, probably his young mistress' attachment is of tenderer sort; when later we see him in the fancier's outfit, the treatment he receives and the uses he is put to may be yet again, and probably are, different. Each of these transformations or stages may mark a veritable epoch in the poodle's existence. And yet, essentially a poodle he was, a poodle he is, and a poodle he will remain. That is *Reform.*

REVOLUTION

BUT WHEN WE LOOK BACK myriads of years, or project ourselves into far-future physical cataclysms, and trace the development of animal life from the invertebrate to the vertebrate, from the lizard to the bird, from the quadruped and mammal till we come to the prototype of the poodle, and finally reach the poodle himself, and so forward, then do we find radical changes at each step, changes from within that alter the very essence of his being and that put, or will put, upon him each time a stamp that alters the very system of his existence. That is *Revolution.*

So with society. Whenever a change leaves the internal mechanism untouched, we have *Reform;* whenever the internal mechanism is changed we have *Revolution.*

Of course, no internal change is possible without external manifestations. The internal changes denoted by the revolution or evolution of the lizard into the eagle go accompanied with external marks. So with society. And therein lies one of the pitfalls into which dilettantism or "Reforms" invariably tumble. They have noticed that ex-

ternals change with internals; and they rest satisfied with mere external changes without looking behind the curtain. But of this more presently.

We Socialists are not Reformers; we are Revolutionists. We Socialists do not propose to change forms. We care nothing for forms. We want a change of the inside of the mechanism of society, let the form take care of itself. We see in England a crowned monarch; we see in Germany a sceptered emperor; we see in this country an uncrowned President, and we fail to see the essential difference between Germany, England, or America. That being the case, we are skeptics as to forms. We are like grown children in the sense we like to look at the inside of things and find out what is there.

One more preliminary explanation. Socialism is lauded by some as an angelic movement; by others it is decried as a devilish scheme. Hence you find the Gomperses blowing hot and cold on the subject; and Harry Lloyd, with whose capers, to your sorrow, you are more familiar than I, pronouncing himself a Socialist in one place and in another running Socialism down. Socialism is neither an aspiration of angels nor a plot of devils. Socialism moves with its feet firmly planted on the ground and its head not lost in the clouds; it takes Science by the hand, asks her to lead, and goes whithersoever she points. It does not take Science by the hand, saying: "I shall follow you if the end of the road please me." No! it takes her by the hand and says: "Whithersoever thou leadest, thither am I *bound* to go." The Socialists, consequently, move as intelligent men; they do not mutiny because, instead of having wings, we have arms and cannot fly as we would wish.

What, then, with an eye single upon the difference between *Reform* and *Revolution,* does Socialism mean? To point out that, I shall take up two or three of what I may style the principal nerve centers of the movement.

GOVERNMENT — THE STATE

ONE OF THESE PRINCIPAL NERVE CENTERS is
the question of "government" or the question of "state." How many of you have not
seen upon the shelves of our libraries books
that treat upon the "History of the State";
upon the "Limitations of the State"; upon
"What the State Should Do and What it
Should Not Do"; upon the "Legitimate
Functions of the State," and so on into
eternity? Nevertheless, there is not one
among all of these, the products, as they all
are, of the vulgar and superficial character
of capitalist thought, that fathoms the question, or actually defines the "state." Not
until we reach the great works of the
American Morgan, of Marx and Engels, and
of other Socialist philosophers, is the matter
handled with that scientific lucidity that
proceeds from facts, leads to sound conclusions, and breaks the way to practical work.
Not until you know and understand the
history of the "state" and "government"
will you understand one of the cardinal
principles upon which Socialist organization
rests and will you be in a condition to organize successfully.

We are told that "government" has always been as it is today, and always will
be. This is the first fundamental error of
what Karl Marx justly calls capitalist vulgarity of thought.

When man started on his career, after
having got beyond the state of the savage,
he realized that cooperation was a necessity
to him. He understood that together with
others he could face his enemies in a better
way than alone; he could hunt, fish, fight
more successfully. Following the instructions of the great writer Morgan — the
only great and original American writer
upon this question — we look to the Indian communities, the Indian settlements as a
type of the social system that our ancestors,
all of them, without exception, went
through at some time.

The Indian lived in the community condition. The Indian lived under a system of
common property. As Franklin described it
in a sketch of the history and alleged sacredness of private property, there was no
such thing as private property among the
Indians. They cooperated, worked together,
and they had a Central Directing Authority
among them. In the Indian communities we
find that Central Directing Authority consisting of the "Sachems." It makes no difference how that Central Directing Authority was elected; there it was. But note this:
its function was to direct the cooperative or
collective efforts of the communities, and, in
so doing, it shared actively in the productive work of the communities. Without it,
its work, the work of the communities,
would not have been done.

When, in the further development of society, the tools of production grew and developed — grew and developed beyond the
point reached by the Indian; when the art
of smelting iron ore was discovered; when
thereby that leading social cataclysm,
wrapped in the mists of ages, yet discern-
ible, took place that rent former communal
society in twain along the line of sex, the
males being able, the females unable to
wield the tool of production — then society
was cast into a new mold; the former community with its democratic equality of
rights and duties vanishes, and a new social
system turns up, divided into two sections
— the one able, the other unable to work
at production. The line that separated these
two sections, being at first the line of sex,
could, in the very nature of things, not yet
be sharp or deep. Yet, notwithstanding, in
the very shaping of these two sections —
one able, the other unable to feed itself —
we have the first premonition of the *classes*,
of class distinctions, of the division of society into the *independent* and the *dependent*,
into *master* and *slaves*, *ruler* and *ruled*.

Simultaneously with this revolution, we
find the first changes in the nature of the

Central Directing Authority, of that body whose original function was to share in, by directing, production. Just as soon as economic equality is destroyed and the economic classes crop up in society, the functions of the Central Directing Authority gradually begin to change, until, finally, when, after a long range of years, moving slowly at first and then with the present hurricane velocity under capitalism proper, the tool has developed further and further and still further, and has reached its present fabulous perfection and magnitude; when, through its private ownership the tool has wrought a revolution within a revolution by dividing society no longer along the line of sex but strictly along the line of ownership or nonownership of the land on and the tool with which to work; when the privately owned, mammoth tool of today has reduced more than 52 percent of our population to the state of being utterly unable to feed without first selling themselves into wage slavery, while it, at the same time, saps the ground from under about 39 percent of our people, the middle class, whose puny tools, small capital, render them certain victims of competition with the large capitalists and makes them desperate; when the economic law that asserts itself upon the system of private ownership of the tool has concentrated these private owners into about 8 percent of the nation's inhabitants, has thereby enabled this small capitalist class to live without toil, and to compel the majority, the class of the proletariat, to toil without living; when, finally, it has come to the pass in which our country now finds itself, that, as was stated in Congress, 94 percent of the taxes are spent in "protecting property" — the property of the trivially small capitalist class — and not in protecting life; when, in short, the privately owned tool has wrought this work, and the classes — the idle rich and the working poor — are in full bloom — then the Central Directing Authority of old stands trans-

formed; its pristine functions of aiding in by directing, production have been supplanted by the functions of holding down the dependent, the slave, the ruled, *i.e.,* the *working class.* Then, and not before, lo, the state, the modern state, the *capitalist state!* Then, lo, the government, the modern government, the *capitalist government* — equipped mainly, if not solely, with the means of suppression, of oppression, of tyranny!

In sight of these manifestations of the modern state, the anarchist — the rosewater and the dirty-water variety alike — shouts: "Away with all Central Directing Authority; see what it does; it can only do mischief; it always did mischief!" But Socialism is not anarchy. Socialism does not, like the chicken in the fable just out of the shell, start with the knowledge of that day. Socialism rejects the premises and the conclusions of anarchy upon the state and upon government. What Socialism says is: "Away with the economic system that alters the beneficent functions of the Central Directing Authority from an aid to production into a means of oppression." And it proceeds to show that, when the instruments of production shall be owned no longer by the minority, but shall be restored to the commonwealth; that when, as the result of this, no longer the minority or any portion of the people shall be in poverty, and classes, class distinctions, and class rule shall, as they necessarily must, have vanished, that then the Central Directing Authority will lose all its repressive functions and is bound to reassume the functions it had in the old communities of our ancestors; become again a necessary aid and assist in production.

The Socialist, in the brilliant simile of Karl Marx, sees that a lone fiddler in his room needs no director; he can rap himself to order, with his fiddle to his shoulder, and start his dancing tune and stop whenever he likes. But just as soon as you have an orchestra, you must also have an orchestra director — a Central Directing Authority. If you don't, you may have a Salvation Army powwow; you may have a Louisiana Negro breakdown; you may have an Orthodox Jewish synagogue where every man sings in whatever key he likes; but you won't have harmony — impossible.

It needs this Central Directing Authority of the orchestra master to rap all the players to order at a given moment; to point out when they shall begin; when to have these play louder, when to have those play softer; when to put in this instrument, when to silence that; to regulate the time of all and preserve the accord. The orchestra director is not an oppressor, nor is his baton an insignia of tyranny; he is not there to bully anybody; he is as necessary or important as any or all of the members of the orchestra.

Our system of production is in the nature of an orchestra. No one man, no one town, no one state can be said any longer to be independent of the other; the whole people of the United States, every individual therein, is dependent and interdependent upon all the others. The nature of the machinery of production; the subdivision of labor which aids cooperation and which cooperation fosters, and which is necessary to the plentifulness of production that civilization requires, compel a harmonious working together of all departments of labor, and thence compel the establishment of a Central Directing Authority, of an orchestra director, so to speak, of the orchestra of the Cooperative Commonwealth.

Such is the state or government that the Socialist revolution carries in its womb. Today, production is left to anarchy, and only tyranny, the twin sister of anarchy, is organized.

Socialism, accordingly, implies organization; organization implies directing authority; and the one and the other are strict reflections of the revolutions undergone by the tool of production. Reform, on the other hand, skims the surface, and with "Referendums" and similar devices limits itself to external tinkerings.

MATERIALISM — MORALITY

THE SECOND NERVE CENTER OF SOCIALISM that will serve to illustrate the difference between Reform and Revolution is its materialistic groundwork.

Take, for instance, the history of slavery. All of our ancestors — this may shock some of you, but it is a fact all the same — all of our ancestors were cannibals at one time. The human race, in its necessity to seek for food, often found it easier to make a raid and take from others the food they had gathered. In those olden, olden days of the barbarism of our ancestors when they conquered a people and took away its property, they had no further use for the conquered; they killed them, spitted them over a good fire, roasted and ate them up. It was a simple and the only profitable way known of disposing of prisoners of war. They did with their captives very much what bees do yet; when they have raided and conquered a hive, they ruthlessly kill every single denizen of the captured hive.

Our ancestors continued cannibals until their social system had developed sufficiently to enable them to keep their prisoners under control. From that moment they found it was more profitable to keep their prisoners of war alive and turn them into slaves to work for them than it was to kill them off and eat them up. With that stage of material development, cannibalism was dropped. From the higher material plane on which our ancestors then stood, their moral vision enlarged and they presently realized that it was immoral to eat up a human being.

Cannibalism disappears to make room for chattel slavery. And what do we see? Watch the process of "moral development" in this country — the classic ground in many ways to study history in, for the reason that the whole development of mankind can be seen here, portrayed in a few years, so to speak. You know how, today, the Northern people put on airs of morality on the score of having "abolished chattel slavery," the "traffic in human flesh," "gone down South and fought, and bled, to free the Negro," etc., etc. Yet we know that just as soon as manufacturing was introduced in the North, the North found that it was too expensive to own the Negro and take care of him; that it was much cheaper not to own the worker; and, consequently, that they "religiously," "humanely" and "morally" sold their slaves to the South, while they transformed the white people of the North, who had no means of production in their hands, into wage slaves, and mercilessly ground them down. In the North, chattel slavery disappeared just as soon as the development of machinery rendered the institution unprofitable. The immorality of chattel slavery became clear to the North just as soon as, standing upon that higher plane that its higher material development raised it to, it acquired a better vision. The benighted South, on the contrary, that had no machinery, remained with eyes shut, and she stuck to slavery till the slave was knocked out of her fists.

Guided by the light of this and many similar lessons of history, Socialism builds upon the principle that the "moral sentiment," as illustrated by the fate of the slave, is not the cause but a powerful aid to revolutions. The moral sentiment is to a movement as important as the sails are to a ship. Nevertheless, important though sails are, unless a ship is well laden, unless she is soundly, properly, and scientifically constructed, the more sails you pile up and spread out, the surer she is to capsize. So with the organizations that are to carry out a revolution. Unless your Socialist organizations are as sound as a bell; unless they are as intolerant as science; unless they will plant themselves squarely on the principle

that two and two make four, and under no circumstances allow that they make five, the more feeling you put into them, the surer they are to capsize and go down. On the contrary, load your revolutionary ship with the proper lading of science; hold her strictly to the lodestar; try no monkeyshines and no dillyings and dallyings with anything that is not strictly scientific, or with any man who does not stand on our uncompromisingly scientific platform; do that, and then unfurl freely the sails of morality; then the more your sails, the better off your ship; but not unless you do that, will you be safe, or can you prevail.

Socialism knows that revolutionary upheavals and transformations proceed from the rockbed of material needs. With a full appreciation of and veneration for moral impulses that are balanced with scientific knowledge, it eschews, looks with just suspicion upon, and gives a wide berth to balloon morality, or be it those malarial fevers that reformers love to dignify with the name of "moral feelings."

THE CLASS STRUGGLE

A THIRD NERVE CENTER OF SOCIALISM by which to distinguish Reform from Revolution is its manly, aggressive posture.

The laws that rule sociology run upon lines parallel with and are the exact counterparts of those that natural science has established prevail in sociology.

In the first place, the central figure in biology is the species, not the individual specimen. Consequently, that is the central figure on the field of sociology that corresponds to and represents the species on the field of biology. In sociology, the economic classes take the place of the species in biology.

In the second place, struggle, and not piping peace; assimilation by the ruthless process of the expulsion of all elements that are not fit for assimilation, and not external coalition — such are the laws of growth in biology, and such they are and needs must be in sociology.

Hence, Socialism recognizes in modern society the existence of a struggle of classes, and the line that divides the combatants to be the economic line that separates the interests of the property-holding capitalist class from the interests of the propertyless class of the proletariat. As a final result of this, Socialism, with the Nazarene, spurns as futile, if not wicked, the method of cajolery and seduction, or the crying of "Peace, peace where there is no peace," and cuts a clean swath, while Reform is eternally entangled in its course of charming, luring, decoying.

24.

William Allen White: What's the Matter with Kansas?

This celebrated editorial, which appeared in William Allen White's Emporia (Kansas) Gazette *on Monday, August 16, 1896, reflected an unhappy experience White had had the previous day as well as his accumulated frustration with the nature of politics in his state of Kansas. During a stroll on Sunday, he had been hooted and jeered by some Populists, a political party that White opposed; and this experience caused him to vent all of his anger against the Populist program, which he considered to be "socialistic." The editorial, which White later described as "pure vitriol," was reprinted in Republican newspapers all over the country and gave him a national reputation. Mark Hanna, the Republican national chairman, claimed that it helped substantially to elect McKinley. The Populists, however, won the state in 1896.*

Source: *Emporia Weekly Gazette,* October 1, 1896.

TODAY the Kansas Department of Agriculture sent out a statement which indicates that Kansas has gained less than 2,000 people in the past year. There are about 125,000 families in the state, and there were about 10,000 babies born in Kansas, and yet so many people have left the state that the natural increase is cut down to less than 2,000 net.

This has been going on for eight years.

If there had been a high brick wall around the state eight years ago and not a soul had been admitted or permitted to leave, Kansas would be a half million souls better off than she is today. And yet the nation has increased in population. In five years, 10 million people have been added to the national population, yet instead of gaining a share of this — say, half a million — Kansas has apparently been a plague spot and, in the very garden of the world, has lost population by 10,000 every year.

Not only has she lost population but she has lost money. Every moneyed man in the state who could get out without great loss is gone. Every month in every community sees someone who has a little money pick up and leave the state. This has been going on for eight years. Money is being drained out all the time. In towns where ten years ago there were three or four or half a dozen money-lending concerns, stimulating industry by furnishing capital, there is now none, or one or two that are looking after the interest and principal already outstanding.

No one brings any money into Kansas anymore. What community knows over one or two men who have moved in with more than $5,000 in the past three years? And what community cannot count half a score of men in that time who have left, taking all the money they could scrape together?

Yet the nation has grown rich; other states have increased in population and wealth — other neighboring states. Missouri has gained nearly 2 million, while Kansas has been losing half a million. Nebraska has gained in wealth and in population, while Kansas has gone downhill. Colorado has gained in every way, while Kansas has lost in every way since 1888.

What is the matter with Kansas?

There is no substantial city in the state. Every big town save one has lost in population. Yet Kansas City, Omaha, Lincoln, St. Louis, Denver, Colorado Springs, Sedalia, the cities of the Dakotas, St. Paul and Minneapolis — all cities and towns in the West — have steadily grown.

Take up the Government Blue Book and you will see that Kansas is virtually off the map. Two or three little scrubby consular places in yellow-fever-stricken communities that do not aggregate $10,000 a year is all the recognition Kansas has. Nebraska draws about $100,000; little old North Dakota draws $50,000; Oklahoma doubles Kansas; Missouri leaves her 1,000 miles behind; Colorado is almost seven times greater than Kansas — the whole West is ahead of Kansas.

Take it by any standard you please, Kansas is not in it.

Go East and you hear them laugh at Kansas; go West and they sneer at her; go South and they "cuss" her; go North and they have forgotten her. Go into any crowd of intelligent people gathered anywhere on the globe and you will find the Kansas man on the defensive. The newspaper columns and magazine pages once devoted to praise of the state, to boastful facts and startling figures concerning her resources, now are filled with cartoons, jibes, and Pefferian speeches. Kansas just naturally isn't in the civilized world. She has traded places with Arkansas and Timbuctoo.

What is the matter with Kansas?

We all know; yet here we are at it again. We have an old mossback Jacksonian who snorts and howls because there is a bathtub in the state house; we are running that old jay for governor. We have another shabby, wild-eyed, rattle-brained fanatic who has said openly in a dozen speeches that "the rights of the user are paramount to the rights of the owner"; we are running him for chief justice so that capital will come tumbling over itself to get into the state. We have raked the ash heap of failure in the state and have found an old human hoopskirt who has failed as a businessman, who has failed as an editor, who has failed as a preacher, and we are going to run him for congressman-at-large. He will help the looks of the Kansas delegation in Washington. Then we have discovered a kid without a law practice and have decided to vote for him as attorney general. Then, for fear some hint that the state had become respectable might percolate through the civilized portions of the nation, we have decided to send three or four harpies out lecturing, telling the people that Kansas is raising hell and letting the corn go to weeds.

Oh, this is a state to be proud of! We are a people who can hold up our heads! What we need here is less money, less capital, fewer white shirts and brains, fewer men with business judgment, and more of these fellows who boast that they are "just ordinary old clodhoppers, but that they know more in a minute about finance than John Sherman"; we need more men who are "posted," who can bellow about the crime of '73, who hate prosperity, and who think that because a man believes in national honor, he is a tool of Wall Street. We have had a few of them — some 150,000 — but we want more.

We need several thousand gibbering idiots to scream about the "Great Red Dragon" of Lombard Street. We don't need population, we don't need wealth, we don't need well-dressed men on the streets, we don't need standing in the nation, we don't need cities on these fertile prairies; you bet we don't! What we are after is the money power. Because we have become poorer and ornerier and meaner than a spavined, distempered mule, we, the people of Kansas, propose to kick; we don't care to build up, we wish to tear down.

"There are two ideas of government," said our noble Bryan at Chicago. "There are those who believe that if you just legislate to make the well-to-do prosperous, their prosperity will leak through on those below. The Democratic idea has been that if you legislate to make the masses prosperous their prosperity will find its way up and through every class and rest upon us."

That's the stuff! Give the prosperous man the dickens! Legislate the thriftless into ease, whack the stuffing out of the creditors, and tell the debtor who borrowed money five years ago, when the money *per capita* was no greater than it is now, that the contraction of the currency gives him a right to repudiate.

Whoop it up for the ragged trousers; put the lazy, greasy fizzle who can't pay his debts on an altar, and bow down and worship him. Let the state ideal be high. What we need is not the respect of our fellowmen but a chance to get something for nothing.

Oh, yes, Kansas is a great state. Here are people fleeing from it by the score every day, capital going out of the state by the hundreds of dollars; and every industry except farming paralyzed, and that crippled because its products have to go across the ocean before they can find a laboring man at work who can afford to buy them. Let's don't stop this year. Let's drive all the decent, self-respecting men out of the state. Let's keep the old clodhoppers who know it all. Let's encourage the man who is "posted." He can talk, and what we need is not mill hands to eat our meat, nor factory hands to eat our wheat, nor cities to oppress the farmer by consuming his butter and eggs and chickens and produce. What Kansas needs is men who can talk, who have large leisure to argue the currency question while their wives wait at home for that nickel's worth of bluing.

What's the matter with Kansas?

Nothing under the shining sun. She is losing wealth, population, and standing. She has got her statesmen, and the money power is afraid of her. Kansas is all right. She has started in to raise hell, as Mrs. Lease advised, and she seems to have an overproduction. But that doesn't matter. Kansas never did believe in diversified crops. Kansas is all right. There is absolutely nothing wrong with Kansas. "Every prospect pleases and only man is vile."

I come from a state that raises corn and cotton and cockleburs and Democrats, and frothy eloquence neither convinces nor satisfies me. I am from Missouri. You have got to show me.

WILLARD D. VANDIVER, speech, 1899

25.

George W. Steevens: The Materialistic Americans

As a journalist sent to this country to report the presidential election of 1896 for the
London Daily Mail, *George W. Steevens had an opportunity to observe American*
habits and characteristics. His views and opinions were incorporated in a book,
The Land of the Dollar *(1897), from which the following selection is taken. Steevens*
was typical of many foreign commentators in interpreting the American love of
concrete accomplishment as a kind of materialism. Although the term "materialistic"
has come to be one of opprobrium, it could be used in 1896 as a fairly benign and
uncritical description of American attitudes and behavior.

Source: *The Land of the Dollar*, New York, 1897, pp. 264-273.

BUSINESS IS BUSINESS all the world over; so, at least, I have been assured by those who ought to know. But it is more emphatically business in the United States than anywhere else. In England, business is business, and there's an end of it; here, business is everything, and there is no end or boundary to it. It affords the one career in the country. Politics is a matter that a citizen must interest himself in one year out of four; but the class which pursues politics day by day and week by week is a small one, and neither very respectable nor very respected. The church, literature, art, the services — they may be all very excellent things in their way if anybody has the curious fancy to make a life of them. But they are hardly regarded as serious careers. The leading men, go where you will — the show citizens that your hospitable entertainer gives you introductions to — are not any of these; they are the first men of business. The first men of business are the first men outright.

It would be idle for me, who do not know the difference between a bill of exchange and a debenture, to attempt to give any idea of the methods on which American business is conducted. I presume that the law of supply and demand, pending its repeal by President Bryan, is much the same here as at home. Yet I seem to notice a keenness, a cutthroat ferocity of competition, in America which is at least less conspicuous in England. With us, the largest and most largely advertised concerns are not necessarily the best, nor even reputed to be the best. If you want to get a bonnet, as I understand, of the one unmistakable and inimitable distinction, you do not go to Peter Robinson's or Marshall & Snellgrove's, but to some little half-lighted shop in Bond Street. So with other commodities. The various supply stores and universal providers are a vast convenience, but I have been told that there are wares a shade better to be got elsewhere. But here everybody goes to the big store of the place, for the little ones cannot live with the prices. In England — of course with limitations — quality rules the market; in America, price.

For instance, in Philadelphia, everybody

goes to Wanamaker's. Mr. Wanamaker was once postmaster general of the republic, and I should think he was a rattling good one. His store was already the largest retail drapery and hosiery and haberdashery, and all that sort of business, in the world, when, by the recent purchase of a giant establishment in New York, he made it larger still. Now, the working of Wanamaker's, as I am informed, is this. It is no use going there to get what you want. You must go to get what Mr. Wanamaker wants to sell. He tells you each morning in the newspapers what he has got today, and if you want it you had better go and get it: the chances are it will be gone tomorrow. The head of each department is entrusted with a certain amount of capital and buys his goods at his own discretion. But woe unto him if he does not turn over his capital quickly. There is a rule that no stock may be in the house more than, I think, three months; after that, off it must go at any sacrifice.

"You can always tell when Mr. Wanamaker's in town," said a shopwalker, "because there's always some change being made." And then he added, in a half voice of awe-stricken worship, "I believe Mr. Wanamaker loves change for its own sake." For the sake of custom, I should say; for this formula of change for change's sake is one of the master keys of American character. Mr. Wanamaker keeps a picture gallery, with some really fine modern French paintings, to beguile his patrons. Today he will have an orchestra playing; tomorrow, a costume exhibition of spinning girls from all the lands of the earth — everyday something new. One day, by moving a table six feet, so that people had to walk round it instead of past it, he increased the sales of an article from three shillings to hundreds of pounds. If that is not genius, tell me what is.

But the really Napoleonic — I was going to say demonic — feature of the Wanamaker system is the unerring skill with which it reaps its profits out of the necessities of others. Fixing his price according to the economic doctrine of final utility — taking no account, that is, of the cost of production, but only of the price at which most people will find it worth their while to buy — Mr. Wanamaker realizes 10 percent for himself and an enormous saving for the consumers. A cargo of rose trees had been consigned from Holland to a firm of florists, which failed while the plants were in mid-ocean. They went a-begging till Mr. Wanamaker bought them up and put them on the market at about half the rate current in Philadelphia. In ten days not one of the 20,000 was left.

A firm which manufactured $100 bicycles found itself without cash to meet its liabilities. Mr. Wanamaker bought up the stock and altered the maker's label as well as one peculiarity of the gear. Then he broke the price to $66, and subsequently to $33. They all went off in a week or so. He bought the plates of a huge edition of the $100 *Century Dictionary*, altered the title page, bound them for himself, and put the article on the market at $51.50. In six weeks he had sold 2,000. A firm in California, which manufactures a particularly excellent kind of blanket, was in difficulties. Mr. Wanamaker bought up the stock and sold it at a third of the normal price in three days.

All this is magnificent for the customer, and apparently not unprofitable to Mr. Wanamaker. But plainly somebody has to pay, and who? The small trader. After the rosetree deal, nobody wanted to buy roses of the florists of Philadelphia. The city is stocked with bicycles and *Century Dictionaries*, and nobody within a radius of miles will want to buy a pair of blankets for a generation. Mr. Wanamaker sends out 365,000 parcels to his customers in the slackest month of the year, and turns over $13 million annually. The small people, it is presumed, are ground to powder against the wall.

Rather similar is the story of Armour's glue factory in Chicago. Mr. Armour's original line in life, as all the world knows, is packing pork. If your tastes lie in the direction of blood, you can spend a happy morning at his place watching dying hogs kick out puncheons of it. Personally, I didn't like it. Not that I object either to blood or to pork; but I resented the way in which the screaming hog, sliding down a rail by one of his hind legs, is unsympathetically put in position for the knife by a hireling: he might at least be allowed to go to the sticker in his own attitude. But the pork-packing business is not what it was, so Mr. Armour had to look to his by-products. Nobody would pay him a profitable price, so he went into the by-product business himself.

He melts the fat in huge vats and runs it down into molds, where it congeals as soap; the soap is run through wires, which cut it, and through machines, which stamp it, and there you are. The fat that is over from the soap runs into the next room and runs out of it as glycerine. The oddments of hide and hoof from the deceased tinned meat are boiled up and cooled and run through wires and come out glue. The hair and bristles are blown about hydraulically, and heated and cooled and curled, and come out ready for sofa pillows. The shinbones reappear as toothbrushes, or go to Japan for imitation ivoryware; the odd bones are ground up into manure. The very drippings of the fat are caught in a trap, on the brink of falling into the river, and brought back captive to the soap kettles. And what results from all this? Mr. Armour, having a worldwide repute and a worldwide business organization, is underselling the firms which cut the price of his fat and bristles. They squeezed him; now he squeezes them. It is the fortune of war.

It is not wonderful that producers try to escape from the mutual butchery of business competition by the construction of trusts and combines. It is even less wonderful that the consumer fiercely resents these. You have only to represent Mr. McKinley as the nominee of the trusts to raise a howl of ex-

ecration. But to what extent America is really cursed with these organizations it is hard to determine. Newspaper agitators see a trust in everything, from bread down to meat skewers. I am hardly competent to criticize the statement, but I doubt it. It must be borne in mind that any such combination to regulate the price of a necessity of life is illegal in this country, and it is hardly credible that if they existed widely evidence would not be found to convict their members, at least occasionally.

For instance, it is fairly certain that there is a trust in anthracite coal. That was as good as proved by the fact that a number of tenders being recently made for coal in Chicago, half a dozen firms quoted widely different figures for bituminous coal, but all the same high price for anthracite. Legal proceedings were pending, or said to be, when I left Chicago. On the other hand, it is urged that the Standard Oil Company, an errant and unblushing trust, has been the means of supplying very excellent oil to everybody at a very low price. It seeks its profits by the extended use of oil rather than by a high price — by making it cheap instead of dear. Of course, this is no justification for leaving trusts unregulated by law; that would be madness in any state. For the more the Standard Oil Trust allures the consumer to make oil a necessity of life, the more helpless he will be delivered into its hands when some day it sees fit to pocket untold millions by raising the price. But I believe — I may be wrong — that the present necessity for such regulation is limited to a very few cases.

But I am straying away from the question. What is the effect of this universality of business in America? It has its murderous side, as we have seen. The weak men who go down are not pitied, and especially not respected. They are dead failures. In Europe there remain some kindly superstitions under which the unsuccessful may take refuge from public contempt. A man may be incompetent, but after all he is of good family; he is well-educated; he is a fine musician; he is a witty fellow. But in America the man who fails in business has failed in the one thing there is to do. The one test of worth in business is to make money, for that is the object of business. Failing in that, his failure is absolute.

But there is another side. In the first place, the preeminence of business is a great clip that holds this unwieldy country together. An active man of business will have interests in every quarter of the States. These interests compel him to know every part of the country, its economic conditions, the habits, pursuits, and character of its inhabitants. But for this bond I verily believe the Union would go to pieces in a twelvemonth. But contact with all parts of the country brings understanding, rubs the edge off prejudice, promotes a candid consideration of the position of others. Prejudiced or uninformed the American may sometimes be; wantonly unjust — I say it deliberately — never.

Another good result, as I take it, of the deification of business is that it keeps democracy fresh and wholesome. Commerce is the most democratic of all pursuits. In the august presence of the dollar, all men are equal. It is not this man who graduated at Harvard against that man who herded swine; it is this man's credit and capital as set down in *Bradstreet* — an amiable little work which gives the money value of every businessman in the States and computes the degree of trust that may be reposed in his signed paper — as against that other man's.

But all this is hideously materialistic. No doubt; only what do you mean by materialistic? In a sense . . . the Americans appear to me the most materialistic people in the world. But as for the love of money, I don't think they are down with it any worse than any other people. I still think, as I said at the very beginning, that it is not

the dollars they worship but the faculties that got them. The man who has made money in this country has attained what is the one aim of ninety-nine out of every hundred of his countrymen. He has had the ability to do what everybody is trying to do. Is it wonderful that he is respected? It would be wonderful indeed if he were not.

Cut off from the hard-won civilization of the Old World, and left to struggle by themselves with the forest and the prairie, it was inevitable that the Americans should prize most highly those less highly organized qualities of the mind which insured success in the struggle. The others may come with time. In the meanwhile, there is this consolation for those who go down. Failure may be complete, but it is never irredeemable. In Europe a boy goes into a bank; he may hate it, but in the bank he usually remains. In America he will next appear in a newspaper office, then behind a draper's counter, then in Congress, then in bankruptcy, and then in a gold mine. You never meet the man who has got a good place and don't mean to lose it.

No place is good enough for the American's estimate of his own deserts — nor is the estimate inexcusable, for no possibility is beyond his legitimate aspiration. Nobody is ever done with. And this applies to the millionaire as well as to the starveling. A man of huge fortune is always breaking out, like Mr. Armour, into some new and unfamiliar trade. I have met a gentleman who made a large fortune as an ironmaster. One day it occurred to him to buy a newspaper. He did not know small pica from nonpareil, and by the time he was mastering the difference, his fortune had melted away, and he had a mortgage on the house his wife and children lived in. He went about his business with an unmoved face. Why not? This was his life. He was playing the great game for the pleasure of playing it; and he played it and won it like a man.

26.

GROVER CLEVELAND: American Interests in the Cuban Revolution

Although the strife in Cuba was not a major issue in the presidential campaign of 1896, its importance for America was already recognized by political leaders. In his final presidential message to Congress on December 7, 1896, Grover Cleveland reviewed the unpleasant history of Spanish-Cuban relations and outlined what he felt were the alternatives open to the United States. Cleveland reflected popular opinion in his earnest attempt to explore every peaceful means for a solution to the Cuban crisis. The President realized that Cuba's proximity to this country bound her fate to ours, but his message, a portion of which appears below, expressed his hope that U.S. intervention would not be necessary.

Source: PRFA, 1896, pp. xxvii-lxii.

THE INSURRECTION IN CUBA still continues with all its perplexities. It is difficult to perceive that any progress has thus far been made toward the pacification of the island or that the situation of affairs as depicted in my last annual message has in the least improved. If Spain still holds Havana and the seaports and all the considerable towns, the insurgents still roam at will over at least two-thirds of the inland country. If the determination of Spain to put down the insurrection seems but to strengthen with the lapse of time and is evinced by her unhesitating devotion of largely increased military and naval forces to the task, there is much reason to believe that the insurgents have gained in point of numbers and character and resources, and are none the less inflexible in their resolve not to succumb without practically securing the great objects for which they took up arms.

. If Spain has not yet reestablished her authority, neither have the insurgents yet made good their title to be regarded as an independent state. Indeed, as the contest has gone on, the pretense that civil government exists on the island, except so far as Spain is able to maintain it, has been practically abandoned. Spain does keep on foot such a government, more or less imperfectly, in the large towns and their immediate suburbs. But, that exception being made, the entire country is either given over to anarchy or is subject to the military occupation of one or the other party. It is reported, indeed, on reliable authority that, at the demand of the commander in chief of the insurgent army, the putative Cuban government has now given up all attempt to exercise its functions, leaving that government confessedly (what there is the best reason for supposing it always to have been in fact) a government merely on paper.

Were the Spanish armies able to meet their antagonists in the open or in pitched battle, prompt and decisive results might be looked for and the immense superiority of the Spanish forces in numbers, discipline, and equipment could hardly fail to tell greatly to their advantage. But they are called upon to face a foe that shuns general engagements, that can choose and does choose its own ground, that, from the nature of the country, is visible or invisible at pleasure, and that fights only from ambuscade and when all the advantages of position and numbers are on its side. In a country where all that is indispensable to life in the way of food, clothing, and shelter is so easily obtainable, especially by those born and bred on the soil, it is obvious that there is hardly a limit to the time during which hostilities of this sort may be prolonged.

Meanwhile, as in all cases of protracted civil strife, the passions of the combatants grow more and more inflamed, and excesses on both sides become more frequent and more deplorable. They are also participated in by bands of marauders, who, now in the name of one party and now in the name of the other, as may best suit the occasion, harry the country at will and plunder its wretched inhabitants for their own advantage. Such a condition of things would inevitably entail immense destruction of property, even if it were the policy of both parties to prevent it as far as practicable. But while such seemed to be the original policy of the Spanish government, it has now apparently abandoned it and is acting upon the same theory as the insurgents, namely, that the exigencies of the contest require the wholesale annihilation of property that it may not prove of use and advantage to the enemy.

It is to the same end that, in pursuance of general orders, Spanish garrisons are now being withdrawn from plantations and the rural population required to concentrate itself in the towns. The sure result would seem to be that the industrial value of the island is fast diminishing, and that unless there is a speedy and radical change in existing conditions, it will soon disappear altogether. That value consists very largely, of course, in its capacity to produce sugar — a capacity already much reduced by the interruptions to tillage which have taken place during the last two years. It is reliably asserted that should these interruptions continue during the current year and practically extend, as is now threatened, to the entire sugar-producing territory of the island, so much time and so much money will be required to restore the land to its normal productiveness that it is extremely doubtful if capital can be induced to even make the attempt.

The spectacle of the utter ruin of an adjoining country, by nature one of the most fertile and charming on the globe, would engage the serious attention of the government and people of the United States in any circumstances. In point of fact, they have a concern with it which is by no means of a wholly sentimental or philanthropic character. It lies so near to us as to be hardly separated from our territory. Our actual pecuniary interest in it is second only to that of the people and government of Spain. It is reasonably estimated that at least from $30 million to $50 million of American capital are invested in plantations and in railroad, mining, and other business enterprises on the island. The volume of trade between the United States and Cuba, which in 1889 amounted to about $64 million, rose in 1893 to about $103 million, and in 1894, the year before the present insurrection broke out, amounted to nearly $96 million.

Besides this large pecuniary stake in the fortunes of Cuba, the United States finds itself inextricably involved in the present contest in other ways, both vexatious and costly. Many Cubans reside in this country and indirectly promote the insurrection through the press, by public meetings, by the purchase and shipment of arms, by the raising of funds, and by other means, which the spirit of our institutions and the tenor of our laws do not permit to be made the subject of criminal prosecutions. Some of them, though Cubans at heart and in all their feelings and interests, have taken out papers as naturalized citizens of the United States, a proceeding resorted to with a view to possible protection by this government and not unnaturally regarded with much indignation by the country of their origin.

The insurgents are undoubtedly encouraged and supported by the widespread sympathy the people of this country always and instinctively feel for every struggle for better and freer government and which, in the case of the more adventurous and restless elements of our population, leads in only too many instances to active and personal participation in the contest. The result is that this government is constantly called upon to protect American citizens, to claim damages for injuries to persons and property, now estimated at many millions of dollars, and to ask explanations and apologies for the acts of Spanish officials, whose zeal for the repression of rebellion sometimes blinds them to the immunities belonging to the unoffending citizens of a friendly power. It follows from the same causes that the United States is compelled to actively police a long line of seacoast against unlawful expeditions, the escape of which the utmost vigilance will not always suffice to prevent.

These inevitable entanglements of the United States with the rebellion in Cuba, the large American property interests affected, and considerations of philanthropy and humanity in general, have led to a vehement demand in various quarters for some sort of positive intervention on the part of the United States. It was at first proposed that belligerent rights should be accorded to the insurgents — a proposition no longer urged because untimely and in practical operation clearly perilous and injurious to our own interests. It has since been and is now sometimes contended that the independence of the insurgents should be recognized. But imperfect and restricted as the Spanish government of the island may be, no other exists there — unless the will of the military officer in temporary command of a particular district can be dignified as a species of government.

It is now also suggested that the United States should buy the island — a suggestion possibly worthy of consideration if there were any evidence of a desire or willingness on the part of Spain to entertain such a proposal. It is urged, finally, that, all other methods failing, the existing internecine strife in Cuba should be terminated by our intervention, even at the cost of a war between the United States and Spain — a war which its advocates confidently prophesy could be neither large in its proportions nor doubtful in its issue.

The correctness of this forecast need be neither affirmed nor denied. The United States has nevertheless a character to maintain as a nation, which plainly dictates that right and not might should be the rule of its conduct. Further, though the United States is not a nation to which peace is a necessity, it is in truth the most pacific of powers and desires nothing so much as to live in amity with all the world. Its own ample and diversified domains satisfy all possible longings for territory, preclude all dreams of conquest, and prevent any casting of covetous eyes upon neighboring regions, however attractive.

That our conduct toward Spain and her dominions has constituted no exception to this national disposition is made manifest by the course of our government, not only thus far during the present insurrection but during the ten years that followed the rising at Yara in 1868. No other great power, it may safely be said, under circumstances of similar perplexity, would have manifested the same restraint and the same patient endurance. It may also be said that this persistent attitude of the United States toward Spain in connection with Cuba unquestionably evinces no slight respect and regard for Spain on the part of the American people.

They in truth do not forget her connection with the discovery of the Western Hemisphere, nor do they underestimate the great qualities of the Spanish people, nor fail to fully recognize their splendid patriotism and their chivalrous devotion to the national honor. They view with wonder and admiration the cheerful resolution with which vast bodies of men are sent across thousands of miles of ocean, and an enormous debt accumulated, that the costly possession of the Gem of the Antilles may still hold its place in the Spanish Crown.

And yet neither the government nor the people of the United States have shut their eyes to the course of events in Cuba or have failed to realize the existence of conceded grievances, which have led to the present revolt from the authority of Spain — grievances recognized by the queen regent and by the Cortes, voiced by the most patriotic and enlightened of Spanish statesmen, without regard to party, and demonstrated by reforms proposed by the executive and approved by the legislative branch of the Spanish government. It is in the assumed temper and disposition of the Spanish government to remedy these grievances, fortified by indications of influential public opinion in Spain, that this government has hoped to discover the most promising and effective means of composing the present strife, with honor and advantage to Spain and with the achievement of all the reasonable objects of the insurrection.

It would seem that if Spain should offer to Cuba genuine autonomy — a measure of home rule which, while preserving the sovereignty of Spain, would satisfy all rational requirements of her Spanish subjects — there should be no just reason why the pacification of the island might not be effected on that basis. Such a result would appear to be in the true interest of all concerned. It would at once stop the conflict. . . .

It would keep intact the possessions of Spain without touching her honor, which will be consulted rather than impugned by the adequate redress of admitted grievances. It would put the prosperity of the island and the fortunes of its inhabitants within their own control without severing the natural and ancient ties which bind them to the mother country, and would yet enable them to test their capacity for self-government under the most favorable conditions.

It has been objected, on the one side, that Spain should not promise autonomy until her insurgent subjects lay down their arms; on the other side, that promised autonomy, however liberal, is insufficient, because without assurance of the promise being fulfilled. But the reasonableness of a requirement by Spain of unconditional surrender on the part of the insurgent Cubans before their autonomy is conceded is not altogether apparent. It ignores important features of the situation — the stability two years' duration has given to the insurrection; the feasibility of its indefinite prolongation in the nature of things and as shown by past experience; the utter and imminent ruin of the island, unless the present strife is speedily composed; above all, the rank abuses which all parties in Spain, all branches of her government, and all her leading public men concede to exist and profess a desire to remove.

Facing such circumstances, to withhold the proffer of needed reforms until the parties demanding them put themselves at mercy by throwing down their arms has the appearance of neglecting the gravest of perils and inviting suspicion as to the sincerity of any professed willingness to grant reforms. The objection on behalf of the insurgents — that promised reforms cannot be relied upon — must of course be considered, though we have no right to assume, and no reason for assuming, that anything Spain undertakes to do for the relief of Cuba will not be done according to both the spirit and the letter of the undertaking.

Nevertheless, realizing that suspicions and precautions on the part of the weaker of two combatants are always natural and not always unjustifiable, being sincerely desirous in the interest of both as well as on its own account that the Cuban problem should be solved with the least possible delay, it was intimated by this government to the government of Spain some months ago that, if a satisfactory measure of home rule were tendered the Cuban insurgents and would be accepted by them upon a guarantee of its execution, the United States would endeavor to find a way not objectionable to Spain of furnishing such guarantee. While no definite response to this intimation has yet been received from the Spanish government, it is believed to be not altogether unwelcome, while, as already suggested, no reason is perceived why it should not be approved by the insurgents.

Neither party can fail to see the importance of early action, and both must realize that to prolong the present state of things for even a short period will add enormously to the time and labor and expenditure necessary to bring about the industrial recuperation of the island. It is therefore fervently hoped on all grounds that earnest efforts for healing the breach between Spain and the insurgent Cubans, upon the lines above indicated, may be at once inaugurated and pushed to an immediate and successful issue. The friendly offices of the United States, either in the manner above outlined or in any other way consistent with our Constitution and laws, will always be at the disposal of either party.

Whatever circumstances may arise, our policy and our interests would constrain us to object to the acquisition of the island or an interference with its control by any other power.

It should be added that it cannot be reasonably assumed that the hitherto expectant attitude of the United States will be indefinitely maintained. While we are anxious to accord all due respect to the sovereignty of Spain, we cannot view the pending conflict in all its features and properly apprehend our inevitably close relations to it and its possible results without considering that, by the course of events, we may be drawn into such an unusual and unprecedented condition as will fix a limit to our patient waiting for Spain to end the contest, either alone and in her own way or with our friendly cooperation.

When the inability of Spain to deal successfully with the insurrection has become manifest, and it is demonstrated that her sovereignty is extinct in Cuba for all purposes of its rightful existence, and when a hopeless struggle for its reestablishment has degenerated into a strife which means nothing more than the useless sacrifice of human life and the utter destruction of the very subject matter of the conflict, a situation will be presented in which our obligations to the sovereignty of Spain will be superseded by higher obligations, which we can hardly hesitate to recognize and discharge. Deferring the choice of ways and methods until the time for action arrives, we should make them depend upon the precise conditions then existing; and they should not be determined upon without giving careful heed to every consideration involving our honor and interest or the international duty we owe to Spain. Until we face the contingencies suggested, or the situation is by other incidents imperatively changed, we should continue in the line of conduct heretofore pursued, thus in all circumstances exhibiting our obedience to the requirements of public law and our regard for the duty enjoined upon us by the position we occupy in the family of nations.

A contemplation of emergencies that may arise should plainly lead us to avoid their creation, either through a careless disregard of present duty or even an undue stimulation and ill-timed expression of feeling. But I have deemed it not amiss to remind the Congress that a time may arrive when a correct policy and care for our interests, as well as a regard for the interests of other nations and their citizens, joined by considerations of humanity and a desire to see a rich and fertile country, intimately related to us, saved from complete devastation, will constrain our government to such action as will subserve the interests thus involved and at the same time promise to Cuba and its inhabitants an opportunity to enjoy the blessings of peace.

1897

27.

John Philip Sousa: "The Stars and Stripes Forever"

Marching bands were immensely popular in the 1890s, and the most famous of all was John Philip Sousa's. The band, a legend in its time, toured the country, and many small towns, as well as large cities, thrilled to its performances. Sousa himself wrote much of the music for the band, and people everywhere danced to the "Sousa two-step," known in Europe as the "Washington Post," after one of his best-known marches. The best known of all was "The Stars and Stripes Forever," with which the band closed every concert. It is still a favorite of marching bands.

THE STARS AND STRIPES FOREVER

Let martial note in triumph float,
And liberty extend its mighty hand.
A flag appears, 'mid thund'rous cheers,
The banner of the Western land.
The emblem of the brave and true,
Its folds protect no tyrant crew,
The red and white and starry blue
Is freedom's shield and hope.

Other nations may deem their flags the best,
And cheer them with fervid elation.
But the flag of the North and South and West
Is the flag of flags, the flag of freedom's nation.

Chorus:
Let eagle shriek from lofty peak
The never-ending watchword of our land.
Let summer breeze waft through the trees
The echo of the chorus grand.
Sing out for liberty and light,
Sing out for freedom and the right.
Sing out for Union and its might,
Oh, patriotic sons!

Hurrah for the flag of the free;
May it wave as our standard forever.
The gem of the land and the sea,
The banner of the right.
Let despots remember the day
When our fathers, with mighty endeavor,
Proclaimed as they marched to the fray,
That by their might, and by their right, it waves forever!

Other nations may deem their flags the best,
And cheer them with fervid elation.
But the flag of the North and South and West
Is the flag of flags, the flag of freedom's nation.

28.

JOHN DEWEY: My Pedagogic Creed

John Dewey's Laboratory School at the University of Chicago put into practice the new educational doctrines of its founder and provided Dewey with a "laboratory" for testing the validity of his ideas. His profound belief in the rightness of his theories prompted him to write about them frequently. The creed that is reprinted below is a succinct and forceful statement of Dewey's early educational beliefs. His emphasis on providing for the social and individual needs for the child in the school environment, as well as on the importance of education as "process" rather than preparation, marked him as one of the great innovators in American education. More people criticized than read Dewey, and the controversy over "progressive education" that he initiated marked American educational literature for the next fifty years.

Source: *Teachers Manuals*, New York, 1897, No. 25, pp. 7-16.

WHAT EDUCATION IS

I BELIEVE that all education proceeds by the participation of the individual in the social consciousness of the race. This process begins unconsciously almost at birth and is continually shaping the individual's powers, saturating his consciousness, forming his habits, training his ideas, and arousing his feelings and emotions. Through this unconscious education the individual gradually comes to share in the intellectual and moral resources which humanity has succeeded in getting together. He becomes an inheritor of the funded capital of civilization. The most formal and technical education in the world cannot safely depart from this general process. . . .

I believe that the individual who is to be educated is a social individual and that society is an organic union of individuals. If we eliminate the social factor from the child, we are left only with an abstraction; if we eliminate the individual factor from society, we are left only with an inert and lifeless mass. Education, therefore, must begin with a psychological insight into the child's capacities, interests, and habits. It must be controlled at every point by reference to these same considerations. These powers, interests, and habits must be continually interpreted — we must know what they mean. They must be translated into terms of their social equivalents — into terms of what they are capable of in the way of social service.

WHAT THE SCHOOL IS

I BELIEVE that the school is primarily a social institution. Education being a social process, the school is simply that form of community life in which all those agencies are concentrated that will be most effective in bringing the child to share in the inherited resources of the race and to use his own powers for social ends.

I believe that education, therefore, is a process of living and not a preparation for future living.

I believe that the school must represent present life — life as real and vital to the child as that which he carries on in the home, in the neighborhood, or on the playground.

I believe that education which does not occur through forms of life, forms that are worth living for their own sake, is always a poor substitute for the genuine reality and tends to cramp and to deaden.

I believe that the school, as an institution, should simplify existing social life; should reduce it, as it were, to an embryonic form. Existing life is so complex that the child cannot be brought into contact with it without either confusion or distraction; he is either overwhelmed by the multiplicity of activities which are going on, so that he loses his own power of orderly reaction, or he is so stimulated by these various activities that his powers are prematurely called into play and he becomes either unduly specialized or else disintegrated.

I believe that as such simplified social life, the school life, should grow gradually out of the homelife; that it should take up and continue the activities with which the child is already familiar in the home.

I believe that it should exhibit these activities to the child and reproduce them in such ways that the child will gradually learn the meaning of them and be capable of playing his own part in relation to them.

I believe that this is a psychological necessity, because it is the only way of securing continuity in the child's growth, the only way of giving a background of past experience to the new ideas given in school.

I believe that it is also a social necessity, because the home is the form of social life in which the child has been nurtured and in connection with which he has had his moral training. It is the business of the school to deepen and extend his sense of the values bound up in his homelife.

I believe that much of present education fails because it neglects this fundamental principle of the school as a form of community life. It conceives the school as a place where certain information is to be given, where certain lessons are to be learned, or where certain habits are to be formed. The value of these is conceived as lying largely in the remote future; the child must do these things for the sake of something else he is to do; they are mere preparation. As a result they do not become a part of the life experience of the child and so are not truly educative.

I believe that the moral education centers upon this conception of the school as a mode of social life, that the best and deepest moral training is precisely that which one gets through having to enter into proper relations with others in a unity of work and thought. The present educational systems, so far as they destroy or neglect this unity, render it difficult or impossible to get any genuine, regular moral training.

I believe that the child should be stimulated and controlled in his work through the life of the community.

I believe that under existing conditions far too much of the stimulus and control proceeds from the teacher because of neglect of the idea of the school as a form of social life.

I believe that the teacher's place and work in the school is to be interpreted from this same basis. The teacher is not in the school to impose certain ideas or to form certain habits in the child, but is there as a member of the community to select the influences which shall affect the child and to assist him in properly responding to these influences.

I believe that the discipline of the school should proceed from the life of the school as a whole and not directly from the teacher.

I believe that the teacher's business is simply to determine on the basis of larger experience and riper wisdom how the discipline of life shall come to the child.

I believe that all questions of the grading of the child and his promotion should be determined by reference to the same standard. Examinations are of use only so far as they test the child's fitness for social life and reveal the place in which he can be of the most service and where he can receive the most help.

THE SUBJECT MATTER
OF EDUCATION

I BELIEVE that the social life of the child is the basis of concentration, or correlation, in all his training or growth. The social life gives the unconscious unity and the background of all his efforts and of all his attainments.

I believe that the subject matter of the school curriculum should mark a gradual differentiation out of the primitive unconscious unity of social life.

I believe that we violate the child's nature and render difficult the best ethical results by introducing the child too abruptly to a number of special studies, of reading, writing, geography, etc., out of relation to this social life.

I believe, therefore, that the true center of correlation on the school subjects is not science, nor literature, nor history, nor geography, but the child's own social activities.

I believe that education cannot be unified in the study of science, or so-called nature study, because, apart from human activity, nature itself is not a unity; nature in itself is a number of diverse objects in space and time, and to attempt to make it the center of work by itself is to introduce a principle of radiation rather than one of concentration.

I believe that literature is the reflex expression and interpretation of social experience; that hence it must follow upon and not precede such experience. It, therefore, cannot be made the basis, although it may be made the summary of unification.

I believe once more that history is of educative value insofar as it presents phases of social life and growth. It must be controlled by reference to social life. When taken simply as history, it is thrown into the distant past and becomes dead and inert. Taken as the record of man's social life and progress, it becomes full of meaning. I believe, however, that it cannot be so taken excepting as the child is also introduced directly into social life.

I believe, accordingly, that the primary basis of education is in the child's powers at work along the same general constructive lines as those which have brought civilization into being.

I believe that the only way to make the

child conscious of his social heritage is to enable him to perform those fundamental types of activity which make civilization what it is.

I believe, therefore, in the so-called expressive or constructive activities as the center of correlation.

I believe that this gives the standard for the place of cooking, sewing, manual training, etc., in the school.

I believe that they are not special studies which are to be introduced over and above a lot of others in the way of relaxation or relief, or as additional accomplishments. I believe, rather, that they represent, as types, fundamental forms of social activity; and that it is possible and desirable that the child's introduction into the more formal subjects of the curriculum be through the medium of these activities.

I believe that the study of science is educational insofar as it brings out the materials and processes which make social life what it is.

I believe that one of the greatest difficulties in the present teaching of science is that the material is presented in purely objective form, or is treated as a new peculiar kind of experience which the child can add to that which he has already had. In reality, science is of value because it gives the ability to interpret and control the experience already had. It should be introduced, not as so much new subject matter, but as showing the factors already involved in previous experience and as furnishing tools by which that experience can be more easily and effectively regulated.

I believe that at present we lose much of the value of literature and language studies because of our elimination of the social element. Language is almost always treated in the books of pedagogy simply as the expression of thought. It is true that language is a logical instrument, but it is fundamentally and primarily a social instrument. Language is the device for communication; it is the tool through which one individual comes to share the ideas and feelings of others. When treated simply as a way of getting individual information, or as a means of showing off what one has learned, it loses its social motive and end.

I believe that there is, therefore, no succession of studies in the ideal school curriculum. If education is life, all life has, from the outset, a scientific aspect, an aspect of art and culture, and an aspect of communication. It cannot, therefore, be true that the proper studies for one grade are mere reading and writing, and that at a later grade reading or literature or science may be introduced. The progress is not in the succession of studies but in the development of new attitudes toward, and new interests in, experience.

I believe, finally, that education must be conceived as a continuing reconstruction of experience; that the process and the goal of education are one and the same thing.

I believe that to set up any end outside of education, as furnishing its goal and standard, is to deprive the educational process of much of its meaning and tends to make us rely upon false and external stimuli in dealing with the child.

THE NATURE OF METHOD

1. I believe that the active side precedes the passive development of the child nature; that expression comes before conscious impression; that the muscular development precedes the sensory; that movements come before conscious sensations. I believe that consciousness is essentially motor or impulsive; that conscious states tend to project themselves in action. . . .

2. I believe that the image is the great instrument of instruction. What a child gets out of any subject presented to him is simply the images which he himself forms with regard to it. . . .

3. I believe that interests are the signs

and symptoms of growing power. I believe that they represent dawning capacities. Accordingly, the constant and careful observation of interests is of the utmost importance for the educator. . . .

4. I believe that the emotions are the reflex of actions.

I believe that to endeavor to stimulate or arouse the emotions apart from their corresponding activities is to introduce an unhealthy and morbid state of mind.

I believe that if we can only secure right habits of action and thought, with reference to the good, the true, and the beautiful, the emotions will for the most part take care of themselves.

I believe that next to deadness and dullness, formalism and routine, our education is threatened with no greater evil than sentimentalism.

I believe that this sentimentalism is the necessary result of the attempt to divorce feeling from action.

THE SCHOOL AND
SOCIAL PROGRESS

I BELIEVE that education is the fundamental method of social progress and reform.

I believe that all reforms which rest simply upon the enactment of law, or the threatening of certain penalties, or upon changes in mechanical or outward arrangements are transitory and futile.

I believe that education is a regulation of the process of coming to share in the social consciousness; and that the adjustment of individual activity on the basis of this social consciousness is the only sure method of social reconstruction.

I believe that this conception has due regard for both the individualistic and socialistic ideals. It is duly individual because it recognizes the formation of a certain character as the only genuine basis of right living. It is socialistic because it recognizes that this right character is not to be formed by mere-

ly individual precept, example, or exhortation, but rather by the influence of a certain form of institutional or community life upon the individual, and that the social organism through the school, as its organ, may determine ethical results.

I believe that in the ideal school we have the reconciliation of the individualistic and the institutional ideals.

I believe that the community's duty to education is, therefore, its paramount moral duty. By law and punishment, by social agitation and discussion, society can regulate and form itself in a more or less haphazard and chance way. But, through education, society can formulate its own purposes, can organize its own means and resources, and thus shape itself with definiteness and economy in the direction in which it wishes to move.

I believe that when society once recognizes the possibilities in this direction and the obligations which these possibilities impose, it is impossible to conceive of the resources of time, attention, and money which will be put at the disposal of the educator.

I believe that it is the business of everyone interested in education to insist upon the school as the primary and most effective interest of social progress and reform in order that society may be awakened to realize what the school stands for and aroused to the necessity of endowing the educator with sufficient equipment properly to perform his task.

I believe that education thus conceived marks the most perfect and intimate union of science and art conceivable in human experience.

I believe that the art of thus giving shape to human powers and adapting them to social service is the supreme art; one calling into its service the best of artists; that no insight, sympathy, tact, executive power is too great for such service.

I believe that with the growth of psychological service, giving added insight into individual structure and laws of growth; and with growth of social science, adding to our knowledge of the right organization of individuals, all scientific resources can be utilized for the purposes of education.

I believe that when science and art thus join hands the most commanding motive for human action will be reached, the most genuine springs of human conduct aroused, and the best service that human nature is capable of guaranteed.

I believe, finally, that the teacher is engaged, not simply in the training of individuals but in the formation of the proper social life.

I believe that every teacher should realize the dignity of his calling; that he is a social servant set apart for the maintenance of proper social order and the securing of the right social growth.

I believe that in this way the teacher always is the prophet of the true God and the usherer in of the true Kingdom of God.

29.

Jane Addams: Foreign-Born Children in the Primary Grades

For Jane Addams, one historian has commented, "education was as broad as experience itself; education was experience." All of her work in settlement houses had convinced her that the formal educational system had divorced itself from life as it really was. Thus she tried to make Hull House a social-educational agency in which people, especially immigrants, could be prepared for the realities of life. Miss Addams' educational philosophy was publicized through her writing and lecturing. Her speech before the National Educational Association's annual meeting in July 1897 is reprinted here in part.

Source: National Educational Association: *Journal of Proceedings and Addresses of the Thirty-Sixth Annual Meeting,* Chicago, 1897, pp. 104-112.

THE FOLLOWING PAPER IS GIVEN with great diffidence. The writer has never been a teacher, nor even a close observer, in primary schools. She only had unusual opportunities for seeing the children of immigrants during and after the period of their short school life. She submits some of the observations and reflections which have come to her concerning the great mass of those children who never get beyond the primary grades in the hope that they may prove suggestive to the educators present. The observations are confined to the children of the Italian colony lying directly east of Hull House, in the 19th Ward of Chicago; although what is said concerning them might be applied, with certain modifications, to the children of Chicago's large Bohemian and Polish colonies.

For the purpose of this paper it will be best to treat of the school as a social institution, within which a certain concentration of social interests takes place for the purpose of producing certain social results. This is certainly legitimate, if we take Dr. Dewey's statement that "the school selects and presents in an organized manner influences and instruments which may expedite and facilitate the socializing of the individual." Certainly, after the child leaves school, his experiences consist of his participation in the social life in the various groups of which he is a member or with which he comes in contact.

Whatever may be our ultimate conception of education, and however much we may differ in definition, as doubtless the members of this convention do widely differ, we shall probably agree that the ultimate aim is to modify the character and conduct of the individual, and to harmonize and adjust his activities; that even the primary school should aim to give the child's own experience a social value; and that this aim too often fails of success in the brief sojourn of the child of the foreign peasant in the public school.

The members of the 19th Ward Italian colony are largely from south Italy, Calabrian and Sicilian peasants, or Neapolitans from the workingmen's quarters of that city. They have come to America with a distinct aim of earning money and finding more room for the energies of themselves and their children. In almost all cases they mean to go back again, simply because their imaginations cannot picture a continuous life away from the old surroundings.

Their experiences in Italy have been that of simple, outdoor activity, and the ideas they have have come directly to them from their struggle with nature, such a hand-to-hand struggle as takes place when each man gets his living largely through his own cultivation of the soil, with tools simply fashioned by his own hands. The women, as in all primitive life, have had more diversified activities than the men. They have cooked, spun, and knitted, in addition to their almost equal work in the fields. Very few of the peasant men or women can either read or write. They are devoted to their children, strong in their family feeling to remote relationships, and clannish in their community life. . . .

Italian parents count upon the fact that their children learn the English language and American customs before they themselves do, and act not only as interpreters of the language about them but as buffers between them and Chicago; and this results in a certain, almost pathetic, dependence of the family upon the child. When a member of the family, therefore, first goes to school, the event is fraught with much significance to all the others. The family has no social life in any structural form and can supply none to the child. If he receives it in the school and gives it to his family, the school would thus become the connector with the organized society about them.

It is the children aged six, eight, and ten who go to school, entering, of course, the primary grades. If a boy is twelve or thirteen on his arrival in America, his parents see in him a wage-earning factor, and the girl of the same age is already looking toward her marriage.

Let us take one of these boys, who has learned in his six or eight years to speak his native language and to feel himself strongly identified with the fortunes of his family.

Whatever interest has come to the minds of his ancestors has come through the use of their hands in the open air; and open air and activity of body have been the inevitable accompaniments of all their experiences. Yet the first thing that the boy must do when he reaches school is to sit still, at least part of the time, and he must learn to listen to what is said to him, with all the perplexity of listening to a foreign tongue. He does not find this very stimulating and is slow to respond to the more subtle incentives of the schoolroom. The peasant child is perfectly indifferent to showing off and making a good recitation. He leaves all that to his schoolfellows who are more sophisticated and who are equipped with better English.

It is not the purpose of this paper to describe the child's life in school, which the audience knows so much better than the writer, but she ventures to assert that if the little Italian lad were supplied, then and there, with tangible and resistance-offering material upon which to exercise his muscle, he would go bravely to work, and he would probably be ready later to use the symbols of letters and numbers to record and describe what he had done; and might even be incited to the exertion of reading to find out what other people had done.

Too often the teacher's conception of her duty is to transform him into an American of a somewhat snug and comfortable type, and she insists that the boy's powers must at once be developed in an abstract direction, quite ignoring the fact that his parents have had to do only with tangible things. She has little idea of the development of Italian life. Her outlook is national and not racial; and she fails, therefore, not only in knowledge of but also in respect for the child and his parents. She quite honestly estimates the child upon an American basis. The contempt for the experiences and languages of their parents which foreign children sometimes exhibit, and which is most damaging to their moral as well as intellectual life, is doubtless due in part to the overestimation which the school places upon speaking and reading in English. This cutting into his family loyalty takes away one of the most conspicuous and valuable traits of the Italian child.

His parents are not specially concerned in keeping him in school and will not hold him there against his inclination, until his own interest shall do it for him. Their experience does not point to the good American tradition that it is the educated man who finally succeeds. The richest man on Ewing Street can neither read nor write — even Italian. His cunning and acquisitiveness, combined with the credulity and ignorance of his countrymen, have slowly brought about his large fortune.

The child himself may feel the stirring of a vague ambition to go on until he is as the other children are; but he is not popular with his schoolfellows, and he sadly feels the lack of dramatic interest. Even the pictures and objects presented to him, as well as the language, are strange.

If we admit that in education it is necessary to begin with the experiences which the child already has, through his spontaneous and social activity, then the city street begins this education for him in a more natural way than does the school. . . .

The school, of course, has to compete with a great deal from the outside in addition to the distractions of the neighborhood. Nothing is more fascinating than that mysterious "downtown," whither the boy longs to go to sell papers and black boots; to attend theaters and, if possible, to stay all night on the pretense of waiting for the early edition of the great dailies. If a boy is once thoroughly caught in these excitements, nothing can save him from overstimulation and consequent debility and worthlessness but a vigorous application of a compulsory education law, with a truant school; which, indeed, should have forestalled the possibility of his ever thus being caught.

It is a disgrace to us that we allow so many Italian boys thus to waste their health in premature, exciting activity, and their mentality in mere cunning, which later leaves them dissolute and worthless men, with no habits of regular work and a distaste for its dullness. These boys are not of criminal descent nor vagrant heritage. On the contrary, their parents have been temperate, laborious, and painstaking, living for many generations on one piece of ground.

Had these boys been made to feel their place in the school community; had they been caught by its fascinations of marching and singing together as a distinct corps; had they felt the charm of manipulating actual material, they might have been spared this erratic development. Mark Crawford, for many years the able superintendent of the Chicago House of Corrections, has said that, in looking over the records of that institution, he found that of 21,000 boys under 17 years of age who had been sent there under sentence less than 80 were schoolboys.

The school is supposed to select the more enduring forms of life and to eliminate, as far as possible, the trivialities and irrelevancies which actual living constantly presents. But, in point of fact, the Italian child has received most of his interests upon the streets, where he has seen a great deal of these trivialities magnified out of all proportion to their worth. He, of course, cares for them very much, and only education could give him a clue as to what to select and what to eliminate.

Leaving the child who does not stay in school, let us now consider the child who does faithfully remain until he reaches the age of factory work, which is, fortunately, in the most advanced of our factory states, fourteen years. . . . The shops and factories all about him contain vivid and striking examples of the high development of the simple tools which his father still uses and of the lessening expenditure of human energy. . . .

No attempt is made to give a boy, who, we know, will certainly have to go into one of them, any insight into their historic significance or to connect them in any intelligible way with the past and future. He has absolutely no consciousness of his social value, and his activities become inevitably perfectly mechanical. Most of the children who are thus put to work go on in their slavish life without seeing whither it tends and with no reflections upon it. The brightest ones among them, however, gradually learn that they belong to a class which does the necessary work of life, and that there is another class which tends to absorb the product of that work.

May we not charge it to the public school that it has given to this child no knowledge of the social meaning of his work? Is it not possible that, if the proper estimate of education had been there; if all the children had been taught to use equally and to honor equally both their heads and hands; if they had been made even dimly to apprehend that for an individual to obtain the greatest control of himself for the performance of social service, and to realize within himself the value of the social service which he is performing, is to obtain the fullness of life, the hateful feeling of class distinction could never have grown up in any of them? It would then be of little moment to himself or to others whether the boy finally served the commonwealth in the factory or in the legislature.

But nothing in this larger view of life has reached our peasant's son. He finds himself in the drudgery of a factory, senselessly manipulating unrelated material, using his hands for unknown ends and his head not at all. Owing to the fact that during his years in school he has used his head mostly and his hands very little, nothing bewilders him so much as the suggestion that the school was intended as a preparation for his work in life. He would be equally amazed to find that his school was supposed to fill his mind with beautiful images and powers of thought, so that he might be able to do this dull mechanical work and still live a real life outside of it. . . .

There is one fixed habit . . . which the boy carries away from school with him to the factory. Having the next grade continually before him as an object of attainment results in the feeling that his work is merely provisional and that its sole use is to get him ready for other things. This tentative attitude takes the last bit of social stimulus out of his factory work, and he pursues it merely as a necessity. His last chance for a realization of social consciousness is gone.

From one point of view the school itself

is an epitome of the competitive system, almost of the factory system. Certain standards are held up and worked for; and, even in the school, the child does little work with real joy and spontaneity. The pleasure which comes from creative effort, the thrill of production, is only occasional and not the sustaining motive which keeps it going. The child in school often contracts the habit of expecting to do his work in certain hours and to take his pleasure in certain other hours; quite in the same spirit as he later earns his money by ten hours of dull factory work and spends it in three hours of lurid and unprofitable pleasure in the evening. Both in the school and the factory his work has been dull and growing duller, and his pleasure must constantly grow more stimulating. Only occasionally, in either place, has he had a glimpse of the real joy of doing a thing for its own sake.

Those of us who are working to bring a fuller life to the industrial members of the community, who are looking forward to a time when work shall not be senseless drudgery but shall contain some self-expression of the worker, sometimes feel the hopelessness of adding evening classes and social entertainments as a mere frill to a day filled with monotonous and deadening drudgery; and we sometimes feel that we have a right to expect more help from the public schools than they now give us.

If the army of schoolchildren who enter the factories every year possessed thoroughly vitalized faculties, they might do much to lighten this incubus of dull factory work which presses so heavily upon so large a number of our fellow citizens. Has our commercialism been so strong that our schools have become insensibly commercialized, rather than that our industrial life has felt the broadening and illuminating effect of the schools?

The boy in the primary grades has really been used as material to be prepared for the grammar grades. Unconsciously, his training, so far as it has been vocational at all, has been in the direction of clerical work. Is it possible that the businessmen, whom we have so long courted and worshiped in America, have really been dictating the curriculum of our public schools, in spite of the conventions of educators and the suggestions of university professors? The businessman has, of course, not said to himself: "I will have the public school train office boys and clerks for me so that I may have them cheap"; but he has thought and sometimes said: "Teach the children to write legibly and to figure accurately and quickly; to acquire habits of punctuality and order; to be prompt to obey and not question why, and you will fit them to make their way in the world as I have made mine."

Has the workingman been silent as to what he desires for his children and allowed the businessman to decide for him there as he has allowed the politician to manage his municipal affairs? Or has the workingman suffered from our universal optimism and really believed that his children would never need to go into industrial life at all but that his sons would all become bankers and merchants?

Certain it is that no sufficient study has been made of the child who enters into industrial life early and remains there permanently, to give him some setoff to its monotony and dullness; some historic significance of the part he is taking in the life of the commonwealth; some conception of the dignity of labor, which is sometimes mentioned to him but never demonstrated. We have a curious notion, in spite of all our realism, that it is not possible for the mass of mankind to have interests and experiences of themselves which are worth anything. We transmit to the children of working people our own skepticism regarding the possibility of finding any joy or profit in their work. We practically incite them to get out of it as soon as possible.

I am quite sure that no one can possibly

mistake this paper as a plea for trade schools, or as a desire to fit the boy for any given industry. Such a specializing would indeed be stupid when our industrial methods are developing and changing, almost day by day. But it does contend that life, as seen from the standpoint of the handwork- er, should not be emptied of all social consciousness and value, and that the school could make the boy infinitely more flexible and alive than he is now to the materials and forces of nature which, in spite of all man's activities, are unchangeable.

30.

Rufus R. Wilson: The Growth of an American School of Sculpture

By the turn of the century it was becoming apparent to native and foreign critics alike that America was coming of age artistically as well as politically. American sculptors of the 1890s were rewarded for their distinctive work by receiving important public commissions. Daniel Chester French, who is mentioned in the following article by Rufus R. Wilson, designed the Lincoln Memorial and sculpted the imposing figure of Lincoln within it. Wilson's article appeared in August 1897.

Source: *Illustrated American*, August 21, 1897.

THE RECENT FAMILIARITY of the public with the sculpture of Augustus St. Gaudens and that of his gifted pupil Frederick Macmonnies enhances interest in the now considerable and constantly growing group of men who, by their work and influence, are creating an American school of sculpture for our sculptors, one and all of them true Americans; and their work has in it a quality that is distinctly national and savors of the soil. This is the result of a change wrought during the last thirty years. America's first sculptors, Powers, Greenough, and the rest, were trained abroad and spent the greater part of their professional careers in Italy, finding their masters among the antique sculptors, with results finished and pleasing in execution, but often so weak and insipid in conception that they leave the observer cold.

The era of imitation, however, soon came to an end, and in Erastus D. Palmer, still living at the ripe age of eighty, there appeared a sculptor who, discarding foreign models and alien ideas, elected with fine independence to work out his art and his career in his own way.

The national note struck by Mr. Palmer is found repeated with added clearness, beauty, and force in the work of J. Q. A. Ward and Augustus St. Gaudens, two men who, more than all others, have influenced the art of sculpture in this country up to the present time. Mr. Ward's long list of admirable statues and symbolic figures have not only shown unswerving devotion to American ideas but have done noble service in creating a receptive and willing audience for the sculptors of a latter day; while Mr. St. Gaudens struck in the splendid "Farragut" of his youth the keynote of a career which, thoroughly American in fiber, is bound to remain one of the glories of our native art. Indeed, it is not too much to say that, without the works and examples of the three men I have named, all of whom have wrought out their destiny among their own people, the brilliant development in American sculpture that has been in progress during the last twenty years would have been impossible.

"We belong to our belongings," Thackeray makes one of his heroines say; and it is only by a glance, however hurried, at the history of American sculpture that one is able to understand and appreciate the careers of such men as Daniel Chester French, F. Edwin Elwell, Herbert Adams, Charles H. Niehaus, Carl Bitter, George G. Barnard, and F. W. Ruckstuhl, who have won fame, and fame that will endure, by taking up and carrying forward the work begun by Palmer, Ward, and St. Gaudens.

Mr. French won his spurs as a sculptor a dozen years or more ago. His "Minute Man" at Concord, where he was born and reared, and his noble "Death and the Sculptor" gave him artistic rank; and this has been confirmed by a number of admirable portrait statues of Cass, Gallaudet, Starr King, and others, and the colossal statue of the "Republic," which was one of the artistic glories of the Columbian Exposition. Today he is at the meridian of his period of productivity, and with his essentially Yankee genius, broadened by foreign travel and observation, is giving forth work that is not only creditable to his native land but would be distinguished in any land.

The little village of Concord, the Concord of Emerson and Alcott, has sent forth another well-equipped sculptor in Mr. Elwell, grandson of Longfellow's "Village Blacksmith," whose artistic career dates from 1879, and who is, so far as I know, the only American sculptor to execute in America a work to be set up abroad. The work referred to is the memorial to F. H. Pont, now in the garden of the old cathedral at Edam, Holland. Mr. Elwell is one of those artists who can work out their ideas only in a burst of what for want of a better word we call inspiration. His finest achievements are the result of a few hours of artistic fervor, and the face of the child in his beautiful and impelling group of "Dickens and Little Nell" was modeled from memory in a single night. However, Mr. Elwell is never guilty of haste or carelessness. His models are the result of many hours of anxious thought, and he is one of those fastidious craftsmen who, by laying fast hold of the present, make the future secure.

The same is true of Mr. Adams and Mr. Barnard. The former, a native of Vermont, who has had his training under Mr. St. Gaudens, supplemented by years of study and residence in Europe, has given proof in his statues of angels, his bas-reliefs and his portrait busts, of an assured command of grace, elegance, and decorative charm very like that possessed by the men who wrought the masterpieces of Renaissance sculpture; and Mr. Barnard, who comes from Pennsylvania, but has studied in France, has done and is doing work so bold and vigorous in conception and execution that, despite his comparative youth, a place in the very front rank of our native sculptors can no longer be denied him.

One of the best things Mr. Barnard has thus far given us is a group in marble showing the end of a struggle between two contestants, in which the victor plants his foot on the prostrate body of his enemy — the whole an effort to symbolize the two natures that struggle for the mastery in every man. Mr. Barnard's technique is still wanting in flexibility and precision, but the figures in his group are well-proportioned and modeled, and when so much has been accomplished, the rest is only a matter of labor and study. We already have enough to be certain that the making of a great sculptor is there.

Ability to depict the nude is always final

proof that a sculptor has mastered the grammar of his art. Measured by this standard, Mr. Niehaus and Mr. Ruckstuhl have proved their calling and election in very splendid fashion. Mr. Niehaus's "Scraper" is a robust piece of realism that has the further charm of technical adequacy; and, it is, perhaps, not too much to say that Mr. Ruckstuhl's "Evening" is the finest female figure that has thus far been credited to our native sculpture.

Mr. Ruckstuhl, who is American in all save the accident of birth, still has his career before him, but Mr. Niehaus has already executed not less than a dozen important pieces of sculpture. These include the masterly standing figure of Garfield now in Cincinnati, an ideal Moses for the new Congressional Library, and a splendid seated figure of Hahnemann, the founder of homeopathy — the last named soon to be set up in Washington — all charged to the full with the simplicity, dignity, and true poetic feeling, which are, I am persuaded, the first requisites of plastic art.

In easy command of all the technical resources of his calling, Mr. Bitter, who is an Austrian by birth and an American by recent adoption, has no superior among the sculptors who live and work on this side of the Western ocean. Most of Mr. Bitter's work has thus far been of a decorative order, but his fine statue of Provost Pepper of the University of Pennsylvania shows the admirable achievement in portrait sculpture of which he is capable when opportunity offers Here his methods, like his theme, are American, and have, moreover, an authoritative charm which only a churl could fail to praise and recognize.

These are only a few of the men who are laboring for the development of our native sculpture. The list could be lengthened indefinitely, but mention must also be made of the veteran Charles Calverley, whose veracious and dignified portrait busts are the best things of their kind produced in any country at the present time; and of J. Scott Hartley, Theodore Baur, Cyrus E. Dallin, John Donoghue, Edward Kemeys, H. A. Lukeman, and Charles A. Lopez. Mr. Hartley's best work, like that of Mr. Calverley, has been done in portraiture — witness his strong and faithful likeness of kindly old John Gilbert, and his admirable portraits of his own and other people's children — and Mr. Baur in such delightful bits of *genre* as his sportive, half-cynical "New Year's Call" stands in a class quite by himself.

Mr. Dallin, who was born in Utah in 1861, and studied under Chapu in Paris, in his "Signal of Peace" and a number of excellent bas-reliefs and portrait busts has proved himself the strongest sculptor that has thus far come out of the farther West; and Mr. Donoghue, who was born in Chicago, and completed his training in Paris and Rome, produced a number of statues and reliefs at once distinguished, dignified, and picturesque, which, though built on Greek foundations, are modern, and his own. Mr. Kemeys' work in animal sculpture, a field which he has made his own, challenges comparison with that of Barye and Fremiet; while the pleasing and sympathetic busts by Mr. Lopez and Mr. Lukeman, the one a pupil of Ward and the other of French . . . prove what may be expected from the men whose careers are just beginning.

Nowhere, save in France, are the sculptors doing better work than they are in America at the present time.

———————◆———————

Noise proves nothing. Often a hen who has merely laid an egg cackles as if she had laid an asteroid.

SAMUEL L. CLEMENS ("MARK TWAIN"), *Following the Equator*

31.

Josiah Quincy: City Government in America

Mayor Josiah Quincy of Boston visited a number of European cities, notably Paris and Berlin, during the early 1890s; and on his return was struck by the comparative inefficiency of American city governments. Inefficiency, as he pointed out, was accompanied by favored treatment of business interests, a charge to be made later by the Progressives. Quincy's suggestions for changing city government to meet the people's needs were contained in an article, "The Development of American Cities," published in March 1897, portions of which are reprinted here.

Source: *Arena*, March 1897.

Observers of modern municipal development on both sides of the Atlantic cannot but be struck with a curious anomaly. In some countries of Europe where the administration of city affairs is controlled only to a very limited extent, or not at all, by the great mass of the citizens, municipal governments are conducted upon broader and more popular lines than in the United States, where universal suffrage prevails. In a certain sense, Berlin and Paris are actually more democratic than New York and Chicago. The people of the former cities have indeed nothing like the direct control over their city governments which those of the latter enjoy, in theory at least; but if we form our judgment, not by the scope of the elective franchise but by that of services rendered, we shall have to award the palm for variety and usefulness of municipal activity, for benefits conferred upon the masses of the people, to the foreign cities.

An intelligent observer, with no other knowledge than that derived from a comparison of work done and results secured, would doubtless conclude that the people ruled more fully in Paris than in New York, in Berlin than in Chicago. In a score of different directions the interests of the average citizen are better and more fully cared for, his wants more fully met in the great city of Europe than in that of America. Municipal government in the Old World seems to be for the people, if not by the people.

My object in calling attention to this curious contrast between the theoretical character of city governments and the results they actually attain is by no means to draw a comparison unfavorable to democratic institutions or universal suffrage. To an American, liberty of thought, of speech, of action is even more desirable than perfection of administration; we would not be the subjects of an imperial master for all the advantages of Berlin. If we must choose, we prefer representative government even to good government. We would not exchange a poor administration representing the will of the whole people, susceptible of improvement as they become wiser, for a better one expressing only the ideas of a ruling class. To slavishly copy the methods of older communities would be as foolish as to decline to give any attention to their experience.

But with the rapid increase in the population of our great cities, and the growing complexity of their life, we may well inquire whether we cannot learn something as to the lines of profitable municipal development in America by a study of the work done abroad. When a European city is found to be promoting the well-being of its people by services of a character not yet undertaken by our municipalities, the question should at once be asked — Why cannot we, in our own way, do as much? The presumption should certainly be that the people of New York are capable of organizing any branch of public service which the city of Berlin finds it for the interest of its people to undertake.

There are three broad classes of municipal services: First, there are those which are of absolute necessity for the existence of a civilized urban community, such as the construction of streets, waterworks, and sewers, or the maintenance of police and fire departments, of hospitals and almshouses. Second, there are those which are now considered indispensable, if not of primary necessity, such as the inspection of certain articles of food, the regulation of the liquor traffic, the protection of the public health, together with the provision, either directly under the control of the city or through the agency of quasi-public corporations, of facilities for passenger transportation through the streets, and of gas and electricity. Third, there are those branches of public activity which provide for wants which are above the primary ones, which supply what may be called municipal conveniences or privileges. Under this heading fall libraries and facilities for higher education, parks, playgrounds, public baths, gymnasia, and facilities for recreation or comfort.

The principles of sound administration are very simple, and they are the same in America as in Europe. To make any executive organization efficient it must have a head — whether elected by universal suffrage, chosen by a select body, or appointed by the central government — who is entrusted with proper powers of control and direction. Perfect men would doubtless make any system of government produce good results; men as we find them only do satisfactory public work when it is properly systematized, coordinated, and controlled. If a large American city wants good government, it must entrust to some one man the full power of executive direction.

The successful performance of any important branch of work in a great city calls for careful and intelligent organization and constant watchfulness. To obtain results as good as those reached abroad we must, through universal suffrage, secure the adoption of the systems and methods best adapted for the purpose, and the appointment of administrative officers of the requisite capacity. The task of directing any important department of a great city calls for ability of a high order. Public opinion must be educated up to the point of demanding that, whatever play may be given to political forces, only men of the requisite qualifications shall be entrusted with high municipal office. This country is as rich as any in the world in capable administrators of large affairs. With proper city charters and the right men entrusted with power under them, we can immensely raise the standard of city administration in a short period of time.

A very large and important part of modern municipal work is of a purely technical character. The engineer, the landscape gardener, the architect, the physician, and other men of professional training have to be entrusted with it, either as regular officials or through special engagements. It is of the first importance to a large city to have a regular and capable professional force, maintained upon a permanent basis, independent of political changes; and this is perfectly possible even when the party system of government prevails. It is cheaper to have a dual organization, one political and one technical, than to forgo the advantages of having trained and experienced experts connected with every branch of work.

When outside professional work or advice is required for special pieces of work, the rule that only the best talent is good enough for the city should be constantly laid down and adhered to. The amount of public money that has been largely wasted in our American cities in erecting buildings designed by second- or third-rate architects is something not pleasant to contemplate. An aroused public opinion can readily control matters of this character.

The question whether such public services as lighting by gas or electricity and passenger transportation in the streets should be entrusted to corporations or performed directly by the municipality is one which is giving rise to a great deal of discussion in this country, and the sentiment in favor of municipal ownership is unquestionably growing. The fact that franchises and locations in the streets have been so universally given to private corporations in our great cities and that an enormous amount of capital has been invested in their securities makes any attempt to inaugurate the European practice of public ownership, with operation either directly by the city or under a lease from it, exceedingly difficult.

But aside from the question of dealing fairly with vested interests, there seems to me to be no reason why an American city should not take up any service of this character which may be recommended by business and financial considerations. There is no principle that stands in the way, for instance, of the municipal ownership and operation of an electric-light plant. It is purely a commercial question in each particular case. The electric-lighting business in particular, with the present improved dynamos and engines, is one which a properly organized city ought to be able to conduct for itself with some economy and advantage.

The argument is sometimes made that new fields of work of this character cannot safely be entered upon until the civil service system is more firmly established in our cities and their general standard of government is higher; but it does not seem to me that such reasoning rests upon a sound basis. Any extension of municipal functions must tend to arouse a public interest which cannot but assist in improving administration and hastening the adoption of a strict civil service system. The indifference of the more intelligent and well-to-do citizens, and their willingness to vote their party tickets blindly, while exercising little or no influence over party nominations, is the curse of many of our cities.

Businessmen of large and unselfish views can control a city government if they will take the pains to do so. If some extension of municipal functions in the directions above indicated would arouse some who are now apathetic to a sense of their vital interest in sound administration, it would do a good work. We should not therefore wait for a perfect municipal organization before we undertake any desirable addition to the services now rendered directly by the city, but should be willing to trust something to the educating and awakening effect of imposing further responsibilities upon a municipal government, and thus bringing it into a new and close relation with the citizens.

It should also be borne in mind that municipal ownership does not necessarily involve municipal operation. Even the highly organized cities of Europe, with their permanent civil service systems, find it better policy to lease certain franchises for a term of years than to operate directly such branches of public service as street-railway systems or gasworks. Many who are alarmed at the suggestion that an American city should manage a great and intricate electric-railway system, with its hundreds or even thousands of employees, are quite willing to consider fairly, as a question chiefly of finance, the proposition that a city should acquire the ownership of the street-railway locations and tracks in its streets, with a view to leasing them on proper terms and conditions for a period of years. It does not follow because municipal operation may be decidedly inexpedient that public ownership and control may not be desirable and beneficial.

In the case of electric-lighting plants, the conditions are such that ownership and operation naturally go together. The comparative simplicity of this service and the present perfection of apparatus make it a peculiarly favorable field for municipal enterprise. There are certainly many considerations in favor of placing the lighting of public streets, grounds, and buildings, at least, upon a municipal basis. Indeed, it seems to me that the case is so clear that the only question for a large city to consider is what legal difficulties or other embarrassments there may be in terminating existing relations with private companies.

In the present state of development of electricity and steam, any competent city engineer should be able to calculate the expense of installing, maintaining, and operating an electric-lighting plant for a given duty. Of course, if a city has not a competent technical and administrative force, it cannot successfully install and operate an electric-light plant; but neither can it properly build and maintain streets without such a force. The latter work calls for scientific and practical knowledge as much as the former; if a city government is properly organized for the one service, it can easily be adapted to the other. If looseness in methods of accounting and bookkeeping is tolerated, of course the real cost of electric lighting will not be shown; but neither will that of other branches of municipal service.

Aside from the question of general public

lighting, every large city should maintain a force of its own for doing all the electrical construction and repair work required in connection with its public buildings and institutions. Electricity must play a large part in the service of every progressive city, and everything pertaining to its use should be brought under the charge of a properly organized department of the city government.

Only the business considerations in favor of municipal ownership have been hitherto touched upon, but the broad political considerations are even stronger. The power now necessarily wielded by the great corporations which control such branches of public service as lighting and transportation often gives them too great an influence over municipal governments. It has been said that the government must either control corporations or be controlled by them. Without fully accepting this sweeping declaration, it must be admitted that there have been many cases in our American cities where corporations have practically dictated the action of city councils.

Their influence over nominations and elections, where they choose to exert it, may often be a determining one. Even a corporation holding a municipal franchise that has nothing further to ask of the city, and only desires to be allowed to prosecute its business without interference, is often drawn into municipal politics by the skillfully planned attacks of politicians who have purposes of their own in view. In short, the connection between quasi-public corporations and the city is necessarily so close that corporate interests are bound to make themselves powerfully felt at times, both by their command of capital and by their influence over large numbers of employees.

The great problem of municipal government under universal suffrage is to reduce the play of purely selfish or individual interests, so that elections may be decided upon broad grounds affecting the great mass of the citizens. The modern municipality touches so many people in such a variety of ways, and is necessarily brought into collision with so many private interests, that any narrowing of the scope of such interests is for the public good. It may be urged, on the other hand, that the influence of the additional city employees made necessary by the taking over of branches of service now performed by corporations will be equally great and equally selfish; but experience proves pretty conclusively that this is not the case.

It has frequently been demonstrated that any influence which may be exerted by municipal employees in favor of a party in power is likely to be fully offset by the opposition of those who have been disappointed in obtaining public office or employment. And even those engaged upon city work are sure to have grievances, real or imaginary, against the administration in power, and are never solidly united in its favor. Moreover, with the extension and firmer establishment of the civil service system, public employees are coming to feel fairly secure of their positions, regardless of political changes.

In respect to the third class of municipal services above mentioned, namely, those falling under the head of conveniences or privileges, the American city has been far behind its European prototype. In the variety and excellence of public facilities for healthful exercise, both indoors and in the open air, for bathing, and for the convenience and recreation of the people, we have much to learn from what has been done abroad; but we are fast waking up to this fact and are beginning to supply these deficiencies. Whatever theories may be entertained as to the proper limits of municipal service, or as to the purposes for which money raised by taxation may properly be spent, the doctrine that a city may advantageously assume any functions generally beneficial to its citizens has in our time become

firmly established in theory and is fast being put into practice.

Steps in the direction of what may fairly be called municipal socialism are undertaken with the full support of strong opponents of state socialism in its broad aspect. The question where to draw the line has now become one of expediency, or of financial limitation, scarcely one of principle. A large degree of paternalism is already an accepted fact in every great and progressive American city, and irresistible forces are constantly tending to widen still further the field of public action.

The wonderful growth of interest in athletics and in various kinds of outdoor sports which has taken place in this country within recent years has naturally directed attention to municipal gymnasia, playgrounds, and baths. The public is awakening to the fact that these can be supplied by municipal agency at an expense which is very small in comparison with that incurred for many other purposes or when measured by the widespread benefits conferred. Facilities for cleanliness, for physical development, and for healthful recreation tend to the social and moral development of the masses of the people. The duty of a city is to promote the civilization, in the fullest sense of the word, of all its citizens. No true civilization can exist without the provision of some reasonable opportunities for exercising the physical and mental faculties, of experiencing something of the variety and of the healthful pleasures of life, of feeling at least the degree of self-respect which personal cleanliness brings with it. The people of a city constitute a community, in all which that significant term implies; their interests are inextricably bound up together, and everything which promotes the well-being of a large part of the population benefits all.

Even from a purely economical standpoint, the provision of the municipal facilities above referred to is fully justifiable through their effect in increasing the capacity of men and women to perform useful service, whether manual or mental. The people of a city live by labor; they grow practically nothing from the soil, but they exchange their products or services for food grown by others, perhaps many thousands of miles away. Everything which increases the efficiency of labor, whether of the head or of the hand, increases the capacity of producing or of serving, and therefore adds to the means of livelihood of the community as a whole. The man or woman who is rested and stimulated by healthful change of occupation and by new ideas, who is afforded some opportunities of development, of enjoyment, and of social contact, becomes a more efficient agency for the production of wealth, to look at the matter from the lowest point of view.

But there is a much higher and truer standpoint. If any civilization is purely material in its aims, if it regards the masses or mankind merely as human machines for doing certain work, or as animals to be housed and fed merely that an appointed task may be performed, it will deservedly perish. The social elevation of man must, indeed, rest upon a secure material foundation. He must work, with all the powers with which he has been endowed, in order that he may have sufficient food, clothing, and shelter. But he does not work for these alone; they are but the foundations upon which he is to build. The object of his existence is the development of all his faculties, physical, mental, and spiritual. Toil is a necessary part of his training, but recreation is a part scarcely less important.

In cities, men are brought more closely together and have a greater number of vital interests in common than in the country. The sentiment of municipal solidarity is constantly growing, and the conception of the true functions of the city government is constantly widening. If socialism is ever attempted, it will come through great cities, not through agricultural settlements. In the great city, universal suffrage is subjected to its most crucial test; the results of that test, so full of import to humanity, will be estimated in the twentieth century. If the nineteenth century — as the period of municipal evolution in the United States — has contributed its full share of waste, inefficiency, and corruption, it can show some great achievements. There are encouraging signs that its closing years will be signalized by the growth of a sounder and broader civic spirit and a higher conception of the duties and opportunities of a great municipality.

For the accomplishment of results of far-reaching beneficence, nothing more is needed than that the same American intelligence, energy, and determination to succeed, which have gained such notable victories in every other field of commercial and intellectual activity, should apply themselves to the special problems presented by city governments. But these must be approached with full confidence that they can be solved. Without shutting our eyes to past failures or existing defects, let us not lose one whit of belief in the beneficent workings of the principle of political equality when it is given a fair chance. Let us set up a high ideal of what a city government should be and of what it should do for all its citizens, and then proceed, with reasonable caution but also with manly courage, to undertake any function or to discharge any duty which tends to promote the well-being of the people.

32.

Susan B. Anthony: The Status of Woman, Past, Present, and Future

By 1897 Susan B. Anthony had labored for over forty years, along with her dear friend Elizabeth Cady Stanton, for the right of women to vote. She was a legend in her own time and was admired for her devotion to and perseverance in the cause of woman suffrage. Girls who were tomboys, one author has noted, were called "Susan B's."
As co-founder of the National Woman Suffrage Association, she worked for the passage of a federal amendment granting women the vote. The amendment, often called the Anthony Amendment, was not ratified until 1920, but Miss Anthony displayed, in this article published in 1897 and reprinted here in part, the confidence and optimism that supported her through the many years of struggle.

Source: *Arena*, May 1897.

Fifty years ago woman in the United States was without a recognized individuality in any department of life. No provision was made in public or private schools for her education in anything beyond the rudimentary branches. An educated woman was a rarity and was gazed upon with something akin to awe. The women who were known in the world of letters, in the entire country, could be easily counted upon the ten fingers. Margaret Fuller, educated by her father, a Harvard graduate and distinguished lawyer, stood preeminently at the head and challenged the admiration of such men as Emerson, Channing, and Greeley. . . .

Such was the helpless, dependent, fettered condition of woman when the first Woman's Rights Convention was called just forty-nine years ago, at Seneca Falls, N.Y., by Elizabeth Cady Stanton and Lucretia Mott. . . .

While there had been individual demands, from time to time, the first organized body to formulate a declaration of the rights of women was the one which met at Seneca Falls, July 19-20, 1848, and adjourned to meet at Rochester two weeks later. In the Declaration of Sentiments and the Resolutions there framed, every point was covered that, down to the present day, has been contended for by the advocates of equal rights for women. Every inequality of the existing laws and customs was carefully considered and a thorough and complete readjustment demanded. . . .

Now, at the end of half a century, we find that, with few exceptions, all of the demands formulated at this convention have been granted. The great exception is the yielding of political rights, and toward this one point are directed now all the batteries of scorn, of ridicule, of denunciation that formerly poured their fire all along the line. Although not one of the predicted calamities occurred upon the granting of the other demands, the world is asked to believe that all of them will happen if this last stronghold is surrendered.

There is not space to follow the history of the last fifty years and study the methods by which these victories have been gained, but there is not one foot of advanced ground upon which women stand today that has not been obtained through the hard-fought battles of other women. The close of this 19th century finds every trade, vocation, and profession open to women, and every opportunity at their command for preparing themselves to follow these occupations.

The girls as well as the boys of a family now fit themselves for such careers as their tastes and abilities permit. A vast amount of the household drudgery that once monopolized the whole time and strength of the mother and daughters has been taken outside and turned over to machinery in vast establishments. A money value is placed upon the labor of women. The ban of social ostracism has been largely removed from the woman wage earner. She who can make for herself a place of distinction in any line of work receives commendation instead of condemnation. Woman is no longer compelled to marry for support, but may herself make her own home and earn her own financial independence.

With but few exceptions, the highest institutions of learning in the land are as freely opened to girls as to boys, and they may receive their degrees at legal, medical, and theological colleges, and practise their professions without hindrance. In the world of literature and art, women divide the honors with men; and our civil service rules have secured for them many thousands of remunerative positions under the government.

It is especially worthy of note that along with this general advancement of women has come a marked improvement in household methods. Woman's increased intelligence manifests itself in this department as conspicuously as in any other. Education, culture, mental discipline, business training develop far more capable mothers and housewives than were possible under the old regime. Men of the present generation give especial thought to comradeship in the

selection of a wife, and she is no less desirable in their eyes because she is a college graduate or has learned the value and the management of money through having earned it.

There has been a radical revolution in the legal status of woman. In most states the old common law has been annulled by legislative enactment, through which partial justice, at least, has been done to married women. In nearly every state they may retain and control property owned at marriage and all they may receive by gift or inheritance thereafter, and also their earnings outside the home. They may sue and be sued, testify in the courts, and carry on business in their own name, but in no state have wives any ownership in the joint earnings.

In six or seven states, mothers have equal guardianship of the children. While in most states the divorce laws are the same for men and women, they never can bear equally upon both while all the property earned during marriage belongs wholly to the husband. There has been such a modification in public sentiment, however, that, in most cases, courts and juries show a marked leniency toward women.

The department of politics has been slowest to give admission to women. Suffrage is the pivotal right, and if it could have been secured at the beginning, women would not have been half a century in gaining the privileges enumerated above, for privileges they must be called so long as others may either give or take them away. If women could make the laws or elect those who make them, they would be in the position of sovereigns instead of subjects. Were they the political peers of man, they could command instead of having to beg, petition, and pray. Can it be possible it is for this reason that men have been so determined in their opposition to grant to women political power?

But even this stronghold is beginning to

yield to the long and steady pressure. In twenty-five states women possess suffrage in school matters; in four states they have a limited suffrage in local affairs; in one state they have municipal suffrage; in four states they have full suffrage, local, state, and national. Women are becoming more and more interested in political questions and public affairs. Every campaign sees greater numbers in attendance at the meetings, and able woman speakers are now found upon the platforms of all parties. Especial efforts are made by politicians to obtain the support of women, and during the last campaign one of the presidential candidates held special meetings for women in the large cities throughout the country.

Some of the finest political writing in the great newspapers of the day is done by women, and the papers are extensively read by women of all classes. In many of the large cities women have formed civic clubs and are exercising a distinctive influence in municipal matters. In most of the states of the Union women are eligible for many offices, state and county superintendents, registers of deeds, etc. They are deputies to state, county, and city officials, notaries public, state librarians, and enrolling and engrossing clerks in the legislatures.

It follows, as a natural result, that in the states where women vote they are eligible to all offices. They have been sent as delegates to national conventions, made presidential electors, and are sitting today as members in both the upper and lower houses of the legislatures. In some towns all the offices are filled by women. These radical changes have been effected without any social upheaval or domestic earthquakes, family relations have suffered no disastrous changes, and the men of the states where women vote furnish the strongest testimony in favor of woman suffrage.

There is no more striking illustration of the progress that has been made by woman than that afforded by her changed position in the church. Under the old regime the Quakers were the only sect who recognized the equality of women. Other denominations enforced the command of St. Paul, that women should keep silence in the churches. A few allowed the women to lift up their voices in class and prayer meetings, but they had no vote in matters of church government. Even the missionary and charity work was in the hands of men.

Now the Unitarians, Universalists, Congregationalists, Wesleyan and Protestant Methodists, Christians, Free-Will Baptists, and possibly a few others, ordain women as ministers, and many parishes, in all parts of the country, are presided over by women preachers. The charitable and missionary work of the churches is practically turned over to women, who raise and disburse immense sums of money. While many of the great denominations still refuse to ordain women, to allow them a seat in their councils, or a vote in matters of church government, yet women themselves are, in a large measure, responsible for this state of affairs.

Forming, as they do, from two-thirds to three-fourths of the membership, raising the greater part of the funds, and carrying on the active work of the church, when they unite their forces and assert their rights, the small minority of men, who have usurped the authority, will be obliged to yield to their just demands. The creeds of the churches will recognize woman's equality before God as the codes of the states have acknowledged it before man and the law.

By far the larger part of the progressive movements just enumerated have taken place during the last twenty-five years, and the progress has been most rapid during the last half of this quarter of a century. With the advantages already obtained, with the great liberalizing of public sentiment, and with the actual proof that the results of enlarged opportunities for women have been for the betterment of society, the next decade ought to see the completion of the struggle for the equality of the sexes.

The hardest of the battles have been

fought, and, while there is still need for both generals and soldiers, the greatest necessity is for the body of women to take possession and hold the ground that has been gained. It is not sufficient that women should fill positions as well as men; they must give vastly better satisfaction in order to prove their claims. There is an urgent demand for women of the highest character and intelligence, because the whole sex will be judged by the few who come forward to assume these new duties.

While by the momentum already gained the reforms demanded would eventually come, women have learned the value of organization and united, systematic work in securing the best and speediest results. It is no longer necessary to make an effort for further educational facilities. The few universities which still close their doors to women will ultimately be compelled to open them by the exigencies of the situation. There are no longer any fences around the industrial field, although men will continue to have the best pickings in the pasture so long as women are disfranchised. There will be a gradual yielding of the laws in recognition of woman's improved position in all departments, but here also there never will be complete equality until women themselves help to make laws and elect lawmakers. In view of this indisputable fact, the advanced thinkers are agreed that the strongest efforts should be concentrated upon this point.

From that little convention at Seneca Falls, with a following of a handful of women scattered through half-a-dozen different states, we have now the great National Association, with headquarters in New York City, and auxiliaries in almost every state in the Union. These state bodies are effecting a thorough system of county and local organizations for the purpose of securing legislation favorable to women, and especially to obtain amendments to their state constitutions. As evidence of the progress of public opinion, more than half

Library of Congress

Susan B. Anthony, who dedicated her life to crusading for equal rights for women

of the legislatures in session during the past winter have discussed and voted upon bills for the enfranchisement of women, and in most of them they were adopted by one branch and lost by a very small majority in the other. The legislatures of Washington and South Dakota have submitted woman-suffrage amendments to their electors for 1898, and vigorous campaigns will be made in those states during the next two years.

For a quarter of a century Wyoming has stood as a conspicuous object lesson in woman suffrage, and is now reinforced by the three neighboring states of Colorado, Utah, and Idaho. With this central group, standing on the very crest of the Rocky Mountains, the spirit of justice and freedom for women cannot fail to descend upon all the Western and Northwestern states. No one who makes a careful study of this question can help but believe that, in a very few years, all the states west of the Mississippi River will have enfranchised their women.

While the efforts of each state are concentrated upon its own legislature, all of the states combined in the national organization are directing their energies toward securing a Sixteenth Amendment to the Constitution of the United States. The demands of this body have been received with respectful and encouraging attention from Congress. Hearings have been granted by the committees of both houses, resulting, in a number of instances, in favorable reports. Upon one occasion the question was brought to a discussion in the Senate and received the affirmative vote of one-third of the members.

Until woman has obtained "that right protective of all other rights — the ballot," this agitation must still go on, absorbing the time and the energy of our best and strongest women. Who can measure the advantages that would result if the magnificent abilities of these women could be devoted to the needs of government, society, home, instead of being consumed in the struggle to obtain their birthright of individual freedom? Until this be gained we can never know, we cannot even prophesy, the capacity and power of woman for the uplifting of humanity.

It may be delayed longer than we think; it may be here sooner than we expect; but the day will come when man will recognize woman as his peer, not only at the fireside but in the councils of the nation. Then, and not until then, will there be the perfect comradeship, the ideal union between the sexes that shall result in the highest development of the race. What this shall be we may not attempt to define, but this we know, that only good can come to the individual or to the nation through the rendering of exact justice.

33.

Songs of Errant Ladies

Singing was a popular pastime in the 1890s, when radio and television did not yet exist and people still found it possible to entertain themselves. Barbershop quartets and choral societies were found in every town, and gathering around the piano to play and sing the popular songs of the day was a common social activity. Many of the songs were sentimental and reflected the romantic and nostalgic feelings that marked the decade. Tales of fallen women and of the dangers of city life were popular, especially in rural areas. "A Bird in a Gilded Cage" and "Just Tell Them That You Saw Me" are examples of the type.

A BIRD IN A GILDED CAGE

The ballroom was filled with fashion's throng,
It shone with a thousand lights;
And there was a woman who passed along,
The fairest of all the sights.
A girl to her lover then softly sighed,
"There's riches at her command."
"But she married for wealth, not for love," he cried,
"Though she lives in a mansion grand.

"She's only a bird in a gilded cage,
A beautiful sight to see.
You may think she's happy and free from care,
She's not, though she seems to be.
'Tis sad when you think of her wasted life,
For youth cannot mate with age;
And her beauty was sold for an old man's gold;
She's a bird in a gilded cage."

I stood in a churchyard just at eve,
When sunset adorned the west;
And looked at the people who'd come to grieve
For loved ones now laid at rest.
A tall marble monument marked the grave
Of one who'd been fashion's queen;
And I thought "She is happier here at rest,
Than to have people say when seen:

"She's only a bird in a gilded cage,
A beautiful sight to see.
You may think she's happy and free from care,
She's not, though she seems to be.
'Tis sad when you think of her wasted life,
For youth cannot mate with age;
And her beauty was sold for an old man's gold;
She's a bird in a gilded cage."

ARTHUR J. LAMB

JUST TELL THEM THAT YOU SAW ME

While strolling down the street one eve upon mere pleasure bent,
'Twas after business worries of the day,
I saw a girl who shrank from me in whom I recognized
My schoolmate in a village far away.
"Is that you, Madge?" I said to her; she quickly turned away.
"Don't turn away, Madge, I am still your friend;
Next week I'm going back to see the old folks and I thought
Perhaps some message you would like to send."

Chorus:
"Just tell them that you saw me," she said. "They'll know the rest.
Just tell them I was looking well, you know.
Just whisper if you get a chance to Mother dear, and say,
I love her as I did long, long ago."

"Your cheeks are pale, your face is thin, come tell me, were you ill?
When last we met your eye shone clear and bright.
Come home with me when I go, Madge, the change will do you good.
Your Mother wonders where you are tonight."
"I long to see them all again, but not just yet," she said;
"'Tis pride alone that's keeping me away.
Just tell them not to worry, for I'm all right, don't you know?
Tell Mother I am coming home some day."

PAUL DRESSER

34.

THEODORE ROOSEVELT: Obstacles to Immediate Expansion

*As assistant secretary of the navy, Theodore Roosevelt tried to implement his
expansionist beliefs. Convinced that a large navy was indispensable to any world
power (a role he desired mightily for the United States), he advocated the building
of a two-ocean navy and the acquisition of bases in the Pacific, specifically Hawaii.
His intellectual mentor, Alfred Thayer Mahan, had supplied him with the theoretical
justification of these views. Opposition to the annexation of Hawaii came from
anti-imperialists in this country as well as from Japan; the population of Hawaii was
one-fourth Japanese, and the government in Tokyo hoped to acquire the islands for
itself. Roosevelt described, in this confidential letter written to Mahan on May 3,
1897, his plan of action.*

Source: *Papers of Theodore Roosevelt*, Manuscript Division, Library of Congress, pp. 225-231.

THIS LETTER MUST, of course, be considered as entirely confidential, because in my position I am merely carrying out the policy of the secretary and the President. I suppose I need not tell you that as regards Hawaii I take your views absolutely, as indeed I do on foreign policy generally. If I had my way we would annex those islands tomorrow. If that is impossible I would establish a protectorate over them.

I believe we should build the Nicaraguan canal at once, and, in the meantime, that we should build a dozen new battleships, half of them on the Pacific Coast; and these battleships should have large coal capacity and a consequent increased radius of action.

I am fully alive to the danger from Japan, and I know that it is idle to rely on any sentimental goodwill toward us.

I think President Cleveland's action was a colossal crime, and we should be guilty of aiding him after the fact if we do not reverse what he did. I earnestly hope we can make the President look at things our way. Last Saturday night Lodge pressed his views upon him with all his strength. I have been getting matters in shape on the Pacific Coast just as fast as I have been allowed.

My own belief is that we should act instantly before the two new Japanese warships leave England. I would send the *Oregon*, and, if necessary, also the *Monterey* (either with a deck load of coal or accompanied by a coaling ship) to Hawaii, and would hoist our flag over the island, leaving all details for after action. I shall press these views upon my chief just so far as he will let me; more I cannot do.

As regards what you say in your letter, there is only one point to which I would take exception. I fully realize the immense importance of the Pacific Coast. Strictly between ourselves, I do not think Admiral Beardslee quite the man for the situation out there; but Captain Barker, of the *Oregon,* is, I believe, excellent in point of decisions, willingness to accept responsibility, and thorough knowledge of the situation.

But there are big problems in the West Indies also. Until we definitely turn Spain out of those islands (and if I had my way that would be done tomorrow), we will always be menaced by trouble there. We should acquire the Danish Islands and, by turning Spain out, should serve notice that no strong European power, and especially not Germany, should be allowed to gain a foothold by supplanting some weak European power. I do not fear England — Canada is a hostage for her good behavior — but I do fear some of the other powers.

I am extremely sorry to say that there is some slight appearance here of the desire to stop building up the Navy until our finances are better. Tom Reed, to my astonishment and indignation, takes this view; and even my chief, who is one of the most high-minded, honorable, and upright gentlemen I have ever had the good fortune to serve under, is a little inclined toward it.

I need not say that this letter must be strictly private. I speak to you with the greatest freedom, for I sympathize with your views, and I have precisely the same idea of patriotism and of belief in and love for our country. But to no one else excepting Lodge do I talk like this.

As regards Hawaii, I am delighted to be able to tell you that Secretary Long shares

Theodore Roosevelt, from a stereograph showing him in the uniform of colonel of the "Rough Riders" following his return from Cuba

our views. He believes we should take the islands, and I have just been preparing some memoranda for him to use at the Cabinet meeting tomorrow. If only we had some good man in the place of John Sherman as secretary of state there would not be a hitch, and even as it is I hope for favorable action. I have been pressing upon the secretary, and through him on the President, that we ought to act now without delay, before Japan gets her two new battleships which are now ready for delivery to her in England. Even a fortnight may make a difference. With Hawaii once in our hands most of the danger of friction with Japan would disappear.

The secretary also believes in building the Nicaraguan canal as a military measure, although I don't know that he is as decided on this point as you and I are; and he believes in building battleships on the Pacific slope.

35.

Philip G. Hubert: The Business of a Factory

In the prolonged conflict between corporate power and labor that characterized the closing years of the nineteenth century, big business often found apologists among writers who gave detailed accounts in praise of factory operations. In this way, the public was informed of the difficulties in managing a big business, of the complexities involved in producing goods, and of the great risks taken by the owners. All in all, the impression given was that capitalists were among the most selfless and patriotic people in the country. Scribner's magazine published a series called "The Conduct of Great Businesses" in 1897, and Philip Hubert wrote an article, reprinted here in part, on the cotton mills.

Source: *Scribner's*, March 1897.

One feature of the manufacturing industries of a country that makes them of perhaps more interest than the agricultural industries is the constant change in the character of the product as well as in the methods of manufacture. The farmers' products seldom or never change. The wheat sealed up in Egyptian tombs 1,500 years before the birth of Christ is found to be identical with that grown in Egypt today, and, upon being planted, yields a similar crop to that now grown.

Not only do manufactured objects change every few years but the field is constantly enlarged by the appearance of new things to make — things not dreamed of a few years ago. Electricity now gives employment to hundreds of thousands of persons whose great-grandfathers never heard of a telegraph, a telephone, an electric light, or a motor. While new farms spring up every day in the wilderness, it is always the same old wheat or corn that results. But every day some new factory begins turning out a product the like of which was never seen

before, and, in some cases, let us hope, may not be seen again. More than this, it is not reasonable to suppose that this stream of novelty which began to flow with the printing press, the steam engine, and the electric spark will ever cease.

It would be strange if we happy possessors of these wonderful tools, unknown to our forefathers, should fail to profit by them and turn out still more wonderful things in the future. The next century ought certainly to give the world gifts as valuable as steam and electricity. The factories of 1997 will make wonders of which we have no conception.

The field is, however, already so large that one branch of manufacture must be taken as a type of all, and I have selected the making of calicoes as offering the best illustrations of this business of manufacturing. The business problems met with by the man who undertakes to buy cotton, weave, print, and sell it as calico are similar in kind with those of the man who makes shoes or lamps or watches. They involve accurate judgment, not only of what the public is asking for but — far more important — what it is going to ask for; the purchase of raw material, the hiring of labor, the judicious management of an army of people so as to avoid laxity on one hand and strikes on the other, the discovery of new and better processes, the choice of designs, the manufacture itself, finally the disposal of the product by a thousand channels, native and foreign.

Let me, therefore, take a big cotton mill making and printing its own calicoes as the type of an American manufacturing business. If a man wants to enter the business of making calicoes, the question of capital is the first consideration. Most of our cotton mills and paper mills are stock corporations, largely because of the vast capital needed. The larger the plant the cheaper the product is an axiom in the cotton business, especially when staple goods, such as sheetings, are to be made. There is always a market here or abroad for American sheeting, and the sales are often made in such vast quantities that the danger of overstocking the market is as nothing compared with fancy dress goods, shoes, or worsted cloths, the fashions of which change from one year to another. It is not unusual to hear of the sale of thousands of bales of sheetings in one operation.

It follows, therefore, that the manufacturer must be ready to take advantage of these periods of profit, so to speak, and be ready with his tens of thousands of bales of goods, where the manufacturer of goods liable to depreciation through change of fashion, such as shoes, hats, fancy printed cloths, etc., does not dare to manufacture much beyond the current demand of the market and is consequently debarred from manufacture upon the vast scale seen in the mills at Fall River, Lowell, and Lawrence. The capital needed for cotton mills being therefore very large — the mill I have selected as a type having a capital of $3 mil-

lion and its property being assessed at nearly $5 million — the ownership is commonly held by a stock company.

Boston is said to depend for its cake upon the profits of the New England cotton mills. When cotton goods sell at a loss, Commonwealth Avenue, metaphorically speaking, is reduced to bread. It speaks well for the business that in the last twenty-five years there have been no failures of importance among the New England cotton mills. . . .

The necessary capital having been subscribed and the manufacture of cotton goods decided upon, the question of site is next to be settled. In the past, good waterpower has been of the chief importance in the selection of a mill site. The splendid waterpower on the Merrimac, at Lowell, Nashua, Lawrence, and elsewhere, explained the existence of gigantic mills at these places. Steam, however, is rapidly replacing waterpower, notwithstanding the improvements made in turbine wheels. In most of the older mills of New England, steam now shares about equally the work with water, while in the new mills it takes almost the whole burden. Of course in factories where the power needed is small, such as in making hats, clothing, shoes, etc., steam has entirely replaced water, the higher cost being of no importance when its greater reliability is considered. As yet electricity has not appeared as motive power, except in small industries. What the tremendous works at Niagara will do in this field remains to be seen. It is easier with electricity to adapt the power to the needs of the day, whether they are great or small, than with steam. Mr. Atkinson foresees the ultimate dispersion of these mill armies to their homes, when electric power can be sent from place to place without loss; then, as before the introduction of steam power, the weaver will work his loom and the spinner his spindles in his own cottage instead of in the big mill.

Whether or not the change will be to the benefit of the operative is still a mooted question among experts. One of the agents of a big mill, a man who has studied the problem at close quarters for twenty years, tells me that the change would be a misfortune for the mill hand. In the mill the worker has the law as his champion in providing good air and light and in limiting the hours of labor; in his own cottage the hours of labor will be measured only by the endurance of the weaker members of the family, while the sanitary arrangements are apt to be defective as compared to those of a modern mill.

It is commonly admitted that while a man or woman who does some small thing in the manufacture of an article — whether it is piecing the broken yarns of a spinning machine or cutting the eye of a needle or gathering matches for boxing — may become marvelously expert, the operator runs the risk of becoming more or less of a machine. The girl who stands at the end of a frame of one hundred spindles and sees a broken thread catches it with lightning-like rapidity and joins it with a touch; the one who cuts the eyes in needles can do the same thing with a human hair; and the girls who pack matches pick up the requisite number for the box, whether it is one hundred, more or less, without counting them, judging simply by touch whether or not the right number is there, and doing it as fast as the eye can follow the hand. Mr. Ruskin contends, probably with reason, that the minute division of labor that makes such wonders possible brutalizes the laborer and that if the girl made the whole article instead of doing one operation out of fifty, she would gain in intelligence if not in expertness.

From an economic, or rather an industrial, point of view, however, manufacturing has to be carried on at present with the greatest subdivision of labor possible. Fierce competition and a small margin of profit

demand it. . . . This minute subdivision of labor which threatens, according to some economists, to make the operative only a part of a machine and needing to be little more intelligent than one of its wheels, may go on at one end of the industry to be counterbalanced at the other end by a process of aggrandizement. Just as in the large cities the department store is absorbing the smaller shops of its neighborhood, so the large factory of the future may absorb its smaller rivals, not only in the same branch of industry but in many others. There are great mills in New England today which not only spin and weave but print, using wool and silk as well as cotton, something unheard of a few years ago. It is an interesting speculation among experts as to how long it will be before the same gigantic mill will turn out cotton goods, woolen goods, silks, shoes, umbrellas, hats and caps, and writing paper. The very process that makes the operative merely the attendant upon a machine favors such a development. . . .

The business organization of most big factories is simple enough. Almost all cotton mill properties are managed by a board of directors elected by the stockholders. These directors appoint officers, among whom the treasurer and the agent are the important personages, the first having charge of the finances, the buying of supplies, payment of expenses, and selling of goods; the second having the actual manufacture of the goods under his control, the hiring of labor, the management of the shops or mills. The treasurer of most New England manufacturing corporations lives in Boston, where the goods are sold, and the agent lives near the mills.

Taking a big cotton mill, the agent employs a head or superintendent for each of the important departments, such as the carding, roving, spinning, weaving, bleaching, printing, and packing. Under these superintendents there may be many or few foremen, according to the character of the work. In some departments where the work is all of the same character, each girl of the 300 in a room doing precisely what her neighbor does, year in and year out, a few foremen suffice. . . .

As in most other trades, strikes are the bane of the factory owner's existence. With a plant worth perhaps $1 million brought to a standstill and perhaps $500,000 worth of raw material in process of manufacture, a strike coming at an awkward time of year means tremendous loss.

Next in importance, or perhaps even of more importance than the character of the hands, comes the character of the machinery in use. The entire machinery of a mill may be said to change every twenty years, just as the entire material of the human body is said to change every seven years, or eleven years — I forget which. I asked one mill superintendent, a veteran who has seen the inside of about every mill in the country, what he looked at most carefully upon entering a rival establishment. "First the machinery, then the hands." . . .

The Rabbeth spindle, invented in 1866 by Francis J. Rabbeth of Ilion, N.Y., has effected a saving of $100 million to this country since its introduction about 1870. . . . What is done today in the new mills just finished at the South would astonish the millhands of twenty years ago. As a rule, these changes in cotton machinery have been introduced without opposition. The spinning and weaving, for instance, are paid for by the piece, so that, the introduction of the Rabbeth spindle, doing twice the work and requiring actually less care and watchfulness on the part of the operator, found its champions as well as its detractors. . . . In a big manufactory it is not everything to invent a laborsaving machine; endless tact must be used to induce the unions to allow its use.

That the purchase of raw material for a big factory requires the services of a dozen experts may well be imagined when the vast sums of money involved are considered. In one cotton mill of New England there was used last year 25,000 bales of cotton, worth about $1 million; 8 million pounds of wool; 50,000 tons of coal; and $100,000 worth of coloring matter and dyes. It is hardly necessary to say that an expert at a liberal salary the year round is essential for each of these purchases. The cotton buyer spends his whole time in the South watching the growing crops, purchasing sometimes a year before the crop is grown, keeping an eye on the stock on hand in different parts of the country, and calculating to a nicety exactly what will be needed and when. All the cotton for a big mill is thus bought where it is grown. . . .

The coloring matter used in printing a yard of calico that sells for 10 cents costs less than the twentieth part of a cent, yet fortunes have been spent in recent years in efforts to reduce this cost. It is said that one mill owner of Rhode Island spent $70,000 inside of three years in experiments to replace madder dyes — the experiments, by the way, leading to nothing valuable in the end. The chemist at one cotton mill I have in mind, a modest man who spends his time mixing colors and testing dyes in his laboratory, receives a salary of $5,000 a year. He has to know not only how to prepare the colors for the printers but how to insure their permanency. "Will it wash?" is about the first question asked by every woman who examines a piece of calico on the dry-goods counter. The chemist is responsible for that.

The labor charge in the cost of a manufactured article varies so much with the character of the product that separate figures, or tables of figures, would be required for each factory. In plain sheeting it is small as compared to fancy prints and fine woolens; in shoes, the more expensive the shoe the greater proportion of cost goes to the workman. For this reason it has been suggested that in parts of the country where labor is cheap, the finest goods, those requiring most hand labor, would be most profitable to make. But as yet the rule is the other way, the older manufacturing communities having a monopoly of expert labor. . . .

A factory having been put up in a suitable spot, equipped with proper machinery, and a force of competent hands engaged, the important question arises: What kind of goods shall be made? This is a question to be decided by the persons who sell the product of the mill — the selling agents. Under the direction of these agents, the art director, so to speak, of the corporation seeks high and low for designs, takes suggestions where he can, employs designers and artists. We can surpass the world at machinery, but as yet we have to go to Paris for our designs. Each of the big mills where printed goods are made keeps its man in Paris watching the new designs and buying the best he can from the professional designers, of which there are a hundred in Paris, some of them earning as high as $20,000 a year. A designer of international reputation commands his own price inasmuch as the design makes or mars the product; it sells or does not sell according to the favor the pattern meets with.

The question is often asked: How do the men who make designs know what kind of goods the public is going to demand? The designs for next winter's goods are already finished. How does the artist know that the fickle public is not going to discard all that it has admired this year and go wild over what it now ignores? This year the colors are faint and suggestive; next year they may be kaleidoscopic in brilliancy. This year ladies' shoes run to a point, next year they may be square-toed. Upon an accurate forecast of the public's whims in these matters depends success. Well, the truth seems to be that, sudden or violent as these fluctuations appear, there is really an evolutionary process involved. Each style or fashion has in it the germs of what is to follow, perhaps visible only to experts but to be discerned. The designer accents the peculiar attributes of a pattern that has found favor one year in order to create his design for the next season. The short life of a design is somewhat surprising. . . .

The element of chance thus enters more or less into any manufacture dependent upon changes of fashion. As the styles for summer have to be made in winter and those for winter in summer, a manufacturer cannot wait to see what the public wants; he has to take his chances. What he has made may or may not meet with favor. If it does not, his whole product will have to be sold at cost or less, to be sent to the confines of civilization. . . .

A factory having produced a stock of goods from the best designs to be obtained by its agents here and abroad, the next step is to sell at a profit. Twenty-five years ago the mill or factory sold all its goods to the jobbers, who in turn distributed them to the retailers throughout the country. Each mill had its selling agents, who undertook to dispose of its product to the jobbers. A retailer could buy nothing directly from the agent of the mill. Within the last ten or fifteen years, the small jobber has been eliminated. In 1850, there were half a hundred dry-goods jobbers in New York City and as many in Boston, all doing a good business. Today, the number has dwindled to half a dozen in each city. The same thing is true of Philadelphia and Chicago. Only a few of the very largest jobbing houses have survived. The selling agents of the mills now go direct to the retailer because the retailers have in many instances become buyers upon a much larger scale than the small jobber of former days.

Go into the Boston or New York office of the agent of any important mill and you will find plenty of samples and clerks but almost no buyers. The agent now goes to the buyer. The agent of the largest cotton mill in western Massachusetts told me that he sent his men to every large dry-goods shop in Boston every day, and his partner in New York did the same thing there. At certain seasons, Boston and New York, twenty-five or thirty years ago, were over-run with the buyers of dry-goods houses from all parts of the country. There were hotels and even newspapers devoted to these buyers and their doings. Much of this business has passed away. Today the travel-ing men, "drummers," of the mills and the few large jobbing houses that have survived, scour the country, taking their samples to the retailer.

A few large jobbers, doing an immense business, still survive in all our large centers because they have the machinery for the distribution of goods in channels where it is not worth the while of the agent to enter — small shops in small towns. The small jobber who gave up business when he found the mills selling directly to the retail shops, who could buy even more goods at a time than he could, had neither the capital nor the army of traveling men necessary to do business upon this scale. The jobber who could buy 5,000 cases of goods at a time and had the machinery and the means for disposing of it survives because the mills sell cheapest to the largest buyer, and the job-ber who buys on this scale is more impor-tant than even the largest retail store. But the small jobber, buying 100 cases of the same goods, gets no better terms than the big retailer and has therefore no excuse for being. Some of the big department stores now obtain a monopoly of certain patterns or designs by taking the whole output of the mill, thus doing what was formerly in the power of only the greatest of job-bers. . . .

The search for a foreign outlet for Ameri-can manufactures began more than half a century ago and still goes on. Every year some new market is discovered. Our old competitor England fights hard, but we can often beat her on her own ground. Every-one may know that we sent our New En-gland cotton cloth to the British colonies by the thousand cases, but it may be news to many that 25,000 American plows went to the Argentine Republic last year, and that the thousands of watches distributed to the Japanese Army as rewards of bravery were made in this country. American trademarks have always been and now are of exception-al value the world over, and this notwith-standing the frequent imitations of them practised by foreign competitors in the past. . . .

It should also be said that nearly all the English houses which had imitated Ameri-can marks, in many cases ignorantly, being instructed to copy certain brands from pat-terns furnished them by their customers abroad, promptly discontinued the practice when the facts were made known to them. No less than twenty-seven imitations of one American brand were thus voluntarily with-drawn. For years past, however, the export of American cotton goods to India and Chi-na has more than resumed its old propor-tions, the shipments for 1896 having ex-ceeded those of any previous year.

Clothes make the man. Naked people have little or no influence in society.

Samuel L. Clemens ("Mark Twain")

36.

Thomas B. Reed: Empire Can Wait

With growing numbers of articulate Americans urging territorial expansion beyond the country's borders, Thomas B. Reed's counsel to postpone the attainment of an empire appeared reactionary to many people. Propagandists for the annexation of Hawaii were impatient; advocates of armed intervention in Cuba demanded action; and spokesmen for the Social Darwinist position argued that it was our destiny to dominate the world. In opposition to these views, Reed, speaker of the House and one of the ablest parliamentarians ever to grace the American political scene, maintained that the United States' strength was in her slow, gradual growth and not in a reckless policy of expansion. His belief was succinctly expressed in this article, published at the end of 1897.

Source: *Illustrated American*, December 4, 1897.

The thing which most engages our attention in history is the growth and decay of empires. There seems to be a natural law operating through all time and through all space. By this law the very extension of an empire seems by its own power and nature to plant the seeds of that decay which has been thus far universal through all time. The Chaldean Empire, the first of all of which there is much record, lived for 450 years and expanded over an area of 500,000 square miles, and then of its own weight fell to pieces.

Assyria succeeded, starting about the size of Nebraska, and after six centuries and a half disappeared as a great empire. Parthia, hardly remembered except from the "Parthian Arrow" in literature, once covered, under the sway of poison-proof Mithridates, 450,000 square miles, a portion of the earth only a little larger than Texas, New Mexico, and the Indian Territory, and 150,000 square miles smaller than the great region of frozen wealth purchased by Mr. Seward of the empire of Russia.

The Roman Empire, symbol even today of grandeur and renown, the greatest nation that has thus far ever lived, comprised at its zenith of power only half of Europe, a portion of Asia, and that strip of Africa which is bounded by most southern waters of the gentle Mediterranean. It also fell of its own weight and greatness, and was conscious that it must fall. The division which was made into the Eastern and the Western Empire, though disguised as a mere administrative division, was a confession, of itself, that the vast regions had become entirely too great for the resources of that year of Our Lord. Nevertheless, no other nation had up to that time laid foundations so permanent, so deep, and so nearly indestructible.

There have been other great empires which have been able to last only a few years, not even completing a century. The military and administrative genius of Napoleon backed up by the great source of his power, the wild enthusiasm of the French Revolution, and the concord between its principles and the general movement of the world outside enabled him to establish an empire which is entitled to no mean comparison with the great structures of the past.

It illustrated, also, within half a lifetime, the process of growth and decay which in more ancient history had required the passing of centuries.

One set of facts runs through all these histories and through all the great displays of generalship and statesmanship: the need of union and the tendency to discord. There were mighty men in all the ages who struggled with a problem, always old, and forever new — the problem of union under one government of diverse nations, giving peace and protection to all, peace within their own borders, and protection against the hordes which ranged themselves outside, pouring from realms unknown, which were teeming with populations, the innumerable vastness of which can hardly be accounted for even by all the discoveries of modern science.

All the genius for war and for statesmanship seems to have been furnished in the due time without fail, as if they were the birth of great necessities and the outcome of the wants of man. When each great empire disappeared, the warring factions and the dismembered governments by the very force of their own disorders were obliged to unite to save themselves from themselves, and from all savage outsiders.

So, on the ruins of one empire arose the monuments of another. But every rapid uprise of empire was the sure precursor of a rapid fall. Had the empire born out of the French Revolution been the slow growth of centuries, centuries would have been needed for its decline. Rome established itself in its long permanence because it understood in some vague way one of the conditions of its life. The great military roads which penetrated into all parts of the broad expanse of the earth's surface conquered by that great people and the distribution of the rank of citizen of Rome are examples of what helped to bind the lands together with more firmness than even the short swords of the trained legionaries.

There are now flourishing still greater empires than those of the past. Rome, when she proclaimed herself the conqueror of the world and sat serenest on her seven hills, had neither the territory nor the population of Russia or of Great Britain, and was in no sense so mighty as either. These modern empires are still pushing forth their arts and arms. Each of the years as they roll by show an enlarged boundary and greater territory. Yet neither of them is at all in a hurry.

By piecemeal the great land of India has been slowly added, and southern Africa is with equal slowness and with equal certainty being gathered in; while Russia waits with a patience which knows no discouragement and will know no defeat for the outlying provinces of Turkey and for Turkey itself.

On the map of 120 years ago, you may see the United States of America as they looked while they were still but the colonies of another country and when they began their struggle for freedom. It is a very empty map. Along the Atlantic Coast, near to the ocean which brought them from the mother lands, only 3 million people found habitations, sustenance, and support. All the great regions beyond the coast stretching to the Mississippi lie out in the wilderness untrodden, save by the exploring foot of the hunters and discoverers. The land was the abode of savages, but was itself more savage than they.

We have added to that little strip of shore and to the undefined wilderness, which might or might not be bounded by the great river of the Mississippi, broad expanse after broad expanse, until we govern under our institutions 4 million square miles and 73 million people.

Turn to the map of 1763 and look at the English colonies which had had the growth of 150 years, and see what a small space they occupy on the map of the country which honors us with its citizenship. It was just a little strip between the mountains and the sea. Where the rivers end, also end all the habitations of those who fought the battles of the Revolution. On the south is Florida, not yet ours. West of us are the broad possessions claimed by the French, which are now the heart of our country, and still further the Spanish claims and the Oregon country, reaching to the Pacific Ocean.

What it took the first 130 years to win and settle is not a tithe of what has come to us in the next 130 years, for the United States of America is not less than 260 years old.

The French and Indian Wars carried us, little dreaming of our greatness or of our independence, to the banks of the great Mississippi, where we found ourselves in 1783 when the Revolution closed. Twenty years more gave us the mouth of the Mississippi and both its banks and almost all its tributary streams with a broad reach toward the North and West, which meant Oregon and the Pacific Ocean.

Texas came to us in 1845, after we had once given it up in 1819 as if of little account. When the Mexican War was over and the Gadsden Purchase had been made, we came to seven-eighths of our present greatness of area, which was completed by the purchase of Alaska in 1868. Since then we have been content to make what we could out of what we have got. What we have done with the lands we own, future history will show us is not the tithe of what we shall do.

Here are three great empires of modern days, each in full life, replete with strength and vigor. Will they have the same fate as the empires of the past? Will the traveler from New Zealand sketch from the ruins of London Bridge the ruins of St. Paul? Will St. Petersburg perish from off the earth? And will New York and Chicago, St. Louis and San Francisco become like Tadmor in the wilderness, or will they flourish and bloom forever?

All history is against the perpetuity of nations. Yet there are modern forces which

seem to be at work to give greater prolongation to the life of empires.

It may be a superficial view of history, but there seems to be but one source of destruction, and that is the failure of each section of a great country to keep abreast of the others, to think the same thoughts, and to promote always the common interest. With such a union the outside hordes might storm in vain.

I have already pointed out the great Roman roads, as binding together the country. Modern science and improvements have added wonderfully to the means of intercommunication, and modern wealth, even in its limited diffusion, has made the stirring about of the people among themselves both frequent and permanent. Frequent intercourse between different regions and the scattering of citizens of one state among all the other states tends to similarity and nurtures mutual understanding.

To think the same things of the republic is a bond of union today of even more importance than in the days of Cicero.

That there are vast differences between the ideas and wants of our separate regions is not so well known as it ought to be, or perhaps so fully taken into account.

In each one of the states themselves there are communities which stand out against their surroundings and refuse to be assimilated and to become one in thought with the others. The geographical differences are real and powerful. Once in our history the danger which comes of internal disagreement has been realized and the destructive War of the Rebellion will always be a warning of possible danger, though its result is a protection also.

These differences are really differences in civilization. It does not matter which section is more advanced or which is less advanced. The only fact of importance is the difference. Similarity is the great want of nations. All the people must be in touch with each other. Modern appliances are all on our side. Lightning, even more than steam, has annihilated space and brought together the uttermost parts of the earth. Both together are the soul of business, and business unites with ties which are deeper than sentiment.

Judging from the teachings of history, the great aim of a nation should be to use all the appliances for advancing knowledge, to assimilate its peoples to a common standard. To that end we must not hasten. Not every opportunity for aggrandizement should be seized. Too much food may mean indigestion, and we are sure not to be hungered while the middle of our empire, perhaps in the future the richest part of it, lies undeveloped. Until that region reaches its growth we are governed and to be governed by a minority.

This will be a heavy strain on our institutions; for unless this power in the Senate, given for the future, is used very sparingly in the present, there will be a sense of injustice which will be very bad for the republic.

There is no need of hurry. As we grow, we will spread fast enough. Our strength grows with our years. Men who are but of yesterday and will never see tomorrow must seize time by the forelock. But those empires which hope for eternity can wait.

37.

WILLIAM McKINLEY: The Alternatives in Cuba

From February 1895, when the insurrection against Spanish rule had begun in Cuba, the American government had tried to maintain a position of neutrality. Neither President Cleveland nor President McKinley wanted war with Spain. But the prolongation of the rebellion led jingoists and interventionists in this country to agitate and propagandize for American involvement. McKinley, in 1897, was heartened by a change within the Spanish government to a more liberal ministry that pledged reform in Cuba. In the following portion of his first annual message to Congress on December 6, 1897, McKinley reviewed the Cuban situation and discussed possible courses of action. He demonstrated a patience that exasperated many of his fellow Republicans; but within a few months McKinley would reverse his stand.

Source: PRFA, 1897, pp. vii-xxxiv.

THE MOST IMPORTANT PROBLEM with which this government is now called upon to deal pertaining to its foreign relations concerns its duty toward Spain and the Cuban insurrection. Problems and conditions more or less in common with those now existing have confronted this government at various times in the past. The story of Cuba for many years has been one of unrest; growing discontent; an effort toward a larger enjoyment of liberty and self-control; of organized resistance to the mother country; of depression after distress and warfare and of ineffectual settlement to be followed by renewed revolt. For no enduring period since the enfranchisement of the continental possessions of Spain in the Western continent has the condition of Cuba or the policy of Spain toward Cuba not caused concern to the United States.

The prospect from time to time that the weakness of Spain's hold upon the island and the political vicissitudes and embarrassments of the home government might lead to the transfer of Cuba to a continental power called forth, between 1823 and 1860, various emphatic declarations of the policy of the United States to permit no disturbance of Cuba's connection with Spain unless in the direction of independence or acquisition by us through purchase; nor has there been any change of this declared policy since upon the part of the government.

The revolution which began in 1868 lasted for ten years, despite the strenuous efforts of the successive peninsular governments to suppress it. Then as now, the government of the United States testified its grave concern and offered its aid to put an end to bloodshed in Cuba. The overtures made by General Grant were refused and the war dragged on, entailing great loss of life and treasure and increased injury to American interests besides throwing enhanced burdens of neutrality upon this government. In 1878, peace was brought about by the Truce of Zanjon, obtained by negotiations between the Spanish commander, Martinez de Campos, and the insurgent leaders.

The present insurrection broke out in February 1895. It is not my purpose at this time to recall its remarkable increase or to characterize its tenacious resistance against the enormous forces massed against it by Spain. The revolt and the efforts to subdue it carried destruction to every quarter of the island, developing wide proportions and defying the efforts of Spain for its suppression. The civilized code of war has been disregarded, no less so by the Spaniards than by the Cubans.

The existing conditions cannot but fill this government and the American people with the gravest apprehension. There is no desire on the part of our people to profit by the misfortunes of Spain. We have only the desire to see the Cubans prosperous and contented, enjoying that measure of self-control which is the inalienable right of man, protected in their right to reap the benefit of the exhaustless treasures of their country. . . .

The instructions given to our new minister to Spain before his departure for his post directed him to impress upon that government the sincere wish of the United States to lend its aid toward the ending of the war in Cuba by reaching a peaceful and lasting result, just and honorable alike to Spain and to the Cuban people. These instructions recited the character and duration of the contest, the widespread losses it entails, the burdens and restraints it imposes upon us, with constant disturbance of national interests, and the injury resulting from an indefinite continuance of this state of things.

It was stated that at this juncture our government was constrained to seriously inquire if the time was not ripe when Spain of her own volition, moved by her own interests and every sentiment of humanity, should put a stop to this destructive war and make proposals of settlement honorable to herself and just to her Cuban colony. It was urged that as a neighboring nation, with large interests in Cuba, we could be required to wait only a reasonable time for the mother country to establish its authority and restore peace and order within the borders of the island; that we could not contemplate an indefinite period for the accomplishment of this result.

No solution was proposed to which the slightest idea of humiliation to Spain could attach, and indeed precise proposals were withheld to avoid embarrassment to that government. All that was asked or expected was that some safe way might be speedily provided and permanent peace restored. It so chanced that the consideration of this offer, addressed to the same Spanish administration, which had declined the tenders of my predecessor and which for more than two years had poured men and treasure into Cuba in the fruitless effort to suppress the revolt, fell to others. Between the departure of General Woodford, the new envoy, and his arrival in Spain the statesman who had shaped the policy of this country fell by the hand of an assassin, and although the cabinet of the late premier still held office and received from our envoy the proposals he bore, that cabinet gave place within a few days thereafter to a new administration, under the leadership of Sagasta.

The reply to our note was received on the 23rd day of October. It is in the direction of a better understanding. It appreciates the friendly purposes of this government. It admits that our country is deeply affected by the war in Cuba and that its desires for peace are just. It declares that the present Spanish government is bound by every consideration to a change of policy that should satisfy the United States and pacify Cuba within a reasonable time. To this end Spain has decided to put into effect the political reforms heretofore advocated by the present premier, without halting for any consideration in the path which in its judgment leads to peace. The military operations, it is said, will continue but will be humane and conducted with all regard for private rights, being accompanied by political action leading to the autonomy of Cuba while guarding Spanish sovereignty.

This, it is claimed, will result in investing Cuba with a distinct personality; the island to be governed by an executive and by a local council or chamber, reserving to Spain the control of the foreign relations, the army and navy, and the judicial administration. To accomplish this, the present government proposes to modify existing legislation by decree, leaving the Spanish Cortes, with the aid of Cuban senators and deputies, to solve the economic problem and properly distribute the existing debt.

In the absence of a declaration of the measures that this government proposes to take in carrying out its proffer of good offices, it suggests that Spain be left free to conduct military operations and grant political reforms, while the United States for its part shall enforce its neutral obligations and cut off the assistance which it is asserted the insurgents receive from this country. The supposition of an indefinite prolongation of the war is denied. It is asserted that the western provinces are already well-nigh reclaimed; that the planting of cane and tobacco therein has been resumed, and that by force of arms and new and ample reforms very early and complete pacification is hoped for.

The immediate amelioration of existing conditions under the new administration of Cuban affairs is predicted, and therewithal the disturbance and all occasion for any change of attitude on the part of the United States. Discussion of the question of the international duties and responsibilities of the United States as Spain understands them is presented, with an apparent disposition to charge us with failure in this regard. This charge is without any basis in fact. It could not have been made if Spain had been cognizant of the constant efforts this government has made at the cost of millions and by the employment of the administrative machinery of the nation at command to perform its full duty according to the law of nations. That it has successfully prevented the departure of a single military expedition or armed vessel from our shores in violation of our laws would seem to be a sufficient answer. But of this aspect of the Spanish note it is not necessary to speak further now. Firm in the conviction of a wholly performed obligation, due response to this charge has been made in diplomatic course.

Throughout all these horrors and dangers to our own peace this government has never in any way abrogated its sovereign prerogative of reserving to itself the determination of its policy and course according to its own high sense of right and in consonance with the dearest interests and convictions of our own people should the prolongation of the strife so demand.

Of the untried measures there remain only: recognition of the insurgents as belligerents; recognition of the independence of Cuba; neutral intervention to end the war by imposing a rational compromise between the contestants, and intervention in favor of one or the other party. I speak not of forcible annexation, for that cannot be thought of. That by our code of morality would be criminal aggression.

Recognition of the belligerency of the Cuban insurgents has often been canvassed as a possible if not inevitable step both in regard to the previous ten years' struggle and during the present war. I am not unmindful that the two houses of Congress in the spring of 1896 expressed the opinion by concurrent resolution that a condition of public war existed, requiring or justifying the recognition of a state of belligerency in Cuba; and, during the extra session, the Senate voted a joint resolution of like import, which however was not brought to a vote in the House of Representatives.

In the presence of these significant expressions of the sentiment of the legislative branch, it behooves the executive to soberly consider the conditions under which so important a measure must needs rest for justification. It is to be seriously considered whether the Cuban insurrection possesses beyond dispute the attributes of statehood, which alone can demand the recognition of belligerency in its favor. Possession, in short, of the essential qualifications of sovereignty by the insurgents and the conduct of the war by them according to the received code of war are no less important factors toward the determination of the problem of belligerency than are the influences and consequences of the struggle upon the internal polity of the recognizing state. . . .

Turning to the practical aspects of a recognition of belligerency and reviewing its inconveniences and positive dangers, still further pertinent considerations appear. In the code of nations there is no such thing as a naked recognition of belligerency unaccompanied by the assumption of international neutrality. Such recognition without more will not confer upon either party to a domestic conflict a status not theretofore actually possessed or affect the relation of either party to other states. The act of recognition usually takes the form of a solemn proclamation of neutrality which recites the *de facto* condition of belligerency as its motive. It announces a domestic law of neutrality in the declaring state. It assumes the international obligations of a neutral in the presence of a public state of war. It warns all citizens and others within the jurisdiction of the proclaimant that they violate those rigorous obligations at their own peril and cannot expect to be shielded from the consequences. The right of visit and search on the seas and seizure of vessels and cargoes and contraband of war and good prize under admiralty law must under international law be admitted as a legitimate consequence of a proclamation of belligerency.

While according the equal belligerent rights defined by public law to each party in our ports disfavors would be imposed on both, which while nominally equal would weigh heavily in behalf of Spain herself. Possessing a navy and controlling the ports of Cuba, her maritime rights could be asserted not only for the military investment of the island but up to the margin of our own territorial waters, and a condition of things would exist for which the Cubans within their own domain could not hope to create a parallel; while its creation through aid or sympathy from within our domain would be even more impossible than now, with the additional obligations of international neutrality we would perforce assume.

The enforcement of this enlarged and

onerous code of neutrality would only be influential within our own jurisdiction by land and sea and applicable by our own instrumentalities. It could impart to the United States no jurisdiction between Spain and the insurgents. It would give the United States no right of intervention to enforce the conduct of the strife within the paramount authority of Spain according to the international code of war.

For these reasons I regard the recognition of the belligerency of the Cuban insurgents as now unwise and therefore inadmissible. Should that step hereafter be deemed wise as a measure of right and duty, the executive will take it.

Intervention upon humanitarian grounds has been frequently suggested and has not failed to receive my most anxious and earnest consideration. But should such a step be now taken when it is apparent that a hopeful change has supervened in the policy of Spain toward Cuba? A new government has taken office in the mother country. It is pledged in advance to the declaration that all the effort in the world cannot suffice to maintain peace in Cuba by the bayonet; that vague promises of reform after subjugation afford no solution of the insular problem; that with a substitution of commanders must come a change of the past system of warfare for one in harmony with a new policy which shall no longer aim to drive the Cubans to the "horrible alternative of taking to the thicket or succumbing in misery"; that reforms must be instituted in accordance with the needs and circumstances of the time, and that these reforms, while designed to give full autonomy to the colony and to create a virtual entity and self-controlled administration, shall yet conserve and affirm the sovereignty of Spain by a just distribution of powers and burdens upon a basis of mutual interest untainted by methods of selfish expediency.

The first acts of the new government lie in these honorable paths. The policy of cruel rapine and extermination that so long shocked the universal sentiment of humanity has been reversed. Under the new military commander a broad clemency is proffered. Measures have already been set on foot to relieve the horrors of starvation. The power of the Spanish armies, it is asserted, is to be used not to spread ruin and desolation but to protect the resumption of peaceful agricultural pursuits and productive industries. That past methods are futile to force a peace by subjugation is freely admitted, and that ruin without conciliation must inevitably fail to win for Spain the fidelity of a contented dependency.

Decrees in application of the foreshadowed reforms have already been promulgated. The full text of these decrees has not been received, but as furnished in a telegraphic summary from our minister are: All civil and electoral rights of peninsular Spaniards are, in virtue of existing constitutional authority, forthwith extended to colonial Spaniards. A scheme of autonomy has been proclaimed by decree, to become effective upon ratification by the Cortes. It creates a Cuban parliament which, with the insular executive, can consider and vote upon all subjects affecting local order and interests, possessing unlimited powers, save as to matters of state, war, and the navy, as to which the governor-general acts by his own authority as the delegate of the central government. This parliament receives the oath of the governor-general to preserve faithfully the liberties and privileges of the colony, and to it the colonial secretaries are responsible. It has the right to propose to the central government, through the governor-general, modifications of the national charter and to invite new projects of law or executive measures in the interest of the colony.

Besides its local powers, it is competent, first, to regulate electoral registration and procedure and prescribe the qualifications of electors and the manner of exercising suffrage; second, to organize courts of justice with native judges from members of the local bar; third, to frame the insular budget both as to expenditures and revenues, without limitation of any kind, and to set apart the revenues to meet the Cuban share of the national budget, which latter will be voted by the national Cortes with the assistance of Cuban senators and deputies; fourth, to initiate or take part in the negotiations of the national government for commercial treaties which may affect Cuban interests; fifth, to accept or reject commercial treaties which the national government may have concluded without the participation of the Cuban government; sixth, to frame the colonial tariff, acting in accord with the peninsular government in scheduling articles of mutual commerce between the mother country and the colonies. Before introducing or voting upon a bill, the Cuban government or the chambers will lay the project before the central government and hear its opinion thereon, all the correspondence in such regard being made public. Finally, all conflicts of jurisdiction arising between the different municipal, provincial, and insular assemblies, or between the latter and the insular executive power, and which from their nature may not be referable to the central government for decision, shall be submitted to the courts.

That the government of Sagasta has entered upon a course from which recession with honor is impossible can hardly be questioned; that in the few weeks it has existed it has made earnest of the sincerity of its professions is undeniable. I shall not impugn its sincerity, nor should impatience be suffered to embarrass it in the task it has undertaken. It is honestly due to Spain and to our friendly relations with Spain that she should be given a reasonable chance to realize her expectations and to prove the asserted efficacy of the new order of things to which she stands irrevocably committed. She has recalled the commander whose brutal orders inflamed the American mind and shocked the civilized world. She has modified the horrible order of concentration and has undertaken to care for the helpless and permit those who desire to resume the cultivation of their fields to do so and assures them of the protection of the Spanish government in their lawful occupations. She has just released the "Competitor" prisoners heretofore sentenced to death and who have been the subject of repeated diplomatic correspondence during both this and the preceding administration.

Not a single American citizen is now in arrest or confinement in Cuba of whom this government has any knowledge. The near future will demonstrate whether the indispensable condition of a righteous peace, just alike to the Cubans and to Spain as well as equitable to all our interests so intimately involved in the welfare of Cuba, is likely to be attained. If not, the exigency of further and other action by the United States will remain to be taken. When that time comes that action will be determined in the line of indisputable right and duty. It will be faced, without misgiving or hesitancy, in the light of the obligation this government owes to itself, to the people who have confided to it the protection of their interests and honor, and to humanity.

Sure of the right, keeping free from all offense ourselves, actuated only by upright and patriotic considerations, moved neither by passion nor selfishness, the government will continue its watchful care over the rights and property of American citizens and will abate none of its efforts to bring about by peaceful agencies a peace which shall be honorable and enduring. If it shall hereafter appear to be a duty imposed by our obligations to ourselves, to civilization and humanity, to intervene with force, it shall be without fault on our part and only because the necessity for such action will be so clear as to command the support and approval of the civilized world.

1898

38.

American Ultimatum to Spain

After McKinley's annual message to Congress in December 1897, the Cuban situation worsened rather than improved. The American battleship Maine *was blown up in Havana Harbor on February 15, 1898, and the newspapers that had been urging war with Spain for the past year stepped up their campaign. The slogan of the hour was: "Remember the* Maine, *to hell with Spain!" In this fiery atmosphere, the State Department sent a series of cablegrams to Stewart L. Woodford, the U.S. ambassador to Spain, stating the American position regarding Cuba. Two messages sent during the last week in March are reprinted here.*

Source: PRFA, 1898, pp. 704, 711-712.

March 26

The President's desire is for peace. He cannot look upon the suffering and starvation in Cuba save with horror. The concentration of men, women, and children in the fortified towns and permitting them to starve is unbearable to a Christian nation geographically so close as ours to Cuba. All this has shocked and inflamed the American mind, as it has the civilized world, where its extent and character are known.

It was represented to him in November that the Blanco government would at once release the suffering and so modify the Weyler order as to permit those who were able to return to their homes and till the fields from which they had been driven. There has been no relief to the starving except such as the American people have supplied. The reconcentration order has not been practically superseded.

There is no hope of peace through Spanish arms. The Spanish government seems unable to conquer the insurgents. More than half of the island is under control of the insurgents. For more than three years our people have been patient and forbearing; we have patrolled our coast with zeal and at great expense, and have successfully prevented the landing of any armed force on the island. The war has disturbed the peace and tranquility of our people.

We do not want the island. The President has evidenced in every way his desire to preserve and continue friendly relations with Spain. He has kept every international obligation with fidelity. He wants an honorable peace. He has repeatedly urged the government of Spain to secure such a peace. She still has the opportunity to do it, and the President appeals to her from every consideration of justice and humanity to do it. Will she? Peace is the desired end.

For your own guidance, the President suggests that if Spain will revoke the reconcentration order and maintain the people until they can support themselves and offer to the Cubans full self-government, with reasonable indemnity, the President will gladly assist in its consummation. If Spain should invite the United States to mediate for peace and the insurgents would make like request, the President might undertake such office of friendship.

March 27

Believed the *Maine* report will be held in Congress for a short time without action. A feeling of deliberation prevails in both houses of Congress. See if the following can be done:

First, armistice until October 1. Negotiations meantime looking for peace between Spain and insurgents through friendly offices of President United States.

Second, immediate revocation of *reconcentrado* order so as to permit people to return to their farms and the needy to be relieved with provisions and supplies from United States cooperating with authorities so as to afford full relief.

Add, if possible, third, if terms of peace not satisfactorily settled by October 1, President of the United States to be final arbiter between Spain and insurgents.

If Spain agrees, President will use friendly offices to get insurgents to accept plan. Prompt action desirable.

39.

Albert Shaw: The Blowing Up of the *Maine*

The battleship Maine *was blown up in Havana Harbor on February 15, 1898, and the American Court of Inquiry published the results of its investigation into the disaster. The court did not assign responsibility but simply concluded that a submarine mine was the cause of the explosion; and whether the explosion was produced by Cuban rebels desiring American intervention, or by irresponsible Spanish loyalists, or simply by an accident, will never be known. But to the newspapers in this country that wanted war with Spain, the guilt was clear. Hearst newspaper headlines read: "Maine Was Destroyed By Treachery!" and "The Whole Country Thrills With War Fever!" Albert Shaw, editorializing in the* Review of Reviews *in April, shared the popular view and expressed great confidence in the war-making potential of the United States.*

Source: *American Monthly Review of Reviews,* April 1898: "The Progress of the World."

THE WEEKS THAT HAVE ELAPSED since that fatal event of February 15th have been making history in a manner highly creditable to the American government and to our citizenship. Captain Sigsbee, the commander of the *Maine,* had promptly telegraphed his desire that judgment should be suspended until investigation had been made. The investigation was set on foot at once, and 75 million Americans have accordingly suspended judgment in the face of a great provocation. For it must be remembered that to suppose the destruction of the *Maine* an ordinary accident and not due to any external agency or hostile intent was, under all the circumstances, to set completely at defiance the law of probabilities.

It is not true that battleships are in the habit of blowing themselves up. When all the environing facts were taken into consideration, it was just about as probable that the *Maine* had been blown up by spontaneous combustion or by some accident in which no hostile motive was concerned, as that the reported assassination of President Barrios of Guatemala, a few days previously, had really been a suicide. . . .

It has been known perfectly well that Spanish hatred might at any time manifest itself by attempts upon the life of the American representative at Havana, Consul General Fitzhugh Lee. This danger was felt especially at the time of the Havana riots in January, and it seems to have had something to do with the sending of the *Maine* to Havana Harbor. The Spaniards themselves, however, looked upon the sending of the *Maine* as a further aggravation of the long series of their just grievances against the United States. They regarded the presence of the *Maine* at Havana as a menace to Spanish sovereignty in the island and as an encouragement to the insurgents. A powerful American fleet lay at Key West and the Dry Tortugas, with steam up ready to follow the *Maine* to the harbor of Havana on a few hours' notice. All this was intensely hateful to the Spaniards, and particularly to the Army officers at Havana who had sympathized with General Weyler's policy and who justly regarded General Weyler's recall to Spain as due to the demand of President McKinley. The American pretense that the *Maine* was making a visit of courtesy seemed to these Spaniards a further example of Anglo-Saxon hypocrisy.

That this intense bitterness against the presence of the *Maine* was felt among the military and official class in Havana was perfectly well known to Captain Sigsbee, his staff, and all his crew; and they were not unaware of the rumors and threats that means would be found to destroy the American ship. It was, furthermore, very generally supposed that the Spanish preparation for the defense of Havana had included mines and torpedoes in the harbor. At the time when the *Maine* went to Havana, it was a notorious fact that the relations between Spain and the United States were so strained that war was regarded as almost inevitable. If war had actually been declared while the *Maine* was at Havana, it is not likely that the Spanish would have permitted the ship's departure without an effort to do her harm.

The Spanish harbor is now and it has been for a good while past under absolute military control; and the American warship, believed by the Spanish authorities to be at Havana with only half-cloaked hostile designs, was obliged to accept the anchorage that was assigned by those very authorities. In view of the strained situation and of the Spanish feeling that no magnanimity is due on Spain's part toward the United States, it is not in the least difficult to believe that the harbor authorities would have anchored the *Maine* at a spot where, in case of the outbreak of war, the submarine harbor defenses might be effectively used against so formidable an enemy.

To understand the situation completely, it must not be forgotten that the Spanish government at first made objection against the *Maine's* intended visit to Havana and, in consenting, merely yielded to a necessity that was forced upon it. All Spaniards regarded the sending of the *Maine* to Havana as really a treacherous act on the part of the United States, and most of them would have deemed it merely a safe and reasonable precautionary measure to anchor her in the vicinity of a submarine mine. Doubtless these suggestions will be read by more than one person who will receive them with entire skepticism. But such readers will not have been familiar with what has been going on in the matter of the Cuban rebellion, or else they will be lacking in memories of good carrying power.

The great majority of the intelligent people of the United States could not, from the first, avoid perceiving that what we may call the self-destruction theory was extremely improbable; while what we may term the assassination theory was in keeping with all the circumstances. Nevertheless, although the probability of guilt was so overwhelming, the American people saw the fairness and the necessity of suspending judgment until proof had been substituted for mere probability. And there was in no part of the country any disposition to take snap judgment or to act precipitately. No other such spectacle of national forbearance has been witnessed in our times.

Unquestionably, the whole community has been intensely eager for news; and it is perhaps true that certain newspapers, which have devoted themselves for a month or more to criticizing the sensational press, might as well have been occupied in a more energetic effort to supply their readers with information. The fact is that the so-called war extras, which for many days were issued from certain newspaper offices at the rate of a dozen or more a day, have not seemed to communicate their hysteria to any considerable number of the American people, East or West, North or South, so far as our observation goes.

The situation has simply been one of a very absorbing and profound interest, while the suspense has been very trying to the nerves. The possibility that our country might soon be engaged in war with a foreign power has been a preoccupying thought not to be dismissed for a single hour. The whole country has known that a fateful investigation was in progress in Havana Harbor; that coast-defense work was being pushed all along our seaboard; that in all the shipyards, public and private, government work was being prosecuted with double or quadruple forces of men, working by night as well as by day; that ammunition factories, iron and steel plants, and every other establishment capable of furnishing any kind of military or naval supplies were receiving orders from the government and were working to the full extent of their capacity; that plans were being made for fitting out merchant ships as auxiliary cruisers; that our naval representatives were negotiating abroad for additional warships; that new regiments of artillerymen were being enlisted for the big guns on the seaboard; that naval recruits were being mustered in to man newly commissioned ships; that the railroads were preparing by order of the War Department to bring the little United States Army from western and northern posts to convenient southern centers; and that while we were making these preparations Spain on her part was trying to raise money to buy ships and to secure allies. All these matters, and many others related to them, have within these past weeks made an immense opportunity for testing the news gathering resources of the American press. . . .

When, therefore, on March 8, the House of Representatives unanimously voted to place $50 million at the unqualified disposal of President McKinley as an emergency fund for the national defense — this action being followed by an equally unanimous vote of the Senate the next day — it was naturally taken for granted all over the country that the situation was believed by the President to be extremely critical. The continued delay of the Board of Inquiry — which had been oscillating between Havana and Key West, conducting its proceedings in secret and mantaining absolute reticence — had naturally served to confirm the belief that its report would show foul play; and it appeared that the President was basing his great preparations of war, in part at least, upon his advance knowledge of the evidence secured by the commission. The unanimity of Congress in support of the President created an excellent impression abroad. Fifty million is a very large sum to place in the hands of one man.

It might have been supposed that there would have been members in both houses who would have insisted upon the appropriation of this money for specific purposes. That not a single man was found to make objection showed a very great capacity for united action in a time of emergency. It also showed, of course, how great is the confidence that Congress and the American people repose in the honor, wisdom, and public spirit of their Presidents. At the time of the Venezuela incident, Congress in similar manner, came unanimously to the support of President Cleveland. In that case, however, there was not the remotest possibility of war; and the episode was merely a diplomatic one in which it was deemed important to show that our government could rely absolutely upon the whole support of the people. The South on all such recent occasions has been foremost in expressions of patriotism.

The vote of $50 million, although an extraordinary measure justified only by the imminent danger of war, was clearly an act that no peace-loving man could reasonably criticize; for preparation is often the means by which conflict is avoided. A larger Navy was in any case greatly desirable for our country, with its long seaboard on the Atlantic and the Pacific and its vast commerce; while the better fortification of our principal ports was an urgent necessity. Since the preparations that have been made so hurriedly during the past few weeks have been of a defensive nature, and since they have been carried out upon lines which had been duly considered in advance, they will have permanent value, and there will have been involved a very small percentage of

waste. If Congress had been wise enough in the past three or four years to lay down more warships in our own yards, it would not have been necessary to contribute millions to foreign shipbuilders.

No part of the $50 million will be squandered by the administration; but it is to be regretted that this emergency fund had not been already expended during the five preceding years by more liberal appropriations for coast defense and naval construction. The great shipyards of the United States, both public and private, are now at the point where, with a sufficient amount of regular work to do, they would speedily be able to compete on equal terms with the best shipbuilding plants of Europe. Iron and steel supplies are now much cheaper in the United States than anywhere else, and it is only the relatively small amount of shipbuilding that has been demanded by our government that has made it more expensive to build a war vessel here than elsewhere.

In a time of real emergency, however, the resources of the United States would prove themselves great enough to supply our own people and the whole world besides. The quickness and inventiveness of American mechanics, engineers, and manufacturers have no parallel in Europe. On a year's notice the United States might undertake to cope even-handed with either the Dual or the Triple Alliance — although we have now only the nucleus of an army and the beginning of a navy, while the European powers have made war preparation their principal business for a whole generation. It is to be suspected that one reason why the American people have bought the newspapers so eagerly during the past weeks is to be found in the satisfaction they have taken in learning how a strictly peaceful nation like ours could if necessary reverse the process of beating swords into plowshares.

It is true, for example, that we have built only a few torpedo boats and only a few vessels of the type known as destroyers; but we have discovered that about a hundred very rich Americans had been amusing themselves within the past few years by building or buying splendid oceangoing, steel-built steam yachts of high speed and stanch qualities, capable of being quickly transformed into naval dispatch boats or armored and fitted with torpedo tubes. Probably not a single private Spanish citizen could turn over to his government such a vessel as the magnificent Goelet yacht, the *Mayflower,* which was secured by our Navy Department on March 16; not to mention scores of other private steam yachts of great size and strength that wealthy American citizens are ready to offer if needed.

It is the prevailing opinion nowadays, it is true, that nothing is to be relied upon in naval war but huge battleships, which take from two to three or four years to build. But if a great war were forced upon us suddenly, it is altogether probable that American ingenuity would devise something wholly new in the way of a marine engine of war, just as American ingenuity improvised the first modern ironclads. We have already in our Navy a dynamite cruiser, the *Vesuvius,* which in actual warfare might prove more dangerous than a half dozen of the greatest battleships of the European navies. There has just been completed, moreover, and offered to our government, a submarine boat, the *Holland,* which seems to be capable of moving rapidly for several miles so completely submerged as to offer no target for an enemy; and it may well be that the torpedoes discharged from an insignificant little vessel capable of swimming below the surface like a fish might prove as fatal to the battleships of an enemy as the alleged mine in the harbor of Havana was fatal to our battleship the *Maine.*

Nowadays, warfare is largely a matter of science and invention; and since a country where the arts of peace flourish and prosper is most favorable to the general advance of science and invention, we stumble upon the paradox that the successful pursuit of peace is after all the best preparation for war. Another way to put it is to say that modern warfare has become a matter of machinery, and that the most highly developed mechanical and industrial nation will by virtue of such development be most formidable in war.

This is a situation that the Spaniards in general are evidently quite unable to comprehend. Their ideas are altogether medieval. They believe themselves to be a highly chivalrous and militant people, and that the people of the United States are really in great terror of Spanish prowess. They think that Spain could make as easy work of invading the United States as Japan made of invading China. Their point of view is altogether theatrical and unrelated to modern facts.

A country like ours, capable of supplying the whole world with electrical motors, mining machinery, locomotive engines, steel rails, and the structural material for modern steel bridges and "skyscrapers," not to mention bicycles and sewing machines, is equally capable of building, arming, and operating an unlimited number of ships of every type, and of employing every conceivable mechanical device for purposes of national defense. In the long run, therefore, even if our preliminary preparations had been of the scantiest character, we should be able to give a good account of ourselves in warfare. . . .

Quite regardless of the responsibilities for the *Maine* incident, it is apparently true that the great majority of the American people are hoping that President McKinley will promptly utilize the occasion to secure the complete pacification and independence of Cuba. There are a few people in the United States — we should not like to believe that more than 100 could be found out of a population of 75 million — who believe that the United States ought to join hands with Spain in forcing the Cuban insurgents to lay down their arms and to accept Spanish sovereignty as a permanent condition under the promise of practical home rule. It needs no argument, of course, to convince the American people that such a proposal reaches the lowest depths of infamy. It is much worse than the proposition made by a few people in Europe last year that the victorious Turks should have the countenance and support of the great nations of Europe in making Greece a part of the Turkish empire. For the Turks had fairly conquered the Greeks; and if Europe had kept hands off, Greece would have been reduced very quickly to the position of an Ottoman province.

But in Cuba it is otherwise. The insurgents, with no outside help, have held their own for more than three years, and Spain is unable to conquer them. The people of the United States do not intend to help Spain hold Cuba. On the contrary, they are now ready, in one way or in another, to help the Cubans drive Spain out of the Western Hemisphere. If the occasion goes past and we allow this Cuban struggle to run on indefinitely, the American people will have lost several degrees of self-respect and will certainly not have gained anything in the opinion of mankind.

40.

WILLIAM McKINLEY: War Message

The Spanish government sincerely wished to avoid war with the United States. But it faced tremendous internal problems coupled with a military situation in Cuba that had gotten out of control. In an effort to appease the Americans without provoking the wrath of opposition groups at home, it agreed to two of the main conditions that the United States had laid down as necessary to gain peace in Cuba: the governor-general of Cuba was instructed by Spain to revoke reconcentration (a brutal policy of committing Cubans to camps); and the commander of the Spanish Army, on April 9, was told to grant an armistice to the insurgents as a prelude to peace. Although McKinley knew of these concessions when he went before Congress on April 11 to ask for a declaration of war, the pressures for war had overwhelmed him and he succumbed to both popular opinion and the views of leading Republican congressmen. Passages from his war message are reprinted below.

Source: PRFA, 1898, pp. 750-760.

OBEDIENT TO THAT PRECEPT of the Constitution which commands the President to give from time to time to the Congress information of the state of the Union and to recommend to their consideration such measures as he shall judge necessary and expedient, it becomes my duty now to address your body with regard to the grave crisis that has arisen in the relations of the United States to Spain by reason of the warfare that for more than three years has raged in the neighboring island of Cuba.

I do so because of the intimate connection of the Cuban question with the state of our own Union and the grave relation the course which it is now incumbent upon the nation to adopt must needs bear to the traditional policy of our government if it is to accord with the precepts laid down by the founders of the republic and religiously observed by succeeding administrations to the present day.

The present revolution is but the successor of other similar insurrections which have occurred in Cuba against the dominion of Spain, extending over a period of nearly half a century, each of which, during its progress, has subjected the United States to great effort and expense in enforcing its neutrality laws, caused enormous losses to American trade and commerce, caused irritation, annoyance, and disturbance among our citizens, and, by the exercise of cruel, barbarous, and uncivilized practices of warfare, shocked the sensibilities and offended the humane sympathies of our people.

Since the present revolution began in February 1895, this country has seen the fertile domain at our threshold ravaged by fire and sword, in the course of a struggle unequaled in the history of the island and rarely paralleled as to the numbers of the combatants and the bitterness of the contest by any revolution of modern times, where a dependent people striving to be free have been opposed by the power of the sovereign state.

Our people have beheld a once prosperous community reduced to comparative want, its lucrative commerce virtually paralyzed, its exceptional productiveness diminished, its fields laid waste, its mills in ruins, and its people perishing by tens of thousands from hunger and destitution. We have found ourselves constrained, in the observance of that strict neutrality which our laws enjoin, and which the law of nations commands, to police our own waters and watch our own seaports in prevention of any unlawful act in aid of the Cubans.

Our trade has suffered; the capital invested by our citizens in Cuba has been largely lost, and the temper and forbearance of our people have been so sorely tried as to beget a perilous unrest among our own citizens, which has inevitably found its expression from time to time in the national legislature; so that issues wholly external to our own body politic engross attention and stand in the way of that close devotion to domestic advancement that becomes a self-contained commonwealth, whose primal maxim has been the avoidance of all foreign entanglements. All this must needs awaken, and has, indeed, aroused the utmost concern on the part of this government, as well during my predecessor's term as in my own.

In April 1896, the evils from which our country suffered through the Cuban war became so onerous that my predecessor made an effort to bring about a peace through the mediation of this government in any way that might tend to an honorable adjustment of the contest between Spain and her revolted colony, on the basis of some effective scheme of self-government for Cuba under the flag and sovereignty of Spain. It failed through the refusal of the Spanish government then in power to consider any form of mediation or, indeed, any plan of settlement which did not begin with the actual submission of the insurgents to the mother country, and then only on such terms as Spain herself might see fit to grant. The war continued unabated. The resistance of the insurgents was in nowise diminished. . . .

By the time the present administration took office a year ago, reconcentration — so called — had been made effective over the better part of the four central and western provinces — Santa Clara, Matanzas, Habana, and Pinar del Rio. . . .

In this state of affairs, my administration found itself confronted with the grave prob-

Library of Congress

William McKinley

jured as we are, deeply and intimately, by its very existence.

Realizing this, it appeared to be my duty, in a spirit of true friendliness, no less to Spain than to the Cubans who have so much to lose by the prolongation of the struggle, to seek to bring about an immediate termination of the war. To this end I submitted, on the 27th ultimo, as a result of much representation and correspondence, through the United States minister at Madrid, propositions to the Spanish government looking to an armistice until October 1 for the negotiation of peace with the good offices of the President.

In addition, I asked the immediate revocation of the order of reconcentration, so as to permit the people to return to their farms and the needy to be relieved with provisions and supplies from the United States, cooperating with the Spanish authorities, so as to afford full relief.

The reply of the Spanish cabinet was received on the night of the 31st ultimo. It offered, as the means to bring about peace in Cuba, to confide the preparation thereof to the insular parliament, inasmuch as the concurrence of that body would be necessary to reach a final result, it being, however, understood that the powers reserved by the constitution to the central government are not lessened or diminished. As the Cuban parliament does not meet until the 4th of May next, the Spanish government would not object, for its part, to accept at once a suspension of hostilities if asked for by the insurgents from the general in chief, to whom it would pertain, in such case, to determine the duration and conditions of the armistice.

The propositions submitted by General Woodford and the reply of the Spanish government were both in the form of brief memoranda, the texts of which are before me, and are substantially in the language above given. The function of the Cuban parliament in the matter of "preparing"

lem of its duty. My message of last December reviewed the situation and narrated the steps taken with a view to relieving its acuteness and opening the way to some form of honorable settlement. The assassination of the prime minister, Canovas, led to a change of government in Spain. The former administration, pledged to subjugation without concession, gave place to that of a more liberal party, committed long in advance to a policy of reform, involving the wider principle of home rule for Cuba and Puerto Rico. . . .

The war in Cuba is of such a nature that short of subjugation or extermination a final military victory for either side seems impracticable. The alternative lies in the physical exhaustion of the one or the other party, or perhaps of both — a condition which in effect ended the ten years' war by the truce of Zanjon. The prospect of such a protraction and conclusion of the present strife is a contingency hardly to be contemplated with equanimity by the civilized world, and least of all by the United States, affected and in-peace and the manner of its doing so are not expressed in the Spanish memorandum; but from General Woodford's explanatory reports of preliminary discussions preceding the final conference it is understood that the Spanish government stands ready to give the insular congress full powers to settle the terms of peace with the insurgents — whether by direct negotiation or indirectly by means of legislation does not appear.

With this last overture in the direction of immediate peace, and its disappointing reception by Spain, the Executive is brought to the end of his effort.

In my annual message of December last I said:

> Of the untried measures there remained only: Recognition of the insurgents as belligerents; recognition of the independence of Cuba; neutral intervention to end the war by imposing a rational compromise between the contestants, and intervention in favor of one or the other party. I speak not of forcible annexation, for that cannot be thought of. That, by our code of morality, would be criminal aggression.

Thereupon I reviewed these alternatives, in the light of President Grant's measured words, uttered in 1875, when, after seven years of sanguinary, destructive, and cruel hostilities in Cuba, he reached the conclusion that the recognition of the independence of Cuba was impracticable and indefensible, and that the recognition of belligerence was not warranted by the facts according to the tests of public law. I commented especially upon the latter aspect of the question, pointing out the inconveniences and positive dangers of a recognition of belligerence which, while adding to the already onerous burdens of neutrality within our own jurisdiction, could not in any way extend our influence or effective offices in the territory of hostilities.

Nothing has since occurred to change my view in this regard, and I recognize as fully now as then that the issuance of a proclamation of neutrality, by which process the so-called recognition of belligerents is published, could, of itself and unattended by other action, accomplish nothing toward the one end for which we labor — the instant pacification of Cuba and the cessation of the misery that afflicts the island. . . .

I said in my message of December last, "It is to be seriously considered whether the Cuban insurrection possesses beyond dispute the attributes of statehood which alone can demand the recognition of belligerency in its favor." The same requirement must certainly be no less seriously considered when the graver issue of recognizing independence is in question, for no less positive test can be applied to the greater act than to the lesser; while, on the other hand, the influences and consequences of the struggle upon the internal policy of the recognizing state, which form important factors when the recognition of belligerency is concerned, are secondary, if not rightly eliminable, factors when the real question is whether the community claiming recognition is or is not independent beyond peradventure.

Nor from the standpoint of expediency do I think it would be wise or prudent for this government to recognize at the present time the independence of the so-called Cuban Republic. Such recognition is not necessary in order to enable the United States to intervene and pacify the island. To commit this country now to the recognition of any particular government in Cuba might subject us to embarrassing conditions of international obligation toward the organization so recognized. In case of intervention our conduct would be subject to the approval or disapproval of such government. We would be required to submit to its direction and to assume to it the mere relation of a friendly ally.

When it shall appear hereafter that there

is within the island a government capable of performing the duties and discharging the functions of a separate nation, and having, as a matter of fact, the proper forms and attributes of nationality, such government can be promptly and readily recognized and the relations and interests of the United States with such nation adjusted.

There remain the alternative forms of intervention to end the war, either as an impartial neutral by imposing a rational compromise between the contestants, or as the active ally of the one party or the other.

As to the first, it is not to be forgotten that during the last few months the relation of the United States has virtually been one of friendly intervention in many ways, each not of itself conclusive, but all tending to the exertion of a potential influence toward an ultimate pacific result, just and honorable to all interests concerned. The spirit of all our acts hitherto has been an earnest, unselfish desire for peace and prosperity in Cuba, untarnished by differences between us and Spain, and unstained by the blood of American citizens.

The forcible intervention of the United States as a neutral to stop the war, according to the large dictates of humanity and following many historical precedents where neighboring states have interfered to check the hopeless sacrifices of life by internecine conflicts beyond their borders, is justifiable on rational grounds. It involves, however, hostile constraint upon both the parties to the contest as well to enforce a truce as to guide the eventual settlement.

The grounds for such intervention may be briefly summarized as follows:

First, in the cause of humanity and to put an end to the barbarities, bloodshed, starvation, and horrible miseries now existing there, and which the parties to the conflict are either unable or unwilling to stop or mitigate. It is no answer to say this is all in another country, belonging to another na-

tion, and is therefore none of our business. It is specially our duty, for it is right at our door.

Second, we owe it to our citizens in Cuba to afford them that protection and indemnity for life and property which no government there can or will afford, and to that end to terminate the conditions that deprive them of legal protection.

Third, the right to intervene may be justified by the very serious injury to the commerce, trade, and business of our people, and by the wanton destruction of property and devastation of the island.

Fourth, and which is of the utmost importance, the present condition of affairs in Cuba is a constant menace to our peace, and entails upon this government an enormous expense. With such a conflict waged for years in an island so near us and with which our people have such trade and business relations; when the lives and liberty of our citizens are in constant danger and their property destroyed and themselves ruined; where our trading vessels are liable to seizure and are seized at our very door by warships of a foreign nation, the expeditions of filibustering that we are powerless to prevent altogether, and the irritating questions and entanglements thus arising — all these and others that I need not mention, with the resulting strained relations, are a constant menace to our peace, and compel us to keep on a semiwar footing with a nation with which we are at peace.

These elements of danger and disorder already pointed out have been strikingly illustrated by a tragic event which has deeply and justly moved the American people. I have already transmitted to Congress the report of the Naval Court of Inquiry on the destruction of the battleship *Maine* in the harbor of Havana during the night of the 15th of February. The destruction of that noble vessel has filled the national heart with inexpressible horror. Two hundred and fifty-eight brave sailors and marines and two officers of our Navy, reposing in the fancied security of a friendly harbor, have been hurled to death, grief and want brought to their homes, and sorrow to the nation.

The Naval Court of Inquiry, which, it is needless to say, commands the unqualified confidence of the government, was unanimous in its conclusion that the destruction of the *Maine* was caused by an exterior explosion, that of a submarine mine. It did not assume to place the responsibility. That remains to be fixed.

In any event, the destruction of the *Maine,* by whatever exterior cause, is a patent and impressive proof of a state of things in Cuba that is intolerable. That condition is thus shown to be such that the Spanish government cannot assure safety and security to a vessel of the American Navy in the harbor of Havana on a mission of peace, and rightfully there. . . .

The long trial has proved that the object for which Spain has waged the war cannot be attained. The fire of insurrection may flame or may smolder with varying seasons, but it has not been, and it is plain that it cannot be, extinguished by present methods. The only hope of relief and repose from a condition which can no longer be endured is the enforced pacification of Cuba. In the name of humanity, in the name of civilization, in behalf of endangered American interests which give us the right and the duty to speak and to act, the war in Cuba must stop.

In view of these facts and of these considerations, I ask the Congress to authorize and empower the President to take measures to secure a full and final termination of hostilities between the government of Spain and the people of Cuba, and to secure in the island the establishment of a stable government, capable of maintaining order and observing its international obligations, insuring peace and tranquillity and the security of its citizens as well as our own, and to use the military and naval forces of the United States as may be necessary for these purposes.

And in the interest of humanity and to aid in preserving the lives of the starving people of the island, I recommend that the distribution of food and supplies be continued, and that an appropriation be made out of the public Treasury to supplement the charity of our citizens.

The issue is now with the Congress. It is a solemn responsibility. I have exhausted every effort to relieve the intolerable condition of affairs which is at our doors. Prepared to execute every obligation imposed upon me by the Constitution and the law, I await your action.

Yesterday, and since the preparation of the foregoing message, official information was received by me that the latest decree of the queen regent of Spain directs General Blanco, in order to prepare and facilitate peace, to proclaim a suspension of hostilities, the duration and details of which have not yet been communicated to me.

This fact with every other pertinent consideration will, I am sure, have your just and careful attention in the solemn deliberations upon which you are about to enter. If this measure attains a successful result, then our aspirations as a Christian, peace-loving people will be realized. If it fails, it will be only another justification for our contemplated action.

Please remain. You furnish the pictures and I'll furnish the war.
WILLIAM RANDOLPH HEARST, telegram to Frederic Remington,
who wished to return home from Cuba, March 1898

"Spanish 'Justice and Honor' be darned!" — Uncle Sam's image in the Hearst press, 1898

THE AMERICAN EMPIRE

The closing of the frontier ended the continental phase of Manifest Destiny; where land was lacking, however, the spirit lingered on. Imperialism in degrees from economic domination to actual possession was the new order; backed by influential segments of the press, by public figures like Senator Henry Cabot Lodge, and finally by President Roosevelt, the movement was an aggressive program to open and consolidate new spheres of economic influence. The campaign rested on a number of justifi- cations. In the Caribbean and Latin America, the Monroe Doctrine, extended later by the Roosevelt Corollary, served as sufficient basis for military occupation of Cuba, Santo Domingo, Haiti, and Nicaragua; economic domination, with police prerogatives similar to the Platt Amendment arrangement with Cuba, lasted considerably longer. In the East, the acquisition of the Philippines raised the notion of turning the Pacific into "an American lake" and plunged the U.S. into the ancient rivalries of Oriental politics.

(Above) Coxey's Army of unemployed men
marching to Washington in 1894; (below)
"King of the Combinations"; caricature of
John D. Rockefeller from "Puck," 1901;
(right) pineapple plantation near Honolulu;
(bottom right) Queen Liliuokalani, deposed
by the pro-annexation faction, 1893

As critics and populists railed against the monopolies, an enlarged vision of American destiny was focused on Hawaii. In 1893, Americans there, led by the sugar growers, overthrew the monarchy and asked for annexation by the United States. Hawaii offered the first opportunity for those urging entrance into "Great Power" competition, but Cleveland, applying a somewhat stricter moral standard, blocked annexation when he found that the U.S. minister had been active in the coup.

Sen. Henry Cabot Lodge; (above) advocates of "Weltpolitik" are depicted as sinister German professors declaiming abstruse theoretical insanity about power and influence

Two steel battleships reflect the new look of the U.S. Navy at the turn of the century

The election of 1896 was the climactic confrontation of Populism with the established powers. Bryan, who could be considered a radical only on the free silver issue, was almost as staunch and conservative as most Republicans. His greatest handicap was his following. McKinley's major asset in the campaign was Mark Hanna, a master at political finance and maneuver. Both Hanna and McKinley were explicitly devoted to business, and strongly identified it with the Republican Party.

(Top) A.F. of L. officers Gompers, Duncan, and Morrison leaving the home of William Jennings Bryan; (center) "A Painful Position for Nurse Mc-Kinley — I've got to take care of this Gold Baby for my political living, but I love my own toot-sey-wootsey the best." (Bottom) President Cleveland and President-elect McKinley enroute to the inauguration ceremony

(Top) "History Repeats Itself — The Robber Barons of the Middle Ages and the Robber Barons of Today," cartoon from "Puck"; (center left) "Mr. Hanna's Stand on the Labor Question"; cartoon by Davenport in "The New York Journal"; (center right) Mark Hanna; (bottom) "He Should Pay Taxes"; Davenport cartoon

Insurrection had convulsed Cuba since 1895. Popular sentiment in the U.S. favored expulsion of the Spanish and pressure for intervention was strong. When the "Maine" exploded in Havana harbor in 1898, widespread and illogical assertions of Spanish culpability induced the President to send an ultimatum to Spain. Despite every indication that Spain would comply, McKinley quickly submitted a war message to Congress and stepped aside. War was declared over strong opposition even from within the Republican Party. House Speaker Reed resigned in opposition to his party's policies.

(Top) The "Maine" in Havana harbor, 1900; troops embarking for Santiago de Cuba, 1898

(Above) Gen. Weyler, Spanish commander in Cuba, was called "Mad Dog" in the press; (below) Thomas Reed, speaker of the House

U.S.S. "New York" bombarding the Aguapores in the Philippines, 1898

(Above) Landing of American troops at Daiquiri, Cuba; photo by William Dinwiddie; (below) Teddy Roosevelt and the Rough Riders at the top of San Juan Hill

(Above) Cavalry of Gen. Gomez' Army at Remedios, Cuba, in 1899; photo by Strohmeyer & Meyer

(Right) Cienfuegos, the last Spanish camp in Cuba; photographed in 1899 by Strohmeyer & Meyer

(Below) Conference of the American Generals Miles, Shafter, and Wheeler, during the siege of Santiago de Cuba, July 1898; photo by William Dinwiddie

Admiral Dewey's Pacific Coast fleet proceeded immediately to Manila, destroyed the Spanish fleet, and then waited for occupation troops to arrive. The United States suddenly found itself in possession of a Pacific empire. Dispatch of Spanish armies in Cuba took only a few months and victory seemed to compensate for earlier doubts. But the noble prospect of bringing civilization to so many unfortunate people was somewhat soiled by revolt in the Philippines. It took three years of vicious war to subdue insurrectionists resisting American "benevolence." An estimated 600,000 Filipinos died in the war.

Scenes from the war against Philippine insurgents: (Top) U.S. troops moving into the back country; Filipino dead at Malals; American attack

(Above) Group of Philippine insurgents; (left) an insurgent outpost in the Philippines; (below) American soldiers pause by bodies of comrades killed in the Philippines

Burning the native district of Manila during the insurrection

(Above) Burning the Palace of Aguinaldo, leader of the insurrection, in Malolos; (below) ruins of Manila after shelling and attack by the American forces, 1899

(Left) Members of the Court of Arbitration, established at the Hague to settle international disputes by judicial means. Few cases ever reached the Court. (Center) Tsar Nicholas II of Russia, who issued the initial call for a peace conference; (bottom) the U.S. delegation to the conference contained a mixture of peace advocates and imperialists, but was dominated by Admiral Mahan

The First Hague Peace Conference in 1899 was championed by peace groups as the first step toward arms control and international cooperation for peace. The national delegations had few such illusions. All measures limiting a nation's freedom to further its interests by any means available were rejected. Admiral Mahan was a chief spokesman for this "realistic" approach to international politics. Symptomatic of the reasons for this failure of the movement for "peace-through-cooperation" was the great power competition for influence in China. Secretary of State Hay enlisted the U.S. in this competition, apropos of no current American interest, by asking for agreement to an "open door" policy in China. Hay hoped to prevent the Europeans from dividing up China to the exclusion of future American trade, but the policy was backed by no real commitment and was ignored.

The U.S. made a further bid for a role in Chinese affairs by gratuitously joining in the suppression of the Boxer Rebellion in 1900. (Top) Peking, a center of Boxer activity, where members of the European community were besieged in the diplomatic compound until rescued by the intervening troops; (left) members of the U.S. 6th Cavalry sent to China; (right) Boxers in Tien Tsin, a Boxer stronghold; (below) English missionary teacher, "heroine of the Siege," and refugee children at the London Mission Schools, Peking

(Top left) Theodore Roosevelt; (top right) "No Wonder He Was Ill," anti-McKinley cartoon; (right) McKinley at the President's Day festivities of the Pan American Exposition (below) held in Buffalo, N.Y., 1901

Roosevelt was made vice-president mainly to keep him safely out of the way. A somewhat overly vigorous and overly conscientious politician in the eyes of the party machine, Roosevelt had made considerable inroads on political corruption as governor of New York. Roosevelt remained safely vice-president for only six months.

41.

Henry Watterson: The Right of Our Might

"Colonel" Henry Watterson was editor of the Louisville Courier-Journal, *one of the most influential newspapers in the South. His interpretation of the Spanish-American War was markedly different from the many apologies for intervention in Cuba. Watterson dismissed the supposed commercial advantages and ignored Manifest Destiny; instead, he spoke of the working out of a "higher law." His April 20, 1898, editorial in support of the war is reprinted here.*

Source: *Louisville Courier-Journal,* April 20, 1898.

THE RESOLUTIONS upon which Congress finally agreed as expressive of our notice to Spain and the causes which impelled it are representative of the mind, heart, and power of the American people. There are some who preferred another phrasing, some who would have written them differently, but all in all they embody the truths and the purposes upon which we rest our case with mankind and appeal to the tribunal of battle. As Congress in the end sank minor differences of declaration and united upon this indictment of Spanish wrong, this proclamation of Cuban independence, this demand for Spanish abdication, this order to the Executive for the enforcement of that demand, and this disclaimer of our own intention to control the sovereignty of Cuba, so the people, ignoring similar differences, proclaim the voice of Congress the voice of themselves, and will make their own the action of the President in giving to their words the force of deeds.

It is given out that the President will to-day sign the resolutions and transmit them along with his ultimatum, allowing Spain a short time — say twenty-four hours — to comply, or take the consequences.

All this, however, is a mere formality. It is the ceremonious preliminary to the duel.

Spain's reply is already discounted. There is no probability — there is hardly a possibility — that it can be anything but a refusal of our demands. That reply received, the war will be on. Within an hour afterward the orders for the movement of our forces against Spain should be issued; by the opening of the coming week Havana should be invested, if not captured.

It is not for the *Courier-Journal* to predict the course of events or to map out the campaign. We shall be surprised, however, if the war, so long in beginning, be not soon over. We doubt if Spain really intends to make much more than a feint at fighting in order to propitiate her belligerent domestic elements, save the throne from the revolutionists, and turn loose Cuba with "honor." If the war should be protracted, it will be either because of serious reverses of our Navy in its first engagements, or because the Spaniards choose to pursue the policy of avoiding direct conflict, and devote their energies to keeping out of the way of our warships, harrying us by privateering depredations, and scattering sallies wherever their cruisers may find a weaker prey. This policy is not altogether improbable unless we should make such quick work of our eviction of Spain from this hemisphere that she may be brought to terms before she fairly begins such a policy.

Certainly we do not expect hostilities to be prolonged by the reverses or destruction of our fleet. Say what one will about Spain's Navy — grant, even, that her ships are a match for ours — we shall never believe that her seamen are a match for ours until they have proved it by a trial of skill. We have never yet met seamen who vanquished ours on equal terms, and we have met and conquered seamen of better fighting blood than any that flows in Latin veins. The American Navy, always unequal in ships to its antagonists, has always defeated its antagonists gloriously, and until it has been demonstrated that its men have sadly degenerated or that they are in no degree the masters of seamanship as applied to the modern development of the man-of-war in its less advanced stages, we shall never believe that they cannot overcome a fleet even much superior to their own manned by the fire-eaters of Spain.

Be that as it may, and whether the war be long or short, it is a war into which this nation will go with a fervor, with a power, with a unanimity that would make it invincible if it were repelling not only the encroachments of Spain but the assaults of every monarch in Europe who profanes the name of divinity in the cause of kingcraft. We do not mean to say that there are not good people in this country, aside from the patriots for revenue only, who are not earnestly and conscientiously opposed to this war. There are many others who believe it could have been averted, with the concession of all our demands, if a stronger hand had been at the helm of our diplomacy before the congressional crisis was reached. But all these will be as one with their countrymen in vigorously prosecuting the war, now that it is inevitable, to a splendid triumph for Americanism, for civilization, for humanity.

And that is what this war means. It is not a war of conquest. It is not a war of envy or enmity. It is not a war of pillage or gain. From the material side it is a war of tremendous loss to us, involving burdens of millions, not one cent of which can we hope to recover. There are those who diet on rice and peer through blue goggles, who whine that on legal grounds we have no right to interfere with Spain's belaboring her own ass, to dispute her sovereignty over Cuba, her own territory. If they had prevailed, America today would be a slaveholding nation. They are deserving of no more serious consideration than the featherheaded maniacs who are bellowing for war only for war's sake. We are not going to the musty records of title archives to find our warrant for this war.

We find it in the law supreme — the law high above the law of titles in lands, in chattels, in human bodies and human souls — the law of man, the law of god. We find it in our own inspiration, our own destiny. We find it in the peals of the bell that rang out our sovereignty from Philadelphia; we find it in the blood of the patriots who won our independence at the cannon's mouth; we find it in the splendid structure of our national life, built up through over a hundred years of consecration to liberty and defiance to despotism; we find it in our own giant strength, attained in the air, and under the skies of freedom and equality, which has not only won and guarded the world's bulwark of liberty and law in our republic, but which has laid down and enforced the decree that liberty and law on this hemisphere shall not be further trespassed on by despotism and autocracy, and which now, in the sight of the powers of the earth and the God of nations, takes one step more and says that liberty and law shall no longer be trampled upon, outraged, and murdered by despotism and autocracy upon our threshold.

That is the right of our might; that is the sign in which we conquer.

42.

WALTER HINES PAGE: The Significance of the War with Spain

The question of America's destiny in world affairs was a relatively new one in the 1890s. With the advent of the Spanish-American War, the United States took her first major step toward world involvement. To Walter Hines Page, editor of the Atlantic Monthly, *the war afforded an occasion to reflect upon the virtues and vices of the new direction in American foreign policy. The following editorial, written in June 1898, soon after Dewey's victory at Manila Bay, is a thoughtful analysis of the subject. The issue of commitment in world affairs, as Page pointed out, demanded a new kind of commitment from Americans also. The editorial is reprinted here in part.*

Source: *Atlantic Monthly*, June 1898: "The War with Spain, and After."

AMERICAN CHARACTER will be still better understood when the whole world clearly perceives that the purpose of the war is only to remove from our very doors this cruel and inefficient piece of medievalism which is one of the two great scandals of the closing years of the century; for it is not a war of conquest. There is a strong and definite sentiment against the annexation of Cuba and against our responsibility for its government further than we are now bound to be responsible. Once free, let it govern itself; and it ought to govern itself at least as well as other Spanish-American countries have governed themselves since they achieved their independence.

The problems that seem likely to follow the war are graver than those that have led up to it; and if it be too late to ask whether we entered into it without sufficient deliberation, it is not too soon to make sure of every step that we now take. The inspiring unanimity of the people in following their leaders proves to be as earnest and strong as it ever was under any form of government; and this popular acquiescence in war puts a new responsibility on those leaders, and may put our institutions and our people themselves to a new test. A change in our national policy may change our very character; and we are now playing with the great forces that may shape the future of the world — almost before we know it.

Yesterday we were going about the prosaic tasks of peace, content with our own problems of administration and finance, a nation to ourselves — "commercials," as our enemies call us in derision. Today we are face to face with the sort of problems that have grown up in the management of world empires, and the policies of other nations are of intimate concern to us. Shall we still be content with peaceful industry, or does there yet lurk in us the adventurous spirit of our Anglo-Saxon forefathers? And have we come to a time when, no more great enterprises awaiting us at home, we shall be tempted to seek them abroad?

The race from which we are sprung is a race that for a thousand years has done the adventurous and outdoor tasks of the world. The English have been explorers, colonizers, conquerors of continents, founders of states. We ourselves, every generation since we came to America, had had great practical enterprises to engage us — the fighting with Indians, the clearing of forests, the War for Independence, the construction of a government, the extension of our territory, the pushing backward of the frontier, the development of an El Dorado (which the Spaniards owned but never found), the long internal conflict about slavery, a great Civil War, the building of railroads, and the compact unification of a continental domain. These have been as great enterprises and as exciting, coming in rapid succession, as any race of men has ever had to engage it — as great enterprises for the play of the love of adventure in the blood as our kinsmen over the sea have had in the extension and the management of their world empire. The old outdoor spirit of the Anglo-Saxon has till lately found wider scope in our own history than we are apt to remember.

But now a generation has come to manhood that has had no part in any great adventure. In politics we have had difficult and important tasks, indeed, but they have not been exciting — the reform of the civil service and of the system of currency, and the improvement of municipal government. These are chiefly administrative. In a sense they are not new nor positive tasks, but the correction of past errors. In some communities politics has fallen into the hands of petty brigands, and in others into those of second-rate men, partly because it has offered little constructive work to do. Its duties have been routine, regulative duties; its prizes, only a commonplace distinction to honest men, and the vulgar spoil of office to dishonest ones.

The decline in the character of our public life has been a natural result of the lack of large constructive opportunities. The best equipped men of this generation have abstained from it and sought careers by criticism of the public servants who owe their power to the practical inactivity of the very men who criticize them.

In literature as well we have well-nigh lost the art of constructive writing, for we work too much on indoor problems and content ourselves with adventures in criticism. It is noteworthy that the three books which have found most readers and had perhaps the widest influence on the masses of this generation are books of utopian social program (mingled with very different proportions of truth), by whose fantastic philosophy, thanks to the dullness of the times, men have tried seriously to shape our national conduct — *Progress and Poverty, Looking Backward,* and *Coin's Financial School.* Apostolic fervor, romantic dreaming, and blatant misinformation have each captivated the idle-minded masses because their imaginations were not duly exercised in their routine toil.

It has been a time of social reforms, of the "emancipation" of women, of national organizations of children, of societies for the prevention of minor vices and for the encouragement of minor virtues, of the study of genealogy, of the rise of morbid fiction, of journals for "ladies," of literature for babes, of melodrama on the stage because we have had melodrama in life also — of criticism and reform rather than of thought and action. These things all denote a lack of adventurous opportunities, an indoor life such as we have never before had a chance to enjoy; and there are many indications that a life of quiet may have become irksome, and may not yet be natural to us. Greater facts than these denote a period also of peace and such well-being as men of our race never before enjoyed — sanitary improvements, the multiplication and the development of universities, the establishment of hospitals, and the application of benevolence to the whole circle of human life — such a growth of goodwill as we had come to think had surely made war impossible.

Is this dream true? Or is it true that with a thousand years of adventure behind us we are unable to endure a life of occupations that do not feed the imagination? After all, it is temperament that tells and not schemes of national policy, whether laid down in Farewell Addresses or in utopian books. No national character was ever shaped by formula or by philosophy; for greater forces than these lie behind it — the forces of inheritance and of events. Are we, by virtue of our surroundings and institutions, become a different people from our ancestors, or are we yet the same race of Anglo-Saxons, whose restless energy in colonization, in conquest, in trade, in "the spread of civilization," has carried their speech into every part of the world and planted their habits everywhere?

Within a week such a question, which we had hitherto hardly thought seriously to ask during our whole national existence, has been put before us by the first foreign war that we have had since we became firmly established as a nation. Before we knew the meaning of foreign possessions in a world ever growing more jealous, we have found ourselves the captors of islands in both great oceans; and from our home-staying policy of yesterday we are brought face to face with worldwide forces in Asia as well as in Europe, which seem to be working, by the opening of the Orient, for one of the greatest changes in human history.

Until a little while ago our latest war dispatches came from Appomattox. Now our latest dispatches (when this is written) come from Manila. The news from Appomattox concerned us only. The news from Manila sets every statesman and soldier in the world to thinking new thoughts about us and to asking new questions. And to nobody has the change come more unexpectedly than to ourselves. Has it come without our knowing the meaning of it? The very swiftness of these events and the ease with which they have come to pass are matter for more serious thought than the unjust rule of Spain in Cuba, or than any tasks that have engaged us since we rose to commanding physical power.

The removal of the scandal of Spain's control of its last American colony is as just and merciful as it is pathetic — a necessary act of surgery for the health of civilization. Of the two disgraceful scandals of modern misgovernment, the one which lay within our correction, will no longer deface the world. But when we have removed it, let us make sure that we stop; for the Old World's troubles are not our troubles, nor its tasks our tasks, and we should not become sharers in its jealousies and entanglements. The continued progress of the race in the equalization of opportunity and in well-being depends on democratic institutions, of which we, under God, are yet, in spite of all our shortcomings, the chief beneficiaries and custodians. Our greatest victory will not be over Spain but over ourselves — to show once more that even in its righteous wrath the republic has the virtue of self-restraint.

At every great emergency in our history we have had men equal to the duties that faced us. The men of the Revolution were the giants of their generation. Our Civil War brought forward the most striking personality of the century. As during a period of peace we did not forget our courage and efficiency in war, so, we believe, during a period of routine domestic politics we have not lost our capacity for the largest statesmanship. The great merit of democracy is that out of its multitudes, who have all had a chance for natural development, there arise, when occasion demands, stronger and wiser men than any class-governed societies have ever bred.

43.

Albert J. Beveridge: The Taste of Empire

*One of the most articulate spokesmen for American commercial imperialism was
Albert Beveridge of Indiana. While campaigning for the Senate, he perfected the
oratorical style that came to characterize his arguments for empire building during
his years on Capitol Hill. Beveridge's position was simple enough: he believed
that the Americans were the chosen people, that our form of government was the
best in the world and should therefore be exported to other countries, and that
it was not only to our commercial and political but also to our moral advantage
to expand beyond our borders. In a campaign speech, given in Indianapolis
on September 16, 1898, and reprinted here in part, Beveridge explained why the
United States should keep the Philippine Islands.*

Source: *Modern Eloquence,* Thomas B. Reed, ed., Vol. XI, Philadelphia, 1903, pp. 224-243.

It is a noble land that God has given us; a land that can feed and clothe the world; a land whose coastlines would enclose half the countries of Europe; a land set like a sentinel between the two imperial oceans of the globe, a greater England with a nobler destiny. It is a mighty people that He has planted on this soil; a people sprung from the most masterful blood of history; a people perpetually revitalized by the virile, man-producing working folk of all the earth; a people imperial by virtue of their power, by right of their institutions, by authority of their heaven-directed purposes — the propagandists and not the misers of liberty.

It is a glorious history our God has bestowed upon His chosen people; a history whose keynote was struck by Liberty Bell; a history heroic with faith in our mission and our future; a history of statesmen who flung the boundaries of the republic out into unexplored lands and savage wildernesses; a history of soldiers who carried the flag across the blazing deserts and through the ranks of hostile mountains, even to the gates of sunset; a history of a multiplying people who overran a continent in half a century; a history of prophets who saw the consequences of evils inherited from the past and of martyrs who died to save us from them; a history divinely logical, in the process of whose tremendous reasoning we find ourselves today.

Therefore, in this campaign, the question is larger than a party question. It is an American question. It is a world question. Shall the American people continue their resistless march toward the commercial supremacy of the world? Shall free institutions broaden their blessed reign as the children of liberty wax in strength, until the empire of our principles is established over the hearts of all mankind?

Have we no mission to perform, no duty to discharge to our fellowman? Has the Almighty Father endowed us with gifts beyond our deserts and marked us as the people of His peculiar favor, merely to rot in our own selfishness, as men and nations must who take cowardice for their companion and self for their deity — as China has, as India has, as Egypt has?

Shall we be as the man who had one talent and hid it, or as he who had ten talents and used them until they grew to riches? And shall we reap the reward that waits on our discharge of our high duty as the sovereign power of earth; shall we occupy new markets for what our farmers raise, new markets for what our factories make, new markets for what our merchants sell — aye, and, please God, new markets for what our ships shall carry?

Shall we avail ourselves of new sources of supply of what we do not raise or make so that what are luxuries today will be necessities tomorrow? Shall our commerce be encouraged until, with Oceanica, the Orient, and the world, American trade shall be the imperial trade of the entire globe? Shall we conduct the mightiest commerce of history with the best money known to man, or shall we use the pauper money of Mexico, of China, and of the Chicago platform?

What are the great facts of this administration? Not a failure of revenue; not a perpetual battle between the executive and legislative departments of government; not a rescue from dishonor by European syndicates at the price of tens of millions in cash and national humiliation unspeakable. These have not marked the past two years — the past two years, which have blossomed into four splendid months of glory.

But a war has marked it, the most holy ever waged by one nation against another — a war for civilization, a war for a permanent peace, a war which, under God, although we knew it not, swung open to the republic the portals of the commerce of the world. And the first question you must answer with your vote is whether you endorse that war. We are told that all citizens and every platform endorse the war, and I admit, with the joy of patriotism, that this is true. But that is only among ourselves, and we are of and to ourselves no longer.

This election takes place on the stage of the world, with all earth's nations for our auditors. If the administration is defeated at the polls, will England believe that we accept the results of the war? Will Germany, that sleepless searcher for new markets for her factories and fields, and therefore the effective meddler in all international complications — will Germany be discouraged from interfering with our settlement of the war if the administration is defeated at the polls? Will Russia, that weaver of the webs of commerce into which province after province and people after people falls, regard us as a steadfast people if the administration is defeated at the polls?

The world is observing us today. Not a foreign office in Europe that is not studying the American republic and watching the American elections of 1898 as it never watched an American election before. Are the American people the chameleon of the nations? "If so, we can easily handle them," say the diplomats of the world. . . .

The world still rubs its eyes from its awakening to the resistless power and sure destiny of this republic. Which outcome of this election will be best for America's future, which will most healthfully impress every people of the globe with the steadfastness of character and tenacity of purpose of the American people — the triumph of the government at the polls or the success of the opposition?

I repeat, it is more than a party question. It is an American question. It is an issue in which history sleeps. It is a situation which will influence the destiny of the republic. . . .

God bless the soldiers of 1898, children

of the heroes of 1861, descendants of the heroes of 1776! In the halls of history they will stand side by side with those elder sons of glory, and the opposition to the government at Washington shall not deny them. No! They shall not be robbed of the honor due them, nor shall the republic be robbed of what they won for their country. For William McKinley is continuing the policy that Jefferson began, Monroe continued, Seward advanced, Grant promoted, Harrison championed, and the growth of the republic has demanded.

Hawaii is ours; Puerto Rico is to be ours; at the prayer of the people, Cuba will finally be ours; in the islands of the East, even to the gates of Asia, coaling stations are to be ours; at the very least the flag of a liberal government is to float over the Philippines, and I pray God it may be the banner that Taylor unfurled in Texas and Frémont carried to the coast — the stars and stripes of glory.

And the burning question of this campaign is whether the American people will accept the gifts of events; whether they will rise as lifts their soaring destiny; whether they will proceed upon the lines of national development surveyed by the statesmen of our past; or whether, for the first time, the American people doubt their mission, question fate, prove apostate to the spirit of their race, and halt the ceaseless march of free institutions.

The opposition tells us that we ought not to govern a people without their consent. I answer: The rule of liberty, that all just government derives its authority from the consent of the governed, applies only to those who are capable of self-government. . . .

They ask us how we will govern these new possessions. I answer: Out of local conditions and the necessities of the case methods of government will grow. If England can govern foreign lands, so can America. If Germany can govern foreign lands, so can America. If they can supervise protectorates, so can America. Why is it more difficult to administer Hawaii than New Mexico or California? Both had a savage and an alien population; both were more remote from the seat of government when they came under our dominion than Hawaii is today.

Will you say by your vote that American ability to govern has decayed; that a century's experience in self-rule has failed of a result? Will you affirm by your vote that you are an infidel to American vigor and power and practical sense; or that we are of the ruling race of the world, that ours is the blood of government, ours the heart of dominion, ours the brain and genius of administration? Will you remember that we do but what our fathers did — we but pitch the tents of liberty farther westward, farther southward — we only continue the march of the flag.

The march of the flag! . . .

Distance and oceans are no arguments. The fact that all the territory our fathers bought and seized is contiguous is no argument. In 1819, Florida was farther from New York than Puerto Rico is from Chicago today; Texas, farther from Washington in 1845 than Hawaii is from Boston in 1898; California, more inaccessible in 1847 than the Philippines are now. Gibraltar is farther from London than Havana is from Washington; Melbourne is farther from Liverpool than Manila is from San Francisco. The ocean does not separate us from lands of our duty and desire — the oceans join us, a river never to be dredged, a canal never to be repaired.

Steam joins us; electricity joins us — the very elements are in league with our destiny. Cuba not contiguous! Puerto Rico not contiguous! Hawaii and the Philippines not contiguous! Our Navy will make them contiguous. Dewey and Sampson and Schley have made them contiguous, and American speed, American guns, American heart and brain and nerve will keep them contiguous forever.

But the opposition is right — there is a difference. We did not need the western Mississippi Valley when we acquired it, nor Florida, nor Texas, nor California, nor the royal provinces of the far Northwest. We had no emigrants to people this imperial wilderness, no money to develop it, even no highways to cover it. No trade awaited us in its savage fastnesses. Our productions were not greater than our trade. There was not one reason for the landlust of our statesmen from Jefferson to Grant, other than the prophet and the Saxon within them.

But today we are raising more than we can consume. Today we are making more than we can use. Today our industrial society is congested; there are more workers than there is work; there is more capital than there is investment. We do not need more money — we need more circulation, more employment. Therefore we must find new markets for our produce, new occupation for our capital, new work for our labor. And so, while we did not need the territory taken during the past century at the time it was required, we do need what we have taken in 1898, and we need it now.

Think of the thousands of Americans who will pour into Hawaii and Puerto Rico when the republic's laws cover those islands with justice and safety! Think of the tens of thousands of Americans who will invade mine and field and forest in the Philippines when a liberal government, protected and controlled by this republic, if not the government of the republic itself, shall establish order and equity there! Think of the hundreds of thousands of Americans who will build a soap-and-water, common-school civilization of energy and industry in Cuba when a government of law replaces the double reign of anarchy and tyranny. Think of the prosperous millions that empress of islands will support when, obedient to the

law of political gravitation, her people ask for the highest honor liberty can bestow, the sacred Order of the Stars and Stripes, the citizenship of the Great Republic!

What does all this mean for every one of us? It means opportunity for all the glorious young manhood of the republic — the most virile, ambitious, impatient, militant manhood the world has ever seen. It means that the resources and the commerce of these immensely rich dominions will be increased as much as American energy is greater than Spanish sloth; for Americans henceforth will monopolize those resources and that commerce. . . .

It means new employment and better wages for every laboring man in the Union. It means higher prices for every bushel of wheat and corn, for every pound of butter and meat, for every item that the farmers of this republic produce. It means active, vigorous, constructive investment of every dollar of moldy and miserly capital in the land.

It means all this tomorrow, and all this forever, because it means not only the trade of the prize provinces but the beginning of the commercial empire of the republic. . . . I said, the commercial empire of the republic. That is the greatest fact of the future. And that is why these islands involve considerations larger than their own commerce. The commercial supremacy of the republic means that this nation is to be the sovereign factor in the peace of the world. For the conflicts of the future are to be conflicts of trade — struggles for markets — commercial wars for existence. And the golden rule of peace is impregnability of position and invincibility of preparation. . . .

Ah! as our commerce spreads, the flag of liberty will circle the globe and the highways of the ocean — carrying trade to all mankind — be guarded by the guns of the republic. And as their thunders salute the flag, benighted peoples will know that the voice of liberty is speaking, at last, for them; that civilization is dawning, at last, for them — liberty and civilization, those children of Christ's gospel, who follow and never precede the preparing march of commerce.

It is the tide of God's great purposes made manifest in the instincts of our race, whose present phase is our personal profit, but whose far-off end is the redemption of the world and the Christianization of mankind. And he who throws himself before that current is like him who, with puny arm, tries to turn the Gulf Stream from its course, or stay, by idle incantations, the blessed processes of the sun.

Shall this future of the race be left with those who, under God, began this career of sacred duty and immortal glory; or shall we risk it to those who would scuttle the ship of progress and build a dam in the current of destiny's large designs? . . .

There are so many real things to be done — canals to be dug, railways to be laid, forests to be felled, cities to be built, unviolated fields to be tilled, priceless markets to be won, ships to be launched, peoples to be saved, civilization to be proclaimed, and the flag of liberty flung to the eager air of every sea. Is this an hour to waste upon triflers with nature's laws? Is this a season to give our destiny over to wordmongers and prosperity wreckers? Is this a day to think of office seekers, to be cajoled by the politician's smile, or seduced by the handshake of hypocrisy? No! No! my fellow citizens!

It is an hour to remember your duty to the home. It is a moment to realize the opportunities fate has opened to this favored people and to you. It is a time to bethink you of the conquering march of the flag. It is a time to bethink you of your nation and its sovereignty of the seas. It is a time to remember that the God of our fathers is our God, and that the gifts and the duties He gave to them, enriched and multiplied, He renews to us, their children.

And so it is an hour for us to stand by the government at Washington, now confronting the enemy in diplomacy, as our loyal hearts on land and sea stood to their guns and stood by the flag when they faced the enemy in war. It is a time to strengthen and sustain that devoted man, servant of the people and of the most high God, who patiently, silently, safely is guiding the republic out into the ocean of world interests and possibilities infinite. It is a time to cheer the beloved President of God's chosen people, till the whole world is vocal with American loyalty to the American government.

Fellow Americans, we are God's chosen people. Yonder at Bunker Hill and Yorktown His providence was above us. At New Orleans and on ensanguined seas His hand sustained us. Abraham Lincoln was His minister, and His was the Altar of Freedom the boys in blue set on a hundred battlefields. His power directed Dewey in the East, and delivered the Spanish Fleet into our hands on the eve of Liberty's natal day, as He delivered the elder Armada into the hands of our English sires two centuries ago. His great purposes are revealed in the progress of the flag, which surpasses the intentions of congresses and cabinets, and leads us like a holier pillar of cloud by day and pillar of fire by night into situations unforeseen by finite wisdom and duties unexpected by the unprophetic heart of selfishness.

The American people cannot use a dishonest medium of exchange; it is ours to set the world its example of right and honor. We cannot fly from our world duties; it is ours to execute the purpose of a fate that has driven us to be greater than our small intentions. We cannot retreat from any soil where Providence has unfurled our banner; it is ours to save that soil for liberty and civilization. For liberty and civilization and God's promise fulfilled, the flag must henceforth be the symbol and the sign to all mankind — the flag!

44.

Henry Holcomb Bennett: "The Flag Goes By"

The Spanish-American War produced a number as well as a variety of songs that was all out of proportion to the war's military importance. One of them was Henry Holcomb Bennett's "The Flag Goes By," which expressed the feelings of many Americans in this period of fervent and — from the point of view of the twentieth century — innocent patriotism.

Source: *An American Anthology, 1787-1900*, Edmund C. Stedman, ed., Cambridge, 1900, Vol. II.

THE FLAG GOES BY

Hats off!
Along the street there comes
A blare of bugles, a ruffle of drums,
A flash of color beneath the sky:
Hats off!
The flag is passing by!

Blue and crimson and white it shines,
Over the steel-tipped, ordered lines.
Hats off!
The colors before us fly;
But more than the flag is passing by.

Sea-fights and land-fights, grim and great,
Fought to make and to save the state:
Weary marches and sinking ships;
Cheers of victory on dying lips;

Days of plenty and years of peace;
March of a strong land's swift increase;
Equal justice, right and law,
Stately honor and reverend awe;

Sign of a nation, great and strong
To ward her people from foreign wrong:
Pride and glory and honor — all
Live in the colors to stand or fall.

Hats off!
Along the street there comes
A blare of bugles, a ruffle of drums;
And loyal hearts are beating high:
Hats off!
The flag is passing by!

Don't cheer, boys; the poor devils are dying.
Captain John Woodward Philip, of the battleship *Texas*, as his ship swept past the burning Spanish ship *Viscaya*, Battle of Santiago, July 3, 1898

45.

Thomas Davidson: Schooling for Breadwinners

Once a group of European immigrants was established in America, it invariably formed an organization to serve its social and cultural needs. Such societies often aided the new immigrants in the process of Americanization by providing libraries and educational facilities. One such society was the New York Educational Alliance, founded by German-born Jews. The Alliance had already accomplished a good deal in the field of education when, in 1898, it sponsored Thomas Davidson's Breadwinners' College on the Lower East Side of New York City. Davidson felt that, in addition to vocational training, working people also needed instruction in the common cultural heritage of the Western world. Such an education could, he thought, bring about a social equality among ethnic groups that would otherwise be unattainable. The following selection from Davidson's book of lectures, The Education of the Wage-Earners, *explains his theories.*

Source: *The Education of the Wage-Earners,* Charles M. Bakewell, ed., Boston, 1904: "The Educational Problems Which the Nineteenth Century Hands Over to the Twentieth."

In one respect, the educational problem in this country is much simpler than the economic one. The people of the United States may be said to have declared unanimously for socialism in education without having, so far as I know, set any limits to the education that may be given. Indeed, having adopted the principle, it cannot logically stop anywhere. All our states, I believe, provide for primary- and common-school education; most of them for high-school education; and many even for college and university education. Indeed, I see no reason to doubt that most of our states would provide for any grade of education for which there was any considerable demand, even for what it might seem their most obvious duty to give — education in statesmanship.

That, however, is not the only condition required, and such education must be given under conditions that can be met by all. Now, at present, all these conditions are, to a large extent, nonexistent. There is no considerable demand for higher education; the higher education given to the few is far from being the sort that is needed for the many; and it is not given under such circumstances that all can take advantage of it. . . .

When a number of young wage earners have acquired habits of study and surrounded themselves with books, they will begin to demand more favorable conditions for study — shorter work hours, college buildings, libraries, instructors — and when the demand becomes strong enough, all these will be accorded. . . . Thus will gradually arise institutions of higher education for the great body of the people, and when these are numerous enough to convince the state that there is among the wage workers a widespread demand for such education, it will take hold of the whole matter and, with public funds, establish a Breadwinners' College or People's University in every city ward and in every country village or township. Then the cause of the higher education of the people will be won and democracy placed on a firm basis. . . .

It is surely clear that the institutions needed in a democracy are such as shall wipe out all the unbrothering distinctions that divide sect from sect, and shall use every effort to secure for the whole body of the people intellectual, moral, political, and economic freedom.

It appears, then, that the People's or Breadwinners' University, which our circumstances demand, must consist of two parts: (1) a College for Culture, and (2) a Polytechnic Institute for Professional Training. Let us consider the nature of (a) the culture, and (b) the training which these must, respectively, give in order to be truly efficient.

CULTURE

CULTURE, IT IS OBVIOUS, MUST EXTEND to the whole human being, body and soul, and to all their functions. It should never be forgotten that it is difference of culture, far more than difference of wealth or position, that separates man from man and class from class.

Body culture includes health, strength, grace, and dexterity, which are acquired, respectively, through hygienics, gymnastics, deportment, and manual training. The whole of these should be taught in the lower schools; but they must be continued in the Breadwinners' University — the first three in the college, the last in the polytechneum.

In the Department of Hygienics, pupils will be taught what to eat and drink, how to prepare it, and when and in what quantities to take it. They will be taught when and how to sleep and how to avoid all those excesses which weaken and break down the nervous system. They will be taught how to avoid the evils of unsanitary homes and unsanitary dressing. No one who has not looked into the matter knows how much the working classes suffer from lack of knowledge of the laws of hygiene.

Ill-fed, ill-clad, accustomed to breathe impure air, they are unable to do their best work, and are wont to be sour and ill-tempered. Look at many of the young people in the streets and note what complexions they have. That means bad food, bad digestion, bad air, bad care. It may be said that good food costs too much; but that is only half-true. There are many inexpensive foods that are excellent; and even dear food is often the cheapest in the long run. All this will be explained in the class in hygienics.

In the class in gymnastics, every exercise will be taught that can impart strength and suppleness to the body, and make it the ready instrument of the soul. The practice of gymnastics should be continued throughout the entire life in order to insure readiness of action. What is more unbecoming than high or stooping shoulders, a sidling or rolling gait, a slow, ungainly movement of hands and feet, a general looseness and feebleness of the whole frame? And these things are not only unbecoming but they also go far to unfit their victims for skilled labor and efficient work. Gymnastics, it should be remembered, are a great aid to hygiene, if they do not degenerate into athletics, which are often extremely unhygienic, not to say brutalizing.

In the class in deportment everything will be done to train the body in ease, dignity, and grace, and impart refinement of manners. It is, to a large extent, the lack of these that unfits the uncultivated man for mingling with cultivated people. In their society he feels awkward and bashful. He feels that everybody is looking at him. He does not know how to act at table, in a drawing room, in a public assembly, and so on. The man of boorish manners who talks loud, uses slang, puts his elbows on the table, and eats with his knife cannot expect to be a welcome guest among refined people.

These, no doubt, seem little things, and they are; but they are big enough to separate class from class, which is not a little thing. There is no reason in the world why men and women who have to earn their living by manual labor should not be as refined in manners and bearing as any other class of the people. It is, largely, the lack of this refinement that makes so many of them willing to live in squalor and that makes the other classes look down upon them as inferiors and their employers treat them as mere "hands."

Soul culture must extend to all the three faculties or aspects of the soul — the intellect, the affections, and the will — and be such as to develop these harmoniously to their full extent. Our present schools and universities do little more than attempt to train the first of these, leaving the other two to take care of themselves. The result is that the affections and wills even of those few who receive a university education remain in the condition of mere caprice, undisciplined and misdirected. In the Breadwinners' University, not only the intellect but also the affections and the will must be educated and trained. Let us consider these faculties in this order.

1. *The Intellect.* What sort of education shall the intellect of the breadwinner receive? In attempting to answer this question, I am assuming that all those who desire higher education have already acquired the lower branches which the state socialistically provides in the common schools: that they can read, write, and cipher; that they know something of geography, physical and political, grammar, physical science, music, drawing, etc. What higher studies shall they undertake? The answer seems obvious: those studies which shall show them their place in the great drama of nature and history and the part they have to play in it. This is what we mean by imparting culture.

The man who knows what he is, whence he is, whither he is going, how he is related to the world and his fellows, is the cultured man. He may not know Sanskrit or Arabic, or even Greek and Latin; he may know very little of chemistry, botany, or astronomy, and nothing of quaternions; yet he will have the essential things. All the studies I have named are important, but they are not essential to culture.

Now, what are the sciences that teach us our place and part in the world? They may all be included under one — the science of evolution. Our place in the world is our place in the process of evolution. What we are consists of what we have done and what we are going to do. But the sciences of what we have done and are going to do are two — history and sociology — the former supplying the facts and the latter the theory of the facts. History includes not merely the evolution of humanity but the whole course of evolution — the story of the world; and sociology, which is the true philosophy, shows the principles by which this evolution is guided, thus enabling us individually to play our part in it.

The facts of history may be classed under various heads, such as natural and cultural; and these again may be subdivided, the former into astronomical, chemical, geological, biological, psychological, etc.; the latter into religious, ethical, political, economic, aesthetic, etc. But all these divisions are made merely for convenience of treatment, and the science of sociology shows that they are all but aspects of one eternal process in which each of us has an eternal part to play.

I know nothing more inspiring than the world view to which a true and exhaustive sociology leads. It is, in truth, religion made scientific; for what else has religion ever been but a view of man's relations to the society of beings that form his environment and of his duties in these relations? In these days when, in the pitiless glare of scientific research, the old unscientific world views which formed the basis of earlier religions are passing away, it is of the utmost importance that they should be replaced by a scientific one. Unless this is done, religion, which lends to life all the sublimity and consecration it has, must disappear, and life become vulgar, sordid, selfish, and frivolous, as, indeed, it is obviously becoming at present, just for want of such a world view. . . .

To draw up a course of study for a Breadwinners' College is not easy; but the following may be regarded as a first attempt:

1. Outline of the course of evolution, including philosophy of evolution.
2. The circle of the sciences (*Encyclopaedie*), including doctrine of method.
3. Outlines of universal history and sociology.
4. Comparative religion, including philosophy of religion.
5. Comparative ethics, including philosophy of ethics.
6. Comparative politics, including political philosophy.
7. Comparative literature, including theory of criticism.
8. Comparative art, including philosophy of aesthetics.
9. History and philosophy of economics.
10. History of discoveries and inventions, and influence of these.
11. History and philosophy of education.
12. Comparative philology, including philosophy of language.
13. History of philosophy and philosophic concepts.
14. Outlines of psychology, including history of psychological theories. . . .

The above curriculum, which would extend over three or four years, might be interspersed with other studies in particular departments of literature and science, care being taken that these entered into integral relations with the whole and contributed to a single world view. Their place in the "circle of the sciences" should be clearly marked.

So much for the culture of the intellect.

2. *The Affections.* It is a well-known law that every faculty is developed through its proper object or "good" — sight by things visible, intelligence by things knowable, will by things doable, and so on. It follows that the affections are developed by things desirable or lovable, and that, if they are to be properly developed, things must be adhered to or appreciated by them in the order of their desirability, that is, their worth for moral life. The question is: How can this be accomplished? Nobility is more desirable than wealth: How can this be brought home to the affections? This is a very different question from: How can an intellectual apprehension or conviction of this be imparted? Intellectual convictions are feeble motives to action compared with affections. A man who loves nobility will be far more noble than the man who knows that nobility is lovable.

How then shall we make people love nobility more than wealth? The answer is: By presenting each in its complete reality. This may be done in various ways — in the home, in the school, in the course of practical life — but the most effective way is through art, whose function it is to present things in such a way as to reveal their true meaning or moral worth. Dante's "Hell" and "Purgatory," by showing the true nature of sin, make it very unlovable, while his "Paradise," by showing the true nature of righteousness, makes it most desirable. How we hate hypocrisy after reading *Measure for Measure;* reckless ambition, after reading *Macbeth;* indecision, after reading *Hamlet;* and so on! Who can intelligently look at the Laocoon group without hating sensual vice; or at the Praxitelean Hermes without loving the spiritual sympathy that longs to educate?

The modern world has rarely realized the function of art, and hence an infinite amount of nonsense and sentimental twaddle has been spoken and written about it;

but the ancients, especially the Greeks, were not so blind. Aristotle saw clearly that art addresses itself to the affections . . . and is calculated to effect their purification, that is, to free them from disorder, obtuseness, and exaggeration. His notions regarding the place of music in education are only now beginning to be appreciated. . . .

We all know to what extent modern life is influenced by literature, and especially by novels and stories which appeal to the affections. Indeed, literature, the most comprehensive of the arts, ought to be the great trainer of the affections, and would undoubtedly be such were it not so stupidly taught in our schools and colleges. In brief, if, following Plato, we distinguish in the human soul a rational part and an irrational part, we may say that, while the former is educated by the sciences, the latter is trained by the fine arts.

But, after all, just as science is only distilled intellectual experience, so the fine arts are only distilled emotional or affectional experience. And just as there is, at the present day, a movement to limit book science, and to accord a considerable space in intellectual education to direct contact with nature, so the affectional culture derivable from the fine arts should be supplemented by emotional training through direct contact with the life of man. The students in the Breadwinners' Colleges, while emotionally realizing the works of Homer, Dante, Shakespeare, Goethe, Phidias, Praxiteles, Da Vinci, and the rest of the mighty, should be using the emotional culture thus gained to penetrate the life about them, its joys and sorrows, its loves and aspirations, and thus to enter into sympathetic, that is normal, relations with their fellowmen.

And no one will have more ample opportunities for this than just these students. More than almost anyone, they are brought face to face with "life's prime needs and agonies," and thus have a chance for a better education than anyone else. There is nothing that is more truly educative, nothing that better insures a correct distribution of the affections than philanthropic work of the right sort, undertaken, not in a spirit of condescension or missionariness but in simple loving kindness and reduced to a habit. The last clause deserves to be emphasized; for it should never be forgotten that, in the training of the affections, habit plays a very important part. We love what we are familiar with and what we can do easily.

3. *The Will.* When the body is strong and healthy, when the intelligence is carefully trained through study and contact with nature, and when the affections are distributed in accordance with the true worth of things, then there will be little need to worry over the training of the will. The will, indeed, is little more than the combined expression of the rational and irrational elements in the soul; in other words, the sum of the irrational impulses directed by rational insight. The breadwinner is a privileged being as far as will training is concerned; for his daily labor calls for almost continual exertion of will.

If in the Breadwinners' Colleges there is to be a will trainer, his chief function will be to select and assign tasks suited to the intellectual and affectional status of his different pupils. Such tasks will be the more effective in proportion to the amount of patience and self-denial they call for; that is, in proportion as they induce the individual to prefer his all-inclusive to his all-exclusive self, and to sacrifice his fragmentary self of the moment to the fully organized self of his entire existence. To live for all men and for eternity is to live a divine life, here and now. . . .

PROFESSIONAL TRAINING

THUS FAR I HAVE SPOKEN OF CULTURE, which opens up to the worker a noble world, invites him to come in, and renders him capable in body and soul of enjoying it and mingling with the best. It is the glory of our nation that no door leading to anything desirable is closed against the man of culture, be he Jew or gentile, rich or poor. But on this earth of ours we need not only culture in order to live a normal human life but also the means of living. We need the former in order to live well, the latter in order to live at all. The higher laws and needs of our being do not abrogate the lower; they come not to destroy but to fulfill.

Culture will make good men and women, good sons and daughters, good husbands and wives, good fathers and mothers, good neighbors and citizens, and so on; but it does not make good mechanics, merchants, bankers, physicians, lawyers, teachers, or artists. For these and many other professions, none of which are essential to us as human beings or citizens, there is needed a special training. Much of this may be, and is, imparted in the actual practice of the different industries; but there is much that cannot be so imparted, and demands special institutions. These are at present demanded for another reason, which cannot but be deplored. The labor unions do their best to prevent apprentices from learning the different trades.

In a special report on *Education in the Industrial and Fine Arts in the United States,* issued by the United States Bureau of Education in 1892, we read:

> The "Unions" welcome foreign-born and bred artisans, but throw every obstacle in the way of training American youths to become skilled artisans. By this policy they force upon the attention of educators and legislators evidences of the pressing need that exists for devising some practical methods whereby the rising generation may have the opportunity hitherto denied them of acquiring definite technical training in skilled industries.

The need of special training schools for the "liberal professions" is universally recognized; but there is no reason why these should be regarded as exceptional among so many. So true is this that, of late years, there have arisen, in considerable numbers, polytechnic institutions and technical schools, offering to certain other professions the needed instruction. . . .

The higher education in this country is not given under such circumstances that all can take advantage of it. Nearly all of its institutions — colleges, universities, polytechnic institutes, technical and industrial schools — are closed against the breadwinners because they are occupied with their work during the day, the only time when these institutions are open. *What the breadwinners need is evening colleges and evening polytechneums.* . . .

Such are a few suggestions toward a solution of the chief educational problem which the nineteenth century hands over to the twentieth. There is little time left for the consideration of minor problems, such as the training of efficient teachers for all grades of education; the arrangements and coordination of studies in view of different ends; the unifying of the whole course of study from the kindergarten up to the university; the establishment of a national university to give tone and direction to the whole national system of education, etc.

The one problem which above all others cries aloud for solution, and which it will be one of the chief tasks of the twentieth century to solve, is the higher education of the breadwinners. This education is absolutely necessary, not only for the well-being of the breadwinners themselves but for the safety of our whole nation and its democratic institutions. A democracy cannot long be sustained by an ignorant demos. This, indeed, is already becoming manifest. Our labor unions have already interfered with the liberty not only of employers and of the public generally but also, and still more, of the individual workman.

Tyranny, socialism, and violent anarchism, with their glittering utopias, are finding adherents among the workingmen. The political boss, with his lying promises and his filthy bribes, finds many of them an easy prey. All these things are fraught with serious dangers to liberty, and they are all due to want of intellectual and moral education. On the other hand, it is to the want of technical training that is due the fact that a very large number of our people are unable by their labor to give to society an equivalent for a decent livelihood, and therefore live in poverty and squalor, which are always powerful incentives to vice, crime, and rebellion. To the lack of the two kinds of education combined is due, in a word, all that we deplore and all that we fear in the condition of the breadwinners.

And for this condition we are all responsible. We leave a large number of them without intellectual and moral culture, and then we despise them because they are ignorant and vicious. We do nothing to refine their manners, and then we complain because they are boorish or brutal. We do not train them in the principles of political economy or sociology, and then we wonder why they become socialists, anarchists, or nihilists. We leave them unacquainted with their political privileges and duties, and then we are indignant because they sell their votes for a glass of whisky. We consign them to dark, cheerless, comfortless homes, and then we berate them because they take refuge in the gilded saloon. We give them no opportunity for the spiritual delights that come from the arts and sciences, and then we scorn them because they seek satisfaction in rum drinking and the other sensual delights of the dive.

To offset the saloon, the dive, and the poolroom, we open quiet reading rooms and chaperoned recreation rooms, and we wonder that they are not attractive to people who have never learned to take delight in reading or in quiet recreation. All these failures and wonderments on our part leave them in a deplorable condition, and build up between us and them a wall of alienation and misunderstanding that not only suggests a "war of classes" in the future but is narrowing and blinding to both classes now. The rich and the learned are poorer and meaner because they cannot enter into brotherly and sisterly relations with the toilers; and these suffer equally because they are sundered from those. Nothing can bring about that sympathy of classes which is so essential to a democracy and so beneficial to all classes but the universal diffusion of culture. The true rivals to the saloon, the dive, and the poolroom are the Breadwinners' College and Polytechneum, with their lectures, their classes, their exhibitions, and their practical work.

There is money enough and talent enough in this city of New York to give a higher education to all the people if they would but demand it. If but half the money that is spent in preaching old fables and obsolete, semibarbarous moralities were devoted to the truly religious purpose of developing the bodies and enlightening the souls of them that sit in darkness, we should soon have a different world about us. Today we need something very different from, and more effective than, the weekly sermon and the catechism. And, above all, we need to learn that the simple doing of our duty in all the relations of life is the only worthy religion. In that religion there are no sects — there is neither Jew nor gentile.

Let us all hope that ere the twentieth century reaches its majority there will be in every city ward and in every country township a People's University, consisting of a college for physical, intellectual, and moral culture and a polytechneum for professional training. So only will it be well with us and our country.

46.

WILLIAM T. HARRIS: Educational Creed

William Torrey Harris, probably the most widely known public school educator in the United States during the late nineteenth century, served as U.S. commissioner of education from 1889 to 1906. As a theorist he was a transitional figure. He advanced and consolidated the ideas of Horace Mann, but he was himself superseded by the progressive educational theorists who centered around John Dewey, some of whose early writing Harris published in the Journal of Speculative Philosophy. *Harris himself was a prolific writer and lecturer and his educational philosophy showed an understanding of educational psychology, as well as the importance of centering school activities around the child and not the teacher. The creed, which is reprinted here in part, was published in 1898.*

Source: *Educational Creeds of the Nineteenth Century,* Ossian H. Lang, ed., New York, 1898, pp. 36-46.

HAVING BEEN ASKED TO WRITE a brief statement of my educational creed, I set down what I consider to be important principles, without, however, taking the pains to arrange them in any systematic order. Many years ago, on being asked for a definition of education, I described it as the process by which the individual is elevated into the species, and explained this brief and technical definition by saying that education gives the individual the wisdom derived from the experience of the race. It teaches him how his species, that is to say, mankind in general, have learned what nature is and what are its processes and laws, and by what means nature may be made useful to man. This lesson of experience is the conquest of nature.

The second and more important lesson is, however, derived from the experience of human nature — the manners and customs of men, the motives which govern human action and especially the evolution or development of human institutions, that is to

say, the combinations of individuals into social wholes. By these combinations the individual man is enabled to exist in two forms. First, there is his personal might, and second, there is the reinforcement which comes to him as an individual through the social unit, the family, civil society, the state, the church. The individuals endow the social unit in which they live with their own strength, and hence the strength of the whole institution is far greater than that of any individual. In fact, the combined strength is greater than the aggregate of the individual strengths which compose it. Ten Robinson Crusoes acting in conjunction are equal not only to ten individual Crusoes but to ten times ten.

It follows from this view of education (as a means of fitting man, the individual, to avail himself of the knowledge of his species or race obtained through two kinds of experience) that I must set a very high value on the accumulated wisdom of the race. I must think that the man as an uneducated individual is infinitely below man as an educated individual. I must think, too, that a system which proposes to let the individual work out his education entirely by himself — Kasper Hauser style — is the greatest possible mistake. Rousseau's doctrine of a return to nature must also seem to me the greatest heresy in educational doctrine. But with this educational principle, so far as stated above, one does not have any protection against a wrong tendency in method which may be justified on the ground that the contribution of the social whole is the essential thing, and the contribution of the individual the unessential thing.

Keeping in view that essential thing, educational method is prone to neglect too much the individual peculiarities and, above all, to undervalue the self-activity of the pupil in gaining knowledge. It does not consult the likes and dislikes of the pupil and cares little or nothing for his interest in his studies. It is content if it secures the substantial thing, namely, that the individual should learn the wisdom of the race and the lesson of subordinating himself to the manners and customs of his fellowmen. It is content if it makes him obedient. He must obey not only the laws of the state but the conventional rules of etiquette. Above all he must obey his parents, his teacher, and his elders. This requirement of obedience carried out to the extent demanded in China, and to a less degree in monarchical countries of Europe and in this country until very recently, is based on a too exclusive contemplation of the social ideal as the chief object of education, and I hasten to add the statements needed to correct its incompleteness.

DEVELOPMENT ACCORDING TO SELF-ACTIVITY

ALL EDUCATION IS BASED on the principle of self-activity. The individual to be educated has the potentiality of perfection in various degrees and can attain this by his self-activity. A material body or a mechanical aggregate of any kind can be modeled or formed or modified externally into some desirable shape. But this external molding is not education. Education implies as an essential condition the activity of a self. It follows from this that while the end of education must be the elevation of the individual into the species, that this can only happen through the self-activity of the individual.

I saw this principle clearly before I saw the entire principle to which it is a part, namely, the relation of the individual to society. I can readily sympathize with scores of my friends and companions in education who see this principle of self-activity but have not yet arrived at the insight into that function of self-activity of the individual which is to so act that it may reinforce itself by the self-activity of institutions or social wholes.

Following this necessity of the individual, I believe that the greatest care should be taken not to arrest the development according to self-activity. Any harsh, mechanical training will tend to arrest development of the child.

There is for human beings as contrasted with lower animals a long period of helpless infancy. This long period is required for the development of man's adaptations to the spiritual environment implied in the habits, modes of behavior, and the arts of the social community into which man is born. Professor John Fiske has shown the importance of this fact to the theory of evolution as applied to man. It is the most important contribution which that doctrine has made to pedagogy.

If the child is at any epoch of his long period of helplessness inured to any habit or fixed form of activity belonging to a lower stage of development, the tendency will be to arrest growth at that standpoint and to make it difficult or next to impossible to continue the growth of the child into higher and more civilized forms of soul activity. Any overcultivation of sense perception in tender years, any severe and long-continued stress upon the exercises of the memory, will prevent the rise of the soul into spiritual insight. I therefore distrust many of the devices invented by teachers of great willpower to secure thoroughness in the learning of the studies in the primary school. . . .

ADJUSTMENT OF INDIVIDUAL TO SOCIETY

SCHOOL EDUCATION and all education is a delicate matter of adjustment, inasmuch as it deals with two factors, spontaneity and prescription. The latter tends to determine the whole individual by the requirements of the social whole; the former tends to make the child a bundle of caprice and arbitrariness by giving full course to his spontaneity or self-activity. The concrete rule of pedagogy is to keep in view both sides and to encourage the child to self-activity only "insofar" as the same is rational, that is to say, insofar as his self-activity enables him to reinforce himself with the self-activity of the social whole, or, to put it in another way, it enforces prescription upon the child only insofar as the same is healthful for the development of his self-activity.

Every pedagogical method must therefore be looked at from two points of view: first, its capacity to secure the development of rationality or of the true adjustment of the individual to the social whole; and, second, its capacity to strengthen the individuality of the pupil and avoid the danger of obliterating the personality of the child by securing blind obedience in place of intelligent cooperation, and by mechanical memorizing in place of rational insight.

I believe that the school does progress and will progress in this matter of adjusting these two sides. But I find and expect to find constantly on the road to progress new theories offered which are more or less neglectful of the delicate adjustment between these two factors of education. . . .

THE FIELD OF CHILD STUDY

FINALLY, A WORD IN MY CREED regarding child study. I have hoped and still hope from the child-study movement a thorough investigation of the question of arrested development. In view of what I have said above regarding the long period of helpless infancy and of the importance of keeping the child open to educative influences as long as possible, it becomes necessary to ascertain the effect of every sort of training or method of instruction upon the further growth of the child. For instance, do methods of teaching arithmetic by the use of blocks, objects, and other illustrative material advance the child or retard him in his ability to master the higher branches of mathematics? What effect upon the pupil's ability to understand motives and actions in history does great thoroughness in arithmetical instruction have; for instance, does it make any difference whether there is only one lesson in arithmetic a day or one each in written arithmetic and in mental arithmetic?

Does a careful training in discriminating fine shades of color and in naming them, continued for twenty weeks to half a year in the primary school, permanently set the mind of the pupil toward the mischievous habit of observing tints of color to such an extent as to make the mind oblivious of differences in form or shape and especially inattentive to relations which arise from the interaction of one object upon another? Questions of this kind are endless in number, and they relate directly to the formation of the course of study and the school program. They cannot be settled by rational or *a priori* psychology, but only by careful experimental study. In the settlement of these questions one would expect great assistance from the laboratories of physiological psychology.

Notwithstanding my firm faith in the efficiency of the school to help the child enter upon the fruits of civilization, I am possessed with the belief that to the school is due very much arrested development. Not very much success in this line can be expected, however, from those enthusiasts in child study who do not as yet know the alphabet of rational psychology. Those who cannot discriminate the three kinds of thinking are not likely to recognize them in their study of children. Those who have no idea of arrested development will not be likely to undertake the careful and delicate observations which explain why certain children stop growing at various points in different studies and require patient and persevering effort on the part of the teacher to help them over their mental difficulties.

The neglected child who lives the life of a street Arab has become cunning and self-helpful, but at the expense of growth in intellect and morals. Child study should take up his case and make a thorough inventory of his capacities and limitations and learn the processes by which these have developed. Child study in this way will furnish us more valuable information for the conduct of our schools than any other fields of investigation have yet done.

47.

Francis W. Parker: Salvation on Earth Through Education

The Cook County Normal School in Chicago, under the direction of Francis W. Parker from 1883 to 1896, became a showplace of progressive education. Implementing the educational theories of Pestalozzi and Froebel, Parker's school placed the child in a position of importance, looked critically at the formal curriculum of the past, and attempted to train children for living in an urban environment. "The center of all movement in education," wrote Parker in his most famous work, Talks on Pedagogics *(1894), "is 'the child.' " The following paper was written by Parker for inclusion in a volume of essays on education.*

Source: *Educational Creeds of the Nineteenth Century*, Ossian H. Lang, ed., New York, 1898, pp. 54-56.

I am obliged to give my pedagogical creed in a very general way.

First, I have unbounded faith in the development of the human race. I believe that the path and goal of mankind is education. The end and aim of education is community life. The child should be a citizen to all intents and purposes the moment he enters the schoolroom; or, in other words, he should become through teaching and training an efficient citizen of his little community.

I believe that the past has given us a vast inheritance of good that we should use for the future. I also believe that, comparatively speaking, we have just begun to study the science of education and apply art; that most things done in the past and that which we are now doing are comparatively crude. I believe that the only consistency in this world worthy the name is constant change in the direction of a better knowledge of humanity and of the means by which humanity rises to higher levels. I believe that the art of teaching is the art of all arts; it surpasses and comprehends all other arts; and that the march of progress is upon the line of the realization of infinite possibilities for the good and growth of mankind.

I believe in personal method in this sense, that each teacher must discover methods by the study of psychology and all that pertains to the development of the human being; that he must apply that which he thinks is for the best good of his pupils, and by supplying the best he will learn something better. The future of education means the closest study and diagnosis of each personality and the application of means to develop that personality into the highest stature of manhood or womanhood. I believe that no teacher, no one, can study the science and art of education and remain in the same place, applying the same methods, more than one day at a time. I believe that what we need in this country today is a close, careful, unprejudiced, thorough study of education as a science. I believe that dog-

matism should have an end and in its place should come scientific methods of study and a tentative mode of application.

I began to keep school forty-two years ago. I began to learn how to teach some twenty-five years ago. And, today, I feel deeply that I have not yet learned the fundamental principles of education. I believe in universal salvation *on earth* through education. I believe that man is the demand, God the supply, and the teacher the mediator; and when the day comes that this mediation shall approach perfection, the human race will enter into new life. I believe that no teaching is worthy the name if it does not have a moral and ethical end.

There are only two things to study, man and nature; there is only one thing to study and that is the Creator of man and nature, God. The study of God's truth and the application of His truth are the highest glory of man. Herein lies the path and the goal of education.

48.

HARRY McCLINTOCK: "Hallelujah, I'm a Bum"

The original of this famous song with its lilting tune is an old English hymn, "Revive Us Again." It was long thought that the irreverent American version had just grown by itself, but Harry McClintock, a Wobblie and sometime hobo, claimed that he had written the words during 1897 or 1898, and his claim seems now to be pretty widely accepted. The song was a favorite of the Industrial Workers of the World (I.W.W.), and it gained new life when thousands of people of a hitherto sedentary disposition went "on the bum" during the Great Depression of the 1930s.

HALLELUJAH, I'M A BUM

Oh, why don't you work, like other men do?
How the hell can I work when there's no work to do?

I went to a house; I knocked on the door;
The lady said, "Scram, bum, you've been here before!"

Chorus:
Hallelujah, I'm a bum,
Hallelujah, bum again!
Hallelujah, give us a handout
To revive us again!

I went to a house; I asked for some bread;
The lady came out, said, "The baker is dead."

Oh, I love my boss; he's a good friend of mine;
That's why I am starving out on the bread line.

Oh, why don't you save all the money you earn?
If I didn't eat, I'd have money to burn.

49.

Josiah Strong: A Nation of Cities

Josiah Strong became something of a national figure after the publication of his book
Our Country *in 1885. Unlike most clergymen of the time, who were careful to*
avoid any public discussion of wages, working conditions, and secular education,
Strong's gospel related religious principles to social needs. He was preoccupied in
many of his writings with the growth of urban areas and their influence on community
life. The following selection is taken from a book published in 1898. Much of the
material had first appeared in the Christian Advocate.

Source: *The Twentieth Century City,* New York, 1898, pp. 33-54.

Foreign immigration has stimulated the growth of cities in the United States, but of course cannot account for the scarcely less surprising growth of European cities. The phenomenal growth of the modern city is due to a redistribution of population. From 1880 to 1890 urban population in the United States increased 61 percent, while rural population increased only 14 percent, and 10,063 townships — 39 percent of the whole number in 1880 — actually lost population. Thus, Chicago more than doubled, while 792 townships in Illinois were depleted.

This redistribution of population is due to three principal causes:

1. The application of machinery to agriculture. A special agent of the government reports that four men with improved agricultural implements now do the work formerly done by fourteen. Inasmuch as the world cannot eat three or four times as much food simply to oblige the farmers, a large proportion of them are compelled to abandon agriculture and are forced into the towns and cities. Simply bearing in mind that the world's capacity to consume food is limited will throw not a little light on eco-

nomic conditions, both present and future. It means that only a limited number of persons can get a living by agriculture, and that when the supply of food has reached the limit of demand, agriculture can increase only as population increases. . . .

2. The second great cause of the modern city's growth was the substitution of mechanical power for muscular, and its application to manufactures. . . .

The springing up of factories in the city to produce agricultural implements and a thousand other things created a demand for labor and attracted to the city the laborers who were being driven from the farms. It should be observed, in this connection, that the application of machinery to agriculture and to manufactures has in one particular produced opposite results. While it has reduced the proportion engaged in the former, it has increased the proportion engaged in the latter. . . . By the close of the century the proportion engaged in manufactures will be twice as large as it was fifty years before.

These opposite effects of machinery upon the two industries are of the greatest importance since they are due to a cause which will continue operative, and will, therefore, shift these proportions more and more, perpetuating the movement of population from country to city. This cause is the fact that there is a natural limit to the world's capacity to consume food, while there is no such limit to its capacity to use the products of the mechanical arts. A family eats no more now than a family of the same size at the beginning of the century (though they eat better food), but their home is supplied with ten times as many manufactured articles, the number and cost of which may be indefinitely increased.

If the world were a hundred times as rich as it is, it could not eat a hundred times as much, nor could it make its food cost a hundredfold more; but it could easily spend a hundred times as much on public buildings and palaces, parks, and private grounds,

equipage and furniture, books and art, dress and ornament. For all these, purse and taste set the only limit of expenditure. The world's agriculture must relatively decrease while its manufactures increase. From 1870 to 1880 the former increased only 8.58 percent, while the latter increased 18.6 percent. Agriculture fell somewhat behind the estimated increase of the world's population, while manufactures increased nearly twice as rapidly.

This harmonizes perfectly with what is known as Engel's economic law. Dr. Engel, formerly head of the Prussian Statistical Bureau, tells us that the percentage of outlay for subsistence grows smaller as the income grows larger, and that the percentage of outlay for sundries becomes greater as income increases.

From all this it follows that, as the world grows richer, which the civilized part of it is doing very fast, an ever increasing proportion of its population must get their livelihood by means of the mechanical and of the fine arts, while an ever decreasing proportion will subsist by agriculture — from which the disproportionate growth of the city follows as a natural inference.

3. The third great cause of the growth of the modern city is the railway, which makes it easy to transport population from country to city and, which is much more important, easy to transport food, thus making it possible to feed any number of millions massed at one point. Prior to railway civilization, local famines were not infrequent; now they are become practically impossible, removing a former check to the growth of great cities.

It should be observed that all these causes are permanent; the tendency which springs from them will, therefore, be permanent. Beyond a peradventure, an ever increasing proportion of the world's population must live in cities. It will not be long before urban population will largely preponderate over rural in the Unites States, and in due time we shall be a nation of cities.

This tremendous migration of millions

from country to city, which marks a new civilization, is creating new social problems, and . . . will soon create most serious political problems. Many are loath to see that the growth of the city is inevitable and are suggesting various ways in which to relieve its congestion.

It is thought that if life on the farm can be rendered less distasteful, the young people, who are now eager to go to the city, may be persuaded to remain. It is true the city is more attractive; human intercourse, multiplied conveniences, greater religious privileges, superior educational advantages, amusements, excitements, an endless variety of happenings — all these appeal strongly to preference and have their influence; but these causes are subordinate. Even if these attractions could be made to preponderate in favor of the country, that would not materially retard the movement cityward. The decisive causes are economic, and they are absolutely compulsory; they do not consult preferences but create necessities.

Some philanthropists think that the congestion of the city might be relieved and the miseries of the slums alleviated by removing families to unoccupied lands; and many are under the impression that if the multitude could be got back to the soil, our most perplexing problems would be solved. But all such fail to appreciate the profound significance of the transition during this century from muscular to mechanical power — the most important change which has ever taken place in the history of the world — one which has already wrought an industrial revolution and is rapidly creating a new civilization. It has separated, as by an impassable gulf, the simple, homespun, individualistic life of the world's past, from the complex, closely associated life of the present and of the future.

In the age of homespun, which, for most of our population, reached nearly to the middle of this century, the typical farmer had little money and little need of it. The industry and ingenuity of himself and of his good wife supplied nearly all the wants of their household. Together they could do in a rude way the work which now represents ten or a dozen trades. They could have reared a family in comparative comfort if they had been cast away on Robinson Crusoe's island. They were practically independent of the whole world.

All this has been radically changed by the substitution of mechanical for muscular power, which has worked two most important results: first, the organization of industry; and second, a vast increase of products.

The organization of industry, of course necessitated the division of labor, by which each of the twenty men, who operate the score of machines which now do the work of a single trade, becomes dependent on the other nineteen. In like manner, the great industries have become allied, each to all the others, constituting together an endless chain of interdependence. Thus have sprung up absolutely new industrial conditions, which are producing equally new social conditions.

Mechanical power, which admits of indefinite increase, together with the organization of industry, which greatly economizes power, has enormously increased production. An excellent statistician estimated a few years since that if the goods made in one year by the 3 million factory workers in the United States at that time had been made by hand, their production would have required the labor of 150 million persons; that is, the machine method may be considered, on the average, about fifty times as productive as the old hand method.

The immense increase of supply greatly stimulated demand and resulted in a remarkable elevation of the standard of living. With the rise of that standard, what at first were regarded as luxuries came to be considered conveniences or comforts and were at length deemed necessities. There are those still living who remember when friction matches were a luxury.

The hand labor of the farmer and his wife, however diversified, soon proved unequal to the multiplying wants of a rising standard of living. They could supply themselves only by purchase, for which money was necessary. The farmer must therefore produce for the market. Thus, agriculture became a part of *organized* industry; and, like manufactures, came under the law of supply and demand; with this important difference, already pointed out, that there is a natural and necessary limit to the world's ability to consume food while its consumption of manufactured articles is determined by purse and taste — a wholly artificial limit, which is constantly being widened.

This natural limit to the world's demand for food, though perfectly obvious when mentioned, necessitates conclusions which are by no means self-evident. It shows that all efforts to relieve the congestion of the city by removing population to unoccupied lands must needs be futile. If 100,000 families could be transferred from city slums to the country and so trained as to become successful farmers, which is more than doubtful, it would not in the slightest degree mitigate poverty or relieve the pressure of population upon the city. These 100,000 farmers could succeed only by getting the market; and as the world would eat no more simply to accommodate them, they could get the market only by driving 100,000 other farmers out of it; who, being forced off the farm, would with their families gravitate to the city.

Farmers could be made independent of the market and so kept on the farm only in one of two ways: viz., by being so ignorant and animal that they would be satisfied simply with food and shelter, content like savages to forgo the comforts of civilized life; or, by being trained to produce for themselves, in the home, the comforts which intelligence demands.

Of course the first alternative is impracticable in this land and in this day. Ignorance and stagnation can solve no problems in a republic. And the second is as impossible as reversing the motion of the earth on its axis and rolling ourselves back into the age of homespun. The man capable of building for himself a comfortable house and of making his own furniture and tools, and the woman who can learn to transform wool and flax into garments and house furnishing are quite too intelligent, ingenious, and competent to spend their lives thus in the midst of modern civilization. They could make a better and easier living by devoting themselves to one of their several trades, which would inevitably take them to the city.

Another conclusion to which we are forced is that all attempts to retard the movement of population from country to city by raising the standard of agriculture will prove worse than futile. It is said that if agriculture were made profitable, as it might be by scientific methods, farmers would not wish to abandon it.

Scientific farming succeeds because a given amount of effort, when more intelligently directed, produces greater results. Inasmuch, then, as the amount of food which the world can consume is limited, the more intelligent or scientific the farming is, the smaller will be the number of farmers required to produce the needed supply, and the larger will be the number driven from country to city. It has already been observed that if scientific methods were universally adopted in the United States, doubtless, one-half of those now engaged in agriculture could produce the present crops, which would compel the other half to abandon the farm.

We may not, therefore, take refuge in unscientific methods. If our agriculture is not improved, we shall endanger our European markets, which were worth to us in 1896 no less than $570 million and gave employment to 1,700,000 farm laborers. We have been able to gain and retain these markets notwithstanding our wasteful and unscientific methods because of free farms of virgin soil. About 2,500,000 farms of 80 acres each have been given away by the government during the past 30 years. This advantage, together with our improved agricultural implements, enabled us to compete so successfully with the farmers of Europe as to produce a general depression of agriculture there, and so to alarm the governments of Europe as to enlist their efforts in behalf of home agriculture. . . .

This widespread revival of agriculture in Europe will force us out of their markets unless we cheapen our produce by more scientific methods, which will of course reduce the number of American farmers. If our agriculture refuses to progress and we thereby lose our foreign markets, the 1,700,000 men now employed in producing our agricultural exports will be forced off the farm. In either case, whether American farmers accept or reject scientific methods, large numbers will be driven to the cities.

We must face the inevitable. The new civilization is certain to be urban; and the problem of the twentieth century will be the city. Many English sovereigns attempted to arrest the growth of London by proclamation. Equally idle will be all attempts to turn back from the modern city the tide of population flowing up to it. One who thinks to circumvent or to successfully resist economic and social laws is fighting against the stars in their courses.

50.

Boss Rule and Ward Politics

Young men and women of the 1890s, filled with idealism and yearning to use their middle- or upper-class education to advantage, frequently worked in settlement houses located in slum areas. The South End House in Boston provided young people with the opportunity to live as well as work with the poor. The City Wilderness, written by these residents of South End House, was a compilation of their observations and investigations. Their findings provided professional sociologists and political reformers with useful insights into the dynamics of the slum. The following excerpt, taken from a chapter entitled "The Roots of Political Power," provides a glimpse of the role of the political machine in a slum area.

Source: *The City Wilderness: A Settlement Study,* by Residents and Associates of the South End House, Robert A. Woods, ed., Boston, 1899, pp. 114-147.

ALMOST EVERY BOY in the tenement-house quarters of the district is member of a gang. The boy who does not belong to one is not only the exception but the very rare exception.

There are certain characteristics in the makeup and life of all gangs. To begin with, every gang has a "corner" where its members meet. This "hangout," as it is sometimes called, may be in the center of a block, but still the gang speak of it as the "corner." The size of a gang varies: it may number five or forty. As a rule, all the boys composing it come from the immediate vicinity of the corner. Every gang has one or more leaders; and of course its character depends very much upon the leaders, for, as one of the boys expressed it, the leader says " 'Come,' and the push move." As a matter of fact, a gang if at all large has two leaders and sometimes three.

In order to show the different kinds of leadership, let me describe the qualities possessed by the three types in a large gang. First of all, there is the gang's "bully." He is the best "scrapper" in the gang. Many a hard-won battle has paved the way to this enviable position; but the position, often attained with so much difficulty, is not a sinecure. The bully not only has to defend the honor of the gang but may have to defend his title at anytime against the ambition of some "growing" member of the gang. Next, there is the gang's "judge"; all matters in dispute are finally submitted to him if no agreement is reached. The boy who enjoys this honor has gained it not by election but by selection. The boys have gradually found out that he does not take sides, but is fair-minded. Finally, there is the gang's "counselor" — the boy whom the gang looks to for its schemes both of pleasure and of mischief. In small gangs the bully may also be the judge and counselor, and even in large gangs it frequently happens that one boy dispenses both the latter functions. Here is the ward boss in embryo. . . .

It is interesting to know what becomes of these various gangs when the boys get to be seventeen or eighteen years old. The more respectable gangs, as a rule, club together and hire a room. The more vicious gangs prefer to use what little money they have in carousing. If by any chance they get a room, their rowdyism will cause their ejection either by the landlord or by the police. Consequently, they have to fall back on the corner or some saloon, as their meeting place. They nearly always seek a back street or the wharves, unfrequented by the police.

Not infrequently these gang connections are tenacious in the case of older men, who sometimes meet in the back of some store to play "forty-five," but more often would be found in a favorite saloon. In numerous cases a saloon serves as a clubroom for one or more gangs of these older men, who are loyally devoted to it. Many of them will walk by saloon after saloon thirsty in order to reach a particular drinking place with enough money to secure the proprietor's welcome.

At this point, it is necessary to give some account of the young men's clubs, in order that the important part that these clubs play in ward politics may be seen; for all this network of social life is taken in hand by the politician. As I said before, the gangs which coalesce and form these clubs are the most respectable ones. They are led to do this partly through a desire to have a warm room and partly because they are tired of standing on the corner and meeting the rebuffs of the policeman. Then such a club opens up the freedom of the district, socially, to them.

The first month or two is a trying time for every new club. Each gang composing it is likely to have a candidate for the principal offices; and frequently the first election is the occasion for a quarrel between the rival gangs, which breaks up the club before it is well begun. There are about eight of these clubs in the particular section which I know best. The dues range from 25 to 50 cents per week, and the club pays usually from $25 to $35 per month for its room. . . .

Each club has its unemployed, who live no one knows exactly how. Some clean up the room and thus save their membership. The fellows who work supply them — in part out of good nature and club feeling — with drinks and tobacco. The room is open in the daytime, and here those out of work can come and play cards and loaf. This contingent is known as the "day club." Very frequently they are the companions of girls who work in factories and receive weekly subsidies out of the girls' earnings. In some cases they impose upon their mothers or sisters who work and thus secure their board at home, and perhaps a little pocket money. . . .

The description thus far of the gang [and] the social club . . . shows that the politician does not need to deal with individuals. Ready at hand are these various social centers for him to make use of.

In addition to these social groups which take on a political character at election time, there are usually in the tenement-house sections several distinctly political clubs. Standing at the head of these clubs is the "machine club." It is now quite the custom of those in control of the party, and known as the "machine," to have such an organization. All the men in the ward having good political jobs are members. In one local club it is estimated that the city employees belonging to it draw salaries to the amount of $30,000 per year; in another club, outside the district, $80,000. It is natural that all the men in these clubs are anxious to maintain the machine. It is a question of bread and butter with them. In addition to city employees, the various machine workers are enrolled. The room of the club is ordinarily very pleasant. There are, of course, in these clubs, the usual social attractions, among other things poker and drinking. At the head of the club stands the boss of the ward.

So much for the organizations which are manipulated for political ends. The various typical actors in ward politics must now be described; first, the boss, his lieutenants, and "heelers." One of the bosses whom the writer knows is fairly typical. He is considered the "prince of jolliers," on account of his alluring ways. He has for many years been in public office of one kind or another. His early opportunities were small. His native abilities, however, enable him to fulfill his official duties with real effectiveness, when political business does not interfere. As he not infrequently plays the role of Warwick in politics, he gets a glimpse of larger worlds to conquer. These, however, can exist for him only as tantalizing dreams, for the lack of that education possessed by many whom he brushes aside and scorns. He does not reap the rich harvest which comes to the members of his craft in other cities. He does not carry with him any of the obvious signs of marked prosperity. He would probably not refuse greater spoils, however.

The possibilities in that direction in Boston are limited mainly to deals in connection with contracts for city works and supplies. The great corporations can only be nettled; they cannot be leeched. Their larger privileges are decided upon by the legislature. Even the licensing and police powers are retained by the state. It is to some extent the love of authority that urges the boss on. He knows his power, his mastery over men.

There is one quality which this typical boss has that gives him a sort of moral leadership. He makes many general promises which he never intends to fulfill, but a specific promise he usually keeps. He is distinguished among the politicians of the city as being a man of his word. This is honesty or sagacity, as you choose to look upon it.

There must be a certain degree of honor in dividing the spoils of politics, and the politician must provide something with which to feed his hungry followers. The jobs that he tries to get for his followers, however, are not secured as the private employer seeks men — for efficiency. The motive of the boss in seeking favors from the city government is to satisfy claims against him and to maintain himself. In this, forsooth, he considers himself as merely going the way of the world. He is to a large extent justified in so thinking. The highly respectable contractor or corporation man, for instance, who directly or indirectly makes corrupt deals with him, does so because "business is business." The boss enters into these deals, and goes through the rest of his program, not because he likes to but because "it's politics." Both are caught in the toils of an evil system.

The boss has reduced to a science the knack of dominating men. If a "jolly" or the "glad hand" will not carry his point, he can quickly frown. The frown of the boss is supposed to carry terror to the hearts of those to whom he has rendered favors or who expect jobs. This is easily accounted for, as without his approval no one in the ward can get a city job.

On the whole, partly for the love of position and power, and partly from a good heart, the boss enjoys doing good turns for men. Stories are told by his admirers of his generous deeds. For instance, he has been known to pay the funeral expenses of poor people who have no insurance. At Christmastime and Thanksgiving he gives turkeys to certain needy families. Dance tickets, baseball passes, tickets to the theater, railway passes, and so forth — which cost him nothing, being simply incidental results of his tools in the Common Council or the legislature voting "right" — are distributed with wise discrimination. He is always ready to treat. Some go so far as to say that if he died tomorrow his friends would have to pay his funeral expenses. This all sounds very generous; but the chief admirers of the boss cannot deny that when the supremacy in the ward is at all endangered, he makes capital of all his good deeds. In other words, every man to whom he has granted a favor is made to feel that the boss expects a vote. . . .

The boss is always strictly orthodox in his politics; he is intensely partisan. Independency is the unpardonable sin in his eyes. He grows really eloquent over "party harmony"; he storms and raves, he plots, he pleads for party harmony. He is really in earnest. His constituency like this loyalty of his, too. He deceives them. Sometimes he deceives himself. He always knows, however, that party harmony brings greater party success, more patronage, larger favors from corporations. Party harmony does not mean to the boss the greater ascendancy of party principles; it stands to him for good business, greater returns. . . .

There are certain lesser figures characteristic of ward politics known as "heelers." They do the dirty work. As a rule, they prefer to serve the well-established boss, as he can best protect them if they are found out and prosecuted in the execution of their villainy. As a rule, a "heeler" is a broken-down "bum," afraid of work, fond of his cups, in touch with loafers and the semi-criminal class, more of a fox than they, energetic enough in a campaign, possessed of a strong dramatic sense, loving the excitement of ward politics with its dark plots and wire pulling, glad to be lifted into temporary importance by having money to spend on the "boys." . . .

Repeaters are important actors in ward politics. It is a curious fact that there are many men belonging to the loafing and semi-criminal class who, because of their nerve, can repeat at a caucus so deftly that they are regarded as "expert repeaters." They are known to the boss or his heelers, and are often employed in close elections. They of course feel fairly secure under the protection of the boss. One fellow whom I know boasted to me that in a certain election he was driven from ward to ward, changing his disguise occasionally, and voting eight times in the course of the day. On inquiry, I found it was in all probability true.

Another man has a city job, but seldom works. He is a "valuable repeater," useful to the boss; the city pays, and the boss is strong enough to make his tenure secure. There are fellows who, without thought of doing wrong, repeat once in a while for some friend up for office. They are accounted respectable young men in the community. They say, "The others do it; we've got to do it to win."

Besides the boss, his lieutenants, and his heelers, there are usually in all tenement-house wards a large number of aspirants for some elective office, together with the incumbents of such positions and some retired politicians. They all have their clientage. Occasionally one will find a man who is honest and really wants to see an honest caucus, honest legislators, and civil service reform. Such men are few in number, however; and while a candidate of that kind will always be lauded in the campaign circulars by his followers for his honesty, his best friends will secretly wonder and shake their heads at his eccentricity. It is impossible to convince the knowing ones that any candidate is not "out for the stuff." . . .

I have spoken of the large number of young men enrolled in social clubs and in describing the activities of the clubs have suggested the character of their members. In these wards there is a large number of men in the employ of the city, chiefly as laborers. I have already referred to the loafers and semi-criminal class. Many of them live in lodging houses. It is a tradition among these men to stand in with the boss. If they get into trouble with the police, he frequently comes to their assistance. Through his help, the case is sometimes quashed or the sentence is abridged. This is the rough contingent that always attends the caucus and drives many respectable citizens away.

In noting the various classes of voters in these wards, it is also necessary to keep steadily in mind the large number of unemployed men. In the study of ward politics this factor has not been sufficiently appreciated. I do not refer now to the loafers but to the honest unemployed. The number of men who are almost ready to fawn upon one for a job is simply appalling. Ask those in the settlements, at the charity headquarters, the mission churches, or the working-

men's resorts, and they will tell you the same story. Some of these men are looking for political jobs. Consider the hold the boss can gain upon them. The few secure a job; the many get promises. Those who get jobs are the slaves of the boss. He does not make the work, and there is no credit in what he does, but you cannot blame them for their slavery. What is the honest use of their suffrage compared with bread? According to the ethics of the district, a man who receives a job is under the most sacred obligations to the politician who bestowed it. The lack of employment, therefore, is one of the most important factors working in the interest of the boss and boss rule.

There is still another group that must be mentioned. There is in these wards a considerable number of young men who regard politics as El Dorado. They are poor but ambitious. Many of them have received a fairly good education. It more and more requires a "friendly pull" in order to secure a good position in business. In business, too, they have to meet strong prejudices of race and religion. Politics, therefore, is for them apparently the easiest way to success in life. In every ward such as we are describing, there are a few conspicuous examples of men living in comfort, who are reported rich and have made their money in politics. It is told you, for instance, that the mother of one of these men lived in a garret and went barefoot out of sheer poverty. Thus the clever young fellow is encouraged to try his hand. Politics means business. Moral scruples are brushed aside. Victory at the caucus is the gateway of fortune. . . .

In nearly all tenement-house wards, one party is strongly in the majority. Such being the case, a nomination at the caucus usually means an election at the polls. The caucus is therefore the place where the real contest occurs. There is no single event in the ward that can equal the caucus for interest. It is a scene where the various gangs meet, as so many tribes, and fight for supremacy; where ambitious young men strive together for a "start" in life; where fortunes are made and lost; where sensational attempts are made to "down" the boss; it is a scene where a strong, rough, "jollying" personality tells as in the good old days of the fighting barons.

Again, it is a busy mart where men are bought and sold, a place where the drunkard can get the price of another drink, a place full of surprises, of unsuspected combinations, of damaging circulars sprung too late for answer, of small leaders fighting under new banners. It is, besides, the great social event for the men of the ward, when they gather in crowds and push and jostle and "jolly" and joke, and yell for their favorite, and bet on him as they might bet on horses. It is, moreover, a leveling event; an event in which the "thug" feels, not as good but better than his more respectable neighbor. Finally, the caucus is a place of action. It is the great ward drama — full of strong human touches, too often potent in tragedy to free institutions and the common welfare.

In case a boss is likely to be strongly opposed at a caucus for the election of ward officers, he can afford to spend a large sum of money in his campaign. How much he can afford to spend is in the main simply a question of business — of addition and subtraction. He stands, aside from the ambition to rule men, to get as much as possible out of politics for himself and the "gang." It is not necessary, usually, to spend much money direct for votes. Beer in the saloons, "beer parties" at the social clubs, and "house parties," getting work for the leaders of doubtful gangs, bailing a member of a tough gang out, employment of heelers to assess and register men falsely, and "circulars" are some of the common methods employed both by the boss and by his opponents, the "mongrels." Beer parties and house parties are time-honored institutions. . . .

Tickets are issued, and sometimes 200 or 300 attend. A beer party is held for the purpose of making the friends of the candidate "solid," and of gaining recruits. There are certain heelers and local leaders who figure largely at such times and are known as "beer-party orators." The speaking of the candidate and his friends amid smoke, sandwiches, and beer is always personal. The fact that the candidate is a "good fellow" is the chief theme. Issues are not referred to.

The house party is a smaller gathering held at the home of the candidate early in the campaign. Those invited are principally his lieutenants. Invitations are issued, however, very seductively, to the certain small leaders who are not "fixed" as yet. The strong camaraderie induced by the beer, sandwiches, and other refreshments makes the planning which is done at such parties much more eager and effective. This social feeling creates temporarily a new gang with all its loyalties; for the sentiment is quite strong in these wards that those who attend such parties shall vote and work for the candidate giving them.

The ward committee usually endorses certain machine candidates before the caucus. This is not always done formally. Sometimes it is simply understood. The cause of such a candidate is then the cause of the boss. The system is of course unfair and undemocratic. In the caucus of the party, all men should be on an equality; none should be ticketed "regular," none "independent." The situation is, however, a natural result of gang rule.

Let us assume that a man is running for office — for the Massachusetts House of Representatives. This will help to bring out in clear relief the advantages possessed by the boss, and the impossibility to a respectable man, not a gang man and without gang connections, of overcoming the start of the machine-endorsed candidate. It takes 400 or 500 votes to win a contest. In such wards there are from 100 to 300 city employees. Then there are a large number of those who are "looking for something." As a result, it would be impossible for a man of strict honor to throw off such a handicap, however able and genial a man he happened to be. In an ethical calculation, those "dead votes" do not count; in reality, they count as much as votes representing honest conviction. These men vote as the boss wishes. Add to their votes those of the men who can be bought with a drink, or who can be falsely registered, and from these sources alone there are 200 or 300 votes, perhaps more. Every such corrupt vote neutralizes an honest one.

In this analysis of machine votes, we have not taken into account the "popularity votes." If the candidate has been the leader of a gang from boyhood up, has graduated from the grammar school, is a good fighter and a good fellow, knows the social code of the saloon, and has a dash of respectability in dress and appearance, he is popular and a successful candidate. In the candidates of these wards, personal popularity is almost essential; the question of fitness for the office cuts little or no figure. Here again the best men of the district must often meet failure.

51.

GEORGE D. HERRON: Christianity and the Use of Private Property

George Herron achieved national recognition in 1890 by virtue of an address delivered in Minnesota on "The Message of Jesus to Men of Wealth." He had a radical view of property rights, emphasizing that Jesus "regarded individual wealth as a moral fall, and as social violence." It was Cain, Herron asserted, who had begun the competitive struggle and he urged a return to the cooperative living and common distribution of property that had prevailed during the first centuries of the Christian era. Herron had great influence at Iowa College (later Grinnell) where he taught from 1893 to 1900, but by 1896 the Congregational Church, in which he was ordained, turned against his teachings. Initially he hoped that the social revolution he envisioned would come about by individual renunciation, but after 1900 he came to agree with Marx that the change would require a long class struggle. The following selection is taken from Lecture Four of a series of eight Monday-noon lectures for the Christian Citizenship League (Chicago) given between October 24 and December 12, 1898. They were published in book form the following year.

Source: *Between Caesar and Jesus*, New York, 1899, pp. 105-140.

But if we say, on the one hand, that the Bible utterly condemns all violence, revolt, fierceness, and self-assertion, then we may safely say, on the other hand, that there is certainly communism in the Bible. The truth is, the Bible enjoins endless self-sacrifice all round; and to any one who has grasped this idea, the superstitious worship of property, the reverent devotedness to the propertied and satisfied classes, is impossible.   — MATTHEW ARNOLD

THE COMMON OWNERSHIP of natural resources follows a clear line of Christian teaching from the beginning of that teaching with Jesus Christ. Nearly all His statements of religious principles are in terms of human relations; and His idea was altogether more communistic than we care to discover. Reduced to economic terms, the realization of His ideal of the kingdom of Heaven could mean nothing less than an all-inclusive, non-exclusive communism of opportunity, use, and service. It may be a debatable matter whether any form of communism is practicable; but it is not open to question that Jesus never contemplated anything else than an organization of human life in which all men should work together for the common good, and each have according to his needs or power to use. . . .

The undeviating hostility of Christ and His witnesses to individual wealth cannot be evaded by following John Wesley's immoral advice to make all one can and then give all one can. The philanthropy of economic extortion is the greatest immediate menace to religion and social progress. The gifts that come not from willful extortion but from as clean hands as the system of things will suffer any man to have are apt to be even more misleading than the benevolence of avarice, because they seem to justify and make Christian what is really anti-Christ. Let us honor such contributions as they deserve to be honored, or concede the economic and historical necessity of individual wealth in the social evolution; but let us not deceive ourselves and become false teachers to the people by speaking of such wealth as Christian.

Wealth is a power in the world, and often a power for good, while a rich man may be very useful and generous, and his motives noble; but, however religious and philanthropic he be, the rich man stands in the antithesis of the Christian attitude toward the world. We cannot honestly imagine one in Christ's state of mind, one feeling as Christ felt, one coming at the world from his point of view giving himself to acquiring individual wealth. Strictly speaking, a rich Christian is a contradiction of terms. This is a hard saying, and it places every one of us in positions of dreadful inconsistency and difficulty; but it is the bald, naked reality of Jesus' teaching.

Let us confess that we are all alike guilty; that none of us are really Christian, if it comes to this; but let us be men enough to look the truth straight in the face. As Charles Kingsley makes one of his characters say, the worm that dieth not and the fire that is not quenched are a great blessing, if one may only know the truth by them at last. The shame and sorrow that the truth brings, I must face with you; for none are guiltier for the existing order of things than those of us who teach in colleges endowed by individual wealth.

Of course, one should not throw away nor destroy nor desecrate any property that is in his hands. He ought not and cannot individually extricate himself from the system that now exists. But the very least that a Christian can do in the existing order is to administer what he possesses for the common good, in the most literal sense of the term. A man cannot be Christian without being practically communistic; as a possessor of property, he is simply a steward having in trust what belongs to others. With this, he must exhaust his possibilities in changing the system from one of private ownership and competition into the common ownership and cooperative service of the kingdom of Heaven. Sometimes I think that a single man of great economic power, accepting such a stewardship, with the heart of Christ in him, could change the world.

The question as to whether economic brotherhood is practicable is a question of whether Christianity is practicable. If Jesus dwelt at the heart of God, and knew the law and secret of the universe, it is not worthwhile trying to establish society on any other basis than that of the universal communism of the Father who maketh His sun to rise on the evil and the good, and sendeth rain on the just and unjust; the Father who, when His children had wasted the abundant resources of life which He had already given them, redeemed them by giving them more resources. Before we dismiss such a social basis as a dream, let us well consider our free schools, the free street railways in the Australian city, the free highways unto the ends of the earth, and many other initiatives in the common life of today, which indicate that we are in the beginnings of a tremendous change upward into communism which Jesus disclosed as universal life and order.

In the fullness of its times, we shall have a new Christian synthesis upon which to base the religious movement which the social spirit seeks, and it will guide society through storm and change. The details of that synthesis do not yet appear; but in the outline emerging from the confusion of our faith, we may behold an economic of the kingdom of Heaven. It will so state the facts and forces which are the sum of Jesus' idea, in such clear terms of present social need, as to afford a definite, tangible, working program of social faith.

It comes, after the long winter of apostolic faith, as a new religion springing up from the seed of Christ in the human soil. It promises a faith for which men will once more be ready to live or die with equal joy.

It will be, as was prophesied by the last words of a beloved teacher, Dr. Edwin Hatch,

> A Christianity which is not new but old, which is not old but new, a Christianity in which the moral and spiritual elements will again hold their place, in which men will be bound together by the bond of mutual service, which is the bond of the sons of God, a Christianity which will actually realize the brotherhood of men, the ideal of its first Christian communities.

The original idea of Jesus once out in the social open as a mode and economy of life, to be seen as it humanly is, will sweep the world. His early standard once lifted amidst the perplexity and strife, and millions will rally to it as if on wings, not one of whom can be changed by our system of religion. His kingdom of Heaven once more at hand, and the Christian conscience that overran the Roman Empire, that wrought the spiritual chivalry of Francis Xavier and Loyola, that went crusading at the call of Hermit Peter and Abbot Bernard, that endured Spanish rack and fire and English gallows and dungeons, that crossed winter seas to found Pilgrim homes and build Puritan states, will arise in a messianic passion vaster than any summoned to change the world by crises past; and our economic problem will dissolve away in its fervent heat, to disclose the friendly stars of the new Heaven lighting the new earth with the everlasting truth that love is law.

———◆———

Do unto the other fellow the way he'd like to do unto you an' do it fust.
EDWARD NOYES WESTCOTT, *David Harum*, 1898

52.

FURNIFOLD M. SIMMONS: For the Restoration of White Supremacy in North Carolina

The Democratic Party, discredited after the Civil War and continuously reminded of its perfidy by the victorious Republicans, rallied throughout the Reconstruction period to regain a majority of voters in the South. In North Carolina a Fusion Party of Republicans, Populists, discontented Democrats, and Negroes was able to hold office for awhile. They had campaigned on the issue of clean and efficient government and had not raised the race issue. The Democrats, however, charged in the 1898 election that the Fusionists were leading the state toward Negro domination. The Negroes were in a majority and controlled the local government in many parts of the state. State Democratic chairman Furnifold Simmons introduced the issue of white supremacy into the campaign in an appeal to the white voters, a portion of which is reprinted here. The Democrats won and remained in power, with few interruptions, until after World War II.

Source: *Raleigh News and Observer,* November 3, 1898.

To the Voters of North Carolina:

The most memorable campaign ever waged in North Carolina is approaching its end. It has been a campaign of startling and momentous developments. The issues which have overshadowed all others have been the questions of honest and economical state government, and WHITE SUPREMACY. These issues were not planned and inaugurated by parties or conventions, but they were evolved out of the extraordinary conditions of the situation. Strenuous efforts have been made by the Fusionist leaders to divert the attention of the people from these conditions and to throw the campaign into other channels, but all their efforts in this direction have proven impotent.

The people of North Carolina are sufficiently intelligent to discriminate between *good and bad* government. They are sufficiently virtuous to want *good and honest* government. They have seen the government of the last two years, and they recog-

nize it to be *bad and corrupt,* and they were not to be seduced from their purpose to sharply arraign the party which has debauched the state before the bar of public opinion.

The horrible condition of affairs in the eastern counties and the progress there of Negro domination over white communities raised the question of whether in any part of North Carolina men of Anglo-Saxon blood should be subjected to the rule and mastery of the Negro, and this issue burned itself into the hearts of the people and kindled a fire of indignation which cannot be smothered by "Executive Proclamation," or by the threat of federal bayonets.

On these two issues, therefore, the Democrats have waged an aggressive and relentless campaign. Our enemies have been on the defensive from the very start. To the charges of extravagance and corruption they at first made denial; then they attempted evasion; then they had recourse to all sorts of subterfuges; but the charges were pressed, the conclusive proofs were offered, the people sat in judgment, and when the evidence was in, rendered their verdict of "Guilty." . . . Here are the material specifications of the bill of indictment:

It was charged and proved that the Fusionists, coming into power under a promise to reduce expenses, had, in three years, increased the expenses of the state government more than *$300,000.*

It was charged and proved that the expenses of the legislature, under Fusion government, had increased in two sessions, *$14,000.*

It was charged and proved that in one year salaries and fees paid the officers and employees of the penitentiary were increased *$9,000.* . . .

To the charge of extravagance was superadded the charge of corruption. . . .

It was charged and proved that public office was made a commercial commodity and bartered and sold for a price, unblushingly, openly, and systematically. . . .

Nor were the scandals and disgraces of the Fusion administration confined to venality, corruption, and pilfering. As the superintendent of the penitentiary was removed for his misconduct in one line, so the physician for the insane at the penitentiary fled the state upon charges of vile conduct too repulsive to name, and the penitentiary farms were shown to be dens of iniquity, too foul to be described. All these and other like charges, one after the other, were presented, and the proofs adduced, the chief witnesses being members of the party in power, the Fusionists attempted to take refuge first behind one cover and then behind another. But all in vain. They were driven from every position by the inexorable logic of FACTS — *facts* that could neither be successfully denied, controverted, nor explained. . . .

In the midst of all this din and conflict, there came a voice from the East, like the wail of Egypt's midnight cry. It was not the voice of despair but of rage. A proud race, which had never known a master, which had never bent the neck to the yoke of any other race, by the irresistible power of Fusion laws and Fusion legislation, had been placed under the control and dominion of that race which ranks lowest, save one, in the human family.

The business of two of the largest and most prosperous cities in the state had been paralyzed by the blight of Negro domination. In another city a white majority had been discriminated against in favor of a black minority, and the white man, who bore all the burdens and expense of government, had been given only one-half the representation of the ignorant and nontaxpaying Negro.

White women, of pure Anglo-Saxon blood, had been arrested upon groundless charges by Negro constables, and arraigned and tried and sentenced by Negro magistrates. . . .

Negro congressmen, Negro solicitors, Negro revenue officers, Negro collectors of customs, Negroes in charge of white institutions, *Negroes* in charge of white schools, *Negroes* holding inquests over the white dead. *Negroes* controlling the finances of great cities, *Negroes* in control of the sanitation and police of cities, *Negro constables* arresting white women and white men, *Negro magistrates* trying white women and white men, white convicts chained to *Negro convicts* and forced to social equality with them. . . .

Before this overwhelming array of evidence, the weak and puny wall of defense set up by the apologists of *Negro* rule crumbled away, and then there came the collapse. They had seen the handwriting on the wall. Everywhere they read in the face of the brave and chivalrous white men of the state a cool, calm, fixed resolution and determination that these things must stop; that hereafter white men should make and administer the laws; that Negro supremacy should forever end in North Carolina. . . .

Driven from every position of defense, disappointed in their hope of intimidating and coercing the people into submitting to their scheme of Negro domination, the desperate men who are now at the head of affairs in North Carolina and who are running the Fusion campaign have still one reliance left. Their last hope is a large corruption fund, which they have extorted from Mark Hanna, the financial agent of the monopolists of the United States, under assurances which they have given him that if they could carry the state this year it will be easier to carry the state for McKinley in 1900. With this corruption fund they still hope to save something from the wreck. They hope to import Negroes from the North and the South of us, to buy up votes . . . and thus block the efforts of the people to reverse the horrible conditions of the past two years. This hope will also prove delusive. If their corruption fund were *tenfold* as large as it is, they could not bribe the sturdy manhood of North Carolina to longer submit to Negro domination.

The battle has been fought, the victory is within our reach. North Carolina is a WHITE MAN's state, and WHITE MEN will rule it, and they will crush the party of Negro domination beneath a majority so overwhelming that no other party will ever again dare to attempt to establish Negro rule here.

53.

WILLIAM McKINLEY: The Acquisition of the Philippines

The foremost issue of the peace negotiations at the end of the Spanish-American War was the disposition of the Philippines, the unexpected conquest of which by Admiral George Dewey left President McKinley in doubt about the future of the islands. There had originally been no intention of retaining the islands, but pressure from commercial and military expansionists eventually persuaded McKinley that there was no suitable alternative. Retention grew even more imperative, when it became clear that Germany would take over the Philippines if the United States relinquished them. On September 16, 1898, McKinley sent instructions to his peace commissioners in Europe, reviewing the American involvement in the war and concluding that cession of the island of Luzon was mandatory. By late October further instructions demanded cession of all the islands. The following selection is from the instructions of September 16. The islands were finally ceded to the United States.

Source: PRFA, 1898, pp. 904-908.

BY A PROTOCOL SIGNED at Washington August 12, 1898 . . . it was agreed that the United States and Spain would each appoint not more than five commissioners to treat of peace, and that the commissioners so appointed should meet at Paris not later than October 1, 1898, and proceed to the negotiation and conclusion of a treaty of peace, which treaty should be subject to ratification according to the respective constitutional forms of the two countries.

For the purpose of carrying into effect this stipulation, I have appointed you as commissioners on the part of the United States to meet and confer with commissioners on the part of Spain.

As an essential preliminary to the agreement to appoint commissioners to treat of peace, this government required of that of Spain the unqualified concession of the following precise demands:

1. The relinquishment of all claim of sovereignty over and title to Cuba.

2. The cession to the United States of Puerto Rico and other islands under Spanish sovereignty in the West Indies.

3. The cession of an island in the Ladrones, to be selected by the United States.

4. The immediate evacuation by Spain of Cuba, Puerto Rico, and other Spanish islands in the West Indies.

5. The occupation by the United States of the city, bay, and harbor of Manila pending the conclusion of a treaty of peace which should determine the control, disposition, and government of the Philippines.

These demands were conceded by Spain, and their concession was, as you will perceive, solemnly recorded in the protocol of the 12th of August. . . .

It is my wish that throughout the negotiations entrusted to the Commission the purpose and spirit with which the United States accepted the unwelcome necessity of war should be kept constantly in view. We took up arms only in obedience to the dictates of humanity and in the fulfillment of high public and moral obligations. We had no design of aggrandizement and no ambition of conquest. Through the long course of repeated representations which preceded and aimed to avert the struggle, and in the final arbitrament of force, this country was impelled solely by the purpose of relieving grievous wrongs and removing long-existing conditions which disturbed its tranquillity, which shocked the moral sense of mankind, and which could no longer be endured.

It is my earnest wish that the United States in making peace should follow the same high rule of conduct which guided it in facing war. It should be as scrupulous and magnanimous in the concluding settlement as it was just and humane in its original action. The luster and the moral strength attaching to a cause which can be

confidently rested upon the considerate judgment of the world should not under any illusion of the hour be dimmed by ulterior designs which might tempt us into excessive demands or into an adventurous departure on untried paths. It is believed that the true glory and the enduring interests of the country will most surely be served if an unselfish duty conscientiously accepted and a signal triumph honorably achieved shall be crowned by such an example of moderation, restraint, and reason in victory as best comports with the traditions and character of our enlightened republic.

Our aim in the adjustment of peace should be directed to lasting results and to the achievement of the common good under the demands of civilization, rather than to ambitious designs. The terms of the protocol were framed upon this consideration. The abandonment of the Western Hemisphere by Spain was an imperative necessity. In presenting that requirement, we only fulfilled a duty universally acknowledged. It involves no ungenerous reference to our recent foe, but simply a recognition of the plain teachings of history, to say that it was not compatible with the assurance of permanent peace on and near our own territory that the Spanish flag should remain on this side of the sea. This lesson of events and of reason left no alternative as to Cuba, Puerto Rico, and the other islands belonging to Spain in this hemisphere.

The Philippines stand upon a different basis. It is nonetheless true, however, that without any original thought of complete or even partial acquisition, the presence and success of our arms at Manila imposes upon us obligations which we cannot disregard. The march of events rules and overrules human action. Avowing unreservedly the purpose which has animated all our effort, and still solicitous to adhere to it, we cannot be unmindful that, without any desire or design on our part, the war has brought us new duties and responsibilities which we must meet and discharge as becomes a great nation on whose growth and career from the beginning the ruler of nations has plainly written the high command and pledge of civilization.

Incidental to our tenure in the Philippines is the commercial opportunity to which American statesmanship cannot be indifferent. It is just to use every legitimate means for the enlargement of American trade; but we seek no advantages in the Orient which are not common to all. Asking only the open door for ourselves, we are ready to accord the open door to others. The commercial opportunity which is naturally and inevitably associated with this new opening depends less on large territorial possession than upon an adequate commercial basis and upon broad and equal privileges. . . .

In view of what has been stated, the United States cannot accept less than the cession in full right and sovereignty of the island of Luzon. It is desirable, however, that the United States shall acquire the right of entry for vessels and merchandise belonging to citizens of the United States into such ports of the Philippines as are not ceded to the United States upon terms of equal favor with Spanish ships and merchandise, both in relation to port and customs charges and rates of trade and commerce, together with other rights of protection and trade accorded to citizens of one country within the territory of another. You are therefore instructed to demand such concession, agreeing on your part that Spain shall have similar rights as to her subjects and vessels in the ports of any territory in the Philippines ceded to the United States.

54.

CHARLES DENBY: The Evident Fitness of Keeping the Philippines

Charles Denby, the former American minister to China, had long been an ardent supporter of American expansion into the Far East. "The Pacific Ocean," he had written to the administration prior to the Spanish-American War, "is destined to bear on its bosom a larger commerce than the Atlantic." Denby was delighted to become a member of McKinley's Commission to study the Philippines after the islands had been acquired as a result of the peace negotiations with Spain. In the following article, published in November 1898, Denby gave further reasons why the United States should retain the islands.

Source: *Forum*, November 1898: "Shall We Keep the Philippines?"

DEWEY'S VICTORY has changed our attitude before the world. We took no part in international questions. We had no standing in the councils of the nations. We were a *quantité négligeable.* So far did the idea that we ought to take no part in foreign questions extend that some of my colleagues at Peking, when I undertook to make peace for China and Japan, deprecated any intervention whatever of the United States in the affairs of the Far East!

The position of absolute indifference to

what is happening in the world is difficult of maintenance; and when it is maintained it is humiliating.

I recognize the existence of a national sentiment in accordance with the supposed teaching of Washington's Farewell Address, which is against the acquisition of foreign territory; but the world has moved and circumstances are changed. We have become a great people. We have a great commerce to take care of. We have to compete with the commercial nations of the world in far-distant markets. Commerce, not politics, is king. The manufacturer and the merchant dictate to diplomacy and control elections. The art of arts is the extension of commercial relations — in plain language, the selling of native products and manufactured goods.

I learned what I know of diplomacy in a severe school. I found among my colleagues not the least hesitation in proposing to their respective governments to do anything which was supposed to be conducive to their interests. There can be no other rule for the government of all persons who are charged with the conduct of affairs than the promotion of the welfare of their respective countries. If it be ascertained or believed that the acquisition of the Philippines would be of advantage to this country then mere sentiment must give way to actual benefit.

It is well known that prophecies of evil have preceded every acquisition we ever made, from the Louisiana Purchase to that of Alaska; and, judging by the results of the various annexations, these prophecies have been misleading.

There is no reason whatever why we cannot administer the Philippines in a manner satisfactory to their people as well as to ourselves. We have recently annexed the Hawaiian Islands. They lie at what are called the "crossroads of the North Pacific." They are near the center of the great lines of commerce from the East to the West. There is little dissent from the policy of their annexation. It is not imagined that their peaceful people will require a great army to control them.

If it could be ascertained today that no army would be necessary, or that a small body of troops at most would be sufficient, to safeguard the Philippines, opposition to their annexation would be greatly diminished. It is simply the dread of a large standing army that causes the body of the people who oppose annexation to withhold their approval. I do not believe that a large army will be necessary in the Philippines; and I am sure that, imitating the policy of England in East India, native troops would serve all purposes.

We have the right as conquerors to hold the Philippines. We have the right to hold them as part payment of a war indemnity. This policy may be characterized as unjust to Spain; but it is the result of the fortunes of war. All nations recognize that the conqueror may dictate the terms of peace. The first answer I received to a telegram sent by me, asking on the part of China that peace negotiations should be commenced and offering to concede the independence of Korea and to pay a reasonable war indemnity, was: "Japan is willing to enter on peace negotiations; but she will dictate the terms."

I am in favor of holding the Philippines because I cannot conceive of any alternative to our doing so, except the seizure of territory in China; and I prefer to hold them rather than to oppress further the helpless government and people of China. I want China to preserve her autonomy, to become great and prosperous; and I want these results, not for the interests of China but for our interests. I am not the agent or attorney of China; and, as an American, I do not look to the promotion of China's interests, or Spain's, or any other country's, but simply of our own.

The whole world sees in China a splendid market for our native products — our timber, our locomotives, our rails, our coal oil, our sheetings, our mining plants, and numberless other articles. We are closer to her than any other commercial country except Japan. There is before us a boundless future which will make the Pacific more important to us than the Atlantic. San Francisco, Seattle, and Tacoma are in their infancy. They are destined to rival New York, Chicago, and Philadelphia.

If we give up the Philippines, we throw away the splendid opportunity to assert our influence in the Far East. We do this deliberately; and the world will laugh at us. Why did we take Manila? Why did we send 20,000 troops to Luzon? Did we do so to emulate the French king who marched his men up the hill and down again? There was no purpose in the conquest of Manila unless we intended to hold it.

The Philippines are a foothold for us in the Far East. Their possession gives us standing and influence. It gives us also valuable trade both in exports and imports.

Should we surrender the Philippines, what will become of them? Will Spain ever conquer the insurgents, and, should she do so, will she retain the islands? To her they will be valueless; and if she sells them to any continental power she will, by that act, light the torches of war.

It is perfectly certain, I think, that England will not stand by and see any other European power take the Philippines. They are on the line to Australia and India. England has stood by and seen Germany, Russia, and France seize portions of China. There is not an Englishman nor an American in the Far East who approves her policy. The taking of the Philippines by any European power other than England would create an explosion in the latter country, and, if unresisted, would lead to the destruction of the ministry and, perhaps, the throne. By holding the Philippines we avert the partition of China, and we postpone at least a general European war.

There is, perhaps, no such thing as manifest destiny; but there is an evident fitness in the happening of events and a logical result of human action.

Dewey's victory is an epoch in the affairs of the Far East. We hold our heads higher. We are coming to our own. We are stretching out our hands for what nature meant should be ours. We are taking our proper rank among the nations of the world. We are after markets, the greatest markets now existing in the world. Along with these markets will go our beneficent institutions, and humanity will bless us.

The little brown brother.

WILLIAM HOWARD TAFT, of the Filipinos when commissioner of the Philippines, 1900. The phrase gave rise to the song, "He may be a brother to Big Bill Taft,/But he's not a brother to me."

1899

55.

Morrison I. Swift: Imperialism and the Threat to Liberty

"We have risen to be one of the great world powers," Henry Cabot Lodge commented on the results of the war with Spain, "and I think we have made an impression upon Europe that will be lasting." But the public was still uneasy about this new departure in American policy. A tremendous amount of literature was produced in 1899 to persuade the American people of the rightness or wrongness of the Philippine adventure. One example of propaganda against new acquisitions was Morrison Swift's book, Imperialism and Liberty. *In this book, portions of which appear here, Swift discussed what he considered the atrocious behavior of the President, businessmen, the newspapers, and the military during the preceding year.*

Source: *Imperialism and Liberty,* Los Angeles, 1899, pp. 34-43, 87-90, 151-154, 171, 375-378.

OUR CRIME IN THE PHILIPPINE ISLANDS

1. The New Policy of Corruption

WE . . . PROPOSE TO SHOW that the new American imperialism is a strict reproduction of . . . British imperialism. . . . If that is lovely and desirable, so is its American imitation. But let us permit American imperialists to speak for themselves and to disclose their own character. . . . This will show whether the Anglo-Saxonism that would be carried to the Philippines and elsewhere is worth carrying, or should be watchfully kept at home and extinguished.

Charles Denby, our one-time minister to China and now a member of McKinley's Commission to study the Philippines, has published a brief paper in answer to the question "Shall we keep the Philippines?" Being a man of prominence and authority among the expansionists, we give his words their due weight. They express the change in American morality toward the world which expansionists are inculcating and practising. This man is the type of those who surround and influence the President. He defines a hard and selfish national policy toward the weak.

Every important thing that has happened, everything that is happening, goes to establish this proposition: *That hard and selfish men and hard and selfish policies will control our imperialist relations; that the kind and well-meaning will be overruled. There is no intention of mildness, humanity, and justice in the forces that are now gaining ascendancy in American life.*

Here is Mr. Denby, the type of the hard

and selfish imperialist politician of the new school, openly impressing upon the country this crass and vulgar European doctrine. Thus Mr. Denby:

> We have become a great people. We have a great commerce to take care of. We have to compete with the commercial nations of the world in far-distant markets. *Commerce, not politics, is king. The manufacturer and the merchant dictate to diplomacy and control elections.* The art of arts is the extension of commercial relations — in plain language, the selling of native products and manufactured goods.
>
> I learned what I know of diplomacy in a severe school. *I found among my colleagues not the least hesitation in proposing to their respective governments to do anything which was supposed to be conducive to their interests. There can be no other rule for the government of all persons who are charged with the conduct of affairs than the promotion of the welfare of their respective countries.*

This then is what expansion and that noble "world diplomacy" with which our ears are being daily tickled bring us to! Here is Mr. Denby, corrupt and confessedly corrupted by this high diplomacy which is to make us a sainted and respected nation before mankind, glorying in the corruption and trying to corrupt his countrymen. If there was ever needed proof that we should keep ourselves unspotted from the filth and foulness of those European and Asiatic complications that territory stealing will assuredly bring, here is that proof. For contact with European codes inflicts those codes upon us. Denby continues his exposure of imperialism, and applies its Christlike morality to the Philippines:

> We have the right as conquerors to hold the Philippines. We have the right to hold them as part payment of a war indemnity. This policy may be characterized as unjust to Spain, but is the result of the fortunes of war. All nations recognize that the conqueror may dictate the terms of peace. . . .
>
> I am in favor of holding the Philippines because I cannot conceive of any alternative to our doing so, *except the seizure of territory in China;* and I prefer to hold them rather than to oppress further the helpless government and people of China. I want China to preserve her autonomy, to become great and prosperous; and *I want these results, not for the interests of China but for our interests. I am not the agent or attorney of China; and, as an American, I do not look to the promotion of China's interests, or Spain's, or any other country's, but simply of our own.*
>
> The whole world sees in China a splendid market for our native products — our timber, our locomotives, our rails, our coal oil, our sheetings, our mining plants, and numberless other articles. . . .
>
> Dewey's victory is an epoch in the affairs of the Far East. We hold our heads higher. We are coming to our own. We are stretching out our hands for what nature meant should be ours. We are taking our proper rank among the nations of the world. *We are after markets, the greatest markets now existing in the world. Along with these markets will go our beneficent institutions, and humanity will bless us.*

This is an exquisite example of the British cant and bathos which is exhibiting itself serenely in the new imperial America. Wherever the basest of international principles of pilfering and freebooting are applied to gain markets, "along with these markets will go our beneficent institutions." The halo of our blessed institutions will pervade and rectify rapacity and wrong! But it will not. We shall not build beneficent institutions on ruffianism and rapacity. "We are after markets, the greatest markets in the world"; we do not care what we do to get them — we will cheerfully rob and kill, we will wrench their fatherland from the weak and call it ours — we admit it in cold blood, but, like the praying professional murderer, we piously declare that God and humanity will bless us in it.

How did our war of humanity to rescue Cuba establish the irrelevant and unheard-of conclusion that unless we take the Philippines there is "no alternative except the seizure of territory in China"? There is no bridge between these two irreconcilable opposites excepting the beneficent institutions of American rapacity. The Philippines have done us no wrong, China has done us no wrong, but because Spain wronged Cuba and we had compassion, we do no wrong in wronging either the Philippines or China. This is the imperialists' creed.

Now, we do not expect to reach such men as Mr. Denby or Mr. Denby's type — the President, the advisers of the President, the whole tribe of commercial, political, and newspaper imperialists who are hounding the nation to crime. "Commerce, not politics, is king. The manufacturer and the merchant dictate to diplomacy *and control elections.*" We realize this. But we turn away from these classes to *the people.* We think that when they realize the brazen fraud being practised on them, *they* will decide to control elections, not only to put an end to the dishonest and ruffianly policy of imperialism but to put an end to the supremacy of commerce over man. . . .

2. McKinley's Proclamation of War

WHEN OUR CONGRESS passed the resolutions which involved us in war with Spain it pledged the following:

> Fourth, that the United States hereby disclaims any disposition or intention to exercise *sovereignty, jurisdiction, or control* over said island [Cuba], except for the pacification thereof, *and asserts its determination, when that is accomplished, to leave the government and control of the island to its people.*

In his message to Congress of December 1897, McKinley recorded and pledged himself in now famous and memorable language. Said he: "I speak not of forcible annexation, because that is not to be thought of, and under our code of morality that would be criminal aggression."

But one year later, on December 21, 1898, this man, on his own initiative, without the authority of Congress or the people, more than a month before the treaty of peace was ratified by the Senate, and when there was no certainty that it would be ratified, issued the following astounding proclamation to the Filipinos:

> With the signature of the treaty of peace between the United States and Spain by their respective plenipotentiaries, at Paris, on the 10th instant, and as the result of the victories of American arms, the future control, disposition, and government of the Philippine Islands are ceded to the United States. In fulfillment of the rights of sovereignty thus acquired and the responsible obligations of government thus assumed, the actual occupation and administration of the entire group of the Philippine Islands becomes immediately necessary, and the military government heretofore maintained by the United States in the city, harbor, and bay of Manila is to be extended with all possible dispatch to the whole of the ceded territory.
>
> In performing this duty the military commander of the United States is enjoined to make known to the inhabitants of the Philippine Islands that in succeeding to the sovereignty of Spain, in severing the former political relations of the inhabitants, and in establishing a new political power, the authority of the United States is to be exerted for the security of the persons and property of the people of the islands, and for the confirmation of all their private rights and relations. It will be the duty of the commander of the forces of occupation to announce and proclaim in the most public manner that we come, not as invaders or conquerors but as friends, to protect the natives in their homes, in their employments, and in their personal and religious rights.
>
> All persons who, either by active aid or by honest submission, cooperate with the government of the United States to

give effect to these beneficent purposes will receive the reward of its support and protection. All others will be brought within the lawful rule we have assumed, with firmness if need be, but without severity so far as may be possible.

Within the absolute domain of military authority, which necessarily is and must remain supreme in the ceded territory until the legislation of the United States shall otherwise provide, etc.

This proclamation drove the Filipinos into war against the United States. There was nothing left for them to do unless they consented to national enslavement. It was not only natural but right that they should go to war against us. Our chief man had notified them by arbitrary decree that if they did not submit to the usurped authority of the United States — "the absolute domain of military authority," he called it — they would be forced into submission by shell and grapeshot. "Honest submission," or death: they had their choice. "Honest submission," or "forcible annexation." All who did not honestly submit to the proclamation of the tyrant were to be "brought within the lawful rule we have assumed, with firmness if need be."

On the 5th of February that firmness began to be applied and 4,000 heroic Filipinos who could not honestly submit to the self-made despot were killed. The man who killed them was William McKinley. The death of each one of them was groundless manslaughter; McKinley was their murderer. He was their self-condemned murderer, convicted by his own words of one year before. "I speak not of forcible annexation, because that is not to be thought of, and *under our code of morality that would be criminal aggression.*"

Under the light of this solemn promise and its bloody repudiation, McKinley reveals himself to be the crowning fraud and hypocrite of the age, who has no right to respect from any honest man in the United States. He originally declared a true American principle, that we cannot take any form of authority over a people that is opposed to that authority without criminal aggression and breaking our code of morality; this code holds of Cuba, of the Philippines, and of every foot of ground not our own under the sun that our cupidity might be disposed to seize. The breaking of this code, consciously held and publicly announced, was therefore an act of detestable piracy, bringing shame and dishonor upon the whole nation.

The administration and the imperialist press have striven to convince our people that the Filipinos are responsible for the war. This is one of the lies that we must tell each other to save a last remnant of our self-respect. But it is nevertheless a lie with no mitigation. McKinley declared war in his proclamation, and the Filipinos began hostilities. The feeble McKinley doubtless honestly hoped that they would honestly submit to his declaration that they were to be as a conquered and subject people to the United States, without the sad necessity of being obliged to forcibly conquer them. The subterfuge did not work. They had never acknowledged the sovereignty of the United States: for the United States to declare sovereignty was therefore for the United States to declare war.

After the "criminal aggression" of McKinley's proclamation that a state of virtual war already existed, that they must submit or be killed, there was nothing for them to do but to fight. And every true American who resents this dastardly aggression by the President upon a harmless race of barbarians should be deeply thankful that they did fight, and must hope that our arms will not be able to subdue them. No honorable American can uphold the criminal attempt of American potentates to deprive a weak race of its liberty in the name of liberty. As liberty-loving American citizens it is our duty to uphold the Filipinos in their righteous and patriotic attempt to keep our yoke from falling on them.

3. All Our Rights Forfeited

FOR THOSE WHO HESITATE at this let us examine the President's rights when he proclaimed honest submission or kind but firm death to the Filipinos: (1) there was no technical, formal, legal, or constitutional sanction for his proclamation; (2) there would have been no right or sanction for it if the peace treaty had been ratified when he issued it.

Let us first consider what rights we had in the Philippines *before* the treaty was approved, remembering that its subsequent approval was not retroactive and could not lend legality to anything that was done before. Now, whether we had any after its ratification, we certainly had no status of authority in the Philippines before that act. We were there purely as opponents of Spain. We were not there as conquerors of the Filipinos but as conquerors of Spain; the Filipinos had helped us drive Spain out. When hostilities ceased, the islands were not ours except by temporary occupation. They were not ours either legally or morally. Spain had not ceded them and we had not decided to accept or even ask for them.

The only power in America that could make our request for them legal and binding, or accept them if offered, was the Senate, and that had not done so. The propositions drawn up by the peace commissioners at Paris were merely an arrangement by which the United States, acting through the Senate as ordered in the Constitution, could request or demand the islands of Spain if it saw fit. The Senate had not acted on the treaty and had consequently not even decided to ask for the Philippines. Our rights even technically were therefore *nil*.

A proclamation of sovereignty from the President when the whole question whether we should take or claim the islands was pending was justified by nothing but the arbitrary will of that ruler. It was no less an outrage than if he should proclaim our sovereignty over Canada, Ireland, or the British Indies. The act was an insult to Spain and a profligate attack upon the Filipinos.

Having issued this unlawful proclamation and so declared war on the Philippine Islanders, we forfeited all further claims over them excepting such as we might win by force if our challenge to war were taken up. After that proclamation the ratification of the treaty was a dead letter, for by our unlawful action all possibility of obtaining the Philippines legally or morally was lost. The question was now between us and them, and was one of force. Of course if they chose to accept the position of a people conquered by us without being conquered, that was their business; but legally and morally they ought not to have accepted that humiliation, and they did not do so. The President's impudent aggression also deserved anything but success.

To recapitulate: As we now stand we have no rights in the Philippines and can obtain none except by brute force. We ruled ourselves out by McKinley's act of usurpation. Spain would have been justified in resenting that act had she been able, and Spain being unable, the natives were justified. Until the acceptance of the treaty by both nations, our policy in the Islands could be only provisional. If Spain finally approved the treaty she transferred to us such rights of sovereignty in the Philippines as she possessed. . . .

BUSINESS ENTERPRISE OF GENERALS

THE WORDS OF OUR FIGHTING CLASSES at home in favor of imperialism likewise lose all their force when we consider who these people are and the motives of selfishness which move them to seek for this country a military future. It is almost enough to name these classes over to understand why they wish expansion. Have we not lately had some deep experiences what a precious set of self-seekers our military officers of all grades and sorts are? Is there anything in the daily conduct of our fire-eating professional politicians to make us think they care for the world, their country, or for aught beyond their own skins and interests? What of our eruptive press? What of great makers of trusts, so disinterested that they are taking all America as their own and damning the people to a hell of poverty and hardship? We charge these classes with seeking their own despicable private ends in painting the glories and profits of expansion.

Let us study them one by one. The trade of officers of war is war. Through schemes of war they promote themselves in the great objects of their lives, salaries, renown, affluence, and influence. All their aspirations and hopes center on military magnification. And it is their trade art to make others see things as they do. They are a species of commercial drummer, whose business success hangs upon their convincing others that wars and rumors and preparations for wars are the most important affairs of human society. They must do this or remain always little people.

They have the galling example of foreign countries. There a general is a truly great man; he is really a god with his clanking sword, his glittering uniform, his awful majesty of mien, his towering disdainment of the common carcasses of mere citizens which creep on the low earth below him. It is a thing to be a general in Europe. Life has character if you can feel yourself reposing on the clouds of power, master of instruments to blow the groveling herd of men to dust if they run amuck the doctrines that you patron. How different in America! How abominable, how degrading! A general is only a mortal here, adored and deified by none — until recently. He swallows

wind into his stomach and swells himself out in vain. He has been kept down in his proper place.

But times have changed and he thinks that if he throws a little more business enterprise into his trade he may win the privilege to expand and swagger and become a tinseled deity. Will he miss such a chance? Will he stint his arguments to convince his darling countrymen how good for them will be the owning of islands and invading of Asia? He looks forward to the time when he will not have to beg and argue to these countrymen, the time when with docile battalions behind his ramrod back he can stride haughty and ferocious across our part of earth and not demean himself by knowing that he has countrymen.

Oh people of America, watch this fellow argue now! Because the Army is still small, see how small and humble he is. With the deferential modesty of impassioned concern for us, he tells us of the danger of our coasts, talks soulfully of universal love, of duty, and of civilization! — this professional murderer, this smasher and preventer of civilization verily talks of duty! But give him his army and what will you hear him talk of then? Go to Russia and listen to the generals; are they talking of love? To civilized Germany, free France, liberal England; are their generals talking as we would wish to give ours liberty to talk?

1. The New Treason

BEWARE. Can you not already note a change of tone, a growing insolence since we took to war and yielded to the importunities of our war lords for a greater body of fighters? When have we before heard such language as this?

> The Army and the Navy are the sword and the shield which this nation must carry if she is to do her duty among the nations of the earth — if she is not to stand merely as the China of the Western Hemisphere.

When before now has anyone dared to use such raw twaddle to us? But the author of this febrile slush says more:

> To no body of men in the United States is the country so much indebted as to the splendid officers and enlisted men of the regular Army and Navy; there is no body from which the country has less to fear, and none of which it should be prouder, none which it should be more anxious to upbuild.

Is not this something wholly new and thunderingly preposterous? Is not the officer that can ooze this foul offense from his self-seeking mind already far on in his dreams toward a European America, where the military swashbuckler will eclipse and terrorize the toiling snail of peace? And yet even this is a lullaby beside the rabid impudence which the same nascent bully already ventures to express.

> As for those in our country who encourage the foe, we can afford contemptuously to disregard them; but it must be remembered that their utterances are saved from being treasonable merely from the fact that they are despicable.

So then, with an army of only 60,000 men, our semi-military gentry dare apply these abusive words to a number of American people so great that it may turn out when counted to be the majority. What will be said and done as time goes on and the Army grows according to the rampant military determination which now neither slumbers nor sleeps? Then those who differ in opinion from our military sheiks will be attended to for treason as they do it in Germany. Treason is something for which men are jailed, hanged, and shot. Treason is anything that displeases those in power, and the number of things that are treasonable increases in proportion to the increase of military force. Treason is merely a political label which those who want to establish their private opinions by force and rule arbitrarily apply to those with different opinions.

The man who says a thing is treason is a tyrant in embryo; he is a person with the blood of the inquisitors in him; he has not learned the smallest lessons of human appreciation, toleration, and progress; he is of that beastly fiber which burned men at the stake in earlier days for thinking as nature ordained them to think. Civilization has been one long and fearful struggle against this cruel beastliness, always betraying itself in new forms. The religious brute has been conquered, but the political brute and the military brute are here still, with the same old mighty will to destroy liberty, the same depraved frenzy to make mankind grovel to them in thought and act, the same aboriginal club with a new name to beat their brains out who resist.

Heresy was the ancient name of the club; the recent name is treason. If you do not believe in God as I do, I will kill you. If you do not believe in my politics, I will kill you. The same foulness in the human mind brings out ever fresh the same hideous deformity of conduct under later conditions, as they say that smallpox is a disease which arose out of syphilis, caused by the lives of abominable nastiness and abandonment of those who lived before us, and which now lives on to infect and injure a cleaner age with its horrid syphilitic substance. So is the cry of treason a recrudescence of the mental syphilis of heresy. . . .

THE BANDIT PRESS

1. As General Hell-Maker

THE PRESS OF THE UNITED STATES vaunts itself the possessor of great power. It has a power similar in many respects to that of the politician. The politician is a representative personage whose force lies in the fact that, after the people have performed the single self-governing act of his election, he does as he pleases. The press is a representative personage for whose erection to influence not even one democratic act is needed or performed. The owner of the press must have money; that answers for the periodic election of the politician. With money the newspaper becomes a representative voice of the people, not because the people chose or established it but because few people have vast sums of money to put into a newspaper and make it stand. The people accept what is given them and it passes for representative because they are unable to put anything really representative in its place.

But the people are thoroughly conscious that the press does not represent them and chafe increasingly under its pretensions to do so. With the concentration of wealth the press becomes less and less representative, less and less truly popular; for it ceases to depend on popular support for existence and depends on bodies of concentrated wealth, its great advertisers. The people recognize this change of the press center of gravity and feel it distinctly in newspaper treatment of popular issues.

The difference that has taken place is this. Formerly, the newspapers sought to discover and vocalize the sentiments of the people, because if they had not done so it would have wrecked their prosperity; now, they coolly give out as popular opinion whatever it suits them to have pass for public opinion; and as they are entirely independent of the will of the people and do not subsist by the people's support, it does not affect them or their interests if what they publish as popular will is the strict reverse of it. It was formerly the boast of the press to mold public opinion by educating it, but now it is able to produce at a moment's notice, overnight, any public opinion that is required without asking or needing the public concurrence. In this sense, public opinion is absolutely controlled by the press. Whatever popular sentiment it desires it manufactures, publishes, announces to be the will of everybody, hears no dissenting voice, and accepts the matter as settled — and so do the people.

The single fault of this process is that the opinion published has no element of the public in it. The popular sentiment which the press thus creates and sends out labeled, "by the people," is always that sentiment which is agreeable not to the masses of people but to the masses of press capital and the other volumes of concentrated riches from which the press draws its current sustenance. But it is as if these utterances were the public mind, for the press holds the avenues of popular speech and the people are obliged to be mute.

It is a circumstance of no slight meaning, this total detachment of the press from the people. Its significance is that public opinion is never really expressed and therefore never really even formed — in short, that public opinion has ceased to be a force or to exist. This is certainly startling when we reflect on the decay of the pulpit and platform, the other leading modes of public expression. Whether the press was the main cause, it was a great cause in the decadence of these institutions, for the audiences reached by the press grew so large that in contrast the number addressed by a pulpit or platform orator seemed hardly worth the labor and machinery of gathering them together. The press has even taken to preaching as a business investment, having a corner in its Sunday edition for compact little sermonlets from the pens of divines, for 5 cents — much less than the rental of a pew — furnishing the public with religion and rescuing it from the Sabbath labor of walking to church.

Rather the greater cause for the decline of the sacred and secular platforms has been the moral shrinkage of those who occupy them. The pastor has declined into an advocate and retainer of the wealthy class, the platform reasoner into a party politician and monger of prejudice, in each instance forfeiting popular confidence and leaving the field in possession of the press, which at least makes thin moral pretensions.

The people are left without a voice. The effect upon them of this loss of speaking power is a paralysis of both thinking and action, while those who command the avenues of expression are able to palm off ready-made, self-interested opinions on the people, making the impression upon each reader that although he does not believe this way others do and leading him to act or acquiesce with what he believes to be the majority view. The main influence of the press comes through this deception. It brazenly proclaims what it calls public sentiment, in which perhaps not a single unit of the public agrees, but all are silent because each dimly fancies that there must be such a sentiment somewhere, not crediting the press with the lying effrontery to declare an absolute fiction so shamelessly.

Each asks himself, too, what will be the use if I protest, since the papers will not spread a dissenting note? The people's mouths are closed with the rivets of necessity for they have no journals of any magnitude through which they are free to speak, the journals that profess to side with the people being conducted by just the same rules and just the same motives as the others, and differing only in the opinions which they publish as public opinion.

The will of the people never governs these publications of a millionaire capitalist — the will of his capital governs; the prosperity of the capital invested in the plant is the pole star of his newspaper policy, and that is never identical with the prosperity of the people, even if the most skillfully educated brains are employed to prove the identity in daily editorials. By them also something which the people are said to want is daily published in lieu of that which they do want, and success, what can succeed, what they think will succeed, not what ought to succeed, is the dominant criterion of everything that is done.

It ought to be made a proverb that the proprietors of none of the great dailies are in the business for principle any more than for their health; they are in it to prosper and they follow the laws of prosperity; so

that a great privately owned sheet which stands out for popular reform is certain to be unsound at the core because of the conditions that govern all private millionaire things. They live by advertisement and sensation. They increase advertisements by increasing sensations. If reform is a prolific sensation, some of them seize upon that as their province, not for the reform itself but for the money that is in it; and their advocacy mutilates it because instead of using it as a grand end they are abusing and degrading it as a means to increase sensation, circulation, and advertisement. . . .

The millionaires fill the papers full of their views daily, the people utter nothing, for not an inch of the papers belongs to them. Is this freedom of speech? It passes for it, yet in fact the people are as much gagged and suppressed as if the heaviest laws and penalties locked their lips.

The millionaires tailor our thoughts for us, as in Russia the government cuts out the thinking of the czar's subjects. There, press autocrats censor what goes in; here, the editors employed by the millionaire owners are the censors. Our way is much better, for it causes no ill feeling; through the marvelous magic of monopoly the people do not feel the hand of censorship, though it works as implacably as if in Russia the czar owned and edited, as he now censors, all the papers of influence. . . .

WITHOUT CONSENT OF THE AMERICAN GOVERNED

THE MOST MOMENTOUS FACT of the century is the *manner* of foisting imperialism upon us. To do it with our consent would have been one thing; to do it without our consent, as it has been done, is the greatest fourth-dimensional marvel of time. The guy of humanity which laid Spain at our feet opened the problem to the millionaire administration how to rob Spain and disarm popular suspicion. The act of confiscating instead of liberating Spain's territory had to be painted as an act of humanity. It was easy enough to say that all the Spanish islands should be liberated from Spain, but the pinch came in showing the humanity of our keeping them, particularly on top of our biblical asseverations not to do so. Our rulers got over that by inventing that the islanders are not fit to govern themselves. It is an invention because it certainly had not and has not been proved. The hardest tussle came when the unselfish trust administration was called on to establish the humanity of exterminating a race to give it liberty. This intention was flatly stated by our war bosses.

During that long, bright period when we had the rebels "well in hand," "Secretary Alger said that the situation was most encouraging and that it was apparent that the Filipinos realized the strength of the United States and saw that resistance would mean extermination for them if they persisted in defying authority." The invention used to clothe this deformity in virtuous humanity was the happiness of unborn future generations to spring from the exterminated. This guy also was soberly perpetrated and soberly received by a people proud of its susceptibility to humor.

Finally the evolution of imperialism reached a stage where the pretense of acting for humanity was an impediment. It prevented steps which were necessary if the juggernaut of progress was to murder on. It was an impediment, yet so tasteful a bait to the pious that it could not be done without. A very daring experiment was tried, that of disclosing the true purpose, territorial conquest for wealth, and painting the stars and stripes of humanity upon it. This plan included the full confession that trade had become the A and Z of the whole matter, but asserting that Yankee trade never went anywhere without carrying a superior article of humanity and civilization in its pack.

If this atrocious humbug found lodgment in the American spleen, every conceivable thing necessary for the world spread of American monopolies would be tolerated by the people, even down to the vivisection of whole savage races for trade experiments. This might be called a dull joke; it is still too early to say whether Americans, renowned among themselves for their biting perception of humor, will be able to see it. Our rulers have conducted their game very artfully, and the work now is to unravel the mesh in which that art has tangled us. How, from the essence of humanity, did the President extract the right to steal? His accomplices in this highwayman's synthesis in commercial chemistry were his politicians and editors.

In their passage from God to greed the steps are as follows. The President began this Fagin performance as soon as Spain was whipped, his instrument was our peace commission at Paris.

Step 1. It would be unhumanitarian to leave the Philippines and Puerto Rico with Spain. *Step 2.* It is our duty to take them away. *Step 3.* We shall not know what to do with them, but duty will always disclose a way. *Step 4.* We have a perfect right to take them. If humanity does not give the right, war does. *Step 5.* Although we fought purely for humanity, we have a right to consider our own good in the settlement incidentally, only incidentally.

Step 6. Considering our own good is in this instance identical with pure humanity, because, as the most generous people on earth, we can do nothing ungenerous. *Step 7.* It may be our duty to appropriate Spain's possessions to save Europe from an unnecessary quarrel. If we do so it will be against our will and for purely humanitarian reasons. *Step 8.* It may be that these possessions would be a great advantage to our trade, but that is not certain, and their climate is bad. *Step 9.* If it should be thrust upon us to take these lands for humanitarian and commercial reasons it will be the best thing that could happen to them. Our use of them for trade purposes would be identical with civilizing them, for this great enlightened nation can do nothing selfishly. We should teach them self-government and liberty, under us. *Step 10.* These semi-savage peoples have all shown themselves worthless and unthankful. Even the Cubans are low and ungrateful. They do not deserve the blood we shed for their liberty, nor much consideration of their wishes. We know better than they do what is best for them. *We must save them from themselves.*

Step 11. Our trade in the East depends on the Philippines. There is no disguising it. We must have the Philippines. It is our right and duty to look after our own interests in the world. That is the only way that we can preserve and spread the light of our enlightenment to others who need it. The dark places of the earth call upon us to trade with them that they may be enlightened. *Step 12.* All human prosperity rests on trade. The powers of Europe will take away our trade if we do not make ourselves a great world power in Army and Navy to protect and extend it. It would be a crime to permit less civilized and humane races than ourselves to capture and people the untilled places of the earth.

By these steps God is hammered into greed and yet retains the image of God. The transition from God to trade is accomplished, but all the trade language remains divine and biblical. The most miraculous part of this miracle is that the people of America had no part in it anywhere.

56.

RUDYARD KIPLING: "The White Man's Burden"

Rudyard Kipling had seen enough of his own country's far-flung colonial ventures to be able to suggest to Americans what the real meaning of their new imperialism might be. While the debate over the Philippines was raging, Kipling addressed to Americans a poem entitled "The White Man's Burden," which, despite its ironic tone, struck a note of nobility that was seized upon by expansionists. It was the title rather than the content of the poem that provided a catch-phrase for imperialists, and the poem, which was first published by S. S. McClure and widely reprinted throughout the country within a week, did much to bolster the expansionist cause.

Source: *McClure's,* February 1899.

THE WHITE MAN'S BURDEN

Take up the white man's burden —
  Send forth the best ye breed —
Go, bind your sons to exile
  To serve your captives' need;
To wait, in heavy harness,
  On fluttered folk and wild —
Your new-caught sullen peoples,
  Half devil and half child.

Take up the white man's burden —
  In patience to abide,
To veil the threat of terror
  And check the show of pride;
By open speech and simple,
  A hundred times made plain,
To seek another's profit
  And work another's gain.

Take up the white man's burden —
  The savage wars of peace —
Fill full the mouth of famine,
  And bid the sickness cease;
And when your goal is nearest
  (The end for others sought)
Watch sloth and heathen folly
  Bring all your hope to nought.

Take up the white man's burden —
  No iron rule of kings,
But toil of serf and sweeper —
  The tale of common things.
The ports ye shall not enter,
  The roads ye shall not tread,
Go, make them with your living
  And mark them with your dead.

Take up the white man's burden,
  And reap his old reward —
The blame of those ye better
  The hate of those ye guard —
The cry of hosts ye humor
  (Ah, slowly!) toward the light:
"Why brought ye us from bondage,
  Our loved Egyptian night?"

Take up the white man's burden —
  Ye dare not stoop to less —
Nor call too loud on Freedom
  To cloak your weariness.
By all ye will or whisper,
  By all ye leave or do,
The silent sullen peoples
  Shall weigh your God and you.

Take up the white man's burden!
  Have done with childish days —
The lightly proffered laurel,
  The easy ungrudged praise:
Comes now, to search your manhood
  Through all the thankless years,
Cold, edged with dear-bought wisdom,
  The judgment of your peers.

57.

George Hoar: The Lust for Empire

Once the Spanish-American War was a fait accompli, *critics of the war turned to its results; should the United States keep Puerto Rico, Cuba, and the Philippine Islands as the fruits of victory? Anti-expansionists said no, while empire builders said yes. The chief congressional spokesman against acquiring an empire was Senator George Hoar. His reasons, given in a speech on January 9, 1899, and reprinted here in part, were largely constitutional; other opponents argued that involvement in the Far East would extend American commitments beyond her capacity to deal with them. Despite their efforts, Puerto Rico and the Philippines became U.S. territories while Cuba was placed under military government. Cuba became a republic in 1902, but the Philippines remained a possession until independence was granted on July 4, 1946. Puerto Rico is still a U.S. possession but citizenship was granted to its inhabitants in 1917. Since 1947 they have chosen their own governor.*

Source: *Record,* 55 Cong., 3 Sess., pp. 493-503.

IT IS NOT MY PURPOSE . . . to discuss the general considerations which affect any acquisition of sovereignty by the American people over the Philippine Islands, which has been or may be proposed. I am speaking today only of the theory of constitutional interpretation propounded by the senator from Connecticut. If at any time hereafter the senator shall seek to put his theories into practice by reducing to subjection a distant people, dwelling in the tropics, aliens in blood, most of them Moslem in faith, incapable to speak or comprehend our language, or to read or to write any language, to whom the traditions and the doctrines of civil liberty are unknown, it will be time to point out what terrible results and penalties this departure from our constitutional principles will bring upon us. . . .

The question is this: Have we the right, as doubtless we have the physical power, to enter upon the government of ten or twelve million subject people without constitutional restraint? Of that question the senator from Connecticut takes the affirmative. And upon that question I desire to join issue.

Mr. President, I am no strict constructionist. I am no alarmist. I believe this country to be a nation, a sovereign nation. I believe Congress to possess all the powers which are necessary to accomplish under the most generous and liberal construction the great objects which the men who framed the Constitution and the people who adopted it desired to accomplish by its instrumentality. I was bred, I might almost say I was born, in the faith which I inherited from the men whose blood is in my veins, of the party of Hamilton and Washington and Webster and Sumner, and not in that of Madison or Calhoun or the strict constructionists. . . .

I affirm that every constitutional power,

whether it be called a power of sovereignty or of nationality — neither of which phrases is found in terms in the Constitution — or whether it be a power expressly declared and named therein, is limited to the one supreme and controlling purpose declared as that for which the Constitution itself was framed: "In order to form a more perfect union, establish justice, insure domestic tranquillity, provide for the common defense, promote the general welfare, and secure the blessings of liberty to ourselves and our posterity."

Now, the liberal constructionists claim that everything which is done to accomplish either of these purposes, unless expressly prohibited, may be constitutionally done by the lawmaking power. And in that I agree with them. The strict constructionist claims, and has claimed from the time of Madison, that these objects can only be accomplished after ways and fashions expressly described in the Constitution or necessarily implied therein. And in that I disagree with him.

But when the senator from Connecticut undertakes to declare that we may do such things not for the perfect union, the common defense, the general welfare of the people of the United States, or the securing of liberty to ourselves and our children, but for any fancied or real obligation to take care of distant peoples beyond our boundaries, not people of the United States, then I deny his proposition and tell him he can find nothing either in the text of the Constitution or the exposition of the fathers, or the judgments of courts from that day to this, to warrant or support his doctrine.

Further, the 1st Article of the Constitution declares: "All legislative powers herein granted shall be vested in a Congress of the United States." What becomes, in the light of that language, of the senator's repeated assertion that powers not denied may be so exercised? Is not legislative power a power of sovereignty? Therefore, according to the senator's logic, every power of legislation

that any foreign government — legislative, constitutional, limited, or despotic — may exercise may be exercised by us. We have heard of limited monarchies, constitutional monarchies, despotisms tempered by assassination; but the logic of the senator from Connecticut makes a pure, unlimited, untempered despotism without any relief from assassins. . . .

But the question with which we now have to deal is whether Congress may conquer and may govern, without their consent and against their will, a foreign nation, a separate, distinct, and numerous people, a territory not hereafter to be populated by Americans, to be formed into American states and to take its part in fulfilling and executing the purposes for which the Constitution was framed, whether it may conquer, control, and govern this people, not for the general welfare, common defense, more perfect union, more blessed liberty of the people of the United States, but for some real or fancied benefit to be conferred against their desire upon the people so governed or in discharge of some fancied obligation to them, and not to the people of the United States.

Now, Mr. President, the question is whether the men who framed the Constitution, or the people who adopted it, meant to confer that power among the limited and restrained powers of the sovereign nation that they were creating. Upon that question I take issue with my honorable friend from Connecticut.

I declare not only that this is not among the express powers conferred upon the sovereignty they created, that it is not among the powers necessarily or reasonably or conveniently implied for the sake of carrying into effect the purposes of that instrument, but that it is a power which it can be demonstrated by the whole contemporaneous history and by our whole history since until within six months they did not mean should exist — a power that our fathers and their descendants have ever loathed and abhorred — and that they believed that no sovereign on earth could rightfully exercise it and that no people on earth could rightfully confer it. They not only did not mean to confer it but they would have cut off their right hands, every one of them, sooner than set them to an instrument which should confer it. . . .

Mr. President, the persons who favor the ratification of this treaty without conditions and without amendment differ among themselves certainly in their views, purposes, and opinions, and as they are so many of them honest and well-meaning persons, we have the right to say in their actual and real opinions. In general, the state of mind and the utterance of the lips are in accord. If you ask them what they want, you are answered with a shout: "Three cheers for the flag! Who will dare to haul it down? Hold onto everything you can get. The United States is strong enough to do what it likes. The Declaration of Independence and the counsel of Washington and the Constitution of the United States have grown rusty and musty. They are for little countries and not for great ones. There is no moral law for strong nations. America has outgrown Americanism."

Mr. President, when I hear from some of our friends this new doctrine of constitutional interpretation, when I hear attributed to men in high places, counselors of the President himself, that we have outgrown the principles and the interpretation which were sufficient for our thirteen states and our 3 million people in the time of their weakness, and by which they have grown to 75 million and forty-five states, in this hour of our strength it seems to me these counselors would have this nation of ours like some prosperous thriving youth who reverses suddenly all the maxims and rules of living in which he has been educated and says to himself, "I am too big for the Golden Rule. I have outgrown the Ten Com-

mandments. I no longer need the straight waistcoat of the moral law. Like Jeshuron, I will wax fat and kick." . . .

In general, the friends of what is called imperialism or expansion content themselves with declaring that the flag which is taken down every night and put up again every morning over the roof of this Senate chamber, where it is in its rightful place, must never be taken down where it has once floated, whether that be its rightful place or not — a doctrine which . . . is not only without justification in international law but, if it were implanted there, would make of every war between civilized and powerful nations a war of extermination or a war of dishonor to one party or the other.

If you cannot take down a national flag where it has once floated in time of war, we were disgraced when we took our flag down in Mexico and in Vera Cruz, or after the invasion of Canada; England was dishonored when she took her flag down after she captured this capital; and every nation is henceforth pledged to the doctrine that wherever it puts its military foot or its naval power with the flag over it, that must be a war to the death and to extermination or the honor of the state is disgraced by the flag of that nation being withdrawn.

I have made a careful analysis of the constitutional argument of the senator from Connecticut. I think I can do it justice. I have not followed the precise order of his statements. But I have put them in logical order. He says:

First, that the United States is a nation, a sovereign.

Second, that as a nation it possesses every sovereign power not reserved in the Constitution to the states or the people.

Third, that the right to acquire territory was not reserved, and is therefore an inherent sovereign right.

Fourth, that it is a right upon which there is no limitation and that in regard to which there is no qualification.

Fifth, that in the right to acquire territory is found the right to govern it.

Sixth, that this right to govern it is also a sovereign right. . . .

Seventh, that it is a right without constitutional limit. . . .

This power to dispose of the territory or other property belonging to the United States and to make all needful rules and regulations respecting it, and the power implied from that provision, to acquire and hold territory or other property, like other constitutional powers, is a power to be exercised only for constitutional purposes. It is like the power to acquire and dispose of ships, or cannon, or public buildings, or a drove of pack mules, or a library, to be exercised in accomplishment of the purposes of the Constitution and not to be exercised where it is not reasonably necessary or convenient for the accomplishment of those purposes.

We have no more right to acquire land or hold it, or to dispose of it for an unconstitutional purpose, than we have a right to fit out a fleet or to buy a park of artillery for an unconstitutional purpose. Among the constitutional purposes for which Congress may acquire and hold territory and other property are the building of forts, and the establishment of post offices and subtreasuries and custom houses. In all these cases it is accomplishing a clearly constitutional purpose.

One of the constitutional purposes is the enlargement of the country by the admission of new states, and therefore Congress may lawfully acquire, hold, and dispose of territory with reference to the accomplishment of that great constitutional purpose, among others. It may also acquire adjoining or outlying territory, dispose of it, make rules and regulations for it for the purposes of national security and defense, although it may not be expected that the territory so acquired, held, and disposed of shall ever come into the Union as a state. That is, as

many people think, the case of Hawaii.

Now, the disposing of and the making rules and regulations for territory acquired for either of these purposes necessarily involves the making laws for the government of the inhabitants — forever, if the territory is not to come in as a state, or during the growing and transition period if and until it shall come in as a state.

But, Mr. President, it is to be observed, and it should not be forgotten, that all this is a constitutional provision which looks chiefly at the land and territory as mere property. And it applies, so far as its terms and its general spirit and purpose are concerned, equally to public lands within a state as to those which are without it. And there is no other provision in the Constitution for making rules and regulations for the territory of the United States or its other property, in the case where the public lands are in Alabama or Florida or Iowa, than where they are in Alaska or Arizona or wherever the public lands are outside any state jurisdiction.

The framers of the Constitution were not thinking mainly and chiefly, when they enacted that clause, of lawmaking, of the government of men, of the rights of citizenship. They were thinking of public property; and although the lawmaking, the rights of men, citizenship have to be recognized from the necessity of the case where the public property is a large tract of land fit for human settlement, yet the language they used and the thought in their minds treated the element of property as the principal, and the element of citizenship as something only temporary and passing, only to last until the property, territory, and inhabitants can be given over to freedom under the jurisdiction of a state, to be admitted as an equal member of our political partnership.

And two things about this clause are quite significant. One is that it is not contained in the article which gives Congress general legislative powers, but is sandwiched in between the section providing for the admission of new states and the section providing for guaranteeing to every state a republican form of government, showing that they were not thinking of conferring a general legislative power over the inhabitants and were only thinking, so far as the inhabitants of a territory were concerned, of the transition or expectant period while they were awaiting admission to statehood. And, Mr. President, you are not now proposing to acquire or own property in the Philippines with dominion as a necessary incident; you are not thinking of the ownership of land there. You propose, now, to acquire dominion and legislative power and nothing else. Where in the Constitution is the grant of power to exercise sovereignty where you have no property? . . .

My proposition, summed up in a nutshell, is this: I admit you have the right to acquire territory for constitutional purposes, and you may hold land and govern men on it for the constitutional purpose of a seat of government or for the constitutional purpose of admitting it as a state. I deny the right to hold land or acquire any property for any purpose not contemplated by the Constitution. The government of foreign people against their will is not a constitutional purpose but a purpose expressly forbidden by the Constitution. Therefore I deny the right to acquire this territory and to hold it by the government for that purpose. . . .

Now, I claim that under the Declaration of Independence you cannot govern a foreign territory, a foreign people, another people than your own; that you cannot subjugate them and govern them against their will, because you think it is for their good, when they do not; because you think you are going to give them the blessings of liberty. You have no right at the cannon's mouth to impose on an unwilling people your Declaration of Independence and your Constitution and your notions of freedom

and notions of what is good. That is the proposition which the senator asserted. He does not deny it now.

If the senator gets up and says, "I will not have those people in Iloilo subdued; I will not govern the Philippine Islands unless the people consent; they shall be consulted at every step," he would stand in a different position. That is what I am complaining of. When I asked the senator during his speech whether he denied that just governments rested on the consent of the governed, he said, in substance, that he did deny it — that is, his answer was "some of them"; and he then went on to specify places where government did not so rest.

The senator says, "Oh, we governed the Indians against their will when we first came here," long before the Declaration of Independence. I do not think so. I am speaking of other people. Now, the people of the Philippine Islands are clearly a nation — a people three and one-third times as numerous as our fathers were when they set up this nation. If gentlemen say that because we did what we did on finding a great many million square miles of forests and a few hundred or thousand men roaming over it without any national life, without the germ of national life, without the capacity for self-government, without self-government, without desiring self-government, was a violation of your principle, I answer, if it was a violation of your principle it was wrong.

It does not help us out any to say that 150 years ago we held slaves or did something else. If it be a violation of your principle, it is wrong. But if, as our fathers thought and as we all think, it was not a violation of the principle because there was not a people capable of national life or capable of government in any form, that is another thing.

But read the account of what is going on in Iloilo. The people there have got a government, with courts and judges, better than those of the people of Cuba, who, it was said, had a right to self-government, collecting their customs; and it is proposed to turn your guns on them, and say, "We think that our notion of government is better than the notion you have got yourselves." I say that when you put that onto them against their will and say that freedom as we conceive it, not freedom as they conceive it, public interest as we conceive it, not as they conceive it, shall prevail, and that if it does not we are to force it on them at the cannon's mouth — I say that the nation which undertakes that plea and says it is subduing these men for their good when they do not want to be subdued for their good will encounter the awful and terrible rebuke, "Beware of the leaven of the Pharisees, which is hypocrisy."

58.

EDWIN MARKHAM: "The Man with the Hoe"

Edwin Markham won national fame in 1899 with the publication in the San Francisco Examiner *of "The Man with the Hoe," his best-known poem. Inspired by Millet's painting, Markham made the French peasant the symbol of the exploited classes throughout the world. The poem so well expressed the feelings of the time that it was published in almost every newspaper in the country and was the subject of innumerable editorial comments. Markham's first successful book of verse,* The Man with the Hoe and Other Poems, *was published in the same year. The version of the poem reprinted here, according to a note in the original, was "revised by the author for the* Outlook," *where it was published in May 1899.*

Source: *Outlook*, May 6, 1899.

❧ THE MAN WITH THE HOE

God created man in His own image,
in the image of God created He him.

Bowed by the weight of centuries he leans
Upon his hoe and gazes on the ground,
The emptiness of ages in his face,
And on his back the burden of the world.
Who made him dead to rapture and despair,
A thing that grieves not and that never hopes,
Stolid and stunned, a brother to the ox?
Who loosened and let down this brutal jaw?
Whose was the hand that slanted back this brow?
Whose breath blew out the light within this brain?

Is this the thing the Lord God made and gave
To have dominion over sea and land;
To trace the stars and search the heavens for power;
To feel the passion of eternity?
Is this the dream He dreamed who shaped the suns
And pillared the blue firmament with light?
Down all the stretch of hell to its last gulf
There is no shape more terrible than this —
More tongued with censure of the world's blind greed —
More filled with signs and portents for the soul —
More fraught with menace to the universe.

What gulfs between him and the seraphim!
Slave of the wheel of labor, what to him
Are Plato and the swing of Pleiades?
What the long reaches of the peaks of song,
The rift of dawn, the reddening of the rose?
Through this dread shape the suffering ages look;
Time's tragedy is in that aching stoop;
Through this dread shape humanity betrayed,
Plundered, profaned, and disinherited,
Cries protest to the judges of the world,
A protest that is also prophecy.

O masters, lords, and rulers in all lands,
Is this the handiwork you give to God,
This monstrous thing distorted and soul-quenched?
How will you ever straighten up this shape;
Touch it again with immortality;
Give back the upward looking and the light;
Rebuild in it the music and the dream;
Make right the immemorial infamies,
Perfidious wrongs, immedicable woes?

O masters, lords, and rulers in all lands,
How will the future reckon with this man?
How answer his brute question in that hour
When whirlwinds of rebellion shake the world?
How will it be with kingdoms and with kings —
With those who shaped him to the thing he is —
When this dumb terror shall reply to God,
After the silence of the centuries?

59.

JOHN DEWEY: The School and Social Progress

As one historian has noted, John Dewey's educational theories "accomplished one of the significant cultural revolutions of his time." Almost single-handedly, Dewey's experiments in his Laboratory School at the University of Chicago showed America what progressive education was all about. One of the major tenets of Dewey's educational philosophy was that education was a social experience, not an individual one. Each child in a school was already in a social context and thereby being educated for a life in a community. In his lectures on school and society, delivered in 1899 to an audience of parents and interested laymen, he explained what the social aspect of his philosophy meant at the Laboratory School.

Source: *School and Society*, Chicago, 1900, Ch. 1.

WE ARE APT TO LOOK at the school from an individualistic standpoint as something between teacher and pupil, or between teacher and parent. That which interests us most is naturally the progress made by the individual child of our acquaintance, his normal physical development, his advance in ability to read, write, and figure, his growth in the knowledge of geography and history, improvement in manners, habits of promptness, order, and industry. It is from such standards as these that we judge the work of the school. And rightly so. Yet the range of the outlook needs to be enlarged.

What the best and wisest parent wants for his own child, that must the community want for all of its children. Any other ideal for our schools is narrow and unlovely; acted upon, it destroys our democracy. All that society has accomplished for itself is put, through the agency of the school, at the disposal of its future members. All its better thoughts of itself it hopes to realize through the new possibilities thus opened to its future self. Here individualism and socialism are at one. Only by being true to the full growth of all the individuals who make it up can society by any chance be true to itself. And in the self-direction thus given, nothing counts as much as the school, for, as Horace Mann said, "Where anything is growing, one former is worth a thousand re-formers."

Whenever we have in mind the discussion of a new movement in education, it is especially necessary to take the broader, or social, view. Otherwise, changes in the school institution and tradition will be looked at as the arbitrary inventions of particular teachers; at the worst, transitory fads, and, at the best, merely improvements in certain details — and this is the plane upon which it is too customary to consider school changes. It is as rational to conceive of the locomotive or the telegraph as personal devices. The modification going on in the method and curriculum of education is as much a product of the changed social situation and as much an effort to meet the needs of the new society that is forming as are changes in modes of industry and commerce.

It is to this, then, that I especially ask your attention: the effort to conceive what roughly may be termed the "New Education" in the light of larger changes in society. Can we connect this "New Education" with the general march of events? If we can, it will lose its isolated character and will cease to be an affair which proceeds only from the overingenious minds of pedagogues dealing with particular pupils. It will appear as part and parcel of the whole social evolution, and, in its more general features at least, as inevitable.

Let us then ask after the main aspects of the social movement; and afterwards turn to the school to find what witness it gives of effort to put itself in line. And since it is quite impossible to cover the whole ground, I shall for the most part confine myself to one typical thing in the modern school movement — that which passes under the name of manual training, hoping if the relation of that to changed social conditions appears, we shall be ready to concede the point as well regarding other educational innovations.

I make no apology for not dwelling at length upon the social changes in question. Those I shall mention are writ so large that he who runs may read. The change that comes first to mind, the one that overshadows and even controls all others, is the industrial one — the application of science resulting in the great inventions that have utilized the forces of nature on a vast and inexpensive scale: the growth of a worldwide market as the object of production, of vast manufacturing centers to supply this market, of cheap and rapid means of communication and distribution between all its parts. Even as to its feebler beginnings, this change is not much more than a century old; in many of its most important aspects it falls within the short span of those now living.

One can hardly believe there has been a revolution in all history so rapid, so extensive, so complete. Through it the face of the earth is making over, even as to its physical forms; political boundaries are wiped out and moved about as if they were indeed only lines on a paper map; population is hurriedly gathered into cities from the ends of the earth; habits of living are altered with startling abruptness and thoroughness; the search for the truths of nature is infinitely stimulated and facilitated and their application to life made not only practicable but commercially necessary. Even our moral and religious ideas and interests, the most conservative because the deepest-lying things in our nature, are profoundly affected. That this revolution should not affect education in other than formal and superficial fashion is inconceivable.

Back of the factory system lies the household and neighborhood system. Those of us who are here today need go back only one, two, or, at most, three generations to find a time when the household was practically the center in which were carried on, or about which were clustered, all the typical forms of industrial occupation. The clothing worn was for the most part not only made in the house but the members of the household were usually familiar with the shearing of the sheep, the carding and spinning of the wool, and the plying of the loom. Instead of pressing a button and flooding the house with electric light, the whole process of getting illumination was followed in its toilsome length from the killing of the animal and the trying of fat to the making of wicks and dipping of candles.

The supply of flour, of lumber, of foods, of building materials, of household furniture, even of metalware, of nails, hinges, hammers, etc., was in the immediate neighborhood, in shops which were constantly open to inspection and often centers of neighborhood congregation. The entire industrial process stood revealed, from the production on the farm of the raw materials till the finished article was actually put to use. Not only this, but practically every member of the household had his own share in the work. The children, as they gained in strength and capacity, were gradually initiated into the mysteries of the several processes. It was a matter of immediate and personal concern, even to the point of actual participation.

We cannot overlook the factors of discipline and of character building involved in this — training in habits of order and of industry, and in the idea of responsibility, of obligation to do something, to produce something, in the world. There was always something which really needed to be done and a real necessity that each member of the household should do his own part faithfully and in cooperation with others. Personalities which became effective in action were bred and tested in the medium of action. Again, we cannot overlook the importance for educational purposes of the close and intimate acquaintance got with nature at first hand, with real things and materials, with the actual processes of their manipulation, and the knowledge of their social necessities and uses. In all this there was continual training of observation, of ingenuity, constructive imagination, of logical thought, and of the sense of reality acquired through first-hand contact with actualities. The educative forces of the domestic spinning and weaving, of the sawmill, the gristmill, the cooper shop, and the blacksmith forge were continuously operative.

No number of object lessons, got up *as* object lessons for the sake of giving information, can afford even the shadow of a substitute for acquaintance with the plants and animals of the farm and garden, acquired through actual living among them and caring for them. No training of sense organs in school, introduced for the sake of training, can begin to compete with the alertness and fullness of sense life that comes through daily intimacy and interest in familiar occupations. Verbal memory can be trained in committing tasks, a certain discipline of the reasoning powers can be acquired through lessons in science and mathematics; but, after all, this is somewhat remote and shadowy compared with the training of attention and of judgment that is

acquired in having to do things with a real motive behind and a real outcome ahead.

At present, concentration of industry and division of labor have practically eliminated household and neighborhood occupations, at least for educational purposes. But it is useless to bemoan the departure of the good old days of children's modesty, reverence, and implicit obedience if we expect merely by bemoaning and by exhortation to bring them back. It is radical conditions which have changed, and only an equally radical change in education suffices. We must recognize our compensations — the increase in toleration, in breadth of social judgment, the larger acquaintance with human nature, the sharpened alertness in reading signs of character and interpreting social situations, greater accuracy of adaptation to differing personalities, contact with greater commercial activities. These considerations mean much to the city-bred child of today. Yet there is a real problem: How shall we retain these advantages and yet introduce into the school something representing the other side of life — occupations which exact personal responsibilities and which train the child with relation to the physical realities of life?

When we turn to the school, we find that one of the most striking tendencies at present is toward the introduction of so-called manual training, shopwork, and the household arts, sewing and cooking. This has not been done "on purpose," with a full consciousness that the school must now supply that factor of training formerly taken care of in the home but rather by instinct, by experimenting and finding that such work takes a vital hold of pupils and gives them something which was not to be got in any other way. Consciousness of its real import is still so weak that the work is often done in a half-hearted, confused, and unrelated way. The reasons assigned to justify it are painfully inadequate or sometimes even positively wrong.

If we were to cross-examine even those

who are most favorably disposed to the introduction of this work into our school system, we should, I imagine, generally find the main reasons to be that such work engages the full, spontaneous interest and attention of the children. It keeps them alert and active instead of passive and receptive; it makes them more useful, more capable, and hence more inclined to be helpful at home; it prepares them to some extent for the practical duties of later life — the girls to be more efficient house managers, if not actually cooks and sempstresses; the boys (were our educational system only adequately rounded out into trade schools) for their future vocations. I do not underestimate the worth of these reasons. Of those indicated by the changed attitude of the children I shall indeed have something to say in my next talk, when speaking directly of the relationship of the school to the child. But the point of view is, upon the whole, unnecessarily narrow.

We must conceive of work in wood and metal, of weaving, sewing, and cooking, as methods of life, not as distinct studies. We must conceive of them in their social significance, as types of the processes by which society keeps itself going, as agencies for bringing home to the child some of the primal necessities of community life, and as ways in which these needs have been met by the growing insight and ingenuity of man; in short, as instrumentalities through which the school itself shall be made a genuine form of active community life instead of a place set apart in which to learn lessons.

A society is a number of people held together because they are working along common lines, in a common spirit, and with reference to common aims. The common needs and aims demand a growing interchange of thought and growing unity of sympathetic feeling. The radical reason that the present school cannot organize itself as a natural social unit is because just this ele-

ment of common and productive activity is absent. Upon the playground, in game and sport, social organization takes place spontaneously and inevitably. There is something to do, some activity to be carried on requiring natural divisions of labor, selection of leaders and followers, mutual cooperation, and emulation. In the schoolroom the motive and the cement of social organization are alike wanting. Upon the ethical side, the tragic weakness of the present school is that it endeavors to prepare future members of the social order in a medium in which the conditions of the social spirit are eminently wanting.

The difference that appears when occupations are made the articulating centers of school life is not easy to describe in words; it is a difference in motive, of spirit and atmosphere. As one enters a busy kitchen in which a group of children are actively engaged in the preparation of food, the psychological difference, the change from more or less passive and inert recipiency and restraint to one of buoyant outgoing energy is so obvious as fairly to strike one in the face. Indeed, to those whose image of the school is rigidly set the change is sure to give a shock. But the change in the social attitude is equally marked. The mere absorption of facts and truths is so exclusively individual an affair that it tends very naturally to pass into selfishness.

There is no obvious social motive for the acquirement of mere learning; there is no clear social gain in success thereat. Indeed, almost the only measure for success is a competitive one, in the bad sense of that term — a comparison of results in the recitation or in the examination to see which child has succeeded in getting ahead of others in storing up, in accumulating the maximum of information. So thoroughly is this the prevalent atmosphere that for one child to help another in his task has become a school crime. Where the schoolwork consists in simply learning lessons, mutual assistance, instead of being the most natural form of cooperation and association, becomes a clandestine effort to relieve one's neighbor of his proper duties.

Where active work is going on all this is changed. Helping others, instead of being a form of charity which impoverishes the recipient, is simply an aid in setting free the powers and furthering the impulse of the one helped. A spirit of free communication, of interchange of ideas, suggestions, results, both successes and failures of previous experiences, becomes the dominating note of the recitation. So far as emulation enters in, it is in the comparison of individuals, not with regard to the quantity of information personally absorbed but with reference to the quality of work done — the genuine community standard of value. In an informal but all the more pervasive way, the school life organizes itself on a social basis.

Within this organization is found the principle of school discipline or order. Of course, order is simply a thing which is relative to an end. If you have the end in view of forty or fifty children learning certain set lessons to be recited to a teacher, your discipline must be devoted to securing that result. But if the end in view is the development of a spirit of social cooperation and community life, discipline must grow out of and be relative to this. There is little order of one sort where things are in process of construction; there is a certain disorder in any busy workshop; there is not silence; persons are not engaged in maintaining certain fixed physical postures; their arms are not folded; they are not holding their books thus and so. They are doing a variety of things, and there is the confusion, the bustle that results from activity. But out of occupation, out of doing things that are to produce results, and out of doing these in a social and cooperative way, there is born a discipline of its own kind and type.

Our whole conception of school discipline changes when we get this point of view. In critical moments we all realize that the only discipline that stands by us, the only training that becomes intuition, is that got through life itself. That we learn from experience, and from books or the sayings of others *only* as they are related to experience, are not mere phrases. But the school has been so set apart, so isolated from the ordinary conditions and motives of life, that the place where children are sent for discipline is the one place in the world where it is most difficult to get experience — the mother of all discipline worth the name. It is only where a narrow and fixed image of traditional school discipline dominates that one is in any danger of overlooking that deeper and infinitely wider discipline that comes from having a part to do in constructive work, in contributing to a result which, social in spirit, is nonetheless obvious and tangible in form — and hence in a form with reference to which responsibility may be exacted and accurate judgment passed.

The great thing to keep in mind, then, regarding the introduction into the school of various forms of active occupation is that through them the entire spirit of the school is renewed. It has a chance to affiliate itself with life, to become the child's habitat, where he learns through directed living, instead of being only a place to learn lessons having an abstract and remote reference to some possible living to be done in the future. It gets a chance to be a miniature community, an embryonic society. This is the fundamental fact, and from this arise continuous and orderly sources of instruction.

Under the industrial *régime* described, the child, after all, shared in the work, not for the sake of the sharing but for the sake of the product. The educational results secured were real, yet incidental and dependent. But in the school the typical occupations followed are freed from all economic stress. The aim is not the economic value of the products but the development of social power and insight. It is this liberation from narrow utilities, this openness to the possibilities of the human spirit that makes these practical activities in the school allies of art and centers of science and history.

The unity of all the sciences is found in geography. The significance of geography is that it presents the earth as the enduring home of the occupations of man. The world without its relationship to human activity is less than a world. Human industry and achievement, apart from their roots in the earth, are not even a sentiment, hardly a name. The earth is the final source of all man's food. It is his continual shelter and protection, the raw material of all his activities, and the home to whose humanizing and idealizing all his achievement returns. It is the great field, the great mine, the great source of the energies of heat, light, and electricity; the great scene of ocean, stream, mountain, and plain, of which all our agriculture and mining and lumbering, all our manufacturing and distributing agencies, are but the partial elements and factors. It is through occupations determined by this environment that mankind has made its historical and political progress. It is through these occupations that the intellectual and emotional interpretation of nature has been developed. It is through what we do in and with the world that we read its meaning and measure its value.

In educational terms, this means that these occupations in the school shall not be mere practical devices or modes of routine employment, the gaining of better technical skill as cooks, sempstresses, or carpenters, but active centers of scientific insight into natural materials and processes, points of departure whence children shall be led out into a realization of the historic development of man. . . .

When occupations in the school are conceived in this broad and generous way, I can only stand lost in wonder at the objections so often heard that such occupations are out of place in the school because they are materialistic, utilitarian, or even menial in their tendency. It sometimes seems to me that those who make these objections must live in quite another world. The world in which most of us live is a world in which everyone has a calling and occupation, something to do. Some are managers and others are subordinates. But the great thing for one as for the other is that each shall have had the education which enables him to see within his daily work all there is in it of large and human significance.

How many of the employed are today mere appendages to the machines which they operate! This may be due in part to the machine itself, or to the regime which lays so much stress upon the products of the machine; but it is certainly due in large part to the fact that the worker has had no opportunity to develop his imagination and his sympathetic insight as to the social and scientific values found in his work. At present, the impulses which lie at the basis of the industrial system are either practically neglected or positively distorted during the school period. Until the instincts of construction and production are systematically laid hold of in the years of childhood and youth, until they are trained in social directions, enriched by historical interpretation, controlled and illuminated by scientific methods, we certainly are in no position even to locate the source of our economic evils, much less to deal with them effectively. . . .

Our school methods, and to a very considerable extent our curriculum, are inherited from the period when learning and command of certain symbols, affording as they did the only access to learning, were all-important. The ideals of this period are still largely in control, even where the outward methods and studies have been changed. We sometimes hear the introduction of manual training, art, and science into the elementary and even the secondary schools deprecated on the ground that they tend toward the production of specialists, that they detract from our present scheme of generous, liberal culture. The point of this objection would be ludicrous if it were not often so effective as to make it tragic.

It is our present education which is highly specialized, one-sided, and narrow. It is an education dominated almost entirely by the medieval conception of learning. It is something which appeals for the most part simply to the intellectual aspect of our natures, our desire to learn, to accumulate information, and to get control of the symbols of learning; not to our impulses and tendencies to make, to do, to create, to produce, whether in the form of utility or of art. The very fact that manual training, art, and science are objected to as technical, as tending toward mere specialism, is of itself as good testimony as could be offered to the specialized aim which controls current education. Unless education had been virtually identified with the exclusively intellectual pursuits, with learning as such, all these materials and methods would be welcome, would be greeted with the utmost hospitality.

While training for the profession of learning is regarded as the type of culture, as a liberal education, that of a mechanic, a musician, a lawyer, a doctor, a farmer, a merchant, or a railroad manager is regarded as purely technical and professional. The result is that which we see about us everywhere — the division into "cultured" people and "workers," the separation of theory and practice. Hardly 1 percent of the entire school population ever attains to what we call higher education; only 5 percent to the grade of our high school; while much more than half leave on or before the completion of the fifth year of the elementary grade. The simple facts of the case are that in the great majority of human beings the distinctively intellectual interest is not dominant. They have the so-called practical impulse and disposition. In many of those in whom by nature intellectual interest is strong, social conditions prevent its adequate realiza-

tion. Consequently, by far the larger number of pupils leave school as soon as they have acquired the rudiments of learning, as soon as they have enough of the symbols of reading, writing, and calculating to be of practical use to them in getting a living.

While our educational leaders are talking of culture, the development of personality, etc., as the end and aim of education, the great majority of those who pass under the tuition of the school regard it only as a narrowly practical tool with which to get bread and butter enough to eke out a restricted life. If we were to conceive our educational end and aim in a less exclusive way, if we were to introduce into educational processes the activities which appeal to those whose dominant interest is to do and to make, we should find the hold of the school upon its members to be more vital, more prolonged, containing more of culture.

But why should I make this labored presentation? The obvious fact is that our social life has undergone a thorough and radical change. If our education is to have any meaning for life, it must pass through an equally complete transformation. This transformation is not something to appear suddenly, to be executed in a day by conscious purpose. It is already in progress. Those modifications of our school system which often appear (even to those most actively concerned with them, to say nothing of their spectators) to be mere changes of detail, mere improvement within the school mechanism, are in reality signs and evidences of evolution. The introduction of active occupations, of nature study, of elementary science, of art, of history; the relegation of the merely symbolic and formal to a secondary position; the change in the moral school atmosphere, in the relation of pupils and teachers — of discipline; the introduction of more active, expressive, and self-directing factors — all these are not mere accidents; they are necessities of the larger social evolution.

It remains but to organize all these factors, to appreciate them in their fullness of meaning, and to put the ideas and ideals involved into complete, uncompromising possession of our school system. To do this means to make each one of our schools an embryonic community life, active with types of occupations that reflect the life of the larger society and permeated throughout with the spirit of art, history, and science. When the school introduces and trains each child of society into membership within such a little community, saturating him with the spirit of service and providing him with the instruments of effective self-direction, we shall have the deepest and best guarantee of a larger society which is worthy, lovely, and harmonious.

60.

Henry A. Rowland: An Appeal for Pure Scientific Research in America

Henry Rowland, according to one scientist, was "the American Helmholtz of the new era in the history of American industries." Rowland worked closely with industry on the Niagara Falls power project at the same time that he was a devoted researcher. As first president of the American Physical Society, one of the many scientific societies that began to appear at the turn of the century, Rowland was considered the acknowledged spokesman of all American physicists. In his presidential address before the second meeting of the Society, delivered October 28, 1899, Rowland described the weaknesses of the American scientific community as well as many of its hopes. Part of the address is reprinted here.

Source: *Bulletin* of the American Physical Society, Vol. I, No. 1: "The Highest Aim of the Physicist."

WE MEET TODAY on an occasion which marks an epoch in the history of physics in America. May the future show that it also marks an epoch in the history of the science which this society is organized to cultivate! For we meet here in the interest of a science above all sciences, which deals with the foundations of the universe, with the constitution of matter from which everything in the universe is made, and with the ether of space by which alone the various portions of matter forming the universe affect each other, even at such distances as we may never expect to traverse whatever the progress of our science in the future.

We who have devoted our lives to the solution of problems connected with physics now meet together to help each other and to forward the interests of the subject which we love — a subject which appeals most strongly to the better instincts of our nature, and the problems of which tax our minds to the limit of their capacity and suggest the grandest and noblest ideas of which they are capable.

In a country where the doctrine of the equal rights of man has been distorted to mean the equality of man in other respects, we form a small and unique body of men — a new variety of the human race, as one of our greatest scientists calls it — whose views of what constitutes the greatest achievement in life are very different from those around us. In this respect we form an aristocracy, not of wealth, not of pedigree, but of intellect and of ideals, holding him in the highest respect who adds the most to our knowledge or who strives after it as the highest good.

Thus we meet together for mutual sympathy and the interchange of knowledge, and may we do so ever with appreciation of the benefits to ourselves and possibly to our science. Above all, let us cultivate the idea of the dignity of our pursuit so that this feeling may sustain us in the midst of a world which gives its highest praise, not to the investigation in the pure ethereal physics which our society is formed to cultivate but to the one who uses for satisfying the physical rather than the intellectual needs of mankind. He who makes two blades of grass grow where one grew before is the benefactor of mankind; but he who obscurely worked to find the laws of such growth is the intellectual superior as well as the greater benefactor of the two.

How stands our country, then, in this respect? My answer must still be now as it was fifteen years ago, that much of the intellect of the country is still wasted in the pursuit of so-called practical science which ministers to our physical needs, and but little thought and money is given to the grander portion of the subject which appeals to our intellect alone. But your presence here gives evidence that such a condition is not to last forever.

Even in the past we have the names of a few whom scientists throughout the world delight to honor: Franklin, who almost revolutionized the science of electricity by a few simple but profound experiments; Count Rumford, whose experiments almost demonstrated the nature of heat; Henry, who might have done much for the progress of physics had he published more fully the results of his investigations; Mayer, whose simple and ingenious experiments have been a source of pleasure and profit to many. This is the meager list of those whom death allows me to speak of and

who have earned mention here by doing something for the progress of our science. And yet the record has been searched for more than a hundred years. How different had I started to record those who have made useful and beneficial inventions!

But I know, when I look in the faces of those before me where the eager intellect and high purpose sit enthroned on bodies possessing the vigor and strength of youth, that the writer of a hundred years hence can no longer throw such a reproach upon our country. Nor can we blame those who have gone before us. The progress of every science shows us the condition of its growth. Very few persons, if isolated in a semicivilized land, have either the desire or the opportunity of pursuing the higher branches of science. Even if they should be able to do so, their influence on their science depends upon what they publish and make known to the world.

A hermit philosopher we can imagine might make many useful discoveries. Yet, if he keeps them to himself, he can never claim to have benefited the world in any degree. His unpublished results are his private gain, but the world is no better off until he has made them known in language strong enough to call attention to them and to convince the world of their truth. Thus, to encourage the growth of any science, the best thing we can do is to meet together in its interest, to discuss its problems, to criticize each other's work, and, best of all, to provide means by which the better portion of it may be made known to the world. Furthermore, let us encourage discrimination in our thoughts and work.

Let us recognize the eras when great thoughts have been introduced into our subject and let us honor the great men who introduced and proved them correct. Let us forever reject such foolish ideas as the equality of mankind and carefully give the greater credit to the greater man. So, in choosing the subjects for our investigation, let us, if possible, work upon those subjects which will finally give us an advanced knowledge of some great subject. I am aware that we cannot always do this; our ideas will often flow in side channels; but, with the great problems of the universe before us, we may sometime be able to do our share toward the greater end. . . .

It is a curious fact that, having minds tending to the infinite, with imaginations unlimited by time and space, the limits of our exact knowledge are very small indeed. In time we are limited by a few hundred or possibly thousand years; indeed, the limit in our science is far less than the smaller of these periods. In space, we have exact knowledge limited to portions of our earth's surface and a mile or so below the surface, together with what little we can learn from looking through powerful telescopes into the space beyond. In temperature, our knowledge extends, from near the absolute zero to that of the sun, but exact knowledge is far more limited. In pressures, we go from the Crookes vacuum still containing myriads of flying atoms to pressures limited by the strength of steel, but still very minute compared with the pressure at the center of the earth and sun, where the hardest steel would flow like the most limpid water. In velocities, we are limited to a few miles per second; in forces, to possibly 100 tons to the square inch; in mechanical rotations, to a few hundred times per second.

All the facts which we have considered, the liability to error in whatever direction we go, the infirmity of our minds in their reasoning power, the fallibility of witnesses and experimenters lead the scientist to be especially skeptical with reference to any statement made to him or any so-called knowledge which may be brought to his attention. The facts and theories of our science are so much more certain than those of history, or of the testimony of ordinary people on which the facts of ordinary history or of legal evidence rest, or of the value of medicines to which we trust when we are ill, indeed, to the whole fabric of supposed truth by which an ordinary person guides his belief and the actions of his life, that it may seem ominous and strange if what I have said of the imperfections of the knowledge of physics is correct.

How shall we regulate our mind with respect to it? There is only one way that I know of and that is to avoid the discontinuity of the ordinary, indeed, the so-called cultivated legal mind. There is no such thing as absolute truth and absolute falsehood. The scientific mind should never recognize the perfect truth or the perfect falsehood of any supposed theory or observation. It should carefully weigh the chances of truth and error and grade each in its proper position along the line joining absolute truth and absolute error.

The ordinary, crude mind has only two compartments, one for truth and one for error; indeed, the contents of the two compartments are sadly mixed in most cases; the ideal scientific mind, however, has an infinite number. Each theory or law is in its proper compartment indicating the probability of its truth. As a new fact arrives the scientist changes it from one compartment to another so as, if possible, to always keep it in its proper relation to truth and error. Thus the fluid nature of electricity was once in a compartment near the truth. Faraday's and Maxwell's researches have now caused us to move it to a compartment nearly up to that of absolute error.

So the law of gravitation within the planetary distances is far toward absolute truth, but may still need amending before it is advanced farther in that direction.

The ideal scientific mind, therefore, must always be held in a state of balance which the slightest new evidence may change in one direction or another. It is in a constant state of skepticism, knowing full well that nothing is certain. It is above all an agnostic with respect to all facts and theories of science as well as to all other so-called beliefs and theories.

Yet it would be folly to reason from this

that we need not guide our life according to the approach of knowledge that we possess. Nature is inexorable; it punishes the child who unknowingly steps off a steep precipice quite as severely as the grown scientist who steps over, with full knowledge of all the laws of falling bodies and the chances of their being correct. Both fall to the bottom and in their fall obey the gravitational laws of inorganic matter, slightly modified by the muscular contortions of the falling object, but not in any degree changed by the previous belief of the person. Natural laws there probably are, rigid and unchanging ones at that. Understand them and they are beneficent; we can use them for our purposes and make them the slaves of our desires. Misunderstand them and they are monsters who may grind us to powder or crush us in the dust.

Nothing is asked of us as to our belief: they act unswervingly and we must understand them or suffer the consequences. Our only course, then, is to act according to the chances of our knowing the right laws. If we act correctly, right; if we incorrectly, we suffer. If we are ignorant, we die. What greater fool, then, than he who states that belief is of no consequence provided it is sincere.

An only child, a beloved wife lies on a bed of illness. The physician says that the disease is mortal; a minute plant called a microbe has obtained entrance into the body and is growing at the expense of its tissues, forming deadly poisons in the blood or destroying some vital organ. The physician looks on without being able to do anything. Daily he comes and notes the failing strength of his patient and daily the patient goes downward, until he rests in his grave. But why has the physician allowed this? Can we doubt that there is a remedy which shall kill the microbe or neutralize its poisons? Why, then, has he not used it? He is employed to cure but has failed. His bill we cheerfully pay because he has done his best and given a chance of cure.

The answer is *ignorance*. The remedy is yet unknown. The physician is waiting for others to discover it or perhaps is experimenting in a crude and unscientific manner to find it. Is not the inference correct, then, that the world has been paying the wrong class of men? Would not this ignorance have been dispelled had the proper money been used in the past to dispel it? Such deaths some people consider an act of God. What blasphemy to attribute to God that which is due to our own and our ancestors' selfishness in not founding institutions for medical research in sufficient numbers and with sufficient means to discover the truth. Such deaths are murder.

Thus the present generation suffers for the sins of the past and we die because our ancestors dissipated their wealth in armies and navies, in the foolish pomp and circumstance of society, and neglected to provide us with a knowledge of natural laws. In this sense they were the murderers and robbers of future generations of unborn millions, and have made the world a charnel house and a place of mourning where peace and happiness might have been. Only their ignorance of what they were doing can be their excuse, but this excuse puts them in the class of boors and savages who act according to selfish desire and not to reason and to the calls of duty. Let the present generation take warning that this reproach be not cast on it, for it cannot plead ignorance in this respect.

This illustration from the Department of Medicine I have given because it appeals to all. But all the sciences are linked together and must advance in concert. The human body is a chemical and physical problem, and these sciences must advance before we can conquer disease.

But the true lover of physics needs no such spur to his actions. The cure of disease is a very important object and nothing can be more noble than a life devoted to its cure. The aims of the physicist, however, are in part purely intellectual. He strives to understand the universe on account of the intellectual pleasure derived from the pursuit, but he is upheld in it by the knowledge that the study of nature's secrets is the ordained method by which the greatest good and happiness shall finally come to the human race.

Where, then, are the great laboratories of research in this city, in this country, nay, in the world? We see a few miserable structures here and there occupied by a few starving professors who are nobly striving to do the best with the feeble means at their disposal. But where in the world is the institute of pure research in any department of science with an income of $100 million per year? Where can the discoverer in pure science earn more than the wages of a day laborer or cook? But $100 million per year is but the price of an army or of a navy designed to kill other people. Just think of it, that 1 percent of this sum seems to most people too great to save our children and descendants from misery and death!

But the 20th century is near; may we not hope for better things before its end? May we not hope to influence the public in this direction?

Let us go forward, then, with confidence in the dignity of our pursuit. Let us hold our heads high with a pure conscience while we seek the truth, and may the American Physical Society do its share now and in generations yet to come in trying to unravel the great problem of the constitution and laws of the universe.

61.

Edwin M. Royle: The Vaudeville Theater

Vaudeville, which began when Tony Pastor opened his New York show in 1881, became family entertainment in the 1890s. Burlesque was replaced in many of the theaters by a more refined variety show that featured continuous performances. Weber and Fields, Sandow the Strong Man, and Lillian Russell singing "Kiss Me Mother, Ere I Die" were the headliners. Before the decade ended, every major city boasted numerous vaudeville theaters and many small towns were treated to traveling shows. The theaters were open all day long and late into the evening; nationwide acts were booked into theaters throughout the country; and for a time vaudeville became the national form of entertainment. Edwin Royle, a vaudevillian and a commentator on his art, published an article in Scribner's *magazine in 1899, which is reprinted here in part.*

Source: *Scribner's,* October 1899.

THE VAUDEVILLE THEATER is an American invention. There is nothing like it anywhere else in the world. It is neither the Café Chantant, the English music hall, nor the German garden. What has been called by a variety of names but has remained always and everywhere pretty much the same — reeky with smoke, damp with libations, gay with the informalities of the half-world — is now doing business with us under the patronage of the royal American family.

Having expurgated and rehabilitated the

tawdry thing, the American invites in the family and neighbors, hands over to them beautiful theaters, lavishly decorated and appointed, nails up everywhere church and army regulations, and in the exuberance of his gaiety passes around ice water. He hasn't painted out the French name, but that is because he has been, as usual, in a hurry. Fourteen years ago this may have been a dream in a Yankee's brain; now it is a part of us. The strictly professional world has been looking for the balloon to come down, for the fad to die out, for the impossible thing to stop, but year by year these theaters increase and multiply, till now they flourish the country over.

Sometimes the vaudeville theater is an individual and independent enterprise; more often it belongs to a circuit. The patronage, expenses, and receipts are enormous. One circuit will speak for all. It has a theater in New York, one in Philadelphia, one in Boston, and one in Providence, and they give no Sunday performances; and yet these four theaters entertain over 5 million people every year, give employment to 350 attachés and to 3,500 actors. Four thousand people pass in and out of each one of these theaters daily. Ten thousand dollars are distributed each week in salaries to the actors and $3,500 to the attachés. Take one theater for example, the house in Boston. It is open the year round and it costs $7,000 a week to keep it open, while its patrons will average 25,000 every week. On a holiday it will play to from 10,000 to 12,000 people. How is it possible?

A holiday to an American is a serious affair, so the doors of the theater are open and the performance begins when most people are eating breakfast; 9:30 A.M. is not too soon for the man who pursues pleasure with the same intensity he puts into business. There are no reserved seats, so one must come first to be first served. One may go in at 9:30 A.M. and stay until 10:30 at night. If he leaves his seat, though, the nearest standing Socialist drops into it and

he must wait for a vacancy in order to sit down again.

Not over 2 percent of an audience remains longer than to see the performance through once, but there are persons who secrete campaign rations about them and camp there from 9:30 A.M. to 10:30 P.M., thereby surviving all of the acts twice and most of them four or five times. The management calculate to sell out the house two and a half times on ordinary days and four times on holidays, and it is this system that makes such enormous receipts possible. Of course I have taken the circuit which is representative of the vaudeville idea at its best, but it is not alone in its standards or success, and what I have said about the houses in New York, Boston, and Philadelphia applies more or less to all the principal cities of the country, and in a less degree, of course, to the houses in the smaller cities.

Some of these theaters are never closed the year round. Some are content with three matinees a week in addition to their night performances. Others open their doors about noon and close them at 10:30 at night. These are called "continuous" houses. It is manifest, I think, that the vaudeville theater is playing an important part in the amusement world and in our national life. Perhaps we should be grateful. At present it would seem that the moral tone of a theater is in the inverse ratio of the price of admission. The higher the price, the lower the tone. It is certain that plays are tolerated and even acclaimed on the New York stage today which would have been removed with tongs half a dozen years ago. . . .

So far as the vaudeville theaters are concerned, one might as well ask for a censorship of a "family magazine." It would be a work of supererogation. The local manager of every vaudeville house is its censor, and he lives up to his position laboriously and, I may say, religiously. The bill changes usually from week to week. It is the solemn duty of this austere personage to sit through the first performance of every week and to let no guilty word or look escape. But this is precautionary only.

"You are to distinctly understand," say the first words of the contracts of a certain circuit, "that the management conducts this house upon a high plane of respectability and moral cleanliness," etc. But long before the performer has entered the dressing rooms, he has been made acquainted with the following legend which everywhere adorns the walls:

NOTICE TO PERFORMERS

You are hereby warned that your act must be free from all vulgarity and suggestiveness in words, action, and costume while playing in any of Mr. —— 's houses, and all vulgar, double-meaning, and profane words and songs must be cut out of your act before the first performance. If you are in doubt as to what is right or wrong, submit it to the resident manager at rehearsal.

Such words as liar, slob, son-of-a-gun, devil, sucker, damn, and all other words unfit for the ears of ladies and children, also any reference to questionable streets, resorts, localities, and barrooms, are prohibited under fine of instant discharge.

——, GENERAL MANAGER.

And this is not merely a literary effort on the part of the management; it is obligatory and final. When we have about accepted as conclusive the time-honored theory that "You must give the public what it wants," and that it *wants* bilge water in champagne glasses, we are confronted with the vaudeville theater no longer an experiment but a comprehensive fact.

The funniest farce ever written could not be done at these houses if it had any of the earmarks of the thing in vogue at many of our first-class theaters. Said a lady to me: "They (the vaudeville theaters) are the only theaters in New York where I should feel absolutely safe in taking a young girl without making preliminary inquiries. Though they may offend the taste, they never offend

one's sense of decency." The vaudeville theaters may be said to have established the commercial value of decency. This is their cornerstone. They were conceived with the object of catering to ladies and children, and, strange to say, a large, if not the larger, part of their audiences is always men. . . .

How careful of the conduct of their patrons the management is may be seen from the following printed *requests* with which the employees are armed:

Gentlemen will kindly avoid the stamping of feet and pounding of canes on the floor, and greatly oblige the management. All applause is best shown by clapping of hands.

Please don't talk during acts, as it annoys those about you and prevents a perfect hearing of the entertainment.

THE MANAGEMENT

When we were playing in Philadelphia, a young woman was singing with what is known as the "song-sheet," at the same theater with us. Her costume consisted of silk stockings, knee breeches, and a velvet coat — the regulation page's dress, decorous enough to the unsanctified eye; but one day the proprietor himself happened in unexpectedly (as is his wont) and the order quick and stern went forth that the young woman was not to appear again except in skirts — her street clothes, if she had nothing else, and street clothes it came about.

These are the chronicles of what is known among the vaudeville fraternity as "The Sunday-school Circuit," and the proprietor of "The Sunday-school Circuit" is the inventor of vaudeville as we know it. This which makes for righteousness, as is usual, makes also for great and abiding cleanliness — physical as well as moral. I almost lost things in my Philadelphia dressing room — it was cleaned so constantly. Paternal, austere perhaps, but clean, gloriously clean!

The character of the entertainment is always the same. There is a sameness even about its infinite variety. No act or "turn" consumes much over thirty minutes. Everyone's taste is consulted, and if one objects to the perilous feats of the acrobats or jugglers he can read his program or shut his eyes for a few moments and he will be compensated by some sweet bell ringing or a sentimental or comic song, graceful or grotesque dancing, a one-act farce, trained animals, legerdemain, impersonations, clay modeling, the biograph pictures, or the stories of the comic monologist.

The most serious thing about the program is that seriousness is barred, with some melancholy results. From the artist who balances a set of parlor furniture on his nose to the academic baboon, there is one concentrated, strenuous struggle for a laugh. No artist can afford to do without it. It hangs like a solemn and awful obligation over everything. Once in a while an artist who juggles tubs on his feet is a comedian, but not always. It would seem as if a serious person would be a relief now and then. But so far the effort to introduce a serious note, even by dramatic artists, has been discouraged. I suspect the serious sketches have not been of superlative merit. Though this premium is put upon a laugh, everyone is aware of the difference between the man who rings a bell at forty paces with a rifle and the man who smashes it with a club, and the loudest laugh is sometimes yoked with a timid salary. The man who said: "Let me get out of here or I'll lose my self-respect — I actually laughed," goes to the vaudeville theaters, too, and must be reckoned with.

So far as the character of the entertainment goes, vaudeville has the "open door." Whatever or whoever can interest an audience for thirty minutes or less, and has passed quarantine, is welcome. The conditions in the regular theaters are not encouraging to progress. To produce a play or launch a star requires capital of from $10,000 upward. There is no welcome and

no encouragement. The door is shut and locked. And even with capital, the conditions are all unfavorable to proof. But if you can sing or dance or amuse people in any way, if you think you can write a one-act play, the vaudeville theater will give you a chance to prove it. One day of every week is devoted to these trials. If at this trial you interest a man who is looking for good material, he will put you in the bill for one performance and give you a chance at an audience, which is much better. The result of this open-door attitude is a very interesting innovation in vaudeville which is more or less recent but seems destined to last — the incursion of the dramatic artist into vaudeville.

The managers of the vaudeville theaters are not emotional persons, and there were some strictly business reasons back of the actor's entrance into vaudeville. We do not live by bread alone but by the saving graces of the art of advertising. It was quite impossible to accentuate sixteen or eighteen features of a bill. Some one name was needed to give it character and meaning at a glance. A name that had already become familiar was preferred. The actor's name served to head the bill and expand the type and catch the eye, and hence arose the vaudeville term, "Headliner."

This word is not used in contracts, but it is established and understood, and carries with it well-recognized rights and privileges, such as being featured in the advertisements, use of the star dressing room, and the favorite place on the bill; for it is not conducive to one's happiness or success to appear during the hours favored by the public for coming in or going out. The manager was not the loser, for many people who had never been inside a vaudeville theater were attracted thither by the name of some well-known and favorite actor and became permanent patrons of these houses.

At first, the actor, who is sentimental rather than practical, was inclined to the belief that it was beneath his dignity to appear on the stage with "a lot of freaks," but he was tempted by salaries no one else could afford to pay (sometimes as high as $500 to $1,000 per week) and by the amount of attention afforded to the innovation by the newspapers. He was told that if he stepped from the sacred precincts of art, the door of the temple would be forever barred against him. The dignity of an artist is a serious thing, but the dignity of the dollar is also a serious thing. None of the dire suppositions happened. The door of the temple proved to be a swinging door, opening easily both ways, and the actor goes back and forth as there is demand for him and as the dollar dictates. Indeed, the advertising secured by association with "a lot of freaks" oiled the door for the actor's return to the legitimate drama at an *increased salary.*

Manifestly, it has been a boon to the "legitimate" artist. To the actor who has starred; who has had the care of a large company, with its certain expenses and its uncertain receipts; who has, in addition, responsibility for his own performance and for the work of the individual members of his company and for the work of the company as a whole, vaudeville offers inducements not altogether measured in dollars and cents. He is rid not only of financial obligation but of a thousand cares and details that twist and strain a nervous temperament. He hands over to the amiable manager the death of the widely mourned Mr. Smith, and prevalent social functions, Lent and the circus, private and public calamities, floods and railroad accidents, the blizzard of winter and the heat of summer, desolating drought and murderous rains, the crops, strikes and panics, wars and pestilences, and opera. It is quite a bunch of thorns that he hands over!

Time and terms are usually arranged by agents, who get 5 percent of the actor's salary for their services. Time and terms arranged, the rest is easy. The actor provides himself and assistants and his play or vehicle. His income and outcome are fixed, and he knows at the start whether he is to be a capitalist at the end of the year; for he runs almost no risk of not getting his salary in the well-known circuits. It is then incumbent on him to forward property and scene plots, photographs, and cast to the theater two weeks before he opens, and on arrival, he plays twenty or thirty minutes in the afternoon and the same at night. There his responsibility ends. It involves the trifling annoyance of dressing and making up twice a day. In and about New York the actor pays the railroad fares of himself and company, but when he goes west or south, the railroad fares (not including sleepers) are provided by the management.

The great circuit which covers the territory west of Chicago keeps an agent in New York and one in Chicago to facilitate the handling of their big interests. These gentlemen purchase tickets, arrange for sleepers, take care of baggage, and lubricate the wheels of progress from New York to San Francisco and back again. The actor's only duty is to live up to the schedule made and provided.

The main disadvantage of the western trip is the loss of a week going and one coming, as there is no vaudeville theater between Omaha and San Francisco. To avoid the loss of a week on my return, I contracted for two nights at the Salt Lake Theater. My company consisted of four people all told, and my ammunition, suited to that caliber, was three one-act plays. To give the entire evening's entertainment at a first-class theater, at the usual prices, with four people, was a novel undertaking.

I finally determined to add to my mammoth aggregation a distinctly vaudeville feature, and while in San Francisco I engaged a young woman who was to fill in the intermissions with her song-and-dance specialty. Scorning painful effort to escape the conventional, I billed her as "The Queen of Vaudeville," whatever that may mean.

We were caught in a tunnel fire at Summit and delayed thirty-six hours. I threatened the railroad officials with various and awful consequences, but the best I could do was to get them to drag my theater trunks around the tunnel by hand over a mile and a half of mountain trail, newly made, and get me into Salt Lake just in time to miss my opening night, with a big advance sale and the heart-rendings incident to money refunded. We were in time to play the second night, but my Queen, starting from 'Frisco on a later train, had shown no signs of appearing when the curtain rose. I made the usual apologies. The evening's entertainment was half over when a carriage came tearing up to the theater and my Queen burst into the theater without music, trunks, costumes, makeup, supper.

She borrowed a gown from my ingenue, which was much too small for her; a pair of slippers from my wife, which were much too big for her; makeup from both ladies; and went on. She leaned over, whispered the key to the leader of the orchestra and began to sing. The orchestra evolved a chord now and then, jiggled and wiggled, stalled, flew the track, crawled apologetically back, did its amiable best individually, but its amiable worst collectively. No mere man could have lived through it. But the young woman justified my billing. She ruled, she reigned, she triumphed. Pluck and good humor always win, and so did the Queen of Vaudeville.

When high-class musical artists and dramatic sketches were first introduced into vaudeville, I understand policemen had to be stationed in the galleries to compel respectful attention, but now these acts are the principal features of every bill, and if they have real merit the gallery gods are the first to appreciate it. So it would seem that vaudeville has torpedoed the ancient superstition that the manager is always forced to give the public just what it wants. At first his efforts were not taken seriously, either by the actor himself or the public, and many well-known artists failed to "make good," as the expression is, largely because they used "canned" or embalmed plays; that is, hastily and crudely condensed versions of well-known plays; but many succeeded, and the result has been a large increase in the number of good one-act farces and comedies and a distinct elevation in the performance and the patronage of the vaudeville theaters. This has been a gain to everybody concerned. . . .

Many of our best comedians, men and women, have come from the variety stage, and it is rather remarkable that some of our best actors have of late turned their attention to it. This interchange of courtesies has brought out some amusing contrasts. A clever comedian of a comic-opera organization was explaining to me his early experience in the "old days," when he was a song-and-dance man. "The tough manager," he said, "used to stand in the wings with a whistle, and if he didn't like your act, he blew it and a couple of stagehands ran in and shut you out from your audience with two flats upon which were painted in huge letters 'N.G.,' and that was the end of your engagement." Then he proceeded to tell with honest pride of his struggles and his rise in the world of art. "And now," said he to me, "I can say *cawn't* as well as you can."

Our first day in vaudeville was rich in experience for us, and particularly for one of the members of my little company. He was already busy at the dressing table making up, when the two other occupants of his room entered — middle-aged, bald-headed, bandy-legged little men, who quickly divested themselves of their street clothes and then mysteriously disappeared from sight. Suddenly a deep-drawn sigh welled up from the floor, and, turning to see what had become of his companions, the actor saw a good-humored face peering up out of a green-striped bundle of assorted legs and arms. He was face to face with the Human Lizard and his partner in the batrachian business, the Human Frog.

"Good Lord! what are you doing?" exclaimed Mr. Roberts.

"Loosenin' up!" laconically.

"But do you always do that?"

"Yes. *Now!*"

"Why *now?*"

"Well, I'm a little older than I was when I began this business, and yer legs git stiff, ye know. I remember when I could tie a knot in either leg without cracking a joint, but now I am four-flushing until I can get enough to retire."

"Four-flushing?"

"Yes, doin' my turn one card shy. You understand."

And the striped bundle folded in and out on itself and tied itself in bows, ascots, and four-in-hands until every joint in the actor's body was cracking in sympathy.

Meanwhile his partner was standing apart, with one foot touching the low ceiling and his hands clutching two of the clothes hooks, striving for the fifth card to redeem *his* four flush.

"Number fourteen!" shouts the callboy through the door.

"That's us!"

And the four-flushers unwound and, gathering their heads and tails under their arms, glided away for the stage.

Presently they were back panting and perspiring, with the information that there was a man in one of the boxes who never turned his head to look at their act; that there was a pretty girl in another box fascinated by it; that the audience had relatives in the ice business and were incapable of a proper appreciation of the double split and the great brother double tie and slide —

whatever that may be; and the two athletes passed the alcohol bottle and slipped gracefully back into their clothes and private life.

This unique and original world has its conventions, too, quite as hard and fast as elsewhere. The vaudeville dude always bears an enormous cane with a spike in the end of it, even though the style in canes may be a bamboo switch. The comedian will black his face, though he never makes the lightest pretense to Negro characterization, under the delusion that the black face and kinky hair and short trousers are necessary badges of the funny man. The vaudeville "artist" and his partner will "slang" each other and indulge in brutal personalities under the theory that they are guilty of repartee; and, with a few brilliant exceptions, they all steal from each other jokes and gags and songs and "business," absolutely without conscience. So that if a comedian has originated a funny story that makes a hit in New York, by the time he reaches Philadelphia he finds that another comedian has filched it and told it in Philadelphia, and the originator finds himself a dealer in second-hand goods.

It is manifest, I think, that vaudeville is very American. It touches us and our lives at many places. It appeals to the businessman, tired and worn, who drops in for half an hour on his way home; to the person who has an hour or two before a train goes, or before a business appointment; to the woman who is wearied of shopping; to the children who love animals and acrobats; to the man with his sweetheart or sister; to the individual who wants to be diverted but doesn't want to think or feel; to the American of all grades and kinds who wants a great deal for his money. The vaudeville theater belongs to the era of the department store and the short story. It may be a kind of lunch-counter art, but then art is so vague and lunch is so real.

And I think I may add that if anyone has anything exceptional in the way of art, the vaudeville door is not shut to that.

62.

BRET HARTE: The Short Story in America

American writers have had conspicuous success in the short story, a genre that is probably French in origin (if it owes its birth to any nation) but that seemed, in the 1920s and 1930s, to have become at least a naturalized citizen of this country. Bret Harte, an early master in the genre, traced the history of the American short story in an article published in a British periodical in July 1899. Harte had been living in England since 1885.

Source: *Cornhill Magazine*, New series, July 1899: "The Rise of the 'Short Story.' "

As it has been the custom of good-natured reviewers to associate the present writer with the origin of the American "short story," he may have a reasonable excuse for offering the following reflections, partly the result of his own observations during the last thirty years and partly from his experience in the introduction of this form of literature to the pages of the Western magazine, of which he was editor at the beginning of that period. But he is far from claiming the invention, or of even attributing its genesis to that particular occasion.

The short story was familiar enough in form in America during the early half of the century; perhaps the proverbial haste of American life was some inducement to its brevity. It had been the medium through which some of the most characteristic work of the best American writers had won the approbation of the public. Poe, a master of the art, as yet unsurpassed, had written; Longfellow and Hawthorne had lent it the graces of the English classics. But it was not the American short story of today. It was not characteristic of American life, American habits, nor American thought. It was not vital and instinct with the experience and observation of the average American; it made no attempt to follow his reasoning or to understand his peculiar form of expres-

sion, which it was apt to consider vulgar; it had no sympathy with those dramatic contrasts and surprises which are the wonders of American civilization; it took no account of the modifications of environment and of geographical limitations; indeed, it knew little of American geography. Of all that was distinctly American it was evasive, when it was not apologetic. And even when graced by the style of the best masters, it was distinctly provincial.

It would be easier to trace the causes which produced this than to assign any distinct occasion or period for the change. What was called American literature was still limited to English methods and upon English models. The best writers either wandered far afield for their inspiration, or, restricted to home material, were historical or legendary; artistically contemplative of their own country, but seldom observant. Literature abode on a scant fringe of the Atlantic seaboard, gathering the drift from other shores and hearing the murmur of other lands rather than the voices of its own; it was either expressed in an artificial treatment of life in the cities, or, as with Irving, was frankly satirical of provincial social ambition.

There was much "fine" writing; there were American Addisons, Steeles, and

Lambs; there were provincial *Spectators* and *Tatlers*. The sentiment was English. Even Irving in the pathetic sketch of "The Wife" echoed the style of *Rosamund Gray*. They were sketches of American life in the form of the English essayists, with no attempt to understand the American character. The literary man had little sympathy with the rough and half-civilized masses who were making his country's history; if he used them at all it was as a foil to bring into greater relief his hero of the unmistakable English pattern.

In his slavish imitation of the foreigner, he did not, however, succeed in retaining the foreigner's quick appreciation of novelty. It took an Englishman to first develop the humor and picturesqueness of American or "Yankee" dialect, but Judge Haliburton succeeded better in reproducing "Sam Slick's" speech than his character. Dr. Judd's *Margaret* — one of the earlier American stories — although a vivid picture of New England farm life and strongly marked with local color, was in incident and treatment a mere imitation of English rural tragedy. It would, indeed, seem that while the American people had shaken off the English yoke in government, politics, and national progression, while they had already startled the Old World with invention and originality in practical ideas, they had never freed themselves from the trammels of English literary precedent. The old sneer "Who reads an American book?" might have been answered by another: "There are no *American* books."

But while the American literary imagination was still under the influence of English tradition, an unexpected factor was developing to diminish its power. It was *humor*, of a quality as distinct and original as the country and civilization in which it was developed. It was at first noticeable in the anecdote or "story," and, after the fashion of such beginnings, was orally transmitted. It was common in the barrooms, the gatherings in the country store, and finally at public meetings in the mouths of stump orators. Arguments were clinched and political principles illustrated by "a funny story." It invaded even the camp meeting and pulpit. It at last received the currency of the public press.

But wherever met it was so distinctly original and novel, so individual and characteristic that it was at once known and appreciated abroad as "an American story." Crude at first, it received a literary polish in the press, but its dominant quality remained. It was concise and condense, yet suggestive. It was delightfully extravagant — or a miracle of understatement. It voiced not only the dialect but the habits of thought of a people or locality. It gave a new interest to slang. From a paragraph of a dozen lines it grew into a half column, but always retaining its conciseness and felicity of statement. It was a foe to prolixity of any kind; it admitted no fine writing nor affectation of style. It went directly to the point. It was burdened by no conscientiousness; it was often irreverent; it was devoid of all moral responsibility — but it was original!

By degrees it developed character with its incident, often, in a few lines, gave a striking photograph of a community or a section, but always reached its conclusion without an unnecessary word. It became — and still exists — as an essential feature of newspaper literature. It was the parent of the American "short story."

But although these beginnings assumed more of a national character than American serious or polite literature, they were still purely comic, and their only immediate result was the development of a number of humorists in the columns of the daily press, all possessing the dominant national quality with a certain individuality of their own. For a while it seemed as if they were losing the faculty of storytelling in the elaboration of eccentric character, chiefly used as a vehicle for smart sayings, extravagant incident, or political satire. They were eagerly received by the public and, in their day, were immensely popular and probably were better known at home and abroad than the more academic but less national humorists of New York or Boston. The national note was always struck even in their individual variations, and the admirable portraiture of the shrewd and humorous showman in "Artemus Ward" survived his more mechanical bad spelling.

Yet they did not invade the current narrative fiction; the short and long storytellers went with their old-fashioned methods, their admirable morals, their well-worn sentiments, their colorless heroes and heroines of the first ranks of provincial society. Neither did social and political convulsions bring anything new in the way of romance. The Mexican War gave us the delightful satires of Hosea Bigelow, but no dramatic narrative. The antislavery struggle before the War of the Rebellion produced a successful partisan political novel — on the old lines — with only the purely American characters of "Topsy," and the New England "Miss Ophelia."

The War itself, prolific as it was of poetry and eloquence, was barren of romance, except for Edward Everett Hale's artistic and sympathetic *The Man Without a Country*. The tragedies enacted, the sacrifices offered, not only on the battlefield but in the division of families and households; the conflict of superb quixotism and reckless gallantry against reason and duty fought out in quiet border farmhouses and plantations; the reincarnation of Puritan and Cavalier in a wild environment of trackless wastes, pestilential swamps, and rugged mountains; the patient endurance of both the conqueror and the conquered — all these found no echo in the romance of the period.

Out of the battle smoke that covered half a continent drifted, into the pages of maga-

zines, shadowy but correct figures of blameless virgins of the North — heroines or fashionable belles — habited as hospital nurses, bearing away the deeply wounded but more deeply misunderstood Harvard or Yale graduate lover who had rushed to bury his broken heart in the conflict. It seems almost incredible that, until the last few years, nothing worthy of that tremendous episode has been preserved by the pen of the romancer.

But if the war produced no characteristic American story, it brought the literary man nearer his work. It opened to him distinct conditions of life in his own country of which he had no previous conception; it revealed communities governed by customs and morals unlike his own, yet intensely human and American. The lighter side of some of these he had learned from the humorists before alluded to; the grim realities of war and the stress of circumstances had suddenly given them a pathetic or dramatic reality. Whether he had acquired this knowledge of them with a musket or a gilded strap on his shoulder, or whether he was later a peaceful "carpetbagger" into the desolate homes of the South and Southwest, he knew something personally of their romantic and picturesque value in story.

Many cultivated aspirants for literature, as well as many seasoned writers for the press, were among the volunteer soldiery. Again, the composition of the Army was heterogeneous: regiments from the West rubbed shoulders with regiments from the East; spruce city clerks hobnobbed with backwoodsmen, and the student fresh from college shared his rations with the half-educated Western farmer. The Union, for the first time, recognized its component parts; the natives knew each other. The literary man must have seen heroes and heroines where he had never looked for them, situations that he had never dreamed of. Yet it is a mortifying proof of the strength of inherited literary traditions that he never dared until quite recently to make a test of them. It is still more strange that he should have waited for the initiative to be taken by a still more crude, wild, and more Western civilization — that of California!

The gold discovery had drawn to the Pacific slope of the continent a still more heterogeneous and remarkable population. The immigration of 1849 and 1850 had taken farmers from the plow, merchants from their desks, and students from their books, while every profession was represented in the motley crowd of gold seekers. Europe and her colonies had contributed to swell these adventurers, for adventurers they were whatever their purpose; the risks were great, the journey long and difficult — the nearest came from a distance of over a thousand miles; that the men were necessarily pre-equipped with courage, faith, and endurance was a foregone conclusion.

They were mainly young; a gray-haired man was a curiosity in the mines in the early days, and an object of rude respect and reverence. They were consequently free from the trammels of precedent or tradition in arranging their lives and making their rude homes. There was a singular fraternity in this ideal republic into which all men entered free and equal. Distinction of previous position or advantages was unknown, even record and reputation for ill or good were of little benefit or embarrassment to the possessor; men were accepted for what they actually were and what they could do in taking their part in the camp or settlement. The severest economy, the direst poverty, the most menial labor carried no shame nor disgrace with it; individual success brought neither envy nor jealousy. What was one man's fortune today might be the luck of another tomorrow.

Add to this utopian simplicity of the people the environment of magnificent scenery, a unique climate, and a vegetation that was marvelous in its proportions and spontaneity of growth; let it be further considered that the strongest relief was given to this picture by its setting among the crumbling ruins of early Spanish possession — whose monuments still existed in Mission and Presidio, and whose legitimate Castilian descendants still lived and moved in picturesque and dignified contrast to their energetic invaders — and it must be admitted that a condition of romantic and dramatic possibilities was created unrivaled in history.

But the earlier literature of the Pacific slope was, like that of the Atlantic seaboard, national and characteristic only in its humor. The local press sparkled with wit and satire, and, as in the East, developed its usual individual humorists. Of these should be mentioned the earliest pioneers of Californian humor: Lieut. [George H.] Derby, a U.S. Army Engineer officer, author of a series of delightful extravagances known as The Squibob Papers; and the later and universally known "Mark Twain," who contributed "The Jumping Frog of Calaveras" to the columns of the weekly press. The San Francisco News Letter, whose whilom contributor, Major Bierce, has since written some of the most graphic romances of the Civil War; The Golden Era, in which the present writer published his earlier sketches, and The Californian, to which, as editor, in burlesque imitation of the enterprise of his journalistic betters, he contributed "The Condensed Novels," were the foremost literary weeklies. These were all more or less characteristically American, but it was again remarkable that the more literary, romantic, and imaginative romances had no national flavor. The better remembered serious work in the pages of the only literary magazine, The Pioneer, was a romance of spiritualism and psychological study, and a poem on the Chandos picture of Shakespeare!

With this singular experience before him, the present writer was called upon to take the editorial control of the Overland Monthly, a much more ambitious magazine venture than had yet appeared in California.

The best writers had been invited to contribute to its pages. But in looking over his materials on preparing the first number, he was discouraged to find the same notable lack of characteristic fiction. There were good literary articles, sketches of foreign travel, and some essays in description of the natural resources of California, excellent from a commercial and advertising viewpoint. But he failed to discover anything of that wild and picturesque life which had impressed him, first as a truant schoolboy and afterwards as a youthful schoolmaster among the mining population.

In this perplexity he determined to attempt to make good the deficiency himself. He wrote "The Luck of Roaring Camp." However far short it fell of his ideal and his purpose, he conscientiously believed that he had painted much that "he saw, and part of which he was," that his subject and characters were distinctly Californian, as was equally his treatment of them. But an unexpected circumstance here intervened. The publication of the story was objected to by both printer and publisher, virtually for not being in the conventional line of subject, treatment, and morals! The introduction of the abandoned outcast mother of the foundling "Luck" and the language used by the characters received a serious warning and protest. The writer was obliged to use his right as editor to save his unfortunate contribution from oblivion. When it appeared at last, he saw with consternation that the printer and publisher had really voiced the local opinion; that the press of California was still strongly dominated by the old conservatism and conventionalism of the East, and that when "The Luck of Roaring Camp" was not denounced as "improper" and "corrupting," it was coldly received as being "singular" and "strange."

A still more extraordinary instance of the "provincial note" was struck in the criticism of a religious paper that the story was strongly "unfavorable to immigration" and decidedly unprovocative of the "investment of foreign capital." However, its instantaneous and cordial acceptance as a new departure by the critics of the Eastern states and Europe enabled the writer to follow it with other stories of a like character. More than that, he was gratified to find a disposition on the part of his contributors to shake off their conservative trammels, and, in an admirable and original sketch of a wandering circus attendant called "Centerpole Bill," he was delighted to recognize and welcome a convert.

The term "imitators," often used by the critics who, as previously stated, had claimed for the present writer the *invention* of this kind of literature, could not fairly apply to those who had cut loose from conventional methods and sought to honestly describe the life around them, and he can only claim to have shown them that it could be done. How well it has since been done, what charm of individual flavor and style has been brought to it by such writers as Harris, Cable, Page, Mark Twain in *Huckleberry Finn,* the author of the *Prophet of the Great Smoky Mountains,* and Miss [Mary E.] Wilkins, the average reader need not be told.

It would seem evident, therefore, that the secret of the American short story was the treatment of characteristic American life, with absolute knowledge of its peculiarities and sympathy with its methods; with no fastidious ignoring of its habitual expression or the inchoate poetry that may be found even hidden in its slang; with no moral determination except that which may be the legitimate outcome of the story itself; with no more elimination than may be necessary for the artistic conception, and never from the fear of the "fetish" of conventionalism. Of such is the American short story of today — the germ of American literature to come.

63.

Paul Dresser and Theodore Dreiser: "On the Banks of the Wabash, Far Away"

Paul Dresser was one of the most successful songwriters of the 1890s, contributing not only the perennial favorite reprinted here but also "My Gal Sal." "On the Banks of the Wabash, Far Away," now the official song of the state of Indiana, was written in 1899 and expressed its author's deep feeling for his native place — he was born in Terre Haute in 1857. The lovely chorus of the song is traditionally supposed to have been written by Dresser's younger brother, Theodore Dreiser (the songwriter changed the family name), who was already a well-known magazine writer but was not yet the author of any of the massive novels that have placed him in the front rank of American literary men.

ON THE BANKS OF THE WABASH, FAR AWAY

Round my Indiana homestead wave the cornfields,
In the distance loom the woodlands clear and cool.
Oftentimes my thoughts revert to scenes of childhood,
Where I first received my lessons, nature's school.
But one thing there is missing in the picture,
Without her face it seems so incomplete.
I long to see my mother in the doorway,
As she stood there years ago, her boy to greet!

Chorus:
Oh, the moonlight's fair tonight along the Wabash,
From the fields there comes the breath of new-mown hay.
Through the sycamores the candlelights are gleaming,
On the banks of the Wabash, far away.

Many years have passed since I strolled by the river,
Arm in arm with sweetheart Mary by my side.
It was there I tried to tell her that I loved her,
It was there I begged of her to be my bride.
Long years have passed since I strolled through the churchyard,
She's sleeping there, my angel Mary dear.
I loved her but she thought I didn't mean it —
Still I'd give my future were she only here.

64.

The Trusts in America

In the 1890s the word "trust" began to take on the sinister connotation that it retains to this day. Farmers, especially, attacked the railroad trusts and the grain trusts as injurious to the agricultural interest and, indeed, as a fundamental anomaly in the free enterprise system that was the economic ideal, if not the practice, of the time. By the turn of the century, no less than forty-two states (out of forty-five) had either adopted constitutional provisions or passed laws inhibiting the activities of the trusts. In September 1899 the Chicago Conference on Trusts, attended by the governors of several Midwestern states as well as by representatives of labor, manufacturers, and the farmers, heard testimony from these and other groups. The following selection includes testimony by the head of the Grangers, by a newspaper editor, by a union leader, by a Socialist, and by a manufacturer.

Source: *Chicago Conference on Trusts*, Chicago, 1900, pp. 218-221, 253-261, 331-340, 569-576.

I.

AARON JONES:
A Farmer's View

EVERY CITIZEN OF THIS REPUBLIC should be free to use his labor as will best contribute to his benefit and happiness; not, however, infringing on the rights of any other citizen.

The right to acquire, own, control, and enjoy the use and income of property is an inalienable right that should be enjoyed by each individual. Governments are organized and laws are enacted to better protect life, liberty, and the ownership and use of property. It is the legitimate function of governments to protect its citizens in the full and free enjoyment of these rights. It is for this security of life and the ownership of property that people are willing to pay taxes for the support of state and national governments.

The tendency of the times is for conduct-

ing large business enterprises and concentration of business into the hands of a few. In the early history of this country, when individuals desired to do a more extended business than they had capital to control, partnerships were formed of two or more, and the business was conducted by them jointly. These partnerships gave them no additional powers or privileges beyond those enjoyed by the individual citizen.

As the demand [grew] for concentration and the conduct of business on a still greater scale, the laws provided for the formation of corporations to conduct certain lines of business, and the state granted them certificates of incorporation with certain defined privileges and the right to conduct business along certain lines; and, in the case of canals and railroads, they were granted the extraordinary power of condemning lands found necessary for the constructions of their roads or canals, and to issue stock, limiting liability within certain limits defined by law, and granting absolute control of the minority of stock by the majority, and many other advantages and privileges not enjoyed by any individual citizen.

These forms of corporation served a useful purpose, but within the past few years . . . these corporations have been consolidating many separate corporations located in one or several states, selling out their plants to a corporation organized for the purpose of buying up all these separate plants and conducting them under one management; and it has been found that the increased power possessed by these large consolidated corporations, or trusts, as they are commonly known, have caused them to pursue a policy that has infringed on the rights of individuals, or have used their influences in restraint of trade, been detrimental to the rights of labor, destroyed the value of other property, and deprived other individuals of the use of their capital, and so far as this has been done, is clearly against public policy; and subversive of the best interests of the republic.

The purpose of this conference, as I understand, is to consider this great question so vitally affecting the property rights of the citizens of the United States and make such recommendation to the Congress of the United States and the several legislatures as will secure such legislation as will in no wise cripple legitimate enterprise and the development of the resources of our country; and yet secure the passage of such laws as will restrain the abuses that have grown up in corporate management of the various corporations now doing business in the United States. This is one of the most important questions now confronting the American people and one that must be met and wisely met, or the republic is drifting on very dangerous grounds, that sooner or later will subvert the liberties of the people. We believe every good and loyal citizen should wisely consider this grave question and cast their influence to secure such legis-

lation, state and national, as will eliminate all the evil practices of these so-called trusts and combinations.

It occurs to me that the first step to be taken in remedial legislation is to pass a well-considered antitrust law by the Congress of the United States, clearly defining what practices on the part of any corporation would be injurious to public policy, and cripple or injure individual enterprise, thrift, and the acquirement and use of the property of any citizen of the republic; and to supplement this law by equally well-considered antitrust laws by each of the several state legislatures to reach and apply to such phases of the matter as could not be reached by the act of Congress of the United States. These laws should have such provisions for their enforcement and provide penalties for violations by fines or imprisonment or both as will insure the compliance and observance of the laws by all corporations and combinations. To make these laws effective, it is absolutely necessary to know what these trusts and combinations are doing; and as these trusts have assumed, so far as appearances go, to be honest, legitimate corporations, it is difficult to ascertain which ones are operating in a way detrimental to public policy.

It would therefore seem that these laws should provide for government and state inspection of their business, of their books, agreements, receipts, and expenditures, and that the state may have full knowledge, the right to examine all vouchers and records of the meetings of directors and managers; in short, full and complete knowledge of all the business of affairs of the corporation. The individuals, in seeking a corporation franchise, have asked the state to help them to a privilege or advantage they did not possess as individuals, or they would not seek to be incorporated as a corporation; and, on account of that advantage granted and to protect the public, this inspection should be rigid and full. The people must know what the specific acts are that are against public policy before the laws can be enforced as against them, and the rights of the public protected.

Corporations may object to this inspection on the ground that it would expose what they claim as their private business. In answer to this it might be said that the rights of the citizens of the state who grant the articles of incorporation or allow them to do business in the state, special privileges, have a right to know that the privilege has not been used against public policy; besides, there is no law now, never has been, never can be any law compelling anyone to form a corporation and invest his money in any corporation enterprise. Those who invest in corporation stock do so voluntarily.

If the corporations are conducting legitimate business, no injury will be done them by inspection. If they are using the powers granted to them by the state to crush out other enterprises and deprive other citizens of the use and value of their property in order to avoid competition; if they are using their power and influence in restraint of trade; if they are using large sums of money to illegitimately control political parties or to control legislation, as was testified before the congressional investigation that the "Sugar Trust made it a rule to make political contributions to the Republican Party in Republican states and to the Democratic Party in Democratic states." Mr. Havemeyer testified that, "We get a good deal of protection for our contributions"; and when asked if his company had not endeavored to control legislation of Congress with a view of making money out of such legislation, he answered: "Undoubtedly. That is what I have been down here for"; and many other cases might be cited. If they have agreements with railroad companies for rebates of freights, as has been shown to be the case in the Standard Oil trust and many others, these practices are most reprehensible and should be punished by such penalties as will effectually stop them. The agreements and conspiracies to depress the prices of raw material and staple products are equally against public policy.

In speaking for the agricultural interests of our country, that great basic industry that produces 70 percent of the wealth of the country, and furnishes 60 percent of the freight on all railroads, lake, river, and coastwise trade, and 69 percent of all exports, and that make it possible for the other industrial interests of our country to prosper, I desire to say, these practices and conditions most seriously and injuriously affect it; and they demand of the legislatures of the several states and of the national Congress well-considered and effective legislation that will prevent the injurious practices of trusts and combinations.

I believe it to be the settled purpose of a majority of the people to hold our representatives in Congress and in the several legislatures personally responsible for the enactment of such laws as will restrain and prevent the continuance of acts of trusts that are against public policy. I do not believe that the people hold any one party as responsible for the present conditions, but I do believe that each individual member holding official position will be, and is, held for his voice and vote and action in the enactment of demanded remedial and protective legislation.

Our country is so vast, its interests so extended, and the constantly increasing wealth in its multiplied forms of the people need carefully considered laws governing the rights and uses of property, that corporations or individuals by agreements may not be able to oppress or destroy any of the great industries of the nation. The demand of the times is for sound, sensible, good businessmen, with broad common sense, to frame the laws of our country, state, and nation.

II.

Benjamin R. Tucker:
An Editor's View

HAVING TO DEAL VERY BRIEFLY with the problem with which the so-called trusts confront us, I go at once to the heart of the subject, taking my stand on these propositions: That the right to cooperate is as unquestionable as the right to compete; that the right to compete involves the right to refrain from competition; that cooperation is often a method of competition, and that competition is always, in the larger view, a method of cooperation; that each is a legitimate, orderly, noninvasive exercise of the individual will under the social law of equal liberty; and that any man or institution attempting to prohibit or restrict either, by legislative enactment or by any form of invasive force, is, insofar as such man or institution may fairly be judged by such attempt, an enemy of liberty, an enemy of progress, an enemy of society, and an enemy of the human race.

Viewed in the light of these irrefutable propositions, the trust, then, like every other industrial combination endeavoring to do collectively nothing but what each member of the combination rightfully may endeavor to do individually, is, *per se*, an unimpeachable institution. To assail or control or deny this form of cooperation on the ground that it is itself a denial of competition is an absurdity. It is an absurdity because it proves too much. The trust is a denial of competition in no other sense than that in which competition itself is a denial of competition. The trust denies competition only by producing and selling more cheaply than those outside of the trust can produce and sell; but in that sense every successful individual competitor also denies competition. And if the trust is to be suppressed for such denial of competition, then the very competition in the name of which the trust is to be suppressed must itself be suppressed also.

I repeat: The argument proves too much. The fact is that there is one denial of competition which is the right of all, and that there is another denial of competition which is the right of none. All of us, whether out of a trust or in it, have a right to deny competition by competing; but none of us, whether in a trust or out of it, have a right to deny competition by arbitrary decree, by interference with voluntary effort, by forcible suppression of initiative.

Again: To claim that the trust should be abolished or controlled because the great resources and consequent power of endurance which it acquires by combination give it an undue advantage, and thereby enable it to crush competition, is equally an argument that proves too much. If John D. Rockefeller were to start a grocery store in his individual capacity, we should not think of suppressing or restricting or hampering his enterprise simply because, with his $500 million he could afford to sell groceries at less than cost, until the day when the accumulated ruins of all other grocery stores should afford him a sure foundation for a profitable business. But, if Rockefeller's possession of $500 million is not a good ground for the suppression of his grocery store, no better ground is the control of still greater wealth for the suppression of his oil trust.

It is true that these vast accumulations under one control are abnormal and dangerous, but the reasons for them lie outside of and behind and beneath all trusts and industrial combinations — reasons which I shall come to presently — reasons which are all, in some form or other, an arbitrary denial of liberty; and but for these reasons, but for these denials of liberty, John D. Rockefeller never could have acquired $500 million, nor would any combination of men be able to control an aggregation of wealth that could not be easily and successfully met by some other combination of men.

Again: There is no warrant in reason for deriving a right to control trusts from the state grant of corporate privileges under which they are organized. In the first place, it being pure usurpation to presume to endow any body of men with rights and exemptions that are not theirs already under the social law of equal liberty, corporate privileges are in themselves a wrong; and one wrong is not to be undone by attempting to offset it with another. But, even admitting the justice of corporation charters, the avowed purpose in granting them is to encourage cooperation, and thus stimulate industrial and commercial development for the benefit of the community. Now, to make this encouragement an excuse for its own nullification by a proportionate restriction of cooperation would be to add one more to those interminable limitations of the task of Sisyphus for which that stupid institution which we call the state has ever been notorious.

Of somewhat the same nature, but rather more plausible at first blush, is the proposition to cripple the trusts by stripping them of those law-created privileges and monopolies which are conferred, not upon trusts as corporate bodies but upon sundry individuals and interests, ostensibly for protection of the producer and inventor, but really for purposes of plunder, and which most trusts acquire in the process of merging the original capitals of their constituent members. I refer, of course, to tariffs, patents, and copyrights.

Now, tariffs, patents, and copyrights either have their foundations in justice, or they have not their foundations in justice. If they have their foundations in justice, why should men guilty of nothing but a legitimate act of cooperation and partnership be punished therefor by having their just rights taken from them? If they have not their foundations in justice, why should men who refrain from cooperation be left in possession of unjust privileges that are denied to men who cooperate? If tariffs are unjust, they should not be levied at all. If patents and copyrights are unjust, they should not be granted to anyone whomsoever. But, if

tariffs and patents and copyrights are just, they should be levied or granted in the interest of all who are entitled to their benefits from the viewpoint of the motives in which these privileges have their origin, and to make such levy or grant dependent upon any foreign motive, such, for instance, as willingness to refrain from cooperation, would be sheer impertinence.

Nevertheless, at this point in the hunt for the solution of the trust problem, the discerning student may begin to realize that he is hot on the trail. The thought arises that the trusts, instead of growing out of competition, as is so generally supposed, have been made possible only by the absence of competition, only by the difficulty of competition, only by the obstacles placed in the way of competition — only, in short, by those arbitrary limitations of competition which we find in those law-created privileges and monopolies of which I have just spoken, and in one or two others, less direct, but still more far-reaching and deadly in their destructive influence upon enterprise. And it is with this thought that anarchism, the doctrine that in all matters there should be the greatest amount of individual liberty compatible with equality of liberty, approaches the case in hand, and offers its diagnosis and its remedy.

The first and great fact to be noted in the case, I have already hinted at. It is the fact that the trusts owe their power to vast accumulation and concentration of wealth, unmatched, and, under present conditions, unmatchable, by any equal accumulation of wealth; and that this accumulation has been effected by the combination of separate accumulations only less vast and in themselves already gigantic, each of which owed its existence to one or more of the only means by which large fortunes can be rolled up — interest, rent, and monopolistic profit. But for interest, rent, and monopolistic profit, therefore, trusts would be impossible. Now, what causes interest, rent, and monopolistic profit? For all three there is but one cause

— the denial of liberty, the suppression of restriction of competition, the legal creation of monopolies.

This single cause, however, takes various shapes.

Monopolistic profit is due to that denial of liberty which takes the shape of patent, copyright, and tariff legislation — patent and copyright laws directly forbidding competition, and tariff laws placing competition at a fatal disadvantage.

Rent is due to that denial of liberty which takes the shape of land monopoly, vesting titles to land in individuals and associations which do not use it, and thereby compelling the nonowning users to pay tribute to the nonusing owners as a condition of admission to the competitive market.

Interest is due to that denial of liberty which takes the shape of money monopoly, depriving all individuals and associations, save such as hold a certain kind of property, of the right to issue promissory notes as currency, and thereby compelling all holders of property, other than the kind thus privileged, as well as all nonproprietors, to pay tribute to the holders of the privileged property for the use of a circulating medium and instrument of credit which, in the complex stage that industry and commerce have now reached, has become the chief essential of a competitive market.

Now, anarchism, which, as I have said, is the doctrine that in all matters there should be the greatest amount of individual liberty compatible with equality of liberty, finds that none of these denials of liberty are necessary to the maintenance of equality of liberty, but that each and every one of them, on the contrary, is destructive of equality of liberty. Therefore it declares them unnecessary, arbitrary, oppressive, and unjust, and demands their immediate cessation.

Of these four monopolies — the banking monopoly, the land monopoly, the tariff monopoly, and the patent and copyright monopoly — the injustice of all but the last

named is manifest even to a child. The right of the individual to buy and sell without being held up by a highwayman whenever he crosses an imaginary line called a frontier; the right of the individual to take possession of unoccupied land as freely as he takes possession of unoccupied water or unoccupied air; the right of the individual to give his IOU, in any shape whatsoever, under any guarantee whatsoever, or under no guarantee at all, to anyone willing to accept it in exchange for something else — all these rights are too clear for argument, and anyone presuming to dispute them simply declares thereby his despotic and imperialistic instincts.

For the fourth of these monopolies, however — the patent and copyright monopoly — a more plausible case can be presented, for the question of property in ideas is a very subtle one. The defenders of such property set up an analogy between the production of material things and the production of abstractions, and on the strength of it declare that the manufacturer of mental products, no less than the manufacturer of material products, is a laborer worthy of his hire. So far, so good. But, to make out their case, they are obliged to go further, and to claim, in violation of their own analogy, that the laborer who creates mental products, unlike the laborer who creates material products, is entitled to exemption from competition.

Because the Lord, in His wisdom, or the devil, in his malice, has so arranged matters that the inventor and the author produce naturally at a disadvantage, man, in his might, proposes to supply the divine or diabolic deficiency by an artificial arrangement that shall not only destroy this disadvantage but actually give the inventor and author an advantage that no other laborer enjoys — an advantage, moreover, which, in practice goes not to the inventor and the author but to the promoter and the publisher and the trust.

Convincing as the argument for property

in ideas may seem at first hearing, if you think about it long enough, you will begin to be suspicious. The first thing, perhaps, to arouse your suspicion, will be the fact that none of the champions of such property propose the punishment of those who violate it, contenting themselves with subjecting the offenders to the risk of damage suits, and that nearly all of them are willing that even the risk of suit shall disappear when the proprietor has enjoyed his right for a certain number of years. Now, if, as the French writer Alphonse Karr remarked, property in ideas is a property like any other property, then its violation, like the violation of any other property, deserves criminal punishment, and its life, like that of any other property, should be secure in right against the lapse of time. And, this not being claimed by the upholders of property in ideas, the suspicion arises that such a lack of the courage of their convictions may be due to an instinctive feeling that they are wrong.

The necessity of being brief prevents me from examining this phase of my subject in detail. Therefore I must content myself with developing a single consideration, which, I hope, will prove suggestive.

I take it that, if it were possible, and if it had always been possible, for an unlimited number of individuals to use to an unlimited extent and in an unlimited number of places, the same concrete things at the same time, there never would have been any such thing as the institution of property. Under those circumstances, the idea of property would never have entered the human mind, or, at any rate, if it had, would have been summarily dismissed as too gross an absurdity to be seriously entertained for a moment. Had it been possible for the concrete creation or adaptation resulting from the efforts of a single individual to be used contemporaneously by all individuals, including the creator or adapter, the realization, or impending realization, of this possibility, far from being seized upon as an excuse for a

law to prevent the use of this concrete thing without the consent of its creator or adapter, and far from being guarded against as an injury to one, would have been welcomed as a blessing to all — in short, would have been viewed as a most fortunate element in the nature of things.

The *raison d'être* of property is found in the very fact that there is no such possibility — in the fact that it is impossible in the nature of things for concrete objects to be used in different places at the same time. This fact existing, no person can remove from another's possession and take to his own use another's concrete creation without thereby depriving that other of all opportunity to use that which he created; and for this reason it became socially necessary, since successful society rests on individual initiative, to protect the individual creator in the use of his concrete creations by forbidding others to use them without his consent. In other words, it became necessary to institute property in concrete things.

But all this happened so long ago that we of today have entirely forgotten why it happened. In fact, it is very doubtful whether, at the time of the institution of property, those who effected it thoroughly realized and understood the motive of their course. Men sometimes do by instinct and without analysis that which conforms to right reason. The institutors of property may have been governed by circumstances inhering in the nature of things, without realizing that, had the nature of things been the opposite, they would not have instituted property. But be that as it may, even supposing that they thoroughly understood their course, we, at any rate, have pretty nearly forgotten their understanding.

And so it has come about that we have made of property a fetish; that we consider it a sacred thing; that we have set up the god of property on an altar as an object of idol worship; and that most of us are not only doing what we can to strengthen and perpetuate his reign within the proper and original limits of his sovereignty but also are mistakenly endeavoring to extend his dominion over things and under circumstances which, in their pivotal characteristic, are precisely the opposite of those out of which his power developed.

All of which is to say, in briefer compass, that from the justice and social necessity of property in concrete things we have erroneously assumed the justice and social necessity of property in abstract things — that is, of property in ideas — with the result of nullifying to a large and lamentable extent that fortunate element in the nature of things, in this case not hypothetical, but real; namely, the immeasurably fruitful possibility of the use of abstract things by any number of individuals in any number of places at precisely the same time, without in the slightest degree impairing the use thereof by any single individual. Thus we have hastily and stupidly jumped to the conclusion that property in concrete things logically implies property in abstract things, whereas, if we had had the care and the keenness to accurately analyze, we should have found that the very reason which dictates the advisability of property in concrete things denies the advisability of property in abstract things. We see here a curious instance of that frequent mental phenomenon — the precise inversion of the truth by a superficial view.

Furthermore, even were the conditions the same in both cases, and concrete things capable of use by different persons in different places at the same time, even then, I say, the institution of property in concrete things, though under those conditions manifestly absurd, would be infinitely less destructive of individual opportunities, and therefore infinitely less dangerous and detrimental to human welfare, than is the institution of property in abstract things. For it is easy to see that, even should we accept the rather startling hypothesis that a single ear of corn is continually and permanently consumable, or rather inconsumable, by an indefinite number of persons scattered over the surface of the earth, still the legal institution of property in concrete things that would secure to the sower of a grain of corn the exclusive use of the resultant ear would not, in so doing, deprive other persons of the right to sow other grains of corn and become exclusive users of their respective harvests; whereas the legal institution of property in abstract things not only secures to the inventor, say, of the steam engine, the exclusive use of the engines which he actually makes, but at the same time deprives all other persons of the right to make for themselves other engines involving any of the same ideas.

Perpetual property in ideas, then, which is the logical outcome of any theory of property in abstract things, would, had it been in force in the lifetime of James Watt, have made his direct heirs the owners of at least nine-tenths of the now existing wealth of the world; and, had it been in force in the lifetime of the inventor of the Roman alphabet, nearly all the highly civilized peoples of the earth would be today the virtual slaves of that inventor's heirs, which is but another way of saying that, instead of becoming highly civilized, they would have remained in a state of semi-barbarism. It seems to me that these two statements, which in my view are incontrovertible, are in themselves sufficient to condemn property in ideas forever.

If, then, the four monopolies to which I have referred are unnecessary denials of liberty, and therefore unjust denials of liberty, and if they are the sustaining causes of interest, rent, and monopolistic profit, and if, in turn, this usurious trinity is the cause of all vast accumulations of wealth — for further proof of which propositions I must, because of the limitation of my time, refer you to the economic writings of the anarchistic school — it clearly follows that the adequate solution of the problem with which the trusts confront us is to be found only in abolition of these monopolies and the consequent guarantee of perfectly free competition.

The most serious of these four monopolies is unquestionably the money monopoly, and I believe that perfect freedom in finance alone would wipe out nearly all the trusts, or at least render them harmless, and perhaps helpful. Mr. Bryan told a very important truth when he declared that the destruction of the money trust would at the same time kill all the other trusts. Unhappily, Mr. Bryan does not propose to destroy the money trust. He wishes simply to transform it from a gold trust into a gold and silver trust. The money trust cannot be destroyed by the remonetization of silver. That would be only a mitigation of the monopoly, not the abolishment of it. It can be abolished only by monetizing all wealth that has a market value; that is, by giving to all wealth the right of representation by currency, and to all currency the right to circulate wherever it can on its own merits. And this is not only a solution of the trust question but the first step that should be taken, and the greatest single step that can be taken, in economic and social reform.

I have tried, in the few minutes allotted to me, to state concisely the attitude of anarchism toward industrial combinations. It discountenances all direct attacks on them, all interference with them, all antitrust legislation whatsoever. In fact, it regards industrial combinations as very useful whenever they spring into existence in response to demand created in a healthy social body. If at present they are baneful, it is because they are symptoms of a social disease originally caused and persistently aggravated by a regimen of tyranny and quackery. Anarchism wants to call off the quacks, and give liberty, nature's great cure-all, a chance to do its perfect work.

Free access to the world of matter, abolishing land monopoly; free access to the world of mind, abolishing idea monopoly; free access to an untaxed and unprivileged market, abolishing tariff monopoly and money monopoly — secure these and all the rest shall be added unto you. For liberty is the remedy of every social evil, and to anarchy the world must look at last for any enduring guarantee of social order.

III.

JOHN W. HAYES:
A Union Leader's View

THE QUESTION which we are invited here to discuss — "Trusts and Combinations" — is fast pressing itself for solution before the highest tribunal in the nation, the court of final resort, for all questions of public policy, the court of public opinion. It is too vital, too important to be confined to the narrow limits of commercial affairs, of mere business operation, or mercenary speculation. It touches the very foundations of our free institutions, involves the liberty of the people, the comfort, happiness and prosperity of millions of freemen, and the stability of our governmental system, established by the fathers to defend and protect coming generations in their inherent rights, which rights were declared by them to be the gift of nature to all her children.

This question, then, involves more than the trivial matter of production and prices. It goes far beyond the profitable operation of the manufacturer. It rises to the high plane of a government policy, involves the question of human rights, of individual liberty, of the status of the citizen, of the dignity of citizenship, the right of defense, a limit to the power of wealth, a point at which the encroachment of mercenary greed must stop, and a barrier created that will enable us to defend our liberties, our manhood, and our independence.

I shall, therefore, discuss this question only as it bears upon the broad field of human rights, and deny at the outset the moral right of any individual, or combination of individuals, to so monopolize any natural field of industry to such an extent as to be able to dictate the conditions which govern the lives of that portion of society which gains its maintenance by the exercise of productive industry in that particular field. I assert that it is contrary to the best interests of society — indeed, that government has not the constitutional power to enact such legislation as will make it possible for any combination of individuals to so limit the volume of production in any natural field for its own particular advantage, or so create conditions that any individual or combination of individuals may have despotic power over the lives of any citizen or number of citizens.

I further assert and maintain that these great combinations are an assault upon the inherent and constitutional rights of the citizen, and that the real and vital advantage to be gained is the despotic control over labor — virtually to own and command the labor engaged in any particular field, and consequently it is an assault upon that portion of the people. If one field may be invaded and reduced to despotic dictation, all may be, and the logical outcome must be the conquest of all fields of production, the establishment of a despotism in each, the enslavement of the people, the overthrow of our free institutions, and the erection of moneyed aristocracy. Thus would our boasted free institutions become a fraud and a pretense, our government perverted, and only used as a machine to enforce the will of the dictators.

The term "trust" is so indefinite, so vague and uncertain, being used many times without a clear conception of its scope or exact reference, that we must secure a definition for it. Webster defines a trust to be "a combination to control production and prices." This definition furnishes us with sufficient grounds to attack them constitutionally, as the control of production involves our inherent rights, the liberty of our citizens — in fact, the very existence of our form of government. Not only does the trust dominate and control production and prices but it controls and cuts off our opportunity to labor, which is one of our inherent rights; and thus the very right to live is denied us, or we are doomed to involuntary servitude for the benefit of a more favored class. This, you see, places the question beyond the profitable operation of the manufacturer and raises one of equity, of justice, and of the rights of man.

An analysis of the character and objects of the trust cannot but convince any unbiased and patriotic mind that they are inimical to our popular form of government, subversive of our institutions, tyrannical in their methods, antagonistic to the common welfare, the common enemy of society, and should be treated as an invader or armed revolutionist aspiring to dictatorial power. Arms are not the only resort of the invader, the despot, or the conqueror. Violence is not the only means of making conquests and enslaving the people; and it can be proven beyond any question of doubt that the methods of the trusts are the methods of the invader, the conqueror, and the despot, and the ends to be accomplished by the instigators of the trusts are exactly those intended to be accomplished by arms directed by military genius. Taking this view of the trusts, which I hold is the correct one, I assert boldly that they are the enemies of society, and as such should be destroyed as any common enemy, and that the financial phase of the question should not come into the subject for consideration, as the liberties of the people are far above the mere question of money.

The definition that a trust is an aggressive combination of private individuals leads naturally to the inquiry, against what or whom this aggression or assault is to be directed? Is it an organization of private individuals formed to attack some similar organization in a competitive rivalry, the result of which will affect the private interests of those immediately concerned, leaving the unsuccessful and unfortunate the ability to recover from any injuries they might suffer from the contest, with their social status unaffected and their capacity and ability to produce unimpaired? Or is it possible that this aggression is against society, against the established social and political conditions, which guarantees to every citizen the right and opportunity to labor in any field of industry he may find most favorable to his pursuit of happiness and the enjoyment of his liberty?

What more nearly concerns the happiness of man than the enjoyment of the full return of his industry, or his liberty, more than the access to any field of industry nature has provided, from which he may gather the necessities and comforts which minister to his happiness and the happiness of those depending upon him? It is the duty of society and government to foster and encourage production, to guard every field of industry for the common good of society, and to develop the producing energy to the greatest extent possible.

There is no fear that a people can produce too much of anything that is serviceable and useful to the community; that the people can become too comfortable or too industrious. The good of society demands that the productive energy be developed to the greatest degree possible; that the fields of industry be not circumscribed; and that free access be guaranteed and preserved to all who require or desire to exercise their productive labor in such fields. The controlling of any field of industry by any individual or combination of individuals is contrary to the declared spirit of our institutions, for it recognizes the power of such individual or combination to restrict production, even to absolutely close the field of opportunity against the citizen, if they consider their personal interests will be benefited thereby.

The great corporations, the trusts, with their capital, their machinery, special privileges, and other advantages, are overwhelming the individual, reducing him to the condition of a mere tool, to be used in their great undertakings for their individual profit, and of no more consequence than a piece of dumb machinery. Man is the slave of necessity, and he who controls the necessities has the power of a despot. The first and prime necessity is the opportunity to exercise his industry in some productive field where he can secure the means of existence. To close this field, to cut off this opportunity, is to sentence him to death. To restrict the exercise of his productive ability, or limit the terms of his access to the opportunity by the will of another, is to make him the slave of another.

It is claimed by short-sighted, selfish, and mercenary men that if the opportunity is closed in one field there are others to which the individual may turn. This is too silly and childish an assertion to merit notice. First, because no such possibility should be allowed to exist under our free institutions; and, next, because were it possible for one field to be monopolized, it is possible for all to be, and the individual would turn from the field closed against him to find all others in the same condition. Even were this not so, his skill, experience, and training in that field would be lost to him, and he would enter a new one at a disadvantage in the competition with trained minds and skilled hands already employed, and an injustice would be done on the one hand, and undue favor extended on the other.

The trust, by monopolizing the field, becomes the dictator of the conditions which govern the life of every individual engaged in the field monopolized. By limiting the extent to which he may exercise his productive energy, limiting his wage, or the possible amount of his earnings, it dictates the quality and quantity of food the worker may eat, the kind of clothes he may wear, the kind of shelter he may provide for his family, the opportunity for education and improvement his children may have, and, by cutting his opportunity to labor, it denies him even the right to live.

The great danger from these great combinations is the fact that they step in between the citizen and the government and levy such tribute as they may choose, imposing the most severe penalties in the form of enforced idleness, destitution, and suffering for refusal to comply with their demands. The individual is thus subjected to the domination of two distinct powers — the one the political government, which taxes him and controls his relations to his fellow citizens, and which power is of his own creation and is submitted to voluntarily; the other controls the necessities by which he exists, and only by permission of the combination which controls his field of industry can he exist at all. This latter is, in its nature, compulsory, and is only submitted to because he is unable to resist it. In this sense he is a slave.

Each field of industry is looked to to supply whatever demand may be made upon it by the necessities of the people, not only of our own country but throughout the world. A larger demand gives greater activity to such industry as is already employed and opportunity to such energy as may at any time be unemployed, the supply being naturally adjusted to the demand and a just and equitable return made to the producing energy. The operation of the trust interrupts this natural adjustment, arbitrarily fixes the volume of production, and demands whatever price necessity may compel the unfortunate consumer to pay, and thus an unjust tax is levied upon all society to fill the purses of the greedy dictators, who dole out whatever pittance they may choose in the form of wages to those unfortunates whose labor they are enabled to command. In this way society is compelled to pay tribute to this speculative freebooter, and submit to his dictation as to the quality and quantity of whatever product he controls which its necessities may demand.

It may be said in reply that this is never done. I answer that it is possible it may be, and it should be so arranged that such a thing would not be possible in any civilized

society. The trust, then, is the enemy of society as well as of the individual.

This surely is enough to condemn it, for whatever is the enemy of society should be exterminated without thought of mercy or charity. But the trust is worse. It is the enemy of free institutions, a breeder of treason against the government, involving the overthrow of our system and the destruction of our liberties. This is a severe charge, but it is capable of clear and undisputable proof.

The great object of human endeavor is the achievement of the greatest degree of human happiness. This is the great aim of all human society, all human governments; and this is the declared and recognized purpose for which our free institutions were devised and established, and the machinery of our government was designed and constructed for the purpose of accomplishing this result in the most effective manner. By preserving the inherent rights and liberties of the individual and defending the dignity of citizenship, it is hoped that the citizen may be protected from the tyranny of more fortunate individuals and classes, and the operation of unjust conditions and influences which may assail him, and he be left untrammeled in his pursuit of that degree of happiness to which he may aspire.

The establishment of the trust renders impossible this preservation and defense, because it transforms the citizen into a servile, dependent upon the despotic will of the corporation, which is governed only by mercenary greed and selfish desire, the trust becoming in its very nature a power far more effective in all things directly pertaining to the individual's comfort and happiness than the government. In this way it usurps the power of government, which it nullifies and overthrows, and so far as the individual affected is concerned, assumes the functions of government. The object and aim of the trust being purely mercenary and selfish, naturally it will seek to establish and maintain conditions which will give it absolute control of the productive energy employed in its field, regardless of the rights of individuals or the common welfare of society.

The legislation enacted by the government, if uninfluenced, naturally would be the expression of the popular will in the interests of individuals and society. This legislation it becomes the interest of the trust to influence and pervert to its own profit and advantage. This opens the door to corruption of the legislative branch of government and the oppression and overawing of the popular will. The representatives of the people are corrupted, and the class dependent on the trust for its employment and maintenance intimidated and practically disfranchised through fear of loss of employment and enforced idleness. They are compelled to support the methods of the trust or neglect to exercise their rights as citizens. In this way the independence of the citizen is destroyed, his manhood degraded, his right to give free expression to his opinions upon public affairs abridged. He becomes a sycophant, a moral coward, a helpless dependent upon the will of his master; and the will of the trusts becomes the only voice heard.

Legislation in this way becomes merely the dictation of the trust, and the pretense that is in the emanation of popular will is false and fraudulent. In this way the power and machinery of government are gradually transferred from the people to the corporation, and that which was founded and intended to protect the citizen and defend his natural and civil rights becomes the means of his oppression. This is unquestionably treason, a conspiracy to usurp and pervert the government, to overthrow free institutions, and to establish a despotism and a favored and dominant class, practically autocratic in its use of power. That this is not only possible but practically in operation at

the present time is proven by the history of our political campaigns for the past two decades, and a review of the legislation enacted in the interests of corporations, which constitute the great bulk of all legislation, municipal, state, and national. It is universally admitted that legislation emanates from the class benefited by it, and, looking over the mass of legislation, one is at no loss to decide what class is benefited. Therefore, there can be no doubt as to what influence brought about its enactment.

The fraud, corruption, and bribery of legislatures; the open defiance of executive authority; the corruption of courts and their officials; the usurpation of power and the legal assumption of rights; the ready appeal to the military and arrogant overriding of the civil authority by this power in controversies between corporations and employees; the defiance of municipal authorities in questions between corporations and municipalities; the employment of armed mercenaries to enforce their decrees; the constant and never ceasing struggle of corporations to compel as many hours of labor and as low a rate of wages as is possible to enforce, are all clearly indicative of the character, desires, and purposes, and show beyond any question such combinations to be the enemies of society and of any form of government which tends to abridge or control their power over the citizen, or the exercise of their will in any undertaking their greed and avarice may suggest, regardless of the rights, interest, liberties, or happiness of the people, or even the interests of the people's government. Their intents are unquestionably treasonable, and if carried to their ultimate results will certainly cause the overthrow of our institutions and government.

In this world all things work in a circle. So it will and must be with trusts if carried to their logical culmination. The inspiring motive which called them into being will prove their destruction, as well as the destruction of our government. They will end by destroying themselves, as well as the government which gave them birth. The very nature of the system proves this.

The trust being an aggressive combination for purely selfish objects attacks the individual, and, by overthrowing his natural rights, seizes upon his field of opportunity and production, appropriating them to its own advantage. This field having been conquered, and the trust strengthened in its financial power, aggressive spirit of selfish greed looks for conquests in allied fields, which are soon invaded and monopolized; or other combinations, seeing the success of the first attempt, enter upon the same campaign of conquest. Soon the individual is overwhelmed and every field of production is monopolized by a trust. Individual enterprise, opportunity, liberty, and individual energy are destroyed; competition for the individual is impossible; and the war between the trusts begins.

The strongest combination in one field attacks the weaker in allied fields, and the overthrow and absorption of this strengthens the victor and makes further conquest possible; which finally ends by the overthrow of all opposition and the monopolizing of all fields of production by one colossal, irresistible combination, instigated by mercenary greed and utter selfishness, which will issue its autocratic decree to a cringing mass of dependent slaves, whose very right to live would depend upon the imperial will of the corporation, which would hold the power of life and death over its subjects. These would represent the citizenship of the pretended republic which might stand for the sham of civil government; for should even a pretense remain, the laws enacted would be merely the will of the corporation. But would such an aggregation of power and wealth be content to allow even a pretense of its subjection to any recognized authority?

It is scarcely reasonable to suppose, but it is far more probable, that all sham and pretense would be thrown aside and the victor openly declare his power, brush aside any futile opposition, set up his aristocracy, and free institutions — the popular government erected by patriotic fathers — would disappear from the face of the earth, and in its stead would arise a despotism born of greed and selfishness, subservient to the interests of an utterly irresponsible group of heartless speculators, ruling their slaves with an iron hand in order to secure to themselves the greatest profit and advantage, and to whom the common welfare would mean only their own mercenary advancement. Beside such conditions the despotism of Russia would be liberty; hereditary monarchy, liberal; the condition of the black slave of the South enjoyable. No more deplorable fate could possibly befall any people than that, which in this case is possible, as the logical outcome of recognizing this heartless, this heathenish, and selfish system.

I do not hesitate to proclaim that in recognizing it at all we are nourishing a serpent, fostering treason, giving aid and comfort to the enemies of society, welcoming an invader, assisting in the overthrow of free institutions and popular government, inviting a dictator, and laying the foundation of despotism. We are sowing the seed of revolution and may reap the harvest upon the bloody fields of civil strife or amid the groans and sighs of fettered slaves — bereft of manhood; wallowing in moral degradation, ignorance, and vice; degraded from the exalted dignity of citizenship in a free and mighty nation to a condition of sycophantic dependence upon the despotic decree of an autocrat.

The slums of Europe have been raked to secure a horde of the most ignorant, the most servile, the most depraved, the lowest element of the most oppressive aristocracies of modern civilization; and these purchased slaves, dependents upon the will of an autocrat, without even the rudiments of education, without even a faint conception of liberty or of human rights, with no conception of the character of our institutions and government. have been injected into our population and employed in the development of some of our most productive fields, where they are worked under conditions almost identical with those under which the convicts of Siberia exist, conditions which no free American citizen could submit to and no man worthy of citizenship should. Thus are these great fields of industry, the inheritance of American children, closed against our own people for the profit of a few speculators, and the industry in these fields ruled despotically by force, and practically a system of slavery established.

Nor does the wrong end here. This mass of ignorance and depravity has been degenerating for centuries under the most iniquitous tyranny, and cannot by any means hope to reach the plane of intelligence our people occupy. They submit willingly and with no sense of humiliation to methods and treatment our own people would not brook, and thus gradually their masters introduce and usurp authority similar to that of European potentates, which, being accepted, gradually comes to be looked upon as legitimate; and so usurped authority comes gradually to be recognized as legal, and our government the executor often of the will of the corporation. Further than this, the influence of this degraded and vicious element upon our own population is bad in the extreme, tending to degrade and lower our own citizens, rather than to elevate those too dense and ignorant to be impressed by moral influences. The result is rather to Europeanize our own people than to Americanize the stolid mass which exists under such degrading influences.

However, it is plain that this grand inheritance of the American people, these great fields of opportunity and production have been closed to their rightful owners and absorbed by a greedy few, who operate them with foreign labor under the most servile and degrading conditions.

That the unrestricted competition of centralized wealth against individual enterprise is fatal to the individual and against the best interests of society is further proven in the commercial field. The small merchant has been forced into the position of a paid servant of the combination. Formerly, young men enjoyed the opportunity of entering this field of occupation with the hope of advancement, if not fortune. Beginning as clerk, they could gain a knowledge of the business and qualify themselves to conduct a business of their own or become partners of their employer, in either case becoming independent, self-reliant, self-supporting, and valuable citizens, maintaining their family in comfort.

Now this opportunity is closed. The field is monopolized by combinations of wealth. The clerk must remain a clerk, without hope in the future, except such increase in his pitiful wages as his master may in his magnanimity see fit to dole out to him. His opportunity is further limited by his being forced into competition with helpless women, driven by necessity to accept any wage in order to exist.

To sum up the whole, this policy of the trusts is an aggressive invasion organized against the best interests of society and destructive to our free institutions and popular government. It is too often the instigator of fraud, corruption, bribery, and treason. It is the ally of despotism, tyranny, mercenary selfishness, and slavery, and is an enemy to the elevation of the race and the equality of man.

IV.

LAURENCE GRONLUND:
A Socialist's View

WE MEAN LEGITIMATE, sound trusts, not fraudulent concerns, such, for instance, where smooth scoundrels sell to gullible people millions worth of worthless common stock, which they know will never produce a dividend. There are plenty of means and of laws to take care of this class. The legitimate trusts are either associations of capital — and to these, department stores belong — or unions of labor. We shall deal with both, though it is the former alone that creates difficulties for us.

Let us at the start understand that it is impossible to crush out either kind of trusts. The politicians who propose that remedy are either supremely ignorant or downright demagogues. In order to find out how to deal with trusts of capital, we must understand their origin.

They are not the outcome of "prohibitive" or other tariffs; neither are they the products of railroad discriminations, though they often are considerably assisted thereby. They are economic necessities, due to our complex civilization. Our commercial and industrial affairs have shown during the last 100 years an ever accelerating tendency to larger schemes, more elaborate organization, more intricate machinery. Our vast iron and steel industry comes down from the village blacksmith, our huge shoe factories from the village cobbler, our textile industry from the village handloom. At one time everyone worked for himself. Then came small, then large, firms, followed by joint-stock companies and corporations. Finally, during the last generation, trusts, more and more extensive and intricate organizations, having for purpose to limit or abolish competition, since it was found to have become highly injurious and unprofitable.

Thus it cannot be too much emphasized that trusts are not due to any casual cause, not to wrong-headedness, not to vicious business principles, often even not to voluntary choice. A brewer in England declared, "We are compelled to take over the other breweries; we don't want to, but we are obliged to." It is an irresistible tendency, of late appalling in its rapidity, to be ascribed to increase of population, scientific discoveries, and mechanical inventions.

Of course, it cannot be stopped. To try to crush the trusts would be like the attempt by a dam to stop the mighty Mississippi. The trusts will go on; the various industries in each line will come under a central management. They will in our country develop in all directions, till finally — some time during the 20th century — all considerable industries will be under the control of trusts, extending from the Atlantic to the Pacific. There is absolutely no help for it.

Still we say the trust is not at all a monster; it is a phenomenon at which to look fearlessly, and to utilize for the public welfare. For this purpose we must fully understand wherein the dangers of the trust consist. It is generally supposed that the only interest the public has is how the trust affects wages and prices. We think this is a great error. We do not believe that trusts as yet have seriously lowered wages or raised prices. They surely need not do it. And we know that in many cases they have lowered prices and raised wages.

But there are two very serious dangers that threaten in the future. Let us assume that the time has come when every considerable industry has come under one head, one manager, whose sway will extend from ocean to ocean. What powers will such a chief not have, what power especially for mischief! Then the trust, indeed, will be capable of seriously affecting the public welfare; then, indeed, it may lower wages and raise prices, if it has a mind to. Can a democracy like ours stand such a state of things? Can it tolerate in its midst a handful of such autocrats, whose aim is simply private greed, and who do not need to care a particle for social need? Already we are now living under an absolutism of capital to which other nations are strangers — but what will it be then?

Again, in every trust, the owners virtually abdicate all their powers in favor of the manager. Hence, when all our industries have become trusts, capital will have had its character completely changed. Formerly, capitalists performed a highly important function, that of directing production; capital had a social character, and was subject to noteworthy social obligations, which sometimes were splendidly discharged. But, in the future, our capital holders will become industrially and economically useless, first superfluous, then harmful; they actually will become rudimentary organs in the social organism, and capital holding will become a pure personal privilege, subject to no social obligation whatever. Can a democracy like ours stand this; will a democracy stand it? No. Such a state of affairs will be simply the last step but one.

Even before trusts arose, when we only had large enterprises that controlled matters of vital interest to the people, the public was forced to step in, in order merely to secure the rights of consumers. Public control has again and again been asserted. Grandmother always has had her way. So with still greater force it will be in the future. The organization of trusts is admirable; it knocks into the heads of all with sledge-hammer blows the patent truth that system is better than planlessness. The machinery of the trust is all ready to the hands of democracy — to public control. No one would think of socializing an industry that was divided into a hundred thousand businesses. But this is a national monopoly. That is why the trust movement is an irreversible step along the path to universal cooperation.

This, we say, is the first answer to the question, what to do with the trusts: Look forward to the future public ownership and management of their enterprises, but let this change proceed slowly. However, prepare for it, make it the ideal of the coming century, and treat the trusts accordingly.

The second thing to do, meanwhile, is to protect labor against the trusts. That they in the future may raise prices arbitrarily is bad enough, but that they arbitrarily may reduce wages is much worse. Oh, if the trusts would believe that it is to their advantage to include their employees in the benefits which they achieve, if they would

conclude to revive the ancient guilds on a higher plane, then the future might be quite bright — but they are too selfish for that!

How, then, protect labor? For our laboring people to help our demagogues in attempting to crush the trust would be suicidal. They would be the first and only ones to feel the blows of such an enterprise. Undoubtedly our trades unions are trusts. Our work people generally do not know what they owe to trades unions, especially what they owe to the old English trades unionists, who kept up their unions in spite of parliamentary terrors. That they now enjoy higher wages and shorter hours is due to the unions. Though strikes often are disastrous to the participants, there never was one, either won or lost, that did not benefit the working people as a class.

It is well that work people are fast coming to look upon the workman as positively immoral who holds aloof from his fellows and refuses to enter the union of his trade. With the arrival of the trust, their ideal has become an organization, controlling the entire labor force of the country, nothing less than a National Syndicate of Labor. They are right. Unless the labor trusts develop equally with trusts of capital, our civilization will soon come to a halt.

But the work people cannot achieve this ideal now with their own unaided efforts — still less when the trusts have gained their giant strength. The state must help them, and a demand is soon to be made on our politicians which they cannot resist. Such a demand has in fact been made by the well-known antisocialist writer, William H. Mallock, to wit: That the trades unions be made an "estate of the realm" by being granted "a privileged status law." Our legislators must persuade every workman, induce him by every practicable motive, to join his union, even to the extent of granting to the unions the privilege of, in last resort, determining all labor questions; thus making the union the representatives of the men on an equal footing with the haughtiest employer. To those who will be horrified at this suggestion, we recommend the words of Thorold Rogers: "I would limit the franchise, parliamentary and local, to those and those only who enter into the guild of labor."

These unions, of course, must be organized in a thorough democratic fashion, so that every workman will have a vote that counts as much as that of everyone else. Moreover, the state, as the representative of the whole community, will rectify the many serious blunders that trades unions in the past have committed, and which sometimes have made them absolutely antisocial institutions, such as the limitation of apprentices and forbidding able workmen to do the best they can.

This is the way to protect adult labor. But we must also protect our growing-up youths against the trusts — both of capital and labor. We must have a new education for our boys — a truly democratic education. Every phase of civilization has had its appropriate education. A good education under the ancient régime was different from a good education during the Middle Ages, and that again very different from a good education for the 20th century. Our boys must be trained into being all-round men, fit to take their places in a perfect democracy. Next, our people now are being forced — especially by the trusts — to take their places according to their capacity, as portions of a great machinery. That is, we are fast becoming a nation of specialists. Specialization evidently is the law that will govern our future. No man will amount to anything unless he becomes a specialist in something useful, and just by becoming such a specialist will he become a valuable member of a perfect democracy.

We must have such an education. Indeed, it has already been started under the name of "The New Education." It will make our boys into capable specialists and all-round men. For that purpose the state must have

control of ten years of the lives of our boys, during which first the principles of the kindergarten and then the principles of manual training should govern. Thus the boys will be trained to take their places in the ranks of the producers, and both the trusts of capital and of labor must be made to submit.

Lastly, we come to the third thing we can do about the trusts. While public control of what is now strictly private business should be merely the ideal for the next century, and not be attempted until its close, there is some business that should immediately be entered upon. That is the so-called public utilities, such as municipal ownership and management of waterworks, of course, of street transportation in every form, of gasworks, and electric-power works. These may not yet be trusts — only large enterprises. But in Brooklyn we find surface and elevated roads already a trust, and in Manhattan they will soon be that. It would be highly desirable, and the best thing for itself, if the new democracy would in its next national platform incorporate a plank demanding municipal control. Nothing would so much convince our people of the blessings of public control, and prove to them that government can do business as well, and even better, than private parties, as such an object lesson.

But here we have still a suggestion to make. It is that the state should have more to say than now it has in municipal enterprises. For them to succeed, they must be undertaken, not with a view of giving labor employment but with the object of furnishing the best and cheapest water, light, and transportation. This the state can effect better than the city. Hence the cry of "local self-government" is wrong. Capitalists might just as properly demand that the legislature shall grant the stockholders of a railroad "self-government free from state interference." The city is a creation of the sovereign state, and when a charter is granted it should safeguard state interests to the same extent that is supposed to be done in granting a charter for a railroad. We say that the state should exercise oversight and have final control, simply because it at least is one step further removed from local pressure, and hence will dare and be able to do things that the local authorities will not dare even attempt.

Then there are public utilities that come under the jurisdiction of the nation, which will furnish splendid opportunities for curbing the trusts. We should have a national express system, to which the late convention with Germany ought to give a great impulse, a national telegraph, national banks of deposit (postal savings banks) and national banks of loans from the funds thus accumulated, and finally national control of railroads. We do at present advocate national ownership and management of these latter; this might as yet be too big a mouthful to digest, but national control of railroad fares and freight rates — this is perfectly practicable, and has been several times recommended to Congress.

It would with one stroke abolish the unjust discrimination, both between localities and between shippers, which the Interstate Commission has been unable to effect. If trusts should ever dare to raise prices, such a national control of freight rates will immediately bring them to their senses. It is perfectly practicable, we contend. Through a committee of Congress it is just as easy to establish schedules of fares and freight rates on all our railroads, and to enforce them, as through the Committee on Ways and Means to establish schedules of duties on imports and to enforce them, as is now done.

This is a practical way, and, we think, a far-seeing way to utilize the trusts for the public welfare, while to attempt to crush the trusts, we repeat, is simply the notion of the demagogues.

In conclusion, we beg those who want more information in this direction to read an English anonymous book entitled, *The Social Horizon,* and this writer's last publication, *The New Economy.*

V.

CLEMENT STUDEBAKER:
A Manufacturer's View

WITHIN CERTAIN REASONABLE LIMITS the combination of agencies for the production of a given article decreases the cost of production. Such combinations enable the use of the latest improved machinery, and the adoption of general facilities to expedite the progress of work usually impossible if the manufacture is carried on with limited capital, or with small productive capacity. Further, it is well known that managerial assistance usually costs little more for a business of great magnitude than for one the output of which is small. On the other hand, however, whenever a business becomes so large that its oversight is impossible by one executive head, then it is often the case that economies are less likely to be successfully practised.

Such, I imagine, would be the case if it were undertaken to operate plants widely separated throughout the country. As to whether the decrease of cost of production ought to be beneficial to society, or the reverse, I think this answers itself in the asking. Morally considered, society ought to be benefited by every honest and proper improvement of conditions in the material world.

To what extent a decrease of the cost of production will profit the consumer will depend largely on the necessity which constrains the purchaser to share with him his saving. If the combination in question were such as to utterly preclude competition, the benefit which would accrue to the consumer by a saving effected by the producer would quite possibly be inappreciable. Most producers under such circumstances would be quite likely to arrogate to themselves credit for the saving effected, and would consider that a division of the benefits under such circumstances would come under the head of philanthropy or benevolences rather than matter-of-fact business.

I would regard a general combination of all of the manufacturing plants for the production of any given article of manufacture as likely to be to some extent disadvantageous to the wage earner. The operation of some factories would perhaps be discontinued in favor of others more eligibly situated, and to the degree that concentration of forces would increase productiveness, there would be a correspondingly diminished demand for laborers. But this, of course, happens whenever improved machinery is introduced, or whenever there is a readjustment of production occasioned by a change in conditions affecting such production.

I do not imagine that combination among industrial enterprises will very seriously affect middlemen. In some cases commercial traveling men could be dispensed with, but the day when the public can be conveniently supplied without the intervention of the merchant is a long ways off.

No true monopoly is possible in this country except that enjoyed by virtue of a patent granted by the United States. If those who undertake to inaugurate trusts had a monopoly of the trust business there would be cause for alarm. But anyone can go into the trust or combination business who is able to find others who will join him. Herein is the safety of society. Combinations of capital build railroads and decrease the cost of travel and transportation. Some part of that saving they keep as profit, but whenever they undertake to keep so much of it from the public as to give them unusually large returns on their capital, a rival road springs up, and down goes the cost to the consumer.

Trusts have undertaken to enfold producers so as to limit competition, but in vain. No sooner have they gathered into the fold all in sight than up springs another. And this will continue to be the case so long as there are profits made which allure outside capital, and outside capital is left free to take a hand in. Sugar refining, the manufacture of tobacco, etc., are cases in point. Whenever these great companies give evidence of making large profits, some powerful rival comes into the field, and competition proceeds to regulate prices on a lower plane.

Combination within reasonable lines is likely to be of benefit. This is already evident in the fact that our products in iron and steel are coming into large demand throughout the world, even in England herself.

The best service which our legislators can render the country, when considering the subject of our productive agencies, is to insure enterprise and home capital a fair field and no favor. It is folly to talk of restraining legitimate combinations. There is scarce a corner grocery in the land that is not witness to a combination of money and brains, a combination for the mutual benefit of the combined. The whole country is built up of combinations. They exist alike in society, in government, and in business; and it is as futile and senseless to talk about restrictions in this particular as it would be to undertake to make Niagara flow upstream into Lake Erie.

As manufacturers, we feel no concern about combinations of capital in our line of business. It is the brainpower of a competitor, rather than his capital in money, which makes him formidable in the struggle.

I am richer than Harriman. I have all the money I want and he hasn't.
JOHN MUIR, in conversation, 1899

Minnesota medicine show offering "long life and good health" by taking Kickapoo Indian Medicine

AFTER THE FRONTIER

The purchase of the Louisiana Territory in 1803 had been an unprecedented act; $15 million had been voted by Congress for the vast land and constitutionality was hopefully assumed. It is a measure of the development of governmental involvement in areas beyond its original competence that in 1904 Congress appropriated $5 million to help finance the Louisiana Purchase Exposition in St. Louis. The Exposition was architecturally small improvement on Chicago's "White City" of eleven years earlier; the display of technology and industry were again very impressive, however, and the crowning feature was the exhibition of 100 automobiles,

the first such sizeable display. Also among the exhibits, to the doubtless delight of the more patriotic fairgoers, was a huge Philippine reservation, displaying for the edification of the customers America's newest acquisition. The fair, though a financial failure, was a demonstration of the development of the West — the successive stages of frontier, settlement, commercial center, and industry, each serving the more forward areas and preparing for the later stages. Just as Chicago had put itself on display earlier, so now was St. Louis and with it the whole Midwest demonstrating its growth into modernity.

(Above) Downtown St. Louis, Mo., at the time of the World's Fair of 1904; (below) Union Railway Station in St. Louis, completed in 1896

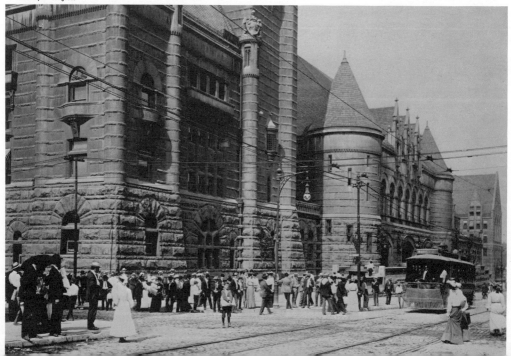

(Above) Two prize winners in the Horse Show at the Livestock Forum; (below) view of the Festival Hall from the Grand Basin of the World's Fair

(Above) Crowds along a street at the fairground in St. Louis, 1904; (below) natives in costume were part of the Philippine exhibit at the Fair

In spite of the determined competition of St. Louis, Chicago remained the metropolis of the Midwest and the Plains, mainly by virtue of its position as a transportation center. Since the demise of the steamboat and with it St. Louis' dominance of river trade, Chicago's access to railroads and to the Great Lakes had become decisive. Commerce and industry brought great wealth to Chicago; though the wise use of wealth was rare, the city could claim the title "Garden City" for its well-developed park system.

(Above) Worker's Parade during the Packinghouse Strike in Chicago in 1904; (left) an unidentified local politician at the scene of a construction project; (below) inspection of a Chicago sweatshop in 1903

(Above left) Company of actors rehearsing for a production of Shakespeare's "As You Like It" in Jackson Park, Chicago; (above right) German building in Jackson Park; (below) elevated train tracks at Chicago Avenue east of Orleans Street, 1900

Horses and buggies along Poyntz Avenue in Manhattan, Kansas, around 1900; photo by S. C. Orr

With the West opened to exploitation and industry, new wealth flowed everywhere. The railroad, having done more to settle the West than any other force, now brought back the gold and silver and copper, the wheat and lumber of the new territories. As wealth and resources spread, so did "culture" — whether in the form of a brass bedstead or a temperance drive or a Chautauqua meeting. The political strength of the West grew slowly through the agrarian movements and culminated in the nomination of Bryan in 1896. Though the uncouth West might still be laughed at, it could never again be ignored.

(Above) Log cabin built by the Swain Finch family on their Custer County, Nebraska, property in the 1880s; (below) the Finch residence in 1892

(Top) View of the trading floor of the Minneapolis Chamber of Commerce building, 1893; (center) crowd watching jack rabbits being trapped in 1893; (left) "constables of the Des Moines Searchers and advance guard of the fighting prohibition army"

(Above) **The Chautauqua Grounds in Galesburg, Ill., early 1900s. The traveling Chautauqua provided lectures, concerts, and recitals for many communities during its summer sessions**

(Above) **Tobacco warehouse damaged in a cyclone that killed 100 persons in Louisville, Ky., 1890; (below) barn-raising on a farm near Paddock's Lake, Kenosha County, Wis., 1891**

(Above left) Miners outside their homes on the ''Street of Rocks'' in Shenandoah, Pa., 1891; (above right) Parade of the Knights Templars during their Triennial Conclave in Pittsburgh, 1898; (below) horse-drawn police cart of the 1890s outside the old Police Station in Detroit, Mich.

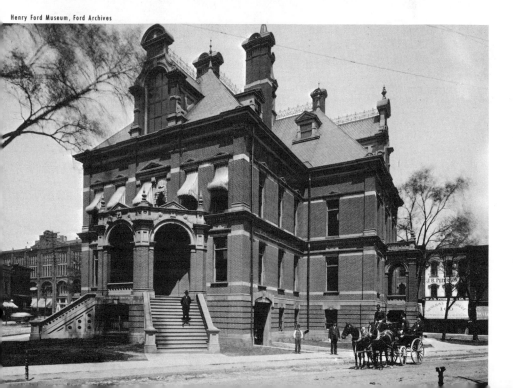

Mahoning Mine, large open pit iron ore mine in northern Minnesota opened in 1895

(Above) Violin trio performing in the cookhouse of a Minnesota lumber camp, 1902; (below) largest load of logs hauled by a four-horse team in 1895

65.

ELBERT HUBBARD: A Message to García

In an 1899 number of the Philistine, *an avant-garde periodical published by Elbert Hubbard at his celebrated Roycroft Press, appeared the following message on the importance of perseverance. It was based on an actual incident in the Spanish-American War: President McKinley had sent Lieutenant Andrew Rowan to meet General Calixto García Iñiquez, leader of the Cuban forces in the fight against Spain. The essay, of course, was designed to inspire loyalty and improve morale among workers, and it was distributed by many industrialists to their employees as well as to all the soldiers in the Russo-Japanese War. It is the most famous single piece Hubbard wrote and its circulation was estimated in 1940 to have reached 40 million copies.*

Source: *A Message to Garcia,* n.p., 1899.

IN ALL THIS CUBAN BUSINESS there is one man stands out on the horizon of my memory like Mars at perihelion. When war broke out between Spain and the United States, it was very necessary to communicate quickly with the leader of the insurgents. Garcia was somewhere in the mountain fastnesses of Cuba — no one knew where. No mail nor telegraph message could reach him. The President must secure his cooperation, and quickly.

What to do!

Someone said to the President, "There's a fellow by the name of Rowan will find Garcia for you, if anybody can."

Rowan was sent for and given a letter to be delivered to Garcia. How "the fellow by the name of Rowan" took the letter, sealed it up in an oilskin pouch, strapped it over his heart, in four days landed by night off the coast of Cuba from an open boat, disappeared into the jungle, and in three weeks came out on the other side of the island, having traversed a hostile country on foot and delivered his letter to Garcia, are things I have no special desire now to tell in detail.

The point I wish to make is this: McKinley gave Rowan a letter to be delivered to Garcia; Rowan took the letter and did not ask, "Where is he at?" By the Eternal! there is a man whose form should be cast in deathless bronze and the statue placed in every college of the land. It is not book learning young men need, nor instruction about this and that, but a stiffening of the vertebrae which will cause them to be loyal to a trust, to act promptly, concentrate their energies; do the thing — "Carry a message to Garcia!"

General Garcia is dead now, but there are other Garcias.

No man who has endeavored to carry out an enterprise where many hands were needed, but has been well-nigh appalled at times by the imbecility of the average man — the inability or unwillingness to concentrate on a thing and do it. Slipshod assistance, foolish inattention, dowdy indifference, and half-hearted work seem the rule; and no man succeeds, unless by hook or crook, or threat, he forces or bribes other men to assist him; or, mayhap, God in His goodness performs a miracle and sends him an Angel of Light for an assistant.

You, reader, put this matter to a test: You are sitting now in your office — six clerks are within call. Summon any one and make this request: "Please look in the encyclopedia and make a brief memorandum for me concerning the life of Correggio."

Will the clerk quietly say, "Yes, sir," and go do the task?

On your life, he will not. He will look at you out of a fishy eye and ask one or more of the following questions:

Who was he?

Which encyclopedia?

Where is the encyclopedia?

Was I hired for that?

Don't you mean Bismarck?

What's the matter with Charlie doing it?

Is he dead?

Is there any hurry?

Shan't I bring you the book and let you look it up yourself?

What do you want to know for?

And I will lay you ten to one that after you have answered the questions, and explained how to find the information, and why you want it, the clerk will go off and get one of the other clerks to help him try to find Garcia — and then come back and tell you there is no such man. Of course I may lose my bet, but according to the law of average, I will not.

Now if you are wise you will not bother to explain to your "assistant" that Correggio is indexed under the C's, not in the K's, but you will smile sweetly and say, "Never mind," and go look it up yourself.

And this incapacity for independent action, this moral stupidity, this infirmity of the will, this unwillingness to cheerfully

catch hold and lift are the things that put pure socialism so far into the future. If men will not act for themselves, what will they do when the benefit of their effort is for all? A first mate with knotted club seems necessary; and the dread of getting "the bounce" Saturday night holds many a worker to his place.

Advertise for a stenographer, and nine out of ten who apply can neither spell nor punctuate — and do not think it necessary to.

Can such a one write a letter to Garcia?

"You see that bookkeeper," said the foreman to me in a large factory.

"Yes, what about him?"

"Well, he's a fine accountant, but if I'd send him uptown on an errand, he might accomplish the errand all right, and, on the other hand, might stop at four saloons on the way, and when he got to Main Street would forget what he had been sent for."

Can such a man be entrusted to carry a message to Garcia?

We have recently been hearing much maudlin sympathy expressed for the "downtrodden denizen of the sweatshop" and the "homeless wanderer searching for honest employment," and with it all often go many hard words for the men in power.

Nothing is said about the employer who grows old before his time in a vain attempt to get frowsy ne'er-do-wells to do intelligent work; and his long, patient striving with "help" that does nothing but loaf when his back is turned. In every store and factory there is a constant weeding-out process going on. The employer is constantly sending away "help" that have shown their incapacity to further the interests of the business, and others are being taken on. No matter how good times are, this sorting continues, only if times are hard and work is scarce, the sorting is done finer — but out and forever out, the incompetent and unworthy go. It is the survival of the fittest.

Self-interest prompts every employer to keep the best — those who can carry a message to Garcia.

I know one man of really brilliant parts who has not the ability to manage a business of his own, and yet who is absolutely worthless to anyone else because he carries with him constantly the insane suspicion that his employer is oppressing or intending to oppress him. He cannot give orders, and he will not receive them. Should a message be given him to take to Garcia, his answer would probably be, "Take it yourself, and be damned!"

Tonight this man walks the streets looking for work, the wind whistling through his threadbare coat. No one who knows him dare employ him, for he is a regular firebrand of discontent. He is impervious to reason, and the only thing that can impress him is the toe of a thick-soled No. 9 boot.

Of course, I know that one so morally deformed is no less to be pitied than a physical cripple; but in our pitying, let us drop a tear, too, for the men who are striving to carry on a great enterprise, whose working hours are not limited by the whistle, and whose hair is fast turning white through the struggle to hold in line dowdy indifference, slipshod imbecility, and the heartless ingratitude which, but for their enterprise, would be both hungry and homeless.

Have I put the matter too strongly? Possibly I have; but when all the world has gone a-slumming I wish to speak a word of sympathy for the man who succeeds — the man who, against great odds, has directed the efforts of others, and, having succeeded, finds there's nothing in it; nothing but bare board and clothes.

I have carried a dinner pail and worked for day's wages, and I have also been an employer of labor, and I know there is something to be said on both sides. There is no excellence, per se, in poverty; rags are no recommendation; and all employers are not rapacious and high-handed, any more than all poor men are virtuous.

My heart goes out to the man who does his work when the "boss" is away as well as when he is at home. And the man who, when given a letter for Garcia, quietly takes the missive, without asking any idiotic questions, and with no lurking intention of chucking it into the nearest sewer, or of doing aught else but deliver it, never gets "laid off," nor has to go on a strike for higher wages. Civilization is one long, anxious search for just such individuals. Anything such a man asks shall be granted; his kind is so rare that no employer can afford to let him go. He is wanted in every city, town, and village — in every office, shop, store, and factory. The world cries out for such; he is needed, and needed badly — the man who can carry a message to Garcia.

———◆———

I wish to preach, not the doctrine of ignoble ease but the doctrine of the strenuous life.
THEODORE ROOSEVELT, speech, Chicago, April 1899

Never put off until to-morrow what should have been done early in the Seventies.
GEORGE ADE, *Fables in Slang*

66.

John D. Rockefeller: On the Advantages of Trusts

The most famous witness before the U.S. Industrial Commission in 1899 was John D. Rockefeller. As head of the vast Standard Oil Company, Rockefeller could speak with authority about the nature of trusts. The Commission's investigation of industrial combinations revealed many abuses, but Rockefeller's testimony, a portion of which appears below, was a clear endorsement of the advantages of consolidating industries. Never mentioning the specific methods he utilized, Rockefeller demonstrated his dogged belief in the rightness of his policy.

Source: 56 Congress, 1 Session, House Document No. 476, Pt. 1, pp. 794-797.

Q. What was the first combination in which you were interested of different establishments in the oil industry?

A. The first combination of different establishments in the oil industry in which I was interested was the union of William Rockefeller & Co., Rockefeller & Andrews, Rockefeller & Co., S. V. Harkness, and H. M. Flagler, about the year 1867.

Q. What were the causes leading to its formation?

A. The cause leading to its formation was the desire to unite our skill and capital in order to carry on a business of some magnitude and importance in place of the small business that each separately had theretofore carried on. As time elapsed and the possibilities of the business became apparent, we found further capital to be necessary, obtained the required persons and capital, and organized the Standard Oil Company with a capital of $1 million. Later we found more capital could be utilized and found persons with capital to interest themselves with us, and increased our capital to $3,500,000. As the business grew and markets were obtained at home and abroad, more persons and capital were added to the business, and new corporate agencies were obtained or organized, the object being always the same — to extend our business by furnishing the best and cheapest products.

Q. Did the Standard Oil Company or other affiliated interests at any time before 1887 receive from the railroads rebates on freight shipped, or other special advantages?

A. The Standard Oil Company of Ohio, of which I was president, did receive rebates from the railroads prior to 1880, but received no special advantages for which it did not give full compensation. The reason for rebates was that such was the railroads' method of business. A public rate was made and collected by the railway companies, but, so far as my knowledge extends, was never really retained in full; a portion of it was repaid to the shippers as a rebate. By this method, the real rate of freight which any shipper paid was not known by his competitors nor by other railway companies, the amount being in all cases a matter of bargain with the carrying company. Each shipper made the best bargain he could, but whether he was doing better than his competitor was only a matter of conjecture.

Much depended upon whether the shipper had the advantage of competition of carriers. The Standard Oil Company of

Ohio, being situated at Cleveland, had the advantage of different carrying lines, as well as of water transportation in the summer and, taking advantage of those facilities, made the best bargains possible for its freights. All other companies did the same, their success depending largely upon whether they had the choice of more than one route.

The Standard sought also to offer advantages to the railways for the purpose of lessening rates of freight. It offered freights in large quantity, carloads and trainloads. It furnished loading facilities and discharging facilities. It exempted railways from liability for fire. For these services it obtained contracts for special allowances on freights. These never exceeded, to the best of my present recollections, 10 percent. But in almost every instance it was discovered subsequently that our competitors had been obtaining as good, and, in some instances, better rates of freight than ourselves.

Q. If so, in what years were these advantages largest, and from what roads were they received?

A. To the best of my recollection, the greatest rebates were paid from 1877 to 1879. During that time we had an agreement for a special 10 percent commission. I think that agreement was made with the Pennsylvania, the Erie, and the New York Central roads. Large rebates were also paid during the summer of 1878, amounting, I believe, to 64½ cents on refined oil to equalize eastern shipments by rail with shipments by Erie Canal. But these rebates were paid to all who shipped by rail. They were not discriminatory rates.

I am not now sure whether any other road than the Pennsylvania collected the full amount and paid these rebates. The Erie and New York Central made the same reductions in rates to meet canal shipments, but my impression is that the Erie at least did not collect the higher rate from shippers and rebate it as did the Pennsylvania.

Q. About what percentage of the profits

of the Standard Oil Company came from special advantages given by the railroads when these were greatest?

A. No percentage of the profits of the Standard Oil Company came from advantages given by railroads at any time. Whatever advantage it received in its constant efforts to reduce rates of freight was deducted from the price of oil. The advantages to the Standard from low freight rates consisted solely in the increased volume of its business arising from the low price of its products.

Q. Did the Standard Oil Company or any of its affiliated companies ever receive, under any name whatever, any income from any railroad for oil shipped over those roads by any of its competitors? If so, give particulars.

A. I know of no such instance. It seems that some arrangement of that nature was entered into by one of our agents in Ohio. . . . When notice of this agreement was brought to the officers of the company for which it was made, it was promptly repudiated, and the money received, some small amount, I think under $300, was refunded. And this was done not because of any action in court or judicial opinion, but promptly as soon as reported, and before we had any knowledge of judicial proceedings.

Q. Has the Standard Oil Company received any financial favors from any railroad since 1887?

A. To my knowledge, none whatever.

Q. Has the ownership of stock in railroad companies by officers of the Standard Oil Company given the Standard advantages with those railroads over its competitors? If so, give particulars.

A. It has not. Stockholders and officers of the Standard have invested in stock of railway companies. But in no instance have they done so for the purpose of influencing the policy of the railway companies, nor to the best of my knowledge and belief has any attempt ever been made through such ownership to influence any railway in favor of the Standard.

Q. To what advantages, or favors, or methods of management do you ascribe chiefly the success of the Standard Oil Company?

A. I ascribe the success of the Standard to its consistent policy to make the volume of its business large through the merits and cheapness of its products. It has spared no expense in finding, securing, and utilizing the best and cheapest methods of manufacture. It has sought for the best superintendents and workmen and paid the best wages. It has not hesitated to sacrifice old machinery and old plants for new and better ones. It has placed its manufactories at the points where they could supply markets at the least expense. It has not only sought markets for its principal products but for all possible byproducts, sparing no expense in introducing them to the public. It has not hesitated to invest millions of dollars in methods for cheapening the gathering and distribution of oils by pipelines, special cars, tank steamers, and tank wagons. It has erected tank stations at every important railroad station to cheapen the storage and delivery of its products.

It has spared no expense in forcing its products into the markets of the world among people, civilized and uncivilized. It has had faith in American oil, and has brought together millions of money for the purpose of making it what it is and holding its markets against the competition of Russia and all the many countries which are producers of oil and competitors against American oil.

Q. What are, in your judgment, the chief advantages from industrial combinations: (a) financially to stockholders; (b) to the public?

A. All the advantages which can be derived from a cooperation of persons and aggregation of capital. Much that one man cannot do alone, two can do together, and once admit the fact that cooperation, or, what is the same thing, combination, is necessary on a small scale, the limit depends solely upon the necessities of business. Two persons in partnership may be a sufficiently large combination for a small business, but if the business grows or can be made to grow, more persons and more capital must be taken in. The business may grow so large that a partnership ceases to be a proper instrumentality for its purposes, and then a corporation becomes a necessity.

In most countries, as in England, this form of industrial combination is sufficient for a business coextensive with the parent country, but it is not so in this country. Our federal form of government, making every corporation created by a state foreign to every other state, renders it necessary for persons doing business through corporate agency to organize corporations in some or many of the different states in which their business is located. Instead of doing business through the agency of one corporation, they must do business through the agencies of several corporations. If the business is extended to foreign countries, and Americans are not today satisfied with home markets alone, it will be found helpful and possibly necessary to organize corporations in such countries, for Europeans are prejudiced against foreign corporations as are the people of many of our states. These different corporations thus become cooperating agencies in the same business and are held together by common ownership of their stocks.

It is too late to argue about advantages of industrial combinations. They are a necessity. And if Americans are to have the privilege of extending their business in all the states of the Union, and into foreign countries as well, they are a necessity on a large scale and require the agency of more than one corporation.

Their chief advantages are: (1) command of necessary capital; (2) extension of limits of business; (3) increase of number of persons interested in the business; (4) economy in the business; (5) improvements and economies which are derived from knowledge of many interested persons of wide experience; (6) power to give the public improved products at less prices and still make a profit for stockholders; (7) permanent work and good wages for laborers.

It is too late to argue about advantages of industrial combinations. They are a necessity. . . .

I speak from my experience in the business with which I have been intimately connected for about forty years. Our first combination was a partnership and afterward a corporation in Ohio. That was sufficient for a local refining business; but dependent solely upon local business, we should have failed years ago. We were forced to extend our markets and to seek for export trade. This latter made the seaboard cities a necessary place of business, and we soon discovered that manufacturing for export could be more economically carried on at the seaboard, hence refineries at Brooklyn, at Bayonne, at Philadelphia, and necessary corporations in New York, New Jersey, and Pennsylvania.

We soon discovered as the business grew that the primary method of transporting oil in barrels could not last. The package often cost more than the contents, and the forests of the country were not sufficient to supply the necessary material for an extended length of time. Hence we devoted attention to other methods of transportation, adopted the pipeline system, and found capital for pipeline construction equal to the necessities of the business.

To operate pipelines required franchises from the states in which they were located, and, consequently, corporations in those states, just as railroads running through different states are forced to operate under separate state charters.

To perfect the pipeline system of transportation required in the neighborhood of $50 million of capital. This could not be obtained or maintained without industrial

Library of Congress

John D. Rockefeller

combination. The entire oil business is dependent upon this pipeline system. Without it, every well would shut down and every foreign market would be closed to us. The pipeline system required other improvements, such as tank cars upon railways, and finally the tank steamer. Capital had to be furnished for them and corporations created to own and operate them.

Every step taken was necessary in the business if it was to be properly developed, and only through such successive steps and by such an industrial combination is America today enabled to utilize the bounty which its land pours forth, and to furnish the world with the best and cheapest light ever known, receiving in return therefor from foreign lands nearly $50 million per year, most of which is distributed in payment of American labor.

I have given a picture rather than a detail of the growth of one industrial combination. It is a pioneer, and its work has been of incalculable value. There are other American products besides oil for which the markets of the world can be opened, and legislators will be blind to our best industrial interests if they unduly hinder by legislation the combination of persons and capital requisite for the attainment of so desirable an end.

Q. What are the chief disadvantages or dangers to the public arising from them?

A. The dangers are that the power conferred by combination may be abused; that combinations may be formed for speculation in stocks rather than for conducting business, and that for this purpose prices may be temporarily raised instead of being lowered. These abuses are possible to a greater or less extent in all combinations, large or small, but this fact is no more of an argument against combinations than the fact that steam may explode is an argument against steam. Steam is necessary and can

be made comparatively safe. Combination is necessary and its abuses can be minimized; otherwise our legislators must acknowledge their incapacity to deal with the most important instrument of industry. Hitherto most legislative attempts have been an effort not to control but to destroy; hence their futility.

Q. What legislation, if any, would you suggest regarding industrial combinations?

A. First, federal legislation under which corporations may be created and regulated, if that be possible. Second, in lieu thereof, state legislation as nearly uniform as possible encouraging combinations of persons and capital for the purpose of carrying on industries, but permitting state supervision, not of a character to hamper industries but sufficient to prevent frauds upon the public.

67.

Samuel M. Jones: A Golden-Rule Government for Cities

While Progressives lamented the corruption in the cities, a few dynamic reform mayors set about the task of removing graft from city government. Samuel Jones, a four-term mayor of Toledo, Ohio, rejected machine politics and established a government based, as he put it, upon the Golden Rule. (He was known as "Golden Rule" Jones.) He instituted public parks, kindergartens, playgrounds, and a municipal golf course. His critics accused him of being a Socialist; he himself asserted that "private ownership is a high crime against democracy." The following article, in which Jones outlined his philosophy of municipal government, was published in September 1899.

Source: *Municipal Affairs*, September 1899: "The New Patriotism: A Golden-Rule Government for Cities."

WE ARE LIVING in one of the most interesting and important epochs in the world's history, thus far — an age that has witnessed more of the marvels of material development than any or all the ages that have preceded it. Steam, electricity, compressed air, liquefied air, and modern inven-

tions in laborsaving machinery have increased the producing power of men twenty-, fifty-, and one hundredfold beyond what was believed to be within the possibilities 100 or even 50 years ago.

Improvement has been the order in every field of human endeavor. So marked and striking have been the changes wrought by these marvelous developments that the thing we call civilization has, as it were, had its head turned, until we have well-nigh lost sight of or forgotten the purpose of life itself, so bewildered have we become with the astounding "successes" (?) that a few have achieved in the fast life of the closing years of this 19th century.

We have well-nigh lost sight of the thing that we call patriotism, and more nearly have we lost any conception of the deep meaning that the word ought to have. As it stands today, it is simple candor to say that the word "patriotism" is to most people a meaningless jingle, the one conception they have of the thing being associated with red fire, bunting, flags, firecrackers, and Fourth of July. The new patriotism, however, is the old patriotism. The flag, the "stars and stripes," still represents the love of millions, but we have been so busy in the chase after wealth that any just conception of patriotism is well-nigh lost in the hurly-burly of the scramble.

It was Lamennais who said: "I love my family more than myself; my village more than my family; my country more than my village; and mankind more than my country." And in this saying he has shown us a just and proper conception of true patriotism, but the narrower conception of life, commonly called selfishness, has well-nigh crushed out this noble ideal and has substituted in its place the brutal maxim that "self-preservation is the first law of nature" (and "to the victors belong the spoils"). It is among wild beasts, but we have reached a point where we are discovering that wild-beast ethics are not good enough upon which to base a permanent and enduring republic. The ethics of the wild beast, the survival of the strongest, shrewdest, and meanest, have been the inspiration of our materialistic lives during the last quarter or half century.

This fact in our national history has brought us today face to face with the inev-itable result. We have cities in which a few are wealthy, a few are in what may be called comfortable circumstances, vast numbers are propertyless, and thousands are in pauperism and crime. Certainly, no reasonable person will contend that this is the goal that we have been struggling for; that the inequalities that characterize our rich and poor represent the ideas that the founders of this republic saw when they wrote that "All men are created equal."

The new patriotism is the love of the millions that is already planning for and opening the way to better things, to a condition of life under this government when every child born in it will have equal opportunity with every other child to live the best possible kind of life that he or she can live. This is the new patriotism — that feeling within one's breast that tells us that there can be no prosperity for some without there is a possibility for some prosperity for all, and that there can be no peace for some without opportunity for some peace for all; that man is a social being, society is a unit, an organism, not a heap of separate grains of sand, each one struggling for its own welfare. We are all so inextricably bound together that there is no possibility of finding the individual good except in the good of all.

These closing years of the century are bringing to us new light upon this subject. We are coming to see that there is a lack of social equilibrium, a lack of balance; that in the struggle for so-called success we have been chasing the *ignis fatuus* [will-o'-the-wisp]. Noble lives by the thousands have been usually wasted in the desperate race after a bauble, and we are discovering that the thing we call "success" is indeed, after all, only a most conspicuous and glaring failure.

A GOLDEN-RULE GOVERNMENT

SOMEWHERE IN GOD'S UNIVERSE there is such a thing as social justice. Equality *is* as brotherhood *is*. It is not a fad of mere theorists or a whim of dreamers but a fact from which there is no more possibility of escape than from the facts of arithmetic.

Daniel Webster stated this fundamental principle when he said:

> Let us hold fast the great truth, that communities are responsible as well as individuals; that no government is respectable which is not just; that without unspotted purity of public faith, without sacred public principle, fidelity, and honor, no mere forms of government, no machinery of laws can give dignity to political society.

I have sometimes tried to picture in my mind the condition of affairs that will prevail when we have a Golden-Rule government, for that is what we are yet to see in this country of ours. It is true that if we think of the obstacles that are in the way of a realization of such a condition, we shall be well-nigh discouraged, but if we have the cause of the people really at heart, we shall be too busy doing the things nearest at hand to let anxiety for signs of visible progress trouble us much. Certainly, we may live in hope that through the agency of the thing we call government we are yet to realize a condition of life among our people that will be less strifeful; a condition in which the people shall have more freedom and liberty; shall at least have liberty to live the life of free men, a privilege that is today denied to by far the greater portion of all humanity.

The steps most likely to contribute to bringing about the better days and the better times for which we all long are to my mind those things that will unify the people, that will serve to weld them together in one common mass, those things that will help them to understand the oneness or solidarity of all society; and the things that are the greatest hindrance to this sort of development are all those agencies that serve to separate the people into fragments, that keep alive the fires of hatred within their bosoms and tend to make them hate rather than to love one another. All these agencies are the enemies of progress and of liberty, and stand directly athwart the path of freedom.

PARTISAN POLITICS THE CHIEF ENEMY OF MUNICIPAL LIBERTY

CHIEF AMONG THEM, and the one agency above all others that the patriot should seek to overcome in the municipality, is partisan politics.

I am sure that I cannot speak too strongly in condemnation of the superstition that we must have parties to carry on the work of the government. To a certain extent the people are quite well-freed from it so far as the municipality is concerned, yet the bosses and the would-be bosses strive to keep the heresy alive in the municipality, the township, and even the village, their argument being that the municipality is the base; and if an organization is allowed to disintegrate there, it will be impossible to keep it alive in the state and the nation. This argument and the superstition so commonly believed that "we must have parties" have served to keep many men in line as partisans who, when it is once shown them that this is only a cunningly devised fable calculated to deceive people in the interest of the few, will quickly step out on the broader plane of privilege as nonpartisans and line themselves along with the element known as the "independent voter," who for years past has been at once the terror of the politicians and the hope of the common people. The hope of American municipalities today lies in augmenting the ranks of the independent, or better, the nonpartisan voter.

From this time forward we shall find the noblest patriots in the ranks of those who dare to be free, who dare to own themselves, who dare to vote for principle and to ignore party. Political parties are a curse to every department of our municipal government; the prime purpose of their existence is to capture the offices and administer every function of government, not in the interest of the municipality, or the state, or the nation, but in the interest of the few managers of the party. It is through the evil influence of these agencies that corruption of every sort is carried into all departments of government and held there as if by a mailed hand. The people have turned in vain from one to the other of these agencies in the hope of relief only to find that the old machine always produced the same old result.

The evil of the contract system that is a festering poison in so many of our municipalities is held and made secure through its contributions to the support of the partisan idea in our politics. The dominant party in any municipality has no trouble in raising funds to carry on its campaigns and making them so exceedingly costly that a canvass for an office is such a luxury that no ordinary man can afford to undertake it. The same thing may be said of franchise grabbing. This is an iniquity that is commonly charged to corrupt politics. There can be no greater error than that the evils of our government are accounted for by corrupt politics. It is corrupt business that creeps in and poisons our political, our social, and — I had almost said — our spiritual life, what little we have left.

John Jay Chapman says on this point:

This political corruption is a mere spur and offshoot of our business corruption. We know more about it because politics cannot be carried on wholly in the dark. Business can. The main facts are known. Companies organize subsidiary companies to which they vote the money of the larger company — cheating their stockholders. The railroad men get up small roads and sell them to the great roads which they control — cheating their stockholders. The purchasing agents of many great enterprises cheat the companies as a matter of course, not by a recognized system of commissions, like French cooks, but by stealth. So, in trade, you cannot sell goods to the retailers unless you corrupt the proper person. It is all politics. All our politics is business and our business is politics.

The fact of the matter is there is little hope for improvement, for progress in the direction of scientific government in our municipalities until we shall first get the people freed from the baneful superstition of partisan politics. The competitive idea at present dominant in most of our political and business life is, of course, the seed root of all the trouble. To think of eradicating this evil, of rooting out this infamy that has kept men for generations facing one another as fighters when their normal condition is that of brothers is a proposition that may well make stout hearts quail, but we know we are gaining ground.

We know that many centuries ago the only form of government was government of the club, that when savagery prevailed the strongest man ruled — his sway was supreme; that that brutal form of government was succeeded by a form less objectionable, by the rule of autocrats and kings; that this unnatural relation among men has now very largely passed away; that today we are ruled to a great extent in America by commerce and industry; that we are rapidly passing to a better and kindlier and a more rational system that will be the rule of the people; coming, indeed, to the time when business will be friendship and government will be love.

The common things of our common life are tending to overthrow the dynasties of the kings of commerce and industry as they have already overthrown the dynasties of the kings of government. Such agencies as public parks, publicly paid for; fire and police departments, serving each and all alike; public streets, which are the common property of the common people; and, above all, the common school, that bulwark of our liberties — these are the fraternal forces that are unifying our life, that are bringing us together as members of one great family having one common interest and one common destiny.

GROWTH OF MUNICIPAL SOCIALISM

THE GROWTH OF THE SENTIMENT favoring municipal socialism in the cities of America is one of the promising signs of the better day. Hundreds of thousands of dollars have been appropriated within the last few years to such humanizing and educating influences as children's playgrounds, free baths, free music in the parks for the people, and in some instances our municipalities have provided free lectures and free concerts for the winter evenings. Every movement of this kind, everything that tends to bring the people together is educating in the right direction, tends toward liberty and the realization of that freedom and equality outlined in the Declaration of Independence and guaranteed by the Constitution.

The only hope of the spoilsman and corruptionist lies in keeping the people apart, in separating them, in leading them to believe that they are natural enemies and not friends; but it is gratifying to note the signs of promise that we have of the better day. There is hardly a city of any importance in America in which the subject of municipal or public ownership has not had more attention and discussion during the last five years than in the twenty, yes, fifty that preceded it.

The people are beginning to understand that we have been pursuing a policy of plundering ourselves, that in the foolish scramble to make individuals rich we have been making all poor. "For a hundred years or so," says Henry D. Lloyd, "our economic theory has been one of industrial government by the self-interest of the individual; political government by the self-interest of the individual we call anarchy." It is one of the paradoxes of public opinion that the people of America, least tolerant of this theory of anarchy in political government, lead in practising it in industry. We are coming to see that the true philosophy of government is to let the individual do what the individual can do best, and let the government do what the government can do best.

Our cities are to be saved by the development of the collective idea. We are coming to understand that every public utility and necessity to the public welfare should be publicly owned, publicly operated, and publicly paid for. Among the properties that according to any scientific conception of the purpose of government should be so owned are waterworks, heating and lighting plants, street railways, telephones, fire alarms, telegraphs, parks, playgrounds, baths, washhouses, municipal printing establishments, and many other industries necessary to the welfare of the whole family that can only be successfully operated by the family in the interest of the whole family.

SOCIAL JUSTICE

IT IS ABSURD TO EXPECT a peacefully ordered and organized community when its government is carried on according to unscientific and unjust principles. There is such a thing as social justice, a justice that is as unerring as any rule in arithmetic, a justice that will discover the exact basis for social relation between every man and every woman; and the first business of a municipality is to see that its affairs are so ordered as to make this justice accessible to the weakest as well as the strongest. When we, the city officials, come to a consideration of the questions of municipal government from this standpoint, we shall begin to have a proper conception of the responsibilities that rest upon us; when we come to understand that the first business of a city is to make such conditions of life as will produce the best-bodied and healthiest fathers and mothers rather than to trifle away valuable time in bartering with an unscientific and bungling contract system of labor in the hope of saving at the spigot while wasting at the bunghole, we shall begin to have a scientific conception of the purpose of government.

The contract system is an infamy, pure and simple, conceived in sin and born in iniquity. It has been bolstered up by the corrupt methods that are the legitimate product and offspring of the wicked and hopeless competitive system. There is but one thing to do with that monstrosity to bring peace and honesty into the work of municipal improvement, and that is to cut it out root and branch, to substitute in its stead the day-labor plan with a stipulated minimum rate in every municipality as a living wage and eight hours to constitute a day's work.

These are in brief the suggestions that have come to mind as to the steps by which we shall give expression to the new patriotism and proceed to realize a Golden-Rule government in which each neighbor will give to the other every right of free thought and free movement which he demands for himself. Only thus shall we realize the community, the republic which, with all its failings, is the highest because the most real application of the spirit of human brotherhood.

68.

Open Letter to President McKinley from Massachusetts Negroes

In the last sixteen years of the nineteenth century, there were 2,500 lynchings in the United States. Most of the victims were Southern Negroes. While states like North and South Carolina were passing laws to disfranchise the Negro, they also succeeded in arousing violent racial hatred. The following letter, written by a group of Massachusetts Negroes in 1899 to President McKinley, effectively expressed the indignation and outrage of Northern Negroes who were helpless to aid their Southern brethren. The unwritten law that Northern politicians, Republican and Democratic alike, should not interfere with local Southern politics precluded any assistance from the North.

Source: *Open Letter to President McKinley by Colored People of Massachusetts,* n.p., n.d.

WE, COLORED PEOPLE of Massachusetts in mass meeting assembled to consider our oppressions and the state of the country relative to the same, have resolved to address ourselves to you in an open letter, notwithstanding your extraordinary, your incomprehensible silence on the subject of our wrongs in your annual and other messages to Congress, as in your public utterances to the country at large. We address ourselves to you, sir, not as suppliants, but as of right, as American citizens, whose servant you are, and to whom you are bound to listen, and for whom you are equally bound to speak, and upon occasion to act, as for any other body of your fellow countrymen in like circumstances.

We ask nothing for ourselves at your hands, as Chief Magistrate of the republic, to which all American citizens are not entitled. We ask for the enjoyment of life, liberty, and the pursuit of happiness equally with other men. We ask for the free and full exercise of all the rights of American freemen guaranteed to us by the Constitution and laws of the Union, which you were solemnly sworn to obey and execute. We ask you for what belongs to us by the high sanction of Constitution and law, and the democratic genius of our institutions and civilization.

These rights are everywhere throughout the South denied to us, violently wrested from us by mobs, by lawless legislatures, and nullifying conventions, combinations, and conspiracies, openly, defiantly, under your eyes, in your constructive and actual presence. And we demand, which is a part of our rights, protection, security in our life, our liberty, and in the pursuit of our individual and social happiness under a government, which we are bound to defend in war, and which is equally bound to furnish us in peace protection, at home and abroad.

We have suffered, sir — God knows how much we have suffered! — since your accession to office, at the hands of a country professing to be Christian, but which is not Christian; from the hate and violence of a people claiming to be civilized, but who are not civilized; and you have seen our sufferings, witnessed from your high place our awful wrongs and miseries, and yet you have at no time and on no occasion opened your lips in our behalf.

Why? we ask. Is it because we are black and weak and despised? Are you silent because without any fault of our own we were enslaved and held for more than two centuries in cruel bondage by your forefathers? Is it because we bear the marks of those sad generations of Anglo-Saxon brutality and wickedness that you do not speak? Is it our fault that our involuntary servitude produced in us widespread ignorance, poverty, and degradation? Are we to be damned and destroyed by the whites because we have only grown the seeds which they planted? Are we to be damned by bitter laws and destroyed by the mad violence of mobs because we are what white men made us? And is there no help in the federal arm for us, or even one word of audible pity, protest, and remonstrance in your own breast, Mr. President, or in that of a single member of your cabinet? Black, indeed, we are, sir, but we are also men and American citizens.

From the year 1619 the Anglo-Saxon race in America began to sow in the mind of the Negro race in America seeds of ignorance, poverty, and social degradation, and continued to do so until the year 1863, when chattel slavery was abolished to save the Union of these states. Then Northern white men began, in order to form a more perfect Union, to sow this self-same mind of the Negro with quite different seeds — seeds of knowledge and freedom; seeds garnered in the Declaration of Independence for the feeding of the nations of the earth, such as the natural equality of all men before the law, their inalienable right to life, liberty, and the pursuit of happiness, and the derivation of the powers of all just governments from the consent of the governed. These seeds of your own planting took root in the mind and heart of the Negro, and the crop of quickening intelligence, desire for wealth, to rise in the social scale, to be as other men, to be equal with them in opportunities and the free play of his powers in the rivalry of life, was the direct and legitimate result.

The struggle of the Negro to rise out of his ignorance, his poverty, and his social degradation, in consequence of the growth of these new forces and ideas within him, to the full stature of his American citizenship, has been met everywhere in the South by the active ill-will and determined race hatred and opposition of the white people of that section. Turn where he will, he encounters this cruel and implacable spirit. He dare not speak openly the thoughts which rise in his breast. He has wrongs such as have never in modern times been inflicted on a people, and yet he must be dumb in the midst of a nation which prates loudly of democracy and humanity, boasts itself the champion of oppressed peoples abroad, while it looks on indifferent, apathetic at appalling enormities and iniquities at home, where the victims are black and the criminals white.

The suppression, the terror wrought at the South is so complete, so ever present, so awful, that no Negro's life or property is safe for a day who ventures to raise his voice to heaven in indignant protest and appeal against the deep damnation and despotism of such a social state. Even teachers and leaders of this poor, oppressed, and patient people may not speak lest their institutions of learning and industry, and their own lives, pay for their temerity at the swift hands of savage mobs. But if the peace of Warsaw, the silence of death reign over our people and their leaders at the South, we of Massachusetts are free, and must and shall raise our voice to you and through you to the country in solemn protest and warning against the fearful sin and peril of such explosive social conditions.

We, sir, at this crisis and extremity in the life of our race in the South, and in this crisis and extremity of the republic as well, in the presence of the civilized world, cry to you to pause, if but for an hour, in pursuit of your national policy of "criminal aggression" abroad to consider the "criminal aggression" at home against humanity and American citizenship which is in the full tide of successful conquest at the South, and the tremendous consequences to our

civilization, and the durability of the Union itself, of this universal subversion of the supreme law of the land, of democratic institutions, and of the precious principle of the religion of Jesus in the social and civil life of the Southern people.

With one accord, with an anxiety that wrenched our hearts with cruel hopes and fears, the colored people of the United States turned to you when Wilmington, N.C., was held for two dreadful days and nights in the clutch of a bloody revolution; when Negroes, guilty of no crime except the color of their skin and a desire to exercise the rights of their American citizenship, were butchered like dogs in the streets of that ill-fated town; and when government of the people, by the people, and for the people perished in your very presence by the hands of violent men during those bitter November days for want of federal aid, which you would not and did not furnish on the plea that you could not give what was not asked for by a coward and recreant governor. And we well understood at the time, sir, notwithstanding your plea of constitutional inability to cope with the rebellion in Wilmington, that where there is a will with constitutional lawyers and rulers there is always a way, and where there is no will, there is no way. We well knew that you lacked the will and, therefore, the way to meet that emergency.

It was the same thing with that terrible ebullition of the mob spirit at Phoenix, S.C., when black men were hunted and murdered, and white men shot and driven out of that place by a set of white savages, who cared not for the Constitution and the laws of the United States any more than they do for the constitution and the laws of an empire dead and buried a thousand years. We looked in vain for some word or some act from you. Neither word nor act of sympathy for the victims was forthcoming, or of detestation of an outrage so mad and barbarous as to evoke even from such an extreme Southern organ as is the *News and Courier*, of Charleston, S.C., hot and stern condemnation.

Hoping against hope, we waited for your annual message to Congress in December last, knowing that the Constitution imposed upon you a duty to give, from time to time, to that body information of the state of the Union. That, at least, we said, the President will surely do; he will communicate officially the facts relative to the tragic, the appalling events, which had just occurred in the Carolinas to the Congress of the United States. But not one word did your message contain on this subject, although it discussed all sorts and conditions of subjects, from the so-called war for humanity against Spain to the celebration of the one hundredth anniversary of the founding of the national capital in 1900. Nothing escaped your eye, at home or abroad, nothing except the subversion of the Constitution and laws of the Union in the Southern states, and the flagrant and monstrous crimes perpetrated upon a weak and submissive race in defiance of your authority, or in virtual connivance therewith. Yes, sir, we repeat, or in virtual connivance therewith.

And, when you made your Southern tour a little later, and we saw how cunningly you catered to Southern race prejudice and proscription; how you, the one single public man and magistrate of the country who, by virtue of your exalted office, ought under no circumstances to recognize caste distinctions and discriminations among your fellow citizens, received white men at the Capitol in Montgomery, Ala., and black men afterward in a Negro church; how you preached patience, industry, moderation to your long-suffering black fellow citizens, and patriotism, jingoism, and imperialism to your white ones; when we saw all these things, scales of illusion in respect to your object fell from our eyes.

We felt that the President of the United States, in order to win the support of the South to his policy of "criminal aggression" in the Far East, was ready and willing to shut his eyes, ears, and lips to the "criminal aggression" of that section against the Constitution and the laws of the land wherein they guarantee civil rights and citizenship to the Negro, whose ultimate reduction to a condition of fixed and abject serfdom is the plain purpose of the Southern people and their laws.

When, several months subsequently, you returned to Georgia, the mob spirit, as if to evince its supreme contempt for your presence and the federal executive authority which you represent, boldly broke into a prison shed where were confined helpless Negro prisoners on a charge of incendiarism and brutally murdered five of them. These men were American citizens, entitled to the rights of American citizens, protection and trial by due process of law. They were, in the eye of the law, innocent until convicted by a jury of their peers. Had they been in legal custody in Russia or Spain or Turkey they had not been slaughtered by a mob under like circumstances; for the Russian military power, or the Spanish or the Turkish, would have guarded those men in their helpless and defenseless condition from the fury of the populace who were seeking their blood.

Sir, they were men; they were your brothers; they were God's children, for whom Jesus lived and died. They ought to have been sacred charges in the hands of any civilized or semi-civilized state and people. But almost in your hearing, before your eyes (and you the Chief Magistrate of a country loudly boastful of its freedom, Christianity, and civilization), they were atrociously murdered. Did you speak? Did you open your lips to express horror of the awful crime and stern condemnation of the incredible villainy and complicity of the constituted authorities of Georgia in the commission of this monstrous outrage, which out-barbarized barbarism and stained through and through with indelible infamy before the world your country's justice, honor, and humanity?

Still later, considering the age, the circumstances and the nation in which the deed was done, Georgia committed a crime unmatched for moral depravity and sheer atrocity during the century. A Negro, charged with murder and criminal assault, the first charge he is reported by the newspapers to have admitted and the second to have denied, was taken one quiet Sunday morning from his captors and burned to death with indescribable and hellish cruelty in the presence of cheering thousands of the so-called best people of Georgia, men, women and children, who had gone forth on the Christian Sabbath to the burning of a human being as to a country festival and holiday of innocent enjoyment and amusement. The downright ferocity and frightful savagery of that American mob at Newnan outdoes the holiday humor and thirst for blood of the tigerlike populace of pagan Rome, gathered to witness Christian martyrs thrown to lions in their roaring arenas.

The death of Hose was quickly followed by that of the Negro preacher Strickland, guiltless of crime, under circumstances and with a brutality of wickedness almost matching in horror and enormity the torture and murder of the first; and this last was succeeded by a third victim, who was literally lashed to death by the wild, beastlike spirit of a Georgia mob, for daring merely to utter his abhorrence of the Palmetto iniquity and slaughter of helpless prisoners.

Did you speak? Did you utter one word of reprobation, of righteous indignation, either as magistrate or as man? Did you break the shameful silence of shameful months with so much as a whisper of a whisper against the deep damnation of such defiance of all law, human and divine; such revulsion of men into beasts, and relapses of communities into barbarism in the very cen-

ter of the republic, and amid the sanctuary of the temple of American liberty itself? You did not, sir, but your attorney general did, and he only to throw out to the public, to your meek and long-suffering colored fellow citizens, the cold and cautious legal opinion that the case of Hose has no federal aspect!

Mr. President, has it any moral or human aspect, seeing that Hose was a member of the Negro race, whom your Supreme Court once declared has no rights in America which white men are bound to respect? Is this infamous dictum of that tribunal still the supreme law of the land? We ask you, sir, since recent events in Arkansas, Mississippi, Alabama, Virginia, and Louisiana, as well as in Georgia and the Carolinas, indeed throughout the South, and your own persistent silence and the persistent silence of every member of your cabinet on the subject of the wrongs of that race in those states, would appear together to imply as much.

Had, eighteen months ago, the Cuban revolution to throw off the yoke of Spain, or the attempt of Spain to subdue the Cuban rebellion, any federal aspect? We believe that you and the Congress of the United States thought that they had, and therefore used, finally, the armed force of the nation to expel Spain from that island. Why? Was it because "the people of the island of Cuba are, and of right ought to be free and independent?" You and the Congress said as much, and may we fervently pray, sir, in passing, that the freedom and independence of that brave people shall not much longer be denied them by our government?

But to resume, there was another consideration which, in your judgment, gave to the Cuban question a federal aspect, which provoked at last the armed interposition of our government in the affairs of that island, and this was "the chronic condition of disturbance in Cuba so injurious and menacing to our interests and tranquillity, as well as shocking to our sentiments of humanity." Wherefore you presently fulfilled "a duty to humanity by ending a situation, the indefinite prolongation of which had become insufferable."

Mr. President, had that "chronic condition of disturbance in Cuba so injurious and menacing to our interests and tranquillity as well as shocking to our sentiments of humanity," which you wished to terminate and did terminate, a federal aspect, while that not less "chronic condition of disturbance" in the South, which is a thousand times more "injurious and menacing to our interests and tranquillity," as well as far more "shocking to our sentiments of humanity," or ought to be, none whatever? Is it better to be Cuban revolutionists fighting for Cuban independence than American citizens striving to do their simple duty at home? Or is it better only in case those American citizens doing their simple duty at home happen to be Negroes residing in the Southern states?

Are crying national transgressions and injustices more "injurious and menacing" to the republic, as well as "shocking to its sentiments of humanity," when committed by a foreign state, in foreign territory, against a foreign people, than when they are committed by a portion of our own people against a portion of our own people at home?

There were those of our citizens who did not think that the Cuban question possessed any federal aspect, while there were others who thought otherwise; and these, having the will and the power, eventually found a way to suppress a menacing danger to the country and a wrong against humanity at the same time. Where there is a will among constitutional lawyers and rulers, Mr. President, there is ever a way; but where there is no will, there is no way.

Shall it be said that the federal government, with arms of Briareus, reaching to the utmost limits of the habitable globe for the protection of its citizens, for the liberation of alien islanders and the subjugation of others, is powerless to guarantee to certain of its citizens at home their inalienable right to life, liberty, and the pursuit of happiness because those citizens happen to be Negroes residing in the Southern section of our country? Do the colored people of the United States deserve equal consideration with the Cuban people at the hands of your administration, and shall they, though late, receive it? If, sir, you have the disposition, as we know that you have the power, we are confident that you will be able to find a constitutional way to reach us in our extremity, and our enemies also, who are likewise enemies to great public interests and national tranquillity.

I'm quite sure that . . . I have no race prejudices, and I think I have no color prejudices nor creed prejudices. Indeed, I know it. I can stand any society. All I care to know is that a man is a human being — that is enough for me; he can't be any worse.

MARK TWAIN

69.

John Hay: The Open Door Policy

In 1899 trade with China amounted to only about 2 percent of the total U.S. trade. Nevertheless, the American government was concerned that China's independence be preserved in the hope that trade might increase. Great Britain, with a much greater stake in China, shared this concern and prodded the United States, behind the scenes, into declaring an Open Door Policy toward China. British interests were served when, on September 6, 1899, Secretary of State John Hay, having informed a few Englishmen of his intention, sent the following "circular letter" to Germany, Russia, and England. Although the provisions of the policy were rather narrow, the letter was followed up the next year by a broader guarantee of China's territorial integrity.

Source: Malloy, I, pp. 246-247.

At the time when the government of the United States was informed by that of Germany that it had leased from His Majesty the Emperor of China the port of Kiaochao and the adjacent territory in the province of Shantung, assurances were given to the ambassador of the United States at Berlin by the Imperial German minister for foreign affairs that the rights and privileges insured by treaties with China to citizens of the United States would not thereby suffer or be in anywise impaired within the area over which Germany had thus obtained control.

More recently, however, the British government recognized by a formal agreement with Germany the exclusive right of the latter country to enjoy in said leased area and the contiguous "sphere of influence or interest" certain privileges, more especially those relating to railroads and mining enterprises; but, as the exact nature and extent of the rights thus recognized have not been clearly defined, it is possible that serious conflicts of interest may at any time arise, not only between British and German subjects within said area but that the interests of our citizens may also be jeopardized thereby.

Earnestly desirous to remove any cause of irritation and to insure at the same time to the commerce of all nations in China the undoubted benefits which should accrue from a formal recognition by the various powers claiming "spheres of interest" that they shall enjoy perfect equality of treatment for their commerce and navigation within such "spheres," the government of the United States would be pleased to see His German Majesty's government give formal assurances and lend its cooperation in securing like assurances from the other interested powers that each within its respective sphere of whatever influence:

First, will in no way interfere with any treaty port or any vested interest within any so-called sphere of interest or leased territory it may have in China.

Second, that the Chinese treaty tariff of the time being shall apply to all merchandise landed or shipped to all such ports as are within said "sphere of interest" (unless they be "free ports"), no matter to what nationality it may belong, and that duties so leviable shall be collected by the Chinese government.

Third, that it will levy no higher harbor dues on vessels of another nationality frequenting any port in such "sphere" than shall be levied on vessels of its own nationality, and no higher railroad charges over lines built, controlled, or operated within its "sphere" on merchandise belonging to citizens or subjects of other nationalities transported through such "sphere" than shall be levied on similar merchandise belonging to its own nationals transported over equal distances.

The liberal policy pursued by His Imperial German Majesty in declaring Kiao-chao a free port and in aiding the Chinese government in the establishment there of a customhouse are so clearly in line with the proposition which this government is anxious to see recognized that it entertains the strongest hope that Germany will give its acceptance and hearty support.

The recent ukase of His Majesty the Emperor of Russia declaring the port of Talien-wan open, during the whole of the lease under which it is held from China, to the merchant ships of all nations, coupled with the categorical assurances made to this government by His Imperial Majesty's representative at this capital at the time, and since repeated to me by the present Russian ambassador, seem to insure the support of the emperor to the proposed measure. Our ambassador at the Court of St. Petersburg has, in consequence, been instructed to submit it to the Russian government and to request their early consideration of it. A copy of my instruction on the subject to Mr. Tower is herewith enclosed for your confidential information.

The commercial interests of Great Britain and Japan will be so clearly served by the desired declaration of intentions, and the views of the governments of these countries as to the desirability of the adoption of measures insuring the benefits of equality of treatment of all foreign trade throughout China are so similar to those entertained by the United States, that their acceptance of the propositions herein outlined and their cooperation in advocating their adoption by the other powers can be confidently expected. I enclose herewith copy of the instruction which I have sent to Mr. Choate on the subject.

In view of the present favorable conditions, you are instructed to submit the above considerations to His Imperial German Majesty's minister for foreign affairs and to request his early consideration of the subject.

Copy of this instruction is sent to our ambassadors at London and at St. Petersburg for their information.

Trust everybody, but cut the cards.
FINLEY PETER DUNNE ("MR. DOOLEY")

70.

Alfred Thayer Mahan: Arbitration and the Moral Aspect of War

To the accompaniment of worldwide publicity, the czar of Russia called a peace conference to be held at The Hague in 1899. Twenty-six nations participated in this international gathering. Disarmament, compulsory arbitration of disputes, and a recodification of the rules of war were slated for discussion. One of the American delegates, Alfred Thayer Mahan, played a major role in limiting the effectiveness of the conference; Mahan voted against compulsory arbitration, arguing that no international machinery could dictate the actions of an individual country. He was also responsible for the U.S. vote against outlawing gas as a military weapon. In the article that is reprinted here in part, Mahan explained his reasons against compulsory arbitration. Andrew White, Mahan's colleague at the conference, summed up his effectiveness in a reluctant tribute: "When he speaks, the millennium fades."

Source: *North American Review*, October 1899: "The Peace Conference and the Moral Aspect of War."

THE VARYING FORTUNES, the ups and downs of the idea of arbitration at the Conference of The Hague, as far as my intelligence could follow them, produced in me two principal conclusions, which so far confirmed my previous points of view that I think I may now fairly claim for them that they have ripened into *opinions,* between which word and the cruder, looser, views received passively as *impressions,* I have been ever careful to mark a distinction.

In the first place, compulsory arbitration stands at present no chance of general acceptance. There is but one way as yet in which arbitration can be compulsory; for the dream of some advanced thinkers, of an International Army, charged with imposing the decrees of an International Tribunal upon a recalcitrant state, may be dismissed as being outside of practical international politics, until at least the nations are ready

for the intermediate step of moral compulsion, imposed by a self-assumed obligation — by a promise. Compulsory arbitration as yet means only the moral compulsion of a pledge taken beforehand, and more or less comprehensive, to submit to arbitration questions which rest still in the unknown future; the very terms of which therefore cannot be foreseen. Although there is a certain active current of agitation in favor of such stipulations, there is no general disposition of governments to accede, except under very narrow and precise limitations, and in questions of less than secondary importance.

Second, there appears to be, on the other hand, a much greater disposition than formerly to entertain favorably the idea of arbitration as a means to be in all cases considered, and where possible to be adopted, in order to solve peaceably difficulties which threaten peace. In short, the consciences of the nations are awake to the wickedness of unnecessary war and are disposed, as a general rule, to seek first, and where admissible, the counterpoise of an impartial judge, where such can be found, to correct the bias of national self-will; but there is an absolute indisposition, an instinctive revolt, against signing away, beforehand, the national conscience by a promise that any other arbiter than itself shall be accepted in questions of the future, the import of which cannot yet be discerned. Of this feeling the vague and somewhat clumsy phrase "national honor and vital interests" has in the past been the expression; for its very indeterminateness reserved to conscience in every case the decision — "May another judge for me here, or must I be bound by my own sense of right?"

Under these circumstances, and having reached so momentous a stage in progress as is indicated by the very calling together of a world conference for the better assuring of peace, may it not be well for us to pause a moment and take full account of the idea — Arbitration, on the right hand and on the left? Noble and beneficent in its true outlines, it too may share, may even now be sharing, the liability of the loftiest conceptions to degenerate into catchwords, or into cant. "Liberty, what crimes have been wrought in thy name!" And does not religion share the same reproach, and conscience also? Yet, will we not away with any of the three?

The conviction of a nation is the conviction of the mass of the individuals thereof, and each individual has therefore a personal responsibility for the opinion he holds on a question of great national, or international, moment. Let us look, each of us — and especially each of us who fears God — into his own inner heart and ask himself how far, in his personal life, he is prepared to accept arbitration. Is it not so that the reply must be, "In doubtful questions of moment,

wherever I possibly can, knowing my necessary, inevitable proneness to one-sided views, I will seek an impartial adviser, that my bias may be corrected; but when that has been done, when I have sought what aid I can, if conscience still commands, it I must obey. From that duty, burdensome though it may be, no man can relieve me. Conscience, diligently consulted, is to the man the voice of God; between God and the man no other arbiter comes."

And if this be so, a pledge beforehand is impossible. I cannot bind myself, for a future of which I as yet know nothing, to abide by the decision of any other judge than my own conscience. Much humor — less wit — has been expended upon the emperor of Germany's supposed carefulness to reject arbitration because of an infringement of his divine rights; a phrase which may well be no more than a blunt expression of the sense that no third party can relieve a man from the obligations of the position to which he is called by God, and that for the duties of that position the man can confidently expect divine guidance and help. Be that as it may, the divine right of conscience will, among Americans, receive rare challenge.

It has been urged, however, that a higher organization of the nations, the provision of a supreme tribunal issuing and enforcing judgments, settling thereby quarrels and disputed rights, would produce for the nations of the earth a condition analogous to that of the individual citizen of the state, who no longer defends his own cause, nor is bound in conscience to maintain his own sense of right, when the law decides against him. The conception is not novel, not even modern; something much like it was put forth centuries ago by the papacy concerning its own functions.

It contains two fallacies: first, the submission of the individual citizen is to force, to the constitution of which he personally contributes little, save his individual and general assent. To an unjust law he submits under protest, doubtless often silent; but he submits, not because he consents to the wrong, whether to himself personally or to others, but because he cannot help it. This will perhaps be denied, with the assertion that willing, intelligent submission to law, even when unjust, is yielded by most, for the general good. One has, however, only to consider the disposition of the average man to evade payment of taxes to recognize how far force daily enters into the maintenance and execution of law.

Nations, on the contrary, since no force exists, or without their volition can exist, to compel them to accept the institution of an authority superior to their own conscience, yield a willing acquiescence to wrong when they so yield in obedience to an external authority imposed by themselves. The matter is not helped by the fact of a previous promise to accept such decisions. The wrongdoing of an individual in consequence of an antecedent promise does not relieve the conscience thus rashly fettered. The ancient rebuke still stands, "Why should thy mouth make thy flesh to sin?" For the individual or the nation, arbitration is not possible where the decision may violate conscience; it therefore can be accepted only when it is known that interest merely, not duty, will be affected by the judgment, and such knowledge cannot exist antecedent to the difficulty arising.

There is a further — a second — fallacy in the supposed analogy between the submission of individuals to law and the advocated submission of states to a central tribunal. The law of the state, overwhelming as is its power relatively to that of the individual citizen, can neither bind nor loose in matters pertaining to the conscience. Still less can any tribunal, however solemnly constituted, liberate a state from its obligation to do right; still less, I say, because the state retains what the individual has in great part lost — the power to maintain what it

The Mariners Museum

Alfred Thayer Mahan, member of the strategy board which directed naval operations during the Spanish-American War

believes to be right. Many considerations may make it more right — I do not say *more expedient* — for a man or for a nation, to submit to, or to acquiesce in, wrong than to resist; but in such cases it is conscience still that decides where the balance of right turns distinctly to the side of wrong.

It is, I presume, universally admitted that occasions may arise where conscience not only justifies but compels resistance to law; whether it be the Christian citizen refusing to sacrifice or the free citizen to subject himself to unconstitutional taxation, or to become the instrument of returning the slave to his master. So also for the Christian state. Existing wrong may have to be allowed lest a greater wrong be done. Conscience only can decide; and for that very reason conscience must be kept free that it may decide according to its sense of right when the case is presented.

There is, therefore, the very serious consideration attendant upon what is loosely styled "compulsory" arbitration — arbitration stipulated, that is, in advance of a question originating or of its conditions being appreciated — that a state may thereby do that which a citizen as toward the state does not do, namely, may voluntarily assume a moral obligation to do, or to allow, wrong. And it must be remembered, also, that many of the difficulties which arise among states involve considerations distinctly beyond and higher than law, as international law now exists; whereas the advocated Permanent Tribunal, to which the ultra-organizers look, to take cognizance of all cases, must perforce be governed by law as it exists. It is not, in fact, to be supposed that nations will submit themselves to a tribunal, the general principles of which have not been crystallized into a code of some sort.

A concrete instance, however, is always more comprehensible and instructive than a general discussion. Let us therefore take the incidents and conditions which preceded our recent war with Spain. The facts, as seen by us, may, I apprehend, be fairly stated as follows. In the island of Cuba, a powerful military force — government it scarcely can be called — foreign to the island, was holding a small portion of it in enforced subjection and was endeavoring, unsuccessfully, to reduce the remainder. In pursuance of this attempt, measures were adopted that inflicted immense misery and death upon great numbers of the population. Such suffering is indeed attendant upon war; but it may be stated as a fundamental principle of civilized warfare that useless suffering is condemned, and it had become apparent to military eyes that Spain could not subdue the island or restore orderly conditions. The suffering was terrible and was unavailing.

Under such circumstances, does any moral obligation lie upon a powerful neighboring state? Or, more exactly, if there is borne in upon the moral consciousness of a mighty people, that such an afflicted community as that of Cuba at their doors is like Lazarus at the gate of the rich man and that the duty of stopping the evil rests upon them, what is to be done with such a case of conscience? Could the decision of another, whether nation or court, excuse our nation from the ultimate responsibility of its own decision?

But, granting that it might have proved expedient to call in other judges, when we had full knowledge of the circumstances, what would have been our dilemma if, conscience commanding one course, we had found ourselves antecedently bound to abide by the conclusions of another arbiter? For let us not deceive ourselves. Absolutely justifiable, nay imperative, as most of us believe our action to have been, when tried at the bar of conscience, no arbitral court acceptable to the two nations would have decided as our own conscience did. A European diplomatist of distinguished reputation, of a small nation likeliest to be unbiased, so said to me personally, and it is known that more than one of our own ablest international lawyers held that we were acting in defiance of international law, as it now exists; just as the men who resisted the Fugitive Slave Law acted in defiance of the statute law of the land.

Decision must have gone against us, so these men think, on the legal merits of the case. Of the moral question, the arbiter could take no account; it is not there, indeed, that moral questions must find their solution, but in the court of conscience. Referred to arbitration, doubtless the Spanish flag would still fly over Cuba.

There is unquestionably a higher Law than law, concerning obedience to which no other than the man himself, or the state, can give account to Him that shall judge. The freedom of the conscience may be fettered or signed away by him who owes to it allegiance, yet its supremacy, though thus disavowed, cannot be overthrown. The

Conference at The Hague has facilitated future recourse to arbitration by providing means through which, a case arising, a court is more easily constituted and rules governing its procedure are ready to hand; but it has refrained from any engagements binding states to have recourse to the tribunal thus created. The responsibility of the state to its own conscience remains unimpeached and independent. The progress thus made and thus limited is to a halting place, at which, whether well chosen or not, the nations must perforce stop for a time; and it will be wise to employ that time in considering the bearings, alike of that which has been done and of that which has been left undone.

Our own country has a special need thus carefully to consider the possible consequences of arbitration, understood in the sense of an antecedent pledge to resort to it; unless under limitations very carefully hedged. There is an undoubted popular tendency in direction of such arbitration, which would be "compulsory" in the highest moral sense — the compulsion of a promise. The world at large and we especially stand at the opening of a new era, concerning whose problems little can be foreseen. Among the peoples, there is manifested intense interest in the maturing of our national convictions, as being, through Asia, newcomers into active international life, concerning whose course it is impossible to predict; and in many quarters, probably in all except Great Britain, the attitude toward us is watchful rather than sympathetic. . . .

Power, force, is a faculty of national life; one of the talents committed to nations by God. Like every other endowment of a complex organization, it must be held under control of the enlightened intellect and of the upright heart; but no more than any other can it be carelessly or lightly abjured without incurring the responsibility of one who buries in the earth that which was entrusted to him for use. And this obligation to maintain right, by force if need be, while

common to all states, rests peculiarly upon the greater in proportion to their means. Much is required of those to whom much is given. So viewed, the ability speedily to put forth the nation's power, by adequate organization and other necessary preparation, according to the reasonable demands of the nation's intrinsic strength and of its position in the world, is one of the clear duties involved in the Christian word "watchfulness" — readiness for the call that may come, whether expectedly or not. Until it is demonstrable that no evil exists, or threatens the world, which cannot be obviated without recourse to force, the obligation to readiness must remain; and, where evil is mighty and defiant, the obligation to use force — that is, war — arises.

Nor is it possible, antecedently, to bring these conditions and obligations under the letter of precise and codified law, to be administered by a tribunal; while legalism, in its spirit, is marked by blemishes as real as those commonly attributed to "militarism," and not more elevated. The considerations which determine good and evil, right and wrong, in crises of national life, or of the world's history, are questions of equity often too complicated for decision upon mere rules, or even principles, of law, international or other.

The instances of Bulgaria, of Armenia, and of Cuba are entirely in point, and it is most probable that the contentions about the future of China will afford further illustration. Even in matters where the interest of nations is concerned, the moral element enters; because each generation in its day is the guardian of those which shall follow it. Like all guardians, therefore, while it has the power to act according to its best judgment, it has no right, for the mere sake of peace, to permit known injustice to be done to its wards.

The present strong feeling throughout the nations of the world in favor of arbitration is in itself a subject for congratulation almost unalloyed. It carries indeed a promise, to the certainty of which no paper covenants can pretend; for it influences the conscience by inward conviction not by external fetter. But it must be remembered that such sentiments, from their very universality and evident laudableness, need correctives, for they bear in themselves a great danger of excess or of precipitancy. Excess is seen in the disposition, far too prevalent, to look upon war not only as an evil but as an evil unmixed, unnecessary, and therefore always unjustifiable; while precipitancy to reach results considered desirable is evidenced by the wish to *impose* arbitration, to prevent recourse to war, by a general pledge previously made.

Both frames of mind receive expression in the words of speakers, among whom a leading characteristic is lack of measuredness and of proportion. Thus an eminent citizen is reported to have said, "There is no more occasion for two nations to go to war than for two men to settle their difficulties with clubs." Singularly enough, this point of view assumes to represent peculiarly Christian teaching; willingly ignorant of the truth that Christianity, while it will not force the conscience by other than spiritual weapons, as "compulsory" arbitration might, distinctly recognizes the sword as the resister and remedier of evil in the sphere "of this world."

Arbitration's great opportunity has come in the advancing moral standards of states, whereby the disposition to deliberate wrongdoing has diminished and consequently the occasions for redressing wrong by force are less frequent to arise. In view of recent events, however, and very especially of notorious, high-handed oppression, initiated since the calling of the Peace Conference and resolutely continued during its sessions in defiance of the public opinion — the conviction — of the world at large, it is premature to assume that such occasions belong wholly to the past. Much less can it be assumed that there will be no further instances of a community believing, conscientiously and entirely, that honor and duty require of it a certain course which another community with equal integrity may hold to be inconsistent with the rights and obligations of its own members. It is quite possible, especially to one who has recently visited Holland, to conceive that Great Britain and the Boers are alike satisfied of the substantial justice of their respective claims.

It is permissible most earnestly to hope that, in disputes between independent states, arbitration may find a way to reconcile peace with fidelity to conscience in the case of both; but if, when friendly suggestion has done its best, the conviction of conscience remains unshaken, war is better than disobedience — better than acquiescence in recognized wrong. The great danger of undiscriminating advocacy of arbitration, which threatens even the cause it seeks to maintain, is that it may lead men to tamper with equity, to compromise with unrighteousness, soothing their conscience with the belief that war is so entirely wrong that beside it no other tolerated evil is wrong. Witness Armenia and witness Crete. War has been avoided; but what of the national consciences that beheld such iniquity and withheld the hand?

71.

Charles Eliot Norton: The Desertion of Ideals

Perhaps the most grief-stricken of all of the patriotic citizens who opposed America's participation in the Spanish-American War and its Philippine aftermath was Charles Eliot Norton, a professor at Harvard who urged his students not to enlist in a war in which, as he put it, "we jettison all that was most precious of our national cargo." In the following letter, written on November 18, 1899, to Charles Waldstein, who had published a book extolling the virtues of expansionism, Norton expressed his dismay at America's desertion of her traditional ideals. His views were summed up in his remark that America "has lost her unique position as a potential leader in the progress of civilization and has taken up her place simply as one of the grasping and selfish nations of the present day."

Source: *Letters of Charles Eliot Norton*, Sara Norton and M. A. DeWolfe Howe, eds., Boston, 1913, pp. 290-291.

I HAVE READ YOUR LITTLE VOLUME on the *Expansion of Western Ideals and the World's Peace* with great interest. As you are aware, your position and my own differ widely on the fundamental question which underlies your essays. But I read with genuine sympathy your very able statement of your own views. I do not think that you do quite justice to the opinions of the men who regard the present policy of America as a misfortune. It is not that we would hold America back from playing her full part in the world's affairs, but that we believe that her part could be better accomplished by close adherence to those high principles which are ideally embodied in her institutions — by the establishment of her own democracy in suchwise as to make it a symbol of noble self-government and by exercising the influence of a great, unarmed, and peaceful power on the affairs and the moral temper of the world.

We believe that America had something better to offer to mankind than those aims she is now pursuing, and we mourn her desertion of ideals which were not selfish nor limited in their application, but which are of universal worth and validity. She has lost her unique position as a potential leader in the progress of civilization and has taken up her place simply as one of the grasping and selfish nations of the present day. We all know how far she has fallen short in the past of exhibiting in her conduct a fidelity to those ideals which she professed, but some of us, at least, had not lost the hope that she would ultimately succeed in becoming more faithful to them.

There are many points in your two papers which, were you here, I should be glad to talk over with you. But it is hardly worthwhile to write of them. Your presentation of the imperialistic position has this great value at least, that it shows that men who hold it are cherishing ideals which, if they can be fulfilled, will make the course on which America has entered less disastrous than we who do not hold them now fear.

1900

72.

Albert J. Beveridge: In Support of an American Empire

The advocates of territorial expansion in the United States represented many ideological positions; there were missionary groups who supported the acquisition of the Philippine Islands from a desire to convert the heathen; there were commercial groups that desired the preferential treatment accorded possessions; there were politicians who envisioned America as a world power. In addition, the rising flood of nationalism could easily be expressed as a desire for wide-flung territories.
Those who tasted empire, for whatever reason, found their champion in U.S. Senator Albert J. Beveridge of Indiana. Beveridge, whose thrilling oratory could be matched only by Bryan, was one of the most aggressive and persistent spokesmen for empire. "Our Navy will make them contiguous!" was Beveridge's response to critics who argued that the Philippines were not part of the American land mass. The following selection comprises portions of a speech given by Beveridge before the Senate on January 9, 1900.

Source: *Record*, 56 Cong., 1 Sess., pp. 704-712.

Mr. President, the times call for candor. The Philippines are ours forever, "territory belonging to the United States," as the Constitution calls them. And just beyond the Philippines are China's illimitable markets. We will not retreat from either. We will not repudiate our duty in the archipelago. We will not abandon our opportunity in the Orient. We will not renounce our part in the mission of our race, trustee, under God, of the civilization of the world. And we will move forward to our work, not howling out regrets like slaves whipped to their burdens but with gratitude for a task worthy of our strength and thanksgiving to Almighty God that He has marked us as His chosen people, henceforth to lead in the regeneration of the world.

This island empire is the last land left in all the oceans. If it should prove a mistake to abandon it, the blunder once made would be irretrievable. If it proves a mistake to hold it, the error can be corrected when we will. Every other progressive nation stands ready to relieve us.

But to hold it will be no mistake. Our largest trade henceforth must be with Asia. The Pacific is our ocean. More and more Europe will manufacture the most it needs, secure from its colonies the most it consumes. Where shall we turn for consumers of our surplus? Geography answers the question. China is our natural customer. She is nearer to us than to England, Germany, or Russia, the commercial powers of the present and the future. They have moved nearer to China by securing permanent bases on her borders. The Philippines give us a base at the door of all the East.

Lines of navigation from our ports to the Orient and Australia, from the Isthmian Canal to Asia, from all Oriental ports to Australia converge at and separate from the Philippines. They are a self-supporting, dividend-paying fleet, permanently anchored at a spot selected by the strategy of Providence, commanding the Pacific. And the Pacific is the ocean of the commerce of the future. Most future wars will be conflicts for commerce. The power that rules the Pacific, therefore, is the power that rules the world. And, with the Philippines, that power is and will forever be the American Republic. . . .

But if they did not command China, India, the Orient, the whole Pacific for purposes of offense, defense, and trade, the Philippines are so valuable in themselves that we should hold them. I have cruised more than 2,000 miles through the archipelago, every moment a surprise at its loveliness and wealth. I have ridden hundreds of miles on the islands, every foot of the way a revelation of vegetable and mineral riches. . . .

Here, then, senators, is the situation. Two years ago there was no land in all the world which we could occupy for any purpose. Our commerce was daily turning toward the Orient, and geography and trade developments made necessary our commercial empire over the Pacific. And in that ocean we had no commercial, naval, or military base. Today we have one of the three great ocean possessions of the globe, located at the most commanding commercial, naval, and military points in the Eastern seas,

within hail of India, shoulder to shoulder with China, richer in its own resources than any equal body of land on the entire globe, and peopled by a race which civilization demands shall be improved. Shall we abandon it?

That man little knows the common people of the republic, little understands the instincts of our race who thinks we will not hold it fast and hold it forever, administering just government by simplest methods. We may trick up devices to shift our burden and lessen our opportunity; they will avail us nothing but delay. We may tangle conditions by applying academic arrangements of self-government to a crude situation; their failure will drive us to our duty in the end.

The military situation, past, present, and prospective, is no reason for abandonment. Our campaign has been as perfect as possible with the force at hand. We have been delayed, first, by a failure to comprehend the immensity of our acquisition; and, second, by insufficient force; and, third, by our efforts for peace. In February, after the treaty of peace, General Otis had only 3,722 officers and men whom he had a legal right to order into battle. The terms of enlistment of the rest of his troops had expired, and they fought voluntarily and not on legal military compulsion. It was one of the noblest examples of patriotic devotion to duty in the history of the world.

Those who complain do so in ignorance of the real situation. We attempted a great task with insufficient means; we became impatient that it was not finished before it could fairly be commenced; and I pray we may not add that other element of disaster, pausing in the work before it is thoroughly and forever done. That is the gravest mistake we could possibly make, and that is the only danger before us. Our Indian wars would have been shortened, the lives of soldiers and settlers saved, and the Indians themselves benefited had we made continuous and decisive war; and any other kind of war is criminal because ineffective. We acted toward the Indians as though we feared them, loved them, hated them — a mingling of foolish sentiment, inaccurate thought, and paralytic purpose. . . .

Mr. President, that must not be our plan. This war is like all other wars. It needs to be finished before it is stopped. I am prepared to vote either to make our work thorough or even now to abandon it. A lasting peace can be secured only by overwhelming forces in ceaseless action until universal and absolutely final defeat is inflicted on the enemy. To halt before every armed force, every guerrilla band opposing us is dispersed or exterminated will prolong hostilities and leave alive the seeds of perpetual insurrection.

Even then we should not treat. To treat at all is to admit that we are wrong. And any quiet so secured will be delusive and fleeting. And a false peace will betray us; a sham truce will curse us. It is not to serve the purposes of the hour, it is not to salve a present situation that peace should be established. It is for the tranquillity of the archipelago forever. It is for an orderly government for the Filipinos for all the future. It is to give this problem to posterity solved and settled, not vexed and involved. It is to establish the supremacy of the American republic over the Pacific and throughout the East till the end of time.

It has been charged that our conduct of the war has been cruel. Senators, it has been the reverse. I have been in our hospitals and seen the Filipino wounded as carefully, tenderly cared for as our own. Within our lines they may plow and sow and reap and go about the affairs of peace with absolute liberty. And yet all this kindness was misunderstood, or rather not understood. Senators must remember that we are not dealing with Americans or Europeans. We are dealing with Orientals. We are dealing with Orientals who are Malays. We are

dealing with Malays instructed in Spanish methods. They mistake kindness for weakness, forbearance for fear. It could not be otherwise unless you could erase hundreds of years of savagery, other hundreds of years of Orientalism, and still other hundreds of years of Spanish character and custom. . . .

Mr. President, reluctantly and only from a sense of duty am I forced to say that American opposition to the war has been the chief factor in prolonging it. Had Aguinaldo not understood that in America, even in the American Congress, even here in the Senate, he and his cause were supported; had he not known that it was proclaimed on the stump and in the press of a faction in the United States that every shot his misguided followers fired into the breasts of American soldiers was like the volleys fired by Washington's men against the soldiers of King George, his insurrection would have dissolved before it entirely crystallized.

The utterances of American opponents of the war are read to the ignorant soldiers of Aguinaldo and repeated in exaggerated form among the common people. Attempts have been made by wretches claiming American citizenship to ship arms and ammunition from Asiatic ports to the Filipinos, and these acts of infamy were coupled by the Malays with American assaults on our government at home. The Filipinos do not understand free speech, and therefore our tolerance of American assaults on the American President and the American government means to them that our President is in the minority or he would not permit what appears to them such treasonable criticism. It is believed and stated in Luzon, Panay, and Cebu that the Filipinos have only to fight, harass, retreat, break up into small parties, if necessary, as they are doing now, but by any means hold out until the next presidential election, and our forces will be withdrawn.

All this has aided the enemy more than

climate, arms, and battle. Senators, I have heard these reports myself; I have talked with the people; I have seen our mangled boys in the hospital and field; I have stood on the firing line and beheld our dead soldiers, their faces turned to the pitiless southern sky, and in sorrow rather than anger I say to those whose voices in America have cheered those misguided natives on to shoot our soldiers down, that the blood of those dead and wounded boys of ours is on their hands, and the flood of all the years can never wash that stain away. In sorrow rather than anger I say these words, for I earnestly believe that our brothers knew not what they did.

But, senators, it would be better to abandon this combined garden and Gibraltar of the Pacific, and count our blood and treasure already spent a profitable loss than to apply any academic arrangement of self-government to these children. They are not capable of self-government. How could they be? They are not of a self-governing race. They are Orientals, Malays, instructed by Spaniards in the latter's worst estate.

They know nothing of practical government except as they have witnessed the weak, corrupt, cruel, and capricious rule of Spain. What magic will anyone employ to dissolve in their minds and characters those impressions of governors and governed which three centuries of misrule has created? What alchemy will change the Oriental quality of their blood and set the self-governing currents of the American pouring through their Malay veins? How shall they, in the twinkling of an eye, be exalted to the heights of self-governing peoples which required a thousand years for us to reach, Anglo-Saxon though we are?

Let men beware how they employ the term "self-government." It is a sacred term. It is the watchword at the door of the inner temple of liberty, for liberty does not always mean self-government. Self-government is a method of liberty — the highest, simplest, best — and it is acquired only after centuries of study and struggle and experiment and instruction and all the elements of the progress of man. Self-government is no base and common thing to be bestowed on the merely audacious. It is the degree which crowns the graduate of liberty, not the name of liberty's infant class, who have not yet mastered the alphabet of freedom. Savage blood, Oriental blood, Malay blood, Spanish example — are these the elements of self-government?

We must act on the situation as it exists, not as we would wish it. I have talked with hundreds of these people, getting their views as to the practical workings of self-government. The great majority simply do not understand any participation in any government whatever. The most enlightened among them declare that self-government will succeed because the employers of labor will compel their employees to vote as their employer wills and that this will insure intelligent voting. I was assured that we could depend upon good men always being in office because the officials who constitute the government will nominate their successors, choose those among the people who will do the voting, and determine how and where elections will be held.

The most ardent advocate of self-government that I met was anxious that I should know that such a government would be tranquil because, as he said, if anyone criticized it, the government would shoot the offender. A few of them have a sort of verbal understanding of the democratic theory, but the above are the examples of the ideas of the practical workings of self-government entertained by the aristocracy, the rich planters and traders, and heavy employers of labor, the men who would run the government. . . .

In all other islands our government must be simple and strong. It must be a uniform government. Different forms for different islands will produce perpetual disturbance because the people of each island would think that the people of the other islands are more favored than they. In Panay I heard murmurings that we were giving Negros an American constitution. This is a human quality, found even in America, and we must never forget that in dealing with the Filipinos we deal with children.

And so our government must be simple and strong. Simple and strong! The meaning of those two words must be written in every line of Philippine legislation, realized in every act of Philippine administration.

A Philippine office in our Department of State; an American governor-general in Manila, with power to meet daily emergencies; possibly an advisory council with no power except that of discussing measures with the governor-general, which council would be the germ for future legislatures, a school in practical government; American lieutenant governors in each province, with a like council about him if possible, an American resident in each district and a like council grouped about him. Frequent and unannounced visits of provincial governors to the districts of their province; periodical reports to the governor-general; an American board of visitation to make semiannual trips to the archipelago without power of suggestion or interference to officials or people, but only to report and recommend to the Philippine office of our State Department; a Philippine civil service, with promotion for efficiency; the abolition of duties on exports from the Philippines; the establishment of import duties on a revenue basis, with such discrimination in favor of American imports as will prevent the cheaper goods of other nations from destroying American trade; a complete reform of local taxation on a just and scientific basis, beginning with the establishment of a tax on land according to its assessed value; the minting of abundant money for Philippine and Oriental use. The granting of franchises and concessions upon the theory of developing the resources of the archipelago, and therefore not by sale, but upon participation in the profits of the enterprise; the formation of a system of public schools everywhere with compulsory attendance rigidly enforced; the establishment of the English language throughout the Islands, teaching it exclusively in the schools and using it, through interpreters, exclusively in the courts; a simple civil code and a still simpler criminal code, and both common to all the islands except Sulu, Mindanao, and Paluan; American judges for all but smallest offenses; gradual, slow, and careful introduction of the best Filipinos into the working machinery of the government, no promise whatever of the franchise until the people have been prepared for it, all this backed by the necessary force to execute it — this outline of government the situation demands as soon as tranquillity is established. Until then military government is advisable. . . .

The men we send to administer civilized government in the Philippines must be themselves the highest examples of our civilization. I use the word "examples," for examples they must be in that word's most absolute sense. They must be men of the world and of affairs, students of their fellowmen, not theorists nor dreamers. They must be brave men, physically as well as morally. They must be as incorruptible as honor, as stainless as purity, men whom no force can frighten, no influence coerce, no money buy. Such men come high, even here in America. But they must be had.

Better pure military occupation for years than government by any other quality of administration. Better abandon this priceless possession, admit ourselves incompetent to do our part in the world-redeeming work of our imperial race; better now haul down the flag of arduous deeds for civilization and run up the flag of reaction and decay than to apply academic notions of self-government to these children or attempt their government by any but the most perfect administrators our country can produce. I assert that such administrators can be found. . . .

Mr. President, self-government and internal development have been the dominant notes of our first century; administration and the development of other lands will be the dominant notes of our second century. And administration is as high and holy a function as self-government, just as the care of a trust estate is as sacred an obligation as the management of our own concerns. Cain was the first to violate the divine law of human society which makes of us our brother's keeper. And administration of good government is the first lesson in self-government, that exalted estate toward which all civilization tends.

Administration of good government is not denial of liberty. For what is liberty? It is not savagery. It is not the exercise of individual will. It is not dictatorship. It involves government, but not necessarily self-government. It means law. First of all, it is a common rule of action, applying equally to all within its limits. Liberty means protection of property and life without price, free speech without intimidation, justice without purchase or delay, government without favor or favorites. What will best give all this to the people of the Philippines — American administration, developing them gradually toward self-government, or self-government by a people before they know what self-government means?

The Declaration of Independence does not forbid us to do our part in the regeneration of the world. If it did, the Declaration would be wrong, just as the Articles of Confederation, drafted by the very same men who signed the Declaration, was found to be wrong. The Declaration has no application to the present situation. It was writ-

ten by self-governing men for self-governing men. It was written by men who, for a century and a half, had been experimenting in self-government on this continent, and whose ancestors for hundreds of years before had been gradually developing toward that high and holy estate.

The Declaration applies only to people capable of self-government. How dare any man prostitute this expression of the very elect of self-governing peoples to a race of Malay children of barbarism, schooled in Spanish methods and ideas? And you who say the Declaration applies to all men, how dare you deny its application to the American Indian? And if you deny it to the Indian at home, how dare you grant it to the Malay abroad?

The Declaration does not contemplate that all government must have the consent of the governed. It announces that man's "inalienable rights are life, liberty, and the pursuit of happiness; that to secure these rights governments are established among men deriving their just powers from the consent of the governed; that when any form of government becomes destructive of those rights, it is the right of the people to alter or abolish it." "Life, liberty, and the pursuit of happiness" are the important things; "consent of the governed" is one of the means to those ends.

If "any form of government becomes destructive of those ends, it is the right of the people to alter or abolish it," says the Declaration. "Any forms" includes all forms. Thus the Declaration itself recognizes other forms of government than those resting on the consent of the governed The word "consent" itself recognizes other forms, for "consent" means the understanding of the thing to which the "consent" is given; and there are people in the world who do not understand any form of government. And the sense in which "consent" is used in the Declaration is broader than mere understanding; for "consent" in the Declaration means participation in the government "consented" to. And yet these people who are not capable of "consenting" to any form of government must be governed.

And so the Declaration contemplates all forms of government which secure the fundamental rights of life, liberty, and the pursuit of happiness. Self-government, when that will best secure these ends, as in the case of people capable of self-government; other appropriate forms when people are not capable of self-government. And so the authors of the Declaration themselves governed the Indian without his consent; the inhabitants of Louisiana without their consent; and ever since the sons of the makers of the Declaration have been governing not by theory but by practice, after the fashion of our governing race, now by one form, now by another, but always for the purpose of securing the great eternal ends of life, liberty, and the pursuit of happiness, not in the savage but in the civilized meaning of those terms — life according to orderly methods of civilized society; liberty regulated by law; pursuit of happiness limited by the pursuit of happiness by every other man.

If this is not the meaning of the Declaration, our government itself denies the Declaration every time it receives the representative of any but a republican form of government, such as that of the sultan, the czar, or other absolute autocrats, whose governments, according to the opposition's interpretation of the Declaration, are spurious governments because the people governed have not "consented" to them.

Senators in opposition are estopped from denying our constitutional power to govern the Philippines as circumstances may demand, for such power is admitted in the case of Florida, Louisiana, Alaska. How, then, is it denied in the Philippines? Is there a geographical interpretation to the Constitution? Do degrees of longitude fix consitutional limitations? Does a thousand miles of ocean diminish constitutional power more than a thousand miles of land?

The ocean does not separate us from the field of our duty and endeavor — it joins us, an established highway needing no repair and landing us at any point desired. The seas do not separate the Philippine Islands from us or from each other. The seas are highways through the archipelago, which would cost hundreds of millions of dollars to construct if they were land instead of water. Land may separate men from their desire; the ocean, never. Russia has been centuries in crossing Siberian wastes; the Puritans cross the Atlantic in brief and flying weeks.

If the Boers must have traveled by land, they would never have reached the Transvaal; but they sailed on liberty's ocean; they walked on civilization's untaxed highway, the welcoming sea. Our ships habitually sailed round the Cape and anchored in California's harbors before a single trail had lined the desert with the whitening bones of those who made it. No! No! The ocean unites us; steam unites us; electricity unites us; all the elements of nature unite us to the region where duty and interest call us.

There is in the ocean no constitutional argument against the march of the flag, for the oceans, too, are ours. With more extended coastlines than any nation of history; with a commerce vaster than any other people ever dreamed of, and that commerce as yet only in its beginnings; with naval traditions equaling those of England or of Greece, and the work of our Navy only just begun; with the air of the ocean in our nostrils and the blood of a sailor ancestry in our veins; with the shores of all the continents calling us, the Great Republic before I die will be the acknowledged lord of the world's high seas. And over them the republic will hold dominion, by virtue of the strength God has given it, for the peace of the world and the betterment of man.

No; the oceans are not limitations of the power which the Constitution expressly gives Congress to govern all territory the nation may acquire. The Constitution declares that "Congress shall have power to dispose of and make all needful rules and regulations respecting the territory belonging to the United States." Not the Northwest Territory only; not Louisiana or Florida only; not territory on this continent only but any territory anywhere belonging to the nation.

The founders of the nation were not provincial. Theirs was the geography of the world. They were soldiers as well as landsmen, and they knew that where our ships should go our flag might follow. They had the logic of progress, and they knew that the republic they were planting must, in obedience to the laws of our expanding race, necessarily develop into the greater republic which the world beholds today, and into the still mightier republic which the world will finally acknowledge as the arbiter, under God, of the destinies of mankind. And so our fathers wrote into the Constitution these words of growth, of expansion, of empire, if you will, unlimited by geography or climate or by anything but the vitality and possibilities of the American people: "Congress shall have power to dispose of and make all needful rules and regulations respecting the territory belonging to the United States."

The power to govern all territory the nation may acquire would have been in Congress if the language affirming that power had not been written in the Constitution; for not all powers of the national government are expressed. Its principal powers are implied. The written Constitution is but the index of the living Constitution. Had this not been true, the Constitution would have failed; for the people in any event would have developed and progressed. And if the Constitution had not had the capacity for growth corresponding with the growth of the nation, the Constitution would and should have been abandoned as the Articles of Confederation were abandoned. For the Constitution is not immortal in itself, is not useful even in itself. The Constitution is immortal and even useful only as it serves the orderly development of the nation. The nation alone is immortal. The nation alone is sacred. The Army is its servant. The Navy is its servant. The President is its servant. This Senate is its servant. Our laws are its methods. Our Constitution is its instrument. . . .

Mr. President, this question is deeper than any question of party politics; deeper than any question of the isolated policy of our country even; deeper even than any question of constitutional power. It is elemental. It is racial. God has not been preparing the English-speaking and Teutonic peoples for a thousand years for nothing but vain and idle self-contemplation and self-admiration. No! He has made us the master organizers of the world to establish system where chaos reigns. He has given us the spirit of progress to overwhelm the forces of reaction throughout the earth. He has made us adepts in government that we may administer government among savage and senile peoples. Were it not for such a force as this the world would relapse into barbarism and night. And of all our race He has marked the American people as His chosen nation to finally lead in the regeneration of the world. This is the divine mission of America, and it holds for us all the profit, all the glory, all the happiness possible to man. We are trustees of the world's progress, guardians of its righteous peace. The judgment of the Master is upon us: "Ye have been faithful over a few things; I will make you ruler over many things."

What shall history say of us? Shall it say that we renounced that holy trust, left the savage to his base condition, the wilderness to the reign of waste, deserted duty, abandoned glory, forget our sordid profit even, because we feared our strength and read the charter of our powers with the doubter's eye and the quibbler's mind? Shall it say that, called by events to captain and command the proudest, ablest, purest race of history in history's noblest work, we declined that great commission? Our fathers would not have had it so. No! They founded no paralytic government, incapable of the simplest acts of administration. They planted no sluggard people, passive while the world's work calls them. They established no reactionary nation. They unfurled no retreating flag.

That flag has never paused in its onward march. Who dares halt it now — now, when history's largest events are carrying it forward; now, when we are at last one people, strong enough for any task, great enough for any glory destiny can bestow? How comes it that our first century closes with the process of consolidating the American people into a unit just accomplished, and quick upon the stroke of that great hour presses upon us our world opportunity, world duty, and world glory, which none but the people welded into an indivisible nation can achieve or perform?

Blind indeed is he who sees not the hand of God in events so vast, so harmonious, so benign. Reactionary indeed is the mind that perceives not that this vital people is the strongest of the saving forces of the world; that our place, therefore, is at the head of the constructing and redeeming nations of the earth; and that to stand aside while events march on is a surrender of our interests, a betrayal of our duty as blind as it is base. Craven indeed is the heart that fears to perform a work so golden and so noble; that dares not win a glory so immortal.

Do you tell me that it will cost us money? When did Americans ever measure duty by financial standards? Do you tell me of the tremendous toil required to overcome the vast difficulties of our task? What mighty work for the world, for humanity, even for ourselves has ever been done with ease? Even our bread must we eat by the sweat of our faces. Why are we charged with power such as no people ever knew if we are not to use it in a work such as no people ever wrought? Who will dispute the divine meaning of the fable of the talents?

Do you remind me of the precious blood that must be shed, the lives that must be given, the broken hearts of loved ones for their slain? And this is indeed a heavier price than all combined. And, yet, as a nation, every historic duty we have done, every achievement we have accomplished has been by the sacrifice of our noblest sons. Every holy memory that glorifies the flag is of those heroes who have died that its onward march might not be stayed. It is the nation's dearest lives yielded for the flag that makes it dear to us; it is the nation's most precious blood poured out for it that makes it precious to us. That flag is woven of heroism and grief, of the bravery of men and women's tears, of righteousness and battle, of sacrifice and anguish, of triumph and of glory. It is these which make our flag a holy thing.

Who would tear from that sacred banner the glorious legends of a single battle where it has waved on land or sea? What son of a soldier of the flag whose father fell beneath it on any field would surrender that proud record for the heraldry of a king? In the cause of civilization, in the service of the republic anywhere on earth, Americans consider wounds the noblest decorations man can win, and count the giving of their lives a glad and precious duty.

Pray God that spirit never fails. Pray God the time may never come when Mammon and the love of ease shall so debase our blood that we will fear to shed it for the flag and its imperial destiny. Pray God the time may never come when American heroism is but a legend like the story of the Cid, American faith in our mission and our might a dream dissolved, and the glory of our mighty race departed.

And that time will never come. We will renew our youth at the fountain of new and glorious deeds. We will exalt our reverence for the flag by carrying it to a noble future as well as by remembering its ineffable past. Its immortality will not pass, because everywhere and always we will acknowledge and discharge the solemn responsibilities our sacred flag, in its deepest meaning, puts upon us. And so, senators, with reverent hearts, where dwells the fear of God, the American people move forward to the future of their hope and the doing of His work.

Mr. President and senators, adopt the resolution offered that peace may quickly come and that we may begin our saving, regenerating, and uplifting work. Adopt it, and this bloodshed will cease when these deluded children of our islands learn that this is the final word of the representatives of the American people in Congress assembled. Reject it, and the world, history, and the American people will know where to forever fix the awful responsibility for the consequences that will surely follow such failure to do our manifest duty. How dare we delay when our soldiers' blood is flowing?

73.

WILLIAM JENNINGS BRYAN: The Paralyzing Influence of Imperialism

In his second campaign for the presidency in 1900, William Jennings Bryan focused his criticism on the Republican administration's imperialistic policy. An avowed pacifist, Bryan had been against the Spanish-American War but had supported the peace treaty; he had hoped that a speedy conclusion to the war would provide the Filipinos with their independence. In his speech of acceptance at Military Park, Indianapolis, August 8, 1900, part of which is reprinted here, Bryan outlined what his objections to imperialism were and what he, as President, would do instead.

In Bryan's opinion, Rudyard Kipling's famous "white man's burden," which was taken up during the Spanish-American War, had to be put down; Bryan hoped to satisfy one anti-imperialistic newspaper, which had asked: "Now will you kindly tell us, Rudyard,/How we may put it down?" The nation, however, went for McKinley, who rolled up an even larger margin over Bryan than in 1896.

Source: *Official Proceedings of the Democratic National Convention Held in Kansas City, Mo., July 4, 5, and 6, 1900*, Chicago, 1900, pp. 205-227.

IF IT IS RIGHT for the United States to hold the Philippine Islands permanently and imitate European empires in the government of colonies, the Republican Party ought to state its position and defend it, but it must expect the subject races to protest against such a policy and to resist to the extent of their ability.

The Filipinos do not need any encouragement from Americans now living. Our whole history has been an encouragement, not only to the Filipinos but to all who are denied a voice in their own government. If the Republicans are prepared to censure all who have used language calculated to make the Filipinos hate foreign domination, let them condemn the speech of Patrick Henry. When he uttered that passionate appeal, "Give me liberty or give me death," he expressed a sentiment which still echoes in the hearts of men.

Let them censure Jefferson; of all the statesmen of history none have used words so offensive to those who would hold their fellows in political bondage. Let them censure Washington, who declared that the colonists must choose between liberty and slavery. Or, if the statute of limitations has run against the sins of Henry and Jefferson and Washington, let them censure Lincoln, whose Gettysburg speech will be quoted in defense of popular government when the present advocates of force and conquest are forgotten.

Someone has said that a truth once spoken can never be recalled. It goes on and on, and no one can set a limit to its ever widening influence. But if it were possible to obliterate every word written or spoken in defense of the principles set forth in the Declaration of Independence, a war of conquest would still leave its legacy of perpetual hatred, for it was God Himself who placed in every human heart the love of liberty. He never made a race of people so low in the scale of civilization or intelligence that it would welcome a foreign master.

Those who would have this nation enter upon a career of empire must consider not only the effect of imperialism on the Filipinos but they must also calculate its effects upon our own nation. We cannot repudiate the principle of self-government in the Philippines without weakening that principle here.

Lincoln said that the safety of this nation was not in its fleets, its armies, its forts, but in the spirit which prizes liberty as the heritage of all men, in all lands, everywhere, and he warned his countrymen that they could not destroy this spirit without planting the seeds of despotism at their own doors.

Even now we are beginning to see the paralyzing influence of imperialism. Heretofore this nation has been prompt to express its sympathy with those who were fighting for civil liberty. While our sphere of activity has been limited to the Western Hemisphere, our sympathies have not been bounded by the seas. We have felt it due to ourselves and to the world, as well as to those who were struggling for the right to govern themselves, to proclaim the interest which our people have, from the date of their own independence, felt in every contest between human rights and arbitrary power. . . .

A colonial policy means that we shall send to the Philippine Islands a few traders, a few taskmasters, and a few officeholders, and an army large enough to support the authority of a small fraction of the people while they rule the natives.

If we have an imperial policy we must have a great standing army as its natural and necessary complement. The spirit which will justify the forcible annexation of the Philippine Islands will justify the seizure of other islands and the domination of other people, and with wars of conquest we can expect a certain, if not rapid, growth of our military establishment.

That a large permanent increase in our regular army is intended by Republican leaders is not a matter of conjecture but a matter of fact. In his message of Dec. 5, 1898, the President asked for authority to increase the standing army to 100,000. In 1896 the army contained about 25,000. Within two years the President asked for four times that many, and a Republican House of Representatives complied with the request after the Spanish treaty had been signed, and when no country was at war with the United States.

If such an army is demanded when an

imperial policy is contemplated but not openly avowed, what may be expected if the people encourage the Republican Party by endorsing its policy at the polls?

A large standing army is not only a pecuniary burden to the people and, if accompanied by compulsory service, a constant source of irritation but it is even a menace to a republican form of government. The army is the personification of force, and militarism will inevitably change the ideals of the people and turn the thoughts of our young men from the arts of peace to the science of war. The government which relies for its defense upon its citizens is more likely to be just than one which has at call a large body of professional soldiers.

A small standing army and a well-equipped and well-disciplined state militia are sufficient at ordinary times, and in an emergency the nation should in the future as in the past place its dependence upon the volunteers who come from all occupations at their country's call and return to productive labor when their services are no longer required — men who fight when the country needs fighters and work when the country needs workers. . . .

The Republican platform promises that some measure of self-government is to be given the Filipinos by law; but even this pledge is not fulfilled. Nearly sixteen months elapsed after the ratification of the treaty before the adjournment of Congress last June and yet no law was passed dealing with the Philippine situation. The will of the President has been the only law in the Philippine Islands wherever the American authority extends.

Why does the Republican Party hesitate to legislate upon the Philippine question? Because a law would disclose the radical departure from history and precedent contemplated by those who control the Republican Party. The storm of protest which greeted the Puerto Rican bill was an indica-

tion of what may be expected when the American people are brought face to face with legislation upon this subject.

If the Puerto Ricans, who welcomed annexation, are to be denied the guarantees of our Constitution, what is to be the lot of the Filipinos, who resisted our authority? If secret influences could compel a disregard of our plain duty toward friendly people living near our shores, what treatment will those same influences provide for unfriendly people 7,000 miles away? If, in this country where the people have a right to vote, Republican leaders dare not take the side of the people against the great monopolies which have grown up within the last few years, how can they be trusted to protect the Filipinos from the corporations which are waiting to exploit the islands?

Is the sunlight of full citizenship to be enjoyed by the people of the United States and the twilight of semi-citizenship endured by the people of Puerto Rico, while the thick darkness of perpetual vassalage covers the Philippines? The Puerto Rico tariff law asserts the doctrine that the operation of the Constitution is confined to the forty-five states.

The Democratic Party disputes this doctrine and denounces it as repugnant to both the letter and spirit of our organic law. There is no place in our system of government for the deposit of arbitrary and irresistible power. That the leaders of a great party should claim for any President or Congress the right to treat millions of people as mere "possessions" and deal with them unrestrained by the Constitution or the Bill of Rights shows how far we have already departed from the ancient landmarks and indicates what may be expected if this nation deliberately enters upon a career of empire.

The territorial form of government is temporary and preparatory, and the chief security a citizen of a territory has is found in the fact that he enjoys the same constitutional guarantees and is subject to the same general laws as the citizen of a state. Take away this security and his rights will be violated and his interests sacrificed at the demand of those who have political influence. This is the evil of the colonial system, no matter by what nation it is applied.

What is our title to the Philippine Islands? Do we hold them by treaty or by conquest? Did we buy them or did we take them? Did we purchase the people? If not, how did we secure title to them? Were they thrown in with the land? Will the Republicans say that inanimate earth has value but that when that earth is molded by the Divine Hand and stamped with the likeness of the Creator it becomes a fixture and passes with the soil? If governments derive their just powers from the consent of the governed, it is impossible to secure title to people, either by force or by purchase.

We could extinguish Spain's title by treaty, but if we hold title we must hold it by some method consistent with our ideas of government. When we made allies of the Filipinos and armed them to fight against Spain, we disputed Spain's title. If we buy Spain's title, we are not innocent purchasers. There can be no doubt that we accepted and utilized the services of the Filipinos and that when we did so we had full knowledge that they were fighting for their own independence; and I submit that history furnishes no example of turpitude baser than ours if we now substitute our yoke for the Spanish yoke. . . .

Some argue that American rule in the Philippine Islands will result in the better education of the Filipinos. Be not deceived. If we expect to maintain a colonial policy, we shall not find it to our advantage to educate the people. The educated Filipinos are now in revolt against us, and the most ignorant ones have made the least resistance to our domination. If we are to govern them without their consent and give them no voice in determining the taxes which they must pay, we dare not educate them lest they learn to read the Declaration of Independence and the Constitution of the United States and mock us for our inconsistency.

The principal arguments, however, advanced by those who enter upon a defense of imperialism are:

First, that we must improve the present opportunity to become a world power and enter into international politics.

Second, that our commercial interests in the Philippine Islands and in the Orient make it necessary for us to hold the islands permanently.

Third, that the spread of the Christian religion will be facilitated by a colonial policy.

Fourth, that there is no honorable retreat from the position which the nation has taken.

The first argument is addressed to the nation's pride and the second to the nation's pocketbook. The third is intended for the church member and the fourth for the partisan.

It is sufficient answer to the first argument to say that for more than a century this nation has been a world power. For ten decades it has been the most potent influence in the world. Not only has it been a world power but it has done more to affect the policies of the human race than all the other nations of the world combined. Because our Declaration of Independence was promulgated, others have been promulgated. Because the patriots of 1776 fought for liberty, others have fought for it. Because our Constitution was adopted, other constitutions have been adopted.

The growth of the principle of self-government, planted on American soil, has been the overshadowing political fact of the 19th century. It has made this nation conspicuous among the nations and given it a place in history such as no other nation has ever enjoyed. Nothing has been able to check the onward march of this idea. I am not willing that this nation shall cast aside the omnipotent weapon of truth to seize again the weapons of physical warfare. I would not exchange the glory of this republic for the glory of all the empires that have risen and fallen since time began.

The permanent chairman of the last Republican National Convention presented the pecuniary argument in all its baldness when he said:

> We make no hypocritical pretense of being interested in the Philippines solely on account of others. While we regard the welfare of those people as a sacred trust, we regard the welfare of the American people first. We see our duty to ourselves as well as to others. We believe in trade expansion. By every legitimate means within the province of government and constitution we mean to stimulate the expansion of our trade and open new markets.

This is the commercial argument. It is based upon the theory that war can be rightly waged for pecuniary advantage and that it is profitable to purchase trade by force and violence. Franklin denied both of these propositions. When Lord Howe asserted that the acts of Parliament which brought on the Revolution were necessary to prevent American trade from passing into foreign channels, Franklin replied:

> To me it seems that neither the obtaining nor retaining of any trade, howsoever valuable, is an object for which men may justly spill each other's blood; that the true and sure means of extending and securing commerce are the goodness and cheapness of commodities, and that the profits of no trade can ever be equal to the expense of compelling it and holding it by fleets and armies. I consider this war against us, therefore, as both unjust and unwise.

I place the philosophy of Franklin against the sordid doctrine of those who would put a price upon the head of an American soldier and justify a war of conquest upon the ground that it will pay. The Democratic Party is in favor of the expansion of trade. It would extend our trade by every legitimate and peaceful means; but it is not willing to make merchandise of human blood.

But a war of conquest is as unwise as it is unrighteous. A harbor and coaling station in the Philippines would answer every trade and military necessity and such a concession could have been secured at any time without difficulty. It is not necessary to own people in order to trade with them. We carry on trade today with every part of the world, and our commerce has expanded more rapidly than the commerce of any European empire. We do not own Japan or China, but we trade with their people. We have not absorbed the republics of Central and South America, but we trade with them. Trade cannot be permanently profitable unless it is voluntary.

When trade is secured by force, the cost of securing it and retaining it must be taken out of the profits, and the profits are never large enough to cover the expense. Such a system would never be defended but for the fact that the expense is borne by all the people while the profits are enjoyed by a few.

Imperialism would be profitable to the Army contractors; it would be profitable to the shipowners, who would carry live soldiers to the Philippines and bring dead soldiers back; it would be profitable to those who would seize upon the franchises, and it would be profitable to the officials whose salaries would be fixed here and paid over there; but to the farmer, to the laboring man, and to the vast majority of those engaged in other occupations, it would bring expenditure without return and risk without reward.

Farmers and laboring men have, as a rule, small incomes, and, under systems which place the tax upon consumption, pay much more than their fair share of the expenses of government. Thus the very people who receive least benefit from imperialism will be injured most by the military burdens which accompany it. In addition to the evils which he and the former share in common, the laboring man will be the first to suffer if Oriental subjects seek work in the United States; the first to suffer if American capital leaves our shores to employ Oriental labor in the Philippines to supply the trade of China and Japan; the first to suffer from the violence which the military spirit arouses, and the first to suffer when the methods of imperialism are applied to our own government. It is not strange, therefore, that the labor organizations have been quick to note the approach of these dangers and prompt to protest against both militarism and imperialism.

The pecuniary argument, though more effective with certain classes, is not likely to be used so often or presented with so much enthusiasm as the religious argument. If what has been termed the "gunpowder gospel" were urged against the Filipinos only, it would be a sufficient answer to say that a majority of the Filipinos are now members of one branch of the Christian Church; but the principle involved is one of much wider application and challenges serious consideration.

The religious argument varies in positiveness from a passive belief that Providence delivered the Filipinos into our hands for their good and our glory to the exultation of the minister who said that we ought to "thrash the natives (Filipinos) until they understand who we are," and that "every bullet sent, every cannon shot, and every flag waved means righteousness."

We cannot approve of this doctrine in one place unless we are willing to apply it everywhere. If there is poison in the blood of the hand, it will ultimately reach the heart. It is equally true that forcible Christianity, if planted under the American flag in the far-away Orient, will sooner or later be transplanted upon American soil. . . .

The argument made by some that it was unfortunate for the nation that it had anything to do with the Philippine Islands, but that the naval victory at Manila made the permanent acquisition of those islands necessary, is also unsound. We won a naval victory at Santiago, but that did not compel us to hold Cuba.

The shedding of American blood in the Philippine Islands does not make it imperative that we should retain possession forever; American blood was shed at San Juan Hill and El Caney, and yet the President has promised the Cubans independence. The fact that the American flag floats over Manila does not compel us to exercise perpetual sovereignty over the islands; the American flag waves over Havana today, but the President has promised to haul it down when the flag of the Cuban republic is ready to rise in its place. Better a thousand times that our flag in the Orient give way to a flag representing the idea of self-government than that the flag of this republic should become the flag of an empire.

There is an easy, honest, honorable solution of the Philippine question. It is set forth in the Democratic platform and it is submitted with confidence to the American people. This plan I unreservedly endorse. If elected, I will convene Congress in extraordinary session as soon as inaugurated and recommend an immediate declaration of the nation's purpose: first, to establish a stable form of government in the Philippine Islands, just as we are now establishing a stable form of government in Cuba; second, to give independence to the Cubans; third, to protect the Filipinos from outside interference while they work out their destiny, just as we have protected the republics of Central and South America, and are, by the

Monroe Doctrine, pledged to protect Cuba.

A European protectorate often results in the plundering of the ward by the guardian. An American protectorate gives to the nation protected the advantage of our strength without making it the victim of our greed. For three-quarters of a century the Monroe Doctrine has been a shield to neighboring republics and yet it has imposed no pecuniary burden upon us. After the Filipinos had aided us in the war against Spain, we could not honorably turn them over to their former masters; we could not leave them to be the victims of the ambitious designs of European nations, and since we do not desire to make them a part of us or to hold them as subjects, we propose the only alternative, namely, to give them independence and guard them against molestation from without.

When our opponents are unable to defend their position by argument, they fall back upon the assertion that it is destiny and insist that we must submit to it no matter how much it violates our moral precepts and our principles of government. This is a complacent philosophy. It obliterates the distinction between right and wrong and makes individuals and nations the helpless victims of circumstances. Destiny is the subterfuge of the invertebrate, who, lacking the courage to oppose error, seeks some plausible excuse for supporting it. Washington said that the destiny of the republican form of government was deeply, if not finally, staked on the experiment entrusted to the American people.

How different Washington's definition of destiny from the Republican definition! The Republicans say that this nation is in the hands of destiny; Washington believed that not only the destiny of our own nation but the destiny of the republican form of government throughout the world was entrusted to American hands. Immeasurable responsibility!

The destiny of this republic is in the hands of its own people, and upon the success of the experiment here rests the hope of humanity. No exterior force can disturb this republic, and no foreign influence should be permitted to change its course. What the future has in store for this nation no one has authority to declare, but each individual has his own idea of the nation's mission, and he owes it to his country as well as to himself to contribute as best he may to the fulfillment of that mission.

Mr. Chairman and Gentlemen of the Committee, I can never fully discharge the debt of gratitude which I owe to my countrymen for the honors which they have so generously bestowed upon me; but, sirs, whether it be my lot to occupy the high office for which the convention has named me or to spend the remainder of my days in private life, it shall be my constant ambition and my controlling purpose to aid in realizing the high ideals of those whose wisdom and courage and sacrifices brought this republic into existence.

I can conceive of a national destiny surpassing the glories of the present and the past — a destiny which meets the responsibilities of today and measures up to the possibilities of the future. Behold a republic, resting securely upon the foundation stones quarried by revolutionary patriots from the mountain of eternal truth — a republic applying in practice and proclaiming to the world the self-evident proposition that all men are created equal; that they are endowed with inalienable rights; that governments are instituted among men to secure these rights, and that governments derive their just powers from the consent of the governed.

Behold a republic in which civil and religious liberty stimulate all to earnest endeavor and in which the law restrains every hand uplifted for a neighbor's injury — a republic in which every citizen is a sovereign, but in which no one cares to wear a crown. Behold a republic standing erect while empires all around are bowed beneath the weight of their own armaments — a republic whose flag is loved while other flags are only feared. Behold a republic increasing in population, in wealth, in strength, and in influence, solving the problems of civilization and hastening the coming of an universal brotherhood — a republic which shakes thrones and dissolves aristocracies by its silent example and gives light and inspiration to those who sit in darkness. Behold a republic gradually but surely becoming a supreme moral factor in the world's progress and the accepted arbiter of the world's disputes — a republic whose history, like the path of the just, "is as the shining light that shineth more and more unto the perfect day."

74.

FINLEY PETER DUNNE: Observations on the Philippines

Satire has had a long life in American political literature. One of the most popular political satirists at the turn of the century was Finley Peter Dunne. Writing for several Chicago newspapers, Dunne discussed a wide range of political subjects. He did it through an artful dialogue between two Irishmen: Mr. Dooley, a fictional saloonkeeper on the South Side of Chicago, and his regular customer Mr. Hennessy. In the following selection these two salty philosophers comment upon the American adventure in the Philippines.

Source: *Observations by Mr. Dooley*, New York, 1902: "The Philippine Peace."

" 'TIS STHRANGE we don't hear much talk about th' Ph'lippeens," said Mr. Hennessy.

"Ye ought to go to Boston," said Mr. Dooley. "They talk about it there in their sleep. Th' raison it's not discussed annywhere else is that ivrything is perfectly quiet there. We don't talk about Ohio or Ioway or anny iv our other possissions because they'se nawthin' doin' in thim parts. Th' people ar-re goin' ahead, garnerin' th' products iv th' sile, sindin' their childher to school, worshipin' on Sundah in th' churches an' thankin' Hiven f'r th' blessin's iv free govermint an' th' protiction iv th' flag above thim.

"So it is in th' Ph'lippeens. I know, f'r me friend Gov'nor Taft says so, an' they'se a man that undherstands con-tintmint whin he sees it. Ye can' thrust th' fellows that comes back fr'm th' jools iv th' Passyfic an' tells ye that things ar-re no betther thin they shud be undher th' shade iv th' cocoanut palm be th' blue wathers iv th' still lagoon. They mus' be satisfied with our rule. A man that isn't satisfied whin he's had enough is a glutton. They're satisfied an' happy an slowly but surely they're acquirin' that love f'r th' govermint that floats over thim that will make thim good citizens without a vote or a right to thrile be jury. I know it. Guv'nor Taft says so.

"Says he: 'Th' Ph'lippeens as ye have

been tol' be my young but speechful frind, Sinitor Bivridge, who was down there f'r tin minyits wanst an' spoke very highly an' at some lenth on th' beauties iv th' scenery, th' Ph'lippeens is wan or more iv th' beautiful jools in th' diadem iv our fair nation. Formerly our fair nation didn't care f'r jools, but done up her hair with side combs, but she's been abroad some since an' she come back with beautiful reddish goolden hair that a tiara looks well in an' that is betther f'r havin' a tiara. She is not as young as she was. Th' simple home-lovin' maiden that our fathers knew has disappeared an' in her place we find a Columbya, gintlemen, with machurer charms, a knowledge iv Euro-peen customs an' not averse to a cigareet. So we have pinned in her fair hair a diadem that sets off her beauty to advantage an' holds on th' front iv th' hair, an' th' mos' lovely pearl in this orny-mint is thim sunny little isles iv th' Passyfic. They are almost too sunny f'r me. I had to come away.

" 'To shift me language suddintly fr'm th' joolry counther an' th' boodore, I will say that nawthin' that has been said even be th' gifted an' scholarly sinitor, who so worthily fills part iv th' place wanst crowded be Hendricks an' McDonald, does justice to th' richness iv thim islands. They raise unknown quantities iv produce, none iv which forchnitly can come into this counthry. All th' riches iv Cathay, all th' wealth iv Ind, as Hogan says, wud look like a second morgedge on an Apache wickeyup compared with th' untold an' almost unmintionable products iv that gloryous domain. Me business kept me in Manila or I wud tell ye what they are. Besides some iv our lile subjects is gettin' to be good shots an' I didn't go down there f'r that purpose.

" 'I turn to th' climate. It is simply hivenly. No other wurrud describes it. A white man who goes there seldom rayturns unless th' bereaved fam'ly insists. It is jus' right. In winter enough rain, in summer plinty iv heat. Gin'rally speakin' whin that thropical sky starts rainin' it doesn't stop till it's impty, so th' counthry is not subjected to th' sudden changes that afflict more northerly climes. Whin it rains it rains; whin it shines it shines. Th' wather frequently remains in th' air afther th' sun has been shinin' a month or more, th' earth bein' a little over-crowded with juice an' this gives th' atmosphere a certain cosiness that is indescribable. A light green mould grows on th' clothes an' is very becomin'. I met a man on th' boat comin' back who said 'twas th' finest winter climate in th' wurruld. He was be profission a rubber in a Turkish bath. As f'r th' summers they are delicious. Th' sun doesn't sit aloft above th' jools iv th' Passyfic. It comes down an' mingles with th' people. Ye have heard it said th' isles was kissed be th' sun. Perhaps bitten wud be a betther wurrud. But th' timprachoor is frequently modified be an eruption iv th' neighborin' volcanoes an' th' inthraduction iv American stoves. At night a coolin' breeze fr'm th' crather iv a volcano makes sleep possible in a hammock swung in th' ice-box. It is also very pleasant to be able to cuk wan's dinner within wan.

" 'Passin' to th' pollytical situation, I will say it is good. Not perhaps as good as ye'ers or mine, but good. Ivry wanst in a while whin I think iv it, an iliction is held. Unforchnitly it usually happens that those ilicted have not yet surrindhered. In th' Ph'lippeens th' office seeks th' man, but as he is also pursooed be th' sojery, it is not always aisy to catch him an' fit it on him. Th' counthry may be divided into two parts, pollytically — where th' insurrection continues an' where it will soon be. Th' brave but I fear not altogether cheery army conthrols th' insurrected parts be martiyal law, but th' civil authorities are supreme in their own house. Th' diff'rence between civil law an' martiyal law in th' Ph'lippeens is what kind iv coat th' judge wears. Th' raysult is much th' same. Th' two branches wurruks in perfect harmony. We bag thim in th' city an' they round thim up in the counthry.

"'It is not always nicessary to kill a Filipino American right away. Me desire is to idjacate thim slowly in th' ways an' customs iv th' counthry. We ar-re givin' hundhreds iv these pore benighted haythen th' well-known, ol'-fashioned American wather cure. Iv coorse, ye know how 'tis done. A Filipino, we'll say, niver heerd iv th' histhry iv this counthry. He is met be wan iv our sturdy boys in black an' blue iv th' Macabebee scouts who asts him to cheer f'r Abraham Lincoln. He rayfuses. He is thin placed upon th' grass an' givin a dhrink, a baynit bein' fixed in his mouth so he cannot reject th' hospitality. Undher th' inflooence iv th' hose that cheers but does not inebriate, he soon warrums or perhaps I might say swells up to a ralization iv th' granjoor iv his adoptive counthry. One gallon makes him give three groans f'r th' constitchoochion. At four gallons, he will ask to be wrapped in th' flag. At th' dew pint he sings Yankee Doodle. Occasionally we run acrost a stubborn an' rebellyous man who wud sthrain at me idee iv human rights an' swallow th' Passyfic Ocean, but I mus' say mos' iv these little fellows is less hollow in their pretintions. Nachrally we have had to take a good manny customs fr'm th' Spanyard, but we have improved on thim. I was talkin' with a Spanish gintleman th' other day who had been away f'r a long time an' he said he wudden't know th' counthry. Even th' faces iv th' people on th' sthreets had changed. They seemed glad to see him. Among th' mos' useful Spanish customs is reconcenthration. Our reconcenthration camps is among th' mos' thickly popylated in th' wurruld. But still we have to rely mainly on American methods. They are always used fin'lly in th' makin' iv a good citizen, th' garotte sildom.

"'I have not considhered it advisable to inthrajooce anny fads like thrile be jury iv ye'er peers into me administhration. Plain sthraight-forward dealin's is me motto. A Filipino at his best has on'y larned half th' jooty iv mankind. He can be thried but he can't thry his fellow man. It takes him too long. But in time I hope to have thim thrained to a pint where they can be good men an' thrue at th' inquest.

"'I hope I have tol' ye enough to show ye that th' stories iv disordher is greatly exaggereated. Th' counthry is progressin' splindidly, th' ocean still laps th' shore, th' mountains are there as they were in Bivridge's day, quite happy apparently; th' flag floats free an' well guarded over th' govermint offices, an' th' cherry people go an' come on their errands — go out alone an' come back with th' throops. Ivrywhere happiness, contint, love iv th' sthepmother counthry, excipt in places where there ar-re people. Gintlemen, I thank ye.'

"An' there ye ar-re, Hinnissy. I hope this here lucid story will quite th' waggin' tongues iv scandal an' that people will let th' Ph'lippeens stew in their own happiness."

"But sure they might do something f'r thim," said Mr. Hennessy.

"They will," said Mr. Dooley. "They'll give thim a measure iv freedom."

"But whin?"

"Whin they'll sthand still long enough to be measured," said Mr. Dooley.

———————◆———————

Many a man that cudden't direct ye to th' dhrug store on th' corner whin he was thirty will get a respectful hearin' whin age has further impaired his mind.
FINLEY PETER DUNNE

75.

William Vaughn Moody: "An Ode in Time of Hesitation"

Acquiring the Philippine Islands from Spain was much easier than pacifying the inhabitants. The Filipinos, who had been in revolt against Spain and saw no advantage in exchanging new masters for old, continued to fight the Americans until March 1902. Although Americans protested indignantly that U.S. rule would be different from Spain's, the argument did not impress the Filipinos. The fighting during two years of rebellion was ruthless and bloody. William Vaughn Moody's poem, "An Ode in Time of Hesitation," a portion of which is reprinted below, dramatically expressed the feelings of anti-expansionists who had protested the original claiming of the islands and who pleaded, in 1900, for the liberation of the Philippines.

Source: *Atlantic Monthly*, May 1900.

AN ODE IN TIME OF HESITATION

IV

Alas! what sounds are these that come
Sullenly over the Pacific seas —
Sounds of ignoble battle, striking dumb
The season's half-awakened ecstasies?
Must I be humble, then,
Now when my heart hath need of pride?
Wild love falls on me from these
    sculptured men;
By loving much the land for which they
    died
I would be justified.
My spirit was away on pinions wide
To soothe in praise of her its passionate
    mood
And ease it of its ache of gratitude.
Too sorely heavy is the debt they lay
On me and the companions of my day.
I would remember now
My country's goodliness, make sweet her
    name.
Alas! what shade art thou
Of sorrow or of blame
Liftest the lyric leafage from her brow,
And pointest a slow finger at her shame?

V

Lies! lies! It cannot be! The wars
    we wage
Are noble, and our battles still are won
By justice for us, ere we lift the gage.
We have not sold our loftiest heritage.
The proud republic hath not stooped to
    cheat
And scramble in the marketplace of war;
Her forehead weareth yet its solemn star.
Here is her witness: this, her perfect son,
This delicate and proud New England
    soul
Who leads despised men, with
    just-unshackled feet,
Up the large ways where death and glory
    meet,
To show all peoples that our shame is
    done,
That once more we are clean and
    spirit-whole.

VIII

Was it for this our fathers kept the law?
This crown shall crown their struggle
    and their ruth?

Are we the eagle nation Milton saw,
Mewing its mighty youth,
Soon to possess the mountain winds of
    truth,
And be a swift familiar of the sun
Where aye before God's face His
    trumpets run?
Or have we but the talons and the maw,
And for the abject likeness of our heart
Shall some less lordly bird be set apart?
Some gross-billed wader where the
    swamps are fat?
Some gorger in the sun? Some prowler
    with the bat?

IX

Ah no!
We have not fallen so.
We are our fathers' sons: let those who
    lead us know!
'Twas only yesterday sick Cuba's cry
Came up the tropic wind, "Now help us,
    for we die!"
Then Alabama heard,
And rising, pale, to Maine and Idaho,
Shouted a burning word;
Proud state with proud impassioned state
    conferred,
And at the lifting of a hand sprang forth,
East, west, and south, and north,
Beautiful armies. Oh, by the sweet blood
    and young
Shed on the awful hill slope at San Juan,
By the unforgotten names of eager boys
Who might have tasted girls' love and
    been stung
With the old mystic joys
And starry griefs, now the spring nights
    come on,

But that the heart of youth is
    generous —
We charge you, ye who lead us,
Breathe on their chivalry no hint of stain!
Turn not their new-world victories to
    gain!
One least leaf plucked for chaffer from
    the bays
Of their dear praise,
One jot of their pure conquest put to
    hire,
The implacable republic will require;
With clamor, in the glare and gaze of
    noon,
Or subtly, coming as a thief at night,
But surely, very surely, slow or soon
That insult deep we deeply will require.
Tempt not our weakness, our cupidity!
For save we let the island men go free,
Those baffled and dislaureled ghosts
Will curse us from the lamentable coasts
Where walk the frustrate dead.
The cup of trembling shall be drainèd
    quite,
Eaten the sour bread of astonishment,
With ashes of the hearth shall be made
    white
Our hair, and wailing shall be in the
    tent:
Then on your guiltier head
Shall our intolerable self-disdain
Wreak suddenly its anger and its pain;
For manifest in that disastrous light
We shall discern the right
And do it, tardily. O ye who lead,
Take heed!
Blindness we may forgive, but baseness
    we will smite.

76.

Charles Sanders Peirce: The Function of a University

Charles S. Peirce, son of the distinguished American mathematician Benjamin Peirce,
was largely educated by his father before entering Harvard. Suffering ills similar to
those suffered a generation before by John Stuart Mill, the younger Peirce, despite
his brilliance in both thought and expression, was not a success in the academic world,
and his last years were spent in serious illness and abject poverty relieved only
by such friends as William James — in whose honor Peirce added "Santiago"
("St. James") to his middle name. The gesture was graceful enough, but Peirce had
nevertheless argued spiritedly, not to say fought, with James for many years about
pragmatism, the philosophical doctrine that they together helped make dominant among
American philosophers for a generation. In the following review of a book about
Clark University's first ten years, Peirce stated some of his convictions about the
academic enterprise.

Source: *Science*, April 20, 1900.

Of the three verbs to *be*, to *do*, and to *know*, the great majority of young men unhesitatingly regard the second as expressing the ultimate purpose and end of life. This is, as a matter of course, the idea of the practical man who knows what he wants and does not desire to want anything else. The average trustee of an American college will think it a very commendable thing for a professor to employ all the time he can possibly save in making money; but if he devotes much energy to any purely theoretical research, the trustees will look upon him askance as a barely respectable squanderer of his opportunities. In England, this notion takes a turn that really makes it a little less gross; yet being foreign, perhaps we can discern its error more easily than in its more familiar guise. Thus, Dr. Karl Pearson, in the introduction to his *Grammar of Science*, deliberately lays down the principle that no end whatever is to be approved without a reason, except the end of the preservation of society; and, applying this rule, declares that the only valid excuse for the encouragement of scientific activity lies in its tending to maintain "the stability of society." This is a truly British phrase, meaning the House of Lords and vested rights and all that.

Only recently, we have seen an American man of science and of weight discuss the purpose of education without once alluding to the only motive that animates the genuine scientific investigator. I am not guiltless in this matter, myself; for, in my youth, I wrote some articles to uphold a doctrine I called Pragmatism; namely, that the meaning and essence of every conception lies in the application that is to be made of it. That is all very well, when properly understood. I do not intend to recant it. But the question arises, *what is* the ultimate application; at that time, I seem to have been inclined to subordinate the *conception* to the *act*, knowing to doing.

Subsequent experience of life has taught me that the only thing that is really desirable without a reason for being so is to render ideas and things reasonable. One cannot well demand a reason for reasonableness itself. Logical analysis shows that reasonableness consists in association, assimilation, generalization, the bringing of items together into an organic whole — which are so many ways of regarding what is essentially the same thing. In the emotional sphere, this tendency toward union appears as Love; so that the Law of Love and the Law of Reason are quite at one.

There was a simple fellow who, in a benighted age and land, wandered about uttering appreciations of the elements of human life which have made an extraordinary impression upon most of us. Of all his sayings, there is none whose truth has been brought home to me more strongly by what I have been able to detect in successful men and women than this: Whoever makes his own welfare his object will simply ruin it utterly. . . . American education, for the most part, is directed to no other object than the welfare of the individual scholars; and thereby incites *them* to pursue that object exclusively.

A great university bears upon its seal the remark of its founder: "I wish to found an institution where any man can learn anything." It was a noble idea; and it would be mean to pick flaws in it, especially as he did not say what ulterior purpose he might have in view. But the university which parades this casual remark as its motto seems to proclaim to its students that their individual well-being is its only aim. Our scientific schools distribute circulars which dwell chiefly upon the handsome incomes their alumni are making, thereby calling up such images as a handsomely laid table, with a pair of Hâvre-de-grace ducks and a bottle of Château Margaux. What comes of such a conception of education and of life, for surely, the purpose of education is not different from the purpose of life?

The result is that, notwithstanding all the devices and tricks of the American teachers' art, it may be doubted whether any teaching ever anywhere did less to make happy men and women. At any rate, the spiritual meagerness of the typical American schoolbook is extreme. The great medieval universities, the modern German universities, the new science colleges of England, which did, and do, great things for their students personally, were never in the least founded for their students' individual advantage, but, on the contrary, because of the expectation that the truths that would be brought to light in such institutions would benefit the State. This end was, and is, so constantly in view that the scholars are led to regard their own lives as having a purpose beyond themselves.

Yet even this is a low view of learning and of science. No reader of this journal is likely to be content with the statement that the searching out of the ideas that govern the universe has no other value than that it helps human animals to swarm and feed. He will rather insist that the only thing that makes the human race worth perpetuation is that thereby rational ideas may be developed and the rationalization of things furthered.

No other occupation of man is so purely and immediately directed to the one end that is alone intrinsically rational as scientific investigation. It so strongly influences those who pursue it to subordinate all motives of ambition, fame, greed, self-seeking of every description that other people, even those who have relatively elevated aspirations, such as theologians and teachers, altogether fail, in many cases, to divine the scientific man's simple motives. The Clark University, in recognizing the pursuit of science as its first object, with teaching — of course, an indispensable means of securing continuity of work — as only a subordinate, or at most a secondary object, has perhaps the most elevated ideal of any university in the world; and I believe it to be so much the better for the individual students.

At any rate, I can only record my personal observation in two visits, after having endeavored, at many universities, to learn to appreciate the atmospheres of such places, that there is a sweetness and a strength there quite exceptional.

I am far from regretting that the institution has been through tribulations and has purged itself of every element alien to its idea. Today the good seed has germinated, so that it can no longer be choked by lower motives if it now only receives what is necessary to its continuance. It is earnestly to be hoped that it may speedily find its Constantine or its Helena. If not, one can but pity the family of its founder, which will have missed so narrowly a crown of high distinction. In that case, one must believe that among the American people, so appreciative of broad ideas, there may be found some thousands of persons, who whether they are quite sure of the immeasurable superiority of the aims of Clark or not, will at any rate feel that one institution of this peculiar kind ought to exist in the land, and will come forward with annual subscriptions to enable it to tide over a prolongation of its period of trial and to wait for the rescue that sooner or later, from some quarter or another, is sure to come.

The volume before us affords indisputable proof of the extraordinary interest and respect which this small institution commands from every genuine man of science the whole world over. Mr. Clark has, at any rate, drawn the eyes of all Europe with expectation upon the city of Worcester. To allow the university, after this, to sink into nothingness would be to make a nasty smirch upon the escutcheon of America that would long remain an offense to all our eyes.

77.

The Evils and Advantages of Industrial Combinations

In June 1898 Congress approved appropriations for an investigation of trusts. The U.S. Industrial Commission, under its chairman, Senator James Kyle of South Dakota, undertook the job and spent over a year gathering data by interviewing representatives from organized labor, the farmers, the manufacturers, and other parties. True to the British and American tradition of conducting exhaustive studies prior to the enactment of new legislation, the Commission's hearings received a good deal of public attention. The conclusions were published on March 1, 1900. A portion of the summary section on the advantages and evils of trusts is reprinted below.

Source: 56 Congress, 1 Session, House Document No. 476, Pt. 1, pp. 32-38.

THOSE WHO ADVOCATE the formation of large industrial combinations claim that they possess over the system of production on a smaller scale by competing plants the following advantages:

1. *Concentration.* By closing individual plants less favorably located or less well equipped and concentrating production into the best plants most favorably located, a great saving can be effected, both in the

amount of capital necessary for the production of a given product and the amount of labor required.

Another advantage of the concentration of industry is that the plants which are kept employed can be run at their full capacity instead of at part capacity, and can largely be run continuously instead of intermittently, so far as the combination happens to control the larger part of the entire output — a material source of saving in certain lines of industry. A still further advantage of this concentration comes in the selling of the product, from the fact that customers, being always sure of ready supply whenever it is wanted, more willingly buy from the large producer; and that there is less loss from bad debts. This readiness to buy from trusts, however, is denied, some witnesses holding that dealers prefer to buy from independent producers. . . .

2. *Freights.* Where the product is bulky, so that the freight forms an essential element of the cost, much can be saved by an organization which has plants established at favorable locations in different sections of the country, so that purchasers can be supplied from nearest plants, thus saving the cross freights, which, of course, must be paid where customers are supplied from single competing plants.

3. *Patents and brands.* Where different establishments, selling separate brands, are brought together into one combination, the use of each brand being made common to all, a great saving is often effected, since the most successful can be more efficiently exploited.

The control also of substantially all patents in one line of industry sometimes enables the combination to secure a monopoly which it could not otherwise secure.

4. *Single management.* The great completeness and simplicity of the operation of a single great corporation or trust is also a source of saving. Where each of the different establishments which are united had be-

fore a president, a complete set of officers, and a separate office force, the combined establishment need have but its one set of chief officers, and subordinates at lesser salaries may take the places of the heads of separate establishments. In this way a material saving is often made in the salaries of the higher officials; while a considerable reduction of the total office force is also possible. It is likewise true that this same form of organization enables one set of traveling salesmen to sell all of the brands or all classes of goods for the separate establishments, and in that way much labor is saved. This is considered a great saving from the standpoint of the producer and consumer, but is likewise naturally considered an evil from the point of view of those who are thus thrown out of work.

The more complete organizations also will distribute the work among the different plants in such a way that to each is given the particular kind of product for which it is specially adapted, and in many cases changes in machinery and changes of workmen from one kind of product to another are avoided, a source often of great saving.

5. *Skilled management.* The bringing into cooperation of leading men from the separate establishments, each having different elements of skill and experience, makes it possible to apply to the business the aggregate ability of all, a factor in many instances doubtless of great advantage. To some degree there may be a finer specialization of business ability, each man being placed at the head of the department for which he is specially fitted; thus giving, of course, the most skilled management possible to the entire industry, whereas before the combination was effected only a comparatively few of the leading establishments would have managers of equal skill.

But this advantage, some think, is limited. The chief managers at the central office are likely to be large stockholders, and thus to have a strong direct interest in the success of the enterprise. This may hold also of many of the superintendents of departments. But others will be hired managers, and, it is claimed, a hired superintendent will not take the same interest in the establishment or be able to exert the same intelligent control as the owner of a comparatively small establishment. Moreover, minute supervision cannot well be exercised in a very large combination.

6. *Export trade.* The control of large capital, also, it is asserted, enables the export trade to be developed to much greater advantage than could be done by smaller establishments with less wealth at their disposal.

Among the evils of the great combinations those most frequently mentioned are:

1. *Employees discharged.* When different establishments come together into one, it is often the case that certain classes of employees are needed in much less numbers than by the independent plants. This is especially true in the case of commercial travelers, and, also, perhaps in the case of superintendents and clerks in the offices. While this is generally admitted, it is considered by many to be an inevitable condition of progress and only a temporary hardship which, like that resulting from the introduction of a new machine, will ultimately result in a greater gain.

2. *Methods of competition.* The large establishments, by cutting prices in certain localities while maintaining the prices in the main, have a decided advantage over the smaller competitors whose market is limited to the one field in which the prices are cut, and consequently can often succeed in driving their rivals out of the business.

Connected with this method of competition is also the use of unfair methods, such as following up rivals' customers, bribing employees of rivals to furnish information, etc.

The sudden raising and lowering of prices by the combinations, without notice and apparently arbitrarily to embarrass their opponents, is also considered a great evil.

3. *Increased prices.* When the combinations have sufficient strength, or for any reason get monopolistic control more or less complete, it is thought that they often raise prices above competitive rates, to the great detriment of the public.

4. *Speculation and overcapitalization.* Another evil often charged against these newer combinations is that the promoter, by virtue of misrepresentations or by the concealment of material facts, is frequently able to secure very large profits for himself at the expense of the people at large who buy the stocks, and that in this way undue speculation is encouraged.

Connected with this evil which comes with the modern method of promotion is that of overcapitalization. Stock is frequently issued to four or five, or even more, times the amount of the cash value of the plants that are brought into the combinations. These stocks then placed upon the market go into the hands of persons ignorant of the real value of the property, who afterward are likely to lose heavily. Pools are sometimes made to control the stock market, or other of the common ways of disposing of the stock by unfair methods are employed.

At times, also, the officers and directors of the large combinations seem to have taken advantage of their inside knowledge of the business to speculate on the stock exchange in their own securities to the great detriment of the other shareholders.

5. *Freight discriminations.* Among the chief evils mentioned are those of freight discriminations in favor of the large companies, which many assert are the chief cause for the growth of the great combinations.

6. *Monopoly; its social effects.* The fact that an organization possesses a practical monopoly and can in that way direct its operations at the expense of its rivals, thereby prevent-

ing competitors from coming into the field, it is thought, takes away from the individual initiative of businessmen and prevents particularly the younger men from going into business independently. The formerly independent heads of establishments entering the combinations are also, it is said, reduced to the position of hired subordinates. By these means, witnesses claim, the trusts are in reality sapping the courage and power of initiative of perhaps the most active and influential men in the community. This evil is denied by many of the members of the large corporations, who think that within those corporations are found opportunities for the exercise of judgment and enterprise and for rising in life which do not exist outside.

REMEDIES

1. *Let-alone policy.* Several of the witnesses are of the opinion that any evils connected with the industrial combinations will be remedied in the ordinary course of business, and that any attempt at regulation by law would be likely to result in more harm than good. Competition, either active or potential, is believed by these witnesses to be a sufficient preventive of monopoly and extortionate prices, while stockholders and investors are believed to be already sufficiently protected by statute and common law, especially in view of the fact that the state cannot guarantee to these persons immunity from carelessness and ignorance on their own part. It is also urged that, under the common law alone, the courts have always held as illegal any monopoly or combination distinctly shown to be in restraint of trade.

While making this general expression of opinion, some of these witnesses afterward admitted that certain measures tending toward giving the public, and particularly the stockholders, more information regarding the nature of the business might be advisable.

2. *Direct suppression of monopolistic combinations.* A few witnesses are inclined to favor the more general enactment of statutes along the lines of those already adopted by numerous states, directly prohibiting the transaction of business by combinations seeking to restrain trade or to control prices. Some witnesses believe that the present statutes, in regard to the states where they have been enacted, in conjunction with the national Antitrust Law of 1890, and the Interstate Commerce Law, would, if vigorously enforced, be all the legislation necessary.

Perhaps a greater number of witnesses, however, directly expressed themselves as opposed to so-called antitrust legislation, while others distinctly imply a similar opposition. These witnesses, including some opponents of individual combinations, as well as lawyers, hold that combination is a natural outgrowth of modern conditions, and that it is practically impossible to suppress it. If any legislation is needed, it should be in the form of regulation and publicity only.

3. *Prohibition of destructive competition.* Two or three witnesses testifying in opposition to the Standard Oil Company advocate legislation to prohibit "destructive competition." The witnesses have in mind especially the cutting of prices in local markets, while retaining them at high figures in other parts of the country. A requirement that, freight rates being considered, prices should be made uniform in all markets is advocated. It is also suggested that general cutting of prices below actual cost of production for the purpose of driving out competitors should, perhaps, be prohibited. No criticism upon these suggestions is offered directly by other witnesses. In connection with this Senator Lee advocated limiting capitalization.

4. *Publicity.* Many of the witnesses, including even representatives of combinations, are of the opinion that a much greater publicity regarding the affairs of such combinations than is now customary would

tend to remove many of the evils. As regards the general public, the knowledge thus secured would avail to prevent the maintenance of extortionate prices as well as unfair methods and conditions of competition. Stockholders and investors would also be protected against abuses by promoters and officers of corporations.

How this publicity should be brought about and the degree to which it should extend is a matter upon which no general agreement existed among the witnesses. Some are inclined to think that it would be wise if somewhat detailed balance sheets of the accounts of the larger combinations could be made public. More of the witnesses, including especially lawyers and officers of corporations, seem rather of the opinion that when the corporation is first organized the details regarding its organization, the values at which plants and other property are taken in, the profits of the promoters, etc., should be made public. After the corporation has been engaged in business, however, while the details of its management should be made known with considerable fullness to the stockholders, the outside public should be given little more information than at present, lest thereby competitors may secure an advantage.

Many of the witnesses believe that publicity, if properly established and enforced, would prove a very efficient remedy. Others think that, while it might be useful, it would not alone be sufficient. At least one of the witnesses is of the opinion that this publicity should be enforced upon all public corporations, such as railways, street railways, etc., but not upon ordinary manufacturing or mercantile corporations.

Strong differences of opinion exist among the different witnesses as to whether legislation along any of the lines suggested, or additional legislation, should be by the individual states or by the federal government. The witnesses also disagree as to the constitutionality of various forms of legislation, both in the case of the states and in the

case of the federal government. Some witnesses were of the opinion that state legislation would be of little service unless practically all of the states adopted uniform laws, and this is considered an impossibility. Others seem to think that legislation, even by a few of the states, if of the right kind, would be very useful. There is perhaps, however, a rather general expression of opinion among those who favor any legislation at all that federal legislation, if constitutional, is desirable, at least to supplement state legislation as to combinations, if not, perhaps, to take entire jurisdiction regarding them.

5. *State legislation.* The chief specific suggestions regarding state legislation were:

(*a*) The classification of corporations should be made much stricter than at present, and each class should be confined closely to the exercise of its specified powers.

(*b*) There should be strict inspection of corporations by state officials, and publicity should be enforced through reports. This, of course, applies primarily to action by the states as regards their own domestic corporations. . . .

(*c*) Combinations, in whatever form (even if it be that of a single corporation), between different corporations, where monopolistic intent can be shown, should be prohibited. . . .

(*d*) Foreign corporations should be forbidden by each state to do business within its borders unless conforming to its laws. As to this last suggestion, the powers of states over foreign corporations, so far as their interstate business is concerned, would be very limited. It appears that the courts would be likely to hold that the states would require a special authorization from Congress to enable them to act with any considerable effectiveness in this regard, even if the power could be secured in that way.

6. *Federal legislation.* The lines of federal legislation suggested fall mainly under the following heads:

(a) Creation of federal corporations under strict federal laws. Some would favor incorporation under federal laws only in case of very large corporations, while from the legal standpoint some others would fix the distinction between state and federal corporations along the line of commerce within the states as distinguished from interstate commerce. The representatives of combinations favoring such federal laws consider that one of their chief advantages would be to prevent unwarranted interference with the business of the corporations by individual states. Some of the witnesses, however, consider that the creation of federal corporations would be harmful as well as unconstitutional.

(b) In connection with federal incorporation, or apart from it, certain witnesses favor a considerable degree of regulation of corporations on the part of the federal government. In this connection, publicity, through reports and inspection, is advocated. A Bureau of Industry is suggested by one witness, having powers somewhat similar to those of the Interstate Commerce Commission. The reports to be made to this body should be of such a nature as to disclose the condition of the business of the corporation, especially as to whether it possessed or was likely to acquire a monopoly or not.

(c) Strengthen Interstate Commerce Commission. Some of the witnesses complain of the inefficiency of the Interstate Commerce Commission. Others urge that it be given greater power, even judicial power, and that pooling among railroads be permitted under its supervision. Especially is it recommended in the testimony taken before the subcommission on transportation that its hands be strengthened by giving it power of audit of railway accounts, power of enforcing its decisions, etc., it being urged that in this way freight discriminations in favor of the large shippers, the combinations, could be prevented.

(d) Two witnesses are inclined to the opinion that unless Congress in some way assumes full control of corporations the United States government should remove, by specific act of Congress, the limitations which now are likely to be laid by the courts, on the basis of the federal Constitution, upon the powers of the states over monopolistic combinations, so far as their interstate business is concerned. It was thought, on the whole, that such an act of Congress would probably be upheld as constitutional by the courts.

(e) Removal or lowering of tariff. Several of the witnesses, though not objecting in the main to the principle of a protective tariff, were of the opinion that in some cases the tariff encouraged, or, even, as one said, was the chief cause of the trust. In such cases they thought it should be lowered or abolished. Mr. Havemeyer expressed himself most strongly in favor of a low horizontal tariff of not over 10 percent, while Mr. Buynitsky proposed that if there were shown to be a monopoly in any protected industry the president might be empowered to lower the tariff on the products of that industry, by executive order, not more than 20 percent, nor for a longer period than five years.

(f) Powers of Congress. Much discussion was presented before the Commission as to the constitutional powers of Congress to enact legislation along any of the lines above suggested. It is admitted that Congress has exclusive control over interstate commerce, and the preponderance of opinion seems to be that it has power to create corporations to carry on such commerce, although this is disputed. Congress is admitted to have no power over purely manufacturing corporations not engaged in interstate business. There is much doubt, however, as to the precise line where business ceases to be domestic and becomes interstate.

Professor Huffcut, at least, is inclined to

think that the courts, even under the present Constitution, would uphold quite general control over the general business of corporations carrying on a widespread business among the several states, on the ground that a large portion, at least, of that business — perhaps most of it — is interstate in character. The control of that would practically control all. In this connection this witness suggests that Congress could probably constitutionally compel such large corporations to submit to federal legislation, and perhaps to incorporate under federal laws, by one of the three following methods:

(1) By forbidding the use of the mails to state corporations engaged in interstate commerce, especially so far as they are shown to be monopolistic and therefore subject to the police power.

(2) By levying a practically prohibitive tax upon state corporations engaged in interstate commerce, as has been done with note issues of state banks. Other witnesses suggest that the government can acquire jurisdiction, in order to compel reports and publicity, by imposing taxes, and some are inclined to suggest that these taxes should be made progressive.

(3) By directly prohibiting state corporations from engaging in interstate commerce.

78.

GEORGE ADE: Two Fables for Moneymakers

George Ade, one of Indiana's most distinguished native sons, was a popular newspaper columnist (he was a mainstay of the old Chicago Record *from 1890 to 1900) and Broadway playwright (he once had three shows running concurrently, which helped to make him a wealthy man), and he was also the author of numerous early movie scripts. His most famous work, however, and the only one that survives today, was his series of "fables in slang," the first volume of which appeared under that title in 1899, to be followed by eleven other collections of short, humorous, and often satiric pieces that made fun of the penchants of his fellow Americans. The two fables reprinted here come from his second volume and are typical of the productions of this master of a genre that has had few proficient practitioners in the last hundred years.*

Source: *More Fables*, Chicago, 1900, pp. 23-35, 61-68.

*The Fable of the Honest
Money-Maker and the
Partner of His Joys,
Such as They Were*

THE PROSPEROUS FARMER LIVED in an Agricultural Section of the Middle West. He commanded the Respect of all his Neighbors. He owned a Section, and had a Raft of big Horses and white-faced Cows and Farm Machinery, and Money in the Bank besides. He still had the first Dollar he ever made, and it could not have been taken away from him with Pincers.

Henry was a ponderous, Clydesdale kind of Man, with Warts on his Hands. He did not have to travel on Appearances, because the whole County knew what he was

Worth. Of course he was Married. Years before he had selected a willing Country Girl with Pink Cheeks, and put her into his Kitchen to serve the Remainder of her Natural Life. He let her have as high as Two Dollars a Year to spend for herself. Her Hours were from 6 A.M. to 6 A.M., and if she got any Sleep she had to take it out of her Time. The Eight-Hour Day was not recognized on Henry's Place.

After Ten Years of raising Children, Steaming over the Washtub, Milking the Cows, Carrying in Wood, Cooking for the Hands, and other Delsarte such as the Respected Farmer usually Frames Up for his Wife, she was as thin as a Rail and humped over in the Shoulders. She was Thirty, and looked Sixty. Her Complexion was like Parchment and her Voice had been worn to a Cackle. She was losing her Teeth, too, but Henry could not afford to pay Dentist Bills because he needed all his Money to buy more Poland Chinas and build other Cribs. If she wanted a Summer Kitchen or a new Wringer or a Sewing Machine, or Anything Else that would lighten her Labors, Henry would Moan and Grumble and say she was trying to land him in the Poorhouse.

They had a dandy big Barn, painted Red with White Trimmings, and a Patent Fork to lift the Hay into the Mow, and the Family lived in a Pine Box that had not been Painted in Years and had Dog-Fennel all around the Front of it.

The Wife of the Respected Farmer was the only Work Animal around the Place that was not kept Fat and Sleek. But, of course, Henry did not count on Selling her. Henry often would fix up his Blooded Stock for the County Fair and tie Blue Ribbons on the Percherons and Herefords, but it was never noticed that he tied any Blue Ribbons on the Wife.

And yet Henry was a Man to be Proud of. He never Drank and he was a Good Hand with Horses, and he used to go to Church on Sunday Morning and hold a Cud of Tobacco in his Face during Services and sing Hymns with Extreme Unction. He would sing that he was a Lamb and had put on the Snow-White Robes and that Peace attended him. People would see him there in his Store Suit, with the Emaciated Wife and the Scared Children sitting in the Shadow of his Greatness, and they said that she was Lucky to have a Man who was so Well Off and lived in the Fear of the Lord.

Henry was Patriotic as well as Pious. He had a Picture of Abraham Lincoln in the Front Room, which no one was permitted to Enter, and he was glad that Slavery had been abolished.

Henry robbed the Cradle in order to get Farm-Hands. As soon as the Children were able to Walk without holding on, he started them for the Corn-Field, and told them to Pay for the Board that they had been Sponging off of him up to that Time. He did not want them to get too much Schooling for fear that they would want to sit up at Night and Read instead of Turning In so as to get an Early Start along before Daylight next Morning. So they did not get any too much, rest easy. And he never Foundered them on Stick Candy or Raisins or any such Delicatessen for sale at a General Store. Henry was undoubtedly the Tightest Wad in the Township. Some of the Folks who had got into a Box through Poor Management, and had been Foreclosed out of House and Home by Henry and his Lawyer, used to say that Henry was a Skin, and was too Stingy to give his Family enough to Eat, but most People looked up to Henry, for there was no getting around it that he was Successful.

When the Respected Farmer had been Married for Twenty Years and the Children had developed into long Gawks who did not know Anything except to get out and Toil all Day for Pa and not be paid anything for it, and after Henry had scraped together more Money than you could load on a Hay-Rack, an Unfortunate Thing happened. His Wife began to Fail. She was now Forty, but the Fair and Fat did not go with it. At that Age some Women are Buxom and just blossoming into the Full Charm of Matronly Womanhood. But Henry's Wife was Gaunt and Homely and all Run Down. She had been Poorly for Years, but she had to keep up and do the Chores as well as the House-Work, because Henry could not afford to hire a Girl. At last her Back gave out, so that she had to sit down and Rest every Once in a While. Henry would come in for his Meals and to let her know how Hearty all the Calves seemed to be, and he began to Notice that she was not very Chipper. It Worried him more than a little, because he did not care to pay any Doctor Bills. He told her she had better go and get some Patent Medicine that he had seen advertised on the Fence coming out from Town. It was only Twenty-Five cents a Bottle, and was warranted to Cure Anything. So she tried it, but it did not seem to restore her Youth and she got Weaker, and at last Henry just had to have the Doctor, Expense or No Expense. The Doctor said that as nearly as he could Diagnose her Case, she seemed to be Worn Out. Henry was Surprised, and said she had not been Complaining any more than Usual.

Next Afternoon he was out Dickering for a Bull, and his Woman, lying on the cheap Bedstead, up under the hot Roof, folded her lean Hands and slipped away to the only Rest she had known since she tied up with a Prosperous and Respected Farmer.

Henry was all Broken Up. He Wailed and Sobbed and made an Awful Fuss at the Church. The Preacher tried to Comfort him by saying that the Ways of Providence were beyond all Finding Out. He said that probably there was some. Reason why the Sister had been taken right in the Prime of her Usefulness, but it was not for Henry to know it. He said the only Consolation he could offer was the Hope that possibly she was Better Off. There did not seem to be much Doubt about that.

In about a Month the Respected Farmer was riding around the Country in his Buck-Board looking for Number Two. He had a business Head and he knew it was Cheaper to Marry than to Hire one. His Daughter was only Eleven and not quite Big Enough as yet to do all the Work for five Men.

Finally he found one who had the Reputation of being a Good Worker. When he took her over to his House to Break Her In, the Paper at the County Seat referred to them as the Happy Couple.

MORAL: *Be Honest and Respected and it Goes.*

The Fable of the Corporation Director and the Mislaid Ambition

ONE OF THE MOST PROMISING BOYS in a Graded School had a Burning Ambition to be a Congressman. He loved Politics and Oratory. When there was a Rally in Town he would carry a Torch and listen to the Spellbinder with his Mouth open.

The Boy wanted to grow up and wear a Black String Tie and a Bill Cody Hat and walk stiff-legged, with his Vest unbuttoned at the Top, and be Distinguished.

On Friday Afternoons he would go to School with his Face scrubbed to a shiny pink and his Hair roached up on one side, and he would Recite the Speeches of Patrick Henry and Daniel Webster and make Gestures.

When he Graduated from the High School he delivered an Oration on "The Duty of the Hour," calling on all young Patriots to leap into the Arena and with the Shield of Virtue quench the rising Flood of Corruption. He said that the Curse of Our Times was the Greed for Wealth, and he pleaded for Unselfish Patriotism among those in High Places.

He boarded at Home for a while without seeing a chance to jump into the Arena, and finally his Father worked a Pull and got him a Job with a Steel Company. He proved to be a Handy Young Man, and the Manager sent Him out to make Contracts. He stopped roaching his Hair, and he didn't give the Arena of Politics any serious Consideration except when the Tariff on Steel was in Danger.

In a little while he owned a few Shares, and after that he became a Director. He joined several Clubs and began to enjoy his Food. He drank a Small Bottle with his Luncheon each Day, and he couldn't talk Business unless he held a Scotch High Ball in his Right Hand.

With the return of Prosperity and the Formation of the Trust and the Whoop in all Stocks he made so much Money that he was afraid to tell the Amount.

His Girth increased — he became puffy under the Eyes — you could see the little blue Veins on his Nose.

He kept his Name out of the Papers as much as possible, and he never gave Congress a Thought except when he talked to his Lawyer of the Probable Manner in which they would Evade any Legislation against Trusts. He took two Turkish Baths every week and wore Silk Underwear. When an Eminent Politician would come to his Office to shake him down he would send out Word by the Boy in Buttons that he had gone to Europe. That's what he thought of Politics.

One day while rummaging in a lower Drawer in his Library, looking for a Box of Poker Chips, he came upon a Roll of Manuscript and wondered what it was. He opened it and read how it was the Duty of all True Americans to hop into the Arena and struggle unselfishly for the General Good. It came to him in a Flash — this was his High School Oration!

Then suddenly he remembered that for several Years of his Life his consuming Ambition had been — to go to Congress!

With a demoniacal Shriek he threw himself at full length on a Leather Couch and began to Laugh.

He rolled off the Sofa and tossed about on a $1,200 Rug in a Paroxysm of Merriment.

His Man came running into the Library and saw the Master in Convulsions. The poor Trust Magnate was purple in the Face.

They sent for a Great Specialist, who said that his Dear Friend had ruptured one of the smaller Arteries, and also narrowly escaped Death by Apoplexy.

He advised Rest and Quiet and the avoidance of any Great Shock.

So they took the High School Oration and put it on the Ice, and the Magnate slowly recovered and returned to his nine-course Dinners.

MORAL: *Of all Sad Words of Tongue or Pen, the Saddest are these, "It Might Have Been."*

[John D. Rockefeller is] *a kind iv society f'r th' prevention iv croolty to money. If he finds a man misusing his money he takes it away fr'm him an' adopts it.*
FINLEY PETER DUNNE ("MR. DOOLEY")

79.

Railroading Songs

Inscribed on a monument in Mount Calvary Cemetery, Jackson, Tennessee, are these words: "John Luther Jones, 1864-1900. To the Memory of the Locomotive Engineer, Whose Name as Casey Jones Became a Part of the Folklore of the American Language." He was called "Casey" because his birthplace was Cayce, Kentucky; he took another engineer's place on the Illinois Central's Cannonball Limited on April 29, 1900, and died in a wreck that day at Vaughn, Mississippi. Of such are legends made. Another "Cannonball Express" — this time on the Wabash (now Norfolk and Western) Railroad — was the inspiration for the second great railroading song reprinted here. Typically, the train is "she" — and the sound of the wheels is in the rhythm of the lines.

♫ CASEY JONES

Come, all you rounders, if you want to
    hear
The story of a brave engineer.
Casey Jones was the rounder's name —
On a six eight wheeler, boys, he won his
    fame.
The caller called Casey at-a half past four,
Kissed his wife at the station door,
Mounted to the cabin with his orders in
    his hand,
And he took his farewell trip to that
    promised land.

    Casey Jones, mounted to the cabin,
    Casey Jones, with his orders in his
        hand,
    Casey Jones, mounted to the cabin,
    And he took his farewell trip to the
        promised land.

"Put in your water and shovel in your coal,
Put your head out the window, watch
    them drivers roll.

I'll run her till she leaves the rail
'Cause I'm eight hours late with that
    western mail."
He looked at his watch and his watch
    was slow,
He looked at the water and the water
    was low,
He turned to the fireman and then he
    said,
"We're goin' to reach Frisco but we'll all
    be dead."

    Casey Jones, goin' to reach Frisco,
    Casey Jones, but we'll all be dead,
    Casey Jones, goin' to reach Frisco,
    We're goin' to reach Frisco, but we'll
        all be dead.

Casey pulled up that Reno Hill,
He whistled for the crossing with an
    awful shrill;
The switchman knew by the engine's
    moan
That the man at the throttle was Casey
    Jones.

He pulled up within two miles of the place
Number Four staring him right in the face,
He turned to the fireman, said, "Boy,
      you better jump,
'Cause there's two locomotives that are
      goin' to bump."

   Casey Jones, two locomotives,
   Casey Jones, that are goin' to bump,
   Casey Jones, two locomotives,
   There's two locomotives that are goin'
         to bump.

Casey said just before he died,
"There's two more roads that I'd like to
      ride."

The fireman said what could they be?
"The Southern Pacific and the Santa Fe."
Mrs. Casey sat on her bed a-sighin',
Just received a message that her Casey
      was dyin'.
Said, "Go to bed, children, and hush
      your cry'n,
Cause you got another papa on the Salt
      Lake Line."

   Mrs. Casey Jones, got another papa,
   Mrs. Casey Jones, on the Salt Lake
         Line,
   Mrs. Casey Jones, got another papa,
   Cause you've got another papa on the
         Salt Lake Line.

✿ WABASH CANNONBALL

I stood on the Atlantic Ocean, on the wide Pacific shore,
Heard the queen of flowing mountains to the South Belle by the door.
She's long, tall, and handsome, she's loved by one and all —
She's a modern combination called the Wabash Cannonball.

   Chorus:
   Listen to the jingle, the rumble, and the roar —
   Riding through the woodlands, to the hill and by the shore.
   Hear the mighty rush of engines, hear the lonesome hobo squall —
   Riding through the jungles on the Wabash Cannonball.

Now the Eastern states are dandies, so the Western people say,
From New York to St. Louis and Chicago by the way,
Through the hills of Minnesota where the rippling waters fall,
No chances can be taken on the Wabash Cannonball.

Here's to Daddy Claxton, may his name forever stand —
He will be remembered through parts of all our land.
When his earthly race is over and the curtain round him falls,
We'll carry him to victory on the Wabash Cannonball.

Gold prospectors trek up Alaska's Chilkoot Pass during the arduous journey to the Yukon, 1899

THE WESTERN ECONOMY

The gold and silver rushes were responsible for opening and settling, however temporarily, large regions of the West. Individual prospectors working simple placer mines and panning the streams constituted the first stage of Western development. For convenience, the turn of the century can be taken to represent an indefinite period during which the economy of the West shifted its emphasis from the purely extractive and generally temporary industries to those more highly evolved and permanent. It was at this point that genuine settlement began, growing in an interdependent relation to economic development of a higher order. Large-scale irrigation projects reclaimed desert and semidesert areas in California and Idaho. The Northwest became the major lumbering area in the country by 1905 when the Douglas fir plywood process was introduced. Puget Sound became a commercial center, exporting wheat from the new farms of the Northwest and serving as the linking market for the next push outward, the Alaska gold rush. The Western economy achieved maturity with the change from the superficial exploitation of a frontier region to a concentrated indigenous development.

Prospectors on the Dyea Trail in the Klondike region of the Yukon Territory, 1897

From the Russian period until the 1890s Alaska was primarily a region of fur trapping and fishing. Some relatively small amount of prospecting and mining had begun in the early 1870s, but it was not until 1896, when gold was discovered on the Klondike River, that mining became a major enterprise. The rush of prospectors in 1897 created new boom settlements — Dawson City had 10,000 inhabitants by 1900 — all around the territory. An estimated $100 million in gold was taken from the Klondike area between 1897 and 1904; the gold strike in Nome in 1898 and additional discoveries of copper and silver assured the development of Alaska.

(Below left) Two Chilkoot Indian guides in 1897; (below right) Sitka, Alaska, about 1896

(Above) The canyon leading south from the Stone House on Chilkoot Pass; photographed in 1897 by La Roche

(Right) "Actresses" bound for the Klondike in 1897; photographed at Happy Camp

(Right) Klondike Trading Company's store

The breakup of the huge Mexican land grants into smaller farms, hastened by the labor shortage following the curtailment of Chinese immigration, ended the dominance of one-crop farming and opened the way to the wide diversification of California agriculture. Large-scale irrigation — 1 million acres by 1890 — and the introduction of warm climate crops such as the seedless orange were the beginning of an agricultural industry that was to lead the nation. After 1895 the production of crude petroleum grew rapidly, stimulated by the successful use of oil in locomotives.

(Top) Members of the Pickwick Club participating in the Tournament of Roses in Pasadena, Calif., 1900; (center) Berkeley, Calif., in 1903; (left) Sunday afternoon in Golden Gate Park, San Francisco, 1902

(Above) Parade for President McKinley during his visit to Los Angeles in 1901; (right) Chinese residents on the street in San Francisco; (below) Avalon Harbor of Catalina Island photographed in 1895

(Above left) Race course at Sacramento; (above right) loggers in a sequoia forest; (below) the superintendent's residence on the Stockdale Ranch in Kern County, California

(Above) More than 10,000 acres of navel orange groves in San Gabriel Valley, Calif., 1903; (right) steam harvester cutting a 25-foot swath on a California farm, 1903; (below left) a ditching machine at Creasy Ranch in Kern County, Calif., 1890; (below right) stock cattle near an irrigation ditch in the pasture of Buena Vista farm

The messianic fervor of the Ghost Dance religion reappeared in 1889 after having been temporarily smothered by the Modoc war of 1873. The Paiute prophet Wovoka revived and developed the cult and under Sitting Bull the Sioux evolved a strong millennial interpretation in which all Indians would be restored to their former independence in a perfect world. The religion was again deemed dangerous by Indian agents and was finally eliminated in the Sioux war of 1889-1890. Nativism among the Southwest and Plains Indians also took a religious turn; from the old peyote complex, a ritualistic use of mescaline dating from the 16th century, a new cult of spiritualism developed, largely contemplative in practice. In the form of a fully organized religion, peyotism probably originated about 1885; it began in Oklahoma, evolving from an earlier Apache rite. Since then, in spite of predictable legal difficulties and hostility on the part of the white culture, the cult has been incorporated as the Native American Church.

(Above and below left) Pueblo Indians of the Isleta tribe, 1890; (right) Indians staging an adaptation of the Passion Play

(Above) Main Street, Lowell, Ariz., about 1900; (left) the plaza in Santa Fe, N.M., early 1900s

(Right) Church of San Miguel, Santa Fe, N.M.; (below) gunfight in Quartzsite, a desert town in Arizona. Man in foreground, holding a six-shooter, is pursuing the other man armed with a rifle turning corner at the fence

(Above) Arkansas Smelter in Leadville, Colorado, 1900

(Left) Flashlight photograph of the underground workings of the Homestake Gold Mine in Lead, S.D., about 1908; (below) climbing the last loop on the mountain railway to Morenci Copper Mines in Arizona, 1908

(Above) The Grand Teton, from a stereograph by Haynes; (right) Blanche Lamont with her school in Hecla, Montana, 1893; (below) view of Manitou, Colorado

(Left) Taking salmon from the trap for the great canneries, Puget Sound, Washington, 1902; (below) view of Portland, Oregon, at the turn of the century, with Mount Ranier in the distance

Like much of the West, the states of the old Oregon Territory had grown rapidly during the gold-fever days of the 1850s and the region had been covered with the temporary placer mines of prospectors. The turn of the century marked a point of departure for the economy of the Northwest; the mining industry fell from dominance as agriculture and lumbering grew behind improvements in transportation. Mining itself became a solid industry as it passed into corporate hands and began to work the deeper and richer lodes.

(Left) Logs fastened loosely together and pulled into Portland harbor enroute to the sawmill

(Top) 38-horse team harvester cutting, threshing, and sacking wheat in Walla Walla, Wash., 1902; (center) threshing with steam power in Oregon; (bottom) sheep shearing in eastern Oregon

(Below) Dill Willis, famous old one-armed hunter of Ashland, Ore.

(Above) Waiting for the signal that Indian lands on the Fort Hall Reservation were open to settlement; Pocatello, Idaho, Land Rush, 1902; (left) The rush to stake claims; (below) settler's temporary home on land acquired during the Rush

80.

Louis Sullivan: The Young Architect

Louis Sullivan's architectural training began at the Massachusetts Institute of Technology and continued at the École des Beaux-Arts, in Paris. The École may have ruined as many fine architects as it has made, but in the case of Sullivan it seemed to emancipate him rather than tie him to past traditions; and his revolutionary idea of skeletal construction, made possible by steel, is the most important architectural advance of modern times. After an immense success early in his career, Sullivan's work was neglected until after his death in 1924, when it enjoyed a revival that continues to this day. In the following selection, taken from a paper he delivered before the Architectural League in June 1900, Sullivan examines the problems of architecture in a democracy.

Source: *Western Architect*, January 1925: "The Young Man in Architecture."

You will remember that it was held that a national style must be generations in forming and that the inference you were to draw from this was that the individual should take no thought for his own natural development because it would be futile so to do, because, as it were, it would be an impertinent presumption. I tell you exactly the contrary: Give all your thought to individual development, which it is entirely within your province and power to control; and let the nationality come in due time as a consequence of the inevitable convergence of thought.

If anyone tells you that it is impossible, within a lifetime, to develop and perfect a complete individuality of expression, a well-ripened and perfected personal style, tell him that you know better and that you will prove it by your lives. Tell him with little ceremony, whoever he may be, that he is grossly ignorant of first principles, that he lives in the dark.

It is claimed that the great styles of the past are the sources of inspiration for this architecture of the present. This fact is the vehement assertion of those who "worship" them. Would you believe it? Really, would you believe it!

So it appears that like can beget its unlike after all. That a noble style may beget, through the agency of an ignoble mind, an ignoble building.

It may be true that a blooded male may beget, through a mongrel female, a cur progeny. But the application of this truth to the above instance wherein occurs the great word "inspiration" implies a brutal perversion of meaning and a pathetic depravity in those who use that word for their sinister ends. For inspiration, as I conceive it, is the intermediary between God and man, the pure fruition of the soul at one with immaculate nature, the greeting of noble minds. To use this word in a tricky endeavor to establish a connection legitimizing the architecture of the present as the progeny of the noblest thought in the past, is, to my mind, a blasphemy, and so it should appear to yours.

In truth, the American architecture of today is the offspring of an illegitimate commerce with the mongrel styles of the past. Do not deceive yourselves for a moment as to this. It is a harsh indictment. But it is warranted by the facts.

Yet, let us not be too severe. Let us remember and make what allowance we may for the depressing, stultifying, paralyzing influence of an unfortunate education. After all, every American man has had to go to school. And everything that he has been taught over and above the three *R*'s has been in essence for his mental undoing. I cannot possibly emphasize this lamentable fact too strongly. And the reason, alas, is so clear, so forcible, so ever present, as you will see.

We live under a form of government called democracy. And we, the people of the United States of America, constitute the most colossal instance known in history of a people seeking to verify the fundamental truth that self-government is nature's law for man. It is of the essence of democracy that the individual man is free in his body and free in his soul. It is a corollary therefrom that he must govern or restrain himself, both as to bodily acts and mental acts; that, in short, he must set up a responsible government within his own individual person.

It implies that highest form of emancipation, of liberty — physical, mental, and spiritual — by virtue whereof man calls the gods to the judgment, while he heeds the divinity of his own soul. It is the ideal of democracy that the individual man should stand self-centered, self-governing — an individual sovereign, an individual god.

Now, who will assert, specifically, that our present system of higher architectural education is in accord with this aspiration? That the form, education, bears any essential relation other than that of antagonism to the function, democracy? It is our misfortune that it does not.

We, as a people, are too youthful. We are too new among the world forces. We are too young. We have not yet had time to discover precisely the trouble, though we feel in our hearts that something is amiss.

Chicago Historical Society

Architect Louis Sullivan; oil portrait by Frank A. Werner, 1919

We have been too busy. And so comes about the incongruous spectacle of the infant democracy taking its mental nourishment at the withered breast of despotism.

To understand it from our point of view, examine! These are the essential points:

We are to revere authority. We are to take everything at second-hand. We are to believe measurements are superior to thought. We are advised not to think. We are cautioned that by no possibility can we think as well as did our predecessors. We are not to examine; *not* to test, *not* to prove. We are to regard ourselves as the elect, because, forsooth, we have been instructed by the elect. We must conform. We are not to go behind the scenes. We are to do as we are told and ask not foolish questions. We are taught that there is a royal road to our art. We are taught hero worship; we are not taught what the hero worshiped. We are taught that nature is one thing, man another thing. We are taught that God is one thing, man another thing.

Does this conform to the ideal of democracy? Is this a fitting overture to the world's greatest drama? Is it not extraordinary that we survive it even in part? Is it a wonder that our representative architecture is vapid, foolish, priggish, insolent, and pessimistic?

Manifestly, you cannot become truly educated in the schools. Ergo, you must educate yourselves. There is no other course, no other hope. For the schools have not changed much in my generation; they will, I fear, not change much in your generation, and soon it will be too late for you.

Strive, strive therefore while you are young and eager, to apply to your mental development the rules of physical development! Put yourselves in training, so to speak. Strive to develop in your minds the agility, flexibility, precision, poise, endurance, and judgment of the athlete. Seek simple, wholesome, nourishing food for the mind. You will be surprised and charmed with the results. The human mind in its natural state, not drowsed and stupefied by a reactionary education, is the most marvelously active agency in all nature. You may trust implicitly in the results of this activity if its surroundings are wholesome.

The mind will inevitably reproduce what it feeds upon. If it feeds upon filth, it will reproduce filth. If it feeds upon dust, it will reproduce dust. If it feeds upon nature, it will reproduce nature. If it feeds upon man, it will reproduce man. If it feeds upon all of these, it will reproduce all of these. It will reproduce infallibly whatever it is fed upon.

It is a wonderful machine; its activity cannot wholly be quenched except by death. It may be slowed down or accelerated, it cannot be stopped. It may be abused in every conceivable way, but it will not stop, even in insanity, even in sleep. So beware how you tamper with this marvelous mechanism, for it will record inevitably, in all its output, whatever you do to it.

81.

FINLEY PETER DUNNE: Troubles of a Candidate

Mr. Dooley, the fictional owner of a South Side Chicago saloon created by Finley Peter Dunne, had opinions on Theodore Roosevelt's hunting habits as well as on presidential campaigns. His frequent listener and participator in his discussions on politics was his regular customer Mr. Hennessy. The presidential campaign of 1900, in which McKinley was running for re-election with Theodore Roosevelt as his running mate, provided Mr. Dooley with an opportunity to discuss the slanderous accusations that were often made during campaigns.

Source: *Mr. Dooley's Philosophy*, New York, 1900, pp. 229-234.

"I WISHT TH' CAMPAIGN was over," said Mr. Dooley.

"I wisht it'd begin," said Mr. Hennessy. "I niver knew annything so dead. They ain't been so much as a black eye give or took in th' ward an' its less thin two months to th' big day."

"'Twill liven up," said Mr. Dooley, "I begin to see signs iv th' good times comin' again. 'Twas on'y th' other day me frind

Tiddy Rosenfelt opened th' battle mildly be insinuatin' that all dimmycrats was liars, horse thieves, an' arnychists. 'Tis thrue he apologized f'r that be explainin' that he didn't mean all dimmycrats but on'y those that wudden't vote f'r Mack but I think he'll take th' copper off befure manny weeks. A ladin' dimmycratic rayformer has suggested that Mack though a good man f'r an idjiot is surrounded be th' vilest scoundhrels iver seen in public life since th' days iv Joolyus Caesar. Th' Sicrety iv th' Threeasury has declared, that Mr. Bryan in sayin' that silver is not convartible be th' terms iv th' Slatthry bankin' law iv 1870, an' th' sicond clause iv th' threaty iv Gansville, has committed th' onpard'nable pollytical sin iv so consthructin' th' facts as to open up th' possibility iv wan not knowin' th' thrue position iv affairs, misundhersthandin' intirely. If he had him outside he'd call him a liar.

"Th' raypublicans have proved that Willum Jennings Bryan is a thraitor be th' letther written be Dr. Lem Stoggins, th' cillybrated antithought agytator iv Spooten Duyvil to Aggynaldoo in which he calls upon him to do nawthin' till he hears fr'm th' doc. Th' letther was sint through th' postal authorities an' as they have established no post-office in Aggynaldoo's hat they cudden't deliver it an' they opened it. Upon r-readin' th' letther Horace Plog iv White Horse, Minnesota, has wrote to Willum Jennings Bryan declarin' that if he (Plog) iver went to th' Ph'lippeens, which he wud've done but f'r th' way th' oats was sproutin' in th' stack, an' had been hit with a bullet he'd ixpict th' Coroner to hold Bryan to th' gran' jury. This was followed be th' publication iv a letther fr'm Oscar L. Swub iv East Persepalis, Ohio, declarin' that his sister heerd a cousin iv th' man that wash'd buggies in a livery stable in Canton say Mack's hired man tol' him Mack'd be hanged befure he'd withdraw th' ar-rmy fr'm Cuba.

"Oh, I guess th' campaign is doin' as well as cud be ixpicted. I see be th' raypublican pa-apers that Andhrew Carnegie has come out f'r Bryan an' has conthributed wan half iv his income or five hundhred millyon dollars to th' campaign fund. In th' dimmycratic pa-apers I r-read that Chairman Jim Jones has inthercipted a letther fr'm the Prince iv Wales to Mack congratulatin' him on his appintmint as gintleman-in-waitin' to th' queen. A dillygation iv Mormons has started fr'm dimmycratic headquarthers to thank Mack f'r his manly stand in favor iv poly-gamy an' th' raypublican comity has undher con-sideration a letther fr'm long term criminals advisin' their colleagues at large to vote f'r Willum Jennings Bryan, th' frind iv crime.

"In a few short weeks, Hinnissy, 'twill not be safe f'r ayether iv the candydates to come out on th' fr-ront porch till th' waitin' dillygations has been searched be a polisman. 'Tis th' divvle's own time th' la-ads that r-runs f'r th' prisidincy has since that ol' boy Burchard broke loose again' James G. Blaine. Sinitor Jones calls wan iv his thrusty hinchman to his side, an' says he: 'Mike, put on a pig-tail, an' a blue shirt an' take a dillygation iv Chinnymen out to Canton an' congratulate Mack on th' murdher iv mission'ries in China. An',' he says, 'ye might stop off at Cincinnati on th' way over an' arrange f'r a McKinley an' Rosenfelt club to ilict th' British Consul its prisidint an' attack th' office iv th' German newspaper,' he says. Mark Hanna rings f'r his sicrety an', says he: 'Have ye got off th' letther fr'm George Fred Willums advisin' Aggynaldoo to pizen th' wells?' 'Yes sir.' 'An' th' secret communication fr'm Bryan found on an arnychist at Pattherson askin' him to blow up th' White House?' 'It's in th' hands iv th' tyepwriter.' 'Thin call up an employmint agency an' have a dillygation iv Jesuites dhrop in at Lincoln, with a message fr'm th' pope proposin' to bur-rn all Protestant churches th' night befure iliction.'

"I tell ye, Hinnissy, th' candydate is kept movin'. Whin he sees a dilly-gation pikin' up th' lawn he must be r-ready. He makes a flyin' leap f'r th' chairman, seizes him by th' throat an' says: 'I thank ye f'r th' kind sintimints ye have conveyed. I am, indeed, as ye have remarked, th' riprisintative iv th' party iv manhood, honor, courage, liberality an' American thraditions. Take that back to Jimmy Jones an' tell him to put it in his pipe an' smoke it.' With which he bounds into th' house an' locks the dure while th' baffled conspirators goes down to a costumer an' changes their disguise. If th' future prisidint hadn't been quick on th' dhraw he'd been committed to a policy iv sthranglin' all the girl babies at birth.

"No, 'tis no aisy job bein' a candydate, an' 'twud be no easy job if th' game iv photygraphs was th' on'y wan th' candydates had to play. Willum Jennings Bryan is photygraphed smilin' back at his smilin' corn fields, in a pair iv blue overalls with a scythe in his hand borrid fr'm th' company that's playin' 'Th' Ol' Homestead,' at th' Lincoln Gran' Opry House. Th' nex' day Mack is seen mendin' a rustic chair with a monkey wrinch, Bryan has a pitcher took in th' act iv puttin' on a shirt marked with th' union label, an' they'se another photygraph iv Mack carryin' a scuttle iv coal up th' cellar stairs.

"An' did ye iver notice how much th' candydates looks alike, an' how much both iv thim looks like Lydia Pinkham? Thim wondherful boardhin'-house smiles that our gifted leaders wears, did ye iver see annything' so entrancin'? Whin th' las' photygrapher has packed his ar-rms homeward I can see th' gr-reat men retirin' to their rooms an' lettin' their faces down f'r a few minyits befure puttin' thim up again in curl-papers f'r th' nex' day display. Glory be, what a relief 'twill be f'r wan iv thim to raysume permanently th' savage or fam'ly breakfast face th' mornin' afther iliction!

"What a raylief 'twill be to no f'r sure that th' man at th' dure bell is on'y th' gas collector an' isn't loaded with a speech iv thanks in behalf iv th' Spanish Gover'mint! What a relief to snarl at wife an' frinds wanst more, to smoke a seegar with th' thrust magnate that owns th' cider facthry near th' station, to take ye'er nap in th' afthernoon undisthurbed be th' chirp iv th' snap-shot! 'Tis th' day afther iliction I'd like f'r to be a candydate, Hinnissy, no matther how it wint."

"An' what's become iv th' vice-prisidintial candydates?" Mr. Hennessy asked.

"Well," said Mr. Dooley, "Th' las' I heerd iv Adly, I didn't hear annythin', an' th' las' I heerd iv Tiddy he'd made application to th' naytional comity f'r th' use iv Mack as a soundin' board."

No matter whether th' Constitution follows th' flag or not, th' Supreme Court follows th' illiction returns.

> FINLEY PETER DUNNE ("MR. DOOLEY"), of a series of decisions by the Supreme Court validating the proceedings of the Congress and the administration, 1900-1904, which in effect denied to the Philippines "equal rights under the Constitution"

1901

82.

The Employment of Women

Since the 1880s the number of women working as well as going to college had been on the rise. To many traditionalists, these facts were alarming. The American home was endangered, they warned; the birth rate would decline (as in fact it was already doing); and women would become masculine. The advocates of enlarged opportunities for women argued that the "ideal of motherhood," as one author put it, "is not to be lessened, but it must be supplemented." The following selections, taken from articles written for the Independent *in 1901, offer a sampling of the conventional views on both sides of the debate: first, the male traditionalist, and then the "emancipated" woman.*

Source: *Independent*, April 11, May 16, 1901.

I.

HENRY T. FINCK: Employments Unsuitable for Women

ONE OF THE MOST IMPORTANT PROBLEMS to be solved in the new century is this: shall women be flowers or vegetables, ornamental or useful? In other words, shall women work, and, if so, what shall their work be and where shall it be — in the garden attached to the home or in the field at large?

Every country is obliged to have its arsenals where rifles, cannon, and other implements of war are manufactured at an enormous cost; yet every civilized person must hope and pray that all these things are made in vain and that the money spent on them is absolutely wasted. The same attitude should be observed by every person of culture toward the question of woman's work away from home. There always will be thousands of poor widows, orphans, and unmarried women who will be compelled to support themselves; and as fortunes are apt to be lost and no one can know whose turn is next, all parents, however wealthy, should have their daughters trained thoroughly in some employment which will enable them, in case of need, to make their own living. But here, again, all should hope and pray that the money thus expended was thrown away.

Instead of recognizing this important truth, a considerable number of agitators are trying hard to persuade women that it is their duty to make themselves independent and self-supporting, not only potentially but actually. Their incessant clamor has dazed and hypnotized many of our girls into the belief that they must not stay under the parental roof, but *must* go out into the world like their brothers to seek their fortunes. The epidemic delusion that home is no place for a girl — a delusion as dangerous to the soul as the plague is to the body — seems to be gaining ground daily. Not long ago a girl, whose father, though not rich is quite able and willing to take care of her, and, in fact, needs her to help with the housework, informed me that her friends were constantly telling her she ought to be ashamed to fall a burden to her father any longer. She had about made up her mind to become a shopgirl when I gave her a piece of my mind on the subject and induced her to stay at home.

An incalculable amount of harm is done by this foolish and criminal warfare on homelife. Instead of being encouraged in the tendency to leave the refining atmosphere of home, girls should be taught that, except under the stress of poverty, it is selfish as well as suicidal on their part to go out and work. Selfish because they take away the work which poor women and men absolutely need for their daily bread; suicidal because, by offering themselves so cheaply to employers, they either drive out the men or, by lowering their wages from the family standard to the individual standard, make it impossible for them to marry; wherefore these same girls who had hoped, by thus going out to work to increase their marriage chances, are left to die as old maids, or "new women," as they now prefer to call themselves.

Had they remained at home and cultivated the graces and refined allurements of femininity, their chances for a good marriage and a happy life would have been much better. Men still prefer, and always will prefer, the home girl to any other kind.

They want a girl who has not marred her beauty and ruined her health by needless work, or rubbed off the peach bloom of innocence by exposure to a rough world — a girl who has been trained by a sensible mother to understand and, if necessary, perform all the various functions and details that make home a comfort and a joy.

The selfishness which prompts the daughters of well-to-do parents to lower the rate of wages for everybody by flooding the market with a competition as ruinous as an invasion of cheap Chinese labor is a most unwomanly quality, which should make men shy of marrying them; though to be sure, many of these girls, like those who encourage the slaughter of birds for their hats, do not know how cruel they are.

It is quite otherwise, of course, with the *poor* girls and women who *must* work. Everything should be done to provide labor opportunities for them; but they should not be allowed, as they are at present, to precipitate themselves blindly into nearly every kind of a job that men have heretofore performed in civilized countries. The agitators take great pleasure in calling attention to women who invade new employments, regardless of the question whether these employments are suitable for them or not. It delights them to point out that whereas a century ago, there were no women in our factories, now about 45 percent of the factory work is done by them. They forget to ask whether the world would not be better off if there were no women at all in the factories, as in the good old times. Is factory work suitable for women? What are womanly employments anyway?

In an article entitled "Are Womanly Women Doomed?" which appeared in the *Independent* of January 31, I said that there were a few simple tests for deciding what kind of work is suitable for women who wish to remain womanly. These tests I shall now consider briefly. The first is a moral test.

The true wealth of a nation lies, as Renan has remarked, in the virtue of its women. Chastity is the most womanly of all virtues, and everything that endangers it should be promptly suppressed. Factory work does this preeminently. Painful revelations on this subject were made some years ago by the Belgian minister of industries, M. de Bruyé. He visited the regions where women shared the factory labor and the mining with the men, and was startled by what he saw. The women predominated over the men, and, instead of improving the men, they had adopted all their vices. In the taverns there were nearly as many carousing women as men, and whole bands of drunken girls sometimes paraded the streets yelling. . . . Perhaps the conditions in this country are not quite so bad as in Europe, but the revelations recently made in connection with a murder trial in a New Jersey factory town showed that we are not far behind.

The fourth *Report of the Commissioner of Labor* (1888) contains some information which should be taken to heart by all parents who recklessly allow their girls to leave home when there is no necessity for it. On page 75 the results are tabulated of an attempt made in fourteen American cities to ascertain the antecedents of 3,866 fallen women. The commissioner himself failed to see the true import of this table, which is that, although there are still six or seven times as many women at home as go out, yet less than one-third (31.97 percent) of the victims of vice came directly from home. Making allowance for children and old women, it will be seen how many times greater are the chances of a girl who stays at home of retaining her virtue. There is a startling lesson in these figures for those who try to create the sentiment that home is no place for a girl. It is, on the contrary, a place which she should not leave unless absolutely compelled by poverty. . . .

Next in importance to the moral test for woman's work comes the hygienic. With his usual keen insight Herbert Spencer has pointed out that "the preservation of health is a duty. Few seem aware that there is such a thing as physical morality." Men, to be sure, need health, too; but they are usually more robust to begin with, and they do not have to provide for that twofold drain on their vital powers which women who are destined to be wives and mothers are subject to. . . .

A man who has for a number of years employed hundreds of women informs me that they may all be divided into two classes — those who are dull and incapable of improvement, and those who have superior ability and can be promoted. These, unfortunately, he says, nearly always break down. Nervous collapse is, indeed, the fate of most women who engage with men in the strenuous competition of mercantile life and otherwise.

Tables have been printed (in the labor report above referred to) showing that a considerable proportion of working women are everywhere doomed to bad health. The damage is, however, much greater than is indicated by the figures in those tables; for a writer in the *British Medical Journal* (September 2, 1899), in discussing the influence of prolonged standing in the production of women's diseases, declares that while only a comparatively small number of factory and shopgirls break down at an early age, 40 percent of married women who have been factory or shopgirls "come under medical attention for pelvic troubles under thirty years of age. The girls are broken down and wearied, but keep at their work by force of circumstances."

Possibly the Rev. S. G. Smith, sociologist of the Minnesota State University, went too far when he said that "for women to work is a sin," and that "the world would be better off if all women were turned out of their jobs tomorrow." But certain it is that the wholesale employment of women in unhealthful work is an evil which calls for more and more stringent legislative interference. It is sapping the vitality of a large proportion of our women, and without healthy women there can be no healthy sons and daughters.

Some employers, when asked why they engage girls, frankly confess that cheapness is the motive (the average earnings of American women workers are under $4.50 a week); others give various fanciful reasons; but that cheapness is the real reason is proved by the increasing tendency toward child labor, which is cheapest of all. There has been an enormous increase within the last decade in the employment of girls under eighteen; and this results in such pitiful spectacles as the recent strike in Paterson of seventy-five factory girls averaging only twelve years of age and compelled, for less than $3 a week, to do work which involves walking up and down a room more than twenty miles a day. The swollen feet, bent forms, and tired faces, prematurely aged, of these girls, who should be playing with their dolls or going to school, are a terrible indictment of a "civilization" which permits such barbarous cruelty.

Besides the moral and hygienic tests for woman's work, there is one more of superlative importance — that of womanliness. "Male and female created He them"; and male and female we want them to remain, not only physically but in the higher qualities of mind and character, which are an acquisition of culture. Whatever tends to unsex women should be frowned on by public opinion, and, if necessary, prohibited by law. The great principle of the division of labor, which is now applied to all human activities, cannot be ignored in the apportionment of work to women and men.

The lowest savages already practised sexual division of labor, but theirs was not based on natural principles but on masculine selfishness. The men reserved for themselves the "honorable" employments of war and the chase, which they looked on as sport, while their wives and daughters were obliged not only to care for the children and do the cooking but to undertake all the hard work of grinding corn, tilling the fields, carrying home the game, cutting and bringing in wood, moving the camp, building huts, and a hundred other things that the men should have done. The result of this cruel doubling of their burdens was that they aged prematurely and lost all traces of such feminine beauty and charm as they might have otherwise developed. They were female men. To the savage the womanly woman was unknown. He was too coarse to appreciate the charms of true femininity.

With a topsy-turviness worthy of a Japanese the impression has been created that the "emancipation of woman" means the liberty to compete with men in all employments whatever. In reality, it means her liberation from the masculine and masculinizing work she was formerly compelled to do. The change came slowly — today millions of European women are still obliged to till the fields — but it came in proportion as men became refined enough to appreciate genuine womanly qualities; and the emancipated women showed their gratitude by becoming more and more unmistakably and delightfully feminine.

Having once discovered the charm of the eternal womanly, men will never allow it to be taken away again, to please a lot of half-women who are clamoring for what they illogically call their "rights." Men will find a way of making these misguided persons understand that it is as unseemly for them to be — as many of them are now — butchers, hunters, carpenters, barbers, stump speakers, iron and steel workers, miners, etc., as it would be for them to try to take the places of our soldiers, sailors, firemen, mail carriers and policemen. All employments which make women bold, fierce, muscular, brawny in body or mind will be more and more rigidly tabooed as unwomanly. Woman's strength lies in beauty and gentleness, not in muscle.

In literature, journalism, art, science (especially electric); in education, charity work, dressmaking; in typewriting (where there is no moral risk), watchmaking, jewelers' work, flower raising or making, and a hundred other branches of work that require no muscular toil, women and girls have all the opportunities for earning a living they need. Let us by all means throw open to them all employments in which their health, their purity, and their womanliness do not suffer; but let this be regarded, not as a special privilege and an indication of social progress, but as a necessary evil to be cured in as many cases as possible by marriage or some other way of bringing the workers back to their deserted homes.

II.

Ida Husted Harper:
Women Ought to Work

THE MOMENT WE ACCEPT THE THEORY that women must enter wage-earning occupations only when compelled to do so by poverty, that moment we degrade labor and lower the status of all women who are engaged in it. This theory prevailed throughout past ages, and it placed a stigma upon working women which is only beginning to be removed by the present generation. As long as a woman advertised her dire necessity by going outside the home to work, she could not avoid a feeling of humiliation and the placing of a barrier between herself and her more favored sisters. The fact that only a few insignificant employments with the most meager wages were permitted added still further to the disgrace of her position.

When, however, in the rapid evolution of the last third of a century, practically all oc-cupations were thrown open and into these poured women of education and social standing belonging to families of ample means, the barriers at once began to fall and the stigma to fade out of sight. The great organizations of women which have been formed during this period freely admit wage earners; all meet on common ground; and frequently, by reason of their superior ability, women engaged in business are elected to the offices. There never was a time when there was such fraternity between women of the leisure and the working classes. To destroy this by barring out from remunerative vocations all except those who must earn their daily bread or become paupers would be a calamity, and this long backward step never will be taken.

Who is to decide just what shall be the size of the family income to entitle a girl to do no outside work? There are some very rich men so niggardly in their allowance to the members of their family that no self-respecting girl, any more than a self-respecting boy, will remain a dependent on their grudging bounty an hour longer than is positively necessary. But if the father of moderate income is generous to the full extent of his means, shall the daughters accept it all until his illness or old age drives them out into the world to work for themselves? Or shall they by their own exertions relieve him of their support and give him a chance to lay aside enough to meet these contingencies?

Those who insist that all the women of the family should confine their labors to the household wholly ignore the vital fact that most of its duties have been carried outside. They note with regret that "while a century ago there were no women in our factories, now 45 percent of their employees are women," but omit to state that far more than 45 percent of the work now done in factories has been taken directly away from the women of the household. They have not left their legitimate work; they simply have followed it from the home to the factory.

The charge is continually made that the entrance of women into the industrial world has lowered men's wages to a ruinous degree. As a matter of fact, there are very few departments of work where men are not receiving higher wages now than ever before. If, however, these were placed at the same figure as before women entered into competition, and the 4 million women now engaged in breadwinning employments were withdrawn and set down in the home, the results would be most disastrous. From necessity they would constitute a vast body of consumers depending upon an inadequate body of producers. It would mean a life of idleness and privation for women, of added labor and sacrifice for men, a situation equally undesirable for both.

Nothing could more effectually destroy the stimulus to exertion in the girls of the high schools and colleges than the knowledge that all progress was to stop on commencement day, that it was to be the end instead of the beginning, that because their fathers were able to support them therefore they must make no use of this education. It is in the households of such that usually there is the least demand for domestic service on their part, as paid servants supply all that is necessary.

Shall these highly trained girls be restricted to the narrow round of social life? Shall they be directed to church, or charity, or reform work, for which they may have neither taste nor capacity? Shall they be forbidden any kind of business because they will take the bread out of the mouth of some poor woman? Why, then, such commendation when the *son* of a Vanderbilt, a Rockefeller, or a Morgan enters actively into business pursuits? Shall only those girls with the good luck to be poor have the chance to develop their talents? How shall

the world ever know the capabilities of woman if she is to be restricted rigidly to one line of action, except when starvation stares her in the face?

Those girls who have the advantage of a home are not wholly responsible for the low wages of the clerks, factory hands, etc. If all such would withdraw from the market it still would be flooded with those capable only of the simplest kind of cheap labor. There is no such thing as a "family standard" or an "individual standard" of wages. It is gauged only by the service performed. A certain price is paid for a certain kind of work. No employer ever asks a man if he has a family, and, if so, pays him more, or if he is unmarried, pays him less. If there were a "family standard," vast numbers of wage-earning women should be paid by it, for they also are supporting others. Women do not "offer themselves cheaply" to employers; they do not underbid; they take all they possibly can get. If they held out for more they would get nothing. Men cannot hope to raise their own wages by driving out this competing element — it has come to stay. They must make common cause with it and both advance together.

If the ranks of bachelors were recruited only from the wage-earning classes, there might be some force in the charge that by lowering wages women made it impossible for men to marry. But the proportion of bachelors is equally as large among the well-to-do and wealthy classes. If the percent of marriage is decreasing, one of the most conspicuous causes is that women themselves are not so anxious to marry as they used to be. This is not on account of any change in the nature of woman, but only because with freedom of industrial opportunity has come that greatest of blessings, freedom of choice in marriage.

Under the old regime the poor girl married because she was obliged to be taken care of; the rich girl because her life was

Ida Husted Harper, journalist and worker in the women's suffrage movement; photographed in 1890

do when the right man makes it, she should accept it with pride and happiness.

Under these circumstances the husband may feel infinitely more honored than if he had been made a choice between two evils — merely preferred to wage earning or an idle, useless existence in a home which had become wearisome. Nothing could be more demoralizing than the injunction to women to "regard their employment as a necessary evil to be cured in as many cases as possible by marriage." It is a sorry compliment to a man to be taken like a dose of medicine.

As a rule, husband and wife should found a home to be supported by the joint labor of both — his without, hers within — each considered of the same value and the proceeds belonging equally to both. Where there are young children, it is most unfortunate for the mother to be compelled to work outside the home. It is even more deplorable for these children themselves to be employed in the mills and factories. There is no difference of opinion on these two points, and a civilization must be striven for which will make such sacrifices unnecessary.

There is not, there never has been, an effort "to create a sentiment that home is no place for a girl." A good home is the one place above all others for a girl, as it is for a boy. It is her rest, her haven, her protection, but this does not necessarily imply that she must not engage in any work outside its limits. Nevertheless, it is a far stretch of the imagination to assume that all girls "leave the refining atmosphere of a home where they might cultivate the graces" to go into ill-smelling, disease-breeding shops and factories. Very few who are employed in such places have homes of refinement, or even of comfort and decency, and oftentimes the factories and stores are far more cheerful and hygienic than the so-called homes they leave. Women among the poor must work if they would live honestly, and the drudgery of factory and shop is no harder than

without aim or occupation and was considered by herself and everybody else a failure until she secured a husband. The necessity was practically the same in both cases. Now the one is enabled to take care of herself, and the other is permitted to follow whatever pursuit she finds most congenial; and, while each expects to marry, each intends to wait until the husband comes whom she can love, respect, and honor until death doth part. Under no other condition should any woman wed.

Marriage should bear the same relation to her life that it does to a man's. She should fit herself to be a useful and agreeable member of society; she should select a vocation — the management of the household, a profession, philanthropy, stenography, factory work — whatever she is best adapted for, and follow it cheerfully and conscientiously. When an offer of marriage comes, she should balance it carefully against the work she has chosen, and if it bring down the scale, as it never will fail to that of the washtub, the scrubbing brush, and the needle; but seldom does the statistician or sociologist devote his time and sympathy to the victims of the heavy and never-ending household tasks.

Far beyond all questions of physical deterioration in its seriousness, however, is the charge that the ranks of vice are recruited from those women who go outside the home to labor. From many directions comes the demand that women seek the shelter of other people's homes if they have none of their own and find safety in housework. But there is no one fact which the statistics demonstrate more unmistakably than that domestic service furnishes a far greater percentage of fallen women than does any other occupation. Helen Campbell makes this unqualified assertion as the result of her thorough researches in several countries, and it is clearly set forth in the reports of Carroll D. Wright and other authorities.

In the investigations of Frances A. Kellor, made in various states in 1899 for Chicago University and published in the *American Journal of Sociology,* she states emphatically that "the domestic class furnishes the most criminals" and that "almost all cases of prostitution resulting from seduction come from this class." Of 1,451 women at Blackwell's Island, 1,298 were domestics, 125 housekeepers, practically all the remainder seamstresses, laundresses, and women following strictly feminine occupations carried on in the home. The rescue missions and maternity hospitals of all cities tell the same story. . . .

It is wholly impracticable to draw a dividing line between the employments which are suitable and those which are unsuitable for women. They have just as much right as men have to decide this question for themselves. Their decision may impose some loss upon man, but this will be compensated by the gain to woman. Nobody can decide just where moral or physical risks are involved.

Typewriting is generally considered a fitting occupation, and yet it may include both. Journalism is usually looked upon as a suitable calling for women, and yet a short time ago the editor of a prominent periodical devoted many columns to show that it was likely to lead to moral and physical destruction.

The countless thousands who have listened to the eloquence of a Willard or an Anthony, and have seen the great reforms they have accomplished, would take issue with him who would characterize them as "stump speakers, misguided and unseemly," or would name theirs as a calling which makes women "bold, fierce, muscular, and brawny in body or mind." It is a mistaken kindness which would doom a woman to inhale the poisonous fumes of "artificial flower making," or to bend her back over a sewing machine, or to depend on the poor rewards of the artist's pencil, rather than engage in some employment which will develop "muscle."

It is no new thing, however, for men to insist that women shall remain physically soft and inactive because it pleases their own aesthetic taste. This was the constant refrain of the Rousseaus and Voltaires of a century ago. In that book of advice which the good old English Dr. Gregory left as a *Legacy to My Daughters,* toward the close of the 18th century, he said: "Should you be so unfortunate as to possess a robust constitution by nature, simulate such sickly delicacy as is necessary to keep up the proper female charm." The Dr. Gregorys of today have advanced a step beyond "sickly delicacy," but they implore women to "show their gratitude to men for relieving them of the heavy work by becoming more and more unmistakably and delightfully feminine." There is simply a difference in expression, but none in the sentiment behind it.

The progressive portion of mankind,

however, is beginning to forget sex occasionally and regard woman as a human being entitled to the same opportunity for healthy physical development as man; and, from the kindergarten to the university, girls now are receiving thorough, scientific training in athletics. The time is past when women can be frightened by an appeal not to become "muscular and brawny," and if it is not objectionable for them to become so by college athletics and outdoor exercise, it certainly is not wrong for them to develop their muscles by work. If, for the good of the world, it should become necessary to decide between "vegetables and flowers, the ox and the antelope," the flowers and the antelope would have to go. But the world needs all of them. It demands men and women of muscle in some departments, and men and women of mind in others. Even in marriage it would be a great sacrifice to hand over to certain classes of men women "whose strength lies in beauty and gentleness."

Neither can women be frightened at the warning that by engaging in occupations outside the home they decrease their chances of marrying. Whatever brings men and women into close association promotes marriage, which is largely the result of propinquity. Those who remain in the seclusion of home find no rivals so dangerous as those who in various outside employments have an opportunity to meet the men, and whom they continually see marrying not only their fellow workmen but frequently their employers. The latter, in all kinds of business, declare that the greatest objection to employing women is that they marry after a few years' service.

It is not intended to argue that every woman should leave the home and go into business, but only that those who wish to do so shall have the opportunity, and that men shall no longer monopolize the gainful occupations. The pleasure of earning money and of enjoying financial independence is just as sweet to a woman as to a man. If men would look upon the household service performed by the women of their family as a wage-earning occupation, entitled to a fixed remuneration, there would be infinitely less desire on their part to engage in outside work. When, however, they receive only board and lodging and must ask for every dollar required for clothes and other necessities, they naturally gaze with longing eyes into more fruitful fields of labor. When men cannot afford to pay their daughters or sisters a fixed sum, then at once the argument falls to the ground that "by studying domestic economy women save as much money at home as they can earn in outside occupations."

It may be that in selecting a wife "men want a girl who has not rubbed off the peach bloom of innocence by exposure to a rough world," but it is not permitted all girls to stay at home and take care of their peach bloom. Those women who make it the object of life to cultivate "refined allurements and soft blandishments to render themselves desirable to future husbands" are not many degrees removed from their sisters who practise the same arts upon the street with a less permanent object. It is no longer practicable to shut women up within four walls to preserve their virtue, and, instead of demanding a return to that medieval custom, it is the duty of society to recognize the new order and, through individual effort, public sentiment, and law, to improve the conditions which surround wage-earning women; to invest them with every right and privilege possessed by workingmen; and in every possible way help them develop strength of character to resist temptation and to fix a higher standard not only for themselves but also for the men with whom they come in contact.

83:

John Bates Clark: The Demos of the Future

With the beginning of a new century, many people speculated about life in twentieth-century America. John Clark, a professor of political economy at Columbia University, contributed his thoughtful observations on "The Society of the Future" to the July 18, 1901, issue of the Independent. *Many of the predictions he made in 1901 became true by mid-century. While some utopians claimed that a radical restructuring of society along communistic lines was inevitable, Clark foresaw the successful and peaceful attainment of wealth and leisure for the majority of Americans without such drastic measures.*

Source: *Independent,* July 18, 1901: "The Society of the Future."

If the goal toward which progress is tending is not socialism, what is it? It must be good or we shall not believe that we are moving toward it. Optimism is the faith of healthy humanity. Without making assertions as to anything that is very remote, we may say that certain changes are undoubtedly going on; that they are taking us in a certain direction and toward a nearer goal that we can define. We shall reach it if economic laws continue to work and the general course of events continues unchanged.

The term "goal," indeed, scarcely describes what is thus before us; for it designates a stopping place, whereas what is before us is a perpetual movement. The halting place of yesterday is the starting point of today, and that of today is to be the starting point of tomorrow. The state that we shall reach in two or, three centuries may contain within itself all the gains that we can now easily imagine; but it will only be the beginning of acquisitions that are beyond the range of our present imaginings. It is easier to define intermediate states. What will society be after fifty years shall have passed, and toward what state will it then be tending? To such a question as this economic movements afford a fairly confident answer.

In the first place, competition will survive. Trusts will not destroy it, and it may even become more effective than it has been. The race for the profits that are to be gained by invention, by chemical discovery, and by business organization will make the work of the world so efficient that its present power of production, great as it is, will, in the retrospect seem like rude first steps in material civilization. We shall improve agriculture and get our living more easily; but we shall make larger gains in producing comforts and luxuries. More and more readily will the earth yield raw materials, and more easily will industry fashion them into fine commodities.

We shall surround ourselves with a profusion of useful things, and so small will be the labor that many of them will cost that it will seem as if genii had a hand in bringing them to us. Machines will become more deft, powerful, rapid, and automatic. They will get their motive power from cheap and abundant sources, and there will be little left for the workers who use them except to touch the buttons that set them moving.

Dwellings and furnishings will improve and vehicles will multiply, till the amount of labor that is now the equivalent of a nickel will give a poor man a longer and more interesting drive than a costly equipage now gives a rich man. . . .

If this is to be the fact, however, it is necessary not only that an abundance of products should be created but that they should be created by and for the workers themselves. The distribution of wealth must be as satisfactory as the production of it is fruitful. It will be so if progress makes labor itself, and not merely industries in which labor is one agent, more and more productive. The empty-handed worker of the future, when he offers himself to an employer for hire, will carry in his hands a potential product for sale, and this product must be larger than the one that the worker of the present tenders. Improvements in method and in organization will enable him to do this.

When a man works with a long lever, the general result is larger than it is when he has a short one; but the important thing is that *that part of the result which is due to labor alone* is greater. A man and a modern machine create a larger product than did a man and an old-fashioned tool; but the essential fact is that what the man himself can claim as his own and actually get is larger than it was in the days of hand labor. When the world shall be filled, as it were, with "genii of the lamp," the man who can call them into action will be a more important factor than is the man of the present, and he can himself create more and get more than can the worker of today.

This means, however, that the struggles of classes that will go on will give them their fair portion of the rich results of industry. In the period that is coming massed forces are to contend with each other. Every occupation, as a whole, will contend with every other occupation; each business will want a high price for its particular product, and can get it only by taxing all who buy the product. Within each business there will be a further struggle, and massed labor will contend with massed capital in the effort to adjust wages. In each line of production both labor and capital will strive to become monopolistic. Capital will try to drive other capital off from its field, and labor will try to drive off other labor.

These attempts cannot fully accomplish their objects. Here and there consolidations of capital will have limited success and will make the position of competing capital perilous. Here and there, also, labor will have the same partial success in guarding its field against the intrusion of competing labor. The effect will be to favor some union laborers at the expense of others and to make the democracy of labor imperfect. Workers will be ranged in strata, representing gradations of well-being; but there is nothing in this that will prevent them all from rising together. They may keep their relative positions and all move upward.

This again requires that the principle of monopoly should everywhere be held in check. The influences that obstruct competition are themselves to be controlled, and if natural tendencies have their way they will be so. When a trust exacts too much, competitors will appear, in spite of all perils that may threaten them. When laborers in any occupation exact too large a premium over ordinary wages, workers will force themselves into their territory in spite of all that can be done to stop them. The imperfections of competition will put some workers into favored classes, but the competition which survives will be dominant and will bring gains to all classes.

That this may be true, the state at least must be democratic. Government by the people must not be allowed to vanish, and those who are ruled must nominate, elect, and control their rulers. If we keep the representative principle at all, as for convenience we must, it will have to be attended by an immense increase of actual self-government. I chance to believe that we are to have the referendum, or what amounts to the referendum, in municipal, state, and federal affairs. The difficulties in the way of this are not trifling, but they weigh far less than the evils that are in store for us if we do not have it.

At the bottom it is for the rescue of competitive industry that we need it. Very insidious is the power that massed capital knows how to use in controlling the so-called representatives of the people, who are often rather the conscienceless substitutes for the people in the work of ruling. Labor should be able to do better than to compete with wealth in this direction. It should have open and honest ways of influencing the acts of the government.

But shall we not, in this political sphere, have too much democracy? Clearly not, and that for several reasons, the chief of which is that the *demos* that will rule will not be the typical one that we think of in connection with the history of democratic states. It will not be a proletariat but will be a body of workmen, most of whom will have a large stake in the industrial order. Their savings will grow and make them conservative wherever the security of property is in question. Their wages will enable them to make accumulations, and the government of the future must be efficient enough to give them safe investments.

Land, under one or another form of title, now affords to laborers their principal medium of investment; and there is little doubt that for laborers, it will continue to be a favorite form of property. The confiscation of rent will not be popular with the coming democracy. Bonds and, in the end, even stocks must also be made available for a similar purpose. If tunnels and canals are dug by means of public funds, the bonds which states will issue will be available as far as they will go; but the society of the future will fall far short of what it ought to be unless the securities of corporations can be safely owned even by the poorer classes.

The world of the near future will not be one with inequalities leveled out of it; and to any person to whom inequality of possessions seems inherently evil, this world will not be satisfactory. It will present a condition of vast and ever growing inequality. With a democracy that depends on a likeness of material possessions, it will have nothing in common. The rich will continually grow richer and the multimillionaires will approach the billion-dollar standard; but the poor will be far from growing poorer. They will surely and not always slowly recede from the poverty line and rise toward the present standard of wealth. As the typical rich man enlarges his holdings — as his fortune increases from $1 million to $10 million, from $10 million to $100 million, and from $100 million to $1 billion — the typical laborer will increase his wages from $1 a day to $2, from $2 to $4, and from $4 to $8. Such gains will mean indefinitely more to him than any possible increase of capital can mean to the rich.

If an earthly Eden is to come through competition, it will come not in spite of but by means of an enormous increase of inequality of outward possessions; but this very change will bring with it a continual approach to equality of genuine comfort. The capitalist may become too rich to sleep, while the laborer becomes so relatively rich that he can live in comfort and rest in peace. Near to the line of maximum happiness may be the lives of the better-paid workers.

The most alluring possibility concerning the democracy of the future lies in the diffusion of culture. The well-paid worker may have any amount of it for himself and his children. No tendency of the present is more marked than that which is slowly obliterating the differences in education which formerly prevailed; and with higher pay and easier labor the worker can more and more avail himself of the new condition. Refinements as well as comforts are to be included in the list of cheap things that can be had as the reward of common labor.

There is a moral effect of progress that is even better. A fraternity of the highest type is among the gains that are well within sight, and, unlike fortunes, so far from perverting it, will bring it to perfection. Brotherly feeling is a weak thing indeed if the condition of its existence is that men shall be equally well-off. Communism does not develop the finer sort of brotherhood; but inequality may develop it if the moral fiber of the race shall grow strong. When men can regard each other with respect and affection in spite of enormous differences of wealth, there will be some virility in their fraternal feeling.

Well within sight is such a condition. As the prizes of political leadership and of social and intellectual eminence shall fall even more often to the man of labor than to the man of mere capital, it may be that very few persons will see in the change any vulgarization of state or society. The *demos* of the future will not win such prizes unless it continues to develop in intellect and character; and if it does so develop, this fact will give it a clear title to any outward prizes it may win. If out of the democracy that is defined by mere possessions there shall come an aristocracy of personal quality, the result will be the best that evolution can give or that imagination can picture.

84.

THOMAS HARDY: "On an Invitation to the United States"

Up to about 1900 the Englishman Thomas Hardy was best known as a novelist, but the failure of Jude the Obscure *(1896), his most thoughtful and original work in that genre but also his most somber, turned him against fiction and he devoted the rest of his life to poetry. In his poetry even more than in his novels he expressed his sense of the darkness and tragedy of all human life — a feeling that is reflected in the poem reprinted here. The response to an invitation to visit the United States was probably written in 1897 and first published in 1901. It is noteworthy that those characteristics of America that attracted many other Europeans — its brightness, newness, and optimism — were just the ones that made Hardy not want to go.*

Source: *Poems of the Past and the Present*, New York, 1901.

ON AN INVITATION TO THE UNITED STATES

My ardors for emprise nigh lost
Since Life has bared its bones to me,
I shrink to seek a modern coast
Whose riper times have yet to be;
Where the new regions claim them free
From that long drip of human tears
Which peoples old in tragedy
Have left upon the centuried years.

For, wonning in these ancient lands,
Enchased and lettered as a tomb,
And scored with prints of perished hands,
And chronicled with dates of doom,
Though my own being bear no bloom
I trace the lives such scenes enshrine,
Give past exemplars present room,
And their experience count as mine.

85.

The Padrone System

The relatively helpless condition — a new land, a different language, and strange customs — of the newly arrived immigrant made him a convenient object of exploitation, especially by employers looking for cheap labor. Among Italian immigrants, most of whom were men, the means of exploitation was the "padrone system" of contract labor, described below in a selection from 1901 reports of the U.S. Industrial Commission.

Source: *Reports of the Industrial Commission on Immigration and Education,* Vol. XV, Washington, 1901, pp. 430-436.

I.

History of Padrone System

In the period of industrial recovery following the Civil War, there was a pressing demand for labor. Special legislation was even invoked to aid in supplying this demand. Thus the act of 1864, for the encouragement of immigration, gave manufacturers and contractors the right to import foreign laborers under contract. Speculation in cheap labor ensued; agents were sent to foreign countries in search for workmen. The unenlightened peasants of Italy were the easiest victims of this speculation. Their coming, in fact, was not of their own accord, as was the case with the people of northern Europe, but they came usually under contract.

This difference between the Italian immigrant and the northern people, and the reason for their having been so easily exploited, is brought out by their illiteracy and ignorance of the English language.

The great bulk of Italian immigration has come from southern Italy, the provinces, Abruzzi, Avellino, Basilicata, Sicily, Calabria, and Naples. Almost the whole number from these provinces are of the peasant class, accustomed to hard work and meager fare. Their illiteracy is very high. In 1899 the illiteracy for all races of immigrants was 22.9 percent, while for the immigrants from southern Italy it was 57.3 percent, and for northern Italy the illiteracy was only 11.4 percent, showing clearly the contrast between this ignorant peasant class of unskilled laborers and the skilled workmen from the manufacturing centers of northern Italy. In 1900 the percentage of illiteracy for these immigrants was 54.5 in contrast to 24.2 for all races and 11.8 for the northern Italians.

This illiteracy is brought out by the investigation of the United States Department of Labor of the Italians in Chicago (*Ninth Special Report*, p. 383). Out of 4,553 persons ten years of age and over, 2,752, or 60.44 percent, were found to be illiterates. Among 2,812 males, 51.96 percent were illiterate; and of 1,741 females, 1,291 or 74.15 percent, were illiterate. As to the literacy itself of the 39.56 percent who were literate, only 18.21 percent could read and write English and Italian, while 54.80 percent could read and write Italian only. More than this, the literate males who could read and write Italian only were 60.55 percent of the literates, which shows how very unfavorably the Italians are situated when they enter industrial activities under American conditions.

The same investigation showed that of the number of persons of foreign birth and ten years of age and over, 58.62 percent were able to speak English and 47.38 percent were not able to speak English. . . .

Some form of contract was then necessary to induce these people to leave their country, for by temperament they were not the self-reliant people of the north who came of their own volition. The dread of change, the fear of coming to a strange and unknown land had to be counteracted by material inducements. It was thus that they came, not in search of work but under contract for several years, and thus were assured in advance of permanent work at what seemed to them high wages.

At this earliest stage in the Italian immigration the padrone was the agent of the contractor or manufacturer. Laborers were demanded, and he acted simply as the agent in supplying specific demands. The manufacturer or contractor was of another nationality, but in looking for cheap labor he had recourse to an Italian already in this country. This Italian, undertaking to supply the number of laborers called for, went or sent to Italy for the number, who entered upon a contract binding themselves to service for from one to three years, and in rare instances even for seven years. At the same time he furnished transportation and took care of them upon landing here until they were sent to the work for which they were contracted. It was thus that the padrone was merely a middleman, the man who stood between the contractor and the men. He was looked upon by the men as their representative, not as their employer, and upon him they depended.

Under this early system there were nu-

merous ways in which the padrone could make money. In the first place, he had a commission from the men as well as from the contractor for furnishing the men, and commission on their passage. Upon getting them here he had a profit from boarding them until they went to work. This was deducted from their prospective earnings. After that the padrone usually furnished food and shelter for them while at work. This privilege was usually given free by the contractor who furnished shelter and for which the padrone charged rent. Then there was also the commission from sending money back to Italy; and finally the commission on the return passage after the contract had been completed.

But the padrone par excellence was not an agent and did not act for the contractor. He acted primarily upon his own initiative and for himself. Instead of waiting for a call for men, he would upon his own responsibility engage Italians to come, and contract for their labor for a certain number of years. After having brought them here he would farm them out to anyone who wanted them. He boarded them, received their wages, and paid them what he saw fit. Sometimes a laborer would receive $40 a year and as often only $40 for two years. Under this system the padrone occasionally would buy outright a minor from his or her parents.

Men, women, and children were thus brought into the country, the boys to become bootblacks, newsboys, or strolling musicians. In this stage the padrone system most closely resembled the system as it existed in Italy, which meant in general the employment of children, or minors, in the "roving professions," such as strolling musicians, performers on the harp or hand organ, and street acrobats. These persons were under the direction of a master or padrone more or less inhuman, to whom belonged all the earnings of these persons.

This system flourished most widely during the decade 1870-1880, and under its influence Italian immigration was stimulated to such an extent that the flow soon equaled the demand. The sphere of the padrone then changed. His work of inducing immigration was no longer necessary; immigrants came without having previously made contracts, and governmental action was aimed at preventing the importation of contract labor. Under these two influences — the great increase in immigration and governmental opposition — the character of the padrone has changed.

As a result of this demand for laborers and the activities of the padroni the Italian immigrants have been largely males, and until recent years have not come by families, as have the other nationalities, notably the German and Scandinavian people. . . .

II.

Present Conditions

UNDER THESE CHANGED CONDITIONS it is probable that the padrone has very little to do with bringing Italians into the country, since it is no longer necessary to have a contract to bring them in, and because it is even unsafe according to federal statutes. The padrone is now nothing more than an employment agent, and exists only because of the immigrants and their illiteracy and ignorance of American institutions. He procures his subjects at the port, upon their landing, by promising them steady work at high wages. If the immigrant does not get under the control of the padrone by this means, the immigrant need only go to the colony of his race in any of the large cities, where he will readily be picked up by one of the padroni and promised employment.

By this means the newcomers are attached to the padrone, who is able to fulfill his promises, because he "stands in" with the contractors, he knows officials and bosses of the railroads, and he is thus in a way to furnish employment for his fellow countrymen who cannot speak English and have no other way of finding employment. It may then be said that the padrone system no longer exists, and that the successor to the padrone is an employment agency, which collects the labor only after it has already arrived in this country, and makes its profit through commissions and keeping boarders.

As Dr. Egisto Rossi, of the Italian Immigration Bureau, has summed up the situation, "The padrone system, or bossism, can be defined as the forced tribute which the newly arrived pays to those who are already acquainted with the ways and language of the country."

Though the character of the padrone is now that of an employment agent, it is undoubtedly true that no Italian has an employment agency license. But it is also true that in nine years there has never been a prosecution of an Italian for carrying on an employment agency without a license. His mode of operation is to go to the regular licensed agencies or to the contractors and furnish the men desired. The padrone also has no office of his own.

But the padrone does not employ the men alone and upon his own responsibility. He works together with the Italian banker, who is a somewhat more responsible party than the padrone; at least the men have more faith in him, because it is through him that they send money back to Italy, and with whom they keep their small savings. It is through the banker that the call is made for the number of men who are wanted, and it is in his office where the arrangements with the men are made. He may advance the money for transportation, and even the commission if the men do not have the money. The padrone takes charge of the men in the capacity of a boss, takes them to the place of work, runs the boardinghouse or shanty store at the place of work, and acts as interpreter for the contractor.

The padroni may be divided into several classes. The first class is the small boss who furnishes many odd jobs for individuals. The next class is the boss who regularly supplies contractors and others with laborers in large numbers. This is the largest class and really stands for the padrone as he at present exists. Finally, there are bosses who at the same time are independent contractors. But this is the exception, for the padrone, it may be said, is never a foreman and just as rarely an independent contractor. His work is to act as an interpreter for the foreman and run the boardinghouse or shanty store.

For furnishing employment he receives a commission from the laborer. This commission depends upon the (1) length of the period of employment; (2) the wages to be received; and (3) whether they board themselves. If they board themselves, the commission is higher and varies from $1 to $10 a head. For a job of five or six months the commission may even rise to $10. In some cases the wages are paid to the padrone, but this is only when the contractor is dishonest and receives a share from the padrone. But if the contractor is honest, he knows that the people are generally cheated, and so he pays the men direct, deducting, however, the board and other charges as shown by the padrone.

Under this system the padrone is in combination with the Italian banker, who furnishes the money to pay for transportation, for the erection of shanties when they are not provided by the contractor, and to buy provisions. All this money is then deducted from the earnings of the men. The profits derived from the venture are finally shared by the padrone with the banker, who, however, finds his chief source of gain in holding the savings of the laborers, sending their money to Italy, and changing the money from American to Italian, in which process great shrinkage usually takes place.

The padrone has a further hold upon these people as a result of irregular employment. During the winter there is almost no employment at all. This means that during the greater part of five months these people are without work. When work is plentiful, the laborer who boards with his boss is said to be fortunate if he can save more than one-half of his earnings. Some of these earnings are sent to Italy or frequently squandered, so that the laborer often finds himself in winter without resources of his own. In such cases he finds it convenient to go [to] the boardinghouse of the boss or banker, where he remains until spring, when it is understood that he shall enter the employ of the boss.

In New York there are large tenements owned by Italian bankers which serve as winter quarters for these laborers. Here the men are crowded together, a dozen or more in one room, under the worst sanitary conditions. It is frequently said that the padrone encourages the men in extravagance in order to have a firmer hold on their future earnings. The employment is even made irregular by the padrone, who furnishes employment for several weeks at a time and then keeps them idle, claiming that the work is not regular.

In the *Ninth Special Report* of the Commissioner of Labor on the condition of Italians in Chicago, it was found that 21.67 percent of persons of whom the question was asked answered that they worked for a padrone. Of this number, 5.96 percent reported that they paid no commission to the padrone for securing the job, while 94.04 percent reported that they paid a commission. It was found that an average of $4.84 per individual, of the number reporting, was paid for the last job at which they worked, and the average time worked on this job was eleven weeks and four days per individual. The average amount paid per week to padrones for employment was thus 42 cents.

The Immigration Investigation Commission of 1895 found that from 500 to 600 laborers employed on sewers and waterworks padroni had deducted from their wages 10 cents and 15 cents each day for procuring employment.

The padrone provides transportation for the men. But in the rates, he overcharges the men, charging for first-class transportation or regular ticket rates, and securing greatly reduced rates because of the large number. If the work is some distance from the city, the padrone often boards the men, and usually buys the privilege from the contractor at a fixed rate per head per month. In some cases the privilege is given by the contractor free, because the padrone saves him trouble in employing men, and is convenient to have around in managing the men. But usually the contractor sells the privilege of furnishing the laborers with board and lodging and wearing apparel, the cost of which is generally deducted from their wages. In consideration of the many advantages which the padroni have in this transaction, they generally have to pay pretty high prices for the privilege, which naturally comes out of the pockets of the immigrants.

If the men board themselves, their food must be bought at the shanty store, which is operated by the padrone. Notices are posted to this effect, and fines are imposed for disobedience. Even dismissal is often the penalty. Occasionally, a fixed daily amount of purchases is required by the padrone, but usually the men are allowed to spend at their pleasure, but only at the padrone store. For example, in 1894, Italian laborers were shipped from New York to Brunswick, Ga., for work on a sewerage contract.

Each man paid the padrone $1 for finding the employment. The passage money, $7 per head, was paid by the banker with the understanding that this was to be deducted from their wages. The agent of the banker paid $25 a month rent for ten huts, but charged each laborer $1 a month, which for 215 men was $215 a month. All supplies had to be bought at the shanty store, the penalty for disobedience being a fine of $5. . . .

Besides the profit from supplying food to the men, the padrone charges from $1 to $3 a head for the shanties in which the men sleep. These shanties are often furnished without charge by the contractor, but the padrone nevertheless charges the men a rent to pay for his boarding privilege. Sometimes he even charges regular fees for medical service, though a regular physician is called in only in very serious cases.

As to the wages, it is seldom in Eastern states that only $1.25 per day is paid, though in 1894, 1895, and 1897 wages were $1, with very little work to be had even at that price. At present they vary from $1.35 to $1.75 per day. In the investigation of the Department of Labor (*Ninth Annual Report, Italians in Chicago*) it was shown that the average weekly earnings for Italian males were $6.41, and the average hours of work per week were 59.4. The highest average weekly wage was $8.25½ in manufactures and mechanical industries, and the next highest was $7.64½ in agriculture, fisheries, and mining.

But this throws no direct light upon the wages or earnings received under the padrone. Under the earlier padrone system, the padrone would import laborers under contract for 75 cents per day for two years' work. But the padrone could get $1.25 per day from railroads and contractors, and this difference would go to him. At present he is only an employment agent, and the wages are usually paid direct to the men, though only after the deductions have been made in favor of the padrone.

In the investigation of the New York Bureau of Labor Statistics into the alien labor employed on state contract work on the Erie Canal (*Report* 1898, p. 1153) it is stated that there were 15,000 common laborers employed, of whom 1,000 were American citizens, 13,500 were Italian aliens, 350 Poles, and 150 Hungarians. The highest wages paid these laborers was $1.75, and the lowest $1.20 per day. Of this number 600, or 4 percent, received $1.20; 4,420, or 30 percent, received $1.25; and 9,794, or 65 percent, received $1.50, which shows that the rate for this labor, of which Italian aliens made up 90 percent, was from $1.20 to $1.50 per day.

As to the amount of employment, the investigation of the Commissioner of United States Department of Labor (*Ninth Special Report, Italians in Chicago*) shows that, out of 2,663 persons employed in remunerative occupations, 1,517, or 56.97 percent, were unemployed some part of the year. The average time unemployed for these 1,517 persons was 7.1 months; for the 109 females in the number it was 6:4 months; and for the 1,408 males, 7.2 months.

The nominally small earnings of these people thus become really very small when it is kept in mind that they are unemployed on an average from five to seven months during the year, and must live during this time on the small savings which they may perhaps have been able to put aside from their earnings.

As to the kind of labor, it may be said that the padrone undertakes to furnish only unskilled labor in the large cities, though the Immigration Investigation Commission of 1895 reported (p. 27 of the report) "that padroni in New York not only guarantee to supply unskilled labor for sewer, railroad, and waterworks construction, but also skilled labor for building trades, and will, furthermore, arrange for their transportation

to a remote point if a small percentage of the passage money is advanced or guaranteed." But in the country and small towns the padroni stand ready to furnish skilled workmen, masons, carpenters, stonecutters, and machinists.

Occasionally, Italians are employed through padroni in the endeavor to break a strike. For example, in the lockout in 1892-93 of the granite cutters, Mr. Duncan testified before the Commission that Italians were employed to take the places of the union men. But he said that they were inefficient and had to drift out of the work because of the minimum wage rate established by the union and the desire of the employer to have only the most profitable men. The general secretary-treasurer of the Granite Cutters' National Union describes a padrone system in New York City which was prepared to supply men to employers in the granite-cutting trade. The union has an eight-hour day with $4 in New York. The padrone gathers the Italians, who comply with the state law by declaring their intentions for citizenship.

These men pay the padrone $12 commission, $6 remaining on deposit as a guaranty that at the end of the week the man supplied with work shall return $6 to the padrone; if not, his employment ceases. These $6 per man per week are paid by the padrone to the contractor, who has thus employed men at $3 under a $4 law in New York, which provides that mechanics employed in the state upon municipal, county, or state work shall be paid the prevailing rate of wages and work the prevailing hours. This is one of the very rare instances where skilled labor is furnished in New York by the padrone system, and it cannot be taken as representative of the system.

The Italian immigrant, however, does not always limit himself to becoming a common laborer on railroad work and other excavations, but often becomes an artisan. Insofar as he becomes an artisan he comes in conflict with American workmen, but the conflict is less sharp than formerly, because the American unions are organizing Italian labor. The Italians themselves are coming to understand the importance of organized labor. This is noticeable especially among the Italian hod carriers, masons, and stonecutters; and where this feeling and sense of organization has developed there is no opportunity for the padrone system.

86.

Frank Lloyd Wright: Art and the Machine

American architects have more often looked backward than forward. Around 1900 architecture and the decorative and industrial arts were especially imitative and derivative; most universities were built in the Gothic style, and public buildings tended to be built either in the colonial or the classical style. Frank Lloyd Wright pleaded for more originality, more verve, more ideas. He urged his fellow architects to make use of the new materials and techniques of the time, and to build buildings that were useful rather than spuriously beautiful. Above all, he asked that buildings fit their environment; a Gothic tower in the midst of a prairie seemed to him almost a monstrosity. Reprinted here is Wright's famous lecture given at Hull House, in Chicago, in 1901, before the Chicago Arts and Crafts Society.

Source: *Catalogue of the Fourteenth Annual Exhibition of the Chicago Architectural Club*, Chicago, 1901.

As we work along our various ways, there takes shape within us, in some sort, an ideal — something we are to become, some work to be done. This, I think, is denied to very few, and we begin really to live only when the thrill of this ideality moves us in what we will to accomplish.

In the years which have been devoted in my own life to working out in stubborn materials a feeling for the beautiful, in the vortex of distorted complex conditions, a hope has grown stronger with the experience of each year, amounting now to a gradually deepening conviction that in the machine lies the only future of art and craft, as I believe, a glorious future; that the machine is, in fact, the metamorphosis of ancient art and craft; that we are at last face to face with the machine — the modern Sphinx — whose riddle the artist must solve if he would that art live — for his nature holds the key. For one, I promise "whatever gods may be" to lend such energy and purpose as I may possess to help make that meaning plain; to return again and again to the task whenever and wherever need be; for this plain duty is thus relentlessly marked out for the artist in this, the Machine Age, although there is involved an adjustment to cherished gods, perplexing and painful in the extreme; the fire of many long-honored ideals shall go down to ashes to reappear, phoenixlike, with new purposes.

The great ethics of the machine are as yet, in the main, beyond the ken of the artist or student of sociology; but the artist mind may now approach the nature of this thing from experience, which has become the commonplace of his field, to suggest, in time, I hope, to prove, that the machine is capable of carrying to fruition high ideals in art — higher than the world has yet seen!

Disciples of William Morris cling to an opposite view. Yet William Morris himself deeply sensed the danger to art of the transforming force whose sign and symbol is the machine, and though of the new art we eagerly seek he sometimes despaired, he quickly renewed his hope.

He plainly foresaw that a blank in the fine arts would follow the inevitable abuse of new-found power and threw himself body and soul into the work of bridging it over by bringing into our lives afresh the beauty of art as she had been, that the new art to come might not have dropped too many stitches nor have unraveled what would still be useful to her.

That he had abundant faith in the new art his every essay will testify. That he miscalculated the machine does not matter. He did sublime work for it when he pleaded so well for the process of elimination its abuse had made necessary; when he fought the innate vulgarity of theocratic impulse in art as opposed to democratic; and when he preached the gospel of simplicity.

All artists love and honor William Morris. He did the best in his time for art and will live in history as the great socialist, together with Ruskin, the great moralist: a significant fact worth thinking about, that the two great reformers of modern times professed the artist.

The machine these reformers protested, because the sort of luxury which is born of greed had usurped it and made of it a terrible engine of enslavement, deluging the civilized world with a murderous ubiquity, which plainly enough was the damnation of their art and craft. It had not then advanced to the point which now so plainly indicates that it will surely and swiftly, by its own momentum, undo the mischief it has made, and the usurping vulgarians as well. Nor was it so grown as to become apparent to William Morris, the grand democrat, that the machine was the great forerunner of democracy.

The ground plan of this thing is now grown to the point where the artist must take it up no longer as a protest: genius must progressively dominate the work of the contrivance it has created; to lend a useful hand in building afresh the "fairness of the earth."

That the machine has dealt art in the grand old sense a deathblow, none will deny. The evidence is too substantial.

Art in the grand old sense — meaning art in the sense of structural tradition, whose craft is fashioned upon the handicraft ideal, ancient or modern; an art wherein this form and that form as structural parts were laboriously joined in such a way as to beautifully emphasize the manner of the joining: the million and one ways of beautifully satisfying bare structural necessities, which have come down to us chiefly through the books as "art."

For the purpose of suggesting hastily and therefore crudely wherein the machine has sapped the vitality of this art, let us assume architecture in the old sense as a fitting representative of traditional art, and printing as a fitting representation of the machine. What printing — the machine — has done for architecture — the fine art — will have been done in measure of time for all art immediately fashioned upon the early handicraft ideal. With a masterful hand Victor Hugo, a noble lover and a great student of architecture, traces her fall in *Notre Dame*. The prophecy of Frollo, that "the book will kill the edifice," I remember was to me as a boy one of the grandest sad things of the world.

After seeking the origin and tracing the growth of architecture in superb fashion, showing how in the Middle Ages all the intellectual forces of the people converged to one point — architecture — he shows how, in the life of that time, whoever was born poet became an architect. All other arts simply obeyed and placed themselves under the discipline of architecture. They were the workmen of the great work. The architect, the poet, the master, summed up in his person the sculpture that carved his facades, painting which illuminated his walls and windows, music which set his bells to pealing and breathed into his organs — there was nothing which was not forced in order to make something of itself in that time, to come and frame itself in the edifice.

Thus, down to the time of Gutenberg, architecture is the principal writing — the universal writing of humanity. In the great granite books begun by the Orient, continued by Greek and Roman antiquity, the Middle Ages wrote the last page. So to enunciate here only summarily a process, it would require volumes to develop; down to the 15th century the chief register of humanity is architecture. In the 15th century everything changes. Human thought discovers a mode of perpetuating itself, not only more resisting than architecture but still more simple and easy. Architecture is dethroned. Gutenberg's letters of lead are about to supersede Orpheus' letters of stone. The book is about to kill the edifice.

The invention of printing was the greatest event in history. It was the first great machine, after the great city. It is human thought stripping off one form and donning another. Printed, thought is more imperishable than ever — it is volatile, indestructible. As architecture, it was solid; it is now alive; it passes from duration in point of time to immortality.

Cut the primitive bed of a river abruptly, with a canal hollowed out beneath its level, and the river will desert its bed. See how architecture now withers away, how little by little it becomes lifeless and bare; how

one feels the water sinking, the sap departing, the thought of the times and people withdrawing from it. The chill is almost imperceptible in the 15th century, the press is yet weak, and at most draws from architecture a superabundance of life; but with the beginning of the 16th century, the malady of architecture is visible. It becomes classic art in a miserable manner; from being indigenous, it becomes Greek and Roman; from being true and modern, it becomes pseudo-classic.

It is this decadence which we call the Renaissance. It is the setting sun which we mistake for dawn. It has now no power to hold the other arts; so they emancipate themselves, break the yoke of the architect, and take themselves off, each in its own direction. One would liken it to an empire dismembered at the death of its Alexander and whose provinces become kingdoms.

Sculpture becomes statuary, the image trade becomes painting, the canon becomes music. Hence Raphael, Angelo, and those splendors of the dazzling 16th century.

Nevertheless, when the sun of the Middle Ages is completely set, architecture grows dim, becomes more and more effaced. The printed book, the gnawing worm of the edifice, sucks and devours it. It is petty, it is poor, it is nothing. Reduced to itself, abandoned by other arts because human thought is abandoning it, it summons bunglers in place of artists. It is miserably perishing.

Meanwhile, what becomes of printing? All the life, leaving architecture, comes to it. In proportion as architecture ebbs and flows, printing swells and grows. That capital of forces which human thought had been expending in building is hereafter to be expended in books; and architecture, as it was, is dead — irretrievably slain by the printed book; slain because it endures for a shorter time; slain because human thought has found a more simple medium of expression which costs less in human effort; because human thought has been rendered volatile and indestructible, reaching uniformly and irresistibly the four corners of the earth and for all.

Thenceforth, if architecture rise again, reconstruct, as Hugo prophesies she may begin to do in the latter days of the 19th century, she will no longer be mistress, she will be one of the arts, never again *the* art; and printing — the machine — remains the second Tower of Babel of the human race.

So the organic process, of which the majestic decline of architecture is only one case in point, has steadily gone on down to the present time, and still goes on, weakening the hold of the artist upon the people, drawing off from his rank poets and scientists, until architecture is but a little, poor knowledge of archaeology; and the average of art is reduced to the gasping poverty of imitative realism; until the whole letter of tradition, the vast fabric of precedent, in the flesh, which has increasingly confused the art ideal while the machine has been growing to power, is a beautiful corpse from which the spirit has flown. The spirit that has flown is the spirit of the new art, but has failed the modern artist, for he has lost it for hundreds of years in his lust for the *letter,* the beautiful body of art made too available by the machine.

So the artist craft wanes. Craft that will not see that human thought is stripping off one form and donning another, and artists are everywhere, whether catering to the leisure class of old England or ground beneath the heel of commercial abuse here in the great West, the unwilling symptoms of the inevitable, organic nature of the machine, they combat, the hell-smoke of the factories they scorn to understand.

And, invincible, triumphant, the machine goes on, gathering force and knitting the material necessities of mankind ever closer into a universal automatic fabric — the engine, the motor, and the battleship — the works of art of the century!

The machine is intellect mastering the drudgery of earth that the plastic art may live; that the margin of leisure and strength by which man's life upon the earth can be made beautiful, may immeasurably widen — its function ultimately to emancipate human expression! It is a universal educator, surely raising the level of human intelligence, so carrying within itself the power to destroy, by its own momentum, the greed which in Morris' time and still in our own time turns it to a deadly engine of enslavement. The only comfort left the poor artist, sidetracked as he is, seemingly is a mean one; the thought that the very selfishness which man's early art idealized, now reduced to its lowest terms, is swiftly and surely destroying itself through the medium of the machine.

The artist's present plight is a sad one; but may he truthfully say that society is less well-off because architecture, or even art, as it was, is dead, and printing, or the machine, lives? Every age has done its work, produced its art with the best tools or contrivances it knew, the tools most successful in saving the most precious thing in the world — human effort. Greece used the chattel slave as the essential tool of its art and civilization. This tool we have discarded, and we would refuse the return of Greek art upon the terms of its restoration because we insist now upon a basis of democracy.

Is it not more likely that the medium of artistic expression itself has broadened and changed, until a new definition and new direction must be given the art activity of the future, and that the machine has finally made for the artist, whether he will yet own it or not, a splendid distinction between the art of old and the art to come? A distinction made by the tool which frees human labor, lengthens and broadens the life of the simplest man, thereby the basis of the democracy upon which we insist.

To shed some light upon this distinction, let us take an instance in the field naturally ripened first by the machine — the commercial field.

The tall modern office building is the machine, pure and simple. We may here sense an advanced stage of a condition surely entering all art for all time; its already triumphant glare in the deadly struggle taking place here between the machine and the art of structural tradition reveals "art" torn and hung upon the steel frame of commerce, a forlorn head upon a pike, a solemn warning to architects and artists the world over.

We must walk blindfolded not to see that all that this magnificent resource of machine and material has brought us so far is a complete, broadcast degradation of every type and form sacred to the art of old; a pandemonium of tin masks, huddled deformities, and decayed methods; quarreling, lying, and cheating, with hands at each other's throats — or in each other's pockets; and none of the people who do these things, who pay for them or use them know what they mean, feeling only — when they feel at all — that what is most truly like the past is the safest and therefore the best; as typical Marshall Field, speaking of his new building, has frankly said: "A good copy is the best we can do."

A pitiful insult, art and craft!

With this mine of industrial wealth at our feet, we have no power to use it except to the perversion of our natural resources? A confession of shame which the merciful ignorance of the yet material frame of things mistakes for glorious achievement.

We half believe in our artistic greatness ourselves when we toss up a pantheon to the god of money in a night or two, or pile up a mammoth aggregation of Roman monuments, sarcophagi, and Greek temples for a post office in a year or two — the patient retinue of the machine pitching in with terrible effectiveness to consummate this unhallowed ambition — this insult to ancient gods. The delicate, impressionable

facilities of terra-cotta becoming imitative blocks and voussoirs of tool-marked stone, badgered into all manner of structural gymnastics, or else ignored in vain endeavor to be honest; and granite blocks, cut in the fashion of the followers of Phidias, cunningly arranged about the steel beams and shafts to look "real" — leaning heavily upon an inner skeleton of steel for support from floor to floor, which strains beneath the "reality" and would fain, I think, lie down to die of shame. The "masters" — ergo, the fashionable followers of Phidias — have been trying to make this wily skeleton of steel seem seventeen sorts of "architecture" at once, when all the world knows — except the "masters" — that it is not one of them.

See, now, how an element — the vanguard of the new art — has entered here, which the structural-art equation cannot satisfy without downright lying and ignoble cheating. This element is the structural necessity reduced to a skeleton, complete in itself without the craftsman's touch. At once the million and one little ways of satisfying this necessity beautifully, coming to us chiefly through the books as the traditional art of building, vanish away — become history.

The artist is emancipated to work his will with a rational freedom unknown to the laborious art of structural tradition — no longer tied to the meager unit of brick arch and stone lintel, nor hampered by the grammatical phrase of their making — but he cannot use his freedom. His tradition cannot think. He will not think. His scientific brother has put it to him before he is ready.

The modern, tall office-building problem is one representative problem of the machine. The only rational solutions it has received in the world may be counted upon the fingers of one hand. The fact that a great portion of our "architects" and "artists" are shocked by them to the point of offense is as valid an objection as that of a child refusing wholesome food because his stomach becomes dyspeptic from overmuch unwholesome pastry — albeit he be the cook himself.

We may object to the mannerism of these buildings, but we can take no exception to their manner nor hide from their evident truth. The steel frame has been recognized as a legitimate basis for a simple, sincere clothing of plastic material that idealizes its purpose without structural pretense. This principle has at last been recognized in architecture, and though the masters refuse to accept it as architecture at all, it is a glimmer in a darkened field — the first sane word that has been said in art for the machine.

The art of old idealized a structural necessity — now rendered obsolete and unnatural by the machine — and accomplished it through man's joy in the labor of his hands. The new will weave for the necessities of mankind, which his machine will have mastered, a robe of ideality no less truthful, but more poetical, with a rational freedom made possible by the machine, beside which the art of old will be as the sweet, plaintive wail of the pipe to the outpouring of full orchestra.

It will clothe necessity with the living flesh of virile imagination, as the living flesh lends living grace to the hard and bony human skeleton. The new will pass from the possession of kings and classes to the everyday lives of all — from duration in point of time to immortality. . . .

Now, let us ask ourselves whether the fear of the higher artistic expression demanded by the machine, so thoroughly grounded in the arts and crafts, is founded upon a finely guarded reticence, a recognition of inherent weakness, or plain ignorance? Let us, to be just, assume that it is equal parts of all three, and try to imagine an arts and crafts society that may educate itself to prepare to make some good impression upon the machine — the destroyer

of their present ideals and tendencies, their salvation in disguise.

Such a society will, of course, be a society for mutual education. Exhibitions will not be a feature of its program for years, for there will be nothing to exhibit except the shortcomings of the society, and they will hardly prove either instructive or amusing at this stage of proceedings. This society must, from the very nature of the proposition, be made up of the people who are in the work — that is, the manufacturers — coming into touch with such of those who assume the practice of the fine arts as profess a fair sense of the obligation to the public such assumption carries with it, and sociological workers whose interests are ever closely allied with art. . . .

Without the interest and cooperation of the manufacturers, the society cannot begin to do its work, for this is the cornerstone of its organization. All these elements should be brought together on a common ground of confessed ignorance, with a desire to be instructed, freely encouraging talk and opinion, and reaching out desperately for anyone who has special experience in anyway connected to address them.

I suppose, first of all, the thing would resemble a debating society, or something even less dignified, until someone should suggest that it was time to quit talking and proceed to do something, which in this case would not mean giving an exhibition but rather excursions to factories and a study of processes in place — that is, the machine in processes too numerous to mention, at the factories with the men who organize and direct them, but not in the spirit of the idea that these things are all gone wrong, looking for that in them which would most nearly approximate the handicraft ideal; not looking into them with even the thought of handicraft, and not particularly looking for craftsmen, but getting a scientific ground plan of the process in mind, if possible, with a view to its natural bent and possibilities.

Some processes and machines would naturally appeal to some, and some to others; there would undoubtedly be among us those who would find little joy in any of them. This is, naturally, not child's play, but neither is the work expected of the modern artist.

I will venture to say, from personal observation and some experience, that not one artist in one hundred has taken pains to thus educate himself. I will go further and say what I believe to be true, that not one educational institution in America has as yet attempted to forge the connecting link between science and art by training the artist to his actual tools, or, by a process of nature study that develops in him the power of independent thought, fitting him to use them properly.

Let us call these preliminaries, then, a process by which artists receive information nine-tenths of them lack concerning the tools they have to work with today — for tools today are processes and machines where they were once a hammer and a gouge. The artist today is the leader of an orchestra, where he once was a star performer.

Once the manufacturers are convinced of due respect and appreciation on the part of the artist, they will welcome him and his counsel gladly and make any experiments having a grain of apparent sense in them. They have little patience with a bothering about in endeavor to see what might be done to make their particular machine medieval and restore man's joy in the mere work of his hands — for this once lovely attribute is far behind.

This proceeding doubtless would be of far more educational value to the artist than to the manufacturer, at least for some time to come, for there would be a difficult adjustment to make on the part of the artist and an attitude to change. So many artists are chiefly "attitude" that some would undoubtedly disappear with the attitude.

But if out of twenty determined students

a ray of light should come to one, to light up a single operation, it would have been worthwhile, for that would be fairly something; while joy in mere handicraft is like that of the man who played the piano for his own amusement — a pleasurable personal accomplishment without real relation to the grim condition confronting us. . . .

Upon this faith in art as the organic heart quality of the scientific frame of things, I base a belief that we must look to the artist brain, of all brains, to grasp the significance to society of this thing we call the machine, if that brain be not blinded, gagged, and bound by false tradition, the letter of precedent. For this thing we call art, is it not as prophetic as a primrose or an oak, therefore, of the essence of this thing we call the machine, which is no more or less than the principle of organic growth working irresistibly the will of life through the medium of man?

Be gently lifted at nightfall to the top of a great downtown office building, and you may see how, in the image of material man, at once his glory and menace, is this thing we call a city. There beneath, grown up in a night, is the monster leviathan, stretching acre upon acre into the far distance. High overhead hangs the stagnant pall of its fetid breath, reddened with the light from its myriad eyes endlessly everywhere blinking. Ten thousand acres of cellular tissue, layer upon layer, the city's flesh, outspreads enmeshed by intricate network of veins and arteries, radiating into the gloom, and there, with muffled, persistent roar, pulses and circulates as the blood in your veins, the ceaseless beat of the activity to whose necessities it all conforms.

Like to the sanitation of the human body is the drawing off of poisonous waste from the system of this enormous creature; absorbed first by the infinitely ramifying, threadlike ducts gathering at their sensitive terminals matter destructive to its life, hurrying it to millions of small intestines, to be collected in turn by larger, flowing to the great sewer, on to the drainage canal, and finally to the ocean.

This 10,000 acres of fleshlike tissue is again knit and interknit with a nervous system marvelously complete, delicate filaments for hearing, knowing, almost feeling the pulse of its organism, acting upon the ligaments and tendons for motive impulse, in all flowing the impelling fluid of man's own life.

Its nerve ganglia! — the peerless Corliss tandems whirling their hundred-ton flywheels, fed by gigantic rows of water-tube boilers burning oil, a solitary man slowly pacing backward and forward, regulating here and there the little feed valves controlling the deafening roar of the flaming gas, while beyond, the incessant clicking, dropping, waiting — lifting, waiting, shifting of the governor gear controlling these modern Goliaths seems a visible brain in intelligent action, registered infallibly in the enormous magnets, purring in the giant embrace of great induction coils, generating the vital current meeting with instant response in the rolling cars on elevated tracks ten miles away, where the glare of the Bessemer steel converter makes a conflagration of the clouds.

More quietly still, whispering down the long, low rooms of factory buildings buried in the gloom beyond, range on range of stanch, beautifully perfected automatons, murmur contentedly with occasional click-clack, that would have the American manufacturing industry of five years ago by the throat today; manipulating steel as delicately as a mystical shuttle of the modern loom manipulates a silk thread in the shimmering pattern of a dainty gown.

And the heavy breathing, the murmuring, the clangor, and the roar! — how the voice of this monstrous thing, this greatest of machines, a great city, rises to proclaim the marvel of the units of its structure, the ghastly warning boom from the deep throats of vessels heavily seeking inlet to the waterway below, answered by the echoing clangor of the bridge bells growing nearer and more ominous as the vessel cuts momentarily the flow of the nearer artery, warning the current from the swinging bridge now closing on its stately passage, just in time to receive in a rush of steam, as a streak of light, the avalanche of blood and metal hurled across it and gone, roaring into the night on its glittering bands of steel, ever faithfully encircled by the slender magic lines tick-tapping its invincible protection.

Nearer, in the building ablaze with midnight activity, the wide white band streams into the marvel of the multiple press, receiving unerringly the indelible impression of the human hopes, joys, and fears throbbing in the pulse of this great activity, as infallibly as the gray matter of the human brain receives the impression of the senses, to come forth millions of neatly folded, perfected news sheets, teeming with vivid appeals to passions, good or evil; weaving a web of intercommunication so far-reaching that distance becomes as nothing, the thought of one man in one corner of the earth one day visible to the naked eye of all men the next; the doings of all the world reflected as in a glass, so marvelously sensitive this wide white band streaming endlessly from day to day becomes in the grasp of the multiple press.

If the pulse of activity in this great city, to which the tremor of the mammoth skeleton beneath our feet is but an awe-inspiring response, is thrilling, what of this prolific, silent obedience?

And the texture of the tissue of this great thing, this forerunner of democracy — the machine — has been deposited particle by particle, in blind obedience to organic law, the law to which the great solar universe is but an obedient machine.

Thus is the thing into which the forces of art are to breathe the thrill of ideality! A SOUL!

87.

Alexander Dowling: The Constitutionality of a Compulsory School Law

Between 1852 and 1918 all the states passed some kind of compulsory school attendance laws. But their effectiveness was often curtailed by the increasing use of child labor, the lack of public support for schools, and sometimes by parents who felt their rights were being invaded. The idea that the state had the right and the obligation to see to the education of youth had not gained unquestioned public acceptance even by the early years of the twentieth century. During the 1890s Indiana passed two compulsory attendance laws that were challenged in the courts in 1901. The following selection is taken from the decision of Judge Dowling in the Indiana Supreme Court, upholding the constitutionality of the laws.

Source: 157 Indiana 324.

Judge Dowling. The appellee was charged upon affidavit before a justice of the peace with having neglected, omitted and, refused to send his child, Vory Bailey, to school in violation of the provisions of the Compulsory Education Law of this state, of March 8, 1897 (Acts 1897, p. 248), as amended by the act of March 6, 1899 (Acts 1899, p. 547). He was convicted before the justice, and, upon an appeal from that judgment to the Circuit Court, the affidavit was quashed. The state appeals.

The constitutionality of the act of March 6, 1899, is assailed by the appellee upon the following grounds: (1) because it is in conflict with §19, Article 4, of the constitution of Indiana; (2) because it is in conflict with §21, Article 4, of the constitution; (3) because it invades the natural right of man to govern and control his own children.

The additional point is made by counsel for the appellee that the facts stated in the affidavit are not sufficient to constitute a public offense.

The title of the act of March 6, 1899, is, "An act entitled an act amending an act concerning the education of children, approved March 8, 1897, and declaring an emergency." It is contended that this title does not conform to that provision of the Constitution which prescribes that every act shall embrace but one subject and matters properly connected therewith, and that such subject shall be expressed in the title. It is also objected that the title of the act is so vague and uncertain as to render it nugatory. It is said that the subject of the act is declared to be the education of children, but that the provisions of the statute relate to subjects of an entirely different nature, such as the duties of parents and guardians concerning the attendance of children at school, the creation of an office, the appointment of a truant officer, and the definition of a misdemeanor.

The law of the case seems to be well settled by the decisions of this court. Such a title as "An act to promote the general welfare of the state"; or "An act to promote good morals," would give no indication of the character of the subject of the statute and, therefore, would fail to meet the requirement that the subject of the act must be expressed in the title. . . .

But the title, "An act concerning drainage," properly embraces legislation authorizing the appointment of a board of drainage commissioners. It is sufficient also to include provisions for the making and collecting of assessments upon the lands benefited by the work, and the recovery of attorney's fees. . . .

The title, "An act to regulate the sale of intoxicating liquors," was held a sufficient expression of the subject of the act, and to authorize provisions prohibiting the sale of liquor, and imposing penalties for violation of the statute. . . . "An act defining felonies, and prescribing punishment therefor," and "An act defining certain felonies, and prescribing punishment therefor," were held sufficiently certain to embrace all felonies mentioned in them with the punishments for the same. . . .

The title of a statute was: "An act to provide for the incorporation of railroad companies"; held a sufficient statement of the subject to embrace a provision for the individual liability of the stockholders. . . .

Bright v. *McCullough*, 27 Ind. 223, contains a luminous and forcible explanation of the meaning of §19 of Article 4 of the constitution:

> The constitution does not assume to divide the general scope of legislation and classify the parts under particular heads or subjects, but, of necessity, has left that power to be exercised by the legislature, as it, in its wisdom and discretion, shall deem proper. The constitution assumes that different subjects of legislation do exist and requires that each act shall embrace but one subject and matters properly connected therewith, which subject shall be expressed in the title.
>
> The purposes of the provision, in view

of the evils intended to be guarded against, can only be effected by requiring that the subject expressed should be reasonably specific, or, in other words, should be such as to indicate some particular branch of legislation, as a head under which the particular provisions of the act might reasonably be looked for. With this restriction, the subject of an act may be enlarged or restricted at the will of the legislature, and the subject must be determined by reference to the language used in the title.

It sometimes occurs that the draftsman, intending to provide a title sufficiently comprehensive to cover various provisions, all, however, relating to a common subject, instead of selecting a subject which is sufficiently comprehensive to embrace all the provisions of the act and expressing it in general terms, attempts to accomplish the desired object by stating in the title, in detail, the character or purpose of the various provisions of sections, thereby often limiting the subject expressed to the particular matters thus specified. But it should be borne in mind that the constitution only requires that a proper subject of legislation should be expressed in the title, and not the particular features or details of the law.

If these relate to the subject expressed, it satisfies the constitutional provisions. The words, "An act concerning highways," would express but a single subject, and yet would constitute a comprehensive title, under which almost any desired provision relating to highways might be enacted, and every effort to express in the title the details of the act would only tend to limit the subject. . . .

We think the title of the statute in question specific enough to guard against the evils intended to be prevented by the constitution. It sufficiently indicates "some particular branch of legislation as a head under which the particular provisions of the act might reasonably be looked for." The subject of the act, as expressed in the title, is "the education of children." Is this any less specific than "drainage" or "highways"? Is it not as definite as "to regulate the sale of intoxicating liquors" or "to provide for the organization of railroad companies"? Yet, each of these has been held a sufficient statement of the subject of the act to which it applied.

The validity of the act of March 6, 1899, is denied, also, because of its supposed conflict with § 21 of Article 4 of the constitution upon the ground that its title does not refer to the title of the act of March 8, 1897, which it purports to amend. The grammatical construction of the title is awkward and inaccurate, but it indicates with sufficient precision that the act of 1899 is an amendment of "An Act Concerning the Education of Children," which was the full title of the act of March 8, 1897. And the statute amended is further identified by reference to the date of its approval.

The rule in such cases is that an act of the legislature is not to be held void because of trivial and unimportant defects in its title. If any reference to the title of the act amended was necessary — as was held in *Feibleman* v. *State*, 98 Ind. 516 — this requirement was sufficiently complied with in the title of the amendatory act of 1899.

The next question presented is whether the statute is an unauthorized invasion of the natural rights of the appellee as a parent.

The natural rights of a parent to the custody and control of his infant child are subordinate to the power of the state and may be restricted and regulated by municipal laws. One of the most important natural duties of the parent is his obligation to educate his child, and this duty he owes not to the child only but to the Commonwealth. If he neglects to perform it, or wilfully refuses to do so, he may be coerced by law to execute such civil obligation. The welfare of the child and the best interests of society require that the state shall exert its sovereign authority to secure to the child the opportunity to acquire an education. Statutes making it compulsory upon the parent, guardian, or other person having the custody and control of children to send them to public or private schools for longer or shorter periods, during certain years of the life of such children, have not only been upheld as strictly within the constitutional power of the legislature but have generally been regarded as necessary to carry out the express purposes of the constitution itself. . . .

To carry out the enlightened and comprehensive system of education enjoined by the constitution of this state, a vast fund, dedicated exclusively to this purpose, has been set apart. Revenues to the amount of more than $2 million annually are distributed among the school corporations of the state. No parent can be said to have the right to deprive his child of the advantages so provided and to defeat the purpose of such munificent appropriations.

In the last place, it is objected that the affidavit is insufficient because it does not allege that the appellee "unlawfully" neglected, etc., to send his child to school. The facts averred sufficiently show that the act of the appellee was unlawful. All of the exceptions and legal excuses named in the statute are negatived in the affidavit, and the conduct of the appellee, as described in that instrument, could not have been lawful.

The rule applicable here is well-stated in Wharton's *Crim. Pl. & Pr.* (8th ed.) § 269, as follows: "The phrase 'unlawful' is in no case essential unless it be a part of the description of the offense as defined by some statute; for, if the fact, as stated, be illegal, it would be superfluous to allege it to be unlawful; if the fact stated be legal, the word 'unlawful' cannot render it indictable."

The affidavit sufficiently charged a public offense.

For the error of the court in sustaining the appellee's motion to quash the affidavit, the judgment is reversed.

88.

IDA B. WELLS BARNETT: Lynching and the Excuse for It

In the twenty years after 1885 there were more lynchings in the United States than legal executions. The great majority of victims were Negroes, who, after a brief period of political power in the South during Reconstruction, by the turn of the century had been disenfranchised and deprived of work and educational opportunities, and, in fact, had almost completely fallen victim to white racism in both North and South. Neither state nor federal governments took any effective action in the matter of lynchings. But the issue was brought before the public by Negro spokesmen, foremost of whom was Ida B. Wells Barnett, head of the antilynch crusade, who lectured throughout the United States and Europe on the subject for several years. In the following article published in 1901, she attacks the premise of whites that lynching was really an extralegal means of securing justice.

Source: *Independent,* May 16, 1901.

IT WAS EMINENTLY BEFITTING that the *Independent's* first number in the new century should contain a strong protest against lynching. The deepest dyed infamy of the 19th century was that which, in its supreme contempt for law, defied all constitutional guarantees of citizenship, and during the last fifteen years of the century put to death 2,000 men, women, and children by shooting, hanging, and burning alive. Well would it have been if every preacher in every pulpit in the land had made so earnest a plea as that which came from Miss Addams' forceful pen.

Appreciating the helpful influences of such a dispassionate and logical argument as that made by the writer referred to, I earnestly desire to say nothing to lessen the force of the appeal. At the same time, an unfortunate presumption used as a basis for her argument works so serious, though doubtless unintentional, an injury to the memory of thousands of victims of mob law that it is only fair to call attention to this phase of the writer's plea. It is unspeakably infamous to put thousands of people to death without a trial by jury; it adds to that infamy to charge that these victims were moral monsters, when, in fact, four-fifths of them were not so accused even by the fiends who murdered them.

Almost at the beginning of her discussion, the distinguished writer says: "Let us assume that the Southern citizens who take part in and abet the lynching of Negroes honestly believe that that is the only successful method of dealing with a certain class of crimes."

It is this assumption, this absolutely unwarrantable assumption, that vitiates every suggestion which it inspires Miss Addams to make. It is the same baseless assumption which influences ninety-nine out of every one hundred persons who discuss this question. Among many thousand editorial clippings I have received in the past five years, 99 percent discuss the question upon the presumption that lynchings are the desperate effort of the Southern people to protect their women from black monsters, and, while the large majority condemn lynching, the condemnation is tempered with a plea for the lyncher — that human nature gives way under such awful provocation and that the mob, insane for the moment, must be pitied as well as condemned. It is strange that an intelligent, law-abiding, and fair-minded people should so persistently shut their eyes to the facts in the discussion of what the civilized world now concedes to be America's national crime.

This almost universal tendency to accept as true the slander which the lynchers offer to civilization as an excuse for their crime might be explained if the true facts were difficult to obtain; but not the slightest difficulty intervenes. The Associated Press dispatches, the press clipping bureau, frequent book publications, and the annual summary of a number of influential journals give the lynching record every year. This record, easily within the reach of everyone who wants it, makes inexcusable the statement and cruelly unwarranted the assumption that Negroes are lynched only because of their assaults upon womanhood.

For an example in point: For fifteen years past, on the first day of each year, the *Chicago Tribune* has given to the public a carefully compiled record of all the lynchings of the previous year. Space will not permit a résumé of these fifteen years, but as fairly representing the entire time, I desire to briefly tabulate here the record of the five years last past. The statistics of the ten years preceding do not vary; they simply emphasize the record here presented.

The record gives the name and nationality of the man or woman lynched, the alleged crime, the time and place of the lynching. With this is given a résumé of the offenses charged, with the number of persons lynched for the offenses named. That enables the reader to see at a glance the causes assigned for the lynchings, and leaves nothing to be assumed. The lynchers, at the time and place of the lynching, are the best authority for the causes which actuate them. Every presumption is in favor of this record, especially as it remains absolutely unimpeached. This record gives the following statement of the colored persons lynched and the causes of the lynchings for the years named.

1896

Murder	24
Attempted murder	4
Rape	31
Incendiarism	2
No cause	2
Alleged rape	2
Cattle stealing	1
Miscegenation	2
Attempted rape	4
Murderous assault	1
Arson	2
Assault	3
Unknown cause	1
Slapping a child	1
Shooting at officer	1
Alleged murder	2
Threats	1
Passing counterfeit money	1
Theft	1

1897

Murder	55
Attempted rape	8
Mistaken identity	1
Arson	3
Murderous assault	2
Running quarantine	1
Burglary	1
Bad reputation	1
Unknown offense	3
Killing white cap	1
Attempted murder	1
Insulting white woman	1
Suspected arson	1
Giving evidence	2
Refusing to give evidence	1
Writing insulting letter	1
Cattle thief	1
Felony	1
Train wrecking	1
Rape	22
Race prejudice	1
Alleged arson	1
Robbery	6
Assault	2
Disobeying federal regulations	1
Theft	2
Elopement	1
Concealing murderer	1

1898

Murder	42
Rape	14
Attempted rape	7
Complicity in rape	1
Highway robbery	1
Burglary	1
Mistaken identity	1
Arson	1
Murderous assault	1
Theft	6
Miscegenation	1
Unknown offense	2
Violation of contract	1
Insults	2
Race prejudice	3
Resisting arrest	1
Suspected murder	13
Assaults upon whites	4

1899

Murder	23
Robbery	6
Inflammatory language	1
Desperado	1
Complicity in murder	3
Rape	11
Attempted rape	8
Arson	8
Unknown offense	4
Resisting arrest	1
Mistaken identity	1
Aiding escape of murderer	3

1900

Murder	30
Rape	16
Attempted assault	12
Race prejudice	9
Plot to kill whites	2
Suspected robbery	1
Giving testimony	1
Attacking white men	3
Attempted murder	4
Threats to kill	1
Suspected murder	2
Unknown offense	2
No offense	1
Arson	2
Suspicion of arson	1
Aiding escape of murderer	1
Unpopularity	1
Making threats	1
Informer	1
Robbery	2
Burglary	4
Assault	2

With this record in view, there should be no difficulty in ascertaining the alleged offenses given as justification for lynchings during the last five years. If the Southern citizens lynch Negroes because "that is the only successful method of dealing with a certain class of crimes," then that class of crimes should be shown unmistakably by this record. Now consider the record.

It would be supposed that the record would show that all, or nearly all, lynchings were caused by outrageous assaults upon women; certainly that this particular offense would outnumber all other causes for putting human beings to death without a trial by jury and the other safeguards of our Constitution and laws.

But the record makes no such disclosure. Instead, it shows that five women have been lynched, put to death with unspeakable savagery, during the past five years. They certainly were not under the ban of the outlawing crime. It shows that men, not a few but hundreds, have been lynched for misdemeanors, while others have suffered death for no offense known to the law, the causes assigned being "mistaken identity," "insult," "bad reputation," "unpopularity," "violating contract," "running quarantine," "giving evidence," "frightening child by shooting at rabbits," etc. Then, strangest of all, the record shows that the sum total of lynchings for these offenses — not crimes — and for the alleged offenses which are only misdemeanors greatly exceeds the lynchings for the very crime universally declared to be the cause of lynching.

A careful classification of the offenses which have caused lynchings during the past five years shows that contempt for law and race prejudice constitute the real cause of all lynching. During the past five years, 147 white persons were lynched. It may be argued that fear of the "law's delays" was the cause of their being lynched. But this is not true. Not a single white victim of the mob was wealthy or had friends or influence to cause a miscarriage of justice. There was no such possibility; it was contempt for law which incited the mob to put so many white men to death without a complaint under oath, much less a trial.

In the case of the Negroes lynched, the mobs' incentive was race prejudice. Few white men were lynched for any such trivial offenses as are detailed in the causes for lynching colored men. Negroes are lynched for "violating contracts," "unpopularity," "testifying in court," and "shooting at rabbits." As only Negroes are lynched for "no offense," "unknown offenses," offenses not criminal, misdemeanors, and crimes not capital, it must be admitted that the real cause of lynching in all such cases is race prejudice, and should be so classified.

Grouping these lynchings under that classification and excluding rape, which in some states is made a capital offense, the record for the five years, so far as the Negro is concerned, reads as follows:

Year	Race prejudice	Murder	Rape	Total lynchings
1896	31	24	31	86
1897	46	55	22	123
1898	39	47	16	102
1899	56	23	11	90
1900	57	30	16	103
Total	229	179	96	504

This table tells its own story and shows how false is the excuse which lynchers offer to justify their fiendishness. Instead of being the sole cause of lynching, the crime upon which lynchers build their defense furnishes the least victims for the mob. In 1896 less than 39 percent of the Negroes lynched were charged with this crime; in 1897, less than 18 percent; in 1898, less than 16 percent; in 1899, less than 14 percent; and in 1900, less than 15 percent were so charged.

No good result can come from any investigation which refuses to consider the facts. A conclusion that is based upon a presumption instead of the best evidence is unworthy of a moment's consideration. The lynching record, as it is compiled from day to day by unbiased, reliable, and responsible public journals, should be the basis of every investigation which seeks to discover the cause and suggest the remedy for lynching. The excuses of lynchers and the specious pleas of their apologists should be considered in the light of the record, which they invariably misrepresent or ignore.

The Christian and moral forces of the nation should insist that misrepresentation should have no place in the discussion of this all important question, that the figures of the lynching record should be allowed to plead, trumpet-tongued, in defense of the slandered dead, that the silence of concession be broken, and that truth, swift-winged and courageous, summon this nation to do its duty to exalt justice and preserve inviolate the sacredness of human life.

───────●───────

America is a hell of a success.
JOSEPH GURNEY ("UNCLE JOE") CANNON

89.

Brooks Adams: War as an Extreme Phase of Economic Competition

Brooks Adams recognized that the acquisition of an overseas empire made the United States the economic competitor of the powerful European nations that held colonial empires. But for Adams, history was on the side of America — the vigorous, emerging power with unlimited potential for economic expansion. Economic supremacy would not come, however, without sacrifice and struggle, and possibly even war, and America, Adams felt, must be ready to pay the price in military preparedness and suitable trade policies. Adams outlined his views in an article entitled "Reciprocity or the Alternative," published in August 1901, and reprinted here in part.

Source: *Atlantic Monthly*, August 1901.

PREVIOUS TO 1890, America had remained chiefly agricultural, buying largely of European manufactures and paying therefor, in part, in evidences of debt. Her own industries, like those of France under Louis XIV, were then organized on too costly a basis for international competition, and were mostly maintained by a system of bounties under the form of a tariff. After 1870, the economic disturbance in Europe caused by the rise of Germany gradually created a stringency in Great Britain; a liquidation of the English loans in America began, and in 1890 this liquidation assumed proportions which culminated in panic.

One method of measuring the pressure to which the United States was subjected during a series of years, and to gauge the change of relations between the Eastern and the Western continent wrought thereby, is to compare the average yearly payments made on balance by America to foreigners from a date antecedent to the catastrophe of 1893 to the present time. If three quin-quennial periods be taken, beginning with 1887, the first will fall substantially before the crisis of the Barings failure.

From 1887 to 1891, the average annual excess of exports over imports amounted to about $44,400,000, a sum certainly not more than sufficient to pay interest due abroad and other like charges. After the failure of the Barings, creditors grew pressing, and the balance rose, between 1892 and 1896, to $185,400,000. In 1896 the United States reached the lowest point in her recent history. Her position then somewhat resembled that of France when Colbert adopted his policy of "selling without buying." The cost of production being too high, Americans could not export manufactures; agricultural supplies alone proved insufficient to yield the sum demanded of her; and the country, in that single year, had to part with $78,880,000 in gold. General insolvency seemed imminent.

When confronted, in 1667, with stagnating commerce and failing industries, Colbert proclaimed his prohibitive tariff, and, finding that this expedient did not correct exchanges, he invaded Holland; but he did not cut the evil he combated at the root, by reorganizing France. In 1897 the United States followed the precedent set by Colbert so far as the tariff was concerned; but Americans, suppler than Frenchmen, did not go to war. They adopted a more effective method of routing the foe. They readjusted their entire system of industry and transportation, bringing the cost of production of the chief articles of modern commerce below the European level. No success has ever been more sudden or more startling.

Between 1897 and 1901 the average excess of American exports over imports has risen to $510 million yearly. The amount tends to increase, and it tends to increase for excellent reasons. Just now America can undersell Europe in agricultural products; she can likewise undersell Europe in minerals as raw material; she can also undersell Europe in most branches of manufactured iron and steel, beside many minor classes of wares. On the present basis, there seems no reason to doubt that, as time goes on, America will drive Europe more and more from neutral markets, and will, if she makes the effort, flood Europe herself with goods at prices with which Europeans cannot compete.

A moment's consideration will disclose the gravity of the situation. Whatever may have been, or may still be, the extent of America's foreign indebtedness, it is certain that, at the present rate of redemption, it must be soon extinguished. Then the time will come when the whole vast burden of payment for American exports will fall upon the annual earnings of foreign nations at the moment when those earnings are cut down by the competition of the very goods for which they must pay.

The inversion of all that has heretofore existed has been so sudden and complete that society has somewhat lost its bearings; nevertheless, the feeling of Europe is apprehension, and that feeling is not without rational foundation. Should the movement of the next decade correspond to the movement of the last, Europe will, at its close, stand face to face with ruin. It is safe to assume, therefore, that Europe will not allow present conditions to remain unchanged, anymore than France did in 1667, or than America did in 1896.

Three avenues seem open by which relief may be obtained. First, Europe may reorganize herself upon a scale to correspond with the organization of the United States; but this solution appears doubtful in view of the decentralization of the continent. Second, the United States may be induced to abandon something of her advantages and ameliorate the situation of Europe by commercial reciprocity. In other words, the United States may prefer to follow somewhat the same policy which Cobden advocated, as opposed to the policy of Colbert and Napoleon. Lastly, Europe may attack the United States and attempt to break her down by arms.

In plain English, Europe finds herself in an impasse. She is pressed on every hand. Her soil, never rich, has been tilled until its culture costs more than that of newer land. Hence, each country must choose between two alternatives: the farmers may be abandoned to their fate, as in the United Kingdom; or they may be protected, as in France and Germany. If the farmers should be abandoned, the military population will disappear, as it has disappeared in Great Britain, and food will have to be bought abroad. If the farmers should be protected, the rest of the country must pay higher for its bread and meat. In either case, the loss will correspond to the sum represented by the inferiority of the European soil and the higher price it bears, as compared with the soil of Argentina or Nebraska.

Prior to 1897, while Europe still held a

substantial monopoly in manufactures, this deterioration of agriculture, if not viewed with pleasure, might be contemplated with equanimity. Not so since 1897, when the Industrial Revolution in North America has brought European mines to a condition of relative exhaustion and European workshops to a position of relative inferiority. Assuming that a satisfactory social readjustment offers, just now, insuperable difficulties, Europeans see but one method of obtaining relief should America retain her tariff: that method is to develop regions abroad containing mines capable of vying with those of Alabama, Pennsylvania, and Lake Superior. And it is precisely here that Europe finds herself propelled toward a collision with the United States, because the United States, for her own protection, has devised a mechanism which holds her rival as in a vise.

America's attack is based not only on her superior resources and her more perfect administration but on her tariff. To make their gigantic industrial system lucrative, Americans have comprehended that it must be worked at the highest velocity and at its full capacity, and they have taken their measures accordingly. To guard against a check, they rely on a practically prohibitive tariff, by which they hope to maintain the home market at a reasonable level; and with the profit thus obtained they expect to make good any loss which may accrue from forcing their surplus upon foreigners at prices with which these cannot cope. No wonder the European regards America as a dangerous and relentless foe; and the fact that Europe has forced on America these measures as a means of self-defense signifies nothing.

The European sees in America a competitor who, while refusing to buy, throws her wares on every market, and who, while she drives the peasant from his land, reduces the profits of industry which support the wage earners of the town. Most ominous of all, he marks a rapidly growing power, which,

while it undersells his mines, closes to him every region of the wide earth where he might find minerals adapted to his needs. Lying like a colossus across the Western continent, with her ports on either ocean, with China opposite and South America at her feet, the United States bars European expansion. South America and China are held to be the only accessible regions which certainly contain the iron, coal, and copper which Europe seeks; and the United States is determined that, if she can prevent it, South America and China shall not be used as bases for hostile competition. Regarding South America, her declarations are explicit, and during the last twelve months her actions in Asia have spoken more emphatically than words.

Moreover, the German considers the theory of the "open door" a mockery. The German avers that no man knows so well as the American that China can never be developed until it is administered by Western methods, and that it is for this reason that America opposes partition. To make Asia pay, the country must be handled as a whole — as America is handled, though not perhaps on so extensive a scale. At all events, in each province the mining, transportation, manufactures, police, and taxation must be controlled by Europeans. To attempt to turn Shansi into a Pennsylvania under Chinese rule would mean ruin.

Thus the continent of Europe finds itself pressed somewhat as Colbert found France pressed in 1667, and, accordingly, Europeans are restive. Evidently, unless all human experience is at fault, that restiveness will grow. Men cannot foresee the future; they can only reason about it by reference to the past; and as they can never know all the forces in operation, their inferences must contain more or less of error. For example, this year, competition appears to be approaching, in intensity, the point of danger; and yet next year an abundant supply of gold may raise prices and thereby allay friction for an indefinite period. Yet, speaking generally and without limit of time, the great question of American economic supremacy remains to be settled; and, as long as Europe continues armed, that question will not be settled peacefully upon America's own terms as America is now organized. There must be compromise or war, or else America must be so strong that war is deemed too hazardous to be attempted. . . .

Assuming, for the moment, for the sake of argument, that the United States is determined to yield nothing but is resolved to push all her advantages to the uttermost, it is clear that an attack upon her would be profitable, if it could be made with reasonable hope of success. Europe believes that it could be made with such hope, provided a coalition could be opportunely formed. In this Europeans may be wrong; but they judge after their own standards, and possibly they may be right. . . .

If a country would live in peace, experience has demonstrated that she must not be too grasping; for excessive greed makes her overthrow a benefit to all, and competitors act accordingly. On the other hand, certain races have felt themselves adapted to win victory in battle, and have prospered; if the American people, after due deliberation, feel aggression to be for their best interest, there is little to be urged by way of precedent against the logic of their decision.

Men inclining to this attitude can point to history and insist that no radical readjustment of the world's economic equilibrium has ever been unaccompanied by war; and that, if war must come, the United States may well face it now. To abandon any advantage would be weakness. The United States is young, strong, rich, and energetic, with an enormous military population. No permanent tranquillity can be hoped for until her supremacy is acknowledged; therefore, the course which will enforce that acknowledgment soonest is the cheapest.

America is as likely now as she will ever be to emerge victorious from any conflict into which she may enter. . . .

If Americans are determined to reject reciprocity in all its forms, to insist on their advantages, to concede nothing to the adversary; if, having driven in the knife, they mean to turn it in the wound, they should recognize that they are provoking reprisals in every form, and accept the situation with its limitations. To carry out an aggressive policy in some security, the United States needs 300,000 trained men whom she can put in the field in 20 days, with an ample reserve of officers and of material. She needs well-fortified coasts and colonies, and an effective transport service. More especially, she needs a Navy. Judging by the example of England, who has always done her best to make her friendship of value, 100 battleships and armored cruisers, equipped and ready for sea, would hardly suffice.

In a word, the experience of ages has demonstrated that alternatives are presented to aspiring nations in regard to the payment they will make for their prize. The one is the alternative of Cobden, the other that of Colbert. There is no middle course. Destruction has awaited the gambler who backs his luck; the braggart who would be at once rich, aggressive, and unarmed. Such a man or such a nation puts a premium on spoliation. It is only necessary to reflect upon the fate of France in 1870 to accept this inference as true.

America enjoys no immunity from natural laws. She can pay for what she takes, or she can fight for it, but she cannot have the earth for nothing. Sooner or later the inexorable tribute will be exacted from her as it has been exacted from every predominant community, from the days of the grandeur of Babylon to those of the glory of London; for, since time began, no race has won for itself supremacy without paying a price in gold or blood to other races as ambitious and almost as powerful as itself.

90.

William McKinley: Reciprocal Trade Agreements

The McKinley Tariff of 1890 was the highest in the nation's history. Yet, eleven years later, while serving his second term as President, McKinley revised his views, and the last speech he made before his assassination was on tariff reform. His attitude reflected a significant shift in the thinking of businessmen during the last decade of the nineteenth century. By 1900 high protective tariffs were no longer the watchword of every Republican politician. McKinley's speech, part of which appears here, was delivered in Buffalo, New York, on September 5, 1901, the day before he was shot.

Source: Richardson, X, pp. 393-397.

TRADE STATISTICS INDICATE that this country is in a state of unexampled prosperity. The figures are almost appalling. They show that we are utilizing our fields and forests and mines, and that we are furnishing profitable employment to the millions of workingmen throughout the United States, bringing comfort and happiness to their homes and making it possible to lay by savings for old age and disability. That all the people are participating in this great prosperity is seen in every American community and shown by the enormous and unprecedented deposits in our savings banks. Our duty is the care and security of these deposits, and their safe investment demands the highest integrity and the best business capacity of those in charge of these depositories of the people's earnings.

We have a vast and intricate business, built up through years of toil and struggle, in which every part of the country has its stake, and will not permit of either neglect or of undue selfishness. No narrow, sordid policy will subserve it. The greatest skill and wisdom on the part of the manufacturers and producers will be required to hold and increase it. Our industrial enterprises, which have grown to such great proportions, affect the homes and occupations of the people and the welfare of the country.

Our capacity to produce has developed so enormously and our products have so multiplied that the problem of more markets requires our urgent and immediate attention. Only a broad and enlightened policy will keep what we have. No other policy will get more. In these times of marvelous business energy and gain, we ought to be looking to the future, strengthening the weak places in our industrial and commercial system, that we may be ready for any storm or strain.

By sensible trade arrangements which will not interrupt our home production, we shall extend the outlets for our increasing surplus. A system which provides a mutual exchange of commodities is manifestly essential to the continued and healthful growth of our export trade. We must not repose in fancied security that we can forever sell everything and buy little or nothing. If such a thing were possible, it would not be best for us or for those with whom we deal. We should take from our customers such of their products as we can use without harm to our industries and labor.

Reciprocity is the natural outgrowth of our wonderful industrial development under the domestic policy now firmly established. What we produce beyond our domestic consumption must have a vent abroad. The excess must be relieved through a foreign outlet, and we should sell everywhere we can and buy wherever the buying will enlarge our sales and productions, and thereby make a greater demand for home labor.

The period of exclusiveness is past. The expansion of our trade and commerce is the pressing problem. Commercial wars are unprofitable. A policy of goodwill and friendly trade relations will prevent reprisals. Reciprocity treaties are in harmony with the spirit of the times; measures of retaliation are not. If perchance some of our tariffs are no longer needed for revenue or to encourage and protect our industries at home, why should they not be employed to extend and promote our markets abroad?

Then, too, we have inadequate steamship service. New lines of steamers have already been put in commission between the Pacific Coast ports of the United States and those on the western coasts of Mexico and Central and South America. These should be followed up with direct steamship lines between the Eastern coast of the United States and South American ports. One of the needs of the times is to direct commercial lines from our vast fields of production to the fields of consumption that we have but barely touched.

Next in advantage to having the thing to sell is to have the convenience to carry it to the buyer. We must encourage our Merchant Marine. We must have more ships. They must be under the American flag, built and manned and owned by Americans. These will not only be profitable in a commercial sense; they will be messengers of peace and amity wherever they go. We must build the Isthmian canal, which will unite the two oceans and give a straight line of water communication with the western coasts of Central and South America and Mexico. The construction of a Pacific cable cannot be longer postponed.

I told William McKinley it was a mistake to nominate that wild man at Philadelphia . . . Now look, that damned cowboy is President of the United States!
    MARK HANNA, on the funeral train carrying McKinley from Buffalo to Washington. The "cowboy" is of course Theodore Roosevelt.

91.

Charter of the United States Steel Corporation

The U.S. Steel Corporation was formed in 1901 as a holding company with complete financial control over several semi-autonomous firms. Prior to 1901 many of the steel-producing facilities in the country, including mining, shipping, manufacturing, and the production of finished products, had come into the hands of trusts, controlled by banker J. P. Morgan and his associates. Their only remaining competitor was Andrew Carnegie. However, Carnegie was no mean adversary; indeed, he almost put Morgan out of business. Carnegie, who was ready to retire anyway, finally decided to sell his company; and although the asking price was high, Morgan agreed to it. The charter of the resulting company, the U.S. Steel Corporation, was signed on February 23, 1901. The corporation was based in New Jersey, whose liberal incorporation laws also drew other large firms.

Source: Horace L. Wilgus, *A Study of the United States Steel Corporation*, Chicago, 1901, pp. 132-137.

Amended Certificate of Incorporation of United States Steel Corporation

WE, THE UNDERSIGNED, in order to form a corporation for the purposes hereinafter stated, under and pursuant to the provisions of the act of the legislature of the state of New Jersey, entitled "An Act Concerning Corporations (Revision of 1896)," and the acts amendatory thereof and supplementary thereto, do hereby certify as follows:

I. The name of the corporation is *United States Steel Corporation.*

II. The location of its principal office in the state of New Jersey is at No. 51 Newark Street, in the city of Hoboken, county of Hudson. The name of the agent therein and in charge thereof, upon whom process against the corporation may be served, is Hudson Trust Company. Said office is to be the registered office of said corporation.

III. The objects for which the corporation is formed are:

To manufacture iron, steel, manganese, coke, copper, lumber, and other materials, and all or any articles consisting, or partly consisting, of iron, steel, copper, wood, or other materials, and all or any products thereof.

To acquire, own, lease, occupy, use, or develop any lands containing coal or iron, manganese, stone or other ores, or oil, and any woodlands or other lands for any purpose of the company.

To mine or otherwise to extract or remove coal, ores, stone, and other minerals and timber from any lands owned, acquired, leased, or occupied by the company, or from any other lands.

To buy and sell or otherwise to deal or to traffic in iron, steel, manganese, copper, stone, ores, coal, coke, wood, lumber, and other materials, and any of the products thereof, and any articles consisting, or partly consisting, thereof.

To construct bridges, buildings, machinery, ships, boats, engines, cars and other equipment, railroads, docks, slips, elevators, waterworks, gasworks and electric works, viaducts, aqueducts, canals and other waterways, and any other means of transportation, and to sell the same, or otherwise dispose thereof, or to maintain and operate the same, except that the company shall not maintain or operate any railroad or canal in the state of New Jersey.

To apply for, obtain, register, purchase, lease, or otherwise to acquire and to hold, use, own, operate, and introduce, and to sell, assign, or otherwise to dispose of, any trademarks, trade names, patents, inventions, improvements, and processes used in connection with, or secured under letters patent of, the United States, or elsewhere, or otherwise; and to use, exercise, develop, grant licenses in respect of, or otherwise turn to account any such trademarks, patents, licenses, processes, and the like, or any such property or rights.

To engage in any other manufacturing, mining, construction, or transportation business of any kind or character whatsoever, and to that end to acquire, hold, own, and dispose of any and all property, assets, stocks, bonds, and rights of any and every kind; but not to engage in any business hereunder which shall require the exercise of the right of eminent domain within the state of New Jersey.

To acquire by purchase, subscription, or otherwise, and to hold or to dispose of stocks, bonds, or any other obligations of any corporation formed for, or then or theretofore engaged in or pursuing, any one or more of the kinds of business, purposes, objects, or operations above indicated, or owning or holding any property of any kind herein mentioned; or of any corporation owning or holding the stocks or the obligations of any such corporation.

To hold for investment, or otherwise to use, sell, or dispose of, any stock, bonds, or other obligations of any such other corporation; to aid in any manner any corporation whose stock, bonds, or other obligations are held or are in any manner guaranteed by the company, and to do any other acts or things for the preservation, protection, improvement, or enhancement of the value of any such stock, bonds, or other obligations, or to do any acts or things designed for any such purpose; and, while owner of any such stock, bonds, or other obligations, to exercise all the rights, powers, and privileges of ownership thereof, and to exercise any and all voting power thereon.

The business or purpose of the company is from time to time to do any one or more of the acts and things herein set forth; and it may conduct its business in other states and in the territories and in foreign countries, and may have one office or more than one office, and keep the books of the company outside of the state of New Jersey, except as otherwise may be provided by law; and may hold, purchase, mortgage, and convey real and personal property either in or out of the state of New Jersey.

Without in any particular limiting any of the objects and powers of the corporation, it is hereby expressly declared and provided that the corporation shall have power to issue bonds and other obligations in payment for property purchased or acquired by it, or for any other object in or about its business; to mortgage or pledge any stock, bonds, or other obligations, or any property which may be acquired by it, to secure any bonds or other obligations by it issued or incurred; to guarantee any dividends or bonds or contracts or other obligations; to make and perform contracts of any kind and description; and in carrying on its business, or for the purpose of attaining or furthering any of its objects, to do any and all other acts and things and to exercise any and all other powers which a copartnership or natural person could do and exercise, and which now or hereafter may be authorized by law.

IV. The total authorized capital stock of the corporation is $1,100,000,000, divided into 11 million shares of the par value of

$100 each. Of such total authorized capital stock, 5,500,000 shares, amounting to $550 million, shall be preferred stock, and 5,500,000 shares amounting to $550 million, shall be common stock.

From time to time, the preferred stock and the common stock may be increased according to law and may be issued in such amounts and proportions as shall be determined by the Board of Directors, and as may be permitted by law.

The holders of the preferred stock shall be entitled to receive, when and as declared from the surplus or net profits of the corporation, yearly dividends at the rate of 7 percent per annum, and no more, payable quarterly on dates to be fixed by the bylaws. The dividends on the preferred stock shall be cumulative and shall be payable before any dividends on the common stock shall be paid or set apart; so that, if in any year dividends amounting to 7 percent shall not have been paid thereon, the deficiency shall be payable before any dividends shall be paid upon or set apart for the common stock.

Whenever all cumulative dividends on the preferred stock for all previous years shall have been declared and shall have become payable and the accrued quarterly installments for the current year shall have been declared, and the company shall have paid such cumulative dividends for previous years and such accrued quarterly installments, or shall have set aside from its surplus or net profits a sum sufficient for the payment thereof, the Board of Directors may declare dividends on the common stock, payable then or thereafter, out of any remaining surplus or net profits.

In the event of any liquidation or dissolution or winding up (whether voluntary or involuntary) of the corporation, the holders of the preferred stock shall be entitled to be paid in full both the par amount of their shares and the unpaid dividends accrued thereon before any amount shall be paid to the holders of the common stock; and after the payment to the holders of the preferred stock of its par value and the unpaid accrued dividends thereon, the remaining assets and funds shall be divided and paid to the holders of the common stock according to their respective shares. . . .

VI. The duration of the corporation shall be perpetual.

VII. The number of directors of the company shall be fixed from time to time by the bylaws. . . .

Unless authorized by votes given in person or by proxy by stockholders holding at least two-thirds of the capital stock of the corporation, which is represented and voted upon in person or by proxy at a meeting especially called for that purpose or at an annual meeting, the Board of Directors shall not mortgage or pledge any of its real property, or any shares of the capital stock of any other corporation; but this prohibition shall not be construed to apply to the execution of any purchase-money mortgage or any other purchase-money lien. As authorized by the Act of the legislature of the state of New Jersey, passed March 22, 1901, amending the 17th Section of the Act Concerning Corporations (Revision of 1896), any action which theretofore required the consent of the holders of two-thirds of the stock at any meeting after notice to them given, or required their consent in writing to be filed, may be taken upon the consent of, and the consent given and filed by the holders of two-thirds of the stock of each class represented at such meeting in person or by proxy. . . .

The Board of Directors shall have power from time to time to fix and to determine and to vary the amount of the working capital of the company; and to direct and determine the use and disposition of any surplus or net profits over and above the capital stock paid in; and in its discretion the Board of Directors may use and apply any such surplus or accumulated profits in purchasing or acquiring its bonds or other obligations, or shares of its own capital stock, to such extent and in such manner and upon such terms as the Board of Directors shall deem expedient; but shares of such capital stock so purchased or acquired may be resold, unless such shares shall have been retired for the purpose of decreasing the company's capital stock as provided by law.

The Board of Directors, from time to time, shall determine whether and to what extent, and at what times and places, and under what conditions and regulations, the accounts and books of the corporation, or any of them, shall be open to the inspection of the stockholders, and no stockholder shall have any right to inspect any account or book or document of the corporation, except as conferred by statute or authorized by the Board of Directors or by a resolution of the stockholders.

Subject always to bylaws made by the stockholders, the Board of Directors may make bylaws, and, from time to time, may alter, amend, or repeal any bylaws; but any bylaws made by the Board of Directors may be altered or repealed by the stockholders at any annual meeting or at any special meeting, provided notice of such proposed alteration or repeal be included in the notice of the meeting.

92.

Theodore Roosevelt: Controlling the Trusts

Theodore Roosevelt's ability to coin the right phrases and to grasp the essence of the public mood made him one of the most popular and effective presidents of this century. Known in the history books as the "trustbuster," Roosevelt, in fact, broke fewer trusts in eight years than his successor did in four. In his first annual message to Congress, delivered on December 3, 1901, Roosevelt devoted some of his remarks to the trusts. As Finley Peter Dunne's Mr. Dooley put it, Roosevelt's attitude toward the trusts was "on wan hand I wud stamp thim undher fut; on th' other hand not so fast." A portion of Roosevelt's message is reprinted below.

Source: Richardson, X, pp. 417-456.

THE TREMENDOUS AND HIGHLY COMPLEX industrial development which went on with ever accelerated rapidity during the latter half of the nineteenth century brings us face to face, at the beginning of the twentieth, with very serious social problems. The old laws and the old customs, which had almost the binding force of law, were once quite sufficient to regulate the accumulation and distribution of wealth. Since the industrial changes which have so enormously increased the productive power of mankind, they are no longer sufficient.

The growth of cities has gone on beyond comparison faster than the growth of the country, and the upbuilding of the great industrial centers has meant a startling increase, not merely in the aggregate of wealth but in the number of very large individual, and especially of very large corporate, fortunes. The creation of these great corporate fortunes has not been due to the tariff nor to any other governmental action but to natural causes in the business world, operating in other countries as they operate in our own.

The process has aroused much antagonism, a great part of which is wholly without warrant. It is not true that as the rich have grown richer, the poor have grown poorer. On the contrary, never before has the average man, the wage worker, the farmer, the small trader, been so well off as in this country and at the present time. There have been abuses connected with the accumulation of wealth; yet it remains true that a fortune accumulated in legitimate business can be accumulated by the person especially benefited only on condition of conferring immense incidental benefits upon others. Successful enterprise, of the type which benefits all mankind, can only exist if the conditions are such as to offer great prizes as the rewards of success.

The captains of industry who have driven the railway systems across this continent, who have built up our commerce, who have developed our manufactures, have, on the whole, done great good to our people. Without them the material development of which we are so justly proud could never have taken place. Moreover, we should recognize the immense importance of this material development of leaving as unhampered as is compatible with the public good the strong and forceful men upon whom the success of business operations inevitably rests. The slightest study of business conditions will satisfy anyone capable of forming a judgment that the personal equation is the most important factor in a business operation; that the business ability of the man at the head of any business concern, big or little, is usually the factor which fixes the gulf between striking success and hopeless failure.

An additional reason for caution in dealing with corporations is to be found in the international commercial conditions of today. The same business conditions which have produced the great aggregations of corporate and individual wealth have made them very potent factors in international commercial competition. Business concerns which have the largest means at their disposal and are managed by the ablest men are naturally those which take the lead in the strife for commercial supremacy among the nations of the world.

America has only just begun to assume that commanding position in the international business world which we believe will more and more be hers. It is of the utmost importance that this position be not jeoparded, especially at a time when the overflowing abundance of our own natural resources and the skill, business energy, and mechanical aptitude of our people make foreign markets essential. Under such conditions it would be most unwise to cramp or to fetter the youthful strength of our nation.

Moreover, it cannot too often be pointed out that to strike with ignorant violence at the interests of one set of men almost inevitably endangers the interests of all. The fundamental rule in our national life — the rule which underlies all others — is that, on the whole, and in the long run, we shall go up or down together. There are exceptions; and in times of prosperity some will prosper far more, and in times of adversity some will suffer far more, than others; but speaking generally, a period of good times means that all share more or less in them, and in a period of hard times all feel the stress to a greater or less degree.

It surely ought not to be necessary to enter into any proof of this statement; the memory of the lean years which began in 1893 is still vivid, and we can contrast them with the conditions in this very year which is now closing. Disaster to great business enterprises can never have its effects limited to the men at the top. It spreads throughout, and while it is bad for everybody, it is worst for those farthest down. The capitalist may be shorn of his luxuries; but the wage worker may be deprived of even bare necessities.

The mechanism of modern business is so delicate that extreme care must be taken not to interfere with it in a spirit of rashness or ignorance. Many of those who have made it their vocation to denounce the great industrial combinations which are popularly, although with technical inaccuracy, known as "trusts" appeal especially to hatred and fear. These are precisely the two emotions, particularly when combined with ignorance, which unfit men for the exercise of cool and steady judgment. In facing new industrial conditions, the whole history of the world shows that legislation will generally be both unwise and ineffective unless undertaken after calm inquiry and with sober self-restraint. Much of the legislation directed at the trusts would have been exceedingly mischievous had it not also been entirely ineffective. In accordance with a well-known sociological law, the ignorant or reckless agitator has been the really effective friend of the evils which he has been nominally opposing.

In dealing with business interests, for the government to undertake, by crude and ill-considered legislation, to do what may turn out to be bad would be to incur the risk of such far-reaching national disaster that it would be preferable to undertake nothing at all. The men who demand the impossible or the undesirable serve as the allies of the forces with which they are nominally at war, for they hamper those who would endeavor to find out in rational fashion what the wrongs really are and to what extent and in what manner it is practicable to apply remedies.

All this is true; and yet it is also true that there are real and grave evils, one of the chief being over-capitalization because of its many baleful consequences; and a resolute and practical effort must be made to correct these evils.

There is a widespread conviction in the minds of the American people that the great corporations known as trusts are in certain of their features and tendencies hurtful to the general welfare. This springs from no spirit of envy or uncharitableness, nor lack of pride in the great industrial achievements that have placed this country at the head of the nations struggling for commercial supremacy. It does not rest upon a lack of intelligent appreciation of the necessity of meeting changing and changed conditions of trade with new methods, nor upon ignorance of the fact that combination of capital in the effort to accomplish great things is necessary when the world's progress demands that great things be done. It is based upon sincere conviction that combination and concentration should be, not prohibited but supervised and within reasonable limits controlled; and in my judgment this conviction is right.

It is no limitation upon property rights or freedom of contract to require that when men receive from government the privilege of doing business under corporate form, which frees them from individual responsibility and enables them to call into their enterprises the capital of the public, they shall do so upon absolutely truthful representations as to the value of the property in which the capital is to be invested. Corporations engaged in interstate commerce should be regulated if they are found to exercise a license working to the public injury.

It should be as much the aim of those who seek for social betterment to rid the business world of crimes of cunning as to rid the entire body politic of crimes of violence. Great corporations exist only because they are created and safeguarded by our institutions; and it is therefore our right and our duty to see that they work in harmony with these institutions.

The first essential in determining how to deal with the great industrial combinations is knowledge of the facts — publicity. In the interest of the public, the government should have the right to inspect and examine the workings of the great corporations engaged in interstate business. Publicity is the only sure remedy which we can now invoke. What further remedies are needed in the way of governmental regulation, or taxation, can only be determined after publicity has been obtained, by process of law, and in the course of administration. The first requisite is knowledge, full and complete — knowledge which may be made public to the world.

Artificial bodies, such as corporations and joint stock or other associations, depending upon any statutory law for their existence or privileges, should be subject to proper governmental supervision, and full and accurate information as to their operations should be made public regularly at reasonable intervals.

The large corporations, commonly called trusts, though organized in one state, always do business in many states, often doing very little business in the state where they are incorporated. There is utter lack of uniformity in the state laws about them; and as no state has any exclusive interest in or power over their acts, it has in practice proved impossible to get adequate regulation through state action. Therefore, in the interest of the whole people, the nation should, without interfering with the power of the states in the matter itself, also assume power of supervision and regulation over all corporations doing an interstate business. This is especially true where the corporation derives a portion of its wealth from the existence of some monopolistic element or tendency in its business.

There would be no hardship in such supervision; banks are subject to it, and in their case it is now accepted as a simple matter of course. Indeed, it is probable that supervision of corporations by the national government need not go so far as is now the case with the supervision exercised over them by so conservative a state as Massachusetts in order to produce excellent results.

When the Constitution was adopted at the end of the eighteenth century, no human wisdom could foretell the sweeping changes, alike in industrial and political conditions, which were to take place by the beginning of the twentieth century. At that time it was accepted as a matter of course that the several states were the proper authorities to regulate, so far as was then necessary, the comparatively insignificant and strictly localized corporate bodies of the day.

The conditions are now wholly different and wholly different action is called for. I believe that a law can be framed which will enable the national government to exercise control along the lines above indicated, profiting by the experience gained through the passage and administration of the Interstate Commerce Act. If, however, the judgment of the Congress is that it lacks the constitutional power to pass such an act, then a constitutional amendment should be submitted to confer the power.

Theodore, if there is one thing more than another for which I admire you, it is your original discovery of the Ten Commandments.

THOMAS B. REED to Theodore Roosevelt

1902

93.

Jacob Riis: The Streets and Alleys of the Poor

Jacob Riis's How the Other Half Lives *(1890) gave Americans a view of slum conditions in New York City. As a police reporter who went into the homes of immigrants and explored the streets and alleys of the poor, Riis exposed the outrageous living conditions he witnessed. In* The Battle With the Slum, *from which the following is taken, Riis dealt with the halting efforts at reform being made in the New York City tenement districts.*

Source: *The Battle With the Slum,* New York, 1902: "The Outworks of the Slum Taken."

HERE I WISH TO MEASURE the stretch we have come since I wrote *How the Other Half Lives* thirteen years ago. Some of it we came plodding and some at full speed; some of it in the face of every obstacle that could be thrown in our way, wresting victory from defeat at every step; some of it with the enemy on the run. Take it all together, it is a long way. Much of it will not have to be traveled over again.

The engine of municipal progress, once started as it has been in New York, may slip many a cog with Tammany as the engineer; it may even be stopped for a season; but it can never be made to work backward. Even Tammany knows that and gropes desperately for a new hold, a certificate of character. In the last election (1901) she laid loud claim to having built many new schools, though she had done little more than to carry out the plans of the previous reform administration, where they could not be upset. As a matter of fact, we had fallen behind again, sadly. But even the claim was significant.

How long we strove for those schools, to no purpose! Our arguments, our anger, the anxious pleading of philanthropists who saw the young on the East Side going to ruin, the warning year after year of the superintendent of schools that the Compulsory Education Law was but an empty mockery where it was most needed, the knocking of uncounted thousands of children for whom there was no room — uncounted in sober fact; there was not even a way of finding out how many were adrift[1] — brought only the response that the tax rate must be kept down. Kept down it was. "Waste" was successfully averted at the spigot; at the bunghole it went on unchecked.

In a swarming population like that, you

1. The first school census was taken in 1895 by order of the legislature. It showed that there were 50,069 children of school age in New York City out of school and unemployed. The number had been variously estimated from 5,000 to 150,000.

Jacob Riis, journalist who used his position as police reporter for the "New York Tribune" to work for reforms in slum and tenement housing

must have either schools or jails, and the jails waxed fat with the overflow. The East Side, that had been orderly, became a hotbed of child crime. And when, in answer to the charge made by a legislative committee (1895) that the father forced his child into the shop, on a perjured age certificate, to labor when he ought to have been at play, that father, bent and heavy-eyed with unceasing toil, flung back the charge with the bitter reproach that we gave him no other choice — that it was either the street or the shop for his boy, and that perjury for him was cheaper than the ruin of the child — we were mute. What, indeed, was there to say? The crime was ours, not his. That was seven years ago. Once since then have we been where we could count the months to the time when every child that knocked should find a seat in our schools; but Tammany came back.

Once again, now, we are catching up. Yesterday, Mayor Low's reform government voted $6 million for new schools. The School Census Law that was forgotten almost as soon as made (the census was to be taken once in two years, but was taken only twice) is to be enforced again so that we know where we stand. In that most crowded neighborhood in all the world, where the superintendent lately pleaded in vain for three new schools, half a dozen have been built, the finest in this or any other land — great, light, and airy structures, with playgrounds on the roof; and all over the city the like are going up.

The briefest of our laws, every word of which is like the blow of a hammer driving the nails home in the coffin of the bad old days, says that never one shall be built without its playground. And not for the child's use only. The band shall play there yet and neighbor meet neighbor in such social contact as the slum has never known to its undoing. Even as I write this the band is tuning up and the children dancing to its strains with shouts of joy. The president of the Board of Education and members of the Board lead in the revolt against the old. Clergymen applaud the opening of the school buildings on Sunday for concerts, lectures, and neighborhood meetings. Common sense is having its day. The streets are cleaned.

The slum has even been washed. We tried that on Hester Street years ago, in the age of cobblestone pavements, and the result fairly frightened us. I remember the indignant reply of a well known citizen, a man of large business responsibility and experience in the handling of men, to whom the office of street-cleaning commissioner had been offered, when I asked him if he would accept. "I have lived," he said, "a blameless life for forty years, and have a character in the community. I cannot afford — no man with a reputation can afford — to hold that office; it will surely wreck it." It made Colonel Waring's reputation. He took the trucks from the streets. Tammany, in a brief interregnum of vigor under Mayor Grant, had laid the axe to the unsightly telegraph poles and begun to pave the streets with asphalt, but it left the trucks and the ash barrels to Colonel Waring as hopeless. Trucks have votes; at least their drivers have. Now that they are gone, the drivers would be the last to bring them back; for they have children, too, and the rescued streets gave them their first playground. Perilous, begrudged by policeman and storekeeper though it was, it was still a playground.

But one is coming in which the boy shall rule unchallenged. The Mulberry Bend Park kept its promise. Before the sod was laid in it, two more were under way in the thickest of the tenement house crowding, and though the landscape gardener has tried twice to steal them, he will not succeed. Play piers and play schools are the order of the day. We shall yet settle the "causes that operated sociologically" on the boy with a lawnmower and a sand heap. You have got your boy, and the heredity of the next one, when you can order his setting.

Social halls for the older people's play are coming where the saloon has had a monopoly of the cheer too long. The labor unions and the reformers work together to put an end to sweating and child labor. The gospel of less law and more enforcement acquired standing while Theodore Roosevelt sat in the governor's chair, rehearsing to us Jefferson's forgotten lesson that "the whole art and science of government consists in being honest." With a back door to every ordinance that touched the lives of the people, if indeed the whole thing was not the subject of open ridicule or the vehicle of official blackmail, it seemed as if we had provided a perfect municipal machinery for bringing the law into contempt with the young, and so for wrecking citizenship by the shortest cut.

Of free soup there is an end. It was never food for free men. The last spoonful was ladled out by yellow journalism with the certificate of the men who fought Roosevelt and reform in the Police Board that it was good. It is not likely that it will ever plague us again. Our experience has taught us a new reading of the old word that charity covers a multitude of sins. It does. Uncovering some of them has kept us busy since our conscience awoke, and there are more left. The worst of them all, that awful parody on municipal charity, the police station lodging room, is gone after twenty years of persistent attack upon the foul dens — years during which they were arraigned, condemned, indicted by every authority having jurisdiction, all to no purpose.

The stale beer dives went with them and with the Bend, and the grip of the tramp on our throat has been loosened. We shall not easily throw it off altogether, for the tramp has a vote, too, for which Tammany, with admirable ingenuity, found a new use, when the ante-election inspection of lodging houses made them less available for colonization purposes than they had been. Perhaps I should say a new way of very old use. It was simplicity itself. Instead of keeping tramps in hired lodgings for weeks at a daily outlay, the new way was to send them all to the island on short commitments during the canvass, and vote them from there *en bloc* at the city's expense. . . .

Thirty-two years have passed since I slept in a police station lodging house, a lonely lad, and was robbed, beaten, and thrown out for protesting; and when the vagrant cur that had joined its homelessness to mine and had sat all night at the door waiting for me to come out — it had been clubbed away the night before, — snarled and showed its teeth at the doorman, raging and impotent, I saw it beaten to death on the step. I little dreamed then that the friendless beast, dead, should prove the undoing of the monstrous wrong done by the maintenance of these evil holes to every helpless man and woman who was without shelter in New York; but it did. It was after an inspection of the lodging rooms, when I stood with Theodore Roosevelt, then president of the Police Board, in the one where I had slept that night, and told him of it, that he swore they should go. And go they did, as did so many another abuse in those two years of honest purpose and effort.

I hated them. It may not have been a very high motive to furnish power for municipal reform; but we had tried every other way, and none of them worked. Arbitration is good, but there are times when it becomes necessary to knock a man down and arbitrate sitting on him, and this was such a time. It was what we started out to do with the rear tenements, the worst of the slum barracks, and it would have been better had we kept on that track. I have always maintained that we made a false move when we stopped to discuss damages with the landlord, or to hear his side of it at all. His share in it was our grievance; it blocked the mortality records with its burden of human woe. The damage was all ours, the profit all his. If there are damages to collect, he should foot the bill, not we. Vested rights are to be protected, but, as I have said, no man has a right to be protected in killing his neighbor.

However, they are down, the worst of them. The community has asserted its right to destroy tenements that destroy life, and for that cause. We bought the slum off in the Mulberry Bend at its own figure. On the rear tenements we set the price, and set it low. It was a long step. Bottle Alley is gone, and Bandits' Roost. Bone Alley, Thieves' Alley, and Kerosene Row — they are all gone. Hell's Kitchen and Poverty Gap have acquired standards of decency; Poverty Gap has risen even to the height of neckties. The time is fresh in my recollection when a different kind of necktie was its pride; when the boy-murderer — he was barely nineteen — who wore it on the gallows took leave of the captain of detectives with the cheerful invitation to "come over to the wake. They'll have a hell of a time." And the event fully redeemed the promise. The whole Gap turned out to do the dead bully honor.

I have not heard from the Gap, and hardly from Hell's Kitchen, in five years. The last news from the Kitchen was when the thin wedge of a column of Negroes, in their uptown migration, tried to squeeze in, and provoked a race war; but that in fairness should not be laid up against it. In certain local aspects it might be accounted a sacred duty; as much so as to get drunk and provoke a fight on the anniversary of the battle of the Boyne. But on the whole the Kitchen has grown orderly. The gang rarely beats a policeman nowadays, and it has not killed one in a long while.

So, one after another, the outworks of the slum have been taken. It has been beaten in many battles; even to the double-decker tenement on the twenty-five foot lot have we put a stop. But its legacy is with us in the habitations of 2 million souls. This is the sore spot, and, as against it all, the rest seems often enough unavailing. Yet it cannot be. It is true that the home, about which all that is to work for permanent progress must cluster, is struggling against desperate odds in the tenement, and that the struggle has been reflected in the morals of the people, in the corruption of the young, to an alarming extent; but it must be that the higher standards now set up on every hand, in the cleaner streets, in the better schools, in the parks and the clubs, in the settlements, and in the thousand and one agencies for good that touch and help the lives of the poor at as many points, will tell at no distant day and react upon the homes and upon their builders. In fact, we know it is so from our experience last fall, when the summons to battle for the people's homes came from the young on the East Side. It was their fight for the very standards I spoke of, their reply to the appeal they made to them. . . .

Some years ago, the United States government conducted an inquiry into the slums of great cities. To its staff of experts was attached a chemist, who gathered and isolated a lot of bacilli, with fearsome Latin names, in the tenements where he went. Among those he labeled were the *Staphylococcus pyogenes albus*, the *Micrococcus fervido-*

sus, the *Saccharomyces rosaceus*, and the *Bacillus buccalis fortuitus*. I made a note of the names at the time because of the dread with which they inspired me. But I searched the collection in vain for the real bacillus of the slum. It escaped science, to be identified by human sympathy and a conscience-stricken community with that of ordinary human selfishness. The antitoxin has been found, and it is applied successfully. Since justice has replaced charity on the prescription the patient is improving. And the improvement is not confined to him; it is general. Conscience is not a local issue in our day.

A few years ago, a United States senator sought reelection on the platform that the Decalogue and the Golden Rule were glittering generalities that had no place in politics, and lost. We have not quite reached the millennium yet, but since then a man was governor in the Empire State, elected on the pledge that he would rule by the 'Ten Commandments. These are facts that mean much or little, according to the way one looks at them. The significant thing is that they are facts, and that, in spite of slipping and sliding, the world moves forward, not backward. The poor we shall have always with us, but the slum we need not have. These two do not rightfully belong together. Their present partnership is at once poverty's worst hardship and our worst blunder.

94.

LYMAN ABBOTT: The Cause and Cure of Anarchism

The anarchist idea of a society without government (because all governments are tyrannical) and without laws (because all laws are oppressive) was "a daydream of romantics," according to one historian, but it was nevertheless seductive enough to bring about the assassination of six heads of state between 1894 and 1912. President McKinley of the United States had been one of them, in 1901; and although American workingmen tended on the whole to be unsympathetic to anarchist agitators, their writings stirred widespread fear among the middle class, which imagined that insurrection was on the verge of breaking out. Lyman Abbott's address before the Nineteenth Century Club of New York, part of which is reprinted here, represented an attempt by an educated American to think clearly about a subject that frightened most people very badly.

Source: *Outlook,* February 22, 1902.

THERE ARE THREE DOCTRINES — if the first can properly be called a doctrine — which are quite distinct, but are often confounded in the public mind: those respectively of assassination, anarchism, and socialism.

The first is the doctrine that all rulers are criminals, robbers of the people, wild beasts, whom any man may kill at sight. To act upon this doctrine is to commit murder. Murder and counseling of murder are crimes; he who does either should be treated by society as either insane or as criminal. Crimes are not to be debated; they are to be prevented or punished. Insane men are not to be reasoned with; they are to be restrained. What methods should be taken to prevent or punish assassination of rulers, and what to punish or to restrain the criminal insane who incite to the assassination of rulers, is a question of criminal law which I do not propose here to discuss. It must suffice to say that this crime is not to be condoned as political, nor this class of criminals given a refuge as patriots, reformers, or even misguided agitators.

Anarchism is defined by E. V. Zenker in his monograph on the subject as "the perfect, unfettered self-government of the individual, and consequently the absence of any kind of external government." It rests upon the doctrine that no man has a right to control by force the action of any other man. In its extreme form it was expressed by the declaration made by an anarchist to me once at a dinner table: "Of course I never think of giving my child a command." By its advocates, anarchism is defended on philosophic grounds: the sanctity of the human will; the inviolability of the personality entrenched in and expressed by that will; the immorality of attempting ever to overawe that will by fear or force of any description.

Anarchism is defended on historic grounds: the evils are recited which have been wrought in human history by the employment of force compelling obedience by one will to another will, as they are seen in political and religious despotism, in the subjugation of women, in every form of brigandage from that of the Italian bands to that of the Napoleonic armies. It is conceded that evils might grow out of the abolition of all government; but it is insisted that they would be insignificant in comparison with the wrongs which have been perpetrated on mankind by the authority of government. Anarchism is defended on religious grounds. Jesus Christ is cited as the first of anarchists; for did he not say, "Resist not evil: if one take away thy coat, give him thy cloak also; and if one smite thee upon the one cheek, turn to him the other

also?" What is this, we are asked, but a denial of the right to use force even in defense of one's simplest and plainest rights?

Socialism, which is curiously confounded by the indiscriminating with anarchism, is its exact opposite. Anarchy is the doctrine that there should be no government control; socialism — that is, state socialism — is the doctrine that government should control everything. State socialism affirms that the state — that is, the government — should own all the tools and implements of industry, should direct all occupations, and should give to every man according to his need and require from every man according to his ability. State socialism points to the evils of overproduction in some fields and insufficient production in others, under our competitive system, and proposes to remedy these evils by assigning to government the duty of determining what shall be produced and what each worker shall produce. If there are too many preachers and too few shoemakers, the preacher will be taken from the pulpit and assigned to the bench; if there are too many shoemakers and too few preachers, the shoemaker will be taken from the bench and assigned to the pulpit.

Anarchy says, no government; socialism says, all government; anarchy leaves the will of the individual absolutely unfettered; socialism leaves nothing to the individual will; anarchism would have no social organism which is not dependent on the entirely voluntary assent of each individual member of the organism at every instant of its history; socialism would have every individual of the social organism wholly subordinate in all his lifework to the authority of the whole body expressed through its properly constituted officers. It is true that there are some writers who endeavor to unite these two antagonistic doctrines by teaching that society should be organized wholly for industry, not at all for government. But how a cooperative industry can be carried on without a government which controls as well as counsels no writer, so far as I have been able to discover, has ever even suggested. . . .

What shall we do with anarchism and the anarchists? We are to protect society from assassins by whatever methods men wise in the penal code can suggest to us. But anarchism is not identical with assassination, and the anarchists are not necessarily assassins; what are we to do with those who are not assassins?

1. We are to treat anarchism seriously; give it a patient hearing; answer it with fair and honest reason. However absurd it may seem to us, it is generally true that he who takes himself seriously is to be taken seriously by his fellowmen.

2. Such serious discussion will discover for us the secret of anarchism in the apotheosis of humanity of which Rousseau was the prophet and of which Thomas Paine was the chiefest literary and Thomas Jefferson the chiefest political exponent in our early national history. If Thomas Paine was right in contending that the less government we have the better, it is not extraordinary that the anarchist concludes that no government would be best of all. If Edmund Burke was right in supposing that the basis of civil society is a convention, the anarchist is logical in concluding that he has a right to disown the convention. If man makes law, man has the power and the right to unmake it; if government rests on the consent of the governed, when the consent is withdrawn the government topples over. We need journalists to affirm, instructors to teach, ministers to preach the sanctity of law — its divine, inviolable, eternal sanctity — especially we need that our legislators should recognize the fact that they are discoverers, not creators; that they are appointed, not to make the laws of the social order but to ascertain what those laws are and to conform the life of the nation thereto. For —

3. Whenever laws are enacted which violate the divine laws of life, they breed anarchy. Anarchism is always a revolt against unjust and unequal laws. Let the legislators recognize the fundamental truth that what is an injury to one is an injury to all, and what is a benefit to the many is a benefit to all; let them seek only the welfare of all by their legislation; let them recognize the truth that law is divine and to set the nation against it is to invite disaster and to conform the nation to it is to insure prosperity, and we shall have little cause to ask — What shall we do with anarchy? It will disappear of itself.

On the contrary, let legislators legislate for special classes; let them encourage by their legislation the spoliation of the many for the benefit of the few; let them protect the rich and forget the poor; let them estimate the prosperity of the nation by the accumulation of its wealth, not by its distribution; let them entrench an industrial system which means long hours, little leisure, and small rewards for the many, and accumulation of unimagined wealth for the few — and men in the bitterness of their hearts will cry out, "If this is government, let us away with it."

4. But just and equal laws will not be enough without just and equal execution of those laws. Let the courts delay to administer justice; let the rich be enabled to keep the poor waiting till their patience and their purses are alike exhausted; let crimes go unpunished until they are forgotten; let the petty gambler be arrested but the rich and prosperous one go free, and anarchism will demand the abolition of all law because it sees in law only an instrument of injustice.

The place in which to attack anarchism is where the offenses grow which alone make anarchism possible. Let us secure the just, speedy, and impartial administration of law; let us elect legislators who seek honestly to conform human legislation to the divine laws of the social order, without fear or favor; let us teach in our churches and our schools and through the press the divine origin, the divine sanctity, and the divine authority of law; and let us, from this vantage ground, meet with fair-minded reason the wild cries of men who have been taught by the monstrous misuse of law to hate all law, both human and divine, and our question will be solved for us; because both anarchy and anarchists will disappear from American society. The way to counteract hostility to law is to make laws which deserve to be respected.

95.

Amos P. Wilder: Governor La Follette and What He Stands For

The leading example of progressivism on the state level was Wisconsin, under its governor, Robert M. La Follette. During his first term, La Follette attracted nationwide attention by his efforts to place more political control in the hands of the people. In his campaign for reelection in 1902, he pledged that he would continue to work for direct primary elections to nominate candidates for state offices. (The measure was passed the next year.) Amos Wilder surveyed the Wisconsin situation in an article for the Outlook *in the spring of 1902, and in the process summed up La Follette's political career to that time.*

Source: *Outlook*, March 8, 1902.

IN WISCONSIN the political issues are two: the direct vote in making nominations, thus bringing political control back to the people; and the forcing of corporations to bear their share of taxation. A most trustworthy state Tax Commission reported a year ago that tax reform should begin by adding over $1,200,000 every two years to the amounts already paid by the railroads. The last legislature refused to enact the increase. Can a legislature be secured that will do its duty?

Wisconsin people are not more Populistic than other well-fed, genial Americans who tolerate bathtubs in their homes and accept Carnegie libraries. But many of them believe that the unfolding life of the nation reveals new dangers to guard against; and it has not escaped attention that the nominating of candidates has become a confused and remote process, and that too often the men of power in political councils are the controlling forces in quasi-public corporations which desire favorable legislation. Wealth seeks to fortify itself with all the concomitants of ability, power, and secrecy. Personality is at work, both coercive and persuasive. There is intrigue, indecision, and the play of vice on weakness. The fighters are taking their posts. There is the cry of challenge and defiance.

Meanwhile, the electorate, a body of over 450,000 voters, mostly agriculturists — men of Wisconsin, sons of New England, Germans, Norwegians, and representatives of many other lands — look confusedly on, waiting for the contest to begin. As in all war, the people pay the bills, carry the burdens, and suffer the distress, but they may also profit by a victory. Governor La Follette, whose reelection is the issue, insists that their interests lie his way. The election occurs in November next. The state Republican convention, which will name the candidate for governor, meets during the summer. The immediate object of the present contest is to secure a majority of the delegates from the seventy counties to this convention and control it.

Governor La Follette is popularly regarded as the standard bearer of reform. He is now serving his first term, and the effort of his opponents is to crush him before he gets any further. Whether one regards this interesting figure as a young David defying the giant of capital and the established order, or brands him as a clever opportunist and a silver-tongued demagogue, will decide one's enrollment, in Wisconsin parlance, as a "half-breed" or a "stalwart." Most of the newspapers are working for his defeat, and not a few of them have shifted their attitude under suspicious circumstances. The adroit opposition has just now complicated the situation and confounded the voters by proposing as their candidate against Governor La Follette a man not only of recognized purity and wisdom but of great determination and aggressive integrity.

Let us consider some of the factors that veil this struggle to get power back to the hands of the people. Governor La Follette is forty-seven years old, but all think of him as young. His family stock was of "the people" and of the soil — a coveted prestige in this Northwest, where farmers control things. La Follette made a reputation in his university days as an orator, but he was too busy earning his living to do much with books. He won the intercollegiate contest when a number of states sent their best college speakers to Iowa City. His oration, an original study of Iago, is still quoted in the district schools. Like many men of the public type, La Follette is strongly endowed with the dramatic instinct. He is short in stature but shapely, with a striking face and head, smooth-shaven, and with abundant dark hair piled up on a high forehead.

He was taken up by the voters when scarcely out of the law school and was made district attorney; then he served six years in Congress — from 1885 to 1891. He was on William McKinley's committee that framed the McKinley tariff, and the Ohio leader thought much of the young man from Wisconsin. For some years, after the Democratic tidal wave of 1890 retired him from Congress, Mr. La Follette practised law. He achieved distinction in jury work, but the attractions of political life were too strong for him, and in 1896 he offered himself to the Republicans for the nomination as governor.

They declined to accept him. In 1898 he tried it again. By this time he had formulated his reforms. He was again defeated, but his platform compelled acceptance. The old-line Republicans, who had long before instinctively felt that he was no longer their kind, were now worried, and their fears were justified. La Follette got out among "the people," spoke to them and with them, and soon had them enthusiastically behind him. In 1900 he received the nomination unanimously, not because the machine wanted him but because it had to take him. He polled the full vote and, with McKinley, secured over a 100,000 Republican majority.

The political methods of any man who can overthrow so well-approved a machine as that which has been built up in Wisconsin merit consideration. He did it by building up an even better machine.

In a campaign, Governor La Follette is a tireless worker, attracting to himself, by his magnetic personality, young men, especially university graduates and young lawyers; and his own law office is a hive of industry. By personal letters and printed documents he reaches great numbers of men of local influence in all the seventy counties of the state. Mrs. La Follette was a classmate of her husband, an unusual woman, interested in advance movements, and an enthusiastic co-worker with him in his public ambition. The governor is a man of blameless personal life, of a sanguine disposition, strong in his likes and dislikes, and styled by his enemies "a dictator" and "vindictive."

He works best with lieutenants who obey without question. It was said of Horatio Seymour that he worked well in any sort of harness. Governor La Follette is not of this class of men. His temperament is on the order of Mr. Bryan's; he is eager to be the people's champion; his mind is aglow with visions of great enactments for the public welfare. Commingled with this is great personal ambition. Men of this stamp wish to be at the head of the procession, not merely in it; and the enactments must bear their name. Only superficial estimators of character and usefulness, however, are dismayed by these outcroppings of human nature. Indeed, one must be prepared to tolerate even cruder forms of human nature to comprehend the potential usefulness of men like La Follette and those who grapple with the modern lions that guard the portals where privilege is entrenched.

With Governor La Follette's stronghold on the common people goes great power as a political organizer and much political adroitness, to which his enemies give a stronger name. This reformer, unlike some others, is not only bold but very shrewd; the children of darkness must look to themselves when pitted against La Follette. His third and successful convention, the one of last summer, is an illustration. After a stormy anti-convention fight, in which La Follette stirred the state as an anti-corporation champion, the remarkable spectacle of a unanimous convention and nomination ensued, and among the workers in the campaign which gave La Follette an unprecedented majority none was more diligent than the railroads. The sudden falling in line of the managers of the railroads and other corporations for La Follette was something of a mystery; some of the other candidates believed that he had come to an understanding with the influential political managers. The friends of the governor assert what I believe to be true, that he had his enemies "on the run"; by brilliant campaign organization in the pivotal counties he routed them. It was then for them a case of "bandwagon."

Governor La Follette does things that weary the patience of the most loyal adherent. So dominant is his personality that many independent men are alienated. He has put men up for office whose characters were objectionable and whose qualifications were pitiful. But through his appointments and policies runs a vein of political purpose. The governor takes all that apply, saints and sinners alike, and there are fishes for the hungry. In his second and successful campaign to secure the governorship, he made a mercilessly persistent attack on Governor Scofield, an excellent executive — one of the honorable order of sawmill owners who have long served Wisconsin in public station. It was hard to see any reason why Scofield should be thrown out and La Follette put in, except that the latter wanted to "lead the people."

And yet, notwithstanding these facts, the man is strong and is really a leader of the people. Why? Because he is honest and fearless and stands for something. Given these qualities and it is amazing how much the electorate will overlook. It suddenly flashes into the minds of the electorate how inspiring is a man with a clear-cut mission, and how rare is the combination of honesty and courage in American public life — so rare when it comes to assailing the castle of privilege and custom that even wisdom is not an indispensable handmaid. It requires some such view of the exigencies of latter-day politics to understand Robert La Follette's position in Wisconsin and why the people cling to him when the ranks of conventionality, wealth, and distinction have pretty generally branded him as a disturber and even a charlatan.

The legislative session of 1900 was stormy almost from the beginning. La Follette sought to crowd through a primary election bill. It was a drastic measure. The party platform promised such a law. It was the one issue about which the entire session of five months raged. The governor was able to pass it in the Assembly by a close vote; but the senators developed opposition to his measure and to him personally, and the feeling ran very high, culminating at the close in a veto of a partial primary measure which the opposition offered him, as he believed, to embarrass him. This veto message scored his enemies in the most scorching language. He charged the opponents of the primary election bill with getting members drunk and tempting them with vice to secure their votes. The *Outlook* said at the time that it was the most vigorous public utterance made in this country for a generation. The opposition senators put on record their assertion that it was insulting.

One of the first steps taken to crush the governor was the purchase of one of the greatest of the Milwaukee dailies, with a circulation throughout the state, its editorial policy being reversed in one day. Soon after the legislature adjourned, the "stalwart" Republican League was formed. On the face of it this call to a reorganization of the party seemed unanswerable; it was signed by eighteen of the thirty-one Republican senators and by eighty-one of the Republican assemblymen, and there were many good men among them. A palatial suite of rooms was engaged in Milwaukee, and for months it has been the headquarters of an anti-La Follette campaign, which for lavish expenditure, bitterness, and persistent effort has rarely been equaled.

State Senator John M. Whitehead (Yale, 1877) has been called upon by the opposition to dispute the nomination with Governor La Follette and has formally accepted the proposition that he should contest the nomination. Mr. Whitehead is a lawyer and a man of the highest character and of unusual force and judgment. He is president of the state Young Men's Christian Association; a big, determined, honest fellow, with no humor, but on intimate terms with grim duty as he sees it. Normally, his would be a candidacy for all well-disposed citizens to get behind. The movement, however, which is urging this candidacy, while statewide in its personnel, will be under "stalwart" auspices; and those who distrust the movement will be tempted to say that Whitehead's candidacy is analogous to Shepard's support and nomination by Tammany Hall.

La Follette is the present hope of "primary elections" in Wisconsin. This interests him more than anything else. Some of his opponents say that it is his scheme to build up a state machine. Many regard the principle as an absurdity; these are the uninformed. The ringsters, of course, are instinctively opposed to allowing the voters to have any more to do with the nominations than necessary. This great reform, which is engaging the attention of thoughtful men in many states, finds its champion in Wisconsin in Governor La Follette. He is eager to further it — not necessarily in the sweeping form in which it was presented to the last legislature but in some fairly advanced way, in order to put the principle on its feet in Wisconsin.

As to the state Tax Commission, all Republicans claim to be its friends; and it is necessary to look beneath the surface. Those interests which object to bigger taxes are in the "stalwart" camp; they presumably pay freely toward the bills of the organization and seek to accomplish their ends largely through its power and machinery. Cooperating with them for the defeat of La Follette are many disinterested citizens who favor aggressive work by the Commission. These are the men who cannot stand for what they call "La Folletteism." They shrink from the governor's methods or question his sincerity. Not a few of the representative men of Wisconsin, including a majority of those who figure in high places at Washington, are of this number. Senator Whitehead, the selected candidate against La Follette, is known as the "Father of the

Tax Commission." I think it can fairly be said that the La Follette forces in the last legislature averaged better as legislators for the people than the stalwarts. It is on this belief that many will support La Follette.

There are times when measures are above men. There are campaigns in which the issue is not the success or overthrow of men but approval or discrediting of a principle. The principle involved in Wisconsin is popular control. The opposition has sneered at primary elections and insists that it was a La Follette scheme to entrench himself, with the aid of typewriters, by sending his literature into the smallest hamlet; but the proposal that citizens get together and indicate on secret ballot whom they would have for mayor and whom they would send to the legislature and to Congress will not down. It commends itself over the present plan of voting for a lot of delegates, whom the citizen does not know, who are to go to some place, perhaps in another county, and vote for some person not specified. La Follette stands for the direct vote.

His opponents say that he has not stood squarely always for vigorous tax reform, but the fact remains that there are now no tax dodgers in his train. For La Follette's political excesses much excuse can be found in the terrific power and wealth pitted against him. He was the one man able to overturn the oligarchy whose rule for years bred recurring restlessness. He may be dictatorial — many leaders are — but it is impossible to conceive him as anyone's tool. The lobby still lives, but it has no hold in the executive chamber.

If he is renominated and reelected, it will be because the voters strike an average, because his merits outweigh his faults, and because the obvious untrustworthiness of the "Republican League" outweighs in the balance the confessed virtue of many of its upholders. The stalwart League will be dominated, not by the many excellent citizens on its outskirts but by the handful of adroit, tireless professionals who find La Follette an obstacle in the way of corporate control of the political machinery of the state.

96.

Daniel Mason: American Composers

There was a running battle throughout much of America's history between those who wanted the arts to imitate traditional European models and those who wished to see them develop a distinctive native style. Daniel Mason belonged to the traditionalists in this debate, which seems rather dated now; he offered his views on American music in an article published in 1902 and reprinted here in part.

Source: *Outlook*, March 15, 1902: "Some American Composers."

When, some years ago, Dr. Dvořák founded upon Negro themes his New World Symphony (which bears in Bohemian the euphonious title "Z nového zveta") and his charming Quartet, Opus 96, and Quintet, Opus 97, there were many ready to proclaim the advent of a veritable American national music. All national music is founded upon folk song, they argued, and American music must be founded on Negro folk song. Others suggested, however, that the Indians were the true aborigines of our continent, and that our music, to be national, must be founded upon their tunes.

It is to be feared that both these theories were based upon a false conception of art, a conception too superficial to be sound. For what is the reason that the music of such nations as Germany, France, Poland, and Russia has been founded upon their primitive folk music, unless that that folk music was the tentative expression of traits deep-founded in the national temperament, and so expressing themselves in greater and greater potency in the later music as it developed? Civilized music is founded upon folk music because, and only because, both spring from deep, unalterable characteristics of the race. The later is merely the evolution of the earlier.

But the American people are not civilized Ethiopians nor civilized red men. They are transplanted Europeans, bearing in their blood a European inheritance of unprecedented multiplicity, and therefore possessed of a mental and moral temper that has little in common with that of Negroes or Indians. The better type of American combines in greater or less degree the practical power of the English, the vivacity of the French, the moral earnestness of the Germans, and many other transatlantic traits; and he adds to the mixture a certain ultimate quality of his own, an indefinable vigor and effervescence of spirit, a big, crude, ardent, democratic enthusiasm. How find the prototype of his appropriate musical expression in the sensuously emotional songs of Negroes or the elementary rhythmic formulae of Indians? Geographical propinquity is a very different relation from community of nature.

Further thought about the matter would lead us to expect from our native musicians a complex and highly varied body of expression, revealing a wide play of influences and voicing a multiplicity of moods and motives. Our music ought to be cosmopolitan rather than narrowly national. It ought to draw freely from all traditions both of thought and technique, and to derive its unity from pertinence to individual expression rather than from limitation to a particular racial convention. We should expect it to be more many-sided than perfect, to fall short not so much in versatility of utterance as in clear fusion of style.

As a matter of fact, this is what we find to be the case when we turn to the work of our composers. They represent many tendencies: the poetically picturesque and imaginative, the warmly romantic and mystical, the intellectual, the brilliant, the richly colored. They have no one pervasive trait that we can point to as distinctively American, as, for example, we can point to the gloomily passionate as Russian or the pseudo-classically finished as French. Their character is individual rather than racial, their technical resources cosmopolitan rather than national. And it is not to be wondered at that, on the whole, their work lacks clearly crystallized style; drawn from so many sources, it is naturally difficult to stamp with unity. There are, accordingly, but few large orchestral works by Americans that impress us as wholly successful and satisfying pieces of art; but there is much vitality and ferment, much that promises a worthy development to come. . . .

Long and various as our list of "legitimate" American composers has grown, it does not enroll two names that are probably more widely known the country over than any of the others. These names are Ethelbert Nevin and John Philip Sousa. The popular success of Nevin's songs and Sousa's marches has been enormous. At the last count Nevin's "'Twas April" had reached 17,000, "One Spring Morning," 19,000, "Little Boy Blue," 24,000, and "The Rosary," 150,000. His ubiquitous piano piece, "Narcissus," has reached the hands of 290,000 pianists, besides being arranged and published for a dozen combinations of instruments. As for Sousa, his marches have been for some years musical pabulum for the entire country. His early attempt, the "Washington Post," is said to have earned him $35, the "Liberty Bell," as many thousands.

The phenomenal success of these two men has been anything but fortuitous, nor is it without a profitable lesson for any composers whose ideals are more recondite than theirs. Nevin and Sousa satisfied two of the perennial needs of musical mankind — the need for the sweetly sentimental and pathetic, and the need for the vigorously rhythmical and stirring. And the "legitimate" American composer, we venture to plead, should not contemn these needs, but seek rather to train the first out of its mawkishness, the second out of its crudity.

For the most part, our composers, whether from defect of vitality or from overestimation of the value of technical subtleties, have failed to utter a forthright word, pealing in all ears with persuasive sincerity and force. Some have refined and intellectualized; some have "written down to the public" — a fatal error; some have followed models over-slavishly; some have become confused by their own facile eclecticism. Whenever they have had something to say, there has been real achievement and advance; but too often they have written with an eye upon the exchequer, or reputation, or the applause of the long-eared populace.

What our national music most needs today appears, then, to be, on the part of the composer, sincerity, open-mindedness, and a resolution never to sully paper with futile ink; on the part of the listener, receptivity, intelligent attention, and superiority to faddism and cant; on the part of the teacher, recognition of the foundation facts of musical instinct, together with a sense of the need of training — in a word, from all who love music or desire its progress, honesty, sensibility, and common sense.

97.

William J. Ghent: The Coming Economic Feudalism

The twentieth century promised many things to many people, most of whom had high hopes for this hundred years that seemed to Americans to coincide with their own rise to world power. One minority critic was not so optimistic; in the view of W. J. Ghent, the future would be characterized by a feudal social order and by the concentration of all political power in the hands of the great industrial barons. We reprint here part of an article published by Ghent in 1902 and later expanded into a book, Our Benevolent Feudalism. *It is interesting to note that many of Ghent's ideas had been expressed by Tocqueville sixty years before.*

Source: *Independent*, April 3, 1902: "The Next Step: A Benevolent Feudalism."

THE NEXT DISTINCT STAGE in the socioeconomic evolution of America may be something entirely different from any of the forms usually predicted. Anarchist prophecies are, of course, futile; and the Tolstoyan Utopia of a return to primitive production, with its prodigal waste of effort and consequent impoverishment of the race, allures but few minds. The Kropotkinian dream of a communistic union of shop industry and agriculture is of a like type; and well-nigh as barren are the Neo-Jeffersonian visions of a general revival of small-farm and small-shop production and the dominance of a middle class democracy. The orthodox economists, with their notions of a slightly modified Individualism, wherein each unit secures the just reward of his capacity and service, are but worshiping an image which they have created out of their books, and which has no real counterpart in life; and finally, the Marxists, who predict the establishment of a cooperative commonwealth, are, to say the least, too sanguine in foreshortening the time of its triumph. Whatever the more distant future may bring to pass, there is but little evidence to prove that collectivism will be the next status of society. Rather, that coming status, of which the contributing forces are now energetically at work and of which the first phases are already plainly observable, will be something in the nature of a Benevolent Feudalism.

That the concentration of capital and the increase of individual holdings of wealth will continue is almost unanimously conceded. Forty years ago, Marx laid down the formula of capitalist accumulation, which has ever since been a fixed article of creed with the orthodox Socialists. "One capitalist always kills many" is its central maxim. And only recently Prof. John B. Clark, doubtless our most distinguished representative of the orthodox economists, declared, in the pages of the *Independent,* that

> the world of the near future . . . will present a condition of vast and ever growing inequality. . . . The rich will continually grow richer, and the multimillionaires will approach the billion dollar standard.

It is a view that needs no particular buttressing of authority, for it is held by most of those who seriously scan the outlook. . . .

The tendencies thus make, on the one hand, toward the centralization of vast power in the hands of a few men — the morganization of industry, as it were — and, on the other, toward a vast increase in the number of those who compose the econom-

ically dependent classes. The latter number is already stupendous. The laborers and mechanics were long ago brought under the yoke through their divorcement from the land and the application of steam to factory operation. They are economically unfree except insofar as their organizations make possible a collective bargaining for wages and hours. The growth of commerce raised up an enormous class of clerks and helpers, perhaps the most dependent class in the community. The growth and partial diffusion of wealth in America has in fifty years largely altered the character of domestic service and increased the number of servants manyfold. Railroad pools and farm-implement trusts have drawn a tightening cordon about the farmers. The professions, too, have felt the change.

Behind many of our important newspapers are private commercial interests which dictate their general policy, if not, as is frequently the case, their particular attitude upon every public question; while the race for endowments made by the greater number of the churches and by all colleges except a few state-supported ones, compels a cautious regard on the part of synod and faculty for the wishes, the views, and prejudices of men of great wealth. To this growing deference of preacher, teacher, and editor is added that of two yet more important classes — the makers and the interpreters of law.

The record of legislation and judicial interpretation regarding slavery previous to the Civil War has been paralleled in recent years by the record of legislatures and courts in matters relating to the lives and health of manual workers, especially in such cases as employers' liability and factory inspection. Thus, with a great addition to the number of subordinate classes, with a tremendous increase of their individual components, and with a corresponding growth of power in the hands of a few score magnates, there is needed little further to make up a socioeconomic status that contains all the essentials of a renascent feudalism.

It is, at least in its beginning, less a personal than a class feudalism. History may repeat itself, as the adage runs; but not by identical forms and events. The great spirals of evolutionary progress carry us for a time back to the general direction of older journeyings but not to the well-worn pathways themselves. The old feudalism exacted faithful service, industrial and martial, from the underling; protection and justice from the overlord. . . .

But, though personal fidelity, in the old sense, is improbable, group fidelity, founded upon the conscious dependence of a class, is already observable, and it grows apace. Out of the sense of class dependence arises the extreme deference which we yield, the rapt homage which we pay — not as individuals but as units of a class — to the men of wealth. We do not know them personally, and we have no sense of personal attachment. But in most things we grant them priority. We send them or their legates to the Senate to make our laws; we permit them to name our administrators and our judiciary; we listen with eager attention to their utterances, and we abide by their judgment. Not always, indeed; for some of us grumble at times and ask angrily where it will all end.

We talk threateningly of instituting referendums to curb excessive power; of levying income taxes or of compelling the government to acquire the railroads and the telegraphs. We subscribe to newspapers and other publications which criticize the acts of the great corporations, and we hail as a new Gracchus the ardent reformer who occasionally comes forth for a season to do battle for the popular cause. But this revolt is, for the most part, sentimental; it is a mental attitude but rarely transmutable into terms of action. It is, moreover, sporadic and flickering; it dies out after a time, and we revert to our usual moods, concerning ourselves with our particular interests and let-

ting the rest of the world wag as it will.

The new feudalism is thus characterized by a class dependence rather than by a personal dependence. But it differs in still other respects from the old. It is qualified and restricted and by agencies hardly operative in medieval times. Democracy tends to restrain it, and ethics to moralize it. Though it has its birth and nurture out of the "rough and unsocialized barbarians of wealth," in Mr. Henry D. Lloyd's phrase, its youth and maturity promise a modification of character. More and more it tends to become a *benevolent* feudalism. On the ethical side it is qualified by a growing and diffusive sense of responsibility and of kinship. The principle of the "trusteeship of great wealth" having found lodgment, like a seed, in the erstwhile barren soil of mammonism, has become a flourishing growth.

The enormous benefactions for social purposes, which have been common of late years and which in 1901 reached a total of $107 million, could come only from men and women who have been taught to feel an ethical duty to society. It is a duty, true enough, which is but dimly seen and imperfectly fulfilled. The greater part of these benefactions is directed to purposes which have but a slight or indirect bearing upon the relief of social distress, the restraint of injustice, or the mitigation of remediable hardships. The giving is even often economically false, and if carried to an extreme would prove disastrous to the community; for in many cases it is a transmutation of wealth from a status of active capital, wherein it makes possible a greater diffusion of comfort, to a status of comparative sterility. But, though often mistaken as is the conception and futile the fulfillment of this duty, the fact that it is apprehended at all is one of far-reaching importance.

The limitation which democracy puts upon the new feudalism is also important; for democracy will endure, in spite of the new order. "Like death," said Disraeli, "it gives back nothing." Something of its substance it gives back, it must be confessed; for it permits the most serious encroachments upon its rights; but of its outer forms it yields nothing, and thus it retains the potentiality of exerting its will in whatever direction it may see fit. And this fact, though now but feebly recognized by the feudal barons, will be better understood by them as time runs on, and they will bear in mind the limit of popular patience. . . .

Macaulay's famous dictum, that the privileged classes, when their rule is threatened, always bring about their own ruin by making further exactions, is likely, in this case, to prove untrue. A wiser forethought begins to prevail among the autocrats of today — a forethought destined to grow and expand and to prove of inestimable value when bequeathed to their successors. Our nobility will thus temper their exactions to an endurable limit; and they will distribute benefits to a degree that makes a tolerant, if not a satisfied, people. They may even make a working principle of Bentham's maxim, and after, of course, appropriating the first and choicest fruits of industry to themselves, may seek to promote the "greatest happiness of the greatest number." For therein will lie their greater security.

Of the particular forms which this new feudalism will take there are already numerous indications which furnish grounds for more or less confident prediction. All societies evolve naturally out of their predecessors. In sociology, as in biology, there is no cell without a parent cell. The society of each generation develops a multitude of spontaneous and acquired variations, and out of these, by a blending process of natural and conscious selection, the succeeding society is evolved. The new feudalism is but an orderly outgrowth of past and present tendencies and conditions. . . .

Of the three underclasses of the old feudalism — subtenants, cotters, and villeins — the first two are already on the ground, and the last is in process of restoration. But the vast complexity of modern society specializes functions, and for the new feudalism still other classes are required. . . .

1. The barons, graded on the basis of possessions.

2. The courtiers and court agents.

3. The workers in pure and applied science, artists and physicians. The new feudalism, like most autocracies, will foster not only the arts but also certain kinds of learning — particularly the kinds which are unlikely to disturb the minds of the multitude. A future Marsh or Cope or Le Conte will be liberally patronized and left free to discover what he will; and so, too, an Edison or a Marconi. Only they must not meddle with anything relating to social science. For obvious reasons, also, physicians will occupy a position of honor and comparative freedom under the new regime.

4. The entrepreneurs, the managers of the great industries, transformed into a salaried class.

5. The foremen and superintendents. This class has heretofore been recruited largely from the skilled workers, but with the growth of technical education in schools and colleges and the development of fixed caste, it is likely to become entirely differentiated.

6. The villeins of the cities and towns, more or less regularly employed, who do skilled work and are partially protected by organization.

7. The villeins of the cities and towns who do unskilled work and are unprotected by organization. They will comprise the laborers, domestics, and clerks.

8. The villeins of the manorial estates, of the great farms, the mines, and the forests.

9. The small-unit farmers (landowning), the petty tradesmen, and manufacturers.

10. The subtenants on the manorial estates and great farms (corresponding to the class of "free tenants" in the old feudalism).

11. The cotters, living in isolated places and on the margin of cultivation.

12. The tramps, the occasionally employed, the unemployed — the wastrels of city and country.

This, then, is the table of socioindustrial rank leading down from the feudatory barons. . . .

There will thus be large displacements of labor and for a time a wide extension of suffering. Popular discontent will naturally follow, and it will be fomented, to some extent, by agitation; but the agitation will be guarded in expression and action, and it will be relatively barren of result. The possible danger therefrom will have been provided against, and a host of economists, preachers, and editors will be ready to show indisputably that the evolution taking place is for the best interests of all; that it follows a "natural and inevitable law"; that those who have been thrown out of work have only their own incompetency to blame; that all who really want work can get it; and that any interference with the prevailing regime will be sure to bring on a panic, which will only make matters worse. Hearing this, the multitude will hesitatingly acquiesce and thereupon subside; and though occasionally a radical journal or a radical agitator will counsel revolt, the mass will remain quiescent. Gradually, too, by one method or another, sometimes by the direct action of the nobility, the greater part of the displaced workers will find some means of getting bread, while those who cannot will be eliminated from the struggle and cease to be a potential factor for trouble.

In its general aspects, shop industry will be carried on much as now. Only the shops will be very much larger, the individual and total output will be greater, the unit cost of production will be lessened. Wages and hours will for a time continue on something like the present level; but, despite the persistence of the unions, no considerable gains in behalf of labor are to be expected. The owners of all industry worth owning, the barons, will laugh at threats of striking and boycotting. No competitor can possibly make capital out of the labor disputes of another, for there will be no competitors, actual or potential. What the barons will most dread will be the collective assertion of the villeins at the polls; but this, from experience, they will know to be a thing of no immediate danger. By the putting forward of a hundred irrelevant issues they can hopelessly divide the voters at each election; or, that failing, there is always to be trusted as a last resort the cry of impending panic.

Practically all industry will be regulated in terms of wages, and the entrepreneurs, who will then have become the chief salaried officers of the nobles, will calculate to a hair the needful production for each year. Waste and other losses will thus be reduced to a minimum. A vast scheme of exact systematization will have taken the place of the old free competition, and industry will be carried on as by clockwork.

Gradually a change will take place in the aspirations and conduct of the younger generations. Heretofore there has been at least some degree of freedom of choice in determining one's occupation, however much that freedom has been curtailed by actual economic conditions. But with the settling of industrial processes comes more and more constraint. The dream of the children of the farms to escape from their drudgery by migrating to the city, and from the stepping stone of a clerkly place at $3 a week to rise to affluence, will be given over, and they will follow the footsteps of their fathers. A like fixity of condition will be observed in the cities, and the sons of clerks and of mechanics and of day laborers will tend to accept their environment of birth and training and abide by it. It is a phenomenon observable in all countries where the economic pressure is severe, and it is certain to obtain in feudal America. . . .

Armed force will, of course, be employed to overawe the discontented and to quiet unnecessary turbulence. Unlike the armed forces of the old feudalism, the nominal control will be that of the State; the soldiery will be regular and not irregular. Not again will the barons risk the general indignation arising from the employment of Pinkertons and other private armies. The worker has unmistakably shown his preference, when he is to be subdued, for the militia and the federal Army. Broadly speaking, it is not an unreasonable attitude; and it goes without saying that it will be respected. The militia of our Benevolent Feudalism will be recruited, as now, mostly from the clerkly class; and it will be officered largely by the sons and nephews of the barons. But its actions will be tempered by a saner policy. Governed by those who have most to fear from popular exasperation, it will show a finer restraint. . . .

This, then, in the rough, is our Benevolent Feudalism to-be. It is not precisely a Utopia, not an "island valley of Avilion"; and yet it has its commendable, even its fascinating, features. "The empire is peace," shouted the partisans of Louis Napoleon; and a like cry, with an equal ardency of enthusiasm, will be uttered by the supporters of the new regime. Peace and stability will be its defensive arguments, and peace and stability it will probably bring. But tranquil or unquiet, whatever it may be, its triumph is assured; and existent forces are carrying us toward it with an ever accelerating speed. One power alone might prevent it — the collective popular will that it shall not be. But of this there is no fear on the part of the barons and but little expectation on the part of the underlings.

98.

George F. Baer: On the Divine Right to Property

Few letters have attracted so much public attention as George F. Baer's reply to W. F. Clark on July 17, 1902. The letter was written during an anthracite coal strike in Pennsylvania. Clark had appealed to Baer, president of the Philadelphia and Reading Railroad, to end the strike. Baer's reply stated in classic, ultraconservative terms the view of the captain of industry concerning the control of wealth. The letter served to intensify the hostile feelings between labor and management and delay any peaceful settlement of the strike.

Source: Caro Lloyd, *Henry Demarest Lloyd*, New York, 1912, p. 190.

I DO NOT KNOW WHO YOU ARE. I see that you are a religious man, but you are evidently biased in favor of the right of the workingman to control a business in which he has no other interest than to obtain fair wages for the work he does.

I beg of you not to be discouraged. The rights and interests of the laboring man will be protected and cared for, not by the labor agitators but by the Christian men to whom God in His infinite wisdom has given the control of the property interests of the country, and upon the successful management of which so much depends.

Do not be discouraged. Pray earnestly that right may triumph, always remembering that the Lord God Omnipotent still reigns, and that His reign is one of law and order and not of violence and crime.

99.

Frank Norris: A Deal in Wheat

Social critics and reformers around the turn of the century put their case before the public in different ways. Jacob Riis presented fully documented reports on slum conditions in New York City. Such authors as Upton Sinclair and Frank Norris used their fiction as a vehicle to express their discontent with social and economic conditions that to them were intolerable. Norris had conceived a major work of social criticism in three volumes to be titled "Epic of the Wheat;" the first volume, The Octopus *(1901), is considered his best book. The following short story, centering around the Chicago grain market, deals with problems more fully explored in* The Pit, *the second volume of the trilogy. Norris died suddenly after an appendectomy in 1902 before writing the third volume.*

Source: *A Deal in Wheat and Other Stories of the New and Old West,* New York, 1903.

I

THE BEAR — WHEAT AT SIXTY-TWO

As Sam Lewiston backed the horse into the shafts of his buckboard and began hitching the tugs to the whiffletree, his wife came out from the kitchen door of the house and drew near, and stood for some time at the horse's head, her arms folded and her apron rolled around them. For a long moment neither spoke. They had talked over the situation so long and so comprehensively the night before that there seemed to be nothing more to say.

The time was late in the summer, the place, a ranch in southwestern Kansas, and Lewiston and his wife were two of a vast population of farmers, wheat growers, who at that moment were passing through a crisis — a crisis that at any moment might culminate in tragedy. Wheat was down to sixty-six.

At length Emma Lewiston spoke.

"Well," she hazarded, looking vaguely out across the ranch toward the horizon, leagues distant; "well, Sam, there's always that offer of brother Joe's. We can quit — and go to Chicago — if the worst comes."

"And give up!" exclaimed Lewiston, running the lines through the torets. "Leave the ranch! Give up! After all these years!"

His wife made no reply for the moment. Lewiston climbed into the buckboard and gathered up the lines. "Well, here goes for the last try, Emmie," he said. "Good-by, girl. Maybe things will look better in town today."

"Maybe," she said gravely. She kissed her husband good-by and stood for some time looking after the buckboard traveling toward the town in a moving pillar of dust.

"I don't know," she murmured at length; "I don't know just how we're going to make out."

When he reached town, Lewiston tied the horse to the iron railing in front of the Odd Fellows' Hall, the ground floor of which was occupied by the post office, and went across the street and up the stairway of a building of brick and granite — quite the most pretentious structure of the town — and knocked at a door upon the first landing. The door was furnished with a pane of frosted glass, on which, in gold letters, was inscribed, "Bridges & Co., Grain Dealers."

Bridges himself, a middle-aged man who wore a velvet skullcap and who was smoking a Pittsburgh stogie, met the farmer at the counter and the two exchanged perfunctory greetings.

"Well," said Lewiston, tentatively, after awhile.

"Well, Lewiston," said the other, "I can't take that wheat of yours at any better than sixty-two."

"Sixty-*two*."

"It's the Chicago price that does it, Lewiston. Truslow is bearing the stuff for all he's worth. It's Truslow and the bear clique that stick the knife into us. The price broke again this morning. We've just got a wire."

"Good heavens," murmured Lewiston, looking vaguely from side to side. "That — that ruins me. I *can't* carry my grain any longer — what with storage charges and — and —— Bridges, I don't see just how I'm going to make out. Sixty-two cents a bushel! Why, man, what with this and with that it's cost me nearly a dollar a bushel to raise that wheat, and now Truslow ——"

He turned away abruptly with a quick gesture of infinite discouragement.

He went down the stairs, and making his way to where his buckboard was hitched, got in, and, with eyes vacant, the reins slipping and sliding in his limp, half-open hands, drove slowly back to the ranch. His wife had seen him coming and met him as he drew up before the barn.

"Well?" she demanded.

"Emmie," he said as he got out of the buckboard, laying his arm across her shoulder, "Emmie, I guess we'll take up with

Joe's offer. We'll go to Chicago. We're cleaned out!"

II

THE BULL — WHEAT AT A DOLLAR-TEN

. . . —— and said Party of the Second Part further covenants and agrees to merchandise such wheat in foreign ports, it being understood and agreed between the Party of the First Part and the Party of the Second Part that the wheat hereinbefore mentioned is released and sold to the Party of the Second Part for export purposes only, and not for consumption or distribution within the boundaries of the United States of America or of Canada.

"Now, Mr. Gates, if you will sign for Mr. Truslow I guess that'll be all," remarked Hornung when he had finished reading.

Hornung affixed his signature to the two documents and passed them over to Gates, who signed for his principal and client, Truslow — or, as he had been called ever since he had gone into the fight against Hornung's corner — the Great Bear. Hornung's secretary was called in and witnessed the signatures, and Gates thrust the contract into his Gladstone bag and stood up, smoothing his hat.

"You will deliver the warehouse receipts for the grain," began Gates.

"I'll send a messenger to Truslow's office before noon," interrupted Hornung. "You can pay by certified check through the Illinois Trust people."

When the other had taken himself off, Hornung sat for some moments gazing abstractedly toward his office windows, thinking over the whole matter. He had just agreed to release to Truslow, at the rate of $1.10 per bushel, 100,000 out of the 2 million and odd bushels of wheat that he, Hornung, controlled, or actually owned. And for the moment he was wondering if, after all, he had done wisely in not goring the Great Bear to actual financial death. He had made him pay $100,000. Truslow was good for this amount. Would it not have been better to have put a prohibitive figure on the grain and forced the Bear into bankruptcy? True, Hornung would then be without his enemy's money, but Truslow would have been eliminated from the situation, and that — so Hornung told himself — was always a consummation most devoutly, strenuously, and diligently to be striven for. Truslow once dead was dead, but the Bear was never more dangerous than when desperate.

"But so long as he can't get *wheat*," muttered Hornung at the end of his reflections, "he can't hurt me. And he can't get it. That I *know*."

For Hornung controlled the situation. So far back as the February of that year an "unknown bull" had been making his presence felt on the floor of the Board of Trade. By the middle of March the commercial reports of the daily press had begun to speak of "the powerful bull clique"; a few weeks later that legendary condition of affairs implied and epitomized in the magic words "Dollar Wheat" had been attained, and by the first of April, when the price had been boosted to $1.10 a bushel, Hornung had disclosed his hand, and in place of mere rumors, the definite and authoritative news that May wheat had been cornered in the Chicago pit went flashing around the world from Liverpool to Odessa and from Duluth to Buenos Aires.

It was — so the veteran operators were persuaded — Truslow himself who had made Hornung's corner possible. The Great Bear had for once over-reached himself, and, believing himself all-powerful, had hammered the price just the fatal fraction too far down. Wheat had gone to sixty-two — for the time, and under the circumstances, an abnormal price. When the reac-

tion came it was tremendous. Hornung saw his chance, seized it, and in a few months had turned the tables, had cornered the product, and virtually driven the bear clique out of the pit.

On the same day that the delivery of the 100,000 bushels was made to Truslow, Hornung met his broker at his lunch club.

"Well," said the latter, "I see you let go that line of stuff to Truslow."

Hornung nodded; but the broker added:

"Remember, I was against it from the very beginning. I know we've cleared up over a hundred thou'. I would have fifty times preferred to have lost twice that and *smashed Truslow dead*. Bet you what you like he makes us pay for it somehow."

"Huh!" grunted his principal. "How about insurance, and warehouse charges, and carrying expenses on that lot? Guess we'd have had to pay those, too, if we'd held on."

But the other put up his chin, unwilling to be persuaded. "I won't sleep easy," he declared, "till Truslow is busted."

III

THE PIT

Just as Going mounted the steps on the edge of the pit the great gong struck, a roar of a hundred voices developed with the swiftness of successive explosions, the rush of a hundred men surging downward to the center of the pit filled the air with the stamp and grind of feet, a hundred hands in eager strenuous gestures tossed upward from out the brown of the crowd, the official reporter in his cage on the margin of the pit leaned far forward with straining ear to catch the opening bid, and another day of battle was begun.

Since the sale of the 100,000 bushels of wheat to Truslow, the "Hornung crowd" had steadily shouldered the price higher, until on this particular morning it stood at $1.50. That was Hornung's price. No one else had any grain to sell.

But not ten minutes after the opening, Going was surprised out of all countenance to hear shouted from the other side of the pit these words:

"Sell May at one-fifty."

Going was for the moment touching elbows with Kimbark on one side and with Merriam on the other, all three belonging to the "Hornung crowd." Their answering challenge of *"Sold"* was as the voice of one man. They did not pause to reflect upon the strangeness of the circumstance. (That was for afterward.) Their response to the offer was as unconscious as reflex action and almost as rapid, and before the pit was well aware of what had happened the transaction of 1,000 bushels was down upon Going's trading card and $1,500 had changed hands. But here was a marvel — the whole available supply of wheat cornered, Hornung master of the situation, invincible, unassailable; yet behold a man willing to sell, a Bear bold enough to raise his head.

"That was Kennedy, wasn't it, who made that offer?" asked Kimbark, as Going noted down the trade — "Kennedy, that new man?"

"Yes; who do you suppose he's selling for; who's willing to go short at this stage of the game?"

"Maybe he ain't short."

"Short! Great heavens, man; where'd he get the stuff?"

"Blamed if I know. We can account for every handful of May. Steady! Oh, there he goes again."

"Sell 1,000 May at $1.50," vociferated the bear-broker, throwing out his hand, one finger raised to indicate the number of "contracts" offered. This time it was evident that he was attacking the Hornung crowd deliberately, for, ignoring the jam of traders that swept toward him, he looked across the pit to where Going and Kimbark were shouting *"Sold! Sold!"* and nodded his head.

A second time Going made memoranda of the trade, and either the Hornung holdings were increased by 2,000 bushels of May wheat or the Hornung bank account swelled by at least $3,000 of some unknown short's money.

Of late — so sure was the bull crowd of its position — no one had even thought of glancing at the inspection sheet on the bulletin board. But now one of Going's messengers hurried up to him with the announcement that this sheet showed receipts at Chicago for that morning of 25,000 bushels, and not credited to Hornung. Someone had got hold of a line of wheat overlooked by the "clique" and was dumping it upon them.

"Wire the Chief," said Going over his shoulder to Merriam. This one struggled out of the crowd, and on a telegraph blank scribbled:

Strong bear movement — New man — Kennedy — Selling in lots of five contracts — Chicago receipts twenty-five thousand.

The message was dispatched, and in a few moments the answer came back, laconic, of military terseness:

Support the market.

And Going obeyed, Merriam and Kimbark following, the new broker fairly throwing the wheat at them in thousand-bushel lots.

"Sell May at 'fifty; sell May; sell May." A moment's indecision, an instant's hesitation, the first faint suggestion of weakness, and the market would have broken under them. But for the better part of four hours they stood their ground, taking all that was offered, in constant communication with the Chief, and from time to time stimulated and steadied by his brief, unvarying command: "Support the market."

At the close of the session they had bought in the 25,000 bushels of May. Hornung's position was as stable as a rock, and the price closed even with the opening figure — $1.50.

But the morning's work was the talk of all La Salle Street. Who was back of the raid? What was the meaning of this unexpected selling? For weeks the pit trading had been merely nominal. Truslow, the Great Bear, from whom the most serious attack might have been expected, had gone to his country seat at Geneva Lake, in Wisconsin, declaring himself to be out of the market entirely. He went bass fishing every day.

IV

THE BELT LINE

ON A CERTAIN DAY toward the middle of the month, at a time when the mysterious Bear had unloaded some 80,000 bushels upon Hornung, a conference was held in the library of Hornung's home. His broker attended it, and also a clean-faced, bright-eyed individual whose name of Cyrus Ryder might have been found upon the payroll of a rather well-known detective agency. For upward of half an hour after the conference began the detective spoke, the other two listening attentively, gravely.

"Then, last of all," concluded Ryder, "I made out I was a hobo, and began stealing rides on the Belt Line Railroad. Know the road? It just circles Chicago. Truslow owns it. Yes? Well, then I began to catch on. I noticed that cars of certain numbers — thirty-one nought thirty-four, thirty-two one ninety — well, the numbers don't matter, but anyhow, these cars were always switched onto the sidings by Mr. Truslow's main elevator D soon as they came in. The wheat was shunted in, and they were pulled

out again. Well, I spotted one car and stole a ride on her. Say, look here, *that car went right around the city on the Belt, and came back to D again, and the same wheat in her all the time*. The grain was reinspected — it was raw, I tell you — and the warehouse receipts made out just as though the stuff had come in from Kansas or Iowa."

"The same wheat all the time!" interrupted Hornung.

"The same wheat — your wheat, that you sold to Truslow."

"Great snakes!" ejaculated Hornung's broker. "Truslow never took it abroad at all."

"Took it abroad! Say, he's just been running it around Chicago, like the supers in 'Shenandoah,' round an' round, so you'd think it was a new lot, an' selling it back to you again."

"No wonder we couldn't account for so much wheat."

"Bought it from us at $1.10, and made us buy it back — our own wheat — at $1.50."

Hornung and his broker looked at each other in silence for a moment. Then all at once Hornung struck the arm of his chair with his fist and exploded in a roar of laughter. The broker stared for one bewildered moment, then followed his example.

"Sold! Sold!" shouted Hornung almost gleefully. "Upon my soul it's as good as a Gilbert and Sullivan show. And we —— Oh, Lord! Billy, shake on it, and hats off to my distinguished friend Truslow. He'll be President some day. Hey! What? Prosecute him? Not I."

"He's done us out of a neat hatful of dollars for all that," observed the broker, suddenly grave.

"Billy, it's worth the price."

"We've got to make it up somehow."

"Well, tell you what. We were going to boost the price to $1.75 next week, and make that our settlement figure."

"Can't do it now. Can't afford it."

"No. Here; we'll let out a big link; we'll put wheat at $2.00, and let it go at that."

"Two it is, then," said the broker.

V

THE BREAD LINE

THE STREET WAS VERY DARK and absolutely deserted. It was a district on the "South Side," not far from the Chicago River, given up largely to wholesale stores, and after nightfall was empty of all life. The echoes slept but lightly hereabouts, and the slightest footfall, the faintest noise, woke them upon the instant and sent them clamoring up and down the length of the pavement between the iron shuttered fronts. The only light visible came from the side door of a certain "Vienna" bakery, where at 1 o'clock in the morning loaves of bread were given away to any who should ask. Every evening about 9 o'clock the outcasts began to gather about the side door. The stragglers came in rapidly, and the line — the "bread line," as it was called — began to form. By midnight it was usually some hundred yards in length, stretching almost the entire length of the block.

Toward ten in the evening, his coat collar turned up against the fine drizzle that pervaded the air, his hands in his pockets, his elbows gripping his sides, Sam Lewiston came up and silently took his place at the end of the line.

Unable to conduct his farm upon a paying basis at the time when Truslow, the "Great Bear," had sent the price of grain down to 62 cents a bushel, Lewiston had turned over his entire property to his creditors, and, leaving Kansas for good, had abandoned farming, and had left his wife at her sister's boarding house in Topeka with the understanding that she was to join him in Chicago as soon as he had found a steady job. Then he had come to Chicago and had turned workman. His brother Joe conducted a small hat factory on Archer Avenue, and for a time he found there a meager employment. But difficulties had occurred, times were bad, the hat factory was involved in debts, the repealing of a certain import duty on manufactured felt overcrowded the home market with cheap Belgian and French products, and in the end his brother had assigned and gone to Milwaukee.

Thrown out of work, Lewiston drifted aimlessly about Chicago, from pillar to post, working a little, earning here a dollar, there a dime, but always sinking, sinking, till at last the ooze of the lowest bottom dragged at his feet and the rush of the great ebb went over him and engulfed him and shut him out from the light, and a park bench became his home and the "bread line" his chief makeshift of subsistence.

He stood now in the enfolding drizzle, sodden, stupefied with fatigue. Before and behind stretched the line. There was no talking. There was no sound. The street was empty. It was so still that the passing of a cablecar in the adjoining thoroughfare grated like prolonged rolling explosions, beginning and ending at immeasurable distances. The drizzle descended incessantly. After a long time midnight struck.

There was something ominous and gravely impressive in this interminable line of dark figures, close-pressed, soundless; a crowd, yet absolutely still; a close-packed, silent file, waiting, waiting in the vast deserted night-ridden street; waiting without a word, without a movement, there under the night and under the slow-moving mists of rain.

Few in the crowd were professional beggars. Most of them were workmen, long since out of work, forced into idleness by long-continued "hard times," by ill luck, by sickness. To them the "bread line" was a godsend. At least they could not starve. Between jobs here in the end was something to hold them up — a small platform, as it were, above the sweep of black water, where for a moment they might pause and take breath before the plunge.

The period of waiting on this night of rain seemed endless to those silent, hungry men; but at length there was a stir. The line moved. The side door opened. Ah, at last! They were going to hand out the bread.

But instead of the usual white-aproned undercook with his crowded hampers there now appeared in the doorway a new man — a young fellow who looked like a book-keeper's assistant. He bore in his hand a placard, which he tacked to the outside of the door. Then he disappeared within the bakery, locking the door after him.

A shudder of poignant despair, an unformed, inarticulate sense of calamity, seemed to run from end to end of the line. What had happened? Those in the rear, unable to read the placard, surged forward, a sense of bitter disappointment clutching at their hearts.

The line broke up, disintegrated into a shapeless throng — a throng that crowded forward and collected in front of the shut door whereon the placard was affixed. Lewiston, with the others, pushed forward. On the placard he read these words:

> Owing to the fact that the price of grain has been increased to two dollars a bushel, there will be no distribution of bread from this bakery until further notice.

Lewiston turned away, dumb, bewildered. Till morning he walked the streets, going on without purpose, without direction. But now at last his luck had turned. Overnight the wheel of his fortunes had creaked and swung upon its axis, and before noon he had found a job in the street-cleaning brigade. In the course of time he rose to be first shift boss, then deputy inspector, then inspector, promoted to the dignity of driving in a red wagon with rubber tires and drawing a salary instead of mere wages. The wife was sent for and a new start made.

But Lewiston never forgot. Dimly he began to see the significance of things. Caught once in the cogs and wheels of a great and terrible engine, he had seen — none better — its workings. Of all the men who had vainly stood in the "bread line" on that rainy night in early summer, he, perhaps, had been the only one who had struggled up to the surface again. How many others had gone down in the great ebb? Grim question; he dared not think how many.

He had seen the two ends of a great wheat operation — a battle between Bear and Bull. The stories (subsequently published in the city's press) of Truslow's countermove in selling Hornung his own wheat, supplied the unseen section. The farmer — he who raised the wheat — was ruined upon one hand; the workingman — he who consumed it — was ruined upon the other. But between the two, the great operators, who never saw the wheat they traded in, bought and sold the world's food, gambled in the nourishment of entire nations, practised their tricks, their chicanery and oblique shifty "deals," were reconciled in their differences, and went on through their appointed way, jovial, contented, enthroned, and unassailable.

When you call me that, smile!
OWEN WISTER, *The Virginian,* 1902

Back country cotton farm photographed by Ray Stannard Baker

THE SOUTH

In 1871 Birmingham, Alabama, was founded at the junction of east-west and north-south railroads; true to the pattern of industrialization, Birmingham gradually became the leading industrial city of the South, producing pig iron, steel, coke, and chemicals. North of Birmingham, the Tennessee Valley was beginning to develop as Chattanooga and Knoxville prospered on Northern capital invested in coal, textiles, and railroads. In 1898 Congress passed a bill authorizing construction of a private hydroelectric project at Muscle Shoals, Alabama; though a dam was not built until 1925 and then under government auspices, its conception indicated a new and promising direction for the Southern economy. In Florida the tourism which the railroad made possible was becoming a major industry; the railroad reached Miami in 1896 and later continued to Key West. At the same time the rest of the country was opened as a market for Florida's citrus and winter truck crops. Despite the slow accumulation of capital in the South, however, the region remained predominantly agricultural, and Southern agriculture continued to consist largely of poor freehold and tenant farmers. As cotton prices fell sharply to seven cents per pound in the early 1890s, it was these classes that filled the membership of the Populist-agrarian movement against both the traditional Bourbons and the newer Southern capitalists.

Canal Street in New Orleans at the turn of the century

(Above) Street scene in New Orleans, about 1900; (below) float in the annual Mardi Gras parade

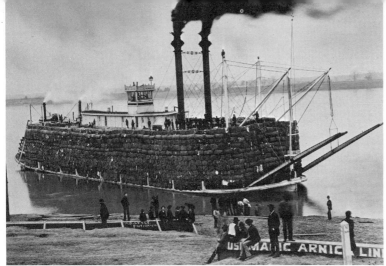

Steamer "Pargoud" loaded with bales of cotton; photo by A. D. Lytle

(Above) Last of the keelboats carrying a load of hoop poles, 1898; (below) goods piled along the levee at Memphis, Tenn., awaiting shipment, 1897

Street scene in New Albany, Miss., photographed by J. L. S. Rogers, about 1900

(Above) Building where cotton is weighed and processed; photo by Ray Stannard Baker; (below) Negroes working as cotton pickers in the South in the 1880s, from a lantern slide

Two scenes in Mississippi photographed by the Detroit Publishing Company in 1901: (Above) Washington Avenue in Ocean Springs and (below) Harry's Villa in Bay St. Louis

Sibley and King Cotton Mills, Augusta, Ga. Textile manufacturing is the city's main industry

(Above) Horse-drawn vehicles crowd the public square of Gainesville, Ga., about 1900; (below) Spanish moss hangs from trees along Sumter Avenue in Summerville, S.C., 1906

(Above) Distilling turpentine in North Carolina in 1908; (left) golfers on the green of the Hampton Terrace course in Augusta, Ga., 1905; (below) Piney Woods resort hotel in Thomasville, Ga., 1890s, photo by Joseph J. Kirkbride

(Above) Memphis Building and Parthenon at the Tennessee Centennial Exposition in Nashville, 1897; (below left) interior of the Negro Building at the Centennial; (below right) President McKinley visiting Negro Building at the Cotton States Exposition in Atlanta, Ga.

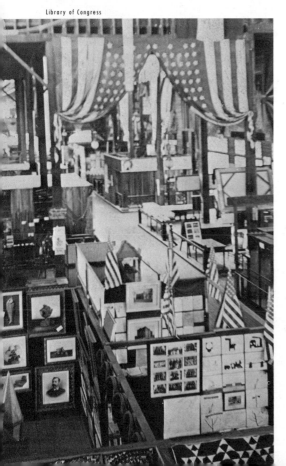

With the return of full sovereignty to Southern state governments by the Hayes agreement in 1877, with the ascendancy of the Populist-racist politicians in the 1890s, and with the Supreme Court's decision in Plessy v. Ferguson in 1896, the Negro was relegated to an inferior status substantially equivalent to that of 1860. By 1910 all Southern states had effectively disfranchised the Negro by law or constitutional amendment; literacy tests, poll taxes, and "grandfather clauses" were popular ways of disqualifying a maximum number of Negroes and a minimum number of whites. After 1900 no Negro was elected to a Southern legislature until 1962.

(Above) Unloading freight from "City of St. Louis" at Dog Tooth Cut-Off; (below left) member of chain gang in Thomasville, Ga.; (below right) Negroes with bloodhounds in Marianna, Ark.

View of Main Street in Strasburg, Va., in the 1890s; photo by Kneisley

(Above) Negro girl leaning against a shock of peanuts; (below) building a road

John Brown's Fort, an abandoned building in Harpers Ferry, West Virginia, in 1882

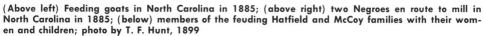

(Above left) Feeding goats in North Carolina in 1885; (above right) two Negroes en route to mill in North Carolina in 1885; (below) members of the feuding Hatfield and McCoy families with their women and children; photo by T. F. Hunt, 1899

Building and grounds of the Ponce de Leon resort hotel in St. Augustine, Fla., 1902; photo by the Detroit Publishing Company

(Above) Patrons relaxing in the court of the Ponce de Leon; (below) man with bicycle on a street in Daytona, Fla., 1904

100.

"The Boll Weevil"

*The nemesis of the Southern farmer was the boll weevil. Feeding on the cotton crop
year after year, this "little black bug" succeeded in overturning the entire economy
of the region. Farmers were forced to plant other crops that were not subject to the
weevil's ravages and to adopt measures designed to eliminate him. The boll weevil
is still around, but he is not feared as he used to be; however, we still sing about him.
There are dozens of versions of the song.*

THE BOLL WEEVIL

The boll weevil is a little black bug
Come from Mexico, they say.
He come over to Texas,
And he thought he better stay,

    A-lookin' for a home,
    Just a-lookin' for a home.
    A-lookin' for a home,
    Just a-lookin' for a home.

The first time I see the boll weevil
He was sitting in the square.
The next time I see the boll weevil
He had all of his family there.

    They're lookin' for a home,
    Just a-lookin' for a home.
    They're lookin' for a home,
    Just a-lookin' for a home.

The farmer took the boll weevil
And he put him in the hot sand.
The boll weevil say to the farmer:
"I'll stand it like a man —

    This'll be my home
    It'll be my home.
    This'll be my home
    It'll be my home."

The farmer took the boll weevil
And he put him in a cake of ice.
The boll weevil say to the farmer:
"This is mighty cool and nice —

    This'll be my home
    It'll be my home.
    This'll be my home
    It'll be my home."

The boll weevil say to the farmer:
"You better leave me alone.
I ate up all your cotton
And now I'll start on the corn,

    Cause I'll have a home,
    I'll have a home.
    Cause I'll have a home,
    I'll have a home."

The merchant got half the cotton,
The boll weevil got the rest;
Didn't leave that farmer's wife
But one old cotton dress,

    And it's full of holes,
    And it's full of holes.
    And it's full of holes,
    And it's full of holes.

The farmer say to the merchant:
"I ain't made but one bale,
And before I give you that one
I'll fight and go to jail —

   I'll have a home,
   I'll have a home.
   I'll have a home,
   I'll have a home."

If anybody should ask you
Who was it wrote this song,
Just tell him it was a dark-skin farmer
With a pair of blue duckins on,

   A-lookin' for a home,
   Just a-lookin' for a home.
   A-lookin' for a home,
   Just a-lookin' for a home.

101.

GEORGE KENNAN: The Vested Rights of Reservation Indians

*Deprived of his land, shunted onto reservations, denied most civil rights, the
American Indian, who by 1900 numbered less than a quarter million, found his
rights even on his reservation often ignored or violated. George Kennan, in the spirit
of a muckraking journalist, described in detail one example of outrageous behavior
to the Sioux in an article that is reprinted here in part.*

Source: *Outlook,* March 29, 1902: "Have Reservation Indians Any Vested Rights?"

JUST WEST OF THE MISSOURI RIVER and south of its tributary the Cannonball, partly in North Dakota and partly in South Dakota, lies an extensive tract of treeless, semiarid land known as the Standing Rock Indian Reservation. It is part of a much larger reservation which was made by virtue of a treaty with the Sioux in 1868, and which, twenty years later, was reduced in area by a partial extinguishment of the Indian title and the throwing open of half the land to white settlement. The Standing Rock Reservation is now the home of about 3,700 Sioux Indians, who live in comfortable houses along the Missouri River and the lower reaches of its tributaries the Grand and Cannonball, and who, with some aid from the government, support themselves by raising cattle — the only industry for which that high prairie country is suited.

These Indians, as described by Mr. James McLaughlin, who was formerly agent at Standing Rock, "are well disposed and obedient to the will of the government; are becoming more and more industrious and provident from year to year; and show a steady advance in civilization. A large number of them labor for themselves and others, not to please the agent in the hope of gaining favors, as formerly, but for the returns that labor brings." Such Indians would seem to be preeminently entitled to sympathy, friendly encouragement, and just treatment.

A year or two ago the Chicago, Milwaukee, and St. Paul Railroad Company constructed a branch line from Roscoe to a point on the Missouri River nearly opposite the southeastern corner of the reservation, and, after having had an understanding, apparently, with certain stockmen of the neighborhood, undertook to persuade the

Indians to lease a large part of their reservation for cattle grazing, which would be profitable to the stockmen and which, at the same time, would increase the business of the railroad. The Indians, however, objected, and, at a grand council summoned by the present agent, Mr. Bingenheimer, and held on the 3rd of May, 1901, they finally refused point-blank to lease any part of their reservation on the ground, primarily, that they already had 15,000 head of cattle and half as many horses of their own, and that they hoped soon to increase their herds to such an extent that all available pasturage — at least in the southern and eastern parts of the reservation — would be utilized.

On the 15th of May, 1901, the Indian commissioner, Mr. W. A. Jones, who was then in New York, wrote to the assistant commissioner in Washington as follows: "I do not see that we can do anything as the situation stands, unless Agent Hatch could persuade those Indians to accept the permit system" [turning cattle into the reservation at a certain stipulated price per head for the grazing privilege]. "I would like very much to have the surplus lands on those reservations" [Standing Rock and Cheyenne River] used for grazing, *but cannot do so without the Indians' consent,* and it seems, at present, that we are unable to secure it. I would suggest that you correspond again by wire with Hatch and Bingenheimer as to whether the Indians have experienced a change of heart in connection with it, and, if so, I would issue permits at once."

Upon receipt of this letter, the assistant commissioner telegraphed Mr. Bingenheimer, the agent at Standing Rock, as follows: "The Commissioner . . . instructs me to again wire you with a view, if possible, of securing consent of Indians for pasturage of 10,000 or 12,000 outside cattle south of Grand River, at the rate of $1 per head. . . . Early action very essential. Wire answer."

The Indians still refused either to lease their lands or to allow cattle to be turned into their reservation on the permit system, and the negotiations, apparently, were dropped.

Five months later, on the 9th of last October, the Indian commissioner, who meanwhile seems himself to have "experienced a change of heart," or at least to have decided upon a different policy, wrote Mr. Bingenheimer, the agent at Standing Rock, as follows: "You are advised that the secretary of the interior, on the 4th inst., granted authority for the permit system . . . of pasturage for outside cattle on the Standing Rock Reservation. . . . The system shall be inaugurated to begin January 1, 1902 . . . the rate shall be $1 per head per annum. . . . The matter should receive immediate attention so that the system shall be in working order on January 1."

' It will be observed that in the interval between May and October the Interior Department changed — or seemed to change — its view of the legal question involved in the case. In May the commissioner wrote his assistant that cattle could not legally be turned into the reservation "without the Indians' consent." In October the Department decided to turn them in without reference to the Indians' consent, and without regard, apparently, to equity or law.

The decision and order were promptly communicated by Agent Bingenheimer to the unfortunate Sioux, who were completely taken by surprise and thrown into a panic. If 10,000 or 15,000 wild Texan cattle were turned into their reservation, without restriction as to range, such cattle would naturally seek the best pasturage in the more settled region; the unfenced fields from which the Indians obtained their winter supply of hay would be overrun; the Texan cattle would mingle with their own, and the latter would be carried away in the roundups; there would be disputes and quarrels over water privileges in the dry season; cowboys would be constantly meddling with their women, and there would inevitably be trouble of all sorts.

Conscious of their inability to make any effective resistance, and more afraid of the turning in of cattle on the permit system than of any other form of invasion, the Indians decided — virtually under compulsion — to lease a pasturing privilege in the unoccupied part of their reservation. They had repeatedly refused, before, to agree to this, and were still opposed to it; but, inasmuch as it would enable them to keep foreign cattle in one place, away from their own homes and fields, while under the permit system such cattle might range anywhere, they decided to consent to it as the lesser of two evils.

The agent, Mr. Bingenheimer, thereupon drew up a form of agreement by which the Indians bound themselves to grant, for a period of five years, a pasturing privilege in "the unoccupied portions" of their reservation, payment for such privilege to be made at the rate of not less than $1 per head for every animal admitted. This agreement contained no stipulation with regard to the area to be leased and no description of its boundaries; but there was a verbal understanding with the agent that the lease or leases should cover only the northwestern part of the reservation, which was then unoccupied, and that the boundaries of the leased tracts should be fixed and staked out by a joint commission composed of the agent and three representative Indian chiefs, including their interpreter, Louis P. Primeau.

The agreement was duly signed and forwarded by the agent to Washington, and the Indian Office at once advertised for bids. The advertisements, however, in open violation and disregard of the written conditions of the Indians' assent, invited bids for grazing lands by the acre and not for pasturage by the head of stock as stipulated. This was clearly disadvantageous for the In-

dians for the reason that, upon lands leased by the acre, the lessees might, without additional expense, put two different lots of cattle in succession every year, while if the lease provided merely for pasturage by the head, payment would have to be made for the first lot, and then in turn for the second lot. It was also disadvantageous for the further reason that land leased by the acre might be overstocked by crowding it with cattle at all seasons of the year and its value as pasturage be thus permanently impaired.

Disregard for the interests of the Indians was also shown in the shortness of the time given stockmen for action. It is customary, in cases of this kind, to allow a month to elapse between advertisement and the opening of bids, in order that competing stockmen may have ample time to inquire, investigate, and make their proposals; but in this particular case there seems to have been some reason for unusual haste, inasmuch as the bids were opened only seventeen days after the appearance of the first advertisement. I shall suggest a possible explanation of this haste when I come to the senatorial investigation of the transaction.

As soon as the bids had been opened, Mr. Bingenheimer, the agent at Standing Rock, proceeded, in behalf and in the name of the Indians, to draw up leases for more than two-thirds of the whole reservation, including not only the unoccupied northwestern part (731,000 acres) but a large tract of nearly 500,000 acres in the central and southern part, where the Indians live and have their winter-hay fields. No attention whatever was paid to the verbal stipulation that the area to be fenced should be surveyed and staked out by a joint commission, nor to the written agreement that it should include only unoccupied land. On the contrary, the Lemmon lease was made without consultation with the Indians as to boundary and without survey, while the Walker lease threw open to the stockmen some of the best and most thickly settled parts of the reservation where the Indians have their homes, their little gardens, their winter-hay fields, and their cattle.

On the 13th of January, 1902, just after the opening of the bids, three of the principal chiefs of the Standing Rock Indians, namely, Thunder Hawk, Walking Shooter, and Weasel Bear, telegraphed Senator Jones, of Arkansas, as follows: "Four hundred families residing within boundary of proposed lease oppose leasing to syndicate. Indians on reservation unanimously protest. Our farms will be overrun and trampled upon. Our efforts at home building and farming will be wasted. We ask you to investigate. Indians desire personal hearing. We are full-blood chiefs."

Upon resolutions offered by senators Rawlins and Jones, the whole question of leasing lands in the Standing Rock reservation was finally brought before the Senate Committee on Indian Affairs, and was discussed by that Committee at a series of meetings held on the 16th and 23rd of January and the 4th of February of the present year. Mr. W. A. Jones, the commissioner of Indian Affairs, made a statement of the case from his point of view; a hearing was given to a delegation of Standing Rock Indians who had come to Washington for the purpose of stopping, if possible, the execution of the Walker lease; and a large number of letters, papers, and documents were submitted for perusal and consideration.

Although the questions, discussions, and proceedings generally of the Committee were so unsystematic, inconsecutive, and inconclusive as to leave almost everything in doubt, some light was thrown upon the policy of the Interior Department and the methods of the Indian Office in dealing with Indian affairs. When, for example, Senator Jones asked the Indian commissioner the direct question, "Did you write a letter to somebody out there saying the permit system would be inaugurated?" — a question that it was impossible to misun-

derstand — the commissioner replied, "No, sir; nor did anybody else." Senator Jones thereupon requested Mr. Primeau, interpreter for the Indians, to read the letter written by the commissioner to Agent Bingenheimer on the 9th of October, 1901 (already quoted, in part, above). That letter expressly directed the agent "to inaugurate the permit system of pasturage for nonresident stock," and to give the matter "immediate attention, so that the system shall be in working order on the 1st of January, 1902."

Inasmuch as this letter, threatening the Indians with the permit system, was the cause and beginning of the whole trouble, one might naturally suppose that the Committee would ask the commissioner a few pertinent questions about it: why, for example, he did in October a thing that he had declared in May he could not do; why a course of procedure that was clearly illegal and impossible in the spring became legal and possible in the fall; and finally, why, in reply to a direct question, he declared he had not written a letter which was immediately afterward produced and read, and which he was then forced to admit was his own? No such questions, however, were propounded, and when the commissioner, in what purported to be an explanation of the letter that he at first denied having written, declared, "There was no intention on my part, nor anyone in the office, to force the permit system or the leasing system upon these Indians," Senator Jones merely remarked, "*I* know you could not violate the law, but the question is whether the *Indians* knew it."

From the statements made before the Committee by the Indians, it is perfectly evident that they did *not* know it; that, as a matter of fact, they *were* forced into a lease of their unoccupied lands; and that they consented to such lease only because they thought it would afford a means of escape from a worse evil in the shape of the permit system, which was about to be "inaugurated" by authority of the secretary of the interior, and in obedience to an unconditional and peremptory order from the commissioner of Indian Affairs.

The provisions and stipulations of the leases that were thus obtained from the Indians by coercion and threat are open to many objections, and they ought to have been made the subject of careful and thorough inquiry when the case came before the Senate Committee.

The Lemmon lease, for example, provides that the lessees shall pay the Indians a certain price per acre for the lands acquired; while the agreement signed by the Indians was that the lessees should pay a certain price per head for the number of cattle pastured in the leased territory. It would be interesting to know why this change was made and what legal authority there is for getting consent to one form of lease and then substituting another.

The agreement with the Indians was for a lease only of "the unoccupied portions of the reservation"; while the Walker lease throws open to the cattlemen a large tract of occupied land, including both banks of the Grand River for a distance of twenty-five miles and taking in the homes, gardens, winter-hay fields, and stock ranges of hundreds of Indian families. Upon what basis of law or equity can an agreement to lease *unoccupied* land be made to justify the virtual confiscation of thousands of acres of *occupied* lands, where the Indians live and where they have made valuable improvements?

The Lemmon lease provides that the cattlemen shall fence in the leased area "with a good, substantial, cattle proof, barbed wire fence . . . such fence to be kept in good repair . . . and to revert to the Indians and become their absolute property at the termination of the lease." The commissioner was evidently aware of the importance to the Indians of such protection as this, because, in reply to a question

from Senator Jones, he said emphatically: "The lessees cannot put a single head on there until they have fenced the land; there is no question about that." At a later period of the investigation, however, it appeared from the commissioner's admissions that in the *occupied* territory covered by the Walker lease, where protection, of course, was most important and essential, the Indians would be expected to do their own fencing — that is, either protect themselves at their own expense from the lessees' cattle or allow the latter to graze over their pastures and trample upon and ruin their improvements.

"I will state," Commissioner Jones says, "as to the families living in the proposed leased tract, that we propose to give them all the wire they will need to fence their holdings, both as to their meadowlands and also whatever other tracts they may want. We insist that they shall do their own fencing, where they are able to do so, but we will give them the material." It is not quite clear whether the word "we" in this statement refers to the commissioner and the cattlemen conjointly or whether it is a plural pronoun standing for a single administrative bureau; but the ambiguity is suggestive rather than practically important. The significant feature of the statement is that the commissioner, after frightening the Indians into an agreement to lease "the *unoccupied* portions" of their reservation, turns the cattle of the stockmen into the *occupied* portions and then coolly informs the occupiers that if they don't want to have their gardens and hayfields trampled over and their improvements ruined, they must, at their own expense, put up fences to keep the foreign cattle out. . . .

It is perfectly clear from the evidence laid before the Committee that certain cattlemen in the neighborhood of the reservation knew what was going on and had formed a "pool" or syndicate to check competition, keep down rates, and, if possible, shut out other bidders. This may be inferred, not only from the shortness of the time allowed between advertisement and award but from the fact that the bids had a very limited range, viz., from a minimum rate of 3 cents to a maximum rate of 3 cents and half a mill per acre; although grazing land in the Cheyenne Reservation, just south of Standing Rock, was leased at that very time for 5 cents per acre, and land on the other side of the Missouri River for 12 cents per acre.

But the existence of this local "pool" or syndicate of stockmen is not merely a matter of inference and conjecture; it is a fact of record. In reply to a question from Senator Harris, Commissioner Jones said: "From the records of the office it appears that they [the local stockmen] have come to some agreement among themselves. The land was divided into two tracts, and those who have cattle near the reservation agreed among themselves to put in a certain number of cattle divided proportionately on some basis. That was an understanding among the lessees." In other words, the local stockmen, who seem to have had early notice of the leasing plan, formed a syndicate and promptly put in their low bids. Then the quick action of the Indian Office in opening these bids protected them from the competition of other stockmen who, perhaps, were not so favorably situated and who did not have time, after the advertisement and before the award, to get their proposals in.

Senator Gamble informed the Committee that he had received complaints based on this ground from other stockmen outside the syndicate, and suggested that "the time for the opening of the bids might have been more extended." The Indian commissioner did not explain why the time was not more extended, and when he was asked by Senator Jones whether 3 cents an acre was an adequate price for the grazing privilege given to the "pool," he replied, "I do not know anything about it."

Mr. William V. Wade, however, of Wade, North Dakota, seems to know something about it, and in a letter to Senator Jones, which was laid before the committee, he says: "Seeing by the papers that you are taking some interest in the wrong being done the Sioux Indians by the renting of their reservation *to a company with which the commissioner of Indian Affairs is connected,* I take the privilege of writing you upon the subject. I think it is all wrong, for the following reasons." After stating his reasons, Mr. Wade adds in conclusion: "A thorough investigation will show up some dark objects only slightly under cover." . . .

Frightened and discouraged by the attitude of the Indian Office, the Sioux decided to make no further opposition to the Lemmon lease, and even offered to extend it so as to take in about 150 square miles of additional territory, provided the commissioner would hold up the Walker lease, which covered the homes and holdings of several hundred families. This, however, the commissioner refused to do, and as no definite action had been taken by the Senate Committee, the Indians finally resolved to carry the case into the courts. Through their counsel, the Hon. William M. Springer, they are now seeking an injunction to restrain the secretary of the interior and the Indian commissioner from proceeding to execute the Walker lease on the ground that it is in flagrant violation of the written agreement by virtue of which, ostensibly, it was authorized. The questions that will be presented in this particular case are:

1. Whether the Indian Office has any legal right to authorize and order the throwing open of a reservation to foreign cattle without the Indians' consent; and

2. Whether, having obtained their consent to one form of lease, the commissioner may legally direct the Indian agent to draw up and execute in their behalf a lease of very different form for which no consent has been given.

The law under which such leases have

hitherto been made is the Act of Congress of February 28, 1891, which provides that leases of Indian lands "may be made by authority of the council speaking for such Indians." The legal presumption would seem to be that Indian leases are not to be made without this specified authority; but, inasmuch as the statute does not expressly forbid the leasing of Indian lands without Indian consent, the Interior Department may now hold that it has power to ignore treaty rights; to regard the Indians as infant or mentally incompetent wards of the government; and to do with their reservations whatever it pleases.

That this view is now being taken, not only by officials and legislators but by the courts, is clearly shown in many recent acts, statements, and decisions. In the discussion of this very case, for example, Senator Platt, of Connecticut, said; "I do not know but what the time has come . . . when we may have to disregard the letter of the treaties which we have made, giving such title as we have given to these Indians, and to proceed upon your [Senator Rawlins'] theory that whatever is best now for the Indians, years having elapsed, we will do."

Senator Rawlins' theory as stated by himself in explanation of a bill to deprive the Indians of the Uintah Reservation of a part of their lands without their consent is as follows: "The legal proposition involved is this: The estates of infants and incompetent persons, incapable of contracting for themselves, are constantly disposed of by the authority of the state, and the proceeds derived are held for their benefit. That is the proposition. These are Indians who cannot intelligently deal with this subject independently. They are wards of the government. This bill does not take away from them anything. It converts their land into a fund which will be applied to their benefit. That is constantly done in the courts of

chancery under an order to sell the land of an infant to which the infant has title in fee simple."

In the case of Lone Wolf and other Indian chiefs against the secretary of the interior which is now pending in the United States Supreme Court, the Court of Appeals of the District of Columbia held last week that "the treaty of 1868" (the same treaty under which the Standing Rock Sioux hold their reservation) "certainly did not vest in the Indians, either in their individual or tribal capacity, anything more than the right to occupy the lands, as against the United States, *until it was found necessary to make other provision for them.* There was no grant of estates, either of freehold or leasehold — only a mere right to occupy and use the lands; but these rights of the Indians were sacred to them, as against every one, *until Congress made provision for assuming control over the lands and making other disposition thereof.*"

If this decision be sustained in the Supreme Court, it will mark the beginning of a new departure in our Indian policy. There will then be no legal bar to the removal of all the American Indians from their reservations and the banishment of every man, woman, and child of them to Alaska or Puerto Rico.

The Sioux ceded 9 million acres of their land to the United States in payment for the reservation they now occupy; but in the light of the decision just rendered by the District Court of Appeals, it appears that they acquired no title, "either of freehold or leasehold." We took their 9 million acres and gave them in return what now seems to have been a "gold brick," made by thinly gilding a metal that the Siberian miners call "zinc-deceit." We have ended one "Century of Dishonor" and are apparently about to begin another.

102.

Lincoln Steffens and Claude H. Wetmore: Corruption and Reform in St. Louis

Corruption was so widespread in many city governments at the turn of the century that bribes were openly given and accepted; legislators proudly represented specific vested interests; and the law was flagrantly ignored. It was in this atmosphere that Lincoln Steffens went to St. Louis in 1902 to see what a crusading young circuit attorney named Joseph Folk was doing to reform the city. His article, written in conjunction with Claude H. Wetmore for McClure's *magazine and reprinted here in part, was the first in a series on municipal corruption that Steffens was to call* The Shame of the Cities.

Source: *McClure's*, October 1902: "Tweed Days in St. Louis."

St. Louis, the fourth city in size in the United States, is making two announcements to the world: one, that it is the worst governed city in the land; the other, that it wishes all men to come and see it. It isn't our worst governed city; Philadelphia is that. But St. Louis is worth examining while we have it inside out.

There is a man at work there, one man, working all alone, but he is the circuit (district or state) attorney, and he is "doing his duty." That is what thousands of district attorneys and other public officials have promised to do and boasted of doing. This man has a literal sort of mind. He is a thin-lipped, firm-mouthed, dark little man, who never raises his voice, but goes ahead doing, with a smiling eye and a set jaw, the simple thing he said he would do. The politicians and reputable citizens who asked him to run urged him when he declined. When he said that if elected he would have to do his duty, they said, "Of course." So he ran, they supported him, and he was elected.

Now some of these politicians are sentenced to the penitentiary, some are in Mexico. The circuit attorney, finding that his "duty" was to catch and convict criminals and that the biggest criminals were some of these same politicians and leading citizens, went after them. It is magnificent, but the politicians declare it isn't politics.

The corruption of St. Louis came from the top. The best citizens — the merchants and big financiers — used to rule the town, and they ruled it well. They set out to outstrip Chicago. The commercial and industrial war between these two cities was at one time a picturesque and dramatic spectacle such as is witnessed only in our country. Businessmen were not mere merchants and the politicians were not mere grafters; the two kinds of citizens got together and wielded the power of banks, railroads, factories, the prestige of the city, and the spirit of its citizens to gain business and population. And it was a close race. Chicago, having the start, always led, but St. Louis had pluck, intelligence, and tremendous energy. It pressed Chicago hard. It excelled in a sense of civic beauty and good government; and there are those who think yet it might have won. But a change occurred. Public spirit became private spirit; public enterprise became private greed.

Along about 1890, public franchises and privileges were sought, not only for legitimate profit and common convenience but for loot. Taking but slight and always selfish interest in the public councils, the big men misused politics. The riff-raff, catching the smell of corruption, rushed into the Municipal Assembly, drove out the remaining respectable men, and sold the city — its streets, its wharves, its markets, and all that it had — to the now greedy businessmen and bribers. In other words, when the leading men began to devour their own city, the herd rushed into the trough and fed also.

So gradually has this occurred that these same citizens hardly realize it. Go to St. Louis and you will find the habit of civic pride in them; they still boast. The visitor is told of the wealth of the residents, of the financial strength of the banks, and of the growing importance of the industries; yet he sees poorly paved, refuse-burdened streets, and dusty or mud-covered alleys; he passes a ramshackle firetrap crowded with the sick and learns that it is the City Hospital; he enters the "Four Courts," and his nostrils are greeted with the odor of formaldehyde used as a disinfectant and insect powder spread to destroy vermin; he calls at the new City Hall and finds half the entrance boarded with pine planks to cover up the unfinished interior. Finally, he turns a tap in the hotel to see liquid mud flow into wash basin or bathtub.

The St. Louis charter vests legislative power of great scope in a Municipal Assembly, which is composed of a Council and a House of Delegates. Here is a description of the latter by the February Grand Jury:

We have had before us many of those who have been, and most of those who are now, members of the House of Delegates. We found a number of these utterly illiterate and lacking in ordinary intelligence, unable to give a better reason for favoring or opposing a measure than a desire to act with the majority. In some, no trace of mentality or morality could be found; in others, a low order of training appeared, united with base cunning, groveling instincts, and sordid desires. Unqualified to respond to the ordinary requirements of life, they are utterly incapable of comprehending the significance of an ordinance and are incapacitated, both by nature and training, to be the makers of laws. The choosing of such men to be legislators makes a travesty of justice, sets a premium on incompetency, and deliberately poisons the very source of the law.

These creatures were well organized. They had a "combine" and legislative institution, which a grand jury has described as follows:

Our investigation, covering more or less fully a period of ten years, shows that, with few exceptions, no ordinance has been passed wherein valuable privileges or franchises are granted until those interested have paid the legislators the money demanded for action in the particular case. Combines in both branches of the Municipal Assembly are formed by members sufficient in number to control legislation. To one member of this combine is delegated the authority to act for the combine and to receive and to distribute to each member the money agreed upon as the price of his vote in support of or opposition to a pending measure. So long has this practice existed that such members have come to regard the receipt of money for action on pending measures as a legitimate perquisite of a legislator.

One legislator consulted a lawyer with the intention of suing a firm to recover an unpaid balance on a fee for the grant of a switch way. Such difficulties rarely occurred, however. In order to insure a regular and indisputable revenue, the combine of each house drew up a schedule of bribery prices for all possible sorts of grants, just such a list as a commercial traveler takes out on the road with him. There was a price for a grain elevator, a price for a short switch; side tracks were charged for by the linear foot, but at rates which varied according to the nature of the ground taken; street improvement cost so much; wharf space was classified and precisely rated.

As there was a scale for favorable legislation, so there was one for defeating bills. It made a difference in the price if there was opposition, and it made a difference whether the privilege asked was legitimate or not. But nothing was passed free of charge. Many of the legislators were saloonkeepers — it was in St. Louis that a practical joker nearly emptied the House of Delegates by getting a boy to rush into a session and call out, "Mister, your saloon is on fire" — but even the saloonkeepers of a neighborhood had to pay to keep in their inconvenient locality a market which public interest would have moved.

From the Assembly, bribery spread into other departments. Men empowered to issue peddler's licenses and permits to citizens who wished to erect awnings or use a portion of the sidewalk for storage purposes charged an amount in excess of the prices stipulated by law and pocketed the difference. The city's money was loaned at interest, and the interest was converted into private bank accounts. City carriages were used by the wives and children of city officials. . . .

Men ran into debt to the extent of thousands of dollars for the sake of election to either branch of the Assembly. One night, on a streetcar to the City Hall, a new member remarked that the nickel he handed the conductor was his last. The next day he deposited $5,000 in a savings bank. A member of the House of Delegates admitted to the February grand jury that his dividends from the combine netted $25,000 in

one year; a councilman stated that he was paid $50,000 for his vote on a single measure. . . .

Then the unexpected happened — an accident. There was no uprising of the people, but they were restive; and the opposition party leaders, thinking to gain some independent votes, decided to raise the cry "reform" and put up a ticket of candidates different enough from the usual offerings of political parties to give color to their platform. These leaders were not in earnest. There was little difference between the two parties in the city; but the Republican rascals had been getting the greater share of the spoils, and the Democrats wanted more than was given to them. "Boodle" was not the issue, no exposures were made or threatened, and the bosses expected to control their men if elected. Simply as part of the game, the Democrats raised the slogan, "reform" and "no more Ziegenheinism."

Mayor Ziegenhein, called "Uncle Henry," was a "good fellow," "one of the boys," and though it was during his administration that the city grew ripe and went to rot, his opponents talked only of incompetence and neglect and repeated such stories as that of his famous reply to some citizens who complained because certain street lights were put out: "You have the moon yet — ain't it?"

When somebody mentioned Joseph W. Folk for circuit attorney, the leaders were ready to accept him. They didn't know much about him. He was a young man from Tennessee; had been president of the Jefferson Club, and arbitrated the railroad strike of 1898. But Folk did not want the place. He was a civil lawyer, had had no practice in criminal law, cared little about it, and a lucrative practice as counsel for corporations was interesting him. He rejected the invitation. The committee called again and again, urging his duty to his party and the city, etc.

"Very well," he said, at last, "I will accept the nomination, but if elected I will do my duty. There must be no attempt to influence my actions when I am called upon to punish lawbreakers."

The committeemen took such statements as the conventional platitudes of candidates. They nominated him, the Democratic ticket was elected, and Folk became circuit attorney for the Eighth Missouri District.

Three weeks after taking the oath of office his campaign pledges were put to the test. A number of arrests had been made in connection with the recent election, and charges of illegal registration were preferred against men of both parties. Mr. Folk took them up like routine cases of ordinary crime. Political bosses rushed to the rescue. Mr. Folk was reminded of his duty to his party and was given to understand that he was expected to construe the law in such a manner that repeaters and other election day criminals who had hoisted Democracy's flag and helped elect him might be either discharged or receive the minimum punishment. The nature of the young lawyer's reply can best be inferred from the words of that veteran political leader Edward R. Butler, Sr., who, after a visit to Mr. Folk, wrathfully exclaimed, "D —— Joe! He thinks he's the whole thing as circuit attorney."

The election cases were passed through the courts with astonishing rapidity; no more mercy was shown Democrats than Republicans, and, before winter came, a number of ward heelers and old-time party workers were behind the bars in Jefferson City. He next turned his attention to grafters and straw bondsmen with whom the courts were infested; and several of these leeches are in the penitentiary today, and the system is broken up because of his activity. But this was little more than the beginning. . . .

Other cities are today in the same condition as St. Louis before Mr. Folk was invited in to see its rottenness. Chicago is cleaning itself up just now; so is Minneapolis; and Pittsburgh recently had a bribery scandal; New York is contented with a respectable outside; Boston is at peace; Cincinnati and St. Paul are satisfied; while Philadelphia is happy in the worst government in the world. As for the small towns and the villages, many of these are as busy as bees at the loot.

St. Louis, indeed, in its disgrace, has a great advantage. It was exposed late; it has not been reformed and caught again and again, until its citizens are reconciled to corruption. But, best of all, the man who has turned St. Louis inside up, turned it, as it were, upside down, too. In all cities, the better classes — the businessmen — are the sources of corruption; but they are so rarely pursued and caught that we do not fully realize whence the trouble comes. And so most cities blame the politicians and the ignorant and vicious poor.

Mr. Folk has shown St. Louis that its bankers, brokers, corporation officers, its businessmen are the sources of evil, so that from the start it will know the municipal problem in its true light. With a tradition for public spirit, it may drop Butler and its runaway bankers, brokers, and brewers, and pushing aside the scruples of the hundreds of men down in blue book and red book and church register, who are lying hidden behind the statutes of limitations, the city may restore good government. Otherwise the exposures by Mr. Folk will result only in the perfection of the corrupt system; for the corrupt can learn a lesson when the good citizens cannot.

The Tweed regime in New York taught Tammany to organize its boodle business; the police exposure taught it to improve its method of collecting blackmail. And both now are almost perfect and safe. The rascals of St. Louis will learn in like manner; they will concentrate the control of their bribery system, excluding from the profit sharing the great mass of weak rascals, and carrying on the business as a business in the interest of a trustworthy few. District Attorney Jerome cannot catch the Tammany men, and Circuit Attorney Folk will not be able another time to break the St. Louis ring. This is St. Louis's one great chance.

But, for the rest of us, it does not matter about St. Louis any more than it matters about Colonel Butler *et al.* The point is, that what went on in St. Louis is going on in most of our cities, towns, and villages. The problem of municipal government in America has not been solved. The people may be tired of it, but they cannot give it up — not yet.

103.

JANE ADDAMS: Industrial Amelioration and Social Ethics

Working in a settlement house among immigrants gave Jane Addams intimate knowledge of the harsh realities of life in an industrial world. She witnessed the bewilderment of new arrivals who did not know how to find a job or even how to go about training for one, and who therefore often stumbled irretrievably in their first attempts at a new life. Her experiences led her to agitate for social reform, and her book Democracy and Social Ethics, *from which the following selection is taken, discussed the kind of social and moral changes that would have to occur before America could live up to its promises.*

Source: *Democracy and Social Ethics*, New York, 1902: "Industrial Amelioration."

THE MAN WHO DISASSOCIATES his ambition, however disinterested, from the cooperation of his fellows, always takes [the] risk of ultimate failure. He does not take advantage of the great conserver and guarantee of his own permanent success which associated efforts afford. Genuine experiments toward higher social conditions must have a more democratic faith and practice than those which underlie private venture. Public parks and improvements, intended for the common use, are after all only safe in the hands of the public itself; and associated effort toward social progress, although much more awkward and stumbling than that same effort managed by a capable individual, does yet enlist deeper forces and evoke higher social capacities.

The successful businessman who is also the philanthropist is in more than the usual danger of getting widely separated from his employees. The men already have the American veneration for wealth and successful business capacity, and, added to this, they are dazzled by his good works. The workmen have the same kindly impulses as he, but while they organize their charity into mutual benefit associations and distribute their money in small amounts in relief for the widows and insurance for the injured, the employer may build model towns, erect college buildings, which are tangible and enduring, and thereby display his goodness in concentrated form.

By the very exigencies of business demands, the employer is too often cut off from the social ethics developing in regard to our larger social relationships and from the great moral life springing from our common experiences. This is sure to happen when he is good "to" people rather than "with" them, when he allows himself to decide what is best for them instead of consulting them. He thus misses the rectifying influence of that fellowship which is so big that it leaves no room for sensitiveness or gratitude. Without this fellowship we may never know how great the divergence between ourselves and others may become, nor how cruel the misunderstandings.

During a recent strike of the employees of a large factory in Ohio, the president of the company expressed himself as bitterly disappointed by the results of his many kindnesses, and evidently considered the employees utterly unappreciative. His state of mind was the result of the fallacy of ministering to social needs from an individual impulse and expecting a socialized return of gratitude and loyalty. If the lunchroom was necessary, it was a necessity in order that the employees might have better food, and, when they had received the better food, the legitimate aim of the lunchroom was met. If baths were desirable, and the fifteen minutes of calisthenic exercise given the women in the middle of each half day brought a needed rest and change to their muscles, then the increased cleanliness and the increased bodily comfort of so many people should of themselves have justified the experiment.

To demand, as a further result, that there should be no strikes in the factory, no revolt against the will of the employer because the employees were filled with loyalty as the result of the kindness, was of course to take the experiment from an individual basis to a social one.

Large mining companies and manufacturing concerns are constantly appealing to their stockholders for funds or for permission to take a percentage of the profits, in order that the money may be used for educational and social schemes designed for the benefit of the employees. The promoters of these schemes use, as an argument and as an appeal, that better relations will be thus established, that strikes will be prevented, and that in the end the money returned to the stockholders will be increased. However praiseworthy this appeal may be in motive, it involves a distinct confusion of issues, and in theory deserves the failure it so often meets with in practice. In the clash which follows a strike, the employees are accused of an ingratitude when there was no legitimate reason to expect gratitude; and useless bitterness, which has really a factitious basis, may be developed on both sides.

Indeed, unless the relation becomes a democratic one, the chances of misunderstanding are increased, when to the relation of employer and employees is added the relation of benefactor to beneficiaries, insofar as there is still another opportunity for acting upon the individual code of ethics.

There is no doubt that these efforts are to be commended, not only from the standpoint of their social value but because they have a marked industrial significance. Failing, as they do, however, to touch the question of wages and hours, which are almost invariably the points of trades union effort, the employers confuse the mind of the public when they urge the amelioration of conditions and the kindly relation existing between them and their men as a reason for the discontinuance of strikes and other trades union tactics. The men have individually accepted the kindness of the employers as it was individually offered, but quite as the latter urges his inability to increase wages unless he has the cooperation of his competitors, so the men state that they are bound to the trades union struggle for an increase in wages because it can only be undertaken by combinations of labor.

Even the much more democratic effort to divide a proportion of the profits at the end of the year among the employees, upon the basis of their wages and efficiency, is also exposed to a weakness, from the fact that the employing side has the power of determining to whom the benefit shall accrue.

Both individual acts of self-defense on the part of the wage earner and individual acts of benevolence on the part of the employer are most useful as they establish standards to which the average worker and employer may in time be legally compelled to conform. Progress must always come through the individual who varies from the type and has sufficient energy to express this variation. He first holds a higher conception than that held by the mass of his fellows of what is righteous under given conditions, and expresses this conviction in conduct, in many instances formulating a certain scruple which the others share but have not yet defined even to themselves.

Progress, however, is not secure until the mass has conformed to this new righteousness. This is equally true in regard to any advance made in the standard of living on the part of the trades unionists or in the improved conditions of industry on the part of reforming employers. The mistake lies, not in overpraising the advance thus inaugurated by individual initiative but in regarding the achievement as complete in a social sense when it is still in the realm of individual action.

No sane manufacturer regards his factory as the center of the industrial system. He knows very well that the cost of material, wages, and selling prices are determined by industrial conditions completely beyond his control. Yet the same man may quite calmly regard himself and his own private principles as merely self-regarding and expect results from casual philanthropy which can only be accomplished through those common rules of life and labor established by the community for the common good.

Outside of and surrounding these smaller and most significant efforts are the larger and irresistible movements operating toward combination. This movement must tend to

decide upon social matters from the social standpoint. Until then it is difficult to keep our 'minds free from a confusion of issues. Such a confusion occurs when the gift of a large sum to the community for a public and philanthropic purpose throws a certain glamor over all the earlier acts of a man and makes it difficult for the community to see possible wrongs committed against it in the accumulation of wealth so beneficently used. It is possible also that the resolve to be thus generous unconsciously influences the man himself in his methods of accumulation. He keeps to a certain individual rectitude, meaning to make an individual restitution by the old paths of generosity and kindness, whereas if he had in view social restitution on the newer lines of justice and opportunity, he would throughout his course doubtless be watchful of his industrial relationships and his social virtues.

The danger of professionally attaining to the power of the righteous man, of yielding to the ambition "for doing good" on a large scale, compared to which the ambition for politics, learning, or wealth are vulgar and commonplace, ramifies through our modern life; and those most easily beset by this temptation are precisely the men best situated to experiment on the larger social lines, because they so easily dramatize their acts and lead public opinion. Very often, too, they have in their hands the preservation and advancement of large vested interests, and often see clearly and truly that they are better able to administer the affairs of the community than the community itself; sometimes they see that if they do not administer them sharply and quickly, as only an individual can, certain interests of theirs dependent upon the community will go to ruin.

The model employer first considered provided a large sum in his will with which to build and equip a polytechnic school, which will doubtless be of great public value. This again shows the advantage of individual management, in the spending as well as in the accumulating of wealth, but this school will attain its highest good, insofar as it incites the ambition to provide other schools from public funds. The town of Zurich possesses a magnificent polytechnic institute, secured by the vote of the entire people and supported from public taxes. Every man who voted for it is interested that his child should enjoy its benefits, and, of course, the voluntary attendance must be larger than in a school accepted as a gift to the community.

In the educational efforts of model employers, as in other attempts toward social amelioration, one man with the best of intentions is trying to do what the entire body of employees should have undertaken to do for themselves. The result of his efforts will only attain its highest value as it serves as an incentive to procure other results by the community as well as for the community.

There are doubtless many things which the public would never demand unless they were first supplied by individual initiative, both because the public lacks the imagination and also the power of formulating their wants. Thus philanthropic effort supplies kindergartens, until they become so established in the popular affections that they are incorporated in the public school system. Churches and missions establish reading rooms, until at last the public library system dots the city with branch reading rooms and libraries. For this willingness to take risks for the sake of an ideal, for those experiments which must be undertaken with vigor and boldness in order to secure didactic value in failure as well as in success, society must depend upon the individual possessed with money, and also distinguished by earnest and unselfish purpose.

Such experiments enable the nation to use the referendum method in its public affairs. Each social experiment is thus tested by a few people, given wide publicity that it may be observed and discussed by the bulk of the citizens before the public prudently makes up its mind whether or not it is wise to incorporate it into the functions of government. If the decision is in its favor and it is so incorporated, it can then be carried on with confidence and enthusiasm.

But experience has shown that we can only depend upon successful men for a certain type of experiment in the line of industrial amelioration and social advancement. The list of those who found churches, educational institutions, libraries, and art galleries is very long, as is again the list of those contributing to model dwellings, recreation halls, and athletic fields. At the present moment factory employers are doing much to promote "industrial betterment" in the way of sanitary surroundings, opportunities for bathing, lunchrooms provided with cheap and wholesome food, clubrooms, and guild halls.

But there is a line of social experiment involving social righteousness in its most advanced form, in which the number of employers and the "favored class" are so few that it is plain society cannot count upon them for continuous and valuable help. This lack is in the line of factory legislation and that sort of social advance implied in shorter hours and the regulation of wages; in short, all that organization and activity that is involved in such a maintenance and increase of wages as would prevent the lowering of the standard of life.

A large body of people feel keenly that the present industrial system is in a state of profound disorder and that there is no guarantee that the pursuit of individual ethics will ever right it. They claim that relief can only come through deliberate corporate effort inspired by social ideas and guided by the study of economic laws, and that the present industrial system thwarts our ethical demands, not only for social righteousness but for social order. Because they believe that each advance in ethics must be made fast by a corresponding advance in politics and legal enactment, they insist upon the right of state regulation and control. While many people representing all classes in a community would assent to this as to a general proposition, and would even admit it as a certain moral obligation, legislative enactments designed to control industrial conditions have largely been secured through the efforts of a few citizens, mostly those who constantly see the harsh conditions of labor and who are incited to activity by their sympathies as well as their convictions.

This may be illustrated by the series of legal enactments regulating the occupations in which children may be allowed to work, also the laws in regard to the hours of labor permitted in those occupations, and the minimum age below which children may not be employed. The first child labor laws were enacted in England through the efforts of those members of Parliament whose hearts were wrung by the condition of the little parish apprentices bound out to the early textile manufacturers of the North; and through the long years required to build up the code of child labor legislation which England now possesses, knowledge of the conditions has always preceded effective legislation.

The efforts of that small number in every community who believe in legislative control have always been reenforced by the efforts of trades unionists rather than by the efforts of employers. Partly because the employment of workingmen in the factories brings them in contact with the children who tend to lower wages and demoralize their trades, and partly because workingmen have no money nor time to spend in alleviating philanthropy, and must perforce seize upon agitation and legal enactment as the only channel of redress which is open to them.

We may illustrate by imagining a row of people seated in a moving streetcar, into which darts a boy of eight, calling out the details of the last murder in the hope of selling an evening newspaper. A comfort-able looking man buys a paper from him with no sense of moral shock; he may even be a trifle complacent that he has helped along the little fellow, who is making his way in the world. The philanthropic lady sitting next to him may perhaps reflect that it is a pity that such a bright boy is not in school. She may make up her mind in a moment of compunction to redouble her efforts for various newsboys' schools and homes that this poor child may have better teaching and, perhaps, a chance at manual training. She probably is convinced that he alone, by his unaided efforts, is supporting a widowed mother, and her heart is moved to do all she can for him.

Next to her sits a workingman trained in trades union methods. He knows that the boy's natural development is arrested and that the abnormal activity of his body and mind uses up the force which should go into growth; moreover, that this premature use of his powers has but a momentary and specious value. He is forced to these conclusions because he has seen many a man, entering the factory at eighteen and twenty, so worn out by premature work that he was "laid on the shelf" within ten or fifteen years. He knows very well that he can do nothing in the way of ameliorating the lot of this particular boy; that his only possible chance is to agitate for proper child labor laws; to regulate, and if possible prohibit, street vending by children in order that the child of the poorest may have his school-time secured to him, and may have at least his short chance for growth.

These three people, sitting in the streetcar, are all honest and upright, and recognize a certain duty toward the forlorn children of the community. The self-made man is encouraging one boy's own efforts; the philanthropic lady is helping on a few boys; the workingman alone is obliged to include all the boys of his class. Workingmen, because of their feebleness in all but numbers, have been forced to appeal to the state in order to secure protection for themselves and for their children. They cannot all rise out of their class, as the occasionally successful man has done; some of them must be left to do the work in the factories and mines, and they have no money to spend in philanthropy.

Both public agitation and a social appeal to the conscience of the community is necessary in order to secure help from the state, and, curiously enough, child labor laws once enacted and enforced are a matter of great pride, and even come to be regarded as a register of the community's humanity and enlightenment. If the method of public agitation could find quiet and orderly expression in legislative enactment, and if labor measures could be submitted to the examination and judgment of the whole without a sense of division or of warfare, we should have the ideal development of the democratic state.

But we judge labor organizations as we do other living institutions, not by their declaration of principles, which we seldom read, but by their blundering efforts to apply their principles to actual conditions, and by the oft-time failure of their representatives, when the individual finds himself too weak to become the organ of corporate action.

The very blunders and lack of organization too often characterizing a union, in marked contrast to the orderly management of a factory, often confuse us as to the real issues involved, and we find it hard to trust uncouth and unruly manifestations of social effort. The situation is made even more complicated by the fact that those who are formulating a code of associated action so often break through the established code of law and order.

As society has a right to demand of the reforming individual that he be sternly held to his personal and domestic claims, so it has a right to insist that labor organizations shall keep to the hardly won standards of public law and order; and the community performs but its plain duty when it registers its protest every time law and order are subverted, even in the interest of the so-called social effort. Yet in moments of industrial stress and strain the community is confronted by a moral perplexity which may arise from the mere fact that the good of yesterday is opposed to the good of today, and that which may appear as a choice between virtue and vice is really but a choice between virtue and virtue. In the disorder and confusion sometimes incident to growth and progress, the community may be unable to see anything but the unlovely struggle itself. . . .

At times of social disturbance the law-abiding citizen is naturally so anxious for peace and order, his sympathies are so justly and inevitably on the side making for the restoration of law, that it is difficult for him to see the situation fairly. He becomes insensible to the unselfish impulse which may prompt a sympathetic strike in behalf of the workers in a nonunion shop because he allows his mind to dwell exclusively on the disorder which has become associated with the strike. He is completely sidetracked by the ugly phases of a great moral movement. It is always a temptation to assume that the side which has respectability, authority, and superior intelligence has therefore righteousness as well, especially when the same side presents concrete results of individual effort as over against the less tangible results of associated effort.

It is as yet most difficult for us to free ourselves from the individualistic point of view sufficiently to group events in their social relations and to judge fairly those who are endeavoring to produce a social result through all the difficulties of associated action. The philanthropist still finds his path much easier than do those who are attempting a social morality. In the first place, the public, anxious to praise what it recognizes as an undoubted moral effort often attended with real personal sacrifice, joyfully seizes upon this manifestation and overpraises it, recognizing the philanthropist as an old friend in the paths of righteousness, whereas the others are strangers and possibly to be distrusted as aliens.

It is easy to confuse the response to an abnormal number of individual claims with the response to the social claim. An exaggerated personal morality is often mistaken for a social morality, and until it attempts to minister to a social situation its total inadequacy is not discovered. To attempt to attain a social morality without a basis of democratic experience results in the loss of the only possible corrective and guide, and ends in an exaggerated individual morality but not in social morality at all. We see this from time to time in the careworn and overworked philanthropist, who has taxed his individual will beyond the normal limits and has lost his clue to the situation among a bewildering number of cases.

A man who takes the betterment of humanity for his aim and end must also take the daily experiences of humanity for the constant correction of his process. He must not only test and guide his achievement by human experience but he must succeed or fail in proportion as he has incorporated that experience with his own. Otherwise, his own achievements become his stumbling block, and he comes to believe in his own goodness as something outside of himself. He makes an exception of himself and thinks that he is different from the rank and file of his fellows. He forgets that it is necessary to know of the lives of our contemporaries, not only in order to believe in their integrity, which is after all but the first beginnings of social morality, but in order to attain to any mental or moral integrity for ourselves or any such hope for society.

104.

Charles H. Vail: Principles of Socialism

The doctrine preached by American socialism around the turn of the century was mainly derived from the theories of European philosophers and economists, and its champions were hard pressed to adapt it to American circumstances. In an effort to make their views palatable to American workers, a group of socialists asked the Reverend Charles Vail to write a pamphlet that would present the doctrine in attractive form. The pamphlet, a part of which appears here, was published in 1902 and was distributed throughout the nation. However, its Marxist terminology remained foreign to American ears.

Source: *The Socialist Movement*, Chicago, 1902.

THE SOCIALIST MOVEMENT is the natural outcome of modern industrial conditions. Like most great movements, it has passed through a utopian phase. This period began early in the 18th century and was characterized by the utopian schemes of Owen, St. Simon, and Fourier. These men were socialists in that their starting point was pro-letarian criticism of the existing social system and their object the overthrow of the capitalist economy and the substitution therefor of collective ownership. They were utopians because they did not grasp the real factors of socialism. They assumed that all that was needed to bring in the new order was enlightenment. They appealed to men as a whole, expecting that, when the matter was rightly understood, all would wish for the change, and those enjoying special privileges would divest themselves of their possessions and usher in the new order!

The utopians ignored the class struggle and consequently failed to recognize the fact that a part of society, the ruling class, was satisfied with the existing order and desired its retention. As the utopians repudiated the class struggle, so they repudiated all political effort. They seemed to think that the preaching of the new gospel was all that was necessary — proclaim aloud the blessings of the new order and it may come, lo! in the twinkling of an eye!

These men were truly children of their age. They did well, grandly well, considering the light they possessed, but they were not in possession of sufficient economic data to enable them to perceive the genesis of capitalist exploitation or comprehend the law of economic evolution. They perceived the evils of our industrial order and depicted the same with clearness and satire, but it was left to the genius of Karl Marx to point out the genesis of surplus value and the law of economic determinism, and thus reduce socialism from utopia to science.

The discoveries of Marx placed socialism upon a solid foundation. It is now no longer a scheme or device of anyone, but a scientific philosophy, and rests upon an historic, economic, and scientific basis.

We need, however, to distinguish between socialism as a future state of society and the socialist movement, which is an effort to realize that state. The socialist movement must, of necessity, be carried on within the confines of the present social order, and so possesses several well-marked characteristics.

1. *It Is a Proletarian Movement*

The class upon which the movement rests is the proletariat — the class of wage and salary workers. The very condition for the existence of modern socialism was the rise of the proletariat class. It is not my purpose here to trace the origin of this class; suffice it to say that every system has given rise to social classes and the capitalist has produced the proletariat. The history of the origin and development of the proletariat is the history of capitalism itself.

The capitalist system necessarily presupposes the rending of society into two classes — the owners of the means of production and those who have nothing but their labor power to sell. The laboring class is thus absolutely dependent upon the capitalist class. The ideal of every proletarian movement must, necessarily, be the emancipation of the workers from this condition of dependence and servitude. Before the proletariat can make much progress toward this end, it must know itself in its historic relations. A clear conception of these relations reveals the program and tactics necessary to success.

For the working class to secure its freedom, it must cease to be dependent upon the capitalist class, and this can only be accomplished by overthrowing the capitalist order. The abolition of modern capitalism can be accomplished in one of two ways: either by reversing the wheels of progress, destroying modern methods and returning to the days of handicraft and individual production, or by retaining modern methods and pushing on the organization of industry to its logical consummation, collective ownership — socialism. The latter method is the only one to which the proletariat can attach itself inasmuch as the proletariat class is the result of the development of the capitalist system, being necessarily associated with production on a large scale. Thus the emancipation of the proletariat must be accomplished by going forward, not backward. Collective ownership of the means of production and distribution is the only solution to the problem. . . .

2. *It Points Out the Necessity of Proletarian Class Consciousness*

Society today is divided into two classes — the propertied and nonpropertied. Every man born into these class conditions inherits, or acquires, a classhood in addition to his manhood. True civilization can never be attained in a class-constituted society, for the members of neither class can reach their highest development in such conditions. The dominance of class interests prevents men from realizing the highest ideal. The socialist recognizes the inevitable result of such conditions and so desires to abolish class distinctions and the class element in character, for he knows that human brotherhood must ever be utopian in a system founded upon antagonistic interests.

While socialists recognize the necessity of abolishing classes, they nevertheless constantly endeavor to awaken the working class to a sense of class consciousness. This appears to many inconsistent. They say, "If you wish to abolish classes, why not begin by ignoring their existence?" We answer, ignoring classes would not alter facts. Classes exist whether we recognize them or not; we may ignore them, but they will not ignore us. Capitalists ignore the existence of classes in order that they may perpetuate them; socialists recognize the existence of classes in order that they may abolish them. Classes will be abolished, not by ignoring their existence but by so changing our economic system that some will not be able to secure an advantage over others.

Today the possessing class, by its ownership of the means of production, is able to maintain its class character. To rid society of classes we must bring these instruments of production and distribution under collective control, for it is the private ownership of these instruments that divides society into two distinct classes. Socialize these instruments, and the possessing or expropriating class will itself be expropriated, or, as Marx expresses it, expropriated of the power of expropriating, and all class distinctions will be abolished.

Now, the only class that has a direct and immediate interest in securing this end is the working class. The interests of this class are diametrically opposed to the interests of the capitalist class. As every class is moved by its material interests, it is necessary to awaken the working class to its interests; in other words, make it class-conscious. This class consciousness carries with it a knowledge of the antagonism of class interests and enables the laborers to see that their emancipation can only be achieved by abolishing the present system and establishing the cooperative commonwealth.

Class consciousness, then, means a consciousness of one's own interests as a member of a class, also a consciousness that his interests can best be subserved by advancing the interests of the class to which he belongs. When a laborer realizes these facts he is said to be class-conscious. He then sees that his interests and the interests of his class are directly opposed to the interests of the capitalist class. He also apprehends the historical fact that the ruling class has always been, since the dawn of private property, the class that owns the dominant factor of production. In feudal times it was the owner of land, today it is the owner of the machine.

Every step in the development of capitalism meant added economic power for the capitalist class, and political supremacy finally resulted from this growth of economic power. While this is true of the capitalist class, the class-conscious laborer realizes that for him political supremacy cannot thus be secured, for the reason that every step in the development of capitalism has meant his greater subjection. Yet with this loss of economic power, due to the development of modern industry, there has come the possibility of political supremacy through the growth of numbers. Upon the political field the working class can become supreme. It overwhelmingly outnumbers the capitalists and its power is sure to increase.

It must be evident to all that the control of the political power is necessary to any class which would permanently improve its economic condition. The first step, then, toward the worker's emancipation is to gain this control. It is thus that socialists, the world over, emphasize the necessity of class-conscious political action upon the part of the working class.

The laborers can here learn a lesson in tactics from the capitalists. The capitalist class is thoroughly class-conscious. It perceives the course of action necessary to maintain its supremacy, and it can always be relied upon to subserve its own interests. . . .

3. It Is Based upon the Class Struggle

Ever since the dawn of private property in the means of production, society has been made up of classes, known at different epochs under various titles — masters and slaves, feudal lords and vassals, capitalists and proletarians — and a struggle is everywhere manifest between these classes of diverse economic interests.

The class struggle is a corollary of the struggle for existence. As the Darwinian law explains organic evolution, so the Marxian law explains social evolution. The struggle between classes reenacts, on the human plane, the drama of the struggle between species. It is the last form of this struggle that we are interested in today. The proletariat, as we have seen, is in a condition of dependence. If it becomes emancipated, it must become supreme, and its supremacy can only be accomplished by a struggle. This struggle for mastery is necessarily a class struggle, a struggle between the proprietary and nonproprietary classes. The subjection of the working class, being due to the fact that the instruments of production are the private property of another class, makes the interests of these two classes antagonistic and a class struggle inevitable. The fact of this class struggle need not be argued; it is evident on every hand by the class legislation, and the strikes, boycotts, and lockouts which are a matter of daily occurrence.

The class struggle is the necessary outcome of class distinctions which involve class interests. The upholding of class interests naturally leads to class opposition and a class struggle. . . .

Although the socialist movement is based upon the class struggle, the triumph of the proletariat class means the abolition of all classes. The reason why previous revolutions resulted in the continuance of class dominance is due to the failure to abolish class ownership in the instruments of production. But the proletariat supremacy will result in the abolition of all dependence, because the tools of production are now social and the working class cannot emancipate itself except by socializing these instruments. When these instruments are owned collectively, the cause of dependence and servitude will be abolished. The abolition of private or corporate ownership means the abolition of all class rule and all class distinctions. . . .

4. It Is a Revolutionary Movement

It must be perfectly clear from the foregoing that the socialist movement is not a reform but a revolution. A reform merely proposes a readjustment of the relations within the present class-organized society. It does not involve a change of economic base but merely a change of externals. Revolution, on the other hand, involves a change from within — a change in the internal mechanism of society without which there could be no progress.

As to whether a measure is socialistic or not depends upon its internal mechanism — upon the standpoint from which it proceeds. A measure may be apparently socialistic; that is, it may be so in outward form, while its internal working may be antisocialistic and designed to serve the interests of some portion of the capitalist class. For example, both the reformer and socialist want to socialize the railways, electric light plants, trolley systems, etc. The former desires to socialize them as a reform, while the latter proposes socialization as a revolution. In either case, there would be a change in external form. The difference is that the reformer would confine the change to externals, while the socialists would cause a change in the internal mechanism. The reformer proceeds from the standpoint of middle class interests as against the interests of the plutocracy; the socialist proceeds from the interests of the working class as against the interests of both the middle and upper class capitalists.

The reformer, for instance, wishes only to abolish the railroad monopoly which is fleecing the middle class; the socialist wishes to abolish all fleecers by abolishing the wage system. The reformers' scheme of socialization would not secure the workers emancipation — they would still be wage slaves and exploited by the capitalist government out of a portion of the wealth they produce. The scheme would undoubtedly reduce the cost of transportation, but there is no evidence that the middle class would reduce the price of their products to consumers. All they are interested in is to transfer the large profits of the railroad magnates into their own pockets. The socialist plan, on the other hand, proposes a change, not only in the external form but in the internal mechanism. It proceeds from the proletarian point of view and has for its object the abolition of all exploitation and the improvement in the condition of the railroad workers. To public ownership we would add democratic management.

Socialism, then, proposes a complete transformation of society — a change so radical as to constitute a social revolution. The term "revolution" is used to describe the final goal to be attained but not the method or tactics employed in its realization. While socialism is revolutionary in its program, it follows the laws of evolution in its method of attainment. . . .

It is true socialism will not spring at once full-fledged into existence — socialists have no magic wand which will effect the social transformation in a single day — but the first step toward that end is the overthrow of the present ruling class through the mastery of the public powers. When socialists are in control of the government, they will then proceed to put their ideals into practice. It will not all be accomplished at once, but as rapidly as possible industry after industry will be socialized, until all businesses are brought under collective control.

Of course, before socialists have captured the national government, they will gain control of municipalities and states, and as fast as they gain control they will carry out, as far as possible, the principles of socialism. But, note, the first step is to gain control — is political supremacy. This has already been accomplished in many European municipalities, and the benefits of a socialist administration, within the limits prescribed by the state, are now being enjoyed.

It is not, however, by reform but by revolutionary methods that results are being realized. We do not eschew taking a step at a time, then, provided the step is in the right direction and tends toward the realization of the final ideal. To the scientific socialist there is no contradiction between the present-day work and the revolutionary agitation. The immediate results which we seek to obtain are merely means for the realization of the ultimate aim. Thus, while not losing sight of the ultimate goal, we propose taking the road that leads to the cooperative commonwealth and capturing en route every outpost on the way.

Labor conditions will improve just in proportion as the outposts are captured by the Socialist Party. Not only this, but any temporary relief that is granted by the capitalist class will be in proportion to the fear caused the class by revolutionary agitation. If labor laws are passed, it is only to pacify the proletariat, but the capitalist class will only see the need of such pacification as the proletariat organize into a class-conscious party. Even then, upon the plea of getting something now, the surest way to secure it is to build up the Socialist vote. *Revolutionary agitation and social reform go hand in hand.*

How many times the laborers have been buncoed! Measures have been passed supposedly designed to benefit labor but afterward were frequently found to be inadequate or ineffective, and, if not, were declared unconstitutional by the capitalist courts. The only way to secure effective labor legislation is to have it backed by a class-conscious labor party. Just in proportion as the Socialist Party gains ascendancy it will secure this end, and will also extend the public service in the interest of the working class. This will not be state socialism or state capitalism, but rather, what has been termed the infiltration of socialism into the state. This would result in immediate benefit to the working class. The public powers would then be an instrument in the hands of the organized proletariat to work for the betterment of social conditions. Even when we have gained complete control, the state will still be a class instrument during the period of transition from private to public ownership — an instrument of the proletariat class to effect its complete emancipation.

It will be the business of the Socialist Party, when in control of the state, to carry out to completeness the legislative task of transformation. But, remember, all changes that tend to leave the present class government intact are mere reforms, and no change that threatens class rule can be introduced until the present class rule itself is subverted. This can only be accomplished by the triumph of the Socialist Party.

105.

WILLIAM RAINEY HARPER: Academic Freedom

The University of Chicago opened its doors in October 1892. Its young president, William Rainey Harper, who was backed by the unlimited financial resources of John D. Rockefeller, had raided the faculties of the leading Eastern universities and brought to the new institution a distinguished group of young professors and intellectuals. John Dewey, Thorstein Veblen, and George Herbert Mead were but three of the many men who quickly established the university as the leading one in the Midwest. In 1902 the university published a report of its first ten years. Volume One included a report, which is reprinted here in part, that commented on the freedom of speech accorded to the faculty.

Source: *The Decennial Publications of the University of Chicago,* Chicago, 1902, 1st series, Vol. I, pp. xxi-xxiv.

THERE ARE TWO POINTS in connection with the work of the members of the staff mention of which I cannot omit. The charge of sensationalism has been made by some unthinking persons against certain instructors in the university. This has had its origin in the misrepresentations of professorial utterances which have appeared in the public press, having come from the pens of irresponsible reporters. An effort has been made in most of these cases to discover the basis of the newspaper statements, and it has generally been found that a remark, entirely innocent, has been twisted either by the reporter or by the editor to subserve a humorous purpose.

I take the liberty of repeating here a statement made at a recent Convocation:

"I am moved to make a statement of fact and opinion concerning two related subjects which quite recently have attracted some attention in the public mind. The first of these is the freedom of opinion enjoyed in these days by members of the university. The second is the use and abuse of this right by professors of the university faculty. Concerning the first, I may be permitted to present a statement adopted unanimously by the members of the Congregation of the university on June 30, 1899:

Resolved:
1. That the principle of complete freedom of speech on all subjects has from the beginning been regarded as fundamental in the University of Chicago, as has been shown both by the attitude of the president and the Board of Trustees and by the actual practice of the president and the professors.
2. That this principle can neither now nor at any future time be called in question.
3. That it is desirable to have it clearly understood that the university, as such, does not appear as a disputant on either side upon any public question; and that the utterances which any professor may make in public are to be regarded as representing his opinions only.

"To this statement of the Congregation I wish to add, first, that whatever may or may not have happened in other universities, in the University of Chicago neither the trustees, nor the president, nor anyone in official position has at any time called an instructor to account for any public utterances which he may have made. Still further, in no single case has a donor to the university called the attention of the trustees

to the teaching of any officer of the university as being distasteful or objectionable. Still further, it is my opinion that no donor of money to a university, whether that donor be an individual or the state, has any right, before God or man, to interfere with the teaching of officers appointed to give instruction in a university.

"When, for any reason, in a university on private foundation, or in a university supported by public money, the administration of the institution or the instruction in any of its departments is changed by an influence from without; when an effort is made to dislodge an officer or a professor because the political sentiment or the religious sentiment of the majority has undergone a change, at that moment the institution has ceased to be a university; and it cannot again take its place in the rank of universities so long as there continues to exist to any appreciable extent the factor of coercion. Neither an individual, nor the state, nor the church has the right to interfere with the search for truth or with its promulgation when found. Individuals, or the state, or the church may found schools for propagating certain special kinds of instruction, but such schools are not universities and may not be so denominated.

"A donor has the privilege of ceasing to make his gifts to an institution if, in his opinion, for any reason, the work of the institution is not satisfactory; but *as donor* he has no right to interfere with the administration or the instruction of the university. The trustees in an institution in which such interference has taken place may not maintain their self-respect and remain trustees. They owe it to themselves and to the cause of liberty of thought to resign their places rather than to yield a principle the significance of which rises above all else in comparison.

"In order to be specific, and in order not to be misunderstood, I wish to say again that no donor of funds to the university —

William Rainey Harper, first president of the new University of Chicago, which was founded under the encouragement of John D. Rockefeller

and I include in the number of donors the founder of the university, Mr. Rockefeller — has ever by a single word or act indicated his dissatisfaction with the instruction given to the students in the university, or with the public expression of opinion made by an officer of the university. I vouch for the truth of this statement, and I trust that it may have the largest possible publicity.

"Concerning the second subject, the use and abuse of the right of free expression by officers of the university staff: As I have said, an instructor in the university has an absolute right to express his opinion. If such an instructor is on an appointment for two or three or four years, and if during these years he exercises this right in such a way as to do himself and the institution serious injury, it is of course the privilege of the university to allow his appointment to lapse at the end of the term for which it was originally made. If an officer on permanent appointment abuses his privilege as a professor, the university must suffer and it is proper that it should suffer. This is only the direct and inevitable consequence of the

lack of foresight and wisdom involved in the original appointment.

"The injury thus accruing to the university is, moreover, far less serious than would follow if, for an expression of opinion differing from that of the majority of the faculty, or from that of the Board of Trustees, or from that of the president of the university, a permanent officer were asked to present his resignation. The greatest single element necessary for the cultivation of the academic spirit is the feeling of security from interference. It is only those who have this feeling that are able to do work which in the highest sense will be beneficial to humanity. Freedom of expression must be given the members of a university faculty, even though it be abused; for, as has been said, the abuse of it is not so great an evil as the restriction of such liberty.

"But it may be asked: In what way may the professor abuse his privilege of freedom of expression? Or, to put the question more largely: In what way does a professor bring reproach and injury to himself and to his institution? I answer: A professor is guilty of an abuse of his privilege who promulgates as truth ideas or opinions which have not been tested scientifically by his colleagues in the same department of research or investigation. A professor has no right to proclaim to the public a truth discovered which is yet unsettled and uncertain. A professor abuses his privilege who takes advantage of a classroom exercise to propagate the partisan views of one or another of the political parties. The university is no place for partisanship. From the teacher's desk should emanate the discussion of principles, the judicial statement of arguments from various points of view, and not the one-sided representations of a partisan character.

"A professor abuses his privilege who in any way seeks to influence his pupils or the public by sensational methods. A professor abuses his privilege of expression of opinion when, although a student and perhaps an authority in one department or group of departments, he undertakes to speak authoritatively on subjects which have no relationship to the department in which he was appointed to give instruction. A professor abuses his privilege in many cases when, although shut off in large measure from the world and engaged within a narrow field of investigation, he undertakes to instruct his colleagues or the public concerning matters in the world at large in connection with which he has had little or no experience.

"A professor abuses his privilege of freedom of expression when he fails to exercise that quality ordinarily called common sense, which, it must be confessed, in some cases the professor lacks. A professor ought not to make such an exhibition of his weakness, or to make an exhibition of his weakness so many times, that the attention of the public at large is called to the fact. In this respect he has no larger liberty than other men.

"But may a professor do all of these things and yet remain an officer in the university? Yes. The professor in most cases is only an ordinary man. Perfection is not to be expected of him. Like men in other professions, professors have their weaknesses. But will a professor under any circumstances be asked to withdraw from the university? Yes. His resignation will be demanded, and will be accepted, when, in the opinion of those in authority, he has been guilty of immorality, or when for any reason he has proved himself to be incompetent to perform the service called for.

"The public should be on its guard in two particulars: The utterance of a professor, however wise or foolish, is not the utterance of the university. No individual, no group of individuals, can speak for the university. A statement, by whomsoever made, is the statement of an individual.

"And further, in passing judgment, care should be taken that the facts are known. It is a habit of modern journalists, and especially of the average student reporter for the newspapers, so to supply facts, so to dress up the real facts, so to magnify and exaggerate, so to belittle and ridicule universities and university men that serious injury is wrought, where perhaps no such injury was intended. It is the fashion to do this sort of thing, and it is done regardless of the consequences. Real regard for the interests of higher education would lead to the adoption of a different policy; but, as matters stand, the professor is often charged with acts and utterances implying an imbecility which is not characteristic of him, and to him there are frequently ascribed startling and revolutionary sentiments and statements of which he is wholly innocent.

"I may sum up the point in three sentences: (1) college and university professors do make mistakes, and sometimes serious ones; but (2) these are to be attributed to the professor and not to the university; and (3) in a large majority of instances the mistake, as published to the world, is misrepresented, exaggerated, or, at least, presented in such a form as to do the professor, the university, and the cause of truth itself gross injustice."

I must mention that beautiful creature, Helen Keller, whom I have known for these many years. I am filled with the wonder of her knowledge, acquired because shut out from all distractions. If I could have been deaf, dumb, and blind I also might have arrived at something.

SAMUEL L. CLEMENS ("MARK TWAIN")

106.

HUGHIE CANNON: "Bill Bailey, Won't You Please Come Home?"

According to one theory of the origin of this famous temperance song, it was a folk song about a railroad man who had deserted his woman that was adapted by Hughie Cannon, a Tin Pan Alley songwriter of the 1890s. Another theory holds that Bill Bailey was a vaudeville performer who had troubles with his wife one night, came to Cannon for sympathy and advice, and inspired the songwriter to create the song. Whatever is the truth of the matter, the song was an instant hit after being first performed in a minstrel show in Newburgh, New York, in 1902.

BILL BAILEY, WON'T YOU PLEASE COME HOME?

On one summer's day, sun was shinin' fine,
The lady honey of old Bill Bailey she hung clothes on the line
  In her backyard,
  And weeping hard.
She married a B & O brakeman who took and throwed her down,
Bellerin' like an old prune-fed calf with a big gang hangin' round,
  And to that crowd
  She yelled out loud:

  "Won't you come home, Bill Bailey, won't you come home?"
    She moans the whole day long.
  "I'll do the cookin', darlin', I'll pay the rent —
    I know I done you wrong.
  'Member that rainy evenin' I drove you out,
  With nothin' but a fine tooth comb?
  I know I'm to blame, well, ain't that a shame,
  Bill Bailey, won't you please come home?"

Bill drove by that door in an automobile,
A great big di-a-mond, coach and footman to hear that big wench squeal.
  "He's all alone,"
  I heard her groan.
She hollered right through that old screen door: "Bill Bailey, are you sore?
Stop a minute and listen to me, won't I see you here no more?"
  Bill winked his eye
  And heard her cry:

  "Won't you come home, Bill Bailey, won't you come home?" etc.

107.

Declaration of the National Woman's Christian Temperance Union

Prohibition was an even more popular cause among the women of the first decades of the twentieth century than the campaign for the suffrage. The National Woman's Christian Temperance Union, founded at Cleveland, Ohio, in 1874, agitated for the passage of laws to prohibit the sale and consumption of alcoholic beverages. By 1902 a few states had prohibition laws, and there were "dry counties" in several others. The following selection is the declaration of principles of the W.C.T.U. as promulgated in 1902.

Source: National Woman's Christian Temperance Union, *Annual Leaflet*, 1902.

WE BELIEVE in the coming of His kingdom whose service is perfect freedom, because His laws, written in our members as well as in nature and in grace, are perfect, converting the soul.

We believe in the gospel of the Golden Rule, and that each man's habits of life should be an example safe and beneficent for every other man to follow.

We believe that God created both man and woman in His own image, and, therefore, we believe in one standard of purity for both men and women, and in the equal right of all to hold opinions and to express the same with equal freedom.

We believe in a living wage; in an eight-hour day; in courts of conciliation and arbitration; in justice as opposed to greed of gain; in "peace on earth and goodwill to men."

We therefore formulate and, for ourselves, adopt the following pledge, asking our sisters and brothers of a common danger and a common hope to make common cause with us in working its reasonable and helpful precepts into the practice of everyday life:

I hereby solemnly promise, *God helping me*, to abstain from all distilled, fermented, and malt liquors, including wine, beer, and cider, and to employ all proper means to discourage the use of and traffic in the same.

To conform and enforce the rationale of this pledge, we declare our purpose to educate the young; to form a better public sentiment; to reform so far as possible, by religious, ethical, and scientific means, the drinking classes; to seek the transforming power of Divine Grace for ourselves and all for whom we work, that they and we may willfully transcend no law of pure and wholesome living; and finally we pledge ourselves to labor and to pray that all of these principles, founded upon the Gospel of Christ, may be worked out into the customs of society and the laws of the land.

1903

108.

WILLIAM GRAHAM SUMNER: An Abomination in Statecraft

William Graham Sumner regarded war in general as an abomination in statecraft, and it was his opinion that America's recent adoption of war as an instrument of national policy (for so it seemed to him) was not only a break with, but also a betrayal of, the principles of the founding fathers. In his essay "War," from which the following selection is taken, he traced the origin and nature of war in human society and expressed his regret at what seemed to him a reversion on the part of the United States to the old bellicose habits of the European nations. "We talk of civilizing lower races," he remarked of the doctrine of the white man's burden, "but we never have done it yet; we have exterminated them." The main brunt of his argument, as reflected in the selection reprinted here, was expressed in the proposition that "if you want war, nourish a doctrine" — which was his way of saying that moral principles should have no part in foreign policy.

Source: *War and Other Essays*, Albert G. Keller, ed., New Haven, 1919.

IF YOU WANT WAR, nourish a doctrine. Doctrines are the most frightful tyrants to which men ever are subject, because doctrines get inside of a man's own reason and betray him against himself. Civilized men have done their fiercest fighting for doctrines. The reconquest of the Holy Sepulcher, "the balance of power," "no universal dominion," "trade follows the flag," "he who holds the land will hold the sea," "the throne and the altar," the revolution, the faith — these are the things for which men have given their lives. What are they all? Nothing but rhetoric and phantasms.

Doctrines are always vague; it would ruin a doctrine to define it, because then it could be analyzed, tested, criticized, and verified; but nothing ought to be tolerated which cannot be so tested. Somebody asks you with astonishment and horror whether you do not believe in the Monroe Doctrine. You do not know whether you do or not, because you do not know what it is; but you do not dare to say that you do not, because you understand that it is one of the things which every good American is bound to believe in. Now, when any doctrine arrives at that degree of authority, the name of it is a club which any demagogue may swing over you at any time and apropos of anything.

In order to describe a doctrine we must have recourse to theological language. A doctrine is an article of faith. It is something which you are bound to believe, not because you have some rational grounds for believing it true but because you belong to such and such a church or denomination. The nearest parallel to it in politics is the "reason of state." The most frightful injustice and cruelty which has ever been perpetrated on earth has been due to the reason of state. Jesus Christ was put to death for the reason of state; Pilate said that he found no fault in the accused, but he wanted to keep the Jews quiet and one man crucified more or less was of no consequence.

None of these metaphysics ought to be tolerated in a free state. A policy in a state we can understand; for instance it was the policy of the United States at the end of the 18th century to get the free navigation of the Mississippi to its mouth, even at the expense of war with Spain. That policy had reason and justice in it; it was founded in our interests; it had positive form and definite scope.

A doctrine is an abstract principle; it is necessarily absolute in its scope and abstruse in its terms; it is a metaphysical assertion. It is never true, because it is absolute, and the affairs of men are all conditioned and relative. The physicists tell us now that there are phenomena which appear to present exceptions to gravitation which can be explained only by conceiving that gravitation requires time to get to work. We are convinced that perpetual motion is absolutely impossible within the world of our experiences, but it now appears that our universe taken as a whole is a case of perpetual motion.

Now, to turn back to politics, just think what an abomination in statecraft an abstract doctrine must be. Any politician or editor can, at any moment, put a new extension on it. The people acquiesce in the doctrine and applaud it because they hear the politicians and editors repeat it, and the politicians and editors repeat it because they think it is popular. So it grows.

During the recent difficulty between England and Germany on one side and Venezuela on the other, some newspapers here began to promulgate a new doctrine that no country ought to be allowed to use its naval force to collect private debts. This doctrine would have given us standing ground for interference in that quarrel. That is what it was invented for. Of course, it was absurd and ridiculous, and it fell dead, unnoticed, but it well showed the danger of having a doctrine lying loose about the house, and one which carries with it big consequences.

It may mean anything or nothing, at any moment, and no one knows how it will be. You accede to it now, within the vague limits of what you suppose it to be; therefore you will have to accede to it tomorrow when the same name is made to cover something which you never have heard or thought of. If you allow a political catchword to go on and grow, you will awaken some day to find it standing over you, the arbiter of your destiny, against which you are powerless, as men are powerless against delusions.

The process by which such catchwords grow is the old popular mythologizing. Your Monroe Doctrine becomes an entity, a being, a lesser kind of divinity, entitled to reverence and possessed of prestige, so that it allows of no discussion or deliberation. The president of the United States talks about the Monroe Doctrine and he tells us solemnly that it is true and sacred, whatever it is. He even undertakes to give some definition of what he means by it; but the definition which he gives binds nobody, either now or in the future, any more than what Monroe and Adams meant by it binds anybody now not to mean anything else. He says that, on account of the doctrine, whatever it may be, we must have a big navy. In this, at least, he is plainly in the right; if we have the doctrine, we shall need a big navy.

The Monroe Doctrine is an exercise of authority by the United States over a controversy between two foreign states, if one of them is in America, combined with a refusal of the United States to accept any responsibility in connection with the controversy. That is a position which is sure to bring us into collision with other states, especially because it will touch their vanity, or what they call their honor — or it will touch our vanity, or what we call our honor, if we should ever find ourselves called upon to "back down" from it. Therefore it is very true that we must expect to need a big navy if we adhere to the doctrine. What can be more contrary to sound statesmanship and common sense than to put forth an abstract assertion which has no definite relation to any interest of ours now at stake, but which has in it any number of possibilities of producing complications which we cannot foresee, but which are sure to be embarrassing when they arise!

What has just been said suggests a consideration of the popular saying, "In time of peace prepare for war." If you prepare a big army and navy and are all ready for war, it will be easy to go to war; the military and naval men will have a lot of new machines and they will be eager to see what they can do with them. There is no such thing nowadays as a state of readiness for war. It is a chimera, and the nations which pursue it are falling into an abyss of wasted energy and wealth.

When the Army is supplied with the latest and best rifles, someone invents a new field gun; then the artillery must be provided with that before we are ready. By the time we get the new gun, somebody has invented a new rifle and our rival nation is getting that; therefore we must have it, or one a little better. It takes two or three years and several millions to do that. In the meantime, somebody proposes a more effective organization which must be introduced; signals, balloons, dogs, bicycles, and every other device and invention must be added, and men must be trained to use them all.

There is no state of readiness for war; the notion calls for never ending sacrifices. It is a fallacy. It is evident that to pursue such a notion with any idea of realizing it would absorb all the resources and activity of the state; this the great European states are now proving by experiment. A wiser rule would be to make up your mind soberly what you want, peace or war, and then to get ready for what you want; for what we prepare for is what we shall get.

———————◆———————

Success four flights Thursday morning all against twenty-one mile wind started from level with engine power alone average speed through air thirty-one miles longest 59 seconds inform press home Christmas.
ORVILLE AND WILBUR WRIGHT, telegram to their father, from Kitty Hawk, North Carolina, Dec. 17, 1903

109.

Treaty with Cuba

After the Spanish-American War, many of the apologists for American intervention insisted that Cuba be given her independence. In 1902 the United States withdrew its troops, and Cuba became a republic. By the provisions of the Platt Amendment, which was included in the Cuban constitution of 1901 and also inserted in the treaty with Cuba in 1903, the United States retained the right to intervene to preserve Cuban independence as well as the right to sanction Cuban concessions to foreign powers. In effect, this made Cuba a protectorate. A portion of the 1903 treaty embodying the amendment, which was not abrogated until 1934, is reprinted below.

Source: Malloy, I, pp. 362-364.

ARTICLE I

The government of Cuba shall never enter into any treaty or other compact with any foreign power or powers which will impair or tend to impair the independence of Cuba, nor in any manner authorize or permit any foreign power or powers to obtain by colonization or for military or naval purposes, or otherwise, lodgment in or control over any portion of said island.

ARTICLE II

The government of Cuba shall not assume or contract any public debt to pay the interest upon which, and to make reasonable sinking fund provision for the ultimate discharge of which, the ordinary revenues of the island of Cuba, after defraying the current expenses of the government, shall be inadequate.

ARTICLE III

The government of Cuba consents that the United States may exercise the right to intervene for the preservation of Cuban independence, the maintenance of a government adequate for the protection of life, property, and individual liberty, and for discharging the obligations with respect to Cuba imposed by the Treaty of Paris on the United States, now to be assumed and undertaken by the government of Cuba.

ARTICLE IV

All acts of the United States in Cuba during its military occupancy thereof are ratified and validated, and all lawful rights acquired thereunder shall be maintained and protected.

ARTICLE V

The government of Cuba will execute and, as far as necessary, extend the plans already devised, or other plans to be mutually agreed upon, for the sanitation of the cities of the island, to the end that a recurrence of epidemic and infectious diseases may be prevented, thereby assuring protection to the people and commerce of Cuba, as well as to the commerce of the Southern ports of the United States and the people residing therein.

ARTICLE VI

The island of Pines shall be omitted from the boundaries of Cuba specified in the constitution, the title thereto being left to future adjustment by treaty.

ARTICLE VII

To enable the United States to maintain the independence of Cuba, and to protect the people thereof, as well as for its own defense, the government of Cuba will sell or lease to the United States lands necessary for coaling or naval stations, at certain specified points, to be agreed upon with the President of the United States.

ARTICLE VIII

The present convention shall be ratified by each party in conformity with the respective constitutions of the two countries, and the ratifications shall be exchanged in the city of Washington within eight months from this date.

In witness whereof, we the respective plenipotentiaries, have signed the same in duplicate, in English and Spanish, and have affixed our respective seals at Havana, Cuba, this 22nd day of May, . . . 1903.

110.

WILLIAM JAMES: The Ph.D. Octopus

William James's career at Harvard University, first as a student and then as a professor of psychology and finally of philosophy, provided him with the background out of which grew the following essay. James was profoundly interested in improving the quality of American teachers. He sadly noted that, although graduate education was still in its infancy in the United States, the Ph.D. degree had already become a necessary badge of employment for university teaching positions. The doctorate and all it entailed held the student, professor, and university in an octopus-like hold. The prestige of a university was determined by the number of faculty members with Ph.D.'s, while graduate schools prided themselves on their difficult standards and withheld the degree from all but the brilliant few.

Source: *Harvard Monthly*, March 1903.

SOME YEARS AGO we had at our Harvard Graduate School a very brilliant student of philosophy, who, after leaving us and supporting himself by literary labor for three years, received an appointment to teach English literature at a sister-institution of learning. The governors of this institution, however, had no sooner communicated the appointment than they made the awful discovery that they had enrolled upon their staff a person who was unprovided with the Ph.D. degree. The man in question had been satisfied to work at philosophy for her

own sweet (or bitter) sake and had disdained to consider that an academic bauble should be his reward.

His appointment had thus been made under a misunderstanding. He was not the proper man; and there was nothing to do but to inform him of the fact. It was notified to him by his new president that his appointment must be revoked, or that a Harvard doctor's degree must forthwith be procured.

Although it was already the spring of the year, our subject, being a man of spirit, took up the challenge, turned his back upon literature (which in view of his approaching duties might have seemed his more urgent concern), and spent the weeks that were left him in writing a metaphysical thesis and grinding his psychology, logic, and history of philosophy up again so as to pass our formidable ordeals.

When the thesis came to be read by our committee, we could not pass it. Brilliancy and originality by themselves won't save a thesis for the doctorate; it must also exhibit a heavy technical apparatus of learning; and this our candidate had neglected to bring to bear. So, telling him that he was temporarily rejected, we advised him to pad out the thesis properly and return with it next year, at the same time informing his new president that this signified nothing as to his merits, that he was of ultra-Ph.D. quality, and one of the strongest men with whom we had ever had to deal.

To our surprise we were given to understand in reply that the quality per se of the man signified nothing in this connection, and that three magical letters were the thing seriously required. The college had always gloried in a list of faculty members who bore the doctor's title, and to make a gap in the galaxy and admit a common fox without a tail would be a degradation impossible to be thought of. We wrote again, pointing out that a Ph.D. in philosophy would prove little anyhow as to one's ability to teach literature; we sent separate letters in which we outdid each other in eulogy of our candidate's powers, for indeed they were great; and at last, *mirabile dictu*, our eloquence prevailed. He was allowed to retain his appointment provisionally, on condition that one year later at the furthest his miserably naked name should be prolonged by the sacred appendage the lack of which had given so much trouble to all concerned.

Accordingly, he came up here the following spring with an adequate thesis (known since in print as a most brilliant contribu-

tion to metaphysics), passed a first-rate examination, wiped out the stain, and brought his college into proper relations with the world again. Whether his teaching, during that first year, of English literature was made any the better by the impending examination in a different subject is a question which I will not try to solve.

I have related this incident at such length because it is so characteristic of American academic conditions at the present day. Graduate schools still are something of a novelty and higher diplomas something of a rarity. The latter, therefore, carry a vague sense of preciousness and honor, and have a particularly "up-to-date" appearance, and it is no wonder if smaller institutions, unable to attract professors already eminent and forced usually to recruit their faculties from the relatively young, should hope to compensate for the obscurity of the names of their officers of instruction by the abundance of decorative titles by which those names are followed on the pages of the catalogues where they appear. The dazzled reader of the list, the parent or student, says to himself, "This must be a terribly distinguished crowd — their titles shine like the stars in the firmament; Ph.D.'s, S.D.'s, and Litt.D.'s bespangle the page as if they were sprinkled over it from a pepper caster."

Human nature is once for all so childish that every reality becomes a sham somewhere, and in the minds of presidents and trustees the Ph.D. degree is in point of fact already looked upon as a mere advertising resource, a manner of throwing dust in the public's eyes. "No instructor who is not a doctor" has become a maxim in the smaller institutions which represent demand; and in each of the larger ones, which represent supply, the same belief in decorated scholarship expresses itself in two antagonistic passions — one for multiplying as much as possible the annual output of doctors; the other for raising the standard of difficulty in passing, so that the Ph.D. of the special institution shall carry a higher blaze of distinction than it does elsewhere. Thus we at Harvard are proud of the number of candidates whom we reject and of the inability of men who are not *distingués* in intellect to pass our tests.

America is thus as a nation rapidly drifting toward a state of things in which no man of science or letters will be accounted respectable unless some kind of badge or diploma is stamped upon him and in which bare personality will be a mark of outcast estate. It seems to me high time to rouse ourselves to consciousness and to cast a critical eye upon this decidedly grotesque tendency. Other nations suffer terribly from the Mandarin disease. Are we doomed to suffer like the rest?

Our higher degrees were instituted for the laudable purpose of stimulating scholarship, especially in the form of "original research." Experience has proved that great as the love of truth may be among men, it can be made still greater by adventitious rewards. The winning of a diploma certifying mastery and marking a barrier successfully passed acts as a challenge to the ambitious; and if the diploma will help to gain breadwinning positions also, its power as a stimulus to work is tremendously increased.

So far, we are on innocent ground; it is well for a country to have research in abundance, and our graduate schools do but apply a normal psychological spur. But the institutionizing on a large scale of any natural combination of need and motive always tends to run into technicality and to develop a tyrannical machine with unforeseen powers of exclusion and corruption. Observation of the workings of our Harvard system for twenty years past has brought some of these drawbacks home to my consciousness, and I should like to call the attention of the readers . . . to this disadvantageous aspect of the picture, and to make a couple of remedial suggestions, if I may.

In the first place, it would seem that to stimulate study, and to increase the *gelehrtes Publikum*, the class of highly educated men

in our country, is the only positive good, and consequently the sole direct end at which our graduate schools, with their diploma-giving powers, should aim. If other results have developed, they should be deemed secondary incidents, and if not desirable in themselves, they should be carefully guarded against.

To interfere with the free development of talent, to obstruct the natural play of supply and demand in the teaching profession, to foster academic snobbery by the prestige of certain privileged institutions, to transfer accredited value from essential manhood to an outward badge, to blight hopes and promote invidious sentiments, to divert the attention of aspiring youth from direct dealings with truth to the passing of examinations — such consequences, if they exist, ought surely to be regarded as drawbacks to the system, and an enlightened public consciousness ought to be keenly alive to the importance of reducing their amount. Candidates themselves do seem to be keenly conscious of some of these evils, but, outside of their ranks or in the general public, no such consciousness so far as I can see exists; or, if it does exist, it fails to express itself aloud. Schools, colleges, and universities appear enthusiastic over the entire system just as it stands and unanimously applaud all its developments.

I beg the reader to consider some of the secondary evils which I have enumerated. First of all, is not our growing tendency to appoint no instructors who are not also doctors an instance of pure sham? Will anyone pretend for a moment that the doctor's degree is a guarantee that its possessor will be successful as a teacher? Notoriously, his moral, social, and personal characteristics may utterly disqualify him for success in the classroom; and of these characteristics his doctor's examination is unable to take any account whatever. Certain bare human beings will always be better candidates for a given place than all the doctor-applicants on hand; and to exclude the former by a rigid rule, and in the end to have to sift the latter by private inquiry into their personal peculiarities among those who know them, just as if they were not doctors at all, is to stultify one's own procedure.

You may say that at least you guard against ignorance of the subject by considering only the candidates who are doctors; but how then about making doctors in one subject teach a different subject? This happened in the instance by which I introduced this article, and it happens daily and hourly in all our colleges. The truth is that the doctor-monopoly in teaching, which is becoming so rooted in American custom, can show no serious grounds whatsoever for itself in reason. As it actually prevails and grows in vogue among us, it is due to childish motives exclusively. In reality it is but a sham, a bauble, a dodge whereby to decorate the catalogues of schools and colleges.

Next, let us turn from the general promotion of a spirit of academic snobbery to the particular damage done to individuals by the system.

There are plenty of individuals so well-endowed by nature that they pass with ease all the ordeals with which life confronts them. Such persons are born for professional success. Examinations have no terrors for them and interfere in no way with their spiritual or worldly interests. There are others, not so gifted, who nevertheless rise to the challenge, get a stimulus from the difficulty, and become doctors, not without some baleful nervous wear and tear and retardation of their purely inner life, but on the whole successfully, and with advantage.

These two classes form the natural Ph.D.'s for whom the degree is legitimately instituted. To be sure, the degree is of no consequence one way or the other for the first sort of man, for in him the personal worth obviously outshines the title. To the second set of persons, however, the doctor-ideal may contribute a touch of energy and solidity of scholarship which otherwise they might have lacked; and were our candidates all drawn from these classes, no oppression would result from the institution.

But there is a third class of persons who are genuinely, and in the most pathetic sense, the institution's victims. For this type of character the academic life may become, after a certain point, a virulent poison. Men without marked originality or native force, but fond of truth and especially of books and study, ambitious of reward and recognition, poor often, and needing a degree to get a teaching position, weak in the eyes of their examiners; among these we find the veritable *chair à canon* [cannon fodder] of the wars of learning, the unfit in the academic struggle for existence. There are individuals of this sort for whom to pass one degree after another seems the limit of earthly aspiration. Your private advice does not discourage them. They will fail, and go away to recuperate, and then present themselves for another ordeal, and sometimes prolong the process into middle life. Or else, if they are less heroic morally they will accept the failure as a sentence of doom that they are not fit, and are broken-spirited men thereafter.

We of the university faculties are responsible for deliberately creating this new class of American social failures, and heavy is the responsibility. We advertise our "schools" and send out our degree requirements, knowing well that aspirants of all sorts will be attracted, and at the same time we set a standard which intends to pass no man who has not native intellectual distinction. We know that there is no test, however absurd, by which, if a title or decoration, a public badge or mark, were to be won by it, some weakly suggestible or hauntable persons would not feel challenged, and remain unhappy if they went without it. We dangle our three magic letters before the eyes of these predestined victims, and they swarm to us like moths to an electric light.

They come at a time when failure can no longer be repaired easily and when the wounds it leaves are permanent; and we say deliberately that mere work, faithfully performed, as they perform it, will not by itself save them, they must in addition put in evidence the one thing they have not got, namely, this quality of intellectual distinction. Occasionally, out of sheer human pity, we ignore our high and mighty standard and pass them. Usually, however, the standard, and not the candidate, commands our fidelity. The result is caprice, majorities-of-one on the jury, and on the whole a confession that our pretensions about the degree cannot be lived up to consistently. Thus, partiality in the favored cases; in the unfavored, blood on our hands; and, in both, a bad conscience, are the results of our administration.

The more widespread becomes the popular belief that our diplomas are indispensable hallmarks to show the sterling metal of their holders, the more widespread these corruptions will become. We ought to look to the future carefully, for it takes generations for a national custom, once rooted, to be grown away from. All the European countries are seeking to diminish the check upon individual spontaneity which state examinations with their tyrannous growth have brought in their train. We have had to institute state examinations, too; and it will perhaps be fortunate if some day hereafter our descendants, comparing machine with machine, do not sigh with regret for old times and American freedom, and wish that the regime of the dear old bosses might be reinstalled, with plain human nature, the glad hand and the marble heart, liking and disliking, and man-to-man relations grown possible again.

Meanwhile, whatever evolution our state examinations are destined to undergo, our universities at least should never cease to regard themselves as the jealous custodians of personal and spiritual spontaneity. They are indeed its only organized and recognized custodians in America today. They ought to guard against contributing to the increase of officialism and snobbery and insincerity as against a pestilence; they ought to keep truth and disinterested labor always in the foreground, treat degrees as secondary incidents, and in season and out of season make it plain that what they live for is to help men's souls and not to decorate their persons with diplomas.

There seem to be three obvious ways in which the increasing hold of the Ph.D. Octopus upon American life can be kept in check.

The first way lies with the universities. They can lower their fantastic standards (which here at Harvard we are so proud of) and give the doctorate as a matter of course, just as they give the bachelor's degree, for a due amount of time spent in patient labor in a special department of learning, whether the man be a brilliantly gifted individual or not. Surely native distinction needs no official stamp, and should disdain to ask for one. On the other hand, faithful labor, however commonplace, and years devoted to a subject always deserve to be acknowledged and requited.

The second way lies with both the universities and colleges. Let them give up their unspeakably silly ambition to bespangle their lists of officers with these doctorial titles. Let them look more to substance and less to vanity and sham.

The third way lies with the individual student and with his personal advisers in the faculties. Every man of native power, who might take a higher degree and refuses to do so because examinations interfere with the free following out of his more immediate intellectual aims, deserves well of his country, and in a rightly organized community would not be made to suffer for his independence. With many men the passing of these extraneous tests is a very grievous interference indeed. Private letters of recommendation from their instructors, which in any event are ultimately needful, ought, in these cases, completely to offset the lack of the breadwinning degree; and instructors ought to be ready to advise students against it upon occasion and to pledge themselves to back them later personally in the market-struggle which they have to face.

It is indeed odd to see this love of titles — and such titles — growing up in a country of which the recognition of individuality and bare manhood have so long been supposed to be the very soul. The independence of the state, in which most of our colleges stand, relieves us of those more odious forms of academic politics which continental European countries present. Anything like the elaborate university machine of France, with its throttling influences upon individuals is unknown here. The spectacle of the "Rath" distinction in its innumerable spheres and grades with which all Germany is crawling today is displeasing to American eyes; and displeasing also in some respects is the institution of knighthood in England, which, aping as it does an aristocratic title, enables one's wife as well as oneself so easily to dazzle the servants at the house of one's friends.

But are we Americans ourselves destined after all to hunger after similar vanities on an infinitely more contemptible scale? And is individuality with us also going to count for nothing unless stamped and licensed and authenticated by some title-giving machine? Let us pray that our ancient national genius may long preserve vitality enough to guard us from a future so unmanly and so unbeautiful!

111.

DAVID PARRY: Organized Labor as the "Great Muscle Trust"

Although union membership was modest at the turn of the century, many manufacturers were worried about the potential strength of organized labor. Using the vocabulary of nineteenth-century liberalism, they argued that the organization of labor prevented the individual worker from exercising his right of free choice. President Theodore Roosevelt's campaign against the trusts, meaning big business monopolies, was, in this view, misplaced. It was irresponsible labor, using brute force to attain its ends, rather than capitalism, which used money, that was the disruptive trust in this country. In his annual message, part of which appears here, the president of the National Association of Manufacturers, David Parry, suggested ways in which the association could combat what he called the "muscle trust."

Source: *Proceedings of the Eighth Annual Convention of the National Association of Manufacturers of the United States of America Held at New Orleans, La., April 14, 15, and 16, 1903*, Indianapolis, 1903: "Annual Report of the President."

THE EIGHTH ANNUAL CONVENTION of the Association meets under auspicious conditions. The country is still in the full enjoyment of that peace and prosperity which have made the last few years so notable, and the coming year gives no indication of reaction in the tide of industrial activity. In the light of the general prosperity it is all the more a pleasure to note the prosperity that has come to the Association. Not only has its membership increased by leaps and bounds but success has attended its efforts in many directions.

With over 2,000 manufacturing establishments of the country on its rolls, as compared to less than 1,000 a year ago, the Association has become more than ever the unrivaled organization of its kind in the world. It stands today as the most efficient mouthpiece of those whose capital is invested in productive enterprise. It stands as a bulwark of progress and as a foe to every agency or force that, through ignorance or deliberate intent, would check industrial development or wreck our free institutions on the rocks of economic fallacy.

The influence the Association has exercised during the past year on the course of national legislation and public thought has been large and wholesome, furnishing signal proof of the power of organization and vindicating its usefulness, not only to its members but to the country as a whole. Largely through its endeavors the new Department of Commerce has been created, and another measure of vast importance, the Isthmian Canal Bill, to which it gave its hearty support, has been enacted into a law since our last convention. The Association also vigorously opposed the eight-hour and anti-injunction bills in the last Congress. The defeat of these measures may, in my opinion, be justly credited to the hearty cooperation of our members in the campaign waged against the bills.

The fight made against these bills involved a contest with organized labor, which fathered them, and an agitation was inaugurated against an organization which would demand such un-American legislation. This agitation has been far-reaching and has produced a distinct change in current sentiment, as indicated by the press and public utterances of prominent men. While the Association has obtained tangible results in other directions aside from those mentioned, yet this contest with organized labor will appear to many to be an overshadowing feature of the past year, and its consideration will, therefore, be given first place in this report.

By its determined opposition to the passage of the eight-hour and the anti-injunction bills, this Association performed what, to my mind, was a great public service, the full significance of which is, perhaps, not realized even by many who were foremost in condemning those measures. The mere defeating of these two bills does not tell the story. What was done that was much more important and far-reaching was to give an opportune check to socialistic impulse. It is impossible to hide our eyes to the fact that a large mass of the people, forgetful of the liberties and blessings they now enjoy, are with reckless ardor striving to force the nation to what must eventually mean industrial disaster, if not anarchy and despotism.

Organized labor, an army presumably 2 million strong, feeling its strength and exultant over many victories it had won, concluded last winter that the time was ripe to make Congress engraft upon the statute books of the nation its sprigs of socialism, legalizing those denials of individual rights which it has heretofore sought to enjoin by force. It drew up and fathered the eight-hour and the anti-injunction bills, the former of which could well have been entitled, "An act to repeal the Bill of Rights guaranteeing the freedom of the individual," and the latter should have been termed, "A bill to legalize strikes and boycotts." . . .

It is well that those who would revolutionize the social order should at the very inception of their national program meet with organized resistance, and it was fortunate that there was an association strong enough to checkmate the influence of organized labor this last winter, and that at a time when, in the full plentitude of its power, it seemed certain of success. Perhaps no proposed act of legislation ever occasioned a greater outpouring of personal appeals to

Congress than did the eight-hour bill. On the one side were the labor unions, sending in countless petitions demanding its passage, and, on the other side, in united array, were the manufacturers, respectfully urging its defeat and setting forth unanswerable arguments why it should be defeated. This conflict — and it was a conflict, and a very momentous one — deserves to go down in history as the first decisive defeat of the socialistic forces which have of late years had such surprising growth. . . .

The chief work that lies within the province of this Association is an educational one. Organized labor owes its present power mainly to the support of public opinion, and this it obtained through constant agitation. The thought and sentiment of thousands who lean toward the cause of labor are based upon *ex parte* consideration. Carried away by the insistent and specious pleas for the "poor workingman," they have lost sight of the grave issues that are at stake. The duty that lies before us is, therefore, a plain one. It is to arouse the great middle class to a realization of what trades unionism really means. It is to show why, in the language of one English writer:

> It is a system that coerces and impoverishes the worker, ruins the capitalist, terrorizes our politicians, and destroys our trade — a system which seems to be hopelessly and irredeemably bad, a bar to all true progress, a danger to the state, and a menace to civilization.

Once thoroughly alive to the true nature of this un-American institution, the people, I firmly believe, will place their stamp of disapproval upon it, and it will dwindle in power faster than it grew. Perhaps a new form of unionism will take its place — a beneficent unionism — for the right of the workmen to organize is not to be disputed, nor is it to be denied that, if conducted along right lines, their organizations have it in their power to accomplish good. The employers of this country have no quarrel

with the men that work for them considered as individuals. The welfare of those who toil in our factories calls for our most earnest consideration. But what we must protest against is the unwarrantable usurpation of rights and the disastrous industrial policy which characterizes them in their present associated capacity.

It remains now to set forth in more detail some of the reasons that give just cause for the denunciation of organized labor.

Organized labor knows but one law, and that is the law of physical force — the law of the Huns and Vandals, the law of the savage. All its purposes are accomplished either by actual force or by the threat of force. It does not place its reliance in reason and justice, but in strikes, boycotts, and coercion. It is, in all essential features, a mob power, knowing no master except its own will, and is continually condemning or defying the constituted authorities. The stronger it grows the greater a menace it becomes to the continuance of free government, in which all the people have a voice. It is, in fact, a despotism springing into being in the midst of a liberty-loving people.

In setting itself up as a power independent of the power of the state, it does not regard itself as bound to observe the Fourteenth Amendment to the Constitution of the United States, which says:

> No state shall make or enforce any law which shall abridge the privileges or immunities of citizens of the United States, nor shall any state deprive any person of life, liberty, or property without due process of law, nor deny to any person within its jurisdiction the equal protection of the laws.

It has not, in times past, hesitated to resort to violence and the destruction of property to compel the acceptance of its demands. Its history is stained with blood and ruin. Many a man whose only fault was that he stood upon his rights has been made to suffer outrage, and even death, and many an employer has been brought face to face with financial ruin. These wrongs cry unto heaven, and yet an unaroused public sentiment too often permits them to go unheeded and unpunished.

It now demands of the public and of Congress the privilege to violate the laws forbidding violence and property destruction that it may continue to maintain its power through terrorism. It extends its tactics of coercion and intimidation over all classes, dictating to the press and the politicians, and strangling independence of thought and American manhood.

It denies to those outside its ranks the individual right to dispose of their labor as they see fit, a right that is one of the most sacred and fundamental of American liberty. It holds a bludgeon over the head of the employer, laying down the terms upon which he shall be permitted to do business. It says to him that he must deal direct with the union; that, while he shall pay the men who work in his factory, they shall be beholden more to the union than to him for their positions; that he cannot employ or discharge men without the endorsement and consent of the union, and that he must pay them the wage fixed by the union, without regard to their individual worth or the economic ability of the employer to pay.

It denies to the individual the right of being his own judge as to the length of time he shall work and as to how much he shall do within the time prescribed. It takes no account of the varying degree of natural aptitude and powers of endurance displayed by individuals, and seeks to place all men in each particular trade on the same dead level, as respects his daily output and his daily wage. Thus a premium is placed on indolence and incompetence, and there is a restriction of human effort, reducing the aggregate production and increasing the cost of the things produced.

This policy amounts to not only a tax upon the consumers, the majority of whom do not belong to organized labor, but it reduces the demands of the trade at home and lessens the chances of successful competition by our manufacturers in foreign markets. The eight-hour law, which it demands, is merely the extension to a wider field of the principle it enforces in trades under its domination.

It drives, unwillingly, men into its ranks by its policy of intimidation. Thousands of its members are such today, not because they sympathize with its purposes but because they fear the consequences of not yielding to its tyranny. These men are, as a class, the more thrifty and capable of its members. They are men who secretly rebel against the system which places them on the level with the incompetent and idle, and would gladly have free conditions established that they might prove their superior worth and thus gain advancement in life. But they dare not openly express their views, for they feel that their employment and peace depend upon their submissive acquiescence to the principles of the union.

While it seeks to compel men already employed in the trades to enlist under its banner, it at the same time seeks to prevent outsiders from entering the trades. It foists upon employers rules limiting the number of apprentices, some unions going so far as to say there shall be no apprentices whatever. The boys from the farms now come to the cities and find the doors to the trades shut against them. While lawyers, doctors, and men in other unorganized vocations are glad to teach young men their knowledge, the trades unionist refuses to do so, and employers are now forced to endow technical schools in the hope of obtaining that supply of new blood for their workshops which is essential to the prevention of dry rot.

Organized labor is an organization of manual labor, trained and untrained, of men who do as they are told and who depend upon the brains of others for guidance. That wide field of labor in which mental capacity is a greater or less requisite on the part of the workers is not represented by it, and cannot be for the obvious impossibility of organizing brains. The rule that organized labor seeks to establish is, therefore, the rule of the least intelligent portion of labor. A comprehension of this fact explains why its leaders are found to be agitators and demagogues, men who appeal to prejudice and envy, who are constantly instilling a hatred of wealth and ability, and who, in incendiary speeches, attempt to stir up men to seize by physical force that which their merit cannot obtain for them.

Composed as it is of the men of muscle rather than the men of intelligence, and commanded by leaders who are at heart disciples of revolution, it is not strange that organized labor stands for principles that are in direct conflict with the natural laws of economics. Its first great principle is that an arbitrary division of production would be better than the division regulated by natural law, provided, however, that it can dictate what this division shall be. It says to capital and to mental and unorganized labor:

> We shall take this proportion of the products of human industry and you may have the balance. If you do not agree to this arrangement you are 'unfair,' you are enemies of the 'poor working man,' you are 'oppressors'; and if you do not peacefully submit to our terms we will compel you to do so by force.

The fixing of arbitrary wage scales by force would result in no benefit to any class of labor if all classes adopted the idea. Suppose that clerks, bookkeepers, lawyers, doctors, managers, businessmen, and, in fact, all workers outside of pure manual labor should organize and should say that they must have such and such wages, or so much profit, or they would go home and stay there. It is within the range of possibility that their demands would be acceded to. Increased wages and profits would thus be accorded to everyone, according to the theory of organized labor, and poverty would be unknown on the earth. What an absurd proposition!

Arbitrary enactments and all the resoluting and demagogy in the world can never create an atom of wealth. Wealth is created by labor, capital, and ability, working together, and there is no other way of creating it. There being a limit to the possible amount of wealth that can be created, and the needs and desires of man being practically unlimited, there follows a natural conflict as to the relative proportion of this wealth going to each factor in production. When one class of men get a bigger share than they formerly got, then there is less for the remaining class of men. It is ridiculous to assert, then, that a universal application of the arbitrary wage-scale scheme would bring about anything but an advance in nominal wages, or, in other words, a decrease in the purchasing power of the dollar. Real wages would remain practically the same. . . .

Organized labor, with characteristic obtuseness, assumes that productive capital has been seized in some piratical manner by those who possess it, and that, therefore, it is legitimate spoils for those who can seize it. It is apparently oblivious to the fact that progress is dependent upon the amount of productive capital in use, for it is capital that multiplies the productive capacity of men, and the more wealth produced the more there is for distribution. It is also an error to assume that all consumable wealth is not distributed as fast as it is produced. The owners or managers of productive capital do not consume that capital. They cannot do it if they would, except by burning it up or otherwise destroying it. Again, they must keep it employed, for idle capital does the owners no good. Now and then we may see some capital not being employed, but it is very small as compared to that which is employed, and in most cases it is merely waiting an opportunity for employment to advantage.

If labor leaders or the state had the management of productive capital it would still have to be kept intact and increased in amount, for if this was not done production would decrease and poverty would increase. It may seriously be doubted if any better plan than that of individual ownership could be devised for the conservation and strenuous employment of capital. That, for the general good of all, it should be increased in amount and efficiently employed ought to be readily recognized.

It is another mistake to assume that capital is lodged in the hands of a few owners. It is true that we find great industries under the guiding hand of one man, but this is not an indication that he alone owns the capital employed. A great part of the capital of the country is owned by the thousands who have a few shares of stock in great concerns, or who have deposited their savings in banks, trust companies, and in insurance companies. The money thus deposited is not idle, but for the time being the owner relinquishes his right to its management, and it all goes to turning the wheels of industry.

Organized labor is particularly denunciatory of trusts, but what greater trust is there than itself? It is the grand trust of the times. It is the muscle trust, the trust of men who make their living by manual labor. It is to be hoped that, in accordance with the Nelson amendment to the Department of Commerce bill, the government, in turning the searchlight of publicity on the trusts, will not forget organized labor. If any institution needs to be exposed to the limelight, it is certainly trades unionism. But it is not only a trust itself; it is a creator of other trusts — of capitalistic trusts as distinguished from labor trusts. One of the leading causes for the formation of a number of the industrial combinations has been the necessity that has confronted employers to unite that the exactions of labor might be more effectively dealt with.

Organized labor is not only seeking to absorb with its tentacles all the manual workers of the cities and factories, but it is also reaching out to take in the farm laborers. Unions of the latter are reported to be rapidly growing in Illinois and Indiana. It is also stated that they are preparing to exact double the wages heretofore paid for this class of labor. If a compact organization of farmhands could be formed, a very serious problem would confront not only the farmers but the entire country. There can be no doubt that such an organization would demand, with all the unreasonableness of ignorance, a wage scale that would greatly enhance the cost of living to each and every one, and would in all likelihood bring about the ruin of our immense export trade in grain and flour.

Organized labor and the Socialist Party differ in one essential respect. The former seeks to bring about socialism by forcible methods, and the latter seeks the same end through the ballot box. The attempt of organized labor to compel the shortening of the hours of labor without regard to the effect on industrial welfare, its dictation of uniform wage scales, which place the indolent and inapt on the same footing with energy and capability, and the absolute power it arrogates to itself over the individual, on the theory that the individual has no rights which the many need respect, are all cardinal principles of socialism. Socialism is a denial of individual and property rights, and so, also, is trades unionism, when reduced to its last analysis.

The bigger they are, the harder they fall.
        Attributed to ROBERT FITZSIMMONS, before his fight with Jeffries, a much larger man, San Francisco, July 25, 1902

112.

W. E. BURGHARDT DU BOIS: What the Black Man Wants

Booker T. Washington and W. E. B. Du Bois were the two leading spokesmen of the Negro in the United States at the turn of the century, but they shared nothing else besides the color of their skin. Washington was the apostle of accommodation to the white man; Du Bois was the revolutionary advocate of Negro rights, who demanded — and who declared that all Negroes really wanted — equal economic and social status. Du Bois' position, of course, came to be the generally accepted one in the later struggle for Negro civil and political rights. The selection reprinted here comprises parts of two chapters of Du Bois' famous book The Souls of Black Folk, *published in 1903.*

Source: *The Souls of Black Folk,* 5th edition, Chicago, 1904, Chs. 1, 3.

I.

The Spiritual Strivings of Black Folk

BETWEEN ME AND THE OTHER WORLD there is ever an unasked question: unasked by some through feelings of delicacy; by others through the difficulty of rightly framing it. All, nevertheless, flutter round it. They approach me in a half-hesitant sort of way, eye me curiously or compassionately, and then, instead of saying directly, How does it feel to be a problem? they say, I know an excellent colored man in my town; or, I fought at Mechanicsville; or, Do not these Southern outrages make your blood boil? At these I smile, or am interested, or reduce the boiling to a simmer, as the occasion may require. To the real question, How does it feel to be a problem? I answer seldom a word.

And, yet, being a problem is a strange experience — peculiar even for one who has never been anything else, save perhaps in babyhood and in Europe. It is in the early days of rollicking boyhood that the revelation first bursts upon one, all in a day, as it were. I remember well when the shadow swept across me. I was a little thing, away up in the hills of New England, where the dark Housatonic winds between Hoosac and Taghkanic to the sea. In a wee wooden schoolhouse, something put it into the boys' and girls' heads to buy gorgeous visiting cards — ten cents a package — and exchange. The exchange was merry, till one girl, a tall newcomer, refused my card, — refused it peremptorily, with a glance. Then it dawned upon me with a certain suddenness that I was different from the others; or like, mayhap, in heart and life and longing, but shut out from their world by a vast veil.

I had thereafter no desire to tear down that veil, to creep through; I held all beyond it in common contempt and lived above it in a region of blue sky and great wandering shadows. That sky was bluest when I could beat my mates at examination time, or beat them at a foot race, or even beat their stringy heads. Alas, with the years all this fine contempt began to fade; for the worlds I longed for, and all their dazzling opportunities, were theirs, not mine. But they should not keep these prizes, I said; some, all, I would wrest from them. Just how I would do it I could never decide —

by reading law, by healing the sick, by telling the wonderful tales that swam in my head — some way.

With other black boys the strife was not so fiercely sunny: their youth shrunk into tasteless sycophancy or into silent hatred of the pale world about them and mocking distrust of everything white; or wasted itself in a bitter cry — Why did God make me an outcast and a stranger in mine own house? The shades of the prison house closed round about us all: walls strait and stubborn to the whitest, but relentlessly narrow, tall, and unscalable to sons of night who must plod darkly on in resignation, or beat unavailing palms against the stone, or steadily, half-hopelessly, watch the streak of blue above.

After the Egyptian and Indian, the Greek and Roman, the Teuton and Mongolian, the Negro is a sort of seventh son, born with a veil, and gifted with second-sight in this American world — a world which yields him no true self-consciousness, but only lets him see himself through the revelation of the other world. It is a peculiar sensation, this double-consciousness, this sense of always looking at oneself through the eyes of others, of measuring one's soul by the tape of a world that looks on in amused contempt and pity. One ever feels his twoness — an American, a Negro; two souls, two thoughts, two unreconciled strivings; two warring ideals in one dark body, whose dogged strength alone keeps it from being torn asunder.

The history of the American Negro is the history of this strife, this longing to attain self-conscious manhood, to merge his double self into a better and truer self. In this merging he wishes neither of the older selves to be lost. He would not Africanize America, for America has too much to teach the world and Africa. He would not bleach his Negro soul in a flood of white Americanism, for he knows that Negro blood has a message for the world. He simply wishes to make it possible for a man to be both a Negro and an American, without being cursed and spit upon by his fellows, without having the doors of opportunity closed roughly in his face.

This, then, is the end of his striving: to be a co-worker in the kingdom of culture, to escape both death and isolation, to husband and use his best powers and his latent genius. These powers of body and mind have in the past been strangely wasted, dispersed, or forgotten. The shadow of a mighty Negro past flits through the tale of Ethiopia the Shadowy and of Egypt the Sphinx. Throughout history, the powers of single black men flash here and there like falling stars, and die sometimes before the world has rightly gauged their brightness.

Here in America, in the few days since Emancipation, the black man's turning hither and thither in hesitant and doubtful striving has often made his very strength to lose effectiveness, to seem like absence of power, like weakness. And yet it is not weakness — it is the contradiction of double aims. The double-aimed struggle of the black artisan — on the one hand to escape white contempt for a nation of mere hewers of wood and drawers of water, and on the other hand to plow and nail and dig for a poverty-stricken horde — could only result in making him a poor craftsman, for he had but half a heart in either cause.

By the poverty and ignorance of his people, the Negro minister or doctor was tempted toward quackery and demagogy; and, by the criticism of the other world, toward ideals that made him ashamed of his lowly tasks. The would-be black savant was confronted by the paradox that the knowledge his people needed was a twice-told tale to his white neighbors, while the knowledge which would teach the white world was Greek to his own flesh and blood. The innate love of harmony and beauty that set the ruder souls of his people a-dancing and a-singing raised but confusion and doubt in the soul of the black artist; for the beauty revealed to him was the soul-beauty of a race which his larger audience despised, and he could not articulate the message of another people. This waste of double aims, this seeking to satisfy two unreconciled ideals has wrought sad havoc with the courage and faith and deeds of ten thousand thousand people — has sent them often wooing false gods and invoking false means of salvation, and at times has even seemed about to make them ashamed of themselves.

Away back in the days of bondage, they thought to see in one divine event the end of all doubt and disappointment; few men ever worshiped Freedom with half such unquestioning faith as did the American Negro for two centuries. To him, so far as he thought and dreamed, slavery was indeed the sum of all villainies, the cause of all sorrow, the root of all prejudice; Emancipation was the key to a promised land of sweeter beauty than ever stretched before the eyes of wearied Israelites. In song and exhortation swelled one refrain — Liberty; in his tears and curses the God he implored had Freedom in His right hand. At last it came, — suddenly, fearfully, like a dream. With one wild carnival of blood and passion came the message in his own plaintive cadences:

Shout, O children!
Shout, you're free!
For God has bought you liberty!

Years have passed away since then — ten, twenty, forty; forty years of national life, forty years of renewal and development, and yet the swarthy specter sits in its accustomed seat at the nation's feast. In vain do we cry to this our vastest social problem:

Take any shape but that, and
my firm nerves
Shall never tremble!

The nation has not yet found peace from its sins; the freedman has not yet found in freedom his promised land. Whatever of good may have come in these years of change, the shadow of a deep disappointment rests upon the Negro people, a disappointment all the more bitter because the unattained ideal was unbounded save by the simple ignorance of a lowly people.

The first decade was merely a prolongation of the vain search for freedom, the boon that seemed ever barely to elude their grasp, like a tantalizing will-o'-the-wisp, maddening and misleading the headless host. The holocaust of war, the terrors of the Ku Klux Klan, the lies of carpetbaggers, the disorganization of industry, and the contradictory advice of friends and foes left the bewildered serf with no new watchword beyond the old cry for freedom. As the time flew, however, he began to grasp a new idea. The ideal of liberty demanded for its attainment powerful means, and these the Fifteenth Amendment gave him. The ballot, which before he had looked upon as a visible sign of freedom, he now regarded as the chief means of gaining and perfecting the liberty with which war had partially endowed him. And why not? Had not votes made war and emancipated millions? Had not votes enfranchised the freedmen? Was anything impossible to a power that had done all this? A million black men started with renewed zeal to vote themselves into the kingdom.

So the decade flew away, the revolution of 1876 came, and left the half-free serf weary, wondering, but still inspired. Slowly but steadily, in the following years, a new vision began gradually to replace the dream of political power — a powerful movement, the rise of another ideal to guide the unguided, another pillar of fire by night after a clouded day. It was the ideal of "book learning"; the curiosity, born of compulsory ignorance, to know and test the power of the cabalistic letters of the white man, the longing to know. Here at last seemed to have been discovered the mountain path to Canaan; longer than the highway of Emancipation and law, steep and rugged, but

W. E. Burghardt Du Bois, early advocate of civil rights for Negroes and founder of the National Association for the Advancement of Colored People

straight, leading to heights high enough to overlook life.

Up the new path the advance guard toiled, slowly, heavily, doggedly; only those who have watched and guided the faltering feet, the misty minds, the dull understandings of the dark pupils of these schools know how faithfully, how piteously this people strove to learn. It was weary work. The cold statistician wrote down the inches of progress here and there, noted also where here and there a foot had slipped or someone had fallen. To the tired climbers, the horizon was ever dark, the mists were often cold, the Canaan was always dim and far away. If, however, the vistas disclosed as yet no goal, no resting place, little but flattery and criticism, the journey at least gave leisure for reflection and self-examination; it changed the child of Emancipation to the youth with dawning self-consciousness, self-realization, self-respect.

In those somber forests of his striving, his own soul rose before him and he saw himself — darkly as through a veil; and yet he saw in himself some faint revelation of his power, of his mission. He began to have a

dim feeling that, to attain his place in the world, he must be himself, and not another. For the first time he sought to analyze the burden he bore upon his back, that deadweight of social degradation partially masked behind a half-named Negro problem.

He felt his poverty; without a cent, without a home, without land, tools, or savings, he had entered into competition with rich, landed, skilled neighbors. To be a poor man is hard, but to be a poor race in a land of dollars is the very bottom of hardships. He felt the weight of his ignorance, not simply of letters but of life, of business, of the humanities; the accumulated sloth and shirking and awkwardness of decades and centuries shackled his hands and feet. Nor was his burden all poverty and ignorance. The red stain of bastardy, which two centuries of systematic legal defilement of Negro women had stamped upon his race, meant not only the loss of ancient African chastity but also the hereditary weight of a mass of corruption from white adulterers, threatening almost the obliteration of the Negro home.

A people thus handicapped ought not to be asked to race with the world, but rather allowed to give all its time and thought to its own social problems. But alas! while sociologists gleefully count his bastards and his prostitutes, the very soul of the toiling, sweating black man is darkened by the shadow of a vast despair. Men call the shadow prejudice and learnedly explain it as the natural defense of culture against barbarism, learning against ignorance, purity against crime, the "higher" against the "lower" races. To which the Negro cries Amen! and swears that to so much of this strange prejudice as is founded on just homage to civilization, culture, righteousness, and progress he humbly bows and meekly does obeisance.

But before that nameless prejudice that leaps beyond all this, he stands helpless, dismayed, and well-nigh speechless; before that personal disrespect and mockery, the ridicule and systematic humiliation, the distortion of fact and wanton license of fancy, the cynical ignoring of the better and the boisterous welcoming of the worse, the all-pervading desire to inculcate disdain for everything black, from Toussaint to the devil — before this there rises a sickening despair that would disarm and discourage any nation save that black host to whom "discouragement" is an unwritten word.

But the facing of so vast a prejudice could not but bring the inevitable self-questioning, self-disparagement, and lowering of ideals which ever accompany repression and breed in an atmosphere of contempt and hate. Whisperings and portents came borne upon the four winds: Lo! we are diseased and dying, cried the dark hosts; we cannot write, our voting is vain; what need of education since we must always cook and serve? And the nation echoed and enforced this self-criticism, saying: Be content to be servants, and nothing more; what need of higher culture for half-men? Away with the black man's ballot, by force or fraud — and behold the suicide of a race! Nevertheless, out of the evil came something of good — the more careful adjustment of education to real life, the clearer perception of the Negroes' social responsibilities, and the sobering realization of the meaning of progress.

So dawned the time of *Sturm und Drang*: storm and stress today rocks our little boat on the mad waters of the world sea; there is within and without the sound of conflict, the burning of body and rending of soul; inspiration strives with doubt, and faith with vain questionings. The bright ideals of the past — physical freedom, political power, the training of brains and the training of hands — all these in turn have waxed and waned, until even the last grows dim and overcast. Are they all wrong — all false? No, not that, but each alone was oversimple and incomplete — the dreams of a credulous race-childhood, or the fond imaginings of the other world which does not know and does not want to know our power. To be really true, all these ideals must be melted and welded into one.

The training of the schools we need today more than ever — the training of deft hands, quick eyes and ears, and, above all, the broader, deeper, higher culture of gifted minds and pure hearts. The power of the ballot we need in sheer self-defense, else what shall save us from a second slavery? Freedom, too, the long-sought, we still seek — the freedom of life and limb, the freedom to work and think, the freedom to love and aspire. Work, culture, liberty, all these we need, not singly but together, not successively but together, each growing and aiding each, and all striving toward that vaster ideal that swims before the Negro people, the ideal of human brotherhood, gained through the unifying ideal of race; the ideal of fostering and developing the traits and talents of the Negro, not in opposition to or contempt for other races but rather in large conformity to the greater ideals of the American republic, in order that some day on American soil two world-races may give each to each those characteristics both so sadly lack.

We, the darker ones, come even now not altogether empty-handed: there are today no truer exponents of the pure human spirit of the Declaration of Independence than the American Negroes; there is no true American music but the wild sweet melodies of the Negro slave; the American fairy tales and folklore are Indian and African; and, all in all, we black men seem the sole oasis of simple faith and reverence in a dusty desert of dollars and smartness. Will America be poorer if she replace her brutal, dyspeptic blundering with lighthearted but determined Negro humility? or her coarse and cruel wit with loving jovial good-humor? or her vulgar music with the soul of the Sorrow Songs?

Merely a concrete test of the underlying principles of the great republic is the Negro Problem, and the spiritual striving of the freedmen's sons is the travail of souls whose burden is almost beyond the measure of their strength, but who bear it in the name of an historic race, in the name of this the land of their fathers' fathers, and in the name of human opportunity.

II.

On Mr. Booker T. Washington

EASILY THE MOST STRIKING THING in the history of the American Negro since 1876 is the ascendancy of Mr. Booker T. Washington. It began at the time when war memories and ideals were rapidly passing; a day of astonishing commercial development was dawning; a sense of doubt and hesitation overtook the freedmen's sons — then it was that his leading began. Mr. Washington came, with a simple, definite program, at the psychological moment when the nation was a little ashamed of having bestowed so much sentiment on Negroes and was concentrating its energies on dollars.

His program of industrial education, conciliation of the South, and submission and silence as to civil and political rights was not wholly original; the free Negroes from 1830 up to wartime had striven to build industrial schools, and the American Missionary Association had from the first taught various trades; and Price and others had sought a way of honorable alliance with the best of the Southerners. But Mr. Washington first indissolubly linked these things; he put enthusiasm, unlimited energy, and perfect faith into this program, and changed it from a bypath into a veritable way of life. And the tale of the methods by which he did this is a fascinating study of human life.

It startled the nation to hear a Negro advocating such a program after many decades of bitter complaint; it startled and won the applause of the South, it interested and won the admiration of the North; and after a confused murmur of protest, it silenced if it did not convert the Negroes themselves.

To gain the sympathy and cooperation of the various elements comprising the white South was Mr. Washington's first task; and this, at the time Tuskegee was founded, seemed, for a black man, well-nigh impossible. And yet ten years later it was done in the word spoken at Atlanta: "In all things purely social we can be as separate as the five fingers, and yet one as the hand in all things essential to mutual progress." This "Atlanta Compromise" is by all odds the most notable thing in Mr. Washington's career.

The South interpreted it in different ways: the radicals received it as a complete surrender of the demand for civil and political equality; the conservatives, as a generously conceived working basis for mutual understanding. So both approved it, and today its author is certainly the most distinguished Southerner since Jefferson Davis, and the one with the largest personal following.

Next to this achievement comes Mr. Washington's work in gaining place and consideration in the North. Others less shrewd and tactful had formerly essayed to sit on these two stools and had fallen between them; but as Mr. Washington knew the heart of the South from birth and training, so by singular insight he intuitively grasped the spirit of the age which was dominating the North. And so thoroughly did he learn the speech and thought of triumphant commercialism and the ideals of material prosperity that the picture of a lone black boy poring over a French grammar amid the weeds and dirt of a neglected home soon seemed to him the acme of absurdities. One wonders what Socrates and St. Francis of Assisi would say to this.

And yet this very singleness of vision and thorough oneness with his age is a mark of the successful man. It is as though nature must needs make men narrow in order to give them force. So Mr. Washington's cult has gained unquestioning followers, his work has wonderfully prospered, his friends are legion, and his enemies are confounded. Today he stands as the one recognized spokesman of his 10 million fellows, and one of the most notable figures in a nation of 70 million.

One hesitates, therefore, to criticize a life which, beginning with so little, has done so much. And yet the time is come when one may speak in all sincerity and utter courtesy of the mistakes and shortcomings of Mr. Washington's career, as well as of his triumphs, without being thought captious or envious, and without forgetting that it is easier to do ill than well in the world.

The criticism that has hitherto met Mr. Washington has not always been of this broad character. In the South, especially, has he had to walk warily to avoid the harshest judgments, and naturally so, for he is dealing with the one subject of deepest sensitiveness to that section. Twice — once when at the Chicago celebration of the Spanish-American War he alluded to the color prejudice that is "eating away the vitals of the South," and once when he dined with President Roosevelt — has the resulting Southern criticism been violent enough to threaten seriously his popularity. In the North the feeling has several times forced itself into words, that Mr. Washington's counsels of submission overlooked certain elements of true manhood, and that his educational program was unnecessarily narrow.

Usually, however, such criticism has not found open expression, although, too, the spiritual sons of the Abolitionists have not been prepared to acknowledge that the schools founded before Tuskegee, by men of broad ideals and self-sacrificing spirit, were wholly failures or worthy of ridicule. While, then, criticism has not failed to follow Mr. Washington, yet the prevailing public opinion of the land has been but too willing to deliver the solution of a wearisome problem into his hands and say, "If that is all you and your race ask, take it."

Among his own people, however, Mr. Washington has encountered the strongest and most lasting opposition, amounting at times to bitterness, and even today continuing strong and insistent even though largely silenced in outward expression by the public opinion of the nation. Some of this opposition is, of course, mere envy; the disappointment of displaced demagogues and the spite of narrow minds. But aside from this, there is among educated and thoughtful colored men in all parts of the land a feeling of deep regret, sorrow, and apprehension at the wide currency and ascendancy which some of Mr. Washington's theories have gained. These same men admire his sincerity of purpose and are willing to forgive much to honest endeavor which is doing something worth the doing. They cooperate with Mr. Washington as far as they conscientiously can; and, indeed, it is no ordinary tribute to this man's tact and power that, steering as he must between so many diverse interests and opinions, he so largely retains the respect of all.

But the hushing of the criticism of honest opponents is a dangerous thing. It leads some of the best of the critics to unfortunate silence and paralysis of effort and others to burst into speech so passionately and intemperately as to lose listeners. Honest and earnest criticism from those whose interests are most nearly touched — criticism of writers by readers, of government by those governed, of leaders by those led — this is the soul of democracy and the safeguard of modern society. If the best of the American Negroes receive by outer pressure a leader whom they had not recognized before, manifestly there is here a certain palpable gain. Yet there is also irreparable loss — a loss of that peculiarly valuable education which a group receives when by search and criticism it finds and commissions its own leaders.

The way in which this is done is at once the most elementary and the nicest problem of social growth. History is but the record of such group leadership; and yet how infinitely changeful is its type and character! And of all types and kinds, what can be more instructive than the leadership of a group within a group? — that curious double movement where real progress may be negative and actual advance be relative retrogression. All this is the social student's inspiration and despair.

Now, in the past, the American Negro has had instructive experience in the choosing of group leaders, founding thus a peculiar dynasty which in the light of present conditions is worthwhile studying. When sticks and stones and beasts form the sole environment of a people, their attitude is largely one of determined opposition to and conquest of natural forces. But when to earth and brute is added an environment of men and ideas, then the attitude of the imprisoned group may take three main forms: a feeling of revolt and revenge; an attempt to adjust all thought and action to the will of the greater group; or, finally, a determined effort at self-realization and self-development despite environing opinion. The influence of all these attitudes at various times can be traced in the history of the American Negro and in the evolution of his successive leaders.

Before 1750, while the fire of African freedom still burned in the veins of the slaves, there was in all leadership or attempted leadership but the one motive of revolt and revenge, typified in the terrible Maroons, the Danish blacks, and Cato of Stono, and veiling all the Americas in fear of insurrection. . . . The slaves in the South . . . made three fierce attempts at insurrection — in 1800 under Gabriel in Virginia, in 1822 under Vesey in Carolina, and in 1831, again in Virginia, under the terrible Nat Turner. . . .

After the war and emancipation, the great form of Frederick Douglass, the greatest of American Negro leaders, still led the host. Self-assertion, especially in political lines, was the main program, and behind Douglass came Elliot, Bruce, and Langston, and the Reconstruction politicians, and, less conspicuous but of greater social significance, Alexander Crummell and Bishop Daniel Payne.

Then came the revolution of 1876, the suppression of the Negro votes, the changing and shifting of ideals, and the seeking of new lights in the great night. Douglass, in his old age, still bravely stood for the ideals of his early manhood — ultimate assimilation *through* self-assertion, and on no other terms. For a time, Price arose as a new leader, destined, it seemed, not to give up but to restate the old ideals in a form less repugnant to the white South. But he passed away in his prime.

Then came the new leader. Nearly all the former ones had become leaders by the silent suffrage of their fellows, had sought to lead their own people alone, and were usually, save Douglass, little known outside their race. But Booker T. Washington arose as essentially the leader, not of one race but of two, a compromiser between the South, the North, and the Negro.

Naturally, the Negroes resented, at first bitterly, signs of compromise which surrendered their civil and political rights, even though this was to be exchanged for larger chances of economic development. The rich and dominating North, however, was not only weary of the race problem but was investing largely in Southern enterprises and welcomed any method of peaceful cooperation. Thus, by national opinion, the Negroes began to recognize Mr. Washington's leadership, and the voice of criticism was hushed.

Mr. Washington represents in Negro thought the old attitude of adjustment and submission; but adjustment at such a peculiar time as to make his program unique. This is an age of unusual economic development, and Mr. Washington's program naturally takes an economic cast, becoming a gospel of Work and Money to such an extent as apparently almost completely to overshadow the higher aims of life. Moreover, this is an age when the more advanced races are coming in closer contact with the less developed races, and the race feeling is therefore intensified; and Mr. Washington's program practically accepts the alleged inferiority of the Negro races.

Again, in our own land, the reaction from the sentiment of wartime has given impetus to race prejudice against Negroes, and Mr. Washington withdraws many of the high demands of Negroes as men and American citizens. In other periods of intensified prejudice, all the Negro's tendency to self-assertion has been called forth; at this period, a policy of submission is advocated. In the history of nearly all other races and peoples the doctrine preached at such crises has been that manly self-respect is worth more than lands and houses, and that a people who voluntarily surrender such respect or cease striving for it are not worth civilizing.

In answer to this, it has been claimed that the Negro can survive only through submission. Mr. Washington distinctly asks that black people give up, at least for the present, three things:

First, political power; second, insistence on civil rights; third, higher education of Negro youth; and concentrate all their energies on industrial education, the accumulation of wealth, and the conciliation of the South.

This policy has been courageously and insistently advocated for over fifteen years, and has been triumphant for perhaps ten years. As a result of this tender of the palm branch, what has been the return? In these years there have occurred:

1. The disfranchisement of the Negro.

2. The legal creation of a distinct status of civil inferiority for the Negro.

3. The steady withdrawal of aid from institutions for the higher training of the Negro. These movements are not, to be sure, direct results of Mr. Washington's teachings; but his propaganda has, without a shadow of doubt, helped their speedier accomplishment.

The question then comes: Is it possible, and probable, that 9 million men can make effective progress in economic lines if they are deprived of political rights, made a servile caste, and allowed only the most meager chance for developing their exceptional men? If history and reason give any distinct answer to these questions, it is an emphatic *No*. And Mr. Washington thus faces the triple paradox of his career:

1. He is striving nobly to make Negro artisans businessmen and property owners; but it is utterly impossible, under modern competitive methods, for workingmen and property owners to defend their rights and exist without the right of suffrage.

2. He insists on thrift and self-respect, but at the same time counsels a silent submission to civic inferiority such as is bound to sap the manhood of any race in the long run.

3. He advocates common-school and industrial training, and depreciates institutions of higher learning; but neither the Negro common schools nor Tuskegee itself could remain open a day were it not for teachers trained in Negro colleges or trained by their graduates.

A man who is good enough to shed his blood for the country is good enough to be given a square deal afterward. More than that no man is entitled to, and less than that no man shall have.

THEODORE ROOSEVELT, Springfield, Illinois, July 4, 1903

113.

Delos O. Kinsman: State Income Taxes

The financial obligations of the state governments increased markedly in the period after the Civil War, owing in part to the expansion of the nation's industrial plant and in part to the growing need for educational and other welfare services for a growing population, and the states were hard pressed to find new sources of revenue. State income taxes were often tried but were widely resisted and usually unsuccessful. The economist Delos Kinsman studied the plans of all the states that had implemented such a tax with a view to comparing them and determining their salient features. His study, the summary chapter of which appears here, included some observations on the general efficacy of an income tax.

Source: *Publications of the American Economic Association: The Income Tax in the Commonwealths of the United States,* New York, November 1903, pp. 110-121.

We shall now give a brief résumé before presenting our conclusion. We cannot charge the commonwealths with slighting the income tax. Of the forty-five states, sixteen have made legislative provision for it, either in a general or special form; of about one hundred constitutions passed by the states, thirteen, representing eight states, have made special provision for its use; and of some forty state tax commissions which have been appointed by the different states, seven have treated it in their reports.

The use of the income tax proper began about 1840 and has continued to the present time. Its history has been marked by three periods of special activity: one from about 1840 to 1850, during which decade six states introduced the tax; another from 1860 to 1870, during which decade seven introduced it; and a third, from about 1895 to the present, which has been marked by a revival of the movement. Of the sixteen states that have employed it, six are still using it — Massachusetts, Virginia, North Carolina, South Carolina, Louisiana, and Tennessee.

Massachusetts has had the longest experience with the tax, extending from 1643 to the present time. South Carolina's experience began in 1701 and, with the exception of about thirty years, has extended to the present. Pennsylvania levied the tax from 1841 to 1871; Maryland, from 1842 to 1850; Virginia, from 1843 to the present; Alabama, from 1843 to about 1886; Florida, from 1845 to 1855; North Carolina, from 1849 to the present time. With but one exception the states introducing the tax between 1860 and 1870 employed it for only very short periods. Missouri employed the tax from 1861 to 1866; Texas, from 1863 to 1868; Georgia, from 1863 to 1866; West Virginia, during 1863; Louisiana, the one exception, from 1865 to the present time; Kentucky, from 1867 to 1872; Delaware, from 1869 to 1872. Tennessee tried the tax in 1883, but then, like Kentucky, only to a very limited extent.

Two causes have led to the introduction of the income tax: the demand for greater justice in the distribution of the burdens of taxation, and the need of increased revenue.

A third cause, a desire to regulate the business from which the income is derived, has operated in a few instances. The need of revenue was the dominant force leading to the introduction of the tax in the period between 1840 and 1850, and also in that between 1860 and 1870. In the first period this need was due to the enormous state debts resulting from extensive internal improvements; in the second period, to the heavy expenses incurred by the Civil War. It must be recognized, however, that the democratic influences which were felt in almost every department of political life about 1840 had not a little influence on the movement during the earlier period. During the present period the demand for justice appears to be the dominant force, although in South Carolina . . . the financial need is having weight.

The states employing the tax have spared neither time nor ingenuity in attempting so to frame the laws as to make the tax effective. Every possible method has been tried. The tax has been levied as a general income tax upon all forms of income and as a special income tax upon one or more forms of income; without regard to the source of the income and modified according to the source; as an apportioned tax, and as a percentage tax. The rate has been made proportional, progressive, and partly proportional and partly progressive. The exemption has been a fixed sum applied to all income and a sum varying with the form of income and with particular classes of individuals. The administration of the law has been under the direct supervision of the central government, and it has been left to the option of the local units. The tax has been employed strictly as a war measure, as a peace measure, and as both.

Of all the states using the tax, six have levied it as a general income tax, affecting all forms of income — rent, interest, wages, and profits. These states are Massachusetts, South Carolina, Virginia, Alabama, North Carolina, and Texas. The scope of the tax in Massachusetts, however, has varied with the different local interpretations placed upon the law. The remaining ten states have each taxed some one or more of the four forms of income. All of them, except Georgia, Tennessee, and Kentucky, have taxed incomes from personal services, salaries being especially mentioned; seven of them, all except Florida, Tennessee, and Kentucky, have taxed profits. Five, Delaware, West Virginia, Kentucky, Tennessee, and Missouri, have taxed interest. The rate of the tax has usually been proportional, although six of the states have made use of the progressive rate.

An exemption has been very generally allowed, varying both in the different states and at different times in the same state. When a fixed sum has been allowed, it has been usually from $300 to $2,500, $500 and $1,000 being the most common amounts. The exemption at present allowed in South Carolina is $2,500. Many of the states have provided for special exemptions, such as the expenses of the business from which the income is derived and the incomes of particular classes of individuals, such as ministers of the gospel, state judges, and certain classes of laborers.

The administration of the tax has been much the same in all the states. It has been assessed, as a rule, by the local assessors and collected by the local tax collectors. The laws have required that the tax should be levied by self-assessment, almost invariably under severe penalties for failure to comply.

The revenue derived from the income tax has been insignificantly small. For instance, Alabama, in 1882, during the period of her most successful experience, received an income tax of only $22,116 out of a state tax of over $600,000. In 1899, North Carolina's income tax amounted to only $4,399 out of a total tax of $723,307. Virginia, in 1899, received only $54,565 from this source, while her state tax amounted to

$2,132,368. South Carolina, in 1898, while levying a state tax of about $1 million, received only $5,190 from her tax upon incomes.

The attitude of the state courts toward the income tax has been one of sympathy. In the few cases upon the subject brought before them, they have upheld the tax. Had all forces been as active in support of the system as the state courts, the tax would undoubtedly have been a success.

Of the thirteen state constitutions providing for the taxation of incomes, Texas has adopted three; one in 1845, a second in 1869, and a third, still in force, in 1876. Louisiana has also adopted three constitutions making special provision for the tax; one in 1845, another in 1852, and a third in 1868. The constitutions of 1879 and of 1898 failed to make such a provision. Virginia has provided for the tax since 1851, the constitution of that year and also that of 1870, still in force, expressly allowing the tax. The next state to provide for the tax in her constitution was North Carolina in 1868. Tennessee, in her constitution of 1870, still in force, incorporated a similar provision. California did likewise in her constitution of 1879, now in operation. Kentucky followed in 1891, and South Carolina, the last of the states to make such provision, in 1895.

Of these thirteen constitutions, seven placed no limitations whatever upon the taxation of incomes — the three constitutions of Texas, the Louisiana constitutions of 1845 and of 1852, the California constitution of 1879, and the Kentucky constitution of 1891. The constitution of Virginia adopted in 1851 provided that in no case should property be taxed when a tax was levied upon the income from it. The constitution of 1870 went to the opposite extreme; although limiting the income tax to the amount in excess of $600, it expressly required the taxation of the capital invested in the business yielding the income. The

Louisiana constitution of 1868, in operation until 1879, required the tax to be levied "pro rata on the amount of income or business done"; the North Carolina constitution of 1868 prohibited the taxation of income from property otherwise taxed; and the Tennessee constitution of 1870 confined it to the taxation of income from stocks and bonds not taxed ad valorem. The present constitution of South Carolina, adopted in 1895, provides that the tax must be graduated.

The states have appointed in all some forty tax commissions, which have given the various tax systems the most careful study, sparing neither time nor pains in their attempt to obtain the most satisfactory system. Eight commissions have treated the income tax in their reports; but only two, the Massachusetts commissions of 1875 and of 1893, have recommended its employment. The principal reason given in each case was that without such a tax some justly subject to taxation would escape. Each report encountered serious opposition; in the commission of 1893 it took the form of a minority report. The chief reasons given by the opposition for their position were that an income tax results in double taxation and that it is impossible justly to administer it. Three minority reports, however, have favored the tax, one by Professor R. T. Ely, a member of the Maryland tax commission of 1886; another by Mr. Wright, a member of the Pennsylvania commission of 1889; and a third by Mr. McNeill, a member of the Massachusetts commission of 1897. The reasons advanced are largely theoretical.

On the other hand, besides the minority report of the Massachusetts commission of 1893, three commissions have expressed their disapproval of the tax; the Maine commission of 1890, the New York commission of 1892, and the Massachusetts commission of 1897. The reason given by the Maine and Massachusetts commissions was that the tax is incapable of practical application; that given by the New York commission was that it is inquisitorial and against the republican spirit. The Texas commission of 1899, to whom the subject of the income tax was referred by the legislature, failed to treat it in their report, probably because it met their disapproval. It is significant that the commissions of Massachusetts, where the tax has been longest tried, have finally recommended its repeal.

The experience of the states with the income tax warrants the conclusion that the tax, as employed by them, has been unquestionably a failure. It has satisfied neither the demands for justice nor the need of revenue. The question arises: Is this failure due to qualities inherent in the nature of the tax, or is it the result of conditions which may be removed? One of the fundamental principles of taxation is that the subjects of a state ought to contribute to the support of the government in proportion to their respective abilities, and it is generally agreed that these abilities are best measured by income. Therefore, theoretically at least, an income tax is unquestionably the fairest system yet proposed. Throughout the history of the tax in the several states the opposition has never seriously attacked it from a theoretical standpoint.

If the failure is to be attributed to the application of the principle, either the laws have failed to embody this principle properly or the administration has been ineffective. While much of the legislation in the states relative to the income tax has been very unsatisfactory, often not appealing to the taxpayers' sense of justice and furnishing excuses for the concealment of property, nevertheless, laws have been passed repeatedly which, if properly administered, would have distributed the burdens with unusual justice. But these laws have failed quite as completely as those with provisions less satisfactory. The failure of the tax, therefore, cannot have been due to the ill success of the laws in embodying the principle.

A careful study of the history of the tax leads one to the conclusion that the failure has been due to the administration of the laws. This conclusion is borne out by both the admissions of the advocates and the assertions of the opponents of the tax, and is corroborated by the reports of tax commissions. The causes operating to produce this failure in administration appear to have been four: the laws themselves have been defective in the provisions for their own administration; the officials have been lax in the enforcement of the laws; the taxpayers have been persistent in evading them; and the nature of some incomes has made them especially difficult to reach.

The income tax laws thus far, failing to recognize the weakness of the average taxpayer, have allowed him to return his own income. Some argue that to employ any other method would be undemocratic and that public sentiment would never submit to it. However, although the public has always opposed any inquisitorial system, the opposition has been often due rather to the fear that it may attain the end sought than that it is counter to the spirit of democracy. Often the taxpayer has something he wishes to conceal and calls on the "spirit of democracy" to help him out. We have yet to learn of a plausible argument in support of the assertion that the income tax is more inquisitorial than other forms of direct taxation.

The income tax has succeeded in nations quite as democratic as the United States. Other methods than self-assessment have been employed successfully, both by foreign nations and to a limited extent by some of our own states. The use of the method of self-assessment has been due, not to public demands but largely to the indifference of legislators. However, it is not to be condemned except that it furnishes the means by which the taxpayer, if he wishes to do so, may escape the tax.

The laxness of the officials in the enforcement of the laws doubtless also has had much to do with the failure of the income tax. Although the laws have usually required the assessors to demand from each taxpayer a full statement of his income and to enforce their demand by a severe penalty, they have not only failed to do this but, in listing the individual's property, have also entirely neglected his income or assessed it so low as to make the tax derived therefrom unimportant. Before we can hope for a successful taxation of incomes, officials must be faithful in the performance of their duty.

The taxpayer also has contributed much to the failure of the income tax. Not only has he taken advantage of every opportunity to escape it but he has also exercised his ingenuity to contrive means of evading it. The taxpayer with an elastic conscience and a good opportunity has usually succeeded in escaping the tax upon such property as could be concealed.

The nature of income is such as to make concealment comparatively easy. Much income is received in such form as to make it quite impossible for anyone except the recipient to know its amount, or at least to make more than a mere estimate, and even the recipient, in many instances, would find it quite impossible to be accurate.

Some of these evils undoubtedly could be corrected. Another method of assessment could be employed; the officials could be compelled to perform their duty; many of the difficulties met with in the determination of income could be removed; even the conscience of the taxpayer could be improved: but so long as the four remain as they are, it is useless to hope for a successful income tax. Indeed, so long as we permit taxpayers possessing dormant consciences to employ the method of self-assessment, failure is almost certain. We must abandon the one or develop the other. Some believe that a heavy fine, rigidly enforced, for failure to return income would make the tax effective; but while this would

doubtless result in great improvement, it would not insure success.

Not a little in the way of changing the attitude of the taxpayer toward the income tax may be done by a more careful framing of the laws so that they will better appeal to his sense of justice. Even more may be done by judicious state expenditures, demonstrating that the payment of taxes is not a waste of money. If this almost universal tendency to escape taxation when possible could be eradicated, the difficulties of enforcing an income tax would disappear. But as this tendency is too deep-seated to make its removal possible, we must turn to a consideration of the other alternative, a change in the mode of assessment.

The English income tax has been satisfactory only where assessment at the source has been employed; where it has been necessary to rely on self-assessment, as it has been in one or two classes, the tax has been a failure. The state of Pennsylvania also has employed the method of assessing income at its source with marked success. Of it one writer says,

> It is the fairest and most economical means of raising value which the state possesses. In 1886 it contributed 53.3 percent of the total revenue from all sources. By reason of it, it became possible in 1867 to release real estate from taxation for state purposes.

The extent to which this method of assessment could be applied to general incomes in this country is uncertain. The Massachusetts tax commission of 1897 considered it practically impossible.

With our present industrial organization, much income is derived from sources not accessible and consequently determinable only by the method of self-assessment. Indeed, it would often be very difficult for the taxpayer himself to determine the exact amount of his income; especially is this true of the agricultural classes and, indeed, of a large portion of the business and professional classes. In England, industry is carried on in such a way that three-fourths of the income can be taxed with no question or demand of the individual taxpayer; this would be impossible in our states. While the method of assessment at the source can be applied to a few forms of income, and insofar as it is possible to do so the income tax would be successful, still we must also say that with our present system of industry the method could not be applied by our states to a large part of the income received and that therefore a general state income tax must be a failure.

As the result of our study we conclude that the state income tax has been a failure, due to the failure of administration, which, in turn, may be attributed to four causes: the method of self-assessment, the indifference of state officials, the persistent effort of the taxpayers to evade the tax, and the nature of the income. The tax cannot be successful so long as taxpayers desirous of evading taxation are given the right of self-assessment. Since all attempts to change the method of self-assessment have failed and the nature of industry in the states is at present such as to make impossible the assessment of a general income tax at the source, we are forced to the conclusion that, even though no constitutional questions should arise, failure will continue to accompany the tax until our industrial system takes on such form as to make possible the use of some method other than self-assessment.

114.

S. S. McClure: The Challenge of the Muckrakers

In the opening decade of the twentieth century several muckraking magazines focused their attention on the inequities and failures of American society: the phenomenal growth of trusts after 1895; corrupt politics; the rise of labor as a potent social force; the evils of the city; failures in education; and numerous other problems. Many Americans in the era of Progressive reform felt that these issues constituted a potential threat to the continued existence of free government, unless public opinion was sufficiently aroused to initiate reforms. One editor, Samuel Sidney McClure, of McClure's magazine, analyzed the challenge to the public conscience offered by one single issue of his magazine, in which there appeared articles by Ida Tarbell, Ray Stannard Baker, and Lincoln Steffens.

Source: *McClure's*, January 1903.

Concerning Three Articles in this Number of McClure's, and a Coincidence that May Set Us Thinking

How many of those who have read through this number of the magazine noticed that it contains three articles on one subject? We did not plan it so; it is a coincidence that the January *McClure's* is such an arraignment of American character as should make every one of us stop and think. How many noticed that?

The leading article, "The Shame of Minneapolis," might have been called "The American Contempt of Law." That title could well have served for the current chapter of Miss Tarbell's History of Standard Oil. And it would have fitted perfectly Mr. Baker's "The Right to Work." All together, these articles come pretty near showing how universal is this dangerous trait of ours. Miss Tarbell has our capitalists conspiring among themselves, deliberately, shrewdly, upon legal advice, to break the law so far as it restrained them, and to misuse it to restrain others who were in their way. Mr. Baker shows labor, the ancient enemy of capital, and the chief complainant of the trusts' unlawful acts, itself committing and excusing crimes. And in "The Shame of Minneapolis" we see the administration of a city employing criminals to commit crimes for the profit of the elected officials, while the citizens — Americans of good stock and more than average culture, and honest, healthy Scandinavians — stood by complacent and not alarmed.

Capitalists, workingmen, politicians, citizens — all breaking the law, or letting it be broken. Who is left to uphold it? The lawyers? Some of the best lawyers in this country are hired, not to go into court to defend cases but to advise corporations and business firms how they can get around the law without too great a risk of punishment. The judges? Too many of them so respect the laws that for some "error" or quibble they restore to office and liberty men convicted on evidence overwhelmingly convincing to common sense. The churches? We know of one, an ancient and wealthy establishment, which had to be compelled by a Tammany holdover health officer to put its tenements in sanitary condition. The colleges? They do not understand.

There is no one left; none but all of us. Capital is learning (with indignation at labor's unlawful acts) that its rival's contempt of law is a menace to property. Labor has shrieked the belief that the illegal power of capital is a menace to the worker. These two are drawing together. Last November, when a strike was threatened by the yardmen on all the railroads centering in Chicago, the men got together and settled by raising wages, and raising freight rates too. They made the public pay. We all are doing our worst and making the public pay. The public is the people.

We forget that we all are the people; that while each of us in his group can shove off on the rest the bill of today, the debt is only postponed; the rest are passing it on back to us. We have to pay in the end, every one of us. And in the end the sum total of the debt will be our liberty.

———————◆———————

Men with the muck-rake are often indispensable to the well-being of society, but only if they know when to stop raking the muck.

THEODORE ROOSEVELT

When Dr. Johnson defined patriotism as the last refuge of a scoundrel, he was unconscious of the then undeveloped capabilities of the word reform.

ROSCOE CONKLING

In uplifting, get underneath.

GEORGE ADE, *Fables in Slang*

1904

115.

IDA M. TARBELL: The Growth of the Standard Oil Company

Ida Tarbell was one of the little group of crusading journalists — muckrakers, as President Roosevelt called them — who in articles and books exposed the social evils and injustice of the time. Miss Tarbell's most sensational series of articles, written for McClure's magazine beginning in 1903, was on John D. Rockefeller and the beginnings of the Standard Oil Company. Her bold denunciation of Rockefeller's techniques shocked many Americans — and pleased others. Rockefeller was the epitome of the self-made man and the national symbol of the free-enterprise system. Miss Tarbell's exposé of the origins of his company and the methods he used to acquire his fortune caused many reflective Americans to consider the virtues and vices of the free-enterprise system itself. In 1904 Miss Tarbell's articles were collected in a book, from which the following selection is taken.

Source: *The History of the Standard Oil Company*, New York, 1904, Vol. II, pp. 256-292.

FEW MEN in either the political or industrial life of this country can point to an achievement carried out in more exact accord with its first conception than John D. Rockefeller; for both in purpose and methods the Standard Oil Company is and always has been a form of the South Improvement Company, by which Mr. Rockefeller first attracted general attention in the oil industry. The original scheme has suffered many modifications. Its most offensive feature, the drawback on other people's shipments, has been cut off. Nevertheless, today, as at the start, the purpose of the Standard Oil Company is the purpose of the South Improvement Company — the regulation of the price of crude and refined oil by the control of the output; and the chief means for sustaining this purpose is still that of the original scheme — a control of oil transportation giving special privileges in rates. . . .

The profits of the present Standard Oil Company are enormous. For five years the dividends have been averaging about $45 million a year, or nearly 50 percent on its capitalization, a sum which capitalized at 5 percent would give $900 million. Of course this is not all that the combination makes in a year. It allows an annual average of 5.77 percent for deficit, and it carries always an ample reserve fund. When we remember that probably one-third of this immense annual revenue goes into the hands of John D. Rockefeller, that probably 90 percent of it goes to the few men who make up the "Standard Oil family," and that it must every year be invested, the Standard Oil Company becomes a much more serious public matter than it was in 1872, when it stamped itself as willing to enter into a conspiracy to raid the oil business — as a much more serious concern than in the years when it openly made warfare of business, and drove from the oil industry by any means it could invent all who had the hardihood to enter it.

For, consider what must be done with the greater part of this $45 million. It must be invested. The oil business does not demand it. There is plenty of reserve for all of its ventures. It must go into other industries. Naturally, the interests sought will be allied to oil. They will be gas, and we have the Standard Oil crowd steadily acquiring the gas interests of the country. They will be railroads, for on transportation all industries depend, and, besides, railroads are one of the great consumers of oil products and must be kept in line as buyers. And we have the directors of the Standard Oil Company acting as directors on nearly all of the great railways of the country, the New York Central; New York, New Haven and Hartford; Chicago, Milwaukee and St. Paul; Union Pacific; Northern Pacific; Delaware, Lackawanna and Western; Missouri Pacific; Missouri, Kansas and Texas; Boston and Maine; and other lesser roads. They will go into copper, and we have the Amalgamated scheme. They will go into steel, and we have Mr. Rockefeller's enormous holdings in the Steel Trust. They will go into banking, and we have the National City Bank and its allied institutions in New York City and Boston, as well as a long chain running over the country.

No one who has followed this history can expect these holdings will be acquired on a rising market. Buy cheap and sell high is a rule of business, and when you control enough money and enough banks you can always manage that a stock you want shall be temporarily cheap. No value is destroyed for you — only for the original owner. This has been one of Mr. Rockefeller's most successful maneuvers in doing business from the day he scared his twenty Cleveland competitors until they sold to him at half price.

You can also sell high, if you have a reputation of a great financier, and control of money and banks. Amalgamated Copper is an excellent example. The names of certain Standard Oil officials would float the most worthless property on earth a few years ago. It might be a little difficult for them to do so today, with Amalgamated so fresh in mind. Indeed, Amalgamated seems today to be the worst "break," as it certainly was one of the most outrageous performances of the Standard Oil crowd. But that will soon be forgotten! The result is that the Standard Oil Company is probably in the strongest financial position of any aggregation in the world. And every year its position grows stronger, for every year there is pouring in another $45 million to be used in wiping up the property most essential to preserving and broadening its power.

And now what does the law of New Jersey require the concern which it has chartered, and which is so rapidly adding to its control of oil the control of iron, steel, copper, banks, and railroads, to make known of itself? It must each year report its name, the location of its registration office, with name of agent, the character of its business, the amount of capital stock issued, and the names and addresses of its officers and directors! . . .

In spite of the Interstate Commerce Commission, the crucial question is still a transportation question. Until the people of the United States have solved the question of free and equal transportation, it is idle to suppose that they will not have a trust question. So long as it is possible for a company to own the exclusive carrier on which a great natural product depends for transportation, and to use this carrier to limit a competitor's supply or to cut off that supply entirely if the rival is offensive, and always to make him pay a higher rate than it costs the owner, it is ignorance and folly to talk about constitutional amendments limiting trusts. So long as the great manufacturing centers of a monopolistic trust can get better rates than the centers of independent effort, it is idle to talk about laws making it a crime to undersell for the purpose of driving a competitor from a market. You must get into markets before you can compete.

So long as railroads can be persuaded to interfere with independent pipelines, to refuse oil freight, to refuse loading facilities, lest they disturb their relations with the Standard Oil Company, it is idle to talk about investigations or antitrust legislation or application of the Sherman Law. So long as the Standard Oil Company can control transportation as it does today, it will remain master of the oil industry, and the people of the United States will pay for their indifference and folly in regard to transportation a good sound tax on oil, and they will yearly see an increasing concentration of natural resources and transportation systems in the Standard Oil crowd.

If all the country had suffered from these raids on competition, had been the limiting of the business opportunity of a few hundred men and a constant higher price for refined oil, the case would be serious enough, but there is a more serious side to it. The ethical cost of all this is the deep concern. We are a commercial people. We cannot boast of our arts, our crafts, our cultivation; our boast is in the wealth we produce. As a consequence, business success is sanctified, and, practically, any methods which achieve it are justified by a larger and larger class. All sorts of subterfuges and sophistries and slurring over of facts are em-

ployed to explain aggregations of capital whose determining factor has been like that of the Standard Oil Company, special privileges obtained by persistent secret effort in opposition to the spirit of the law, the efforts of legislators, and the most outspoken public opinion. How often does one hear it argued, the Standard Oil Company is simply an inevitable result of economic conditions; that is, given the practices of the oil-bearing railroads in 1872 and the elements of speculation and the over-refining in the oil business, there was nothing for Mr. Rockefeller to do but secure special privileges if he wished to save his business.

Now, in 1872 Mr. Rockefeller owned a successful refinery in Cleveland. He had the advantage of water transportation a part of the year, access to two great trunk lines the year around. Under such able management as he could give it, his concern was bound to go on, given the demand for refined oil. It was bound to draw other firms to it. When he went into the South Improvement Company, it was not to save his own business but to destroy others. When he worked so persistently to secure rebates after the breaking up of the South Improvement Company, it was in the face of an industry united against them.

It was not to save his business that he compelled the Empire Transportation Company to go out of the oil business in 1877. Nothing but grave mismanagement could have destroyed his business at that moment; it was to get every refinery in the country but his own out of the way. It was not the necessity to save his business which compelled Mr. Rockefeller to make war on the Tidewater. He and the Tidewater could both have lived. It was to prevent prices of transportation and of refined oil going down under competition. What necessity was there for Mr. Rockefeller trying to prevent the United States Pipe Line doing business? Only the greed of power and money. Every great campaign against rival interests which the Standard Oil Company

Ida M. Tarbell

has carried on has been inaugurated, not to save its life but to build up and sustain a monopoly in the oil industry. These are not mere affirmations of a hostile critic; they are facts proved by documents and figures.

Certain defenders go further and say that if some such combination had not been formed the oil industry would have failed for lack of brains and capital. Such a statement is puerile. Here was an industry for whose output the whole world was crying. Petroleum came at the moment when the value and necessity of a new, cheap light was recognized everywhere. Before Mr. Rockefeller had ventured outside of Cleveland, kerosene was going in quantities to every civilized country. Nothing could stop it, nothing check it but the discovery of some cheaper light or the putting up of its price. The real "good of the oil business" in 1872 lay in making oil cheaper. It would flow all over the world on its own merit, if cheap enough.

The claim that only by some such aggregation as Mr. Rockefeller formed could

enough capital have been obtained to develop the business falls utterly in face of fact. Look at the enormous amounts of capital, a large amount of it speculative, to be sure, which the oil men claim went into their business in the first ten years. It was estimated that Philadelphia alone put over $168 million into the development of the Oil Regions, and New York, $134 million, in their first decade of the business. How this estimate was reached the authority for it does not say. It may have been the total capitalization of the various oil companies launched in the two cities in that period. It shows very well, however, in what sort of figures the oil men were dealing.

When the South Improvement Company trouble came in 1872, the producers launched a statement in regard to the condition of their business in which they claimed that they were using a capital of $200 million. Figures based on the number of oil wells in operation or drilling at that time of course represent only a portion of the capital in use. Wildcatting and speculation have always demanded a large amount of the money that the oil men handled. The almost conservative figures in regard to the capital invested in the Oil Regions in the early years were those of H. E. Wrigley, of the Geological Survey of Pennsylvania. Mr. Wrigley estimates that in the first twelve years of the business $235 million was received from wells. This includes the cost of the land, of putting down and operating the well, also the profit on the product. This estimate, however, makes no allowance for the sums used in speculation; an estimate, indeed, which it was impossible for one to make with any accuracy.

The figures, unsatisfactory as they are, are ample proof, however, that there was plenty of money in the early days to carry on the oil business. Indeed, there has always been plenty of money for oil investment. It did not require Mr. Rockefeller's capital to develop the Bradford oilfields, build the first seaboard pipeline, open West Virginia, Texas, or Kansas. The oil business would no more have suffered for lack of capital without the Standard combination than the iron or wheat or railroad or cotton business. The claim is idle, given the wealth and energy of the country in the forty-five years since the discovery of oil.

Equally well does both the history and the present condition of the oil business show that it has not needed any such aggregation to give us cheap oil. The margin between crude and refined was made low by competition. It has rarely been as low as it would have been had there been free competition. For five years even the small independent refineries, outside of the Pure Oil Company, have been able to make a profit on the prices set by the Standard, and this in spite of the higher transportation they have paid on both crude and refined, and the wall of seclusion the railroads build around domestic markets.

Very often people who admit the facts, who are willing to see that Mr. Rockefeller has employed force and fraud to secure his ends, justify him by declaring, "It's business." That is, "it's business" has come to be a legitimate excuse for hard dealing, sly tricks, special privileges. It is a common enough thing to hear men arguing that the ordinary laws of morality do not apply in business. Now, if the Standard Oil Company were the only concern in the country guilty of the practices which have given it monopolistic power, this story never would have been written. Were it alone in these methods, public scorn would long ago have made short work of the Standard Oil Company. But it is simply the most conspicuous type of what can be done by these practices. The methods it employs with such acumen, persistency, and secrecy are employed by all sorts of businessmen, from corner grocers up to bankers. If exposed, they are excused on the ground that this is business. If the point is pushed, frequently

the defender of the practice falls back on the Christian doctrine of charity, and points that we are erring mortals and must allow for each other's weaknesses! — an excuse which, if carried to its legitimate conclusion, would leave our businessmen weeping on one another's shoulders over human frailty, while they picked one another's pockets.

One of the most depressing features of the ethical side of the matter is that instead of such methods arousing contempt they are more or less openly admired. And this is logical. Canonize "business success," and men who make a success like that of the Standard Oil Trust become national heroes! The history of its organization is studied as a practical lesson in money-making. It is the most startling feature of the case to one who would like to feel that it is possible to be a commercial people and yet a race of gentlemen. Of course such practices exclude men by all the codes from the rank of gentlemen, just as such practices would exclude men from the sporting world or athletic field. There is no gaming table in the world where loaded dice are tolerated, no athletic field where men must not start fair. Yet Mr. Rockefeller has systematically played with loaded dice, and it is doubtful if there has ever been a time since 1872 when he has run a race with a competitor and started fair. Business played in this way loses all its sportsmanlike qualities. It is fit only for tricksters.

The effects on the very men who fight these methods on the ground that they are ethically wrong are deplorable. Brought into competition with the trust, badgered, foiled, spied upon, they come to feel as if anything is fair when the Standard is the opponent. The bitterness against the Standard Oil Company in many parts of Pennsylvania and Ohio is such that a verdict from a jury on the merits of the evidence is almost impossible! A case in point occurred a few years ago in the Bradford field. An oil producer was discovered stealing oil from the National Transit Company. He had tapped the main line and for at least two years had run a small but steady stream of Standard oil into his private tank. Finally, the thieving pipe was discovered, and the owner of it, after acknowledging his guilt, was brought to trial.

The jury gave a verdict of "Not guilty!" They seemed to feel that though the guilt was acknowledged, there probably was a Standard trick concealed somewhere. Anyway, it was the Standard Oil Company and it deserved to be stolen from! The writer has frequently heard men, whose own business was conducted with scrupulous fairness, say in cases of similar stealing that they would never condemn a man who stole from the Standard! Of course such a state of feeling undermines the whole moral nature of a community.

The blackmailing cases of which the Standard Oil Company complains are a natural result of its own practices. Men going into an independent refining business have for years been accustomed to say: "Well, if they won't let us alone, we'll make them pay a good price." The Standard complains that such men build simply to sell out. There may be cases of this. Probably there are, though the writer has no absolute proof of any such. Certainly there is no satisfactory proof that the refinery in the famous Buffalo case was built to sell, though that it was offered for sale when the opposition of the Everests, the managers of the Standard concern, had become so serious as later to be stamped as criminal by judge and jury, there is no doubt. Certainly nothing was shown to have been done or said by Mr. Matthews, the owner of the concern which the Standard was fighting, which might not have been expected from a man who had met the kind of opposition he had from the time he went into business.

The truth is, blackmail and every other business vice is the natural result of the pe-

culiar business practices of the Standard. If business is to be treated as warfare and not as a peaceful pursuit, as they have persisted in treating it, they cannot expect the men they are fighting to lie down and die without a struggle. If they get special privileges they must expect their competitors to struggle to get them. If they will find it more profitable to buy out a refinery than to let it live, they must expect the owner to get an extortionate price if he can. And when they complain of these practices and call them blackmail, they show thin sporting blood. They must not expect to monopolize hard dealings, if they do oil.

These are considerations of the ethical effect of such business practices on those outside and in competition. As for those within the organization, there is one obvious effect worth noting. The Standard men as a body have nothing to do with public affairs, except as it is necessary to manipulate them for the "good of the oil business." The notion that the businessman must not appear in politics and religion save as a "standpatter" — not even as a thinking, aggressive force — is demoralizing, intellectually and morally.

Ever since 1872 the organization has appeared in politics only to oppose legislation obviously for the public good. At that time the oil industry was young, only twelve years old, and it was suffering from toorapid growth, from speculation, from rapacity of railroads, but it was struggling manfully with all these questions. The question of railroad discriminations and extortions was one of the "live questions" of the country. The oil men as a mass were allied against it. The theory that the railroad was a public servant bound by the spirit of its charter to treat all shippers alike, that fair play demanded open equal rates to all, was generally held in the oil country at the time Mr. Rockefeller and his friends sprung the South Improvement Company. One has only to read the oil journals at the time of the oil war of 1872 to see how seriously all phases of the transportation question were considered. The country was a unit against the rebate system. Agreements were signed with the railroads that all rates henceforth should be equal. The signatures were not on before Mr. Rockefeller had a rebate, and gradually others got them, until the Standard had won the advantages it expected the South Improvement Company to give it.

From that time to this Mr. Rockefeller has had to fight the best sentiment of the oil country and of the country at large as to what is for the public good. He and his colleagues kept a strong alliance in Washington fighting the Interstate Commerce Bill from the time the first one was introduced in 1876 until the final passage in 1887. Every measure looking to the freedom and equalization of transportation has met his opposition, as have bills for giving greater publicity to the operations of corporations. In many of the great state legislatures one of the first persons to be pointed out to a visitor is the Standard Oil lobbyist. Now, no one can dispute the right of the Standard Oil Company to express its opinions on proposed legislation. It has the same right to do this as all the rest of the world. It is only the character of its opposition which is open to criticism, the fact that it is always fighting measures which equalize privileges and which make it more necessary for men to start fair and play fair in doing business.

Of course the effect of directly practising many of their methods is obvious. For example, take the whole system of keeping track of independent business. There are practices required which corrupt every man who has a hand in them. One of the most deplorable things about it is that most of the work is done by youngsters. The freight clerk who reports the independent oil shipments for a fee of $5 or $10 a month is probably a young man learning his first lessons in corporate morality. If he happens to sit in Mr. Rockefeller's church on Sundays, through what sort of a haze will he receive the teachings? There is something alarming to those who believe that commerce should be a peaceful pursuit, and who believe that the moral law holds good throughout the entire range of human relations, in knowing that so large a body of young men in this country are consciously or unconsciously growing up with the idea that business is war and that morals have nothing to do with its practice.

And what are we going to do about it, for it is *our* business? We, the people of the United States, and nobody else, must cure whatever is wrong in the industrial situation, typified by this narrative of the growth of the Standard Oil Company. That our first task is to secure free and equal transportation privileges by rail, pipe, and waterway is evident. It is not an easy matter. It is one which may require operations which will seem severe; but the whole system of discrimination has been nothing but violence, and those who have profited by it cannot complain if the curing of the evils they have wrought bring hardship in turn on them. At all events, until the transportation matter is settled, and settled right, the monopolistic trust will be with us — a leech on our pockets, a barrier to our free efforts.

As for the ethical side, there is no cure but in an increasing scorn of unfair play, an increasing sense that a thing won by breaking the rules of the game is not worth the winning. When the businessman who fights to secure special privileges, to crowd his competitor off the track by other than fair competitive methods, receives the same summary disdainful ostracism by his fellows that the doctor or lawyer who is "unprofessional," the athlete who abuses the rules, receives, we shall have gone a long way toward making commerce a fit pursuit for our young men.

116.

LINCOLN STEFFENS: The Shame of Our Cities

Throughout 1902 and 1903 Lincoln Steffens traveled to many U.S. cities to collect material for his famous articles on city government for McClure's *magazine. The experience turned out to be an eye-opening one for Steffens, who was amazed at the extent of corruption he discovered. The articles received a good deal of publicity and even worried some, but not many, local politicians. Much to Steffens' surprise the readers' interest in his articles did not move them to sincere and continuing efforts to reform their city governments. In 1904 Steffens collected the articles in a book,* The Shame of the Cities. *The following excerpt is taken from his Introduction, which was both a summary of his findings and a challenge to the reader.*

Source: *The Shame of the Cities*, New York, 1904: "Introduction; and Some Conclusions."

THE MISGOVERNMENT of the American people is misgovernment by the American people.

When I set out on my travels, an honest New Yorker told me honestly that I would find that the Irish, the Catholic Irish, were at the bottom of it all everywhere. The first city I went to was St. Louis, a German city. The next was Minneapolis, a Scandinavian city, with a leadership of New Englanders. Then came Pittsburgh, Scotch Presbyterian, and that was what my New York friend was. "Ah, but they are all foreign populations," I heard. The next city was Philadelphia, the purest American community of all, and the most hopeless. And after that came Chicago and New York, both mongrel-bred, but the one a triumph of reform, the other the best example of good government that I had seen. The "foreign element" excuse is one of the hypocritical lies that save us from the clear sight of ourselves.

Another such conceit of our egotism is that which deplores our politics and lauds our business. This is the wail of the typical American citizen. Now, the typical American citizen is the businessman. The typical businessman is a bad citizen; he is busy. If he is a "big businessman" and very busy, he does not neglect, he is busy with politics, oh, very busy and very businesslike. I found him buying boodlers in St. Louis, defending grafters in Minneapolis, originating corruption in Pittsburgh, sharing with bosses in Philadelphia, deploring reform in Chicago, and beating good government with corruption funds in New York.

He is a self-righteous fraud, this big businessman. He is the chief source of corruption, and it were a boon if he would neglect politics. But he is not the businessman that neglects politics; that worthy is the good citizen, the typical businessman. He too is busy, he is the one that has no use and therefore no time for politics. When his neglect has permitted bad government to go so far that he can be stirred to action, he is unhappy, and he looks around for a cure that shall be quick so that he may hurry back to the shop. Naturally, too, when he talks politics, he talks shop. His patent remedy is quack; it is business.

"Give us a businessman," he says ("like me," he means). "Let him introduce business methods into politics and government; then I shall be left alone to attend to my business."

There is hardly an office from United States senator down to alderman in any part of the country to which the businessman has not been elected; yet politics remains corrupt, government pretty bad, and the selfish citizen has to hold himself in readiness, like the old volunteer firemen, to rush forth at any hour, in any weather, to prevent the fire; and he goes out sometimes and he puts out the fire (after the damage is done) and he goes back to the shop sighing for the businessman in politics.

The businessman has failed in politics as he has in citizenship. Why? Because politics is business. That's what's the matter with it. That's what's the matter with everything — art, literature, religion, journalism, law, medicine — they're all business, and all — as you see them. Make politics a sport, as they do in England, or a profession, as they do in Germany, and we'll have — well, something else than we have now — if we want it, which is another question. But don't try to reform politics with the banker, the lawyer, and the dry-goods merchant, for these are businessmen and there are two great hindrances to their achievement of reform: one is that they are different from, but no better than, the politicians; the other is that politics is not "their line."

There are exceptions both ways. Many politicians have gone out into business and done well (Tammany ex-mayors and nearly all the old bosses of Philadelphia are prominent financiers in their cities), and businessmen have gone into politics and done well (Mark Hanna, for example). They haven't reformed their adopted trades, however, though they have sometimes sharpened

them most pointedly. The politician is a businessman with a specialty. When a businessman of some other line learns the business of politics, he is a politician and there is not much reform left in him. Consider the United States Senate, and believe me.

The commercial spirit is the spirit of profit, not patriotism; of credit, not honor; of individual gain, not national prosperity; of trade and dickering, not principle. "My business is sacred," says the businessman in his heart. "Whatever prospers my business, is good; it must be. Whatever hinders it, is wrong; it must be. A bribe is bad, that is, it is a bad thing to take; but it is not so bad to give one, not if it is necessary to my business." "Business is business" is not a political sentiment, but our politician has caught it. He takes essentially the same view of the bribe, only he saves his self-respect by piling all his contempt upon the bribe giver, and he has the great advantage of candor. "It is wrong, maybe," he says, "but if a rich merchant can afford to do business with me for the sake of a convenience or to increase his already great wealth, I can afford, for the sake of a living, to meet him halfway. I make no pretensions to virtue, not even on Sunday." And as for giving bad government or good, how about the merchant who gives bad goods or good goods, according to the demand?

But there is hope, not alone despair, in the commercialism of our politics. If our political leaders are to be always a lot of political merchants, they will supply any demand we may create. All we have to do is to establish a steady demand for good government. The bosses have us split up into parties. To him parties are nothing but means to his corrupt ends. He "bolts" his party, but we must not; the bribe giver changes his party from one election to another, from one county to another, from one city to another, but the honest voter must not. Why? Because if the honest voter cared no more for his party than the politician and the grafter, then the honest vote would govern, and that would be bad — for graft.

It is idiotic, this devotion to a machine that is used to take our sovereignty from us. If we would leave parties to the politicians, and would vote not for the party, not even for men, but for the city, and the state, and the nation, we should rule parties, and cities, and states, and nation. If we would vote in mass on the more promising ticket, or, if the two are equally bad, would throw out the party that is in and wait till the next election and then throw out the other party that is in, then, I say, the commercial politician would feel a demand for good government and he would supply it. That process would take a generation or more to complete, for the politicians now really do not know what good government is. But it has taken as long to develop bad government, and the politicians know what that is. If it would not "go," they would offer something else, and, if the demand were steady, they, being so commercial, would "deliver the goods."

But do the people want good government? Tammany says they don't. Are the people honest? Are the people better than Tammany? Are they better than the merchant and the politician? Isn't our corrupt government, after all, representative?

President Roosevelt has been sneered at for going about the country preaching, as a cure for our American evils, good conduct in the individual, simple honesty, courage, and efficiency. "Platitudes!" the sophisticated say. Platitudes? If my observations have been true, the literal adoption of Mr. Roosevelt's reform scheme would result in a revolution, more radical and terrible to existing institutions, from the Congress to the church, from the bank to the ward organization, than socialism or even than anarchy. Why, that would change all of us — not alone our neighbors, not alone the grafters, but you and me.

No, the contemned methods of our despised politics are the master methods of our braggart business, and the corruption that shocks us in public affairs we practise ourselves in our private concerns. There is no essential difference between the pull that gets your wife into society or for your book a favorable review and that which gets a heeler into office, a thief out of jail, and a rich man's son on the board of directors of a corporation; none between the corruption of a labor union, a bank, and a political machine; none between a dummy director of a trust and the caucus-bound member of a legislature; none between a labor boss like Sam Parks, a boss of banks like John D. Rockefeller, a boss of railroads like J. P. Morgan, and a political boss like Matthew S. Quay. The boss is not a political, he is an American institution, the product of a freed people that have not the spirit to be free.

And it's all a moral weakness; a weakness right where we think we are strongest. Oh, we are good — on Sunday — and we are "fearfully patriotic" on the Fourth of July. But the bribe we pay to the janitor to prefer our interests to the landlord's is the little brother of the bribe passed to the alderman to sell a city street, and the father of the air-brake stock assigned to the president of a railroad to have this lifesaving invention adopted on his road. And as for graft, railroad passes, saloon and bawdy-house blackmail, and watered stock, all these belong to the same family.

We are pathetically proud of our democratic institutions and our republican form of government, of our grand Constitution and our just laws. We are a free and sovereign people, we govern ourselves and the government is ours. But that is the point. We are responsible, not our leaders, since we follow them. We *let* them divert our loyalty from the United States to some "party"; we *let* them boss the party and turn our municipal democracies into autocracies and our republican nation into a plutocracy. We cheat our government and we let our leaders loot it, and we let them wheedle and bribe our sovereignty from us.

True, they pass for us strict laws, but we are content to let them pass also bad laws, giving away public property in exchange; and our good, and often impossible, laws we allow to be used for oppression and blackmail. And what can we say? We break our own laws and rob our own government, the lady at the customhouse, the lyncher with his rope, and the captain of industry with his bribe and his rebate. The spirit of graft and of lawlessness is the American spirit. . . .

The Fourth of July oration is the "front" of graft. There is no patriotism in it, but treason. It is part of the game. The grafters call for cheers for the flag, "prosperity," and "the party," just as a highwayman commands "hands up," and while we are waving and shouting, they float the flag from the nation to the party, turn both into graft factories, and prosperity into a speculative boom to make "weak hands," as the Wall Street phrase has it, hold the watered stock while the strong hands keep the property. "Blame us, blame anybody, but praise the people," this, the politician's advice, is not the counsel of respect for the people but of contempt. By just such palavering as courtiers play upon the degenerate intellects of weak kings, the bosses, political, financial, and industrial, are befuddling and befooling our sovereign American citizenship; and, likewise, they are corrupting it. . . .

The people are not innocent. That is the only "news" in all the journalism of these articles, and no doubt that was not new to many observers. It was to me. When I set out to describe the corrupt systems of certain typical cities, I meant to show simply how the people were deceived and betrayed. But in the very first study, St. Louis, the startling truth lay bare that corruption was not merely political; it was financial, commercial, social; the ramifications of boodle were so complex, various, and far-reaching that one mind could hardly grasp them, and not even Joseph W. Folk, the tireless prosecutor, could follow them all.

This state of things was indicated in the first article which Claude H. Wetmore and I compiled together, but it was not shown plainly enough. Mr. Wetmore lived in St. Louis, and he had respect for names which meant little to me. But when I went next to Minneapolis alone, I could see more independently, without respect for persons, and there were traces of the same phenomenon. The first St. Louis article was called "Tweed Days in St. Louis," and though the "better citizen" received attention the Tweeds were the center of interest. In "The Shame of Minneapolis," the truth was put into the title; it was the Shame of Minneapolis; not of the Ames administration, not of the Tweeds, but of the city and its citizens. And yet Minneapolis was not nearly so bad as St. Louis; police graft is never so universal as boodle. It is more shocking, but it is so filthy that it cannot involve so large a part of society.

So I returned to St. Louis, and I went over the whole ground again, with the people in mind, not alone the caught and convicted boodlers. And this time the true meaning of "Tweed Days in St. Louis" was made plain. The article was called "The Shamelessness of St. Louis," and that was the burden of the story. In Pittsburgh also the people was the subject, and though the civic spirit there was better, the extent of the corruption throughout the social organization of the community was indicated. But it was not till I got to Philadelphia that the possibilities of popular corruption were worked out to the limit of humiliating confession. That was the place for such a study. There is nothing like it in the country, except possibly, in Cincinnati. Philadelphia certainly is not merely corrupt but corrupted, and this was made clear. Philadelphia was charged up to — the American citizen.

It was impossible in the space of a magazine article to cover in any one city all the phases of municipal government, so I chose cities that typified most strikingly some particular phase or phases. Thus, as St. Louis exemplified boodle; Minneapolis, police graft; Pittsburgh, a political and industrial machine; and Philadelphia, general civic corruption; so Chicago was an illustration of reform, and New York of good government. All these things occur in most of these places. There are, and long have been, reformers in St. Louis, and there is today police graft there. Minneapolis has had boodling and council reform, and boodling is breaking out there again. Pittsburgh has general corruption, and Philadelphia a very perfect political machine. Chicago has police graft and a low order of administrative and general corruption, which permeates business, labor, and society generally. As for New York, the metropolis might exemplify almost anything that occurs anywhere in American cities, but no city has had for many years such a good administration as was that of Mayor Seth Low.

That which I have made each city stand for is that which it had most highly developed. It would be absurd to seek for organized reform in St. Louis, for example, with Chicago next door; or for graft in Chicago with Minneapolis so near. After Minneapolis, a description of administrative corruption in Chicago would have seemed like a repetition. Perhaps it was not just to treat only the conspicuous element in each situation. But why should I be just? I was not judging; I arrogated to myself no such function. I was not writing about Chicago for Chicago, but for the other cities, so I picked out what light each had for the instruction of the others.

But, if I was never complete, I never exaggerated. Every one of those articles was an understatement, especially where the conditions were bad, and the proof thereof is that while each article seemed to astonish other cities, it disappointed the city which was its subject. Thus, my friends in Philadelphia, who knew what there was to know, and those especially who knew what I knew, expressed surprise that I reported so little. And one St. Louis newspaper said that "the facts were thrown at me and I fell down over them." There was truth in these flings. I cut 20,000 words out of the Philadelphia article and then had not written half my facts. I know a man who is making a history of the corrupt construction of the Philadelphia City Hall, in three volumes, and he grieves because he lacks space. You can't put all the known incidents of the corruption of an American city into a book.

Our so-called civilization has shown its movement, even at the center, arrested. It has failed to concentrate further. Its next effort may succeed, but it is more likely to be one of disintegration, with Russia for the eccentric on one side and America on the other.

HENRY ADAMS, letter to Brooks Adams

Scene along the Boardwalk in Atlantic City, N.J., 1902

"THE GOOD OLD DAYS"

America's Golden Age — that period that is held up in the national folklore as our closest approach to perfection — is a vague period beginning sometime in the 1880s and lasting perhaps until World War I. The era is most conveniently represented, however, by a single decade, the "Gay Nineties." These, more than any others, are the years of small towns lined with stately elms, of band concerts at the park pavilion, of ice cream parlors and circuses. The cities were full of fashionable gentlemen and Gibson Girls. Lillian Russell and Sarah Bernhardt entertained the nation when the nation wasn't busily entertaining itself. Theodore Roosevelt was himself something of a symbol; his doctrine of the "strenuous" life fit in perfectly with the generation that made bicycling and football national pastimes and Sandow the Strong Man a national hero. Of necessity, generalizations like "the Good Old Days" ignore much that was unfortunately true of the period. The appalling conditions of slums and poor rural areas, widespread though they were, were rather quickly and easily overlooked by a nation bent on exploiting its new wealth and strength; they were much more so as the period receded into a historical golden glow. The same generation that would in decades to come be envied for its easy, pleasant life and carefree society was capable of pursuing gleefully the "splendid little war" of 1898. The belief that pain and death were un-American dominated the home front in this war; in this there may be the last full expression of American innocence.

Farmers with a hay wagon on a Pennsylvania country road in 1900

Crowd watching the harness racing at the fair in Middlebury, Vermont

(Top) Looking east down Main Street in Nantucket village, 1897; family gathered on Sunday afternoon on a farm near Philadelphia; (below) Town Square, Monmouth, Ill., 1900

(Above) Crowds assembling in Rocky Ford, Colo., for the annual Melon Day celebration, 1904; (center) watermelons before and after the picnic; (bottom) "Melon Pile Rush"

Views of Southbridge, Mass.: (Above) St. Mary's and Notre Dame Churches, as seen from the cliff

(Above) American Optical Company's works; (below) Hartwell's Block to (left) Universalist Church

Interior of a canal boat out from Philadelphia on an excursion

(Below) Two vacationers in Maine photographed in wooded settings by Joseph J. Kirkbride, 1885-1886

(Above) Capt. Scott and his family, a Maine family photographed by Kirkbride; (right) boy with a cart, platinum print by Clarence H. White of his oldest son, 1898; (below) Lena Gibson, photographed by Kirkbride in Maine while on vacation; (bottom) NCO's from Company "B," 11th infantry, stationed on Bedloe's Island, N.Y.

Home of E. C. Stotesbury, a Philadelphia financier, photographed in 1885

(Above) Asbury Park Beach, N.J., 1903; (below) hunting lodge of the 1880s

(Above) Dartmouth football team, 1901; (below left) John L. Sullivan and Ryan at the "Arena" in Philadelphia, 1897; (below right) Cornell playing football against Rochester

Jeffries-Sharkey contest in 1899; enlargement from newsreel film

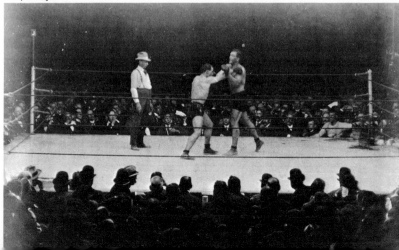

The circus comes to town: (Top) Barnum's parade down Pennsylvania Avenue, Washington, about 1890; (center) circus tents erected in Monument Square by the Court House in Racine, Wis.; (left) bareback rider performing, 1905

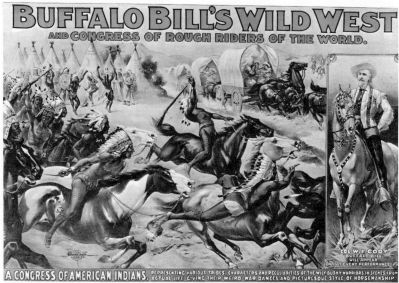

(Above) Poster advertising Buffalo Bill's Wild West Show, 1899; (right) Buffalo Bill in costume; (below) gun fight between cowboys and Indians in the London performance of 1905

The traveling circus reached the peak of its popularity around the turn of the century — at that time there were over 100 of them working around the country. While circuses were about the same everywhere, William Cody assembled a show that was distinctively American and successfully toured the United States, Europe, and Great Britain. A combination of circus and rodeo, Buffalo Bill's "Wild West" exhibition starred himself, famed scout and buffalo hunter; Annie Oakley, lady marksman; and, briefly, Sitting Bull.

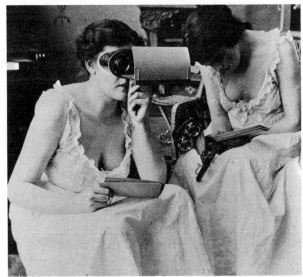

(Top) The Temple of Music at the Pan American Exposition in Buffalo in 1901; (center left) Sandow the Strong Man; photo by Napoleon Sarony, 1893; (center right) "An interesting picture" a suggestive bit of restrained Victorian sex; (left) one of the more grotesque exhibits at the Buffalo Exposition. Similar exhibits were an attraction at every fair until World War II

117.

George Washington Plunkitt: Practical Politics

George Washington Plunkitt used shrewd judgment, common sense, and intuition to build a successful political career. A veteran politician with forty-five years of experience in the affairs of New York State, he was one of the stalwarts of Tammany Hall. During his lifetime he amassed a large personal fortune, but he also managed to benefit his constituents, thereby developing a loyal following. Plunkitt was one of the most forthright of officeholders when it came to expressing his views to the public on the workings of machine politics. During several years prior to 1905 he gave a series of candid interviews to reporter William L. Riordon summing up his philosophy of practical politics. Four of these interviews are reprinted here, the last of which is Plunkitt's reaction to Lincoln Steffens' The Shame of the Cities, published in 1904.

Source: *Plunkitt of Tammany Hall*, William L. Riordon, ed., New York, 1905.

HONEST GRAFT AND DISHONEST GRAFT

EVERYBODY IS TALKIN' these days about Tammany men growin' rich on graft, but nobody thinks of drawin' the distinction between honest graft and dishonest graft. There's all the difference in the world between the two. Yes, many of our men have grown rich in politics. I have myself. I've made a big fortune out of the game, and I'm gettin' richer every day, but I've not gone in for dishonest graft — blackmailin' gamblers, saloonkeepers, disorderly people, etc. — and neither has any of the men who have made big fortunes in politics.

There's an honest graft, and I'm an example of how it works. I might sum up the whole thing by sayin': "I seen my opportunities and I took 'em."

Just let me explain by examples. My party's in power in the city, and it's goin' to undertake a lot of public improvements.

Well, I'm tipped off, say, that they're going to lay out a new park at a certain place.

I see my opportunity and I take it. I go to that place and I buy up all the land I can in the neighborhood. Then the board of this or that makes its plan public, and there is a rush to get my land, which nobody cared particular for before.

Ain't it perfectly honest to charge a good price and make a profit on my investment and foresight? Of course, it is. Well, that's honest graft.

Or, supposin' it's a new bridge they're goin' to build. I get tipped off and I buy as much property as I can that has to be taken for approaches. I sell at my own price later on and drop some more money in the bank.

Wouldn't you? It's just like lookin' ahead in Wall Street or in the coffee or cotton market. It's honest graft, and I'm lookin' for it every day in the year. I will tell you frankly that I've got a good lot of it, too.

I'll tell you of one case. They were goin' to fix up a big park, no matter where. I got on to it, and went lookin' about for land in that neighborhood.

I could get nothin' at a bargain but a big piece of swamp, but I took it fast enough and held on to it. What turned out was just what I counted on. They couldn't make the park complete without Plunkitt's swamp, and they had to pay a good price for it. Anything dishonest in that?

Up in the watershed I made some money, too. I bought up several bits of land there some years ago and made a pretty good guess that they would be bought up for water purposes later by the city.

Somehow, I always guessed about right, and shouldn't I enjoy the profit of my foresight? It was rather amusin' when the condemnation commissioners came along and found piece after piece of the land in the name of George Plunkitt of the Fifteenth Assembly District, New York City. They wondered how I knew just what to buy. The answer is — I seen my opportunity and I took it. I haven't confined myself to land; anything that pays is in my line. . . .

I've told you how I got rich by honest graft. Now, let me tell you that most politicians who are accused of robbin' the city get rich the same way.

They didn't steal a dollar from the city treasury. They just seen their opportunities and took them. That is why, when a reform administration comes in and spends a half million dollars in tryin' to find the public robberies they talked about in the campaign, they don't find them.

The books are always all right. The money in the city treasury is all right. Everything is all right. All they can show is that the Tammany heads of departments looked after their friends, within the law, and gave them what opportunities they could to make honest graft. Now, let me tell you that's never goin' to hurt Tammany with the people. Every good man looks after his friends, and any man who doesn't isn't likely to be popular. If I have a good thing to hand out in private life, I give it to a friend. Why shouldn't I do the same in public life?

Another kind of honest graft. Tammany has raised a good many salaries. There was an awful howl by the reformers, but don't you know that Tammany gains ten votes for every one it lost by salary raisin'?

The Wall Street banker thinks it shameful to raise a department clerk's salary from $1,500 to $1,800 a year, but every man who draws a salary himself says: "That's all right. I wish it was me." And he feels very much like votin' the Tammany ticket on election day, just out of sympathy. . . .

The fact is that a reformer can't last in politics. He can make a show for a while, but he always comes down like a rocket. Politics is as much a regular business as the grocery or the dry-goods or the drug business. You've got to be trained up to it or you're sure to fail. Suppose a man who knew nothing about the grocery trade suddenly went into the business and tried to conduct it according to his own ideas. Wouldn't he make a mess of it? He might make a splurge for a while, as long as his money lasted, but his store would soon be empty. It's just the same with a reformer. He hasn't been brought up in the difficult business of politics and he makes a mess of it every time.

I've been studyin' the political game for forty-five years, and I don't know it all yet. I'm learnin' somethin' all the time. How, then, can you expect what they call "businessmen" to turn into politics all at once and make a success of it? It is just as if I went up to Columbia University and started to teach Greek. They usually last about as long in politics as I would last at Columbia.

You can't begin too early in politics if you want to succeed at the game. I began several years before I could vote, and so did every successful leader in Tammany Hall.

When I was twelve years old I made myself useful around the district headquarters and did work at all the polls on election day. Later on, I hustled about gettin' out voters who had jags on or who were too lazy to come to the polls. There's a hundred ways that boys can help, and they get an experience that's the first real step in statesmanship. Show me a boy that hustles for the organization on election day, and I'll show you a comin' statesman.

That's the a, b, c of politics. It ain't easy work to get up to y and z. You have to give nearly all your time and attention to it. Of course, you may have some business or occupation on the side, but the great business of your life must be politics if you want to succeed in it. A few years ago Tammany tried to mix politics and business in equal quantities, by havin' two leaders for each district, a politician and a businessman. They wouldn't mix. They were like oil and water. The politician looked after the politics of his district; the businessman looked after his grocery store or his milk route, and whenever he appeared at an executive meeting, it was only to make trouble. The whole scheme turned out to be a farce and was abandoned mighty quick.

Do you understand now why it is that a reformer goes down and out in the first or second round, while a politician answers to the gong every time? It is because the one has gone into the fight without trainin', while the other trains all the time and knows every fine point of the game.

THE CURSE OF CIVIL SERVICE REFORMS

THIS CIVIL SERVICE LAW is the biggest fraud of the age. It is the curse of the nation. There can't be no real patriotism while it lasts. How are you goin' to interest our young men in their country if you have no offices to give them when they work for their party? Just look at things in this city today. There are 10,000 good offices, but we can't get at more than a few hundred of them. How are we goin' to provide for the thousands of men who worked for the Tammany ticket? It can't be done. These men were full of patriotism a short time ago. They expected to be servin' their city, but when we tell them that we can't place them, do you think their patriotism is goin' to last? Not much. They say: "What's the use of workin' for your country anyhow? There's nothin' in the game." And what can they do? I don't know, but I'll tell you what I do know. I know more than one young man in past years who worked for the ticket and was just overflowin' with patriotism, but when he was knocked out by the civil service humbug he got to hate his country and became an Anarchist.

This ain't no exaggeration. I have good reason for sayin' that most of the Anarchists in this city today are men who ran up against civil service examinations. Isn't it enough to make a man sour on his country when he wants to serve it and won't be allowed unless he answers a lot of fool questions about the number of cubic inches of water in the Atlantic and the quality of sand in the Sahara Desert? There was once a bright young man in my district who tackled one of these examinations. The next I heard of him he had settled down in Herr Most's saloon smokin' and drinkin' beer and talkin' socialism all day. Before that time he had never drank anything but whisky. I knew what was comin' when a young Irishman drops whisky and takes to beer and long pipes in a German saloon. That young man is today one of the wildest Anarchists in town. And just to think! He might be a patriot but for that cussed civil service.

Say, did you hear about that Civil Service Reform Association kickin' because the tax commissioners want to put their fifty-five deputies on the exempt list and fire the outfit left to them by Low? That's civil service for you. Just think! Fifty-five Republicans and mugwumps holdin' $3,000 and $4,000 and $5,000 jobs in the Tax Department when 1,555 good Tammany men are ready and willin' to take their places! It's an outrage! What did the people mean when they voted for Tammany. What is representative government, anyhow? Is it all a fake that this is a government of the people, by the people, and for the people? If it isn't a fake, then why isn't the people's voice obeyed and Tammany men put in all the offices?

When the people elected Tammany, they knew just what they were doin'. We didn't put up any false pretenses. We didn't go in for humbug civil service and all that rot. We stood as we have always stood, for rewardin' the men that won the victory. They call that the spoils system. All right; Tammany is for the spoils system, and when we go in we fire every anti-Tammany man from office that can be fired under the law. It's an elastic sort of law and you can bet it will be stretched to the limit.

Of course the Republican State Civil Service Board will stand in the way of our local Civil Service Commission all it can; but say! — suppose we carry the state sometime; won't we fire the up-State Board all right? Or we'll make it work in harmony with the local board, and that means that Tammany will get everything in sight. I know that the civil service humbug is stuck into the constitution, too, but, as Tim Campbell said: 'What's the constitution among friends?'

Say, the people's voice is smothered by the cursed civil service law; it is the root of all evil in our government. You hear of this thing or that thing goin' wrong in the nation, the state, or the city. Look down beneath the surface and you can trace everything wrong to civil service. I have studied the subject and I know. The civil service humbug is underminin' our institutions and if a halt ain't called soon this great republic will tumble down like a Park Avenue house when they were buildin' the subway, and on its ruins will rise another Russian government.

This is an awful serious proposition. Free silver and the tariff and imperialism and the Panama Canal are triflin' issues when compared to it. We could worry along without any of these things, but civil service is sappin' the foundation of the whole shootin' match. Let me argue it out for you. I ain't up on sillygisms, but I can give you some arguments that nobody can answer.

First, this great and glorious country was built up by political parties; second, parties can't hold together if their workers don't get the offices when they win; third, if the parties go to pieces, the government they built up must go to pieces, too; fourth, then there'll be h —— to pay.

Could anything be clearer than that? Say, honest now; can you answer that argument? Of course you won't deny that the government was built up by the great parties. That's history, and you can't go back of the returns. As to my second proposition, you can't deny that either. When parties can't get offices, they'll bust. They ain't far from the bustin' point now, with all this civil service business keepin' most of the good things from them. How are you goin' to keep up patriotism if this thing goes on? You can't do it. Let me tell you that patriotism has been dying out fast for the last twenty years. Before then when a party won, its workers got everything in sight. That was somethin' to make a man patriotic. Now, when a party wins and its men come forward and ask for their reward, the reply is, "Nothin' doin'," unless you can answer a list of questions about Egyptian mummies and how many years it will take for a bird to wear out a mass of iron as big as the earth by steppin' on it once in a century.

I have studied politics and men for forty-five years, and I see how things are driftin'.

Sad indeed is the change that has come over the young men, even in my district, where I try to keep up the fire of patriotism by gettin' a lot of jobs for my constituents, whether Tammany is in or out. The boys and men don't get excited any more when they see a United States flag or hear the "Star Spangled Banner." They don't care no more for firecrackers on the Fourth of July. And why should they? What is there in it for them? They know that no matter how hard they work for their country in a campaign, the jobs will go to fellows who can tell about the mummies and the bird steppin' on the iron. Are you surprised then that the young men of the country are beginnin' to look coldly on the flag and don't care to put up a nickel for firecrackers?

Say, let me tell of one case. After the battle of San Juan Hill, the Americans found a dead man with a light complexion, red hair, and blue eyes. They could see he wasn't a Spaniard, although he had on a Spanish uniform. Several officers looked him over, and then a private of the Seventy-first Regiment saw him and yelled, "Good Lord, that's Flaherty." That man grew up in my district, and he was once the most patriotic American boy on the West Side. He couldn't see a flag without yellin' himself hoarse.

Now, how did he come to be lying dead with a Spanish uniform on? I found out all about it, and I'll vouch for the story. Well, in the municipal campaign of 1897, that young man, chockful of patriotism, worked day and night for the Tammany ticket. Tammany won, and the young man determined to devote his life to the service of the city. He picked out a place that would suit him and sent in his application to the head of department. He got a reply that he must take a civil service examination to get the place. He didn't know what these examinations were, so he went, all lighthearted, to the Civil Service Board. He read the

questions about the mummies, the bird on the iron, and all the other fool questions — and he left that office an enemy of the country that he had loved so well. The mummies and the bird blasted his patriotism. He went to Cuba, enlisted in the Spanish Army at the breakin' out of the war, and died fightin' his country.

That is but one victim of the infamous civil service. If that young man had not run up against the civil examination, but had been allowed to serve his country as he wished, he would be in a good office today, drawin' a good salary. Ah, how many young men have had their patriotism blasted in the same way!

Now, what is goin' to happen when civil service crushes out patriotism? Only one thing can happen — the republic will go to pieces. Then a czar or a sultan will turn up, which brings me to the fourthly of my argument; that is, there will be h —— to pay. And that ain't no lie.

TO HOLD YOUR DISTRICT: STUDY HUMAN NATURE AND ACT ACCORDIN'

THERE'S ONLY ONE WAY TO HOLD A DISTRICT: you must study human nature and act accordin'. You can't study human nature in books. Books is a hindrance more than anything else. If you have been to college, so much the worse for you. You'll have to unlearn all you learned before you can get right down to human nature, and unlearnin' takes a lot of time. Some men can never forget what they learned at college. Such men may get to be district leaders by a fluke, but they never last.

To learn real human nature you have to go among the people, see them and be seen. I know every man, woman, and child in the Fifteenth District, except them that's been born this summer — and I know some of them, too. I know what they like and what they don't like, what they are strong at and what they are weak in, and I reach them by approachin' at the right side.

For instance, here's how I gather in the young men. I hear of a young feller that's proud of his voice, thinks that he can sing fine. I ask him to come around to Washington Hall and join our Glee Club. He comes and sings, and he's a follower of Plunkitt for life. Another young feller gains a reputation as a baseball player in a vacant lot. I bring him into our baseball club. That fixes him. You'll find him workin' for my ticket at the polls next election day. Then there's the feller that likes rowin' on the river, the young feller that makes a name as a waltzer on his block, the young feller that's handy with his dukes — I rope them all in by givin' them opportunities to show themselves off. I don't trouble them with political arguments. I just study human nature and act accordin'.

But you may say this game won't work with the high-toned fellers, the fellers that go through college and then join the Citizens' Union. Of course it wouldn't work. I have a special treatment for them. I ain't like the patent medicine man that gives the same medicine for all diseases. The Citizens' Union kind of a young man! I love him! He's the daintiest morsel of the lot, and he don't often escape me.

Before telling you how I catch him, let me mention that before the election last year, the Citizens' Union said they had 400 or 500 enrolled voters in my district. They had a lovely headquarters, too, beautiful rolltop desks and the cutest rugs in the world. If I was accused of havin' contributed to fix up the nest for them, I wouldn't deny it under oath. What do I mean by that? Never mind. You can guess from the sequel, if you're sharp.

Well, election day came. The Citizens' Union's candidate for senator, who ran against me, just polled 5 votes in the district, while I polled something more than 14,000 votes. What became of the 400 or

500 Citizens' Union enrolled voters in my district? Some people guessed that many of them were good Plunkitt men all along and worked with the Cits just to bring them into the Plunkitt camp by election day. You can guess that way, too, if you want to. I never contradict stories about me, especially in hot weather. I just call your attention to the fact that on last election day 395 Citizens' Union enrolled voters in my district were missin' and unaccounted for.

I tell you frankly, though, how I have captured some of the Citizens' Union's young men. I have a plan that never fails. I watch the City Record to see when there's civil service examinations for good things. Then I take my young Cit in hand, tell him all about the good thing and get him worked up till he goes and takes an examination. I don't bother about him any more. It's a cinch that he comes back to me in a few days and asks to join Tammany Hall. Come over to Washington Hall some night and I'll show you a list of names on our rolls marked "C.S." which means, "bucked up against civil service."

As to the older voters, I reach them, too. No, I don't send them campaign literature. That's rot. People can get all the political stuff they want to read — and a good deal more, too — in the papers. Who reads speeches, nowadays, anyhow? It's bad enough to listen to them. You ain't goin' to gain any votes by stuffin' the letter boxes with campaign documents. Like as not you'll lose votes, for there's nothin' a man hates more than to hear the letter carrier ring his bell and go to the letter box expectin' to find a letter he was lookin' for, and find only a lot of printed politics. I met a man this very mornin' who told me he voted the Democratic state ticket last year just because the Republicans kept crammin' his letter box with campaign documents.

What tells in holdin' your grip on your district is to go right down among the poor families and help them in the different ways they need help. I've got a regular system for this. If there's a fire in Ninth, Tenth, or Eleventh Avenue, for example, any hour of the day or night, I'm usually there with some of my election district captains as soon as the fire engines. If a family is burned out, I don't ask whether they are Republicans or Democrats, and I don't refer them to the Charity Organization Society, which would investigate their case in a month or two and decide they were worthy of help about the time they are dead from starvation. I just get quarters for them, buy clothes for them if their clothes were burned up, and fix them up till they get things runnin' again. It's philanthropy, but it's politics, too — mighty good politics. Who can tell how many votes one of these fires bring me? The poor are the most grateful people in the world, and, let me tell you, they have more friends in their neighborhoods than the rich have in theirs.

If there's a family in my district in want, I know it before the charitable societies do, and me and my men are first on the ground. I have a special corps to look up such cases. The consequence is that the poor look up to George W. Plunkitt as a father, come to him in trouble — and don't forget him on election day.

Another thing, I can always get a job for a deservin' man. I make it a point to keep on the track of jobs, and it seldom happens that I don't have a few up my sleeve ready for use. I know every big employer in the district and in the whole city, for that matter, and they ain't in the habit of sayin' no to me when I ask them for a job.

And the children — the little roses of the district! Do I forget them? Oh, no! They know me, every one of them, and they know that a sight of Uncle George and candy means the same thing. Some of them are the best kind of vote-getters. I'll tell you a case. Last year a little Eleventh Avenue rosebud, whose father is a Republican, caught hold of his whiskers on election day

and said she wouldn't let go till he'd promise to vote for me. And she didn't.

ON *THE SHAME OF THE CITIES*

I'VE BEEN READIN' A BOOK by Lincoln Steffens on *The Shame of the Cities*. Steffens means well but, like all reformers, he don't know how to make distinctions. He can't see no difference between honest graft and dishonest graft and, consequent, he gets things all mixed up. There's the biggest kind of a difference between political looters and politicians who make a fortune out of politics by keepin' their eyes wide open. The looter goes in for himself alone without considerin' his organization or his city. The politician looks after his own interests, the organization's interests, and the city's interests all at the same time. See the distinction? For instance, I ain't no looter. The looter hogs it. I never hogged. I made my pile in politics, but, at the same time, I served the organization and got more big improvements for New York City than any other livin' man. And I never monkeyed with the penal code.

The difference between a looter and a practical politician is the difference between the Philadelphia Republican gang and Tammany Hall. Steffens seems to think they're both about the same; but he's all wrong. The Philadelphia crowd runs up against the penal code. Tammany don't. The Philadelphians ain't satisfied with robbin' the bank of all its gold and paper money. They stay to pick up the nickels and pennies and the cop comes and nabs them. Tammany ain't no such fool. Why, I remember, about fifteen or twenty years ago, a Republican superintendent of the Philadelphia almshouse stole the zinc roof off the buildin' and sold it for junk. That was carryin' things to excess. There's a limit to everything, and the Philadelphia Republicans go beyond the limit. It seems like they can't be cool and moderate like real politicians. It ain't fair, therefore, to class Tammany men with the Philadelphia gang. Any man who undertakes to write political books should never for a moment lose sight of the distinction between honest graft and dishonest graft, which I explained in full in another talk. If he puts all kinds of graft on the same level, he'll make the fatal mistake that Steffens made and spoil his book.

A big city like New York or Philadelphia or Chicago might be compared to a sort of Garden of Eden, from a political point of view. It's an orchard full of beautiful apple trees. One of them has got a big sign on it, marked; "Penal Code Tree — Poison." The other trees have lots of apples on them for all. Yet the fools go to the Penal Code Tree. Why? For the reason, I guess, that a cranky child refuses to eat good food and chews up a box of matches with relish. I never had any temptation to touch the Penal Code Tree. The other apples are good enough for me, and O Lord! how many of them there are in a big city!

Steffens made one good point in his book. He said he found that Philadelphia, ruled almost entirely by Americans, was more corrupt than New York, where the Irish do almost all the governin'. I could have told him that before he did any investigatin' if he had come to me. The Irish was born to rule, and they're the honestest people in the world. Show me the Irishman who would steal a roof off an almhouse! He don't exist. Of course, if an Irishman had the political pull and the roof was much worn, he might get the city authorities to put on a new one and get the contract for it himself, and buy the old roof at a bargain — but that's honest graft. It's goin' about the thing like a gentleman, and there's more money in it than in tearin' down an old roof and cartin' it to the junkman's — more money and no penal code.

One reason why the Irishman is more honest in politics than many Sons of the Revolution is that he is grateful to the country and the city that gave him protection and prosperity when he was driven by oppression from the Emerald Isle. Say, that sentence is fine, ain't it? I'm goin' to get some literary feller to work it over into poetry for next St. Patrick's Day dinner.

Yes, the Irishman is grateful. His one thought is to serve the city which gave him a home. He has this thought even before he lands in New York, for his friends here often have a good place in one of the city departments picked out for him while he is still in the old country. Is it any wonder that he has a tender spot in his heart for old New York when he is on its salary list the mornin' after he lands?

Now, a few words on the general subject of the so-called shame of cities. I don't believe that the government of our cities is any worse, in proportion to opportunities, than it was fifty years ago. I'll explain what I mean by "in proportion to opportunities." A half a century ago, our cities were small and poor. There wasn't many temptations lyin' around for politicians. There was hardly anything to steal, and hardly any opportunities for even honest graft. A city could count its money every night before goin' to bed, and if three cents was missin', all the fire bells would be rung. What credit was there in bein' honest under them circumstances? It makes me tired to hear of old codgers back in the thirties or forties boastin' that they retired from politics without a dollar except what they earned in their profession or business. If they lived today, with all the existin' opportunities, they would be just the same as 20th century politicians. There ain't any more honest people in the world just now than the convicts in Sing Sing. Not one of them steals anything. Why? Because they can't. See the application?

Understand, I ain't defendin' politicians of today who steal. The politician who steals is worse than a thief. He is a fool. With the grand opportunities all around for the man with a political pull, there's no excuse for stealin' a cent. The point I want to make is that if there is some stealin' in politics, it don't mean that the politicians of 1905 are, as a class, worse than them of 1835. It just means that the old-timers had nothin' to steal, while the politicians now are surrounded by all kinds of temptations and some of them naturally — the fool ones — buck up against the penal code.

118.

GEORGE M. COHAN: Nostalgia for Broadway

Broadway as an institution and as a symbol was largely created by a group of dramatists and songwriters around the turn of the twentieth century, among whom George M. Cohan was probably the leading figure. The following songs are typical of his productions — romantic, sentimental, and patriotic, they nevertheless retain the ability to make the heart beat a little faster at the mention of what came to be called, a generation later, "The Great White Way."

THE YANKEE DOODLE BOY

I'm the kid that's all the candy,
I'm a Yankee Doodle Dandy.
I'm glad I am —
So's Uncle Sam.
I'm a real live Yankee Doodle,
Made my name and fame and boodle
Just like Mister Doodle did
By riding on a pony.
I love to listen to the Dixie strain,
"I long to see the girl I left behind me";
And that ain't a josh,
She's a Yankee, by gosh.
Oh, say can you see
Anything about a Yankee that's a phony?

Chorus:
I'm a Yankee Doodle Dandy,
A Yankee Doodle, do or die;
A real live nephew of my Uncle Sam,
Born on the Fourth of July.

I've a Yankee Doodle sweetheart,
She's my Yankee Doodle joy.
Yankee Doodle came to London just to
  ride the ponies —
I am the Yankee Doodle Boy.

Father's name was Hezekiah,
Mother's name was Ann Maria —
Yanks through and through,
Red, white, and blue.
Father was so Yankee-hearted,
When the Spanish War was started,
He slipped on his uniform
And hopped upon a pony.
My mother's mother was a Yankee true,
My father's father was a Yankee, too —
And that's going some,
For the Yankees, by gum.
Oh, say can you see
Anything about a Yankee that's a phony?

❧ GIVE MY REGARDS TO BROADWAY

Did you ever see two Yankees part
Upon a foreign shore;
When the good ship's just about to start
For old New York once more?
With tear-dimmed eye they say good-
    bye,
They're friends, without a doubt;
When the man on the pier shouts, "Let
    them clear!"
As the ship strikes out:

Chorus:
"Give my regards to Broadway,
Remember me to Herald Square.
Tell all the gang at 42nd Street

That I will soon be there.
Whisper of how I'm yearning
To mingle with that old-time throng.
Give my regards to old Broadway
And tell them I'll be there e'er long.

Say hello to dear old Coney Island,
If there you chance to be;
When you're at the Waldorf,
Have a smile and charge it up to me;
Mention my name every place you go,
As round the town you roam;
Wish you'd call on my gal, now
    remember, old pal,
When you get back home."

119.

THORSTEIN VEBLEN: Business and the Community

*Thorstein Veblen wrote about economics from an anthropological viewpoint and with a
mordant wit. Although more erudite than crusading journalists like Lincoln Steffens
and Ida Tarbell, Veblen shared their zeal to expose the evils in American society.
Veblen saw the business ethos as permeating all segments of American life. The
belief in unfettered competition and in the accumulation and display of wealth, and
reverence for private property — all were American business values held firmly
by laborers and capitalists alike. In the following selection, which is taken from
a book published in 1904, Veblen analyzed the loss of natural liberty in modern
industrial society.*

Source: *The Theory of Business Enterprise*, New York, 1904: "Business Principles in Law and Politics."

POPULAR WELFARE is bound up with the conduct of business, because industry is managed for business ends; and also because there prevails throughout modern communities a settled habit of rating the means of livelihood and the amenities of life in pecuniary terms. But apart from their ef-fect in controlling the terms of livelihood from day to day, these principles are also in great measure decisive in the larger affairs of life, both for the individual in his civil relations and for the community at large in its political concerns. Modern (civilized) in-stitutions rest, in great part, on business principles. This is the meaning, as applied to the modern situation, of the current phrases about the Economic Interpretation of History, or the Materialistic Theory of History.

Because of this settled habit of seeing all the conjunctures of life from the business point of view, in terms of profit and loss, the management of the affairs of the community at large falls by common consent into the hands of businessmen, and is guided by business considerations. Hence, modern politics is business politics, even apart from the sinister application of the phrase to what is invidiously called corrupt politics. This is true both of foreign and domestic policy. Legislation, police surveillance, the administration of justice, the military and diplomatic service, all are chiefly concerned with business relations, pecuniary interests, and they have little more than an incidental bearing on other human interests. All this apparatus is also charged with the protection of life and personal liberty, but its work in this bearing has much of a pecuniary color. . . .

Courts speak more unequivocally for the metaphysical principles and apply them with a surer and firmer touch. In the view of these higher adepts of the law, free contract is so inalienable a natural right of man that not even a statutory enactment will enable a workman to forego its exercise and its responsibility. By metaphysical necessity its exercise attaches to the individual so indefeasibly that it cannot constitutionally be delegated to collective action, whether legislative or corporate. This extreme consequence of the principle of natural liberty has at times aroused indignation in the vulgar; but their grasp of legal principles is at fault. The more closely the logical sequence is followed up, the more convincingly does the legitimacy of such a decision stand out. . . .

Representative government means, chiefly, representation of business interests. The government commonly works in the interest of the businessmen with a fairly consistent singleness of purpose. And in its solicitude for the businessmen's interests, it is borne out by current public sentiment, for there is a naïve, unquestioning persuasion abroad among the body of the people to the effect that, in some occult way, the material interests of the populace coincide with the pecuniary interests of those businessmen who live within the scope of the same set of governmental contrivances. . . .

The ground of sentiment on which rests the popular approval of a government for business ends may be summed up under two heads: patriotism and property. Both of these terms stand for institutional facts that have come down out of a past which differed substantially from the present situation. The substance of both is of the nature of unreasoning sentiment, in the sense that both are insisted on as a matter of course, as self-legitimating grounds of action which, it is felt, not only give expedient rules of conduct but admit of no question as to their ulterior consequences or their value for the life purposes of the community.

The former of these fundamental institutional habits of thought (perhaps better, habits of mind) runs back to the discipline of early barbarism, through the feudal days of fealty, to the earlier days of clan life and clannish animosity. It has, therefore, the deep-rooted strength given by an extremely protracted discipline of predation and servitude. Under modern conditions it is to be rated as essentially an institutional survival, so ingrained in the populace as to make any appeal to it secure of a response irrespective of the material merits of the contention in whose behalf the appeal is made.

By force of this happy knack of clannish fancy, the common man is enabled to feel that he has some sort of metaphysical share in the gains which accrue to the businessmen who are citizens of the same "commonwealth"; so that whatever policy furthers the commercial gains of those businessmen, whose domicile is within the national boundaries, is felt to be beneficial to all the rest of the population.

The second institutional support of business politics, viz., property, is similarly an outgrowth of the discipline of the past, and similarly, though perhaps in a less degree, out of touch with the discipline of the more recent cultural situation. In the form in which it prevails in the current popular animus, the principle of ownership comes down from the days of handicraft industry and petty trade. . . . As it is of less ancient and less unbroken descent, so it seems also to be a less secure cultural heritage than the sense of patriotic solidarity. It says that the ownership of property is the material foundation of human well-being, and that this natural right of ownership is sacred, after the manner in which individual life, and more especially national life, is sacred. The habits of life and thought inculcated by joint work under the manorial system and by joint rules under the handicraft system have apparently contributed much to the notion of a solidarity of economic interests, having given the notion such a degree of consistency as has enabled it to persist in the face of a visible discrepancy of interests in later, capitalistic times.

Under this current, business regime, business gains are the basis of individual wealth, and the (pseudo) notion of joint acquisition has taken the place of the manorial notion of joint work. The institutional animus of ownership, as it took shape under the discipline of early modern handicraft, awards the ownership of property to the workman who has produced it. By a dialectical conversion of the terms, this metaphysical dictum is made to fit the circumstances of later competitive business by construing acquisition of property to mean production of wealth; so that a businessman is looked upon as the putative producer of whatever wealth he acquires. By force of this sophistication the acquisition of property by any person is held to be, not only expedient for the own-

er but meritorious as an action serving the common good. Failure to bargain shrewdly or to accumulate more goods than one has produced by the work of one's own hands is looked upon with a feeling of annoyance, as a neglect, not only of opportunity, but of duty. The pecuniary conscience commonly does not, of course, go to quixotic lengths in a public-spirited insistence on everybody's acquiring more than an aliquot part of the aggregate wealth on hand, but it is felt that he best serves the common good who, other things equal, diverts the larger share of the aggregate wealth to his own possession. His acquiring a defensible title to it makes him the putative producer of it.

The natural-rights basis of ownership is by this paralogism preserved intact, and the common man is enabled to feel that the businessmen in the community add to the aggregate wealth at least as much as they acquire a title to; and the successful businessmen are at least as well persuaded that such is their relation to the aggregate wealth and to the material well-being of the community at large. So that both the businessmen whose gains are sought to be enhanced by business politics and the populace by whose means the business gains are secured work together in good faith toward a well-advised business end — the accumulation of wealth in the hands of those men who are skilled in pecuniary matters. . . .

The ring of business interests which secures the broadest approval from popular sentiment is, under constitutional methods, put in charge of the government establishment. This popular approval may be secured on the ground of a sound business platform or (in part) on some ground extraneous to business policy proper, such as a wave of national animosity, a popular candidate, a large grain crop, etc. But the only secure basis of an enduring party tenure of the government machinery is a business policy which falls in with the interests or the prejudices of the effective majority.

120.

George F. Roesch: The Constitutionality of a New York Child Labor Law

New York was one of the industrial states that responded to the demands of urban reformers of the late nineteenth century for social welfare legislation. One law, passed in 1897, which prohibited children under fourteen from working during school hours, brought protests from the business community on the grounds that it encroached on the right of contract. In what proved to be an important test of the law, a New York state court in 1904 upheld its constitutionality in City of New York v. Chelsea Jute Mills. *The court ruled (a portion of Judge Roesch's opinion is reprinted here) that the Constitution provides the states with the police powers to protect the health and welfare of their citizens.*

Source: 88 New York Supplement 1085 (1904).

Judge Roesch. This is an action to recover a statutory penalty. As it is a test case, upon the outcome of which many others depend, and is the first of its kind in this state, a full examination of the questions involved will be attempted. . . .

The language of the statute follows:

> It shall be unlawful for any person, firm, or corporation to employ any child under fourteen years of age, in any business or service whatever, during any part of the term during which the public schools of the district in which the child resides are in session . . . and any person who shall employ any child contrary to the provisions of this section . . . shall, for each offense, forfeit and pay to the treasurer of the city or village, or to the supervisor of the town in which such child resides, a penalty of $50.

The act prescribes a comprehensive system of public education, and other sections provide for instruction elsewhere, if desired, than at a public school. The salient facts are not disputed.

Annie Ventre resides with her parents in this city, borough of Brooklyn, in which the defendant, a domestic corporation organized under the laws of our state, transacts its business of manufacturing and selling seamless jute bags and other jute fabrics. She was but twelve years of age on July 29, 1903. She began to work in the factory of the defendant on April 7, 1903, and continued until the day preceding the trial. She worked at emptying "bobbins," beginning her labors at 7 o'clock A.M. and stopping at 6:15 o'clock P.M., with an intermission from noon until 12:45 o'clock for lunch, except that on Saturdays, with the same hours otherwise, she ceased work at 2:15 o'clock P.M.

When she applied for work on April 7, 1903, she stated she was "sixteen passed," and gave the forelady an affidavit, signed and sworn to by her father on April 6, 1903, before a commissioner of deeds, to the effect that she was born "on April 4, 1887, and that she was sixteen years old on April 4, 1903." The father testified that the affidavit was not in fact true, but that July 29, 1903, was her twelfth birthday. The mother testified positively that her daughter was twelve years old on July 29, 1903. There was no objection to this testimony as to age. It is admitted of record that the terms of the public schools are uniform throughout the city and that these were in session during the period the child worked as stated.

The statute is assailed for unconstitutionality. No particular provision of the state or federal Constitution is assigned. It is claimed to be "an unwarranted, illegal, and unconstitutional deprivation of the liberties of the defendant." The defendant also urges immunity from the penalty on account of the alleged "good faith, absence of intent to violate the statute, nonemployment of Annie Ventre since her age was established in court." The integrity of the statute is upheld under the police power of the state. A statute should not be declared unconstitutional unless required by the most cogent reasons, or compelled by unanswerable grounds. . . .

Every presumption is in favor of the constitutionality of a statute. . . . It is difficult to satisfactorily define the police power to cover every case. But it includes such legislative measures as promote the health, safety, or morals of the community. . . . It is true that the legislature must respect freedom of contract and the right to live and work where and how one will. . . . Yet the weal of the people is the supreme law. The legislature may not disregard it; private interests are subordinated to the public good, and even a statute opposed to natural justice and equity, requiring vigilance or causing vexation or annoyance, will be upheld if within constitutional limitations. . . .

Much more potent, if possible, is a statute seeking the protection of children. They are the wards of the state, which is particularly interested in their well-being as future members of the body politic, and has an inherent right to protect itself and them against the baneful effects of ignorance, infirmity, or danger to life and limb. . . .

Legislation is replete with enactments of such a character. We have a most enlightened code for the prevention of cruelty to children. The Penal Code (Section 288) requires that a minor child shall be furnished with "medical attendance." In *People* v. *Pierson* . . . it was held that the medical attendance required is the authorized medical attendance of a duly licensed practitioner and not that of representatives of irregular therapeutics, as Christian Scientists and the like. In *People* v. *Ewer* . . . a statute was held to be within the police power which prohibited the appearance of a child under fourteen years of age in public on any stage. It was declared that the legislature had the right and power to exercise its judgment as to what would be detrimental to the best interests of the children of the state, and, having done so, such judgment should not be impeached by the court, and that

> it cannot be disputed that the interest which the state has in the physical, moral, and intellectual well-being of its members warrants the implication and the exercise of every just power which will result in preparing the child in future life to support itself, to serve the state, and in all relations and duties of adult life to perform well and capably its part.

So statutes have been passed providing for compulsory vaccination of children, and have been upheld as within the police power. . . .

Again, the factory legislation of our state, from that of May 18, 1886, to Chapter 173, p. 298, Laws 1893, aimed at the protection of children. We were in accord therein with advanced steps in similar legislation throughout the civilized world. In *Fitzgerald* v. *Alma Furniture Company* . . . there will be found an historical summary of such acts in our own and foreign countries, from which it will appear that every civilized state has passed such enactments. The Court of Appeals showed in a striking manner its purpose to maintain such legislation in deciding that a corporation which violates the statute is practically an insurer of the safety of the child, and a child who is injured, irrespective of any negligence on the part of the corporation, is not, as matter of law, chargeable with contributory negligence or with having assumed the risks of employment. The employment itself is sufficient evidence of the employer's negligence in such case, as the employment is itself a civil wrong. . . .

The test of such legislation is to determine whether on its face it serves a public purpose, reaches all persons of a reasonably ascertained class indiscriminately, and is cognate to the objects it proposes to subserve. Unless these questions are negatived, the court must declare the act constitutional. . . .

The court [has] held an act restricting the hours of labor in bakeries a valid exercise of the police power, in view of the unwholesome character of the work. The statute under consideration does not discriminate, is auxiliary to the primary purpose to enforce education and elevate future citizenship, is not arbitrary, puts no unnecessary restriction upon freedom of action, and resorts to no unnecessary rigor, because it would be impossible, otherwise than by an absolute prohibition of employment of all children under fourteen years of age, to accomplish its beneficent ends. Nor does it constitute any improper infringement of any right a parent may have in a child or to its labor, or a child may have to labor. . . . Nor is the court, in its efforts to test the validity of an act, confined to the statute itself, its general scope and trend, or literal provisions. The court may resort to facts and circumstances of which it can take judicial notice, and evidence may even be introduced to enlighten the judicial mind. . . .

So, in *People* v. *Lochner* . . . Judge Vann strengthens judicial knowledge with elaborate quotations from scientific literature, and maintains the judicial right to "resort to such sources of information as were open to the legislature." There is no dearth of medical testimony to the evils of child labor. Many medical authorities could be quoted. But the legislature had in its own archives ample testimony in the premises. Governors Hill, Black, and Odell had, in annual messages, explained the situation and earnestly urged legislation. The annual reports of the factory inspectors called attention in strong terms to the evils of child labor and the necessity of compulsory education. In fact, the legislature merely heeded the recommendations of an able committee of its own body, known as the Reinhard Committee, of which Hon. Julius M. Mayer was counsel. The committee was specially charged with the investigation of existing conditions.

Its report is a powerful document. An extract from it will suffice to show its general import and disclose the origin and reason of the law in question:

> The committee stamps the employment of child labor under the statutory age as one of the most extensive evils now existing in the city of New York, and an evil which is a constant and grave menace to the welfare of its people. . . . These children were undersized, poorly clad, and dolefully ignorant, unacquainted with the simplest rudiments of a common-school education, having no knowledge of the simplest figures, and unable in many cases to write their own names in the native or any other language. Parents and corrupt notaries alike connive at the employment of children under the statutory age. . . . No child under the age should be permitted to work in any manufacturing establishment without a health certificate. . . . The legislation, however, must be collaterally supported by a vigilant carrying out of the Compulsory Education Law. . . .

Congress has likewise taken up the subject. Similar recommendations will be found in the Report of the Industrial Commission of 1900 (vol. 5). In the light of such overpowering evidence, the legislature might, indeed, have been charged with criminal neglect of the welfare of the people had it failed to act as it did.

It is further objected that the section under consideration is foreign to the scope of the school law, in no way aids the school authorities in their work, and has no legitimate place in that statute. The objection is not tenable. The provisions of the Child Labor Law (Laws 1897, p. 477, c. 415 §70) must be read in connection with the section in question, which is complementary to and a necessary concomitant of the former. They but emphasize the intent of the legislature to prohibit the labor and enforce the education of children under the stated age. In no other way could its salutary purpose have been more effectually encompassed. It is directly germane to the chief end of the school law, which is a general law, and not a private or local statute that might fall within Article 3, §16, of the state constitution, confining such a bill to but one subject, which must be expressed in the title.

The strong language of Chief Judge Parker in *People* v. *Lochner* . . . may well be applied here:

> Does the label or the body of the statute prevail? Does calling a statute names deprive it of its intended and real character? If a statute relating principally to banking happens, in the course of codification, to be incorporated as an article in the general corporation law, does it cease to operate on the banking business? I submit without argument that the questions answer themselves.

So here the section is not invalidated merely because embodied in the school law. The legislature thus reaffirmed its mandate against child labor to foster education upon the benign theory that representative government can be safe only when future suffrage is enlightened by education. Legisla-

tion providing for compulsory education of children has been specifically held valid in other states under the general police power. . . . From the foregoing the conclusion is irresistible that the section assailed is a just and valid exercise of the police power of the state.

Nor may the defendant assert exemption from liability on account of "good faith, want of intent to violate the statute, and nonemployment of the child since the trial." Assuredly the last ground is not seriously urged. If it were countenanced, the extent and duration of violations of the statute would only be measured by a defendant's successful appeal to the "law's delay." Nor is the good faith of defendant or absence of intent an excuse. The defendant was not active in its quest after the age of the child. It was passive. It complacently received the affidavit of the father upon that point. The forelady testified that she made no other inquiries, but rested entirely upon the affidavit and the statement of the girl that she was "sixteen passed."

She was in court. To the most casual observer the very appearance of the child refuted her statement. When she made it she was but eleven years and nine months old, and her daily toil dragged through 10½ hours. She showed the effects in her maldevelopment and stunted growth. She was a living picture of the results of child labor in a factory at a delicate age, when womanhood and manhood are in a stage of development. Impelled solely by principles conservative of the supreme welfare, the law should be upheld, thus making it impossible to enfeeble and deteriorate the future citizenship of the state.

The school law makes no mention of any certificate or affidavit as to age. Nor does the Child Labor Law as to children under fourteen. But the Child Labor Law does permit the employment of children between fourteen and sixteen years of age, if a certificate executed by a health officer is filed in

the office of the employer. The affidavit in question would not even have answered the requirements of the labor law.

The case cited, *Mayor v. Bigelow* . . . has no application. The defendant was a reputable physician who had neglected to file his license properly. The statute itself gave him leave to rectify his error, and, after he had done so, the court very properly refused to inflict the penalty. The present statute is absolute. It must necessarily be so to accomplish its object. The employer acts at his peril. The fact of employment makes him liable. The contention of the defendant would require judicial legislation and render the statute nugatory, for good faith could easily be alleged and seldom disproved. It would, furthermore, put a premium on perjury to obtain employment. The decisions are adverse to the position of the defendant. So in abduction cases, the accused determines at his peril whether or not the female is or is not over the statutory age. . . .

Where a statute provides a penalty for the doing of an act not in itself criminal, it is not necessary for the penalty to be incurred that the act be done willfully and maliciously. . . . The point is very strongly illustrated in the cases prohibiting the sale of liquors to minors, where it is held that the fact that the seller supposed the minor was over the age, and had even been so informed by his father, did not relieve him from the penalty. . . . The rule is well established that, unless a statute makes knowledge and intent elements of its violation, neither the want of knowledge nor the absence of intent can be shown as a defense. . . .

As is pointedly said in *People* v. *Kibler* . . . "Experience has taught the lesson that repressive measures which depend for their efficiency upon proof of the dealer's knowledge and of his intent to deceive and defraud are of little use and rarely accomplish their purpose."

The legislature must be presumed to have had such lessons in mind, and to have deliberately passed an act that would not nullify itself. If this law be declared invalid, the door will be thrown wide open to the most noxious kinds of child labor. Upon the whole case, then, there must be judgment for the plaintiff against the defendant for the penalty of $50, together with the costs and disbursements of this action.

Judgment for plaintiff for the penalty of $50, together with costs and disbursements.

We like little children because they tear out as soon as they get what they want.
FRANK McKINNEY ("KIN") HUBBARD

I conceive that the right way to write a story for boys is to write so that it will not only interest boys but strongly interest any man who has ever been a boy. That immensely enlarges the audience.
SAMUEL L. CLEMENS ("MARK TWAIN")

121.

JOHN M. HARLAN AND OLIVER WENDELL HOLMES, JR.: Northern Securities Company v. United States

In the decade from 1890 to 1900, various court decisions had reduced the Sherman Anti-Trust Act almost to a dead letter. But in 1901 there was a new President who was suspicious of the power of great wealth and willing to use the antitrust statute where necessary. In 1902 Theodore Roosevelt ordered his attorney general, Philander Knox, to prosecute the Northern Securities Company, a holding company that had been formed in 1901 to control the Northern Pacific, the Chicago, Burlington and Quincy, and the Great Northern Railway. The U.S. Supreme Court ruled (in a 5 to 4 decision) on March 14, 1904, that Northern Securities did come within the scope of the Sherman Act and was, therefore, an illegal combination in restraint of trade. The door to increased government regulation of business was opened, and Roosevelt was hailed, somewhat undeservedly, as the "trustbuster." The following selection contains passages from Justice Harlan's opinion for the majority and from the dissent by Justice Holmes.

Source: 193 U.S. 197.

Mr. Justice Harlan announced the affirmance of the decree of the Circuit Court, and delivered the following opinion. . . .

We will not encumber this opinion by extended extracts from the former opinions of this Court. It is sufficient to say that from the decisions in the above cases certain propositions are plainly deducible and embrace the present case. Those propositions are:

That although the act of Congress known as the Anti-Trust Act has no reference to the mere manufacture or production of articles or commodities within the limits of the several states, it does embrace and declare to be illegal every contract, combination, or conspiracy, in whatever form, of whatever nature, and whoever may be parties to it, which directly or necessarily operates *in restraint* of trade or commerce *among the several states or with foreign nations;*

That the act is not limited to restraints of interstate and international trade or commerce that are unreasonable in their nature, but embraces *all* direct *restraints* imposed by any combination, conspiracy, or monopoly upon such trade or commerce;

That railroad carriers engaged in interstate or international trade or commerce are embraced by the act;

That combinations even among *private* manufacturers or dealers whereby *interstate or international commerce* is restrained are equally embraced by the act;

That Congress has the power to establish *rules* by which *interstate and international* commerce shall be governed, and, by the Anti-Trust Act, has prescribed the rule of free competition among those engaged in such commerce;

That *every* combination or conspiracy which would extinguish competition between otherwise competing railroads engaged in *interstate trade or commerce,* and which would *in that way* restrain *such* trade or commerce, is made illegal by the act;

That the natural effect of competition is to increase commerce, and an agreement whose direct effect is to prevent this play of competition restrains instead of promotes trade and commerce;

That to vitiate a combination, such as the act of Congress condemns, it need not be shown that the combination, in fact, results or will result in a total suppression of trade or in a complete monopoly, but it is only essential to show that by its necessary operation it tends to restrain interstate or international trade or commerce or tends to create a monopoly in such trade or commerce and to deprive the public of the advantages that flow from free competition;

That the constitutional guarantee of liberty of contract does not prevent Congress from prescribing the rule of free competition for those engaged in *interstate and international* commerce; and,

That under its power to regulate commerce among the several states and with foreign nations, Congress had authority to enact the statute in question. . . .

Underlying the argument in behalf of the defendants is the idea that as the Northern Securities Company is a state corporation, and as its acquisition of the stock of the Great Northern and Northern Pacific Railway companies is not inconsistent with the powers conferred by its charter, the enforcement of the act of Congress, as against those corporations, will be an unauthorized interference by the national government with the internal commerce of the states creating those corporations.

This suggestion does not at all impress us. There is no reason to suppose that Congress had any purpose to interfere with the internal affairs of the states, nor, in our opinion, is there any ground whatever for the contention that the Anti-Trust Act regulates their domestic commerce. By its very terms the act regulates only commerce among the states and with foreign states.

Viewed in that light, the act, if within the powers of Congress, must be respected; for, by the explicit words of the Constitution, that instrument and the laws enacted by Congress in pursuance of its provisions are the supreme law of the land, "anything in the constitution or laws of any state to the contrary notwithstanding" — supreme over the states, over the courts, and even over the people of the United States, the source of all power under our governmental system in respect of the objects for which the national government was ordained.

An act of Congress constitutionally passed under its power to regulate commerce among the states and with foreign nations is binding upon all; as much so as if it were embodied, in terms, in the Constitution itself. Every judicial officer, whether of a national or a state court, is under the obligation of an oath so to regard a lawful enactment of Congress. Not even a state, still less one of its artificial creatures, can stand in the way of its enforcement. . . .

It is said that whatever may be the power of a state over such subjects Congress cannot forbid single individuals from disposing of their stock in a state corporation, even if such corporation be engaged in interstate and international commerce; that the holding or purchase by a state corporation, or the purchase by individuals, of the stock of another corporation, for whatever purpose, are matters in respect of which Congress has no authority under the Constitution; that, so far as the power of Congress is concerned, citizens or state corporations may dispose of their property and invest their money in any way they choose; and that in regard to all such matters, citizens and state corporations are subject, if to any authority, only to the lawful authority of the state in which such citizens reside, or under whose laws such corporations are organized.

It is unnecessary in this case to consider such abstract, general questions. The Court need not now concern itself with them. They are not here to be examined and determined, and may well be left for consideration in some case necessarily involving their determination.

In this connection, it is suggested that the contention of the government is that the acquisition and *ownership* of stock in a state railroad corporation is itself interstate commerce if that corporation be engaged in interstate commerce. This suggestion is made in different ways, sometimes in express words, at other times by implication. For instance, it is said that the question here is whether the power of Congress over interstate commerce extends to the regulation of the ownership of the stock in state railroad companies by reason of their being engaged in such commerce. Again, it is said that the only issue in this case is whether the Northern Securities Company can acquire and hold stock in other state corporations. Still further, is it asked, generally, whether the organization or ownership of railroads is not under the control of the states under whose laws they came into existence?

Such statements as to the issues in this case are, we think, wholly unwarranted and are very wide of the mark; it is the setting up of mere men of straw to be easily stricken down. We do not understand that the government makes any such contentions or takes any such positions as those statements imply. It does not contend that Congress may control the mere acquisition or the mere ownership of stock in a state corporation engaged in interstate commerce. Nor does it contend that Congress can control the organization of state corporations authorized by their charters to engage in interstate and international commerce.

But it does contend that Congress may protect the freedom of interstate commerce by any means that are appropriate and that are lawful and not prohibited by the Constitution. It does contend that no state corporation can stand in the way of the enforcement of the national will, legally expressed. What the government particularly complains of, indeed, all that it complains of here, is the existence of a combination among the stockholders of competing railroad companies which, in violation of the act of Congress, restrains interstate and international commerce through the agency of a common corporate trustee designated to act for both companies in repressing free competition between them. . . .

The means employed in respect of the combinations forbidden by the Anti-Trust Act, and which Congress deemed germane to the end to be accomplished, was to prescribe as *a rule for interstate and international* commerce (not for domestic commerce) that it should not be vexed by combinations, conspiracies, or monopolies which restrain commerce by destroying or restricting competition. We say that Congress has prescribed such a rule, because in all the prior cases in this Court the Anti-Trust Act has been construed as forbidding any combination which by its necessary operation destroys or restricts free competition among those engaged in interstate commerce; in other words, that to destroy or restrict free competition in interstate commerce was to restrain such commerce.

Now, can this Court say that such a rule is prohibited by the Constitution or is not one that Congress could appropriately prescribe when exerting its power under the commerce clause of the Constitution? Whether the free operation of the normal laws of competition is a wise and wholesome rule for trade and commerce is an economic question which this Court need not consider or determine. Undoubtedly, there are those who think that the general business interests and prosperity of the country will be best promoted if the rule of competition is not applied. But there are others who believe that such a rule is more necessary in these days of enormous wealth than it ever was in any former period of our history.

Be all this as it may, Congress has, in effect, recognized the rule of free competition by declaring illegal every combination or conspiracy in restraint of interstate and international commerce. As in the judgment of Congress the public convenience and the general welfare will be best subserved when the natural laws of competition are left undisturbed by those engaged in interstate commerce, and as Congress has embodied that rule in a statute, that must be, for all, the end of the matter if this is to remain a government of laws and not of men.

It is said that railroad corporations created under the laws of a state can only be consolidated with the authority of the state. Why that suggestion is made in this case we cannot understand, for there is no pretense that the combination here in question was under the authority of the states under whose laws these railroad corporations were created. But even if the state allowed consolidation, it would not follow that the stockholders of two or more state railroad corporations, having *competing lines and engaged in interstate commerce,* could lawfully combine and form a distinct corporation to hold the stock of the constituent corporations, and, by destroying competition between them, in violation of the act of Congress, restrain commerce among the states and with foreign nations. . . .

We reject any such view of the relations of the national government and the states composing the Union as that for which the defendants contend. Such a view cannot be maintained without destroying the just authority of the United States. It is inconsistent with all the decisions of this Court as to the powers of the national government over matters committed to it. No state can, by merely creating a corporation, or in any other mode, project its authority into other states and across the continent so as to prevent Congress from exerting the power it possesses under the Constitution over interstate and international commerce, or so as to exempt its corporation engaged in interstate commerce from obedience to any rule lawfully established by Congress. . . .

Every corporation created by a state is necessarily subject to the supreme law of the land. And yet the suggestion is made that to restrain a state corporation from interfering with the free course of trade and commerce among the states in violation of an act of Congress is hostile to the reserved rights of the states. The federal court may not have power to forfeit the charter of the Securities Company; it may not declare how its shares of stock may be transferred on its books, nor prohibit it from acquiring real estate, nor diminish or increase its capital stock. All these and like matters are to be regulated by the state which created the company. But to the end that effect be given to the national will, lawfully expressed, Congress may prevent that company, in its capacity as a holding corporation and trustee, from carrying out the purposes of a combination formed in restraint of interstate commerce.

The Securities Company is itself a part of the present combination; its head and front; its trustee. It would be extraordinary if the Court, in executing the act of Congress, could not lay hands upon that company and prevent it from doing that which, if done, will defeat the act of Congress. Upon like grounds the Court can, by appropriate orders, prevent the two competing railroad companies here involved from cooperating with the Securities Company in restraining commerce among the states. In short, the Court may make any order necessary to bring about the dissolution or suppression of an illegal combination that restrains interstate commerce. All this can be done without infringing in any degree upon the just authority of the states.

The affirmance of the judgment below will only mean that no combination, however powerful, is stronger than the law or will be permitted to avail itself of the pretext that to prevent it doing that which, if done, would defeat a legal enactment of Congress, is to attack the reserved rights of the states. It would mean that the government which represents all can, when acting within the limits of its powers, compel obedience to its authority. It would mean that no device in evasion of its provisions, however skillfully such device may have been contrived, and no combination, by whomsoever formed, is beyond the reach of the supreme law of the land if such device or combination by its operation directly restrains commerce among the states or with foreign nations in violation of the act of Congress. . . .

The judgment of the Court is that the decree below be and hereby is *affirmed,* with liberty to the Circuit Court to proceed in the execution of its decree as the circumstances may require.

Mr. Justice Holmes . . . dissenting.

I am unable to agree with the judgment of the majority of the Court, and although I think it useless and undesirable, as a rule, to express dissent, I feel bound to do so in this case and to give my reasons for it.

Great cases like hard cases make bad law. For great cases are called great, not by reason of their real importance in shaping the law of the future but because of some accident of immediate, overwhelming interest which appeals to the feelings and distorts the judgment. These immediate interests exercise a kind of hydraulic pressure which makes what previously was clear seem doubtful, and before which even well-settled principles of law will bend. . . .

The question to be decided is whether, under the act of July 2, 1890 . . . it is unlawful, at any stage of the process, if several men unite to form a corporation for the purpose of buying more than half the stock of each of two competing interstate railroad companies, if they form the corporation and the corporation buys the stock. I will suppose further that every step is taken, from the beginning, with the single intent of ending competition between the companies. I make this addition, not because it may not be and is not disputed but because, as I shall try to show, it is totally unimportant

under any part of the statute with which we have to deal.

The statute of which we have to find the meaning is a criminal statute. The two sections on which the government relies both make certain acts crimes. That is their immediate purpose and that is what they say. It is vain to insist that this is not a criminal proceeding. The words cannot be read one way in a suit which is to end in fine and imprisonment and another way in one which seeks an injunction. The construction which is adopted in this case must be adopted in one or the other sort. I am no friend of artificial interpretations because a statute is of one kind rather than another, but all agree that before a statute is to be taken to punish that which always has been lawful it must express its intent in clear words. So I say we must read the words before us as if the question were whether two small exporting grocers should go to jail. . . .

This act is construed by the government to affect the purchasers of shares in two railroad companies because of the effect it may have, or, if you like, is certain to have, upon the competition of these roads. If such a remote result of the exercise of an ordinary incident of property and personal freedom is enough to make that exercise unlawful, there is hardly any transaction concerning commerce between the states that may not be made a crime by the finding of a jury or a court. The personal ascendancy of one man may be such that it would give to his advice the effect of a command if he owned but a single share in each road. The tendency of his presence in the stockholders' meetings might be certain to prevent competition, and thus his advice, if not his mere existence, become a crime.

I state these general considerations as matters which I should have to take into account before I could agree to affirm the decree appealed from, but I do not need them for my own opinion, because when I read the act I cannot feel sufficient doubt as to the meaning of the words to need to fortify my conclusion by any generalities. Their meaning seems to me plain on their face.

The 1st Section makes "every contract, combination in the form of trust or otherwise, or conspiracy in restraint of trade or commerce among the several states, or with foreign nations" a misdemeanor, punishable by fine, imprisonment, or both. Much trouble is made by substituting other phrases assumed to be equivalent, which then are reasoned from as if they were in the act. The court below argued as if maintaining competition were the expressed object of the act. The act says nothing about competition. I stick to the exact words used.

The words hit two classes of cases, and only two — contracts in restraint of trade and combinations, or conspiracies in restraint of trade, and we have to consider what these respectively are. Contracts in restraint of trade are dealt with and defined by the common law. They are contracts with a stranger to the contractor's business (although in some cases carrying on a similar one) which wholly or partially restrict the freedom of the contractor in carrying on that business as otherwise he would. The objection of the common law to them was primarily on the contractor's own account. The notion of monopoly did not come in unless the contract covered the whole of England. . . .

If the statute applies to this case it must be because the parties, or some of them, have formed, or because the Northern Securities Company is, a combination in restraint of trade among the states, or, what comes to the same thing in my opinion, because the defendants, or some or one of them, are monopolizing or attempting to monopolize some part of the commerce between the states. But the mere reading of those words shows that they are used in a limited and accurate sense. According to popular speech, every concern monopolizes whatever business it does, and if that business is trade between two states, it monopolizes a part of the trade among the states.

Of course, the statute does not forbid that. It does not mean that all business must cease. A single railroad down a narrow valley or through a mountain gorge monopolizes all the railroad transportation through that valley or gorge. Indeed every railroad monopolizes, in a popular sense, the trade of some area. Yet I suppose no one would say that the statute forbids a combination of men into a corporation to build and run such a railroad between the states.

I assume that the Minnesota charter of the Great Northern and the Wisconsin charter of the Northern Pacific both are valid. Suppose that, before either road was built, Minnesota, as part of a system of transportation between the states, had created a railroad company authorized singly to build all the lines in the states now actually built, owned, or controlled by either of the two existing companies. I take it that that charter would have been just as good as the present one, even if the statutes which we are considering had been in force. In whatever sense, it would have created a monopoly the present charter does. It would have been a large one, but the act of Congress makes no discrimination according to size. Size has nothing to do with the matter. A monopoly of "any part" of commerce among the states is unlawful. The supposed company would have owned lines that might have been competing — probably the present one does. But the act of Congress will not be construed to mean the universal disintegration of society into single men, each at war with all the rest, or even the prevention of all further combinations for a common end.

There is a natural feeling that somehow or other the statute meant to strike at combinations great enough to cause just anxiety on the part of those who love their country more than money, while it viewed such little ones as I have supposed with just indifference. This notion, it may be said, somehow breathes from the pores of the act, although it seems to be contradicted in every way by the words in detail. And it has occurred to me that it might be that when a combination reached a certain size it might have attributed to it more of the character of a monopoly merely by virtue of its size than would be attributed to a smaller one. I am quite clear that it is only in connection with monopolies that size could play any part. But my answer has been indicated already.

In the first place, size in the case of railroads is an inevitable incident and if it were an objection under the act, the Great Northern and the Northern Pacific already were too great and encountered the law. In the next place, in the case of railroads it is evident that the size of the combination is reached for other ends than those which would make them monopolies. The combinations are not formed for the purpose of excluding others from the field. Finally, even a small railroad will have the same tendency to exclude others from its narrow area that great ones have to exclude others from a greater one, and the statute attacks the small monopolies as well as the great. The very words of the act make such a distinction impossible in this case, and it has not been attempted in express terms.

If the charter which I have imagined above would have been good notwithstanding the monopoly, in a popular sense, which it created, one next is led to ask whether and why a combination or consolidation of existing roads, although in actual competition, into one company of exactly the same powers and extent, would be any more obnoxious to the law. . . . The monopoly would be the same as if the roads were consolidated after they had begun to compete — and it is on the footing of monopoly that I now am supposing the objection made.

But to meet the objection to the prevention of competition at the same time, I will

suppose that three parties apply to a state for charters; one for each of two new and possibly competing lines respectively, and one for both of these lines, and that the charter is granted to the last. I think that charter would be good, and I think the whole argument to the contrary rests on a popular instead of an accurate and legal conception of what the word "monopolize" in the statute means. I repeat, that in my opinion there is no attempt to monopolize, and what, as I have said, in my judgment amounts to the same thing, that there is no combination in restraint of trade, until something is done with the intent to exclude strangers to the combination from competing with it in some part of the business which it carries on.

Unless I am entirely wrong in my understanding of what a "combination in restraint of trade" means, then the same monopoly may be attempted and effected by an individual, and is made equally illegal in that case by § 2. But I do not expect to hear it maintained that Mr. Morgan could be sent to prison for buying as many shares as he liked of the Great Northern and the Northern Pacific, even if he bought them both at the same time and got more than half the stock of each road. . . .

A partnership is not a contract or combination in restraint of trade between the partners unless the well-known words are to be given a new meaning invented for the purposes of this act. It is true that the suppression of competition was referred to in *United States* v. *Trans-Missouri Freight Association*, 166 U. S. 290, but, as I have said, that was in connection with a contract with a stranger to the defendant's business — a true contract in restraint of trade. To suppress competition in that way is one thing, to suppress it by fusion is another. The law, I repeat, says nothing about competition, and only prevents its suppression by contracts or combinations in restraint of trade, and such contracts or combinations derive their character as restraining trade from other features than the suppression of competition alone.

To see whether I am wrong, the illustrations put in the argument are of use. If I am, then a partnership between two stage drivers who had been competitors in driving across a state line, or two merchants once engaged in rival commerce among the states, whether made after or before the act, if now continued is a crime. For, again I repeat, if the restraint on the freedom of the members of a combination caused by their entering into partnership is a restraint of trade, every such combination, as well the small as the great, is within the act.

In view of my interpretation of the statute, I do not go further into the question of the power of Congress. That has been dealt with by my brother White, and I concur in the main with his views. I am happy to know that only a minority of my brethren adopt an interpretation of the law which in my opinion would make eternal the *bellum omnium contra omnes* and disintegrate society so far as it could into individual atoms. If that were its intent I should regard calling such a law a regulation of commerce as a mere pretense. It would be an attempt to reconstruct society. I am not concerned with the wisdom of such an attempt, but I believe that Congress was not entrusted by the Constitution with the power to make it, and I am deeply persuaded that it has not tried.

122.

Mark Hanna: Socialism and the Labor Unions

In the early years of the century, most businessmen held one of two attitudes toward organized labor. They were either openly hostile and willing to use force to suppress unionization, or they believed in trying to meet some though not all of labor's demands. The National Association of Manufacturers was strongly antilabor, but it used lobbying techniques in Congress, rather than force, to weaken labor unions. The National Civic Federation, another business association, represented the second position. Mark Hanna, a conservative millionaire associated with the federation, believed that respectful treatment of labor leaders, such as Samuel Gompers, would lead to harmonious capital-labor relations. Hanna was instrumental in bringing the obdurate coal owners to the bargaining table in October 1902, during the national anthracite coal strike. In the following selection, taken from a book published in 1904, the year of his death, Hanna discusses socialism in the labor movement.

Source: *Mark Hanna: His Book*, Boston, 1904, pp. 30-45.

It must never be forgotten that organized labor is an older institution than organized capital. The instinct of workingmen to band together to protect themselves is no more to be wondered at than the same instinct when shown on the part of capital. Now, my plan is to have organized union labor Americanized in the best sense and thoroughly educated to an understanding of its responsibilities, and in this way to make it the ally of the capitalist, rather than a foe with which to grapple. . . .

Many of the ills that have crept into labor organizations are importations from older countries and will not live here because they are not fitted to our conditions. While labor unions may have been a curse to England, I believe that they will prove a boon to our own country, when a proper basis of confidence and respect is established. We have, perhaps, been too busy and too engrossed in our rapid expansion to look upon the ethical side of this question, and forgot that two factors contributed to the prosperity of our nation — the man who works with his hands and the man who works with his head — partners in toil who ought to be partners also in the profits of that toil. . . .

The menace of today, as I view it, is the spread of a spirit of socialism, one of those things which is only half understood and is more or less used to inflame the popular mind against all individual initiative and personal energy, which has been the very essence of American progress. While this spirit of socialism has caused apprehension in some quarters, it has been joyfully received by a certain class of people who do not desire to acquire competence in the ordinary and honest manner and gladly seize any excuse for agitating the public mind on the chance of putting money in their own pockets — the men who are described as having "no stake in the country."

My own impression is confirmed by information from laboring men that socialism, in the European sense of the word, will never find a firm footing in America. There is a spirit of cooperation or community of interests which some people may confound with socialism that is making headway with us; but when anyone attempts, for political or financial reasons, to advocate the whole program of European socialism, he will find little prospect of the seed taking root in American soil. This, I think, was demonstrated very conclusively in the Ohio campaign, where higher socialism was brought forth as an issue.

When the people understand this subject in its fullest sense and some of the mysteries and the fascinating glamor connected with the mysterious that now shroud the subject are torn away and it is seen plainly, it will be found to be repellent to American ideas of integrity and honesty. Its objects will be seen to be the very opposite of those desired both by labor and capital, since it gives no aid toward the building up and development of the country, nor does it guarantee each man a chance to make a home for himself. Fairness and justice will never agree to the confiscation of the products of one man's toil in order to insure comfort to the idle and worthless.

The old law of compensation is operative now as ever. No "ism" is wanted by the American people that will take from any citizen the just and equitable reward of his labor. There is always a likelihood of movements of this kind fascinating people who have met with a degree of failure in their own efforts; but it is a shortsighted policy to destroy the fabric of national union in order to promulgate a doctrine the very essence of which is selfishness. I believe a single vigorous campaign of agitation would quickly show what support these doctrines may expect from the American people, as has been proven over and over along these lines. As a general rule, the American people are pretty levelheaded.

Now, I do not mean that those who have taken up socialism should be roundly scored and abused, for a great many of these are honest and sincere in their belief, which belief arises from not really understanding the matter, having been misled by misrepresentation. It is usually said that there are only two sides to a question, but in this matter there are two sides and two ends, and by the time our socialist has surveyed the two sides and the big end and the little one, he will not find that socialism is going to benefit him much in America.

It seems to me more reasonable to take up the difficulties of labor and capital case by case, and situation after situation, as they come up, and try to adjust them in a manner at once permanent and peaceful; in this way the inherent rights of the individual will be better served than by an attempt to demolish a system of government which is so well suited to the needs of the American people and which has so well withstood the attacks of the dreamer and the agitator in the years that are past.

If there is any one superb virtue that the American people possess it is courage in grappling with the issues of the future, and I do not think there will ever be a faltering note in this respect, no matter what the obstacle, no matter what the difficulty may be. But we must get right down to the belief that life is a matter of mutual interest between labor and capital; we cannot separate the two great factors which underlie our development; it is not possible for one to prosper permanently unless the other shares in that prosperity.

There must be a common ground where all can meet with the honest determination to do what is right, meeting bravely the conditions as they change and seizing the opportunity as it offers for the betterment of all the people. The movement already inaugurated among large employers looking toward the utmost comfort and convenience of their employees is not carried out altogether from philanthropic motives but is a matter of business also, and it is one of the most hopeful signs of the times.

This is essentially a great economic age — an age when energy, materials, and purposes are all being utilized for the best. When a man loses his day's work and is compelled to spend that time in absolute idleness, the whole community suffers a loss as well as he, and it is something that is lost forever to the commonwealth; this would be found entirely unnecessary were the honest motives of both sides given proper consideration. And we feel convinced that we have a very great duty to perform in resisting the onslaught of the socialistic tendency which helps to bring this state of affairs into being. Both capital and labor must yield in time to the great law of fair dealing, man to man.

In proportion to a man's ambitions and his ability to earn for himself a betterment of his condition, there will be a striving on his part to attain his ideals, and this, in itself, is the germ of progress; and just as far as that encroaches on others who are working for the same object, there will be a natural resistance. But there are few citizens in this country who would condone any interference with the personal rights of a neighbor. There always will be a neutral ground where conflicting interests can meet and confer and adjust themselves — a sort of Hague tribunal, if you please, in the everyday affairs of life.

The American labor unions are becoming more and more conservative and careful in their management and are not likely to be led away from the straight road by hotheaded members.

Businessmen, too, have found that fighting does not pay in trade. There is an old saying that the best lawyer is he who keeps his client out of lawsuits, and the best leader is he who can avoid difficulties; but the greater experience and intelligence which necessarily exist among employers, owing to the fact of their longer training in the forum of business, places upon them an important responsibility.

I wish I could impress upon every American the individual responsibility that rests upon each one of us. Every year of experience, every dollar of accumulated capital, every talent we possess should be regarded as a sacred charge for the good of the nation, to help in uniting the interests of rich and poor, learned and unlearned.

123.

Robert Hunter: Ten Million in Poverty

The modern view of poverty is one result of the emergence in the 1890s of a group of highly articulate social workers who investigated the actual living conditions of the poor and reached conclusions about its causes very different from those popular a generation before. Jane Addams of Hull House in Chicago, Lillian Wald at the Henry Street Settlement in New York City, and Robert Hunter, a New York settlement worker, were but three who declared that it was social and economic conditions, not individual weakness, that produced poverty. Hunter wrote a book on the subject that expressed many of the professional social worker's views. A portion of its concluding chapter is reprinted here.

Source: *Poverty*, New York, 1904, pp. 318-340.

We are perhaps too prone to think of those in poverty as effortless beings who make no fight for themselves and wait in misery until someone comes to assist them. Such an opinion is without any foundation. It is based upon knowledge gained by acquaintance with the pauper and vagrant, and is in nowise applicable to the workers in poverty. It is small wonder that workers who are underfed, underclothed, and poorly housed are sometimes won from their hard and almost hopeless toil by sensual pleasures. Nor is it surprising that they are driven to despair by the brutal power of the economic forces which dominate their lives.

Without the security which comes only with the ownership of property, without a home from which they may not be evicted, without any assurance of regular employment, without tools with which they may employ themselves, they are pathetically dependent upon their physical efficiency — their health and strength — and upon the activity of machinery, owned by others, and worked or left idle as the owners consider it wise or profitable. In their weak and unorganized condition, they are unlike the skilled workers, made powerful by their unions and by their methods of collective bargaining; they are fighting alone, each one against another. . . .

Having been drawn, about twelve years ago, to some interest in the problems of poverty, there happened to me the common experience of all those of like interests. The poor in the broader sense of that word were busily at work and trying rather to conceal than to make evidence of their poverty; while the beggars, vagrants, idlers, and dependents of all sorts were more or less always pressing forward their necessities. It was natural, therefore, for me to confuse the problem of poverty with that of pauperism and to take up with some enthusiasm the ideas which are a part of the propaganda of many useful charitable organizations. To the charitable workers these problems of vagrancy and pauperism seem possible of solution.

Many reforms — among which wise giving, friendly visiting, workrooms, work tests, model lodging houses, rent collecting, etc., are a few — were, in the early '90s, making rapid headway. They were, at that time, ranked first in importance in the category of organized movements for diminishing the evils of pauperism. Many committees were at work promoting these reforms, and in different cities I was able to help in their efforts. The result of their work was not discouraging, but in every instance they came hard up against one almost insurmountable obstacle.

The pauper and the vagrant were not dissatisfied; they clamored for alms, but they did not wish to alter their way of living. Even those who possessed the capacity for industrial usefulness and who might have become self-supporting did not wish to go back again into the factories, mills, or mines. In fact, so far as one could see, they were as unwilling as the others to alter their ways of living. However miserable their lot seemed to those of us on the committees, to them it seemed to be, on the whole, acceptable enough to bring a certain sort of content. However malarious and poisonous and undrained, they loved their valley of idleness and quiet; they hated the hill upon which they were constrained to toil; they shrank from its disappointments, its bruises, its weariness and bitterness, while its meanness and ugliness of life were but slightly less mean and ugly than their own.

The children, bred into the ways of pauperism, nearly always took up the vices of their parents. They were pleasure loving, and whatever was toilsome seemed abhorrent to them. The girls took the easier path; it appeared unquestionably more desirable to their childish standards, and for a time at least it gave them more of everything, for which most human beings seem to hunger — finery, leisure, and a kind of pleasure. The men and boys liked vagrancy, and those who were not attracted to these ways settled down into a satisfied, imperturbable

pauperism. They lived in God only knows what misery. They ate when there were things to eat; they starved when there was lack of food. But, on the whole, although they swore and beat each other and got drunk, they were more contented than any other class I have happened to know.

It took a long time to understand them. Our committees were busy from morning until night in giving them opportunities to take up the fight again and to become independent of relief. They always took what we gave them; they always promised to try; but as soon as we expected them to fulfill any promises, they gave up in despair, and either wept or looked ashamed, and took to misery and drink again — almost, so it seemed to me at times, with a sense of relief.

I am reminded now of a vagrant whom I knew well and for many years believed to be sincerely trying to become "a man," as we used to say. He has turned up wherever I have happened to be — in Chicago or New York. He has always looked me up, and together we have conspired to overcome his vagrant instincts. We have always failed, and, after a few weeks' work, Jerry disappears, and I know what has become of him. At last, in his case as in many others, I have become convinced that he is more satisfied and content with the life of a vagrant than with the miserable lot of an unskilled, underpaid workman.

But as long as one works with, or observes only, the dependent classes, the true, or at least what seems to me the true, explanation of this apparent satisfaction of vagrants and paupers remains in the dark. It was not until I had lived for several years among the toilers in a great industrial community that the reason for the content of the dependent classes became clear to me. In this community of workers, several thousand human beings were struggling fiercely against want. Day after day, year after year, they toiled with marvelous persistency and perseverance. Obnoxious as the simile is, they worked from dawn until nightfall, or from sunset until dawn, like galley slaves under the sting of want and under the whip of hunger. On cold, rainy mornings, at the dusk of dawn, I have been awakened, two hours before my rising time, by the monotonous clatter of hobnailed boots on the plank sidewalks as the procession to the factory passed under my window. Heavy, brooding men; tired, anxious women; thinly dressed, unkempt little girls; and frail, joyless little lads passed along, half-awake, not one uttering a word as they hurried to the great factory. From all directions, thousands were entering the various gates — children of every nation of Europe.

Hundreds of others — obviously a hungrier, poorer lot than those entering the gates, some were most ragged and almost shoeless, but all with eager faces — waited in front of a closed gate, until finally a great red-bearded man came out and selected twenty-three of the strongest, best-looking of the men. For these the gates were opened, and the others, with downcast eyes, marched off to seek employment elsewhere or to sit at home, or in a saloon, or in a lodging house, until the following morning, when they came wistfully again to some factory gate.

In this community, the saddest in which I have ever lived, fully 50,000 men, women, and children were all the time either in poverty or on the verge of poverty. It would not be possible to describe how they worked and starved and ached to rise out of it. They broke their health down; the men acquired in this particular trade a painful and disabling rheumatism, and consumption was very common. The girls and boys followed in the paths of their parents. The wages were so low that the men alone often could not support their families, and mothers with babies toiled in order to add to the income. They gave up all thought of joyful living, probably in the hope that by

tremendous exertion they could overcome their poverty; but they gained while at work only enough to keep their bodies alive. Theirs was a sort of treadmill existence with no prospect of anything else in life but more treadmill. When they were not given work in the mill, they starved; and when they grew desperate, they came to my office and asked for charity.

Here was a mass of men whose ways of living were violently opposed to those of the vagrant or the pauper. They were distorting themselves in the struggle to be independent of charity and to overcome poverty. That they hated charity must be taken without question. The testimony of scores of men is proof of it, even if, indeed, their very lives were not. But, despite all their efforts, they lived in houses but little, if any, better than those of the paupers; they were almost as poorly dressed; they were hardly better fed.

In other words, these men, women, and children were, to my mind, struggling up the face of a barren precipice . . . sometimes in hope, sometimes in despair, yet bitterly determined; the abyss of vice, crime, pauperism, and vagrancy was beneath them, a tiny ray of hope above them. Flitting before them was the leopard, persistently trying to win them from their almost hopeless task by charms of sensuality, debauch, and idleness. The lion, predatory and brutal, threatened to devour them; the she-wolf (Greed), hungry for them, enriched herself by their labors. Some were won from their toil by sensual pleasures, some were torn from their footholds by economic disorders, others were too weak and hungry to keep up the fight, and still others were rendered incapable of further struggle by diseases resulting from the unnecessary evils of work or of living. . . .

However merciful and kind and valuable the works of the charitable and the efforts of those who would raise up again the pauper and the vagrant, they are not remedial.

Insofar as the work of the charitable is devoted to reclamation and not to prevention, it is a failure. Not that anyone could wish that less were done in the direction of reclamation. The fact only is important that effort is less powerful there than in overcoming the forces which undermine the workers and those who are struggling against insurmountable difficulties. It is an almost hopeless task to regenerate the degenerate, especially when, if the latter are to succeed, they must be made to take up again the battle with those very destructive forces which are all the time undermining stronger, more capable, and more self-reliant men than they.

The all-necessary work to be done is not so much to reclaim a class which social forces are ever active in producing, as it is to battle with the social or economic forces which are continuously producing recruits to that class. The forces producing the miseries of pauperism and vagrancy are many, but none are so important as those conditions of work and of living which are so unjust and degrading that men are driven by them into degeneracy. When the uncertainties, hardships, trials, sorrows, and miseries of a self-supporting existence become so painful that good, strong, self-reliant men and women are forced into pauperism, then there is but little use in trying to force the paupers and the vagrants back into the struggle.

It is not necessary to debate the relative importance of individual or social forces, or of heredity or environment upon the extent of poverty in order to prove that social forces are constantly and everywhere active in bringing poverty to a great mass of people. Leaving all such questions out of the discussion, we can nevertheless be certain that obstacles can be too great for even the strongest of men to overcome. And this is almost precisely what happens to the masses in poverty.

As a class they have the longest hours of work, they have the lowest pay — often not even living wages; they have competition of the severest kind to face — unskilled workers from every land come to seek their employment; they are oppressed by sweating methods, their employment is irregular; their tenements are the most unsanitary, and their rents relatively the highest that any class pay; the prices for food and fuel are exorbitant because they must buy in small quantities; when they find it necessary to go into debt they are fleeced by loan sharks; they are most often ill; they bear the burden of more deaths than any other class; and, being without savings, they are in actual distress as soon as they are unable to work, or as soon as they are unemployed as a result of economic or other causes.

Furthermore, the children are prevented from having fair opportunities to master the difficulties which ruined their fathers. Their health is imperiled and not seldom destroyed by unsanitary homes; they are injured morally and otherwise by a *necessary* street life; their food is in many cases so poor that it will not feed the brain, and they are consequently unable to learn; they are early pressed to do a man's labor and are often ruined physically and blighted in other ways by this early and unnatural toil. With all of these and many other obstacles and disadvantages working their ruin, only the strongest and most fortunate are able to put forth the struggle necessary to master their fate. For the others, their life's course lies up an almost baffling precipice. . . .

There are probably, in fairly prosperous years, no less than 10 million persons in poverty; that is to say, underfed, underclothed, and poorly housed. Of these, about 4 million persons are public paupers. Over 2 million workingmen are unemployed from four to six months in the year. About 500,000 male immigrants arrive yearly and seek work in the very districts where unemployment is greatest. Nearly half of the families in the country are propertyless.

Over 1,700,000 little children are forced to become wage earners when they should still be in school. About 5 million women find it necessary to work, and about 2 million are employed in factories, mills, etc. Probably no less than 1 million workers are injured or killed each year while doing their work, and about 10 million of the persons now living will, if the present ratio is kept up, die of the preventable disease, tuberculosis.

We know that many workmen are overworked and underpaid. We know in a general way that unnecessary disease is far too prevalent. We know some of the unsanitary evils of tenements and factories; we know of the neglect of the street child, the aged, the infirm, the crippled. Furthermore, we are beginning to realize the monstrous injustice of compelling those who are unemployed, who are injured in industry, who have acquired diseases due to their occupation, or who have been made widows or orphans by industrial accidents to become paupers in order that they may be housed, fed, and clothed. Something is known concerning these problems of poverty, and some of them at least are possible of remedy.

To deal with these specific problems, I have elsewhere mentioned some reforms which seem to me preventive in their nature. They contemplate mainly such legislative action as may enforce upon the entire country certain minimum standards of working and of living conditions. They would make all tenements and factories sanitary; they would regulate the hours of work, especially for women and children; they would regulate and thoroughly supervise dangerous trades; they would institute all necessary measures to stamp out unnecessary disease and to prevent unnecessary death; they would prohibit entirely child labor; they would institute all necessary edu-

cational and recreational institutions to replace the social and educational losses of the home and the domestic workshop; they would perfect, as far as possible, legislation and institutions to make industry pay the necessary and legitimate cost of producing and maintaining efficient laborers. They would institute, on the lines of foreign experience, measures to compensate labor for enforced seasons of idleness, due to sickness, old age, lack of work, or other causes beyond the control of the workman; they would prevent parasitism on the part of either the consumer or the producer and charge up the full costs of labor in production to the beneficiary, instead of compelling the worker at certain times to enforce his demand for maintenance through the tax rate and by becoming a pauper; they would restrict the power of employer and of shipowner to stimulate for purely selfish ends an excessive immigration, and in this way to beat down wages and to increase unemployment.

Reforms such as these are not ones which will destroy incentive, but rather they will increase incentive by more nearly equalizing opportunity. They will make propertied interests less predatory, and sensuality, by contrast with misery, less attractive to the poor. . . .

This does not mean that there is to be no struggle . . . but rather that the life of the poorest toiler shall not be a hopeless thing from which many must turn in despair. In other words, the process of Justice is to lift stony barriers against which the noblest beat their brains out, and from which the ignoble (but who shall say not more sensible?) turn away in despair. Let it be this, rather than a barren relief system, administered by those who must stand by, watching the struggle, lifting no hand to aid the toilers, but ever succoring those who flee and those who are bruised and beaten.

124.

Hugo Münsterberg: The American Passion for Money Explained

Hugo Münsterberg, a German psychologist, came to America as a professor at Harvard University in 1897 and, like so many visitors before him, published a book about the country. The Americans, which appeared in 1904 and from which the following selection is taken, contained observations on America's political institutions, its economy, and its popular culture. Münsterberg was particularly interested in the American character, and in a chapter titled "The Spirit of Self-Initiative," he defended the proposition that Americans were not really greedy materialists, as many European critics maintained, but were instead the world's greatest idealists.

Source: *The Americans,* translated by Edwin B. Holt, New York, 1905, pp. 229-254.

ONE WHO WISHES TO UNDERSTAND the almost fabulous economic development of the United States must, indeed, not simply consider its ore deposits and gold mines, its coal- and oilfields, its wheatlands and cotton districts, its great forests and the supplies of water. The South Americans live no less in a country prospered by nature, and so also do the Chinese. South Africa offers entirely similar conditions to those of the North American continent, and yet its development has been a very different one; and, finally, a consideration of the peculiar forms of American industrial organization, as, for instance, the trusts, reveals merely symptoms and not the real causes which have been at work.

The colossal industrial successes, along with the great evils and dangers which have come with them, must be understood from the makeup of the American character. . . . The pressure to be up and doing has opened the earth, tilled the fields, created industries, and developed such technical skill as today may even dream of dominating the world.

But to grant that the essentials of such movements are not to be found in casual external circumstances, but must lie in the mental makeup of the nation, might lead in this case to ascribing the chief influence to quite a different mental trait. The average European, permeated as he is with Old World culture, is, in fact, convinced that this intense economic activity is the simple result of unbounded greed. The search for gold and the pursuit of the dollar, we often hear, have destroyed in the American soul every finer ambition; and since the American has no higher desire for culture, he is free to chase his Mammon with undisguised and shameless greed. The barbarity of his soul, it is said, gives him a considerable economic advantage over others who have some heart as well as a pocketbook and whose feelings incline to the humane.

Whether such a contemptuous allegation is a useful weapon in the economic struggle is not here in question. One who desires to understand the historical development of events in the New World is bound to see in all such talk nothing but distortion and to realize that Europe could face its own economic future with less apprehension if it would estimate the powers of its great competitor more temperately and justly, and would ask itself honestly if it could not learn a thing or two here and there.

Merely to ape American doings would, in the end, avail nothing; that which proceeds from intellectual and temperamental traits can be effectively adopted by others only if they can acquire the same traits. It is useless to organize similar factories or trusts without imitating in every respect the men who first so organized themselves. Whether this last is necessary, he alone can say who has understood his neighbors at their best and has not been contented to make a merely thoughtless and uncharitable judgment.

A magnificent economic life such as that of America can never spring from impure ethical motives, and the person is very naïve who supposes that a great business was ever built up by mere impudence, deception, and advertising. Every merchant knows that even advertisements benefit only a solid business, and that they run a bad one into the ground. And it is still more naïve to suppose that the economic strength of America has been built up through underhanded competition without respect to law or justice, and impelled by nothing but a barbarous and purely material ambition. One might better believe that the twenty-story office buildings on Lower Broadway are supported merely by the flagstones in the street; in point of fact, no mere passerby who does not actually see the foundations of such colossal structures can have an idea of how deep down under the soil these foundations go in order to find bedrock. Just so the colossal fabric of American industry is able to tower so high only because it has its foundation on the hard rock of honest conviction.

In the first place, we might look into the American's greed for gold. A German observes immediately that the American does not prize his possessions much unless he has worked for them himself; of this there are innumerable proofs, in spite of the opposite appearances on the surface. One of the most interesting of these is the absence of the bridal dower. . . . Even when the parents of the bride are prosperous, it is unusual for a young couple to live beyond the means of the husband. Everywhere one sees the daughters of wealthy families stepping into the modest homes of their husbands, and these husbands would feel it to be a disgrace to depend on their prosperous fathers-in-law. An actual dowry received from the bride's parents during their lifetime is virtually unknown.

Another instance of American contempt for unearned wealth, which especially contrasts with European customs, is the disapproval which the American always has for lotteries. If he were really bent on getting money, he would find the dower and the lottery a ready means; whereas, in fact, the lottery is not only in all its forms forbidden by law but public opinion wholly disapproves of games of chance. The president of Harvard University, in a public address given a short time since, in which he spoke before a large audience of the change in moral attitude, was able to give a striking illustration of the transformation in the fact that two generations ago the city of Boston conducted a lottery in order to raise money for rebuilding a university structure which had been destroyed by fire. He showed vividly how such a transaction would be entirely unthinkable today, and how all American feelings would revolt at raising money for so good a cause as an educational institution by so immoral a means as a public lottery. The entire audience received this as a matter of course, apparently without a suspicion as to how many cathedrals are being built in Europe today from tickets at half a dollar.

It was amusing to observe how Carnegie's friend Schwab, who had been the greatly admired manager of the steelworks, fell in public esteem when news came from the Riviera that he was to be seen at the gaming tables of Monaco. The true American despises anyone who gets money without working for it. Money is not the thing which is considered, but the manner of getting it. This is what the American cares for, and he prizes the gold he gets primarily as an indication of his ability.

At first sight it looks as if this disinclination to gambling were not to be taken seriously. It would signify nothing that the police discover here and there a company of gamblers who have barricaded the door; but a European might say that there is another sort of speculative fever which is very prevalent. Even Americans on the Stock Exchange often say, with a smile: We are a gambling nation; and from the point of view of the broker it would be so. He sees how all classes of people invest in speculative securities, and how the public interests itself in shares which are subject to the greatest fluctuations; how the cab driver and the hotel waiter pore nervously over the quotations, and how new mining stocks and industrial shares are greedily bought by schoolteachers and commercial clerks. The broker sees in this the people's desire for gambling, because he is himself thoroughly aware of the great risks which are taken and knows that the investors can see only a few of the factors which determine prices.

But in the public mind all this buying and selling looks very different. The small man, investing a few dollars in such doubtful certificates, never thinks of himself as a gambler; he thinks that he understands the market; he is not trusting to luck, but follows the quotations day by day for a long time and asks his friends for "tips," until he is convinced that his own discretion and cunning will give him an advantage. If he were to think of his gain as matter of chance, as the broker thinks it is, he would not only not invest his money but would be no longer attracted by the transactions. And whenever he loses, he still goes on, believing that he will be able the next time to figure out the turn of the market more accurately.

The same is true of the wagers which the Anglo-Saxon is always making because he loves excitement. For him a wager is not a true wager when it is merely a question of chance. Both sides make calculations and have their special considerations which they believe will determine the outcome, and the winner feels his gain to be earned by his shrewdness. An ordinary game of chance does not attract the American, a fact which may be seen even in the grotesque game of poker. In a certain sense, the American's aversion to tipping servants reveals, perhaps, the same trait. The social inferiority which he feels to be implied in the acceptance of a fee goes against the self-respect of the individual; but there is the additional disinclination here to receiving money which is not strictly earned.

There are positive traits corresponding to these negative ones; and especially among them may be noticed the use to which money is put after it is gotten. If the American were really miserly, he would not distribute his property with such a free hand. Getting money excites him, but keeping it is less interesting, and one sees not seldom the richest men taking elaborate precautions that only a small part of their money shall fall to their children, because they think that the possession of money which is not self-earned is not a blessing. From these motives one may understand at once the magnificent generosity shown toward public enterprises.

Public munificence cannot well be gauged by statistics, and especially not in America. Most of the gifts are made quietly, and of course the small gifts which are never heard about outweigh the larger ones; and, nevertheless, one can have a fair idea of American generosity by considering only the large gifts made for public ends. If we consider only the gifts of money which are greater than $1,000, and which go to public institutions, we have in the year 1903 the pretty sum of $76,935,000. There can be no doubt that all the gifts under $1,000 would make an equal sum. . . .

One sees clearly, again, that the real attraction which the American feels for moneymaking does not lie in the having but only in the getting, from the perfect equanimity, positively amazing to the European, with which he bears his losses. To be sure, his irrepressible optimism stands him in good stead; he never loses hope, but is confident that what he has lost will soon be made up. But this would be no comfort to him if he did not care much less for the possession than for the getting of it. The American chases after money with all his might, exactly as on the tennis court he tries to hit the ball, and it is the game he likes and not the prize. If he loses he does not feel as if he had lost a part of himself, but only as if he had lost the last set in a tournament.

When, a short time ago, there was a terrific crash in the New York stock market and hundreds of millions were lost, a leading Parisian paper said: "If such a financial crisis had happened here in France, we should have had panics, catastrophes, a slump in *rentes,* suicides, street riots, a ministerial crisis, all in one day; while America is perfectly quiet, and the victims of the battle are sitting down to collect their wits. France and the United States are obviously two entirely different worlds in their civilization and in their way of thinking."

As to the estimation of money and its acquirement, France and the United States are indeed as far apart as possible, while Germany stands in between. The Frenchman prizes money as such; if he can get it without labor, by inheritance or dowry, or by gambling, so much the better. If he loses it, he loses a part of himself; and when he has earned enough to be sure of a livelihood, he retires from moneymaking pursuits as soon as possible.

It is well known that the ambition of the average Frenchman is to be a *rentier.* The American has exactly the opposite idea. Not only does he endure loss with indifference and despise gain which is not earned, but he would not for any price give up the oc-

cupation of making money. Whether he has much or little, he keeps patiently at work; and, as no scholar or artist would ever think of saying that he had done enough work, and would from now on become a scientific or literary *rentier* and live on his reputation, so no American, as long as he keeps his health, thinks of giving up his regular business.

The profession of living from the income of investments is virtually unknown among men, and the young men who take up no moneymaking profession because they "don't need to" are able to retain the social respect of their fellows only by undertaking some sort of work for the commonwealth. A man who does not work at anything, no matter how rich he is, can neither get nor keep a social status.

This also indicates, then, that the American does not want his money merely as a means for material comfort. Of course, wealthy Americans are becoming more and more accustomed to provide every thinkable luxury for their wives and daughters. Nowhere is so much expended for dresses, jewelry, equipages and service, for country houses and yachts, works of art and private libraries; and many men have to keep pretty steadily at work year in and year out in order to meet their heavy expenditures. And the same thing is repeated all down the social scale. According to European standards, even the workingman lives luxuriously. But, in spite of this, no person who has really come into the country will deny that material pleasures are less sought after for themselves in the New World than in the Old.

It always strikes the European as remarkable how very industrious American society is and how relatively little bent on pleasure. It has often been said that the American has not yet learned how to enjoy life; that he knows very well how to make money but not how to enjoy it. And that is quite true; except that it leaves out of account the main point — which is, that the American takes the keenest delight in the employment of all his faculties in his work and in the exercise of his own initiative. This gives him more pleasure than the spending of money could bring him.

It is, therefore, fundamentally false to stigmatize the American as a materialist and to deny his idealism. A people is supposed to be thoroughly materialistic when its sphere of interests comprises problems relating only to the world of matter, and fancies itself to be highly idealistic when it is mainly concerned with intangible objects. . . . But it is merely play on words to call nations realistic or idealistic on the strength of these metaphysical conceptions, instead of using the words in their social and ethical significations. . . .

This is the main point: The economic life means to the American a realizing of efforts which are in themselves precious. It is not the means to an end, but is its own end. If two blades of grass grow where one grew before, or two railroad tracks where there was but one; if production, exchange, and commerce increase and undertaking thrives, then life is created, and this is, in itself, a precious thing. The European of the Continent esteems the industrial life as honest but not as noble; economic activities seem to him good for supporting himself and his family, but his duty is merely to supply economic needs which are now existing. . . .

A nation can never do its best in any direction unless it believes thoroughly in the intrinsic value of its work; whatever is done merely through necessity is never of great national significance, and second-rate men never achieve the highest things. If the first minds of a nation look down with contempt on economic life, if there is no real belief in the ideal value of industry, and if creative minds hold aloof from it, that nation will necessarily be outdone by others in the economic field. But where the ablest strength engages with idealistic enthusiasm in the service of the national economic problems, the nation rewards what the

people do as done in the name of civilization, and the love of fame and work together spur them on more than the material gain which they will get. Indeed, this gain is itself only their measure of success in the service of civilization.

The American merchant works for money in exactly the sense that a great painter works for money; the high price which is paid for his picture is a very welcome indication of the general appreciation of his art; but he would never get this appreciation if he were working for the money instead of his artistic ideals. Economically, to open up this gigantic country, to bring the fields and forests, rivers and mountains into the service of economic progress, to incite the millions of inhabitants to have new needs and to satisfy these by their own resourcefulness, to increase the wealth of the nation, and, finally, economically, to rule the world and within the nation itself to raise the economic power of the individual to undreamed-of importance, has been the work which has fascinated the American. And every individual has felt his cooperation to be ennobled by his firm belief in the value of such an aim for the culture of the world. . . .

The spirit of self-initiative does not know pettiness. . . . The boundless prairies and towering mountains which the pioneers saw before them inspired them to undertake great things and to overlook small hindrances, and in laying out their first plans to overlook small details. American captains of industry often say that they purposely pay no attention to a good many European methods because they find such pedantic endeavor to economize and to achieve minute perfections to be wasteful of time and unprofitable.

The same spirit is found, as well, in fields other than the industrial. When the American travels he prefers to pay out round sums rather than to haggle over the price of things, even although he pays considerably more thereby than he otherwise would. And nothing makes him more angry than to find that instead of stating a high price at the outset, the person with whom he is dealing ekes out his profit by small additional charges. This large point of view involves such a contempt of petty detail as to astonish Europeans. Machines costing hundreds of thousands of dollars, which were new yesterday, are discarded today because some improvement has been discovered; and the best is everywhere found none too good to be used in this magnificent industrial system. If the outlay is to correspond to the result, there must be no parsimony.

A similar trait is revealed in the way in which every man behaves toward his neighbor. It is only the petty man who is envious, and envy is a word which is not found in the American vocabulary. If one's own advantage is not the goal, but general economic progress, then the success of another man is almost as great a pleasure as one's own success. It is for the American an aesthetic delight to observe, and in spirit to cooperate with, economic progress all along the line; and the more others accomplish, the more each one realizes the magnificence of the whole industrial life.

Men try to excel one another, as they have to do wherever there is free competition; and such rivalry is the best and surest condition for economic progress. Americans use every means in their power to succeed, but if another man comes out ahead they neither grumble nor indulge in envy, but rather gather their strength for a new effort. Even this economic struggle is carried on in the spirit of sport. The fight itself is the pleasure. The chess player who is checkmated in an exciting game is not sorry that he played and does not envy the winner.

125.

Theodore Roosevelt: No Empire Without a Navy

The global involvement of the United States following the Spanish-American War had greatly expanded the nation's commerce. President Roosevelt, convinced that protection of America's international interests required a powerful and efficient navy, recommended its expansion in the Congress of 1903-1904. Unexpected opposition to Roosevelt came from some influential fellow Republicans, including Representative Theodore Burton of Ohio, who spoke in Congress on February 22, 1904, against the naval program. Roosevelt replied to Burton on February 23 with the letter reprinted here.

Source: Papers of Theodore Roosevelt, Manuscript Division, Library of Congress, pp. 461-464.

My Dear Mr. Burton:

I respect your character and ability so highly and believe so in your power for good, and therefore, as a corollary, in your power for evil if it is misused, and I am so confident in your good judgment, that I write you a word in reference to your speech on the Navy.

As you can imagine, this speech was a genuine shock to me. To have Mr. Gorman and Mr. Williams advocate policies which, if carried out, mean jeopardy to the nation's interests and honor is what we must expect; but that you should take what seems to me such a course is a matter of grave concern.

Let me point out very briefly what I regard as the fundamental error in the position of those who now wish to stop our building up the Navy, and who nevertheless belong to the Republican Party. The one unforgivable crime is to put oneself in a position in which strength and courage are needed and then to show lack of strength and courage. This is precisely the crime committed by those who advocate or have acquiesced in the acquisition of the Philippines, the establishment of naval stations in Cuba, the negotiation of the treaty for building the Panama Canal, the taking of Puerto Rico and Hawaii, and the assertion of the Monroe Doctrine; and who nevertheless decline to advocate the building of a navy such as will alone warrant our attitude in any one, not to say all, of these matters.

It is perfectly allowable, although I think rather ignoble, to take the attitude that this country is to occupy a position in the New World analogous to that of China in the Old World, to stay entirely within her borders, not to endeavor to assert the Monroe Doctrine, incidentally to leave the Philippines, to abandon the care of the Panama Canal, to give up Hawaii and Puerto Rico, etc., etc., and therefore to refuse to build up any navy. It is also allowable, and as I think, in the highest degree far-sighted and honorable, to insist that the attitude of the Republican Party in all these matters during the last eight years has been the wise and proper attitude, and to insist therefore that the Navy shall be kept up and built up as required by the needs of such an attitude. But any attempt to combine the two attitudes is fraught with the certainty of hopeless and ignominious disaster to the nation. To be rich, aggressive, and yet helpless in war, is to invite destruction.

If everything that the Republican Party has done during the past eight years is all wrong; if we ought not to have annexed Hawaii, or taken the Philippines, or established a kind of protectorate over Cuba, or started to build the Panama Canal, then let us reverse these policies and give up building a navy; but to my mind it is to inflict a great wrong on the generations who come after us if we persevere in these policies and do not back them up by building a navy.

Mr. Williams, for instance, is against the fortification of Subic Bay. He affects to regard the fortification of Subic Bay as a menace to the independence of the Philippines, with which it has nothing in the world to do. I do not know how much his attitude is due to sheer ignorance, or unwillingness, or inability to think things out, or how much it is mere affectation. Of course, in any event, for him, coming from a state where his party supremacy and his own political success rest wholly and exclusively on the basis of governing the majority of his fellow citizens, who happen to have different colored skins, without their consent, it is hypocritical and base to make the false plea that he does for the Filipinos.

An honest but misguided enthusiast can make such a plea and retain his self-respect, when it is known that at home he is equally sincere in insisting that all men, of whatever race, however incompetent, shall have equal chances to govern themselves. But for a man by his life and by every act which gratifies his own ambitions at home to prove the negation of what he asserts in reference to people abroad is even more base than it is foolish. Without regard to this, however, Mr. Williams' attitude about Subic Bay is monstrous in view of what we have seen happen before our eyes to the Russians at Port Arthur because of their unpreparedness.

If we are to have a naval station in the Philippines; if we are to have a fleet in Asiatic waters, or to exert the slightest influence in eastern Asia where our people hope to find a market, then it is of the highest importance that we have a naval station at Subic Bay. If we are not to have that station, and are not to have a navy, then we should be manly enough to say that we intend to abandon the Philippines at once; not to try to keep a naval station there; and not to try to exercise that influence in foreign affairs which comes only to the just man armed who wishes to keep the peace.

China is now the sport and plaything of stronger powers because she has constantly acted on her belief in despising and making little of military strength afloat or ashore, and is therefore powerless to keep order within or repel aggression from without. The little powers of Europe, although in many cases they lead honorable and self-respecting national lives, are powerless to accomplish any great good in foreign affairs, simply and solely because they lack the element of force behind their good wishes.

We, on the contrary, have been able to do so much for The Hague tribunal and for the cause of international arbitration; we have been able to keep the peace in the waters south of us; to put an end to bloody misrule and bloody civil strife in Cuba, in the Philippines, and at Panama; and we are able to exercise a pacific influence in China, because, and only because, together with the purpose to be just and to keep the peace, we possess a navy which makes it evident that we will not tamely submit to injustice or tamely acquiesce in breaking the peace.

This letter is for you personally. I write it because I respect you and like you.

126.

ANDREW B. STERLING: "Meet Me in St. Louis, Louis"

The centenary of the Louisiana Purchase occurred in 1904, and it was celebrated by an international exposition held at St. Louis. The official song of the fair was "Meet Me in St. Louis, Louis," the idea for which lyricist Andrew B. Sterling reputedly had while sitting in a Broadway café. A customer asked a waiter, whose name was Louis, for a glass of St. Louis beer. "Another Louis, Louis!" the customer called out, whereupon Sterling, struck by the rhythm of the phrase, wrote down the words of the song. Millions sang it at the fair in 1904, and it was revived by Judy Garland in the movie Meet Me in St. Louis *in 1944.*

MEET ME IN ST. LOUIS, LOUIS

When Louis came home to the flat,
He hung up his coat and his hat.
He gazed all around, but no wifey he found,
So he said, "Where can Flossie be at?"
A note on the table he spied,
He read it just once, then he cried.
It ran: "Louis, dear, it's too slow for me here,
So I think I will go for a ride.

"Meet me in St. Louis, Louis,
Meet me at the fair,
Don't tell me the lights are shining
Any place but there.
We will dance the Hoochee Koochee,
I will be your tootsie wootsie,
If you will meet me in St. Louis, Louis,
Meet me at the fair."

The dresses that hung in the hall
Were gone; she had taken them all.
She took all his rings and the rest of his things;
The picture he missed from the wall.
"What! moving?" the janitor said,
"Your rent is paid three months ahead."
"What good is the flat?" said poor Louis. "Read that."
And the janitor smiled as he read:

"Meet me in St. Louis, Louis,
Meet me at the fair,
Don't tell me the lights are shining
Any place but there.
We will dance the Hoochee Koochee,
I will be your tootsie wootsie,
If you will meet me in St. Louis, Louis,
Meet me at the fair."

Index of Authors

*The numbers in brackets
indicate selection numbers
in this volume.*

ABBOTT, LYMAN (Dec. 18, 1835-Oct. 22, 1922), Congregational clergyman, author, and editor. Edited (1876-1922) *Christian Union* (from 1893 *The Outlook*); pastor (1888-99) of Plymouth Congregational Church, Brooklyn; wrote *The Spirit of Democracy* (1910). **[94]**

ADAMS, BROOKS, (June 24, 1848-Feb. 13, 1927), lawyer and historian. Son of Charles Francis Adams and brother of Henry Adams; wrote *Law of Civilization and Decay* (1895), *America's Economic Supremacy* (1900), *The New Empire* (1902), *The Theory of Social Revolutions* (1913). **[89]**

ADDAMS, JANE (Sept. 6, 1860-May 21, 1935), social reformer. Founder and first director (1889-1935) of Hull House, a pioneer social settlement house in Chicago; president (1919) of the Women's International League for Peace and Freedom; received Nobel Peace Prize (1931); wrote *Democracy and Social Ethics* (1902), *Twenty Years at Hull House* (1910). **[29, 103]**

ADE, GEORGE (Feb. 9, 1866-May 16, 1944), author, playwright, and humorist. Wrote *Fables in Slang* (in series, from 1899), *The Old Time Saloon* (1931), and plays including *The College Widow* (1904). **[78]**

ANTHONY, SUSAN B. (Feb. 15, 1820-March 13, 1906), social reformer. Agent (1856-61) of the American Anti-Slavery Society; published (1868-70) the liberal weekly, *The Revolution;* organized and led (1869-90) the National Woman Suffrage Association; president (1890-1906) of the National American Woman Suffrage Association. **[32]**

BAER, GEORGE F. (Sept. 26, 1842-April 26, 1914), lawyer and industrialist. President (from 1901) of the Philadelphia and Reading Railway; led resistance to the United Mine Workers of America in the anthracite strike of 1902. **[98]**

BARNETT, IDA B. WELLS (fl. 1901), social reformer. Editor (*c.* 1892) of the *Memphis Free Press;* on the staff of *Chicago Conservator;* chairman (*c.* 1901) of the Anti-Lynching Bureau of the National Afro-American Council. **[88]**

BATES, KATHARINE LEE (Aug. 12, 1859-March 28, 1929), educator, author, and poetess. Professor of English (1891-1925) at Wellesley College; wrote several volumes of poetry, including U.S. national hymn, "America the Beautiful" (1911). **[1]**

BENNETT, HENRY HOLCOMB (Dec. 5, 1863-April 30, 1924), writer. Author of military stories and of illustrated articles on birds; watercolorist; wrote articles on National Guard (1898-99), stories of army life (1898-1901). **[44]**

BEVERIDGE, ALBERT J. (Oct. 6, 1862-April 27, 1927), historian, political leader, and public official. U.S. senator from Ohio

(1899-1911); wrote *The Russian Advance* (1903), *The Life of John Marshall* (4 vols., 1916-19). **[43, 72]**

BREWER, DAVID J. (June 20, 1837-March 28, 1910), jurist. Judge (1865-69) of the first judicial district of Kansas; justice (1870-84) of the Kansas Supreme Court; associate justice (1889-1910) of the U.S. Supreme Court; president (1895-98) of the Venezuela boundary and arbitration commissions. **[7]** See also Author Index, Vol. 11.

BROWN, HENRY B. (March 2, 1836-Sept. 4, 1913), jurist. Associate justice (1890-1906) of the U.S. Supreme Court. **[21]**

BRYAN, WILLIAM JENNINGS (March 19, 1860-July 26, 1925), lawyer and political leader. U.S. representative from Nebraska (1891-95); free-silver advocate; thrice defeated (1896, 1900, 1908) candidate for President of the United States; edited (from 1901) the weekly *Commoner;* secretary of state (1913-15) under Wilson; a prosecuting attorney in the Scopes "monkey trial" at Dayton, Tenn. (1925). **[22, 73]** See also Author Index, Vol. 13.

CANNON, HUGHIE (fl. 1902), songwriter. **[106]**

CLARK, JOHN BATES (Jan. 26, 1847-March 21, 1938), economist. Professor of economics and history (1877-81) at Carleton College, (1882-93) at Smith College, (1892-95) at Amherst, and (1895-1923) at Columbia; editor (1895-1911) of *Political Science Quarterly;* wrote *The Philosophy of Wealth* (1885), *The Distribution of Wealth* (1899). **[83]**

CLEVELAND, GROVER (March 18, 1837-June 24, 1908), lawyer, political leader, and statesman. Twenty-second (1885-89) and twenty-fourth (1893-97) President of the United States; mayor of Buffalo, N.Y. (1881-82); governor of New York (1883-85). **[26]** See also Author Index, Vol. 11.

COHAN, GEORGE M. (July 3, 1878-Nov. 5, 1942), actor, playwright, and producer. Wrote and acted in plays (*Little Johnny Jones,* 1904; *The Song and Dance Man,* 1923) and composed popular songs ("I'm 'a Yankee Doodle Dandy," "You're a Grand Old Flag," "Give My Regards to Broadway," "Over There"). **[118]** See also Author Index, Vols. 13, 14.

DAVIDSON, THOMAS (Oct. 25, 1840-Sept. 14, 1900), philosopher and scholar. Founded (1883) the Fellowship of the New Life, of which the Fabian Society was an offshoot; organized Breadwinners' College in New York City for the education of working people; wrote *A History of Education* (1900). **[45]**

DE LEON, DANIEL (Dec. 14, 1852-May 11, 1914), lawyer and labor leader. Lecturer in Latin-American diplomacy (1883-89) at Columbia University; founded (1895) the Socialist Trade and Labor Alliance; editor (from 1900) of the Socialist Labor Party organ, *The People.* **[23]** See also Author Index, Vol. 13.

DENBY, CHARLES (June 16, 1830-Jan. 13, 1904), lawyer and diplomat. Minister to China (1885-98); member (1899) of U.S. Philippines Commission. **[54]**

DEWEY, JOHN (Oct. 20, 1859-June 1, 1952), philosopher, psychologist, and educator. Professor of philosophy (1894-1904) at the University of Chicago and (1904-30) at Columbia University; founder and director (1896-1904) of the University of Chicago Laboratory School; wrote many works, including *Democracy and Education* (1916), *Problems of Men* (1946). **[28, 59]** See also Author Index, Vol. 17.

DOWLING, ALEXANDER (Dec. 19, 1839-Dec. 11, 1917), jurist. Associate justice (1898-1904) of the Indiana Supreme Court. **[87]**

DREISER, THEODORE (Aug. 27, 1871-Dec. 28, 1945), author and editor. Brother of songwriter Paul Dresser; editor (1907-10) for Butterick publications; wrote travel books, short stories, essays, and novels, including *Sister Carrie* (1900), *An American Tragedy* (1925). **[63]**

DRESSER, PAUL (1857-1911), songwriter. Brother of novelist Theodore Dreiser; wrote the words and music for "On the Banks of the Wabash," "Sweet Savannah," "The Blue and the Gray," and "My Gal Sal." **[33, 63]**

DU BOIS, W. E. BURGHARDT (Feb. 23, 1868-Aug. 27, 1963), educator, editor, and author. Professor of economics and history (1897-1910) and of sociology (1932-44) at Atlanta University; a found-

HARTE, BRET (Aug. 25, 1836-May 5, 1902), author and editor. Edited (1868-70) the *Overland Monthly;* U.S. consul in Germany (1878-80) and in Scotland (1880-85); wrote *The Luck of Roaring Camp and Other Sketches* (1870), *Tales of the Argonauts* (1875). [62] See also Author Index, Vol. 10.

HAY, JOHN (Oct. 8, 1838-July 1, 1905), poet, journalist, historian, and diplomat. Private secretary to President Lincoln; assistant secretary of state (1879-81) under Hayes; ambassador to Great Britain (1897-98); secretary of state (1898-1905) under McKinley and Theodore Roosevelt; wrote *Poems* (1890) and, with John Nicolay, *Abraham Lincoln: A History* (10 vols., 1890). [69]

HAYES, JOHN W. (Dec. 26, 1854-Nov. 24, 1942), labor leader. An officer (from 1884) of the Knights of Labor. [64]

HERRON, GEORGE D. (Jan. 21, 1862-Oct. 9, 1925), Congregational clergyman and Socialist author. Founder (1906), with Mrs. E. D. Rand, of the Rand School of Social Sciences, New York City; wrote *Why I Am a Socialist* (1900), *The Menace of Peace* (1917). [51]

HOAR, GEORGE (Aug. 29, 1826-Sept. 30, 1904), lawyer and public official. U.S. representative from Massachusetts (1869-77); U.S. senator (1877-1904). [57]

HOLMES, OLIVER WENDELL, JR. (March 8, 1841-March 6, 1935), jurist. Son of physician and author Oliver Wendell Holmes; professor of law (1882) at Harvard Law School; associate justice (1883-99) and chief justice (1899-1902) of the Massachusetts Supreme Court; associate justice (1902-32) of the U.S. Supreme Court. [121] See also Author Index, Vols. 13, 14.

HUBBARD, ELBERT (June 19, 1856-May 7, 1915), author, editor, and printer. Founded (1895) the Roycroft Shop for artistic printing; founded and edited (1895-1915) *The Philistine* and (1908-15) *The Fra;* wrote *A Message to Garcia* (1899) and other short stories and sketches. [65]

HUBERT, PHILIP G. (Jan. 9, 1852-Jan. 3, 1925), journalist. Music critic (1877-90) for the *New York Evening Post* and (1890-94) for the *New York Herald;* an editor (1906-11) for the *Herald;* wrote *Inventors* (1893), *The Stage as a Career* (1900). [35]

HUNTER, ROBERT (April 10, 1874-May 15, 1942), social worker. Head worker (1902-03) in University Settlement, N.Y.; chairman (1902-06) of the New York Child Labor Commission; wrote *Tenement Conditions in Chicago* (1901), *Poverty* (1904), *Violence and the Labor Movement* (1914). [123]

JAMES, WILLIAM (Jan. 11, 1842-Aug. 26, 1910), psychologist and philosopher. Son of Henry James, Sr., and brother of Henry James; professor (1872-1907) at Harvard; established (1875) the first psychological research laboratory in U.S.; leading advocate of pragmatism; wrote *The Principles of Psychology* (1890), *The Will to Believe and Other Essays* (1897), *The Varieties of Religious Experience* (1902), *Pragmatism* (1907), *The Meaning of Truth* (1909). [110] See also Author Index, Vol. 13.

JONES, AARON (fl. 1899), Grand Master (*c.* 1899) of the National Grange. [64]

JONES, SAMUEL M. (Aug. 8, 1846-July 12, 1904), industrialist, politician, and reformer. Born Wales; established manufacturing plant at Toledo, Ohio; advocated labor policies based on the Golden Rule, becoming known as "Golden Rule" Jones; reform mayor of Toledo (1897-1904). [67]

KENNAN, GEORGE (Feb. 16, 1845-May 10, 1924), explorer, journalist, and author. Assistant manager (1877-85) of Associated Press, Washington, D.C.; correspondent (1885-86) in Russia and Siberia for Century Co. and (1898) in Cuba for *The Outlook;* wrote *Siberia and the Exile System* (2 vols., 1891), *Campaigning in Cuba* (1899). [101]

KINGSBURY, F. J. (fl. 1895), social scientist and author. President (*c.* 1895) of the American Social Science Association. [13]

KINSMAN, DELOS O. (Aug. 30, 1868-May 2, 1948), economist. Professor of social sciences (1901-16) at State Teachers College, Whitewater, Wis.; professor of economics (1916-26) at Lawrence College and (1926-39) at American University; member of the American Economic Association and opponent of the income tax; author of several books on economics and government. [113]

KIPLING, RUDYARD (Dec. 30, 1865-Jan. 18, 1936), British author. Born of British parents in India; an editor (1882-89) of *Civil & Military Gazette and Pioneer*, Lahore, India; began writing verse and novels in India and (from *c.* 1889) in England; received Nobel Prize for Literature (1907); wrote *Plain Tales From the Hills* (1887), *Barrack-Room Ballads* (1892), *Captains Courageous* (1897), *Kim* (1901). [56]

LAMB, ARTHUR J. (1870-1928), lyricist. Wrote "Asleep in the Deep" and "A Bird in a Gilded Cage." [33]

LAUGHLIN, JAMES LAURENCE (April 2, 1850-Nov. 28, 1933), economist. Professor of political economy (1890-92) at Cornell and (1892-1916) at the University of Chicago; edited (1892-1933) the *Journal of Political Economy*; wrote *Study of Political Economy* (1885), *Reciprocity* (1903). [16]

LODGE, HENRY CABOT (May 12, 1850-Nov. 9, 1924), public official and author. U.S. representative from Massachusetts (1887-93); U.S. senator (from 1893); wrote *The Story of the American Revolution* (2 vols., 1898), *The Senate and the League of Nations* (1925), and several biographies. [2, 19, 20] See also Author Index, Vols. 13, 14.

McCLINTOCK, HARRY (fl. 1897-1926), songwriter. [48] See also Author Index, Vol. 13.

McCLURE, S. S. (Feb. 17, 1857-March 21, 1949), editor and publisher. Born Ireland; founder (1884) of McClure Syndicate, first newspaper syndicate in the U.S.; founder and editor (1893-1914) of *McClure's* magazine. [114]

McKINLEY, WILLIAM (Jan. 29, 1843-Sept. 14, 1901), lawyer and statesman. Twenty-fifth President of the United States (1897-1901); U.S. representative from Ohio (1877-83, 1885-90); governor

(1892-96); assassinated by Leon Czolgosz, an anarchist (Sept. 6, 1901). [37, 40, 53, 90]

MAHAN, ALFRED THAYER (Sept. 27, 1840-Dec. 1, 1914), naval officer and historian. President (1886-89, 1892-93) of the Naval War College, Newport, R.I.; delegate to The Hague Peace Conference (1899); wrote *The Influence of Sea Power Upon History, 1660-1783* (1890). [70] See also Author Index, Vol. 11.

MARKHAM, EDWIN (April 23, 1852-March 7, 1940), poet. Wrote *The Man With the Hoe and Other Poems* (1899), *Lincoln and Other Poems* (1901), *Gates of Paradise* (1920). [58]

MASON, DANIEL (Nov. 20, 1873-Dec. 4, 1953), teacher and composer. Professor of music at Columbia University; composed two symphonies, a string quartet, and piano pieces; wrote *Contemporary Composers* (1919). [96]

MOODY, WILLIAM VAUGHN (July 8, 1869-Oct. 17, 1910), poet and playwright. Teacher of English (1894) at Harvard and (1895-1901) at the University of Chicago; wrote *Poems* (1901), three poetic dramas, and plays. [75]

MÜNSTERBERG, HUGO (June 1, 1863-Dec. 16, 1916), psychologist. Born Germany; professor of psychology (1892-95, 1897-1916) at Harvard University; Harvard laboratory for experimental psychology built under his direction; pioneer in field of applied psychology. [124]

NORRIS, FRANK (March 5, 1870-Oct. 25, 1902), journalist and novelist. War correspondent (1895) in South Africa for *San Francisco Chronicle* and (1898) in Cuba for *McClure's* magazine; wrote *McTeague* (1899), *The Octopus* (1901), *The Pit* (1903). [99]

NORTON, CHARLES ELIOT (Nov. 16, 1827-Oct. 21, 1908), editor, author, and educator. Co-editor (1864-68) with James Russell Lowell of the *North American Review*; a founder (1865) of the *Nation*; lecturer in history of art (1874-98) at Harvard; translated Dante's *Divine Comedy*, and edited *Poems of John Donne* (1895, 1905) and *Poems of Mrs. Anne Bradstreet* (1897). [71]

OLNEY, RICHARD (Sept. 15, 1835-April 8, 1917), lawyer and public official. Attorney general (1893-95) and secretary of state (1895-97) under Cleveland. [3] See also Author Index, Vol. 11.

PAGE, WALTER HINES (Aug. 15, 1855-Dec. 21, 1918), journalist, diplomat, and publisher. Wrote (1887-95) for the *Forum;* wrote (1895-98) for and edited (1898-1900) the *Atlantic Monthly;* partner (from 1900) in Doubleday, Page & Co., publishers; founder and editor (1900-13) of the *World's Work;* ambassador to Great Britain (1913-18). [42]

PARKER, FRANCIS W. (Oct. 9, 1837-March 2, 1902), educator. A leader of the progressive education movement; school superintendent in Quincy, Mass.; head of Cook County Normal School, Chicago; wrote *Talks on Pedagogics* (1894), *Talks on Teaching* (1896). [47] See also Author Index, Vol. 11.

PARRY, DAVID (March 26, 1852-May 12, 1915), manufacturer. Worked in hardware businesses in Indiana; president of Parry Auto Co.; president (*c.* 1903) of the National Association of Manufacturers and of Citizen's Industrial Association of America; wrote *The Scarlet Empire* [111]

PEIRCE, CHARLES SANDERS (Sept. 10, 1839-April 19, 1914), philosopher, logician, and scientist. Staff member (1861-91) of U.S. Coast Survey; lecturer in logic (1879-84) at Johns Hopkins University; founder of American pragmatism. [76]

PLUNKITT, GEORGE WASHINGTON (fl. 1904), politician. District boss in the New York City Tammany Hall organization; his political memoirs were published as *Plunkitt of Tammany Hall* (1905). [117]

QUINCY, JOSIAH (Oct. 15, 1859-Sept. 8, 1919), public official. Massachusetts legislator; assistant secretary of state (1893) under Cleveland; mayor of Boston (1895-99). [31]

REED, THOMAS B. (Oct. 18, 1839-Dec. 7, 1902), lawyer and public official. U.S. representative from Maine (1877-99) and speaker of the House (1889-91, 1895-99); sponsored a series of rules (adopted

Feb. 14, 1890) increasing the speaker's power. [36]

RIIS, JACOB (May 3, 1849-May 26, 1914), journalist, author, and social reformer. Wrote (1877-88) for the *New York Tribune* and (1888-99) for the *New York Evening Sun;* established (1888-89) Riis Neighborhood House (N.Y.C.) for social work; wrote *How the Other Half Lives* (1890) and other works. [93] See also Author Index, Vol. 11.

ROCKEFELLER, JOHN D. (July 8, 1839-May 23, 1937), industrialist and financier. Founder (1870) and president of Standard Oil Co.; organized (1882) the Standard Oil trust, which was dissolved by Ohio Supreme Court (1892); organized Standard Oil Co. of New Jersey, holding company dissolved by Supreme Court (1911); established and endowed four large charitable corporations (Rockefeller Foundation, General Education Board, Laura Spelman Rockefeller Memorial, and Rockefeller Institute for Medical Research). [66] See also Author Index, Vol. 13.

ROESCH, GEORGE F. (June 10, 1855-Dec. 21, 1917), jurist and public official. Member (1889-94) of New York Senate; justice (1893-1909) of the 4th U.S. District Court; assistant district attorney for New York (from *c.* 1910). [120]

ROOSEVELT, THEODORE (Oct. 27, 1858-Jan. 6, 1919), soldier, historian, and statesman. Twenty-sixth President of the United States (1901-09); assistant secretary of the navy (1897-98) under McKinley; served in Cuba (1898) as colonel of "Roosevelt's Rough Riders" voluntary cavalry regiment; governor of New York (1899-1900); Vice-President of the United States (1901) under McKinley; succeeded to the presidency upon McKinley's death (Sept. 14, 1901); received Nobel Peace Prize (1906); wrote *The Naval War of 1812* (1882), *The Winning of the West* (4 vols., 1889-96). [14, 18, 34, 92, 125] See also Author Index, Vols. 11, 13, 14.

ROWLAND, HENRY A. (Nov. 27, 1848-April 16, 1901), physicist. First professor of physics (1875-1901) at Johns Hopkins University; first president (1899-1900) of the American Physical Society. [60]

ROYLE, EDWIN M. (March 2, 1862-Feb. 16, 1942), actor and playwright. Wrote *Friends, The Winning of Barbara Worth, The Conqueror, Her Way Out.* [61]

SCHUYLER, MONTGOMERY (Aug. 19, 1843-July 16, 1914), journalist and architectural critic. Wrote (1865-83) for the *New York World* and (1883-1907) for the *New York Times;* managing editor (1885-87) of *Harper's Weekly;* a founder (1891) of the *Architectural Record;* wrote *Studies in American Architecture* (1892), *Westward the Course of Empire* (1906). [11]

SHAW, ALBERT (July 23, 1857-June 25, 1947), editor. Founded and edited (1891-1937) the *American Review of Reviews;* edited (1937-39) *Literary Digest;* wrote *Political Problems of American Development* (1907), *Abraham Lincoln* (2 vols., 1929). [39]

SIMMONS, FURNIFOLD M. (Jan. 20, 1854-April 30, 1940), lawyer and public official. U.S. representative from North Carolina (1887-89); U.S. senator (1901-31); co-sponsor of Underwood-Simmons Tariff Act (1913). [52]

SOUSA, JOHN PHILIP (Nov. 6, 1854-March 6, 1932), bandmaster and composer. Bandmaster (1880-92) of U.S. Marine Band; toured U.S. and abroad with own band (from 1892); composed marches ("Semper Fidelis" 1888, "Washington Post" 1889, "The Stars and Stripes Forever" 1897) and comic operas (*El Capitán,* 1896). [27]

SPALDING, JOHN L. (June 2, 1840-Aug. 25, 1916), Roman Catholic clergyman. Bishop (1877-1908) of Peoria, Ill.; wrote books on religion, philosophy, education, and social issues, and several volumes of verse (*America and Other Poems,* 1885, and *The Poet's Praise,* 1887). [17]

STEEVENS, GEORGE W. (1869-1900), English journalist. Special correspondent for the *London Daily Mail* in U.S., Greece, Germany, Egypt, India, South Africa, and at the Dreyfus trial. [25]

STEFFENS, LINCOLN (April 6, 1866-Aug. 9, 1936), journalist. Editor (1898-1902) of the *New York Commercial Advertiser,* (1902-06) of *McClure's* magazine, and (1906-11) of *American Magazine* and *Everybody's Magazine;* a leader of the "muckrakers"; wrote *The Shame of the Cities* (1904), *Upbuilders* (1909), *Autobiography* (1931). [102, 116]

STERLING, ANDREW B. (1874-Aug. 11, 1955), lyricist. Wrote the words for "Meet Me in St. Louis, Louis," "Wait Till the Sun Shines, Nellie," and "When My Baby Smiles at Me." [126]

STRONG, JOSIAH (Jan. 19, 1847-April 28, 1916), Congregational clergyman, author, and social reformer. Secretary (1881-84) of the Congregational Home Missionary Society; founded (1898) the League for Social Service, later (1902) the American Institute for Social Service; wrote *Our Country* (1885), *The New Era* (1893). [49] See also Author Index, Vol. 11.

STUDEBAKER, CLEMENT (March 12, 1831-Nov. 27, 1901), manufacturer. Founded (1852) the blacksmith and wagon-making firm of H. and C. Studebaker; president (1868-1901) of Studebaker Brothers Co., world's largest wagon and carriage manufacturer. [64]

SULLIVAN, LOUIS (Sept. 3, 1856-April 14, 1924), architect. Father of modernism in architecture and employer of the concept that "form follows function"; designer of the Auditorium, Gage, and Stock Exchange buildings in Chicago, the Union Trust Building in St. Louis, and the Bayard Building in New York; wrote *The Autobiography of an Idea* (1924). [80] See also Index, Vols. 11, 14.

SUMNER, WILLIAM GRAHAM (Oct. 30, 1840-April 12, 1910), Episcopal clergyman, social scientist, and economist. Professor of social and political science (1872-1909) at Yale; advocate of laissez faire economics and personal liberty; wrote *The Forgotten Man* (1919), *The Science of Society* (1927). [108] See also Author Index, Vols. 10, 11.

SWIFT, MORRISON I. (fl. 1899), author. [55]

TARBELL, IDA M. (Nov. 5, 1857-Jan. 6, 1944), author and editor. Editor (1883-91) of the *Chautauquan,* (1894-1906) of *McClure's* magazine, and (1906-15) of the *American Magazine;* wrote *The History of the Standard Oil Company* (2 vols., 1904) and several biographies of business leaders. [115]

TAYLOR, FREDERICK (March 20, 1856-March 21, 1915), inventor and efficiency engi-

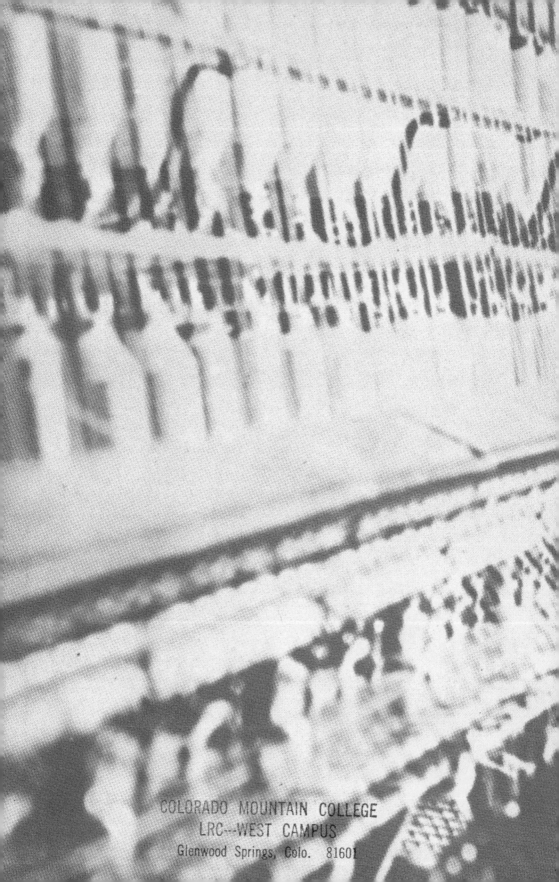

COLORADO MOUNTAIN COLLEGE
LRC--WEST CAMPUS
Glenwood Springs, Colo. 81601